Philosophical Foundations of Medical Law

Philosophical Foundations of Medical Law

Edited by

ANDELKA M PHILLIPS
THANA C DE CAMPOS
JONATHAN HERRING

OXFORD
UNIVERSITY PRESS

OXFORD
UNIVERSITY PRESS

Great Clarendon Street, Oxford, OX2 6DP,
United Kingdom

Oxford University Press is a department of the University of Oxford.
It furthers the University's objective of excellence in research, scholarship,
and education by publishing worldwide. Oxford is a registered trade mark of
Oxford University Press in the UK and in certain other countries

First Edition published in 2019

Impression: 1

Published in the United States of America by Oxford University Press
198 Madison Avenue, New York, NY 10016, United States of America

British Library Cataloguing in Publication Data
Data available

Library of Congress Control Number: 2019945715

ISBN 978–0–19–879655–8

Printed and bound by
CPI Group (UK) Ltd, Croydon, CR0 4YY

Contents

List of Contributors

Thana C de Campos, Assistant Professor, Escuela de Gobierno, Pontificia Universidad Católica de Chile.

Pip Coore, DPhil candidate, Faculty of Law, University of Oxford.

Donna Dickenson, Emeritus Professor of Medical Ethics and Humanities, University of London.

Charles Foster, Professor, University of Oxford.

Robert Gay OP, Blackfriars Hall, University of Oxford.

Robert P George, McCormick Professor of Jurisprudence; and Professor of Politics, Princeton University.

Imogen Goold, Associate Professor, Faculty of Law, University of Oxford; and Tutorial Fellow, St Anne's College.

Kate Greasley, Associate Professor, Faculty of Law, University of Oxford; and Tutorial Fellow, Hertford College.

Jonathan Herring, DM Wolfe-Clarendon Fellow in Law, Exeter College; and Professor of Law and Vice-Dean of the Faculty of Law, University of Oxford.

Kirsty Horsey, Kent Law School, University of Kent.

Pia Jolliffe, Blackfriars Hall, University of Oxford.

William Jolliffe, independent scholar.

David Albert Jones, Director, The Anscombe Bioethics Centre.

John Keown, Professor, Kennedy Institute of Ethics, Georgetown University.

Camillia Kong, Senior Research Fellow and Principal Investigator for the Judging Values and Participation in Mental Capacity Law Project, Institute for Criminal Policy Research, Birkbeck College University of London; and Research Associate, Ethox Centre, University of Oxford.

Andelka M Phillips, Senior Lecturer at Te Piringa Faculty of Law, University of Waikato; and Research Associate at the Centre for Health, Law, and Emerging Technologies (HeLEX), University of Oxford.

Heloise Robinson, DPhil candidate, Faculty of Law, University of Oxford.

Benedict Rumbold, Assistant Professor, University of Nottingham.

Julian Savulescu, Director of the Oxford Uehiro Centre for Practical Ethics; Uehiro Professor of Practical Ethics; and Fellow of St Cross College.

Trevor Stammers, Director, Centre for Bioethics and Emerging Technologies (CBET), St Mary's University.

Christopher O Tollefsen, Department of Philosophy, University of South Carolina.

Francisco J Urbina, Pontificia Universidad Catolica de Chile.

Carissa Véliz, Research Fellow, Uehiro Centre for Practical Ethics; and Research Fellow, Wellcome Centre for Ethics and Humanities.

Jesse Wall, Senior Lecturer, Faculty of Law, University of Auckland.

Daniel Wang, Lecturer in Health and Human Rights, Queen Mary University of London.

Dominic Wilkinson, Consultant Neonatologist, John Radcliffe Hospital Oxford; and Professor of Medical Ethics, Oxford Uehiro Centre for Practical Ethics, University of Oxford.

Introduction

Andelka M Phillips, Thana C de Campos, and Jonathan Herring

Today's world is one of rapid technological change and the practice of medicine has not escaped its reach. The rise of personalized medicine, precision medicine, Big Data, and the Quantified Self movement (including wearable technology and mobile health technology), as well as new consumer-focused services, such as personal genomics, are challenging existing paradigms in medical law and governance frameworks. All of these developments have led to medical law experiencing transformation and this trend is likely to continue. Lawyers and ethicists working in this context must now be ever ready to grapple with new and complex medical and ethical issues.

In particular, the advent of personalized medicine is changing the nature of the traditional doctor–patient relationship. Patients can now simultaneously be consumers and doctors can now simultaneously be service providers. At a fundamental level, this changes the nature of the doctor–patient relationship. If trust was the ethical value guiding the traditional relationship, now other considerations, such as market efficiency, are aggregated to the considerations of the relationship between the patient and the health-care provider. Also, if medical law traditionally focused on the regulation of the doctor–patient relationship, nowadays medical law also encompasses the regulation of institutional relationships involving health-care providers of different sorts and at various levels. This includes a myriad of health-care institutions, such as local hospitals, national public health-care systems, pharmaceutical companies, civil society organizations, and global health organizations (such as the World Health Organization and its regional offices).

Some new services also pose challenges for medical lawyers and ethicists, because they are not being offered within the traditional clinical setting and thus sit outside the traditional governance frameworks established in medical settings. For example, personal genomics services, which allow for DNA tests to be ordered online without medical intermediaries, have created a new market for DNA tests that exists outside the health-care sector, as tests are available for recreational purposes, as well as health conditions. Many of these new services have also increased the range of entities involved in providing health care, which in turn has meant that medical law now needs to address who is said to fall within the doctor–patient framework. We now need to consider tensions between trust-based and market-based relationships, together with questions of the rationing, prioritization, provision, and allocation of public health-care resources both nationally and globally. This also requires consideration of questions related to caring for the ill privately at home, and other intractable questions related to the beginning and ending of life, which have only grown in complexity, as medical innovations have progressed.

This book does not purport to promote a single view of how these challenges should be addressed. It seeks, rather, to show how philosophical thinking can provide ways of examining the questions. As will be clear, the writers in this collection are coming from a range

Andelka M Phillips, Thana C de Campos, and Jonathan Herring, *Introduction* In: *Philosophical Foundations of Medical Law*.
Edited by: Andelka M Phillips, Thana C de Campos, and Jonathan Herring, Oxford University Press (2019).
DOI: 10.1093/oso/9780198796558.003.0001

of perspectives and we have deliberately sought to ensure that a broad range of opinion is reflected.

I. Part A: Philosophical Foundations of Medical Law—General Theories

The fast-paced transformations in medical law and ethics prompted by the unprecedented progress in medical innovations calls for scholars to revisit their views, so as to provide ethical justifications that are current, more sophisticated, and are more capable of providing better guidance for decision making on medical issues. Questions on medical law and bioethics are often analysed according to six main philosophical perspectives. These together can be viewed as forming the philosophical foundations of medical law. The first part of this book covers these main philosophical approaches, namely: virtue ethics; consequentialism; deontology; natural law; ethics of care; and feminism.

The first philosophical approach to medical law explored in Chapter 1 of this volume is the virtue ethics theory. Virtue ethics is a way of viewing the moral life in terms of the necessary dispositions, which shape human action towards the good, and towards human flourishing. It was the dominant approach to moral philosophy in ancient and medieval thought, and it has recently experienced a revival. The Hippocratic tradition provides a virtue ethics framework for medicine, and the revival of virtue ethics has led, as Gay's chapter explores, to further work to explore the importance of virtue in medical practice. Gay argues that, in the morally and technically complex world of medical practice, the virtues of prudence, justice, fortitude, and temperance are necessary for the doctor to act according to the best interests of the patient, which are in line with the proper ends of medicine. In this respect, he contends that the law has a role in prohibiting acts that are not in accordance with the ends of medicine, and which cannot be virtuous. In other words, the law has a role in helping to arrive at prudential decisions in cases where there are disputes between patients or their families and medical teams about a best course of action. Gay's chapter concludes by emphasizing that medical law should have a role in cultivating virtue within medicine for the benefit of patients and doctors.

The second main philosophical theory applicable to the context of medical law and ethics is consequentialism, according to which the right act is the act that brings the best consequences. Savalescu and Wilkinson's chapter provides a definition of consequentialism. They then describe some examples of the influence of consequentialism over current medical law, by outlining the areas where consequentialism is at odds with current medical law and how medical law should evolve according to consequentialism.

Consequentialism is typically defined in stark contrast with deontology, which is the third main philosophical theory applicable to the context of medical law and ethics. Deontological ethics is typically traced back to Immanuel Kant and is for this reason also called Kantian ethics. For deontology (from Greek *deon*, meaning 'duty'), actions should be taken (or not taken) not primarily because of their consequences, but because the agent has a responsibility to act in that particular way. De Campos's chapter introduces Kant's theory in the context of the human right to health, which is relevant to discussions on medical law and bioethics. Her chapter first discusses the problems of the current state of affairs, where justice and human rights (including the human right to health) have become tantamount to unconstrained rights to choose autonomously according to one's individual preferences. This is the modern conception of justice, reduced to autonomy rights. After explaining how the relationship between rights-holders and duty-bearers in the context of human rights in general and the human right to health in particular has been lost, she proceeds to argue that deontology's emphasis on responsibilities can be capable of restoring the lost balance between rights and duties. De Campos's chapter discusses the deontological understanding of the human right to health (and its correlated core duties). She then applies these theoretical discussions to typical debates of medical law and bioethics, particularly the doctrine of the minimum core obligations that spur from the human right to health.

A fourth approach to medical law and bioethics is offered by Natural Law Theory. It is grounded on the Aristotelian tradition of virtue ethics put forth by Thomas Aquinas. However, it takes into consideration the consequences of one's actions while also placing particular importance on duties (as correlatives to rights) and on some moral absolutes (that Kantians call 'categorical imperatives'). Natural law's foundational principles are derived from the identification of basic human goods. George and Tollefsen's chapter first discusses these foundational principles of natural law, as well as the derived set of moral norms that emerge from consideration of the integral directiveness or prescriptivity of such principles. Their chapter then proceeds to discuss the implications of these moral norms for medical practice and medical law. They focus on four themes: (1) the intentional taking of human life; (2) authority for medical decision making; (3) the distribution of health-care resources in society and the existence of a 'right to health care'; and (4) the rights of 'physician conscience' in medical practice and medical law.

In the context of medical law and bioethics, at the core of all these philosophical schools of thought is the idea of care. Ethics of Care is therefore the fifth philosophical approach presented by this book. For an ethics of care approach, with its starting point being that people are relational, then the supposition is that there will be responsibilities for others. The emphasis here will be on relations and responsibilities, thus: we are born into relationships which carry responsibilities with them. This seems to be a common ground among ethics of care, virtue ethics, deontology, and natural law, in their responses to a utilitarian individualistic approach to medical law and bioethics. Herring's chapter summarizes the nature as well as the intellectual history of the Ethics of Care school of thought, by providing a definition of the concept of care. It then sets out the main themes of the approach and considers some of the objections that have been raised to it. In doing so, the chapter discusses the ways in which ethics of care could be used to resolve difficult issues that arise in medical law and ethics.

Although the ethics of care approach is not necessarily feminist in nature, it has found considerable support among feminist commentators. Greasley's chapter discusses the feminist approach to medical law and bioethics (the sixth philosophical approach in the book) by focusing on the ethics of abortion. For Greasley, feminist ethics approaches to abortion tend to be critical of the methodology employed by mainstream philosophical treatments of the abortion problem. In particular, she argues, they impugn the latter's reliance on abstract theorizing and general principles, advising that only focus on the particular and concrete details of real-life ethical problems such as abortion can direct us towards the truth of the matter. Greasley's chapter provides a defence of so-called 'traditional' abortion ethics from such criticisms. More precisely, she explains and vindicates the aim of mainstream abortion ethics to discern and apply more general moral principles to the particular case of abortion, as well as the centrality of foetal moral status to many of those accounts. Greasley's chapter seeks to demonstrate that mainstream and feminist ethical approaches are more aligned in both their methods and their claims than might first appear.

These are the six main philosophical foundations of medical law and ethics. In legal reasoning, each of these six schools of thought justifies and provides a particular interpretation of certain concepts and themes of medical law and ethics. Wall's chapter recaps these different philosophical approaches to medical law and ethics by discussing the different legal reasoning processes that each of them provides. For Wall, because legal reasoning is not a hermetically sealed process, foreign objects such as philosophy can influence it and become part of it. His chapter explores how philosophy gets in, and then considers a 'deflationary' account of the role of philosophy in legal reasoning. He then discusses two ways in which philosophy gets into the law. First, philosophy gets in through our reasoning *about* the law; it gets in through our explanations, criticisms, and recommended reforms of the law. Second, philosophy gets into our reasoning *according* to the law; it gets in when we ascribe meaning to a legal standard, substantiate its content, and qualify its scope. He then considers the suggestion that, in all these instances, it is not philosophy that gets into the law, but it is the law borrowing philosophical materials to put to its owns distinct use.

II. Part B: How These Six Philosophical Schools of Thought Illuminate Specific Contemporary Discussions of Medical Law and Ethics

The second part of this volume addresses the application of these six different philosophical schools of thought to illuminate specific contemporary discussions of medical law and ethics. These chapters explore how, in different scenarios, particular philosophical theories are applied in order to justify a certain course of action in the context of health care.

For many jurists, at the core of both beginning- and end-of-life questions lies the concept of dignity. For Foster, however suspicious or dismissive of the notion of dignity one is, the concept is unavoidable. Although the idea of dignity is embodied in many national and international legal instruments (particularly those on human rights in general and the human right to health in particular, as discussed in Chapter 5), it also sometimes does legal and philosophical work that no other concept can do. For Foster, there are classically two broad ways in which dignity has been understood: as an inalienable status; and as an aspiration. While one cannot lose 'status' dignity, common to all humans, one may not only fail to acquire 'aspirational' dignity, but one can even lose it. Foster argues that these two ways of seeing dignity are really two sides of the same coin, and that dignity should be seen instead as *humanization*: as objective human thriving. Seen that way, dignity escapes its critics, and can take its place as the foundational principle in medical law and ethics, from which all other principles are ultimately derived.

As Keown remarks, the concept of dignity in medical law and ethics has historically been informed by the principle of the 'sanctity' or 'inviolability' of human life. Although English law has over the last half century departed from that principle by accommodating utilitarian thinking (see Chapter 4, this volume), Keown argues that the lines it has drawn are both arbitrary and liable to further erosion. Keown's chapter explores some of those arbitrary and philosophically incoherent aspects of medical law. First, his chapter contends that it is philosophically incoherent for the law to calibrate its protection of human life according to arbitrary stages of human development, such as birth, viability, the fourteenth day after fertilization, and implantation. Second, it contends that to the extent that the law permits life-sustaining treatment to be withheld or withdrawn from incompetent patients on the basis that their 'quality of life' is insufficient, even with an intent to hasten death, it again displays ethical incoherence. Third, Keown's chapter maintains that, were the law to endorse intentionally assisting suicidal refusals of treatment or food and water, or to permit physician-assisted suicide for the 'terminally ill', its ethical incoherence would be aggravated.

Building on virtue theory (see Chapter 1, this volume), and focusing on the end-of-life question of withholding or withdrawing medical treatment or care, Jones's chapter explores the idea of the virtuous physician who should seek a golden balance between overtreatment and undertreatment. This requires not only clinical judgment (*techne*), but an overall best-interest decision (*phronesis*). For Jones, medical law has means to prevent undertreatment due to negligence, but is less well-adapted to preventing overtreatment. For him, the Law Lords in the *Bland* case seemingly approved the withdrawal of tube-feeding even with intent to end life, and this would mark a radical departure from Hippocratic virtue ethics. Subsequent legal developments have restored consistency to the law by prohibiting omissions with that intent, but they have not, Jones argues, remedied the error of condoning undertreatment through neglect of the objective goods of health and life.

Urbina's chapter provides another take on the assisted suicide and euthanasia debate. His discussion sheds light on the use of the principle of proportionality in medical law and ethics. The chapter pays particular attention to some significant human rights cases concerning assisted suicide and euthanasia, which constitute a paradigmatic example of the use of the principle of proportionality in the domain of medical law. Urbina analyses the different requirements entailed by proportionality and highlights some potential deficiencies or dangers of proportionality reasoning in the domain of medical law. He concludes that, though the use of proportionality in human rights cases is open to important challenges, other uses of proportionality in medical law and ethics can be acceptable.

Wang and Rumbold also discuss the role of courts in questions pertaining to medical law and bioethics. Their discussion is centred around justice-related questions pertaining to the allocation of scarce health-care resources and priority setting. For them, the justification for the judicial review of priority-setting decisions in the NHS is premised upon a distinction between substantive policy decisions and matters of procedural fairness, with courts themselves perceiving their function as restricted primarily to assessments of procedure. They highlight that this approach finds normative ground in the 'procedural turn' in the philosophical literature on justice in health, in particular in the influential idea of 'accountability for reasonableness'. However, their chapter argues that relying on the substance/procedure distinction to identify the appropriate role for the courts in the control of allocative decisions in health will attract to judicial review a series of concerns raised in the philosophical literature with regard to the idea of securing just priority-setting through procedural means.

Another justice-related question that arises in the context of medical law and bioethics is related to organ transplantation, the formation of an organ market, and the increase of organ trafficking and transplant tourism. For Stammers, if organs become a commodity, their shortage opens up the possibility of illegal markets developing. Supporters of regulated organ markets are, he argues, understandably keen to distance themselves from organ trafficking and transplant tourism and indeed most argue that regulated organ markets would reduce the incidence of both. However, Stammers's chapter argues that harm to vendors is involved in all three.

Stammers's discussion of organ market, organ trafficking, and transplant tourism deals not only with questions of justice regarding the regulation of such market, it also introduces the discussion of property in body parts, which is more fully explored by Dickenson. In common law, the understanding has been that there is no property in excised human tissue. However, in an era of widespread commodification of tissue, for Dickenson, the practical reasons behind this position are increasingly outdated, while the philosophical grounds are paradoxical. For her, this no-property rule has been construed so as to deprive tissue providers of ongoing rights, whereas researchers, universities, and biotechnology companies are prone to assume that once they acquire proprietary rights, those rights are complete and undifferentiated. Dickenson contends that that position can and should be remedied. She argues for a modified Lockean concept of property (as the fruit of one's labour) and a more sophisticated jurisprudential understanding of property in the body as a bundle of rights. Particularly in the case of women's tissues, such as ova and umbilical cord blood, this model can offer, Dickenson argues, more effective protection against the global 'enclosures' of bodily tissue.

The question of property in the body, particularly in the case of women's bodies, also arises in the context of surrogacy. Horsey's chapter discusses and argues for the need of re-regulation of surrogacy. For Horsey, the law does not currently serve the interests of those involved in surrogacy to the extent it should, including intended parents, surrogates, and—importantly—children. Partly, as Horsey claims, this is due to the bulk of the legislation regulating surrogacy being developed in the 1980s, when family laws and policies were significantly different, and when the tone of the law was permissive, yet discouraging of surrogacy. A direct outcome of this, Horsey claims, was an increase in intended parents seeking surrogacy overseas. Horsey concludes that a reform of the laws on surrogacy should carefully and pragmatically consider the exact message that the reformed law would send, so as to maximize its utilitarian potential, while minimizing ethical concerns. Defending a utilitarian approach (and therefore building on Chapter 4) to the reform of surrogacy laws, Horsey argues that a balancing and proportionality assessment is needed. This should balance the ideals of reproductive liberty and autonomy and of the welfare interests of children and surrogates, and all of these should be carefully weighted.

Surrogacy is a form of 'Assisted Reproductive Technologies' (ARTs). ARTs cover an array of methods and technologies that enable the conception of children that would not previously have been possible. ART access therefore enables the infertile to have children, whether via IVF, the use of donor gametes, full surrogacy, or a combination of these. ARTs, specifically IVF, also enable embryo selection. Prenatal genetic diagnosis can be undertaken prior to implantation to make a diagnosis of any suspected genetic conditions. As Goold's chapter remarks, the assumed benefit is the avoidance of a life affected by that condition. However, with the use of ARTs come some concerns. For Goold, the expansion in both the possibilities and our desires about how to deploy ARTs raises questions about how far one should restrict the use of ARTs. Goold's chapter considers the philosophical question of whether merely because one *can* do something, one *should* do it, and the question about *who* should be permitted to use ARTs and to *what ends*. Goold's chapter explores these questions by engaging with what reproductive liberty and autonomy mean, and considers whether, if at all, constraints on either can be justified.

The ethics of prenatal genetic diagnosis and embryo selection based on suspected genetic conditions and disabilities also arise in the context of abortion. Robinson's chapter discusses the permissibility of abortion of disabled persons, as compared to abortion for any other reasons. As Robinson's chapter demonstrates, there is significant support in the literature both for the perspective that abortion on the basis of a risk of disability is *less* morally objectionable, and for the view that it is *more* morally objectionable. Robinson's chapter reviews these different ethical perspectives to examine how arguments are strongly linked to whose interests are considered – especially those of the parents, those of the foetus, and those of others, such as disabled people living with the same condition which can be detected prenatally. Robinson's chapter explores the extent of the apparent conflict between the interests of various stakeholders—in particular, between the interests of the parents and those of others. She argues that the parents' interests are often only superficially understood: when the nature of the parents' choice is analysed more fully, and when the consequences and the costs of choice are taken into consideration, the parents' interests become, Robinson argues, more aligned with the interests of others than they may at first appear to be.

The use of ARTs is also debated and justified within the modern context of fertility decline and population ageing. Jolliffe and Jolliffe's chapter provides some helpful context that situates the relationship between fertility and population ageing, discussing the 'demographic deficit' and its economic consequences. They then turn to address the legal and ethical issues related to these demographic developments. In particular, they discuss how population control and family-planning policies attempt to enhance or curb fertility through the use of laws, stipends, and regulations. Jolliffe and Jolliffe's chapter focuses on reproductive medicine and more specifically on the moral issues that may shape fertility decisions at the individual level of society, by providing a reflection on these issues in the light of a Christian take on reproduction.

Population ageing also brings up questions of elder care. Coore's chapter examines the increased reliance on families to care for their older relatives, and the choice made by these families to enter into Family Care Agreements for legal protection. Coore's chapter illuminates this little-known area of family care to better understand whether (if at all) Family Care Agreements are adequately protecting older people and their caregiving adult child from harmful outcomes. In doing so, Coore's chapter provides some examples of the manner in which the law has already responded to the ageing population and identifies areas that require further attention. Coore largely deals with the relationship of care between an older parent and their adult child ('the Caring Relationship'). This chapter also raises questions about the scope of medical law in exploring how informal family relationships can constitute an important part of health-care provision.

The theme of elder care raises questions on the right to make one's own decisions about care and treatment, the concept of personal autonomy, and the concept of mental capacity functions. Under the Mental Capacity Act 2005 in England and Wales (MCA), mental capacity is decided according to a functional test based on the ability to (1) understand, (2) retain, (3) use and weigh, and (4) communicate information that is relevant to a specific decision. For Kong, in theory, these value-neutral criteria are designed such that assessors refrain from judging the wisdom and goodness of individuals' decisions. However, she argues that these functional criteria are in reality problematic in their presumption of an individualistic model of autonomy and value-neutral. For her, procedural focus precludes explicit engagement with certain evaluative judgments that are needed to articulate what may be incapacitous in the decision making expressive of self-harming egosyntonic disorders. Kong argues that a relational approach to the question of mental capacity helps to clarify the substantive evaluative judgments needed in such cases. Specifically, Kong suggests that the concept of capacity should operationalize a model of relational autonomy that illuminates the importance of *mutual recognition* in the development of self-narratives that are consistent with autonomy.

Questions on autonomy in the context of health care often bring up questions on other individual rights, such as medical privacy. Véliz's chapter explores the challenge that Big Data brings to medical privacy. She first offers a brief overview of the role of privacy in medical settings. Véliz understands privacy as having one's personal information and one's personal sensorial space (what she calls *autotopos*) unaccessed. Her chapter then discusses how the challenge of Big Data differs from other risks to medical privacy, and what can be done to minimize that risk. Véliz argues that the most effective way of protecting people from suffering unfair medical consequences is by having public universal health-care coverage where citizens contribute to the system through taxes, and not through dues based on personal data.

Finally, Phillips's chapter explores how electronic contracts and website design can impact upon the exercise of an individual's autonomy. She uses the example of personal genomics to highlight some of the challenges that arise in offering DNA tests outside a clinical setting. Previously, genetic tests were typically only offered in a medical context and, when individuals undergo testing in a clinic, they are typically required to provide informed consent and also undergo both pre- and post-test genetic counselling. In contrast, personal genomics allows for tests to be purchased through the internet without medical intermediaries and companies often rely on their electronic contracts and privacy policies to govern their relationship with consumers and the provision of these services. Phillips draws upon other work by Frischmann and Selinger, as well as the Norwegian Consumer Council, which suggests that the current design of websites and electronic contracts may be exerting a negative influence on people's ability to make an informed choice and exercise their autonomy. Specifically, interface design often encourages people to make quick decisions and may also lead to people clicking agreement to electronic contracts automatically. Phillips's chapter seeks to shed some light on how our interaction with electronic contracts and the designed environment of websites may be negatively impacting our autonomy and the need to consider how the electronic contracting environment could be improved for medical services.

PART A
GENERAL THEORIES

1

Virtue Ethics and Medical Law

Robert Gay OP

I. Virtue Theory Compared to Autonomy and Utility-Based Ethics

The concept of virtue is often compared unfavourably with the concepts of autonomy or utility in relation to its usefulness as a guide to action. The principle of respect for autonomy, that is, the duty and thus the right of each person to take responsibility for his or her own decisions, seems to provide clear guidance for action or inaction.[1] Autonomy means different things to different people, including 'liberty ... dignity, integrity, individuality, independence, responsibility and self-knowledge ... self-assertion ... critical reflection ... freedom from obligation ... absence of external causation ... and knowledge of one's own interests'.[2] Respect for autonomy implies that a person can freely choose what should be done on his or her behalf, and have that choice respected or, at the very least, implies allowing the person to refuse that something be done to him or to her in the context of health care. We might suggest that a paradigm example of the application of this principle is the ethical and legal requirement for sufficiently informed consent, whereby 'anyone capable of making decisions has an absolute right to accept or refuse medical treatment, regardless of the wisdom or consequences of the decision'.[3] Invasive treatment cannot ethically or legally be imposed on a competent adult who refuses to accept it, since to do so would be to commit the offence of battery.[4] An apparent exception to this rule, in English law, is the compulsory treatment of people with a mental illness.[5] However, even here, the rationale seems to be related to autonomy, since mental illness compromises autonomy, but the provision of compulsory treatment, under strictly limited conditions, could enable the patient to return to a situation where he or she might be able to make a more authentically autonomous decision. The principle of utility, that is, the need to consider potentially harmful and potentially beneficial consequences when evaluating human laws and practices, also seems, prima facie, to provide clear guidance for action or inaction. This principle implies a duty to maximize benefit, or at least, a duty to prefer the more beneficial or less harmful of available alternatives, all other things being equal.[6] In the context of health care, a form of utilitarianism is evident in the use of the Quality Adjusted Life Year (QALY) as a measure of health benefit.[7]

[1] TL Beauchamp and JF Childress, *Principles of Biomedical Ethics* (6th edn, Oxford University Press, 2009), 99; JF Childress, 'The Place of Autonomy in Bioethics' in S Holland (ed), *Arguing about Bioethics* (Routledge, 2012), 310

[2] G Dworkin, *The Theory and Practice of Autonomy* (Cambridge University Press, 1988), 4.

[3] Peter Jackson J in *Heart of England NHS Trust v JB* [2104] EWHC 302 (COP), also *Re B (Consent to Treatment: Capacity)* [2002] EWHC 429.

[4] J Herring, *Medical Law and Ethics* (7th edn, Oxford University Press, 2018), 150.

[5] As described in the Mental Health Act 1983. Ibid 587.

[6] RM Hare, 'A Utilitarian Approach' in H Kuhse and P Singer (eds), *A Companion to Bioethics* (Wiley-Blackwell, 2012), 85.

[7] E Nord, *Cost Value Analysis in Health Care: Making Sense of QALYs* (Cambridge University Press, 1999).

Robert Gay OP, *Virtue Ethics and Medical Law* In: *Philosophical Foundations of Medical Law*. Edited by: Andelka M Phillips, Thana C de Campos, and Jonathan Herring, Oxford University Press (2019).
DOI: 10.1093/oso/9780198796558.003.0002

In seeming contrast to the clear and applicable principles of autonomy and utility shown in the above examples, the concept of virtue is often presented merely as a recommendation of certain personal character traits specified in very general terms.[8] The promotion of such generic virtues as courage, temperateness, and practical good sense seems desirable, but by the same token they often seem to add little to the discussion of specific ethical or legal questions.[9] Furthermore, the internal subjective focus of virtue theory is often thought to offer no contribution to discussion of the external objective requirements of professional ethics and law. Why is it of any concern to patients how the doctor subjectively feels about a given treatment or procedure, or what general disposition he or she has?

II. Historical Background to Framing Virtue between Autonomy and Beneficence

This unfavourable assessment of virtue theory is shaped to a large extent by an intellectual framework according to which all ethical systems are divided between deontological rights-based approaches and teleological consequence-based approaches. Dividing the ethical world in this way takes the principles of autonomy and utility as primary and, indeed, as architectonic for how we think about ethics. However, the attempt to understand all ethical systems, theories, and concepts in relation to the ethical dichotomy of deontology-versus-teleology is a form of ethical dualism that is inadequate to the diverse historical, theoretical, and experiential reality of human action.

It is useful to remember that this neat dichotomy is a very recent innovation in Western moral philosophy. Indeed, it can be dated to a particular time and place, with the publishing in 1930 of two influential text books on ethics: one by the Cambridge philosopher CD Broad, *Five Types of Ethical Theory*, and the other by his Oxford contemporary WD Ross, *The Right and the Good*. Broad's work consists of a historical survey of contributions in moral philosophy from Spinoza to Sidgwick. In his summing-up of what he saw as the main problems of ethics during the covered period, he noted that ethical systems fell into two different classes: those which were based on 'Concepts of Obligation', which relied on notions such as ' "right", "ought", "duty" etc.', which he called deontological; and those which were based on 'Concepts of Value', which relied on notions such as ' "goodness", "merit", etc.', which he called teleological.[10] Ross's exploration of the concepts of 'right' and 'good' was influential in reinforcing this bipartite division, where moral theories would either be concerned with what is right, in terms of rules, duties, and obligations, or with what is good, in terms of consequences, utility, and value.[11] These two texts had a huge influence on the teaching of moral philosophy in the Anglophone world until the late twentieth century, but also, especially in the case of Ross, had a direct influence on the way in which medical ethics was thought about and taught from the late 1970s onwards. Ross's work, for example,

[8] For a discussion of these issues, see RB Louden, 'On Some Vices of Virtue Ethics' in R Crisp and M Slote (eds), *Virtue Ethics* (Oxford University Press, 1997), 201.

[9] N Tonti-Filippini, *About Bioethics: Philosophical and Theological Approaches* (Connor Court Publishing, 2011), 115.

[10] CD Broad, *Five Types of Ethical Theory* (Routledge, 2014), 277.

[11] See especially Stratton-Lake's introduction to D Ross, *The Right and the Good* (Oxford University Press, 2002), ix.

proposes a list of prima facie duties, which are the ground moral reasons for action.[12] These duties are fidelity, reparation, gratitude, justice, beneficence, self-improvement, and non-maleficence.[13] These provided a basis for the text book written by Thomas Beauchamp and James Childress: *Principles of Biomedical Ethics*. Beauchamp and Childress proposed four 'prima facie' principles (a concept they took from Ross) to guide ethical decision making in medicine.[14] Of these principles, two—namely autonomy and non-maleficence—are deontological, with two—beneficence and justice (understood primarily in relation to resource allocation)—having a teleological basis. The four principles, or as it has been termed, 'Principlism', has dominated medical ethics education for a generation, and while it has attracted criticism, especially from philosophers,[15] it remains influential because it seems to provide physicians with useful rules of thumb within an easily memorized schema.

III. The Need for Virtue

Elizabeth Anscombe pointed out the inadequacies of the dominant strands of Anglophone moral philosophy in the mid-twentieth century in her essay 'Modern Moral Philosophy' (MMP). The paper proposed three theses, namely that moral philosophy should cease until an adequate 'philosophy of psychology' could be described; ethics described in terms of obligation and duty should be jettisoned; and from Sidgwick onwards, the differences between the theories proposed by moral philosophers lacked importance.[16] From the outset, Anscombe notes the striking difference between Aristotle's work and that of modern moral philosophers and those who represented their work, such as Broad and Ross (who do not consider pre-Enlightenment philosophers in their studies), and in particular how different the language and concepts of modern moral philosophy are to Aristotle.[17] In MMP, Anscombe argues that there is a notable plurality of approaches in modern moral philosophy, such that each philosopher seems to have their own alternative theory of human action, or 'philosophy or psychology', with its own emphasis and, for Anscombe at least, their own problematic features.[18] In particular, the utilitarian philosophers fail to see some of the serious problems with using the notion of 'pleasure' as the guide for action. For example, in practice, no moralist attempts to calculate all the possible consequences of every one of his or her actions and omissions, since this would be impossible. Instead, the utilitarian assumes a standard of behaviour and then makes an exception where the likely consequences would otherwise cause some obvious or identifiable harm, and does so 'from the standards current in his society or his circle'.[19] Anscombe also found utilitarian thought problematic because it does not uphold that certain actions (such as the killing of the innocent) are always and everywhere wrong; this, for her, was a sign of a 'corrupt mind'.[20]

[12] Ibid 21.
[13] Ibid.
[14] Beauchamp and Childress (n 1) 99ff.
[15] See eg: Tonti-Filippini (n 9) 19; ED Pellegrino, *The Philosophy of Medicine Reborn* (University of Notre Dame Press, 2008), 204.
[16] GEM Anscombe, *Human Life, Action and Ethics* (Imprint Academic, 2005), 169.
[17] Ibid.
[18] Ibid 170.
[19] Ibid 192.
[20] Ibid 198.

In contrast to what seems to be the arbitrariness of consequentialist thinking (both in its conventional standards and in its exceptions), appeal to exceptionless moral rules might seem to provide a clear and defensible decision-making framework. However, rule-based approaches also face great challenges. In MMP, Anscombe was highly critical of the language of obligation in modern moral philosophy, including Kant's 'legislating for oneself', since the absence of a higher lawgiver (by which was meant a Divine lawgiver) renders such language senseless. Further problems with deontological ethics were pointed out by Anscombe's friend and mentor Wittgenstein, who saw rule-based ethics as resulting in a paradox, namely that 'no course of action could be determined by a rule, because every course of action can be made out to accord with the rule'.[21] He resolved this paradox by appeal to the idea of a practice, 'and hence also "obeying a rule" is a practice'.[22] What this indicated is that a practice is learned and is shaped by, but also shapes, habits or dispositions of mind. In the case of practical reasoning, the person with the correct dispositions is the virtuous person, whose good character is shaped by the goods inherent in a practice, who knows how to apply the ethical rules of justice to a particular situation.

Anscombe's paper received a variety of critical responses. Nevertheless, it paved the way for a reassessment and rehabilitation of virtue ethics as a normative approach in moral philosophy. Perhaps the most comprehensive attempt at this comes from Alistair MacIntyre. Like Anscombe before him, MacIntyre attempts to describe the unsatisfactory nature of the status quo in moral philosophy. His own critique looks especially at the 'fragmentation of the language of morality', whereby moral philosophy has 'fragments of a conceptual scheme' without the 'context from which they derive'.[23] For MacIntyre, fragmentation explains why such a wide variety of positions can be argued with regard to a given moral problem, all of which seem to be logically valid, and yet are incommensurable, with no easy way of deciding between them.[24] He is also clear that post-Enlightenment philosophy's abandonment of an Aristotelian teleological framework for ethics, with an overarching sense of what human beings are and how that shapes human life, has been a key part of the fragmentation of moral discourse.[25] The blame for the abandonment of a teleological framework is often placed with Hume and GE Moore, though the fact that human nature as grounding ethics is anathema for so many scholars suggests a more complicated history than that. One need only think, for example, of the effect of the theory of evolution on a teleological account of nature as an important post-Enlightenment influence in both science and ethics.[26]

MacIntyre is as adept at deconstruction as Anscombe, and provides a lengthy and detailed account of the origins and development of the status quo. Furthermore, he tries to construct a positive framework as a solution, a coherent framework for moral discourse. He proposes that the antidote to the fragmentation of moral discourse should be anchored in socially established human practices, and a description of virtues and their function in bringing about human excellence and flourishing within that framework.[27] For MacIntyre,

[21] L Wittgenstein, *Philosophical Investigations* (GEM Anscombe, PMS Hacker, and J Sculte (trs), 4th edn, Wiley-Blackwell, 2009), § 201.
[22] Ibid § 202.
[23] A MacIntyre, *After Virtue* (2nd edn, Duckworth, 1985), 2.
[24] Ibid 8.
[25] Ibid 55.
[26] For a more detailed account of some of these issues, see T Chapell, 'Virtue Ethics in the Twentieth Century' in DC Russell (ed), *The Cambridge Companion to Virtue Ethics* (Cambridge University Press, 2013).
[27] MacIntyre (n 23) 193.

a practice is defined as a 'socially established cooperative activity through which goods internal to that form of activity are realised'.[28] The range of possible practices is large, and incorporates 'arts, sciences, games, politics ... the making and sustaining of family life', all of which involve cooperation, sets of skills, common language and standards, and so on.[29] Furthermore, within those practices, there are 'goods', which are internal to them, and those goods are both aimed at and achieved by those involved in the practice; this both requires and develops 'human powers' to achieve excellence.[30] These human powers are the virtues, dispositions which help achieve those goals, and which transform those within that practice who seek to achieve them.

IV. The Main Features of Virtue Ethics

Through the combination of the critique and positive framework for virtue outlined above, we can see that an advantage of virtue ethics as a normative approach is that, rather than ask questions that cannot be answered (in relation to all the possible consequences of an action and every possible assessment of every possible rule of action), it directs our attention to the practices of human life within which people flourish. The advantage of MacIntyre's insights is clear for medical ethics if we understand medicine as a practice according to his definition, and one which has a clear aim and a noble purpose. To practice medicine successfully, a doctor requires scientific knowledge and technical skills, acquired through study of the appropriate theoretical knowledge and detailed practical training. However, medicine is not confined to theoretical information and practical skills. There are other dimensions to medicine which mean that the doctor also requires the appropriate moral dispositions to, say, be trustworthy with confidential information, to carry out examinations appropriately and sensitively, to be emotionally in control under pressure, and to use medical tools and drugs which can cause serious physical harm when misused.

In his Nichomachean Ethics, Aristotle saw a strong analogy between skill (*techne*), such as the skills that are acquired by a musician through years of practice, and virtue (*arete*), the good dispositions of character that are acquired by upbringing and education.[31] Technical skills, like playing a musical instrument, are acquired through practice, and perhaps also shaped by instruction from a good musician. Once those skills have been acquired, however, their use is limited, because they only make us good at a specific and narrow range of tasks associated with that activity. Like skills, the virtues are also acquired through training and practice of what is in accordance with human flourishing, are needed for the broader and more open-ended task of living life well, and shape the person's activity in this wider pursuit. Thus, virtues, such as honesty or courage, are not confined to just some activities, but, if we possess them, will shape all our actions. Aristotle argued that everyone needs the intellectual and moral virtues if they are to fulfil the fundamental task or function (*ergon*) of being human, which is determined by human nature.[32]

[28] Ibid 187.
[29] Ibid 188.
[30] Ibid 187.
[31] Aristotle, *Nichomachean Ethics* (C Rowe (tr), Oxford University Press, 2002), II.4 1105a17.
[32] Ibid I.7 1097b23.

That aim of human function is something which he describes as *eudaimonia*, which is translated variously as happiness, flourishing or human fulfilment, which is what is 'worth pursuing for itself'.[33] It is the fundamental task of human beings to seek fulfilment, and this forms the overarching purpose, *telos*, of human life, and shapes everything else about human action.

Aristotle gives a definition of a virtue as 'a disposition issuing in decisions, depending on intermediacy of the kind relative to us, this being determined by rational prescription and in the way in which the wise person would determine it'.[34] From this definition, we can see that an important element of Aristotle's account of the virtues is his view that virtue typically exists as a middle way between vices of excess and defect, 'the intermediacy' in the definition above. This can be understood more clearly using examples. The virtue of courage is not only opposed to the vice of cowardice, but is also opposed to the opposite vice of being rash. Likewise, temperance is not only opposed to gluttony, but to excessive dieting. It is important to realize that the use of the term 'mean' does not imply that the middle way is the mathematical average. The mean can be thought of as a rule for action, but the identification of the mean is not determined by a rule or a set of rules, but rather will depend on the circumstances, the person's roles and responsibilities, and the more general requirements of human flourishing. Thus, the mean with regard to alcohol for an alcohol-dependent person will be no alcohol, rather than, say, the recommended maximum weekly intake.

If virtue consists in moderation between extremes, then it might be thought that nothing is forbidden absolutely. However, Aristotle was clear that some kinds of action are inherently contrary to virtue, since 'in some cases they have been named in such a way that they are combined with badness from the start'.[35] Aristotle himself gives examples of such things, including 'malice, shamelessness, grudging ill will ... fornication, theft and murder'. All of these are examples of actions which Aristotle argued are not defective as excesses or deficiencies according to a mean, but rather are inherently wrong, since 'one goes astray however one does them'.[36] It is therefore the case that virtue typically will lie between opposite vices, as the middle term between extremes, but also, and independently, some kinds of action will be contrary to virtue because they are contrary to certain human goods. To take two of Aristotle's examples, neither adultery nor murder can be virtuous if done in moderation. The act of adultery is always contrary to virtue because it stands in contradiction to marital fidelity, which is an inherent aspect of the good of that practice. Likewise, murder is contrary to the good of life itself. It can be argued that it may not always be easy to identify which kinds of actions are inherently wrong in this way, and indeed this is seen as one of the weaknesses of virtue ethics, one which has often led to its abandonment as a useful moral theory which can guide and direct human action. What is clear is that, on an Aristotelian account, some actions are contrary to virtue inherently, because of the kinds of actions they are, and other actions are contrary to virtue not inherently, but through excess or defect.

[33] Ibid I.7 1097a31.
[34] Ibid II.6 1106b36.
[35] Ibid II.6 1107a8.
[36] Ibid II.6 1107a25.

V. The Origins of the Application of Virtue Ethics to Medicine

Virtues, in Aristotle's understanding, are required for all worthwhile roles in life. As has been discussed, this is what distinguishes virtues from technical skills. However, the virtues may take particular forms or have particular significance in different roles. To take some examples, the honesty of the judge or the courage of the soldier can be described in more detail and have very specific functions within their professions. We might also say that for certain roles, certain virtues become central, as indeed is the case for the honesty of the judge and the courage of the soldier, and their absence renders effective fulfilment of those roles impossible. Looking at medicine in a similar way, we see that it is a discipline, a body of knowledge, and a set of skills. However, it is also a profession, an ethical undertaking shaped by a particular commitment to certain virtues. For example, within the medical profession, the tact and sensitivity that are needed to communicate clearly with patients are different from the kind of communication needed by a barrister or a journalist, a politician, or a school teacher. In each case, the context of the communication shapes which aspects of communication will be more important and which failures will be more harmful. The context for the communication between a doctor and a patient is distinguished by inequality of knowledge, sensitive personal information, emotional vulnerability, and sometimes impaired capacity on the part of the patient, and all of this often coupled with an urgent need for a decision. Managing such an inequality of vulnerability, requirement for trust, and decision making well is therefore far from straightforward, since the doctor has considerable moral and technical demands placed on his or her shoulders. The practice of medicine is therefore difficult, and requires the virtues if it is to be done well, for the benefit of the patient and the well-being of the doctor.

The practice of reflecting ethically on medicine has a long history, going back certainly as far as Hippocrates, or at least to the oath attributed to him.[37] Regardless as to whether the oath is actually his, or simply an acknowledgement of his status as one of the founding fathers of medicine, what is clear is that Hippocrates was a philosopher–physician, and saw the intimate connection between his role as a physician and his need to reflect philosophically on what he was doing as a physician. In fact, philosophy would seem to have been at the heart even of the birth of medicine as a separate discipline.[38] The Hippocratic Oath, and its variants, have been used as a framework for the ethics of medical practice for three millennia. When we look at the Hippocratic Oath in its earliest form, we see a text which gives an ethical framework to a code of practice for the physician.[39] The text itself has this ethical framework expressed in terms of practices which should not or should be carried out, such as, 'I will not give a drug that is deadly to anyone if asked for it' and 'into as many houses as I will enter, I will go for the benefit of the ill'. Such expressions have the characteristics of a rule-based, deontological ethical system, but might also be argued as consistent with an Aristotelian teleological framework with the end goal of medicine stated, and with exceptionless norms which are in accordance with that framework.[40] We likewise see an

[37] For examples of the works of Hippocrates, the oath attributed to him, and its analysis, see WHS Jones, ET Withington, WD Smith, et al (trs), *Hippocrates* (Harvard University Press, 2014); and SH Miles, *The Hippocratic Oath and the Ethics of Medicine* (Oxford University Press, 2005).

[38] Pellegrino (n 15) 401–23.

[39] Miles (n 37) xiii–ix.

[40] Ibid.

emphasis on the character of the physician as one who is viewed as trustworthy by those who are treated by him. Such an emphasis has a distinctly virtue-based ethic for the practice of medicine.

Similarly, when we look at Thomas Percival's highly influential early eighteenth-century work, 'Medical Ethics', we find a concern almost exclusively with professional conduct of medical professionals. Indeed, the work itself is subtitled 'A Code of Institutes and Precepts Adapted to the Professional Conduct of Physicians and Surgeons'.[41] Percival provides descriptions of the character and disposition of doctors and surgeons, so that they might best serve their patients through the good exercise of their craft. Besides those characteristics which mark excellence in particular skills, the doctor should also exhibit dispositions such as tenderness, steadiness, condescension, authority, and temperance, so that they might inspire confidence in their patients.[42] The fact that his ethical framework contains these kinds of dispositions as important perhaps owes much to the Hippocratic framework, which is relatively untouched by post-Enlightenment concerns found in the moral philosophy of that time.

While Hippocrates and Percival are only two examples, they give an insight into the preoccupations of medical ethics before the rise of bioethics in the second half of the twentieth century. And we also see the main preoccupation as the relationship between the physician and the patient, and the expression of codes to regulate the interactions. The concern is to do with the physician and that physician's action. The language is influenced by ideas of dispositions of character, and both technical and moral rectitude of the practitioner of medicine. The patient is arguably a silent, vulnerable recipient of treatment and care; albeit one who is protected by codes which recognize that vulnerability and seek to promote good practice and character among practitioners.

VI. Virtue in Medical Ethics in Contemporary Thought: The Ends of Medicine and the Cardinal Virtues

To date, the most significant attempts to bring virtue theory and medical ethics to the forefront, and specifically the ethics of medical practice, have come from the work of Edmund Pellegrino and his collaborators, in particular David Thomasma. The framework chosen by Pellegrino for his virtue ethics is the Aristotelian one already outlined, though supplemented by insights from the work of Thomas Aquinas. We can also see hints of the importance of elements of MacIntyre's work, *After Virtue*, and especially his understanding of the importance of medicine as a practice in the setting of virtue ethics. Pellegrino and Thomasma's application of virtue ethics to the practice of medicine is based on an understanding of the nature of medical practice and, in particular, a philosophical account of the nature of medicine, and its technical and moral components. A key part of the development of their understanding of the role of virtue in medicine comes from their examination of the reality of illness and the vulnerabilities that it brings about in the patient.[43] This is allied to a

[41] T Percival, *Medical Ethics, or, A Code of Institutes and Precepts, Adapted to the Conduct of Physicians and Surgeons* (Cambridge University Press, 2014).

[42] Ibid ch 1.

[43] ED Pellegrino and DC Thomasma, *The Virtues in Medical Practice* (Oxford University Press, 1993), 35.

sense of the privileged position of the medical practitioner as one who has specialist training and knowledge which that practitioner is duty-bound to use for the benefit of the patient; specifically to be used to assist the patient in regaining health, as much as that is possible.[44] They acknowledge that medical practice involves negotiating the clear inequality between the patient and practitioner, the importance of a relationship of trust between them, and the responsibility for making medical decisions which have a moral character and which morally involve the medical practitioner in the outcome of any intervention which that practitioner may carry out on a patient.[45]

The ethical framework which they outline has a teleological structure which shapes the virtues required to carry out the task well. The end they suggest is the restoration and improvement of health through the cure of underlying pathologies, and where this is not possible, the care and relief of suffering of the patient. Because of this, the overarching principle of medicine is the good of the patient—their best interests. Every intervention is to be carried out in accordance with this end, and the virtues have a role in guiding the action of the medical practitioner towards it.[46] Pellegrino and Thomasma propose a set of eight key virtues which guide the action of a medical practitioner in line with the end or purpose of medicine, and give an account of how each of them guides action in the relationship between the practitioner and the patient. They are fidelity to trust, compassion, phronesis, justice, fortitude, temperance, integrity, and self-effacement. In what follows, the four cardinal virtues will be presented as they occur in Pellegrino and Thomasma's thought, supplemented with other thinkers.

The key virtue of medical practice is Aristotle's *phronesis*, or prudence as it is commonly known. Prudence has a negative association with caution and inaction in common parlance, yet in reality it sits as the 'capstone' of the virtues in medical practice because, as for Aquinas and others before them, it shapes and guides the formation and development of the other virtues.[47] This virtue is important because it is the disposition by which reasoning about what should be done in a given situation is perfected. It has a key role in medical practice because it brings together the intellectual, technical, and moral aspects of medicine, linking knowledge, technical skill, and judgement with a moral evaluation of the good of the patient in their specific situation, and guides clinical judgement accordingly.[48] As such, it is not simply a virtue which guides things solely from the medical practitioner's viewpoint, but also takes into account the relevant features of the patient's view of their situation. We might therefore say that it includes reasoning about the patient's diagnosis; the medical and surgical means available to assist the burdens, risks, and side effects of using such means; and the various factors of importance to the patient, such as their psychological condition, values and beliefs, family circumstances, and so on.[49] Prudence does what a simple principle-based ethic cannot achieve, namely, enables a dynamic dispositional response to the technical and moral challenges presented by a given patient in their unique circumstances.[50]

44 Ibid.
45 Ibid 42.
46 Ibid 53.
47 Ibid 84.
48 Ibid 86.
49 Ibid 88.
50 Ibid 89.

Several scholars have commented on the importance of prudence in medical practice. For example, Devettere develops an account of prudence as the archetypal virtue of the doctor, and like Pellegrino and Thomasma uses the thought of Aristotle and Aquinas to this end.[51] In acknowledging the importance of the details of specific situations in prudential reasoning, he uses prudence as a way of analysing specific cases, as a way of determining a course of right action. Similarly, Montgomery sees prudence in a similar light, as a way of navigating the contingency and moral complexity of real clinical situations, while Marcum develops a similar line to Pellegrino and Thomasma.[52] There have also been some critical accounts of seeing prudence as the most important of the virtues for medicine. Hofman has suggested that Pellegrino and Thomasma have misunderstood the Aristotelian notion of prudence, and that what they describe as prudence could be more adequately described by the idea of *techne* in the Hippocratic tradition.[53] Kristjánsson has also noted the variety of ways in which Aristotelian *phronesis* is understood in the literature, and how that has led to a divergence of use in the medical ethical literature.[54] The fact that such divergence is present shows how a deeper understanding of the idea of prudence is required to improve its usefulness in medical ethics.

When it comes to the interaction between prudence and medical law, there are several possible points of interaction. One such point of interaction comes from the law related to medical negligence. The key case which informs medical negligence is that of *Bolam v Friern Hospital Management Committee*, which led to the development of what is now referred to as the 'Bolam test', whereby a 'doctor is not guilty of negligence if he has acted in accordance with a practice accepted as proper by a responsible body of medical men skilled in that particular art'.[55] One might argue that the features of medical treatment and the actions of doctors in cases of medical negligence are assessments not only of skills, but also of the exercise of prudential reasoning in decision making and execution. Perhaps one might suggest that the additional weight of *Bolitho v City and Hackney Health Authority*, which indicates that scrutiny of the logical structure of medical decision making in negligence cases should be made, further opens questions of alleged medical negligence to scrutiny at the level of prudential reasoning on the part of the doctor who stands accused of that negligence.[56] What is clear is that the virtue of prudence itself, which perfects reasoning about what should be done in a given situation, is one which helps doctors to act in such a way as to prevent negligence and therefore harm to patients.

The virtue of justice can be defined as the 'strict habit of rendering what is due to others'.[57] In common parlance, justice has a whole range of meanings, and the virtue itself often is subdivided into justice towards individuals (commutative justice) and as it relates to the common good (distributive justice).[58] Justice is often thought of more as a principle with normative implications rather than as a virtue, and in medical ethics we see this in the fact

[51] RJ Devettere, *Practical Decision Making in Healthcare Ethics: Cases, Concepts and the Virtue of Prudence* (4th edn, Georgetown University Press, 2016).

[52] K Montgomery, *How Doctors Think: Clinical Judgment and the Practice of Medicine* (Oxford University Press, 2005), 4; JA Marcum, *The Virtuous Physician* (Springer, 2012), 60.

[53] B Hofman, 'Medicine as Practical Wisdom (Phronesis)' (2002) 1 Poiesis & Praxis 135.

[54] K Kristjánsson, 'Phronesis as an Ideal in Professional Medical Ethics: Some Preliminary Positionings and Problematics' (2015) 36 Theoretical Medicine and Bioethics 299.

[55] [1957] 2 All ER 118, 112.

[56] [1997] 3 WLR 1151.

[57] Pellegrino and Thomasma (n 43) 92.

[58] Ibid 93.

that it is given as one of Beauchamp and Childress's principles.[59] For the doctor, justice is not simply a normative principle for action, but is the disposition which makes sure that the doctor acts in such a way that each patient is given what they are due. It is rooted in a profound sense of both the worth of the patient and their dignity, and thus regulates the relationship with the patient in many ways. The virtue of justice shapes the one-to-one interaction between the doctor and the patient (commutative justice), and also wider questions of the fair allocation of finite resources (distributive justice). The fact that a virtue is required to act well towards the patient and give them what they are due is not surprising, given how difficult a task being just is. Many factors can come into play which might jeopardize the giving of appropriate time, attention, treatments, and resources to patients, including the 'self-interest, comfort and preferences of the doctor'.[60] However, as the doctor negotiates these complexities and decides in favour of what is just for the patient, the virtue of justice can be cultivated. Justice is a key example of where virtue ethics, in the Hippocratic and Aristotelian traditions, has something to say about certain actions as excluded, because they are incompatible with virtue.

The oath attributed to Hippocrates gives a clear statement that actions which are unjust and cause harm are incompatible with the role of the doctor. Such acts which are specifically mentioned are counselling a patient to take a drug with the purpose of ending their life, providing such a drug with the purpose of ending life (ie assisting suicide), actions which lead to an abortion, and the breaking of patient confidentiality.[61] In Aristotelian terms, such actions have no mean, are incompatible with the good of the patient, and are therefore unjust. We might also extend the Hippocratic logic to include within the category of inherently unjust actions such harms as treatments or procedures which have not been consented to by the patient, or failing to provide adequate information about risks of treatment and procedures.[62] The virtue of justice is required to ensure that a doctor has the right disposition to avoid such actions. It is a point of departure from traditional Hippocratic medical ethics that a system of justice might allow some actions which until recent times have been seen as inherently unjust, and therefore incompatible with justice as a virtue, such as is the case with the Abortion Act 1967. The debate both for and against the moral permissibility of abortion is well known, and can be examined in a variety of sources.[63] The law in England and Wales as it currently stands does not allow a doctor to advise a patient on actions which would lead to their killing themselves, although attempts have been made to introduce legislation to allow assisted suicide for those who have a terminal illness, are over 18, and have capacity.[64]

Justice conceived as a 'strict habit of rendering what is due to others' has much to say about other aspects of medical law, not least as a way of reflecting on how finite financial and human resources are allocated within medicine.[65] The QALY metric enables health-care

59 Beauchamp and Childress (n 1) 240.
60 Pellegrino and Thomasma (n 43).
61 Miles (n 37) xiii.
62 For an example case of the former, see *R v Healy* [2003] 2 Cr App R (S) 87; for the latter, see *Montgomery v Lanarkshire Health Board* [2015] UKSC 11.
63 See eg: CR Kaczor, *The Ethics of Abortion: Women's Rights, Human Life, and the Question of Justice* (2nd edn, Routledge, 2015); K Greasley and CR Kaczor, *Abortion Rights: For and Against* (Cambridge University Press, 2018).
64 See eg the Assisted Dying Bill 2016–2017. For law concerning the end of life, see *R (On the application of Nicklinson) v Ministry of Justice* [2014] UKSC 38, [225]; also Herring (n 4) 500.
65 Pellegrino and Thomasma (n 43) 92.

economists to conduct a cost/benefit analysis of new treatments which can be used to inform allocation decisions. As the principle of autonomy can be invoked by patients to demand the provision of a desired treatment or procedure, or can be used to refuse an unwanted treatment or procedure, likewise the principle of utility can be invoked by doctors, or by Hospital Trusts, to justify withholding expensive treatments that would offer the patient only marginal benefit.[66] While QALY-based decisions are not per se part of medical law, they are used by the National Institute of Health and Clinical Excellence (NICE) as a basis for assessing resource allocation decisions, which are themselves often subject to judicial review, and such reviews are an opportunity for assessment of the decisions made in the light of what is according to the virtue of justice.[67]

The virtue of fortitude, often known as courage, has a key role to play in medical practice. Such a term as courage is used in a whole variety of ways, depending on context. However, not all such actions are necessarily courage as a moral virtue. We might consider, for example, the person taking life-threatening risks for the sake of taking a 'selfie' as a case in point. An action might be described as fearless, but this does not make it virtuous, because the risk is entirely disproportionate to the benefits, and therefore does not conform with the appropriate mean between allowing fear to overcome a person, leading to the extreme of cowardice, and of a fearless rash behaviour at the other extreme. For doctors, this is an extremely important virtue, since doing what is right for patients is not simple.[68] There is often, for example, the threat of disease and its possible transmission to the doctor, which might cause a doctor to fail to care for the patient properly out of an excessive fear. In the other direction, the doctor might not give due attention to the risks involved with such patient, thereby exposing him- or herself, or indeed others, to unnecessary risks.[69] Here, we can see the strong reliance of courage on prudence, which helps to set the mean, taking into consideration all the specific features of the case.

Another example of the need for the virtue of courage comes from consideration of the relationship between the doctor and the patient, and specifically as regards communication with the patient. The obvious example is the need for the virtue of courage when breaking bad news to patients, or speaking to patients who are volatile or hostile for some reason. The temptation to shrink back in such situations, or even to speak indirectly, such as hiding behind technical language, is understandable. Perhaps also a brusque and very direct approach might also be tempting, not allowing the fear of a negative reaction to enter into consideration. However, the virtuous doctor will be able to moderate between these two extremes. In a similar way, the virtue of courage will be required to negotiate the bureaucratic and administrative landscape of medicine as it impacts on the ends of medicine with regard to patient care.[70] The virtue of courage has a particular interaction with law in the question of whistle-blowing, whereby a doctor needs to report problems relating to patient care which are critical of a colleague or a group of colleagues. Many have commented that raising such concerns is far from simple, both in terms of procedure and in terms of the

[66] J McKie, J Richardson, PD Singer, et al, *The Allocation of Health Care Resources: An Ethical Evaluation of the 'QALY' Approach* (Ashgate, 1998).

[67] See eg: *R (Servier) v National Institute of Health and Clinical Excellence* [2009] EWHC 281 (Admin); *R (Fraser) v National Institute of Health and Clinical Excellence* [2009] EWHC 452 (Admin).

[68] Pellegrino and Thomasma (n 43) 111.

[69] Ibid.

[70] Ibid 113.

risks involved for the whistle-blower themselves.[71] Such an activity involves a prudential assessment of the situation, and the courage to take a risk in order that what is seen as right for the sake of patient safety and well-being is carried out.

The final cardinal virtue for consideration is temperance. This virtue, like prudence, suffers from an image problem, because of an association exclusively with abstinence from alcohol. However, in virtue ethics it has a much richer understanding which includes, more broadly, the idea of self-integration and self-mastery.[72] This might include, therefore, the correct disposition as regards bodily pleasures such as food and drink and sexual desire, but also broader concerns to do with the wider issues of self-control and restraint, including patience, a civility in communication, humility, and other allied qualities, which have obvious importance within the practice of medicine.[73] Even in the narrower sense of the virtue of temperance as regards their own relationship to, say food and drink, a doctor who is self-integrated in these aspects has the advantage of being well disposed to a healthy attitude to themselves which should facilitate the relationship with the patient. There are many examples of cases involving what might be termed intemperate behaviour by doctors in their personal lives or professional lives which have been seen as having a bearing on their fitness to practice, such as sexual misconduct, issues of anger management, or issues with alcohol and other substances.[74] Some such behaviour is not only an issue of professional misconduct, but also of criminal conduct, and was specifically prohibited in the original Hippocratic framework.[75]

The broader sense of temperance, which includes humility, civility, and patience, clearly concerns qualities, which if absent, could lead to serious problems in the relationship with patients, families, and, of course, colleagues. One key problem with medical practice has been identified as the issue of paternalism, which at its worst can take the form of 'playing God', whereby the doctor's knowledge and technical ability, and the status and power that these may bring, are not used for the patient's benefit.[76] Thus, temperance allows the self-mastery necessary to have the clarity of mind to recognize the condition of the patient, to communicate effectively with them and their families, and to use the interventions necessary for their good, and in conformity with their wishes, rather than to be driven by self-interest. It is possible to see that the virtue of temperance is a key virtue in ensuring that the doctor keeps him- or herself responsive to his or her patient's needs.

VII. Conclusion

Given the framework and the account of the virtues presented above, it is clear not only that virtue ethics has an important contribution to make in moral philosophy, but also that

[71] See eg *Day v Health Education England* [2017] ICR 917.

[72] Pellegrino and Thomasma (n 43) 118.

[73] C Peterson and MEP Seligman, *Character Strengths and Virtues: A Handbook and Classification* (Oxford University Press, 2004), 386; E Telfer, 'Temperance' (1990) 16 Journal of Medical Ethics 157.

[74] See R Harris, 'Analysis of Cases Resulting in Doctors Being Erased or Suspended from the Medical Register' (2015), https://www.gmc-uk.org/-/media/documents/Analysis_of_cases_resulting_in_doctors_being_suspended_or_erased_from_the_medical_register_FINAL_REPORT_Oct_2015.pdf_63534317.pdf accessed 15 July 2019.

[75] Miles (n 37) 139.

[76] Pellegrino and Thomasma (n 43) 120.

virtue has occupied a place in the tradition of ethical reflection on medicine, and can continue to contribute and enhance medical ethical reflection. Virtue ethics as a normative approach has much to offer to the debates surrounding some of the most important issues in medical ethics. Virtue ethics also recognizes and gives due weight to the fact that doctors work in a complex environment, and that their task is not simply a question of deploying knowledge and skills, but of making moral judgements. Making judgements about what is a correct course of action for the good of the patient and putting it into practice is often difficult, and the virtues are required for the doctor to judge and act well in accordance with the good of the patient, judged according to the ends of medicine. Virtue ethics not only makes a contribution to the key normative questions of our time, but also provides an emphasis on dispositions and the character of doctors as they navigate the complex theoretical, technical, and moral landscape that is the reality of modern medical practice.

In terms of the interaction between virtue and medical law, it has been shown that virtue ethics forbids certain actions which are inherently contrary to virtue, because they do not have a mean between vices of excess and defect. Where those actions are clearly harmful to the common good, the law has a role in discouraging them through threat of punishment and sanctions. Furthermore, virtue ethics can be used to provide a method of critically analysing legal judgements related to medical disputes, and the extent to which they have promoted and upheld virtuous action in each case. An example of such analysis is provided by Jones in this present volume with regard to a virtue ethics approach to finding the mean appropriate to treatment and care, and the extent to which case law has facilitated this (see Chapter 8, this volume). Finally, medical law can be seen as a tool in helping to sustain and shape an ethos in medicine which makes a positive contribution to cultivating virtue. Given what has been outlined in this chapter, it is clear that virtue ethics is highly relevant to medical ethics, and medical law can help to shape medical practice by promoting virtue and deterring vice. However, examination of the interaction between medical law and virtue remains an area which is largely unexplored.

Bibliography

Anscombe, GEM, *Human Life, Action and Ethics* (Imprint Academic, 2005).

Aristotle, *Nichomachean Ethics* (C Rowe (tr), Oxford University Press, 2002).

Beauchamp, TL and Childress, JF, *Principles of Biomedical Ethics* (6th edn, Oxford University Press, 2009).

Broad, CD, *Five Types of Ethical Theory* (Routledge, 2014).

Chapell, T, 'Virtue Ethics in the Twentieth Century' in DC Russell (ed), *The Cambridge Companion to Virtue Ethics* (Cambridge University Press, 2013).

Childress, JF, 'The Place of Autonomy in Bioethics' in S Holland (ed), *Arguing about Bioethics* (Routledge, 2012).

Devettere, RJ, *Practical Decision Making in Healthcare Ethics: Cases, Concepts and the Virtue of Prudence* (4th edn, Georgetown University Press, 2016).

Dworkin, G, *The Theory and Practice of Autonomy* (Cambridge University Press, 1988).

General Medical Council, 'Good Medical Practice' (2013), https://www.gmc-uk.org/-/media/documents/good-medical-practice---english-1215_pdf-51527435.pdf accessed 15 July 2019.

Greasley, K and Kaczor, CR, *Abortion Rights: For and Against* (Cambridge University Press, 2018).

Hare, RM, 'A Utilitarian Approach' in H Kuhse and P Singer (eds), *A Companion to Bioethics* (Wiley-Blackwell, 2012).

Herring, *Medical Law and Ethics* (7th edn, Oxford University Press, 2018).

Hofman, B, 'Medicine as Practical Wisdom (Phronesis)' (2002) 1 Poiesis & Praxis 135.
Jones, WHS, Withington, ET, Smith, WD, and Potter, P (trs) *Hippocrates* (Harvard University Press, 2014).
Kaczor, CR, *The Ethics of Abortion: Women's Rights, Human Life, and the Question of Justice* (2nd edn, Routledge, 2015).
Kristjánsson, K, 'Phronesis as an Ideal in Professional Medical Ethics: Some Preliminary Positionings and Problematics' 36 Theoretical Medicine and Bioethics 299.
Louden, RB, 'On Some Vices of Virtue Ethics' in R Crisp and M Slote (eds), *Virtue Ethics* (Oxford University Press, 1997).
MacIntyre, A, *After Virtue* (2nd edn, Duckworth, 1985).
Marcum, JA, *The Virtuous Physician* (Springer, 2012).
McKie, J, Richardson, J, Singer, PD, and Kuhse, H, *The Allocation of Health Care Resources: An Ethical Evaluation of the 'QALY' Approach* (Ashgate, 1998).
Miles, SH, *The Hippocratic Oath and the Ethics of Medicine* (Oxford University Press, 2005).
Montgomery, K, *How Doctors Think: Clinical Judgment and the Practice of Medicine* (Oxford University Press, 2005).
Nord, E, *Cost Value Analysis in Health Care: Making Sense of QALYs* (Cambridge University Press, 1999).
Pellegrino, ED, *The Philosophy of Medicine Reborn* (University of Notre Dame Press, 2008).
Pellegrino, ED and Thomasma, DC, *The Virtues in Medical Practice* (Oxford University Press, 1993).
Percival, T, *Medical Ethics, or, A Code of Institutes and Precepts, Adapted to the Conduct of Physicians and Surgeons* (Cambridge University Press, 2014).
Peterson, C and Seligman, MEP, *Character Strengths and Virtues: A Handbook and Classification* (Oxford University Press, 2004).
Ross, D, *The Right and the Good* (Oxford University Press, 2002).
Telfer, E, 'Temperance' 16 Journal of Medical Ethics 157.
Tonti-Filippini, N, *About Bioethics: Philosophical and Theological Approaches* (Connor Court Publishing, 2011).
Wittgenstein, L, *Philosophical Investigations* (GEM Anscombe, PMS Hacker, and J Sculte (trs), 4th edn, Wiley-Blackwell, 2009).

2

Feminism, Ethics of Care, and Medical Ethics

Jonathan Herring

I. Introduction

Care ethics has become a highly influential approach to ethical questions. It has found considerable support among feminist commentators, although it is not inevitably feminist in nature. This chapter will describe its main themes and then explore its significance for medical law.

The literature on ethics of care is voluminous.[1] It is sometimes assumed that ethics of care is just about interpersonal relationships of a certain kind and so not of 'broader' significance. That may have been true in the early literature, but now ethics of care is used to consider issues ranging from international relations to environmental policies.[2] It has been developed into a fully-fledged moral theory in its own right.

II. The Origins of an Ethic of Care

Contemporary understandings of an ethic of care are normally traced back to Carol Gilligan's *In a Different Voice*,[3] although no doubt its origins lie much further back than that.[4] That book was a critique of Lawrence Kohlberg's suggestion that women, on average, had a lower moral development than men. His argument was that moral maturity involved a progression from a 'pre-conventional level', where the actor was motivated by a desire to please authority figures, through to a 'convention level', where the motivation was to conform to the rules of a group; and finally a 'post-convention level', where the individual used abstract universal principles to evaluate conventional rules. Kohlberg argued that relying on that approach, more men than women were found in the post-conventional level. Women,

[1] Leading works on an ethic of care include: C Gilligan, *In a Different Voice* (Harvard University Press, 1982); J Tronto, *Moral Boundaries* (Routledge, 1993); S Sevenhuijsen, *Citizenship and the Ethics of Care* (Routledge, 1998); N Noddings, *Starting at Home: Caring and Social Policy* (University of California Press, 2002); E Feder Kittay, *Love's Labour: Essays on Women, Equality and Dependency* (Routledge, 1999); R Groenhout, *Connected Lives: Human Nature and an Ethics of Care* (Rowman & Littlefield, 2004); V Held, *The Ethics of Care* (Oxford University Press, 2006); D Engster, *The Heart of Justice: Care Ethics and Political Theory* (Oxford University Press, 2007); J Bridgeman, *Parental Responsibility, Young Children and Healthcare Law* (Cambridge University Press, 2009); J Herring, *Caring and the Law* (Hart, 2013) (from which material for this chapter is taken); S Collins, *The Core of Care Ethics* (Palgrave, 2015); M Barnes, T Brannelly, L Ward, et al, *Ethics of Care: Critical Advances in International Perspective* (Policy Press, 2015); R Harding, R Fletcher, and C Beasley, *Revaluing Care in Theory, Law and Policy* (Routledge, 2016); C Rogers, *Intellectual Disability and Being Human: A Care Ethics Model* (Routledge, 2016); R Harding, *Duties to Care* (Cambridge University Press, 2017); J Herring, *Law and the Relational Self* (Cambridge University Press, 2019).

[2] eg Held (n 1).

[3] Gilligan (n 1).

[4] eg Groenhout (n 1) draws on the writing of Augustine.

Jonathan Herring, *Feminism, Ethics of Care, and Medical Ethics* In: *Philosophical Foundations of Medical Law*. Edited by: Andelka M Phillips, Thana C de Campos, and Jonathan Herring, Oxford University Press (2019).
DOI: 10.1093/oso/9780198796558.003.0003

he claimed, typically did not move beyond the conventional level. In particular, he argued that generally women focused on their conflicting responsibilities to people, rather than looking at their position in terms of abstract principles.

Gilligan in reply challenged Kohlberg's assumptions about which forms of moral reasoning were superior. She rejected the assumption that using universal abstract principles revealed more moral sophistication than reasoning using emotional and relational arguments. She suggested that women using this form of thinking were speaking with a 'different voice'—one that emphasized relationships, connections, and nurturing over rational thought and competing rights. Women focused on the importance of preserving ongoing relationships and balancing their responsibilities. Individuals were understood primarily in the context of their relationships.

There are now few who claim that ethics of care are a particularly female method of thinking. For example, Nel Noddings's influential book, *Caring*, was subtitled *A Feminine Approach to Ethics and Moral Education* in its 1984 edition, but subtitled *A Relational Approach to Ethics and Moral Education* in its 2013 edition. Indeed, even Gilligan herself later made it clear that her point was to question the assumptions about which kinds of moral reasoning are superior, rather than distinguishing between the way in which men and women think.[5] Her primary argument was that ethics of care provides a helpful alternative to standard moral approaches.

Before exploring the theory in detail, a brief overview of the theory will be provided. Ethics of care is summarized by Maria Drakopoulou as embracing

> a vision of human relationships and of society grounded upon the primacy of human connectedness, wherein care and compassion are seen as fundamental and where emotions, peaceful co-operation, empathy, friendship and responsibility are aspired to rather than universal, abstract, rational principles (autonomy, freedom, justice, equality and rights).[6]

Under an ethic of care, caring would become the most highly valued activity in society. Caring relationships would be seen as fulfilling an essential societal obligation. Social support systems would encourage and enable caring relationships to take place.[7]

An ethics of care would challenge the traditional legal tools of rights and responsibilities. The law and many ethical theories assume that we are competent, detached, independent people who are entitled to have our rights of self-determination and autonomy fiercely protected.[8] These key rights protect the individual from interference form others. An ethic of care approach, however, would argue that a more accurate picture of the self is that we are ignorant, vulnerable, interdependent individuals, whose strength and reality is not in our autonomy, but in our relationships with others.

This highlights the key difference between an ethic of care approach and alternative approaches. While traditional approaches start with individuals and determine what rights an individual has or what course of action will promote the well-being of individuals, an

5 Gilligan (n 1).

6 M Drakopoulou, 'The Ethic of Care, Female Subjectivity and Feminist Legal Scholarship' (2000) 8 Feminist Legal Studies 199.

7 O Hankivsky, *Social Policy and the Ethic of Care* (University of British Columbia Press, 2004).

8 J Herring, *Vulnerable Adults and the Law* (Oxford University Press, 2016), ch 2; Herring, *Law and the Relational Self* (n 1).

ethic of care approach starts with caring relationships and asks what interventions would promote those relationships. Legal interventions, rights, and interests are not designed to protect individuals per se, so much as upholding and maintaining networks of relationships of care. As Tove Petersen explains, at the heart of most ethical theory is a core value: 'deontology accentuates rights; the theories of justice emphasize justice; and the utilitarian tradition values the society's overall well-being'.[9] For ethics of care, the core value is care. It is, therefore, essential to have a sufficient definition of care.

III. The Definition of Care

Defining care has proved not straightforward and some of the critics of ethics of care have, understandably, complained that the ambiguity over the nature of care makes the approach unworkable. One of the most cited definitions of care is that of Bernice Fischer and Joan Tronto:

> a species of activity that includes everything we do to maintain, contain, and repair our 'world' so that we can live in it as well as possible. That world includes our bodies, ourselves, and our environment.[10]

That seems a very wide definition and could potentially cover so many activities that it would rob care ethics of a distinctive focus.

The UK Government has used the following definition of a carer:

> A carer spends a significant proportion of their life providing unpaid support to family or potentially friends. This could be caring for a relative, partner or friend who is ill, frail, disabled or has mental health or substance misuse problems.[11]

In 2018, the UK Government in its action plan on carers updated the definition:

> a carer is considered to be anyone who spends time looking after or helping a friend, family member or neighbour who, because of their health and care needs, would find it difficult to cope without this help regardless of age or whether they identify as a carer.[12]

There are some notable differences with the more recent definition. First, the 2018 definition seems to apply without any restriction as to the time: a few minutes of care would, technically, fall within this definition. By contrast, the 2008 definition required the carer to show they spent a significant proportion of their life caring. Second, the 2018 definition it is not limited to those who care for adults, but would seem to include child care within the

[9] T Pettersen, 'The Ethic of Care: Normative Structures and Empirical Implications' (2011) 54 Health Care Analysis 51.

[10] B Fisher and J Tronto, 'Towards a Feminist Theory of Caring' in D Cheal (ed), *Family: Critical Concepts in Sociology* (Routledge, 1999), 34.

[11] HM Government, *Carers at the Heart of 21st-Century Families and Communities* (The Stationery Office, 2008), 18.

[12] Department of Health and Social Care, *Carers Action Plan 2018–2020* (DoHSC, 2018), 4.

definition.[13] Third, the 2018 definition is broad in terms of those who receive care. There is no need to show that the person is disabled or ill, as required in the 2008 definition, but simply that they will find it difficult to cope without the care. Finally, the 2008 definition only applied to family members and only 'potentially' friends. The 2018 definition clearly covers friends, and indeed neighbours. However, it should be noted that it is designed not to apply to 'professional carers'.

Other definitions seek to list the kinds of activities which might be regarded as care:

> washing, feeding, getting in and out of bed, assistance with toileting, giving medication, changing dressings, giving injections or catheritistaion, dealing with incontinence, assisting with paperwork and personal business including managing money, negotiation and liaison with 'professional' caring agencies and staff, providing transport and undertaking household tasks.[14]

As is clear from the definitions discussed so far, there is dispute over the extent to which care should be seen as a practice, a value, or a virtue. It is perhaps best understood as a combination of these. Virginia Held[15] has suggested that care is best seen as a cluster of practices and values. Tronto appears to take a similar approach and identifies four sub-elements of care: (1) attentiveness, aware of need; (2) responsibility, a willingness to respond and take care of need; (3) competence, providing effective care; and (4) responsiveness, considering the views of others and avoiding abuse.[16] Developing these and other writings, I have developed an approach to defining care as being categorized under four key markers:[17]

- meeting needs;
- respect;
- responsibility; and
- relationality.

These may be exhibited in different degrees. While not providing a definition as such, they provide an indication of the extent to which an activity is or is not care. Where all four markers are clearly present, there is undoubtedly care. When these markers are shown to a lesser extent, the behaviour moves away from the central understanding of care. The terms need further explanation.

A. Meeting Needs

Caring relationships involve meeting the needs of others. Care is not therefore a feeling, but an activity. One that produces a good. Hence, many care ethicists distinguish between caring *about* and caring *for*.[18] Caring about something can be seen as essentially an attitude

[13] The 2008 document makes it clear that although unclear on its face, the definition was not intended to apply to children.
[14] M Barnes, *Caring and Social Justice* (Palgrave, 2006), 6.
[15] Held (n 1) 34, 40.
[16] Tronto (n 1) 125–35.
[17] These are developed in more detail in Herring, *Caring and the Law* (n 1) ch 2.
[18] Tronto (n 1) 127–34.

of mind, whereas caring for involves doing something. Seeing it simply as a virtue or disposition loses sight of the fact that care is labour of political and economic significance.[19] The fact that caring involves meeting a need is in line with Joan Tronto's somewhat controversial point that caring in an incompetent way may not constitute caring.[20] However, as emphasized below, care must be seen in terms of a relationship and so there may be a caring relationship even if there is the occasional burnt meal or blouse!

But if care is about meeting needs, what is a need? I argue that they should be understood in a broad way to cover those things that give life meaning and value. They can cover basic biological needs (eg food and shelter), but also emotional and relational needs. So understood, care ranges from managing financial issues and working through bureaucracies, to a cosy chat or playing a game. My understanding is, therefore, broader than that of Daniel Engster, who restricts care to helping people meet their basic needs, which includes 'everything we do to help individuals to meet their vital biological needs, develop or maintain their basic capabilities, and avoid or alleviate unnecessary or unwanted pain and suffering, so that they can survive, develop, and function in society'.[21] I think Engster's list does not pay sufficient weight to the meeting of emotional needs, which are important for human flourishing.

B. Respect

Respect involves treating the other person as an individual and not simply as an object: seeking to identify and respond to the other's unique needs and not following a tick box set of procedures. Robin Dillon[22] captures this with the word 'attention' and argues:

> The term 'care' denotes here an epistemic attitude, understood as a moral ideal of attention: a commitment to attend, with intensely focused perception to all aspects of the irreducible particularity of individual human persons in their concrete contexts.

Respectful care requires empathy, seeking to identify the individual's perception and to anticipate their needs. It involves ensuring there is proper consent. It also involves treating the person in a dignified way. This may involve, for example, ensuring more intimate aspects of care are done in private and showing due respect for the person's abilities. It also involves being alert to how the other person is experiencing the care. It certainly means that to amount to care, there must be no exploitation or abuse.

C. Responsibility

Good care involves accepting responsibility towards another. That means not just caring when it is convenient to do so. For many people, however, there must be a balancing of

[19] Hence, those who see an ethic of care as a form of virtue ethics are misguided in failing to appreciate its political significance.
[20] Tronto (n 1) 127–34.
[21] Engster (n 1) 28.
[22] R Dillon, 'Respect and Care' (1992) 22 Canadian Journal of Philosophy 105, 128.

caring responsibilities. Responsibility is important in care because parties need to rely on care and need to have care that is consistent and if it is to be respectful, given by someone who has got to know the other. People need to arrange care and balance responsibilities, and that may require depending on others to provide care.

Responsibilities to care arise from our relationships to others. The significance of referring to responsibilities is that it challenges the emphasis that is placed on autonomy and choice in much current thinking. As Ruth Groenhout points out:

> The problem is that many of the most morally weighty relationships we find ourselves in are often both unchosen and constitutive of identity in crucial ways. In such relationships, weighing aggregate interests to determine whether one does (or does not) have a responsibility to another seems a deeply flawed method of determining normative status. Deciding whether or not to get up at night to comfort my infant by calculating whether her interests or mine are weightier seems perverse.[23]

There are, however, dangers in this kind of argument. Simply because two people are in a caring relationship does not thereby deprive others of any responsibility. The state and others have an obligation to intervene if they were aware that the relationship was abusive and to ensure an appropriate sharing of the burdens of care. Joan Tronto[24] uses the phrase 'privileged irresponsibility', which captures the idea that the most advantaged in society often ignore their caring responsibilities or purchase care services to delegate them.

D. Relationality

At the heart of caring is relationship. Too much academic writing and the public discourse divide people up into 'carers' and 'cared for'. Charitable groups focus on promoting the rights of carers. Governments produce documents promoting policies for carers.[25] This creates an artificial divide between those who are carers and those who receive care. Rather than promoting the interests of carers, an ethic of care should seek to promote caring relationships.

Peter Beresford has captured the concerns over the idea of care well:

> The reality seems to be that while care might be regarded by many of us as a good idea in principle and something that some people might need at some time, few of us identify with it for ourselves and actually want to be 'cared for' in this sense. There is a strong reluctance to see ourselves or to be in this position, because it implies dependence. Care is a concept that is primarily associated with children. Models for adult caring have tended to be borrowed from childcare and grow out of the unequal relationships associated with looking after children. This has been the basis for many people's assumptions and understanding of such care.[26]

[23] R Groenhout, 'Book Review' (2017) 43 Social Theory and Practice 214, 215.

[24] Tronto (n 1) 125.

[25] eg HM Government, *Recognised, Valued and Supported: Next Steps for the Carers Strategy* (HM Government, 2010).

[26] P Beresford, *What Future for Care?* (Joseph Rowntree Foundation, 2008), 4.

It is important, therefore, for caring relationships to require both (or all) parties to be open to receiving the support and help of the other. Caring should be about a reciprocal relationship. As Carol Gilligan writes: 'The ideal of care is thus an activity of relationships, of seeing and responding to need, taking care of the world by sustaining the web of connection so that no one is left alone.'[27] In a caring relationship, the parties are contributing care to the other: be that in terms of a psychological, emotional, or physical sense. Michael Fine and Caroline Glendinning capture this importance of the relational aspect of care in these words:

> Recent studies of care suggest that qualities of reciprocal dependence underlie much of what is termed 'care'. Rather than being a unidirectional activity in which an active caregiver does something to a passive and dependent recipient, these accounts suggest that care is best understood as the product or outcome of the relationship between two or more people.[28]

This relational aspect is also important because it puts the activities within their context, a context which provides those acts with meaning. The provision of care only makes sense and can be properly understood when placed in the context of the parties' relationships. An act of caring for the parties can have a meaning well beyond the here and now. It may reflect a long-standing commitment or a mutual responsibility. The act may have overtones recalling aspects of the relationship many years ago.

A critic of relational care may claim it idealizes the situation, especially with those with profound needs.[29] Diemut Bubeck argues that a key element of caring is that it

> involves ... a one-sided dependency of the person in need of care on the prospective carer. Their relationship is not one between equals or of equal bargaining strength since the carer has the power to withhold care and the cared for's needs have to be met. This power differential is irreducible since the needs to be met cannot be met by those in need themselves.[30]

This raises an important concern about my approach. However, the nature of power in a caring relationship is not straightforward. A study of 'carers' of patients with Alzheimer's found recipients of care resisting the attempts of others to provide care.[31] Some caregivers felt powerless in the situation. The pressures they face can mean they feel far from in charge in the relationship. There is a mutual powerlessness in the relationship. I repeat, this is not to say abuse cannot take place under the 'guise' of a relationship, but in a good caring relationship the issue of who has power over who is a non-question.

I suspect critics of the relational approach to care over-emphasize the rational and physical aspects of a relationship. A severely disabled patient might not readily be able to offer care in the traditional sense of offering services to the other. Objectively comprehensible

[27] Gilligan (n 1) 73.

[28] M Fine and C Glendinning, 'Dependence, Independence or Inter-Dependence? Revisiting the Concepts of Care and Dependency' (2005) 25 Ageing and Society 601, 619.

[29] E Feder Kittay, 'Dependency, Difference and the Global Ethic of Longterm Care' (2005) 13 Journal of Political Philosophy 433.

[30] D Bubeck, *Care, Gender and Justice* (Clarendon Press, 1995), 141.

[31] C Chorn Dunham and J Harms Cannon, '"They're Still in Control Enough to Be in Control": Paradox of Power in Dementia Caregiving' (2008) 22 Journal of Aging Studies 45.

communication may even be difficult. But relationships are made up of more than the doing of deeds and the saying of words. A touch, an expression, the slightest smile, can convey great warmth. Further, the care needs to be seen in the context of the whole relationship between the parties and while appearing more one-sided at this point in time, when looked at in the context of the whole relationship between the parties, it will be viewed differently.

IV. Central Themes in an Ethic of Care Approach

Having discussed the definition of care, some of the key themes in ethics of care will now be explored.

A. The Centrality of Care

At the heart of an ethic of care is the claim that caring is the highest good and of the greatest social value. It is a universal experience, which is an inevitable part of being human and necessary for our survival. Daniel Engster claims that humans have an innate evolutionary disposition to care.[32] The importance of care rests in part on an acknowledgement that we are all vulnerable. That claims needs more explanation.

Selma Sevenhuijsen claims that 'all people are vulnerable, dependent and finite, and that we all have to find ways of dealing with this in our daily existence and in the values which guide our individual and collective behaviour'.[33] It is because of this innate vulnerability that our care of each other is so important. Martha Fineman is a leading proponent of this vulnerability approach. She argues:

> The vulnerability approach recognizes that individuals are anchored at each end of their lives by dependency and the absence of capacity. Of course, between these ends, loss of capacity and dependence may also occur, temporarily for many and permanently for some as a result of disability or illness. Constant and variable throughout life, individual vulnerability encompasses not only damage that has been done in the past and speculative harms of the distant future, but also the possibility of immediate harm. We are beings who live with the ever-present possibility that our needs and circumstances will change. On an individual level, the concept of vulnerability (unlike that of liberal autonomy) captures this present potential for each of us to become dependent based upon our persistent susceptibility to misfortune and catastrophe.[34]

We are all profoundly dependent on others for our physical and psychological well-being. Part of our vulnerability leads from our embodiment. We like to present our bodies as self-contained and secure structures. In fact, our bodies are leaky and in a constant change of

[32] D Engster, 'Care in the State of Nature' in D Engster and M Hamington (eds), *Care Ethics and Political Theory* (Oxford University Press, 2015).

[33] Sevenhuijsen (n 1).

[34] M Fineman, 'The Vulnerable Subject: Anchoring Equality in the Human Condition' in M Fineman (ed), *Transcending the Boundaries of Law: Generations of Feminism and Legal Theory* (Routledge, 2011), 168. See also Herring, *Law and the Relational Self* (n 1).

flux.[35] Our bodies are insecure and vulnerable. Our society has built up a wide range of structures and forms of assistance which disguise our vulnerability.

Susan Dodds also argues that we need a legal and social system which is not premised on individualistic conceptions of autonomy, but on an acceptance of our vulnerability:

> A vulnerability-centered view of the self and of persons is better able to capture many of our moral motivations and intuitions than can be captured by an autonomy-focused approach. We are all vulnerable to the exigencies of our embodied, social and relational existence and, in recognizing this inherent human vulnerability, we can see the ways in which a range of social institutions and structures protect us against some vulnerabilities, while others expose us to risk. We do not have to view our obligations towards those who lack the capacity to develop or retain autonomy as having a different source from our obligations towards those whose autonomy is made vulnerable due to a degree of dependency. It may be easier to recognize the social value of provision of care if it is viewed as something on which we all have been dependent and on which we are all likely to be dependent at different points in our lives, rather than altruistic behaviour extended to those who lack 'full personhood.'[36]

In summary, ethics of care criticizes other general approaches to ethics as 'modelled on the experience of men in public life and in the marketplace'[37] and not appropriate for the lives of those caring. While the marketplace model is based on assumptions of our independence and need to pursue our own goals, an ethics of care has at its heart an acknowledgement of our vulnerability from which flows an acknowledgement of the importance of interdependency and care. The law and society should above all be seeking to uphold and maintain caring relationships. It is because we are, have been, and will be dependent on others that caring is so important.[38]

B. Intermingled Interests

At the heart of an ethic of care is a belief that people are relational. Our identities and interests are tied up with others. This means that separating out the interests of parties in an intimate relationship is problematic, if not impossible. If good things happen to someone in a positive relationship with another, then that is good for both of them. Similarly, harming someone harms those with whom they are in relationship. Supporters of an ethic of care do not need to reject entirely the notion of an individual self, but simply recognize that its identity and nature can only be appreciated through relation to others.[39] As Catriona Mackenzie writes: 'To be a person is to be a temporally extended embodied subject whose identity is constituted in and through one's lived bodily engagement with the world and others.'[40]

[35] J Herring and P-L Chau, 'My Body, Your Body, Our Bodies' (2007) 15 Medical Law Review 54.
[36] S Dodds, 'Depending on Care: Recognition of Vulnerability and the Social Contribution of Care Provision' (2007) 21 Bioethics 500, 507.
[37] Held (n 1) 23–4.
[38] Engster (n 1) 40.
[39] C Foster and J Herring, *Identity, Personhood and the Law* (Springer, 2017).
[40] C Mackenzie, 'Personal Identity, Narrative Integration and Embodiment' in S Campbell, L Meynell, and S Sherwin (eds), *Embodiment and Agency* (Pennsylvania State University Press, 2009).

C. The Importance of Responsibilities

Ethics of care emphasizes the importance of responsibilities within caring relationships. While not necessarily opposed to the idea of legal rights, it is wary of their dominance in the legal discourse, and the dangers that rights are used in an individualistic way. Supporters of ethics of care argue that rather than the primary focus of the legal or ethical enquiry being whether 'is my right to do X?', the question should be: 'What is my proper obligation within the context of this relationship?'[41] Rather than the law promoting people's freedom from responsibility, the focus should be on how the law can enable people to fulfil their responsibilities. Rights should primarily exist to enable people to carry out their responsibilities.[42] As Eva Feder Kittay puts it:[43]

> Responsibilities are usually understood to derive from conceptions of the good, while duties are derived from a concept of the right. Instead, in a theory of justice guided by an ethics of care, responsibilities are based not only on individual conceptions of the good, but also on the legitimate (i.e., non-coercive)—even if not fully chosen—connections that we bear to one another.

The understanding of responsibilities within care ethics is very different from the standard understanding. The classic liberal perspective is that one is 'born free' and that any responsibilities one takes must be in some sense voluntarily assumed. However, for an ethic of care approach, with its starting point being that people are relational, then the supposition is that there will be responsibilities for others. We are born into relationships which carry responsibilities with them. So, the response to a person in need is not an assessment of the extent you might owe them an obligation to assist, but rather an assessment of how one can meet that need, giving other caring responsibilities.[44] This approach is captured by Noddings:

> an ethic of caring implies a limit on our [moral] obligation. Our obligation is limited and delimited by relation. We are never free, in the human domain, to abandon our preparedness to care; but, practically, if we are meeting those in our inner circles adequately as ones-caring and receiving those linked to our inner circles by formal chains of relation, we shall limit the calls upon our obligation quite naturally. We are not obliged to summon the 'I must' if there is no possibility of completion in the other. I am not obliged to care for starving children in Africa, because there is no way for this caring to be completed in the other unless I abandon the caring to which I am obligated.[45]

Therefore, the question is not 'is there a good reason to restrict my freedom?', but rather: 'Is it possible to have some freedom, given the responsibilities of those I am connected to?' This might, to some, seem shocking. Surely, they say, we should start with a presumption

[41] Held (n 1) 15.
[42] F Williams, 'The Presence of Feminism in the Future of Welfare' (2002) 31 Economy and Society 502.
[43] E Feder Kittay, 'A Theory of Justice as Fair Terms of Social Life Given Our Inevitable Dependency and Our Inextricable Interdependency' in D Engster and M Harrington (eds), *Care Ethics and Political Theory* (Oxford University Press, 2015).
[44] S Sevenhuisen, 'Caring in the Third Way: The Relation between Obligation, Responsibility and Care in *Third Way* Discourse' (2000) 20 Critical Social Policy 5.
[45] Noddings (n 1) 86.

of freedom, rather than responsibility. However, I suggest two reasons why we should not. First, that reflects the reality of life for most people. Our lives are not marked by freedom, but by our responsibilities to others. Second, it is in our responsibilities that relationships flourish and in our relationships that we flourish. As Polona Curk puts it: 'We take responsibility for each other because we continue to need each other and because we establish meaningful relationships through taking responsibility for each other.'[46]

D. The Importance of Non-Abstraction

Ethics of care rejects abstract moral rules. The particular context and concrete reality of the individual, their relationships, and their histories need to be taken into account. What might work for one group of people in one situation will not work in another. Hence, those taking an ethics of care approach will often say in the face of an ethical dilemma, 'well it all depends on the circumstances of the case'. As Nel Noddings writes: 'Since so much depends on the subjective experience of those involved in ethical encounters, conditions are rarely "sufficiently similar" for me to declare that you must do what I must do.'[47]

E. Emotions

Much of the law emphasizes the importance of rationality and intellect. The concepts of mental capacity, informed consent, and compliance with standards expected by a responsible body of opinion all privilege in legal discourse logical thought and sound judgment. There is nothing wrong in that, but the emotional side of humanity is lost. The love which goes on caring and caring; the grief, disappointment, frustration, anger, and despair, which are all part of life, find no place. This means in legal cases the law can struggle to develop a response to issues which are not readily reducible to an economic value nor expressed in terms of individualized rights. That can be seen, for example, in the law of tort, where damages for an economic loss are readily recoverable, whereas loss for distress, unwanted pregnancy, or bereavement finds the courts struggling to produce a coherent response. An ethic of care seeks to acknowledge the role that both emotion and rationality play in relationships.

F. Justice and Care

Carol Gilligan contrasted an ethic of care with an ethic of justice.[48] She was not advocating that there was no role for justice in an ethic of care, but the relationship between the two concepts has proved controversial among care ethicists. Without some conception of justice, care ethics could be used to justify harmful or manipulative activities. We have

[46] P Curk, 'Passions, Dependencies, Selves: A Theoretical Psychoanalytic Account of Relational Responsibility' in C Lind, H Keating, and J Bridgeman (eds), *Taking Responsibility, Law and the Changing Family* (Routledge, 2011).
[47] Noddings (n 1) 5.
[48] Gilligan (n 1).

talked about ensuring that care obligations are distrusted fairly, but that inevitably involves some notions of justice.

Most contemporary care ethicists agree that there needs to be some kind of 'meshing of care and justice'.[49] Virginia Held writes particularly persuasively on this issue. She explains the differences between the concepts in this way:

> An ethic of justice focuses on questions of fairness, equality, individual rights, abstract principles, and the consistent application of them. An ethic of care focuses on attentiveness, trust, responsiveness to need, narrative nuance, and cultivating caring relations. Whereas an ethic of justice seeks a fair solution between competing individual interests and rights, an ethic of care sees the interest of carers and cared-for as importantly intertwined rather than as simply competing.[50]

However, she then makes it clear that an ethic of care incorporates justice:

> There can be care without justice. There has historically been little justice in the family, but care and life have gone on without it. There can be no justice without care, however, for without care no child would survive and there would be no persons to respect.[51]

Significantly, this understanding argues that care and justice actually need to work together. Held explains that care is the 'basic moral value' and justice needs to fit within that. Care is essential for people to survive and justice must not prevent care, but enable it and ensure a fair sharing of its burdens.[52] Without care, talk of justice would be meaningless. This means that justice must be understood in terms of care. As Selma Sevenhuijsen explains:

> Justice should be based on values such as reconciliation, reciprocity, diversity and responsibility, and on the willingness and ability of citizens to accept responsibility for each other's well-being. Justice, thus conceived, explicitly opens up discursive space for deliberating about what constitutes injustice or, in other words, for continuous reflection on which 'social evils' we need to address.[53]

G. Gender and Ethic of Care

There is debate over whether it is useful to see an ethic of care as necessarily feminist. There can be no doubt that anyone asking 'the women's question' (to adopt one definition of feminism) should be concerned about care.[54] Women undertake the vast majority of care work and therefore suffer, particularly from the inadequate weight placed on care in society's allocation of resources. Throughout history, care has been regarded as the work of 'slaves, servants, and women'.[55] Through the lowly treatment of care, the privileged position of men has

[49] Held (n 1) 128.
[50] Ibid 15.
[51] Ibid 17.
[52] Ibid 71–2.
[53] Sevenhuijsen (n 1) 145.
[54] Pe Bowden, *Caring: Gender Sensitive Ethics* (Routledge, 1997), 2.
[55] Tronto (n 1) 21.

been maintained.[56] The lack of attention paid to care is, therefore, one aspect of patriarchy.[57] For Joan Tronto, 'care is deeply implicated in existing structures of power and inequality'.[58]

While that does, I argue, make an ethic of care particularly appealing for feminists and, when seen in the broader feminist context, can provide a further argument in favour of adopting an ethic of care approach, there is no reason why a non-feminist could not also be attracted to an ethic of care approach. One could be drawn to an ethic of care independently of any feminist approach via, for example, virtue ethics[59] or religious belief.

As already mentioned, care work disadvantages participants in a range of ways. However, when considering the gender impact, there are complex intersections with race, disability, and other grounds of disadvantage. These mean that the lack of value of care impacts in a unique way on black women and disabled women, for example.[60]

H. Political Theory

In its early days, ethics of care may have appeared to have a narrow focus and be of particular relevance for dealing with intimate relationships, such as those of parent–child. However, as care ethics has developed, it is clear that its horizons are far wider than this. Indeed, an ethic of care has a considerable amount to say about politics and indeed international relationships.[61]

At Feder Kittay makes clear, valuing care requires state support:

> Without adequate care and assistance that has institutional support and protection, the possibilities of having a flourishing life under conditions of dependency are greatly diminished. Principles of justice that begin with an ethic of care and with inevitable human dependency will be ones that form around non-exploitation, non-deprivation or neglect, non-abuse, and sustaining bonds of care and assistance.[62]

If we start with the universal vulnerability and the obligation to meet the needs of those around us, this places responsibilities not only on individuals, but also on the state to support care and provide the facilities and framework that care needs.[63] The state has a further responsibility to ensure that care work is assigned fairly. Indeed, Fiona Robinson sees this as a key aspect of an ethics of care:

> Care ethics is a critical feminist theory that seeks to reveal the different forms of power that keep the values and activities of care hidden from 'public' view, and to demonstrate the devastating effects that ensue when care is consistently devalued, sidelined, and subordinated to the higher values of profit and military power.[64]

[56] Ibid.
[57] Ibid 7–8.
[58] Ibid 21.
[59] M Slote, *The Ethics of Care and Empathy* (Routledge, 2007), 172–3.
[60] O Hankivsky, 'Rethinking Care Ethics' (2014) 108 American Political Science Review 252.
[61] Engster and Hamington (n 32).
[62] Feder Kittay (n 43).
[63] Rogers (n 1) 34.
[64] F Robinson, 'Care Ethics, Political Theory, and the Future of Feminism' in Engster and Hamington (n 32).

Understood in this way, ethics of care is certainly not simply the ethics of private relations.[65] Indeed, a growing body of literature shows that care is an international issue. Barnes and colleagues write of:

> A greater awareness of the interconnectedness of humanity across national boundaries as well as within interpersonal networks requires a politics and practices that encompass care and justice . . .[66]

I. Disability

A major critique of an ethic of care is found in disability studies.[67] Many writers on care have presented the issue from the carer's perspective, such as the calls for 'carers' rights'. There is a danger in some ethic of care writing of assuming that a disability must be 'remedied' by care. Care involves interfering in the body of the individual, rather than changing societal provisions. Care certainly can be experienced in a negative way. Richard Woods contends:

> Disabled people have never demanded or asked for care! We have sought independent living, which means being able to achieve maximum independence and control over our own lives. The concept of care seems to many disabled people a tool through which others are able to dominate and manage our lives.[68]

As this quote indicates, care should not be seen as something a 'carer' does to the other, but as a tool used by the disabled person to achieve independence.[69] The focus should be on empowerment, control, and choice for those with disabilities. Some disability rights activists have argued for the use of the term 'helper' or 'personal assistant'.[70] Julia Twigg's recent qualitative research on older people's experiences of being bathed highlights this quite clearly:

> One person, strong and able, stands above and over another who is frail and physically vulnerable, forced to rely on their strength and goodwill. Being naked in the face of someone who is not, contains a powerful dynamic of domination and vulnerability, and it is often used in situations of interrogation and torture as a means of subjugating the individual.[71]

This is a powerful critique of care.[72] The best response to it from an ethic of care approach is to reiterate the importance of the relational model of care, and therefore to talk of caring relationships, rather than carers. The traditional division between the carer and person

65 Engster and Hamington (n 32).

66 M Barnes, T Brannelly, L Ward, et al, 'Introduction: The Critical Significance of Care' in Barnes et al (n 1) 7.

67 B Hughes, L McKie, D Hopkins, et al, 'Love's Labours Lost? Feminism, the Disabled People's Movement and an Ethic of Care' (2005) 39 Sociology 259.

68 Quoted in T Shakespeare, *Help* (Venture Press, 2000), 63.

69 J Morris, 'Impairment and Disability: Constructing an Ethics of Care that Promotes Human Rights' (2001) 16 Hypatia 1.

70 C Kelly, 'Making "Care" Accessible: Personal Assistance for Disabled People and the Politics of Language' (2011) 31 Critical Social Policy 562.

71 J Twigg, 'Carework as a Form of Bodywork' (2000) 20 Ageing and Society 389.

72 J Herring, 'The Disability Critique of Care' (2014) 8 Elder Law Review 2.

receiving care fails to capture the dynamic in caring relationships. It tends to emphasize the vulnerability of some, rather than recognizing the vulnerability of all. It paints the 'cared for' as passive. By seeing caring relationships, we can recognize that we are all givers and receivers of care—maybe in different ways, and the kinds of care involved are different. The language of caring relationships can capture the dynamic nature of relationships. Caregiving relationships change over time so that pigeonholing the parties into categories of carer and care receiver become artificial.

There is another important point here: the division of 'carer' is not only false because it imagines that one party to the relationship is the provider of the care, it also overlooks the point that the 'carer' may themselves be receiving care from others.[73] Further, negative attitudes about disability are reflected in negative attitudes about care. As Bill Hughes and colleagues[74] put it:

> the parties involved in the caring relationship are perpetually invalidated because the value of care is measured against the autonomous adult male who neither requires nor delivers care. To be a carer or cared for—male or female, disabled or non-disabled in either role—is to be found wanting, to be other in relation to the masculine subject of modernity, to be reduced to 'the other of the same'. Those who give and receive care are marginalized, 'used and wasted' bodies, existing, by and large, on the margins of what counts as the truly human community.

V. Ethics of Care and Medical Law

I move on now to expand on the particular issues for medical law gained by adopting an ethic of care perspective. Clearly, in the space available, I can do no more than highlight a few.[75] Before doing that, a little more needs to be said about the relationship between ethics of care and law more generally.

A. Ethics of Care and Law

It might be thought that the relationship between law and ethics of care is somewhat uneasy. Lawyers are called upon when relationships break down. Is not an approach based on promoting caring relations particularly inappropriate in a legal system which is trying to resolve disputes between people whose relationship has broken down? Indeed, legal solutions are typically designed to enable parties to move apart, rather than help them to continue their relationship. That is a fair point, but I suggest that this underplays the potential for law to use an ethic of care.

It is important to note that the law has a far greater influence on behaviour than cases which come to court. To take a trivial example, the law on illegal parking impacts on a far

73 N Watson, L McKie, B Hughes, et al, '(Inter)Dependence, Needs and Care: The Potential for Disability and Feminist Theorists to Develop an Emancipatory Model' (2010) 38 Sociology 221.

74 Hughes et al (n 67).

75 See Herring, *Caring and the Law* (n 1) ch 6; Herring (n 8) ch 7.

larger range of people than simply those who receive parking fines. Hence, the civil and criminal laws which respond to malpractice from medical professionals has a far greater impact in its encouragement of professionals' good conduct, than the very few cases that come to court.

Law can therefore be used powerfully to encourage people to act in a way which will promote caring relationships. A particularly good example might be the law dealing with how those lacking mental capacity will be treated. The Mental Capacity Act 2005 requirement that if someone is making a decision on behalf of a person who lacks capacity (P), then it should be made based on an assessment of P's behaviour, sends a powerful message about the treatment of those lacking capacity.

The public law can also do much to encourage and enable caring relationships. The laws on welfare payments, employment rights, and legal protections for those in caring relationships are an important part of enabling and encouraging care in a practical sense and in sending a powerful message about the way in which society values care.[76]

That said, there are dangers here. The more the public good of caring is emphasized, the more the danger that it becomes subject to legal and social regulation, inspection, and supervision. Caring relationships in their nature should be spontaneous, free, and individualized. These values will all be challenged by the kind of regime which could be attached to caring if the arguments of the public importance of care are recognized.

B. Autonomy and Ethics of Care

Autonomy plays a key role in medical law. To some medical ethicists, it is the most significant ethical principle, but even to those who would disagree with that, they would agree it is an important one. Joseph Raz defines it in this way:

> The ruling idea behind the ideal of personal autonomy is that people should make their own lives. The autonomous person is a (part) author of his own life. The ideal of personal autonomy is the vision of people controlling, to some degree, their own destiny, fashioning it through successive decisions throughout their lives.[77]

This individualist conception of autonomy is linked to a whole set of other ideas: self-sufficiency, self-sovereignty, moral independence, self-government, pluralism, and liberty.[78]

In terms of English medical law and ethics, this has led to a powerful protection for the right to bodily integrity: not to be given medical treatment without your consent, providing you have capacity.[79] Importantly, that right persists however foolish or immoral doctors or others may find your decision to be. The right of autonomy means that medical professionals should inform patients of the risks attached to operations and reasonable alternative procedures so they can exercise their right to choose whether or not to consent to the treatment.[80]

[76] A Stewart, 'Carers as Legal Subjects' in R Harding, R Fletcher, and C Beasley, *Revaluing Care in Theory, Law and Policy* (Routledge, 2016).

[77] J Raz, *The Morality of Freedom* (Oxford University Press, 1986), 369.

[78] M Fineman, *The Autonomy Myth* (New Press, 2004), 263.

[79] J Herring, *Medical Law and Ethics* (6th edn, Oxford University Press, 2016), ch 3.

[80] *Montgomery v Lanarkshire Health Board* [2015] UKSC 11.

Ethics of care supporters have been somewhat sceptical of autonomy, or at least the version presented above. An ethics of care would seek a more relational account of autonomy: one that recognizes that our plans, interests, and identities are constituted through our relationships with others.[81] Therefore, talking about making 'my decision' about 'my body' or 'my life' would be a perplexing idea for many ethic of care supporters. Our lives, interests, and plans are deeply entwined. Decisions must be made cooperatively in the context of and through these relationships, in a way which promotes their flourishing.

Lorraine Code argues that for supporters of individualized autonomy:

> Autonomous man is—and should be—self-sufficient, independent, and self-reliant, a self-realizing individual who directs his efforts towards maximizing his personal gains. His independence is under constant threat from other (equally self-serving) individuals: hence he devises rules to protect himself from intrusion. Talk of right, rational self-interest, expedience, and efficiency permeates his moral, social, and political discourse. In short, there has been a gradual alignment of autonomy with individualism.[82]

By contrast, at the heart of relational autonomy is a 'shared conviction ... that persons are socially embedded and that agents' identities are formed within the context of social relationships and shaped by a complex of intersecting social determinants, such as race, class, gender, and ethnicity'.[83] We are not constantly clashing rights with those we live with; rather, our interests are intertwined. People in close relationships seek a compromise which is good for 'us' and do not see it as a matter of weighing up competing interests. The intertwining of identities and interests means that to discuss 'my decision' is simply a fiction. Our decisions are constrained by the responsibilities and realities of our lives and the relationships within which we are embedded.[84]

Three consequences flow from this in a practical sense. The first is that assessments of capacity should be made in a relational way. Rather than a single individual being assessed by a medical professional alone to see if they have the capacity to make decisions, we should be aware that decision making should be seen as a relational matter and hence whether those involved in this network of caring relationships can make the decision.[85] Second, and an important caveat to that point, while an ethics of care is keen to promote caring relationships, it is also particularly alert to the dangers of abuse within relationships. Because it emphasizes the importance of relationships in establishing flourishing, they are particularly aware of how abusive relationships can be used to harm flourishing. This means that the law should be alert to not giving effect to decisions which are the product of an abusive, rather than a caring, relationship. Third, we need to balance the weight attached to autonomy with the responsibilities that flow from relationships.[86] People have freedom in their caring

[81] J Herring, *Relational Autonomy and Family Law* (Springer, 2015).

[82] L Code, 'Second Persons' in L Code (ed), *What Can She Know? Feminist Theory and the Construction of Knowledge* (Cornell University Press, 1991), 78.

[83] Ibid 4.

[84] J Nedelsky, 'Reconceiving Autonomy: Sources, Thoughts and Possibilities' (1989) 1 Yale Journal of Law and Feminism 7.

[85] R Harding, 'Care and Relationality: Supported Decision-Making under the UNCRPD' in R Harding, R Fletcher, and C Beasley, *Revaluing Care in Theory, Law and Policy* (Routledge, 2016).

[86] C Kong, 'The Convention for the Rights of Persons with Disabilities and Article 12: Prospective Feminist Lessons against the "Will and Preferences" Paradigm' (2015) 4 Laws 709.

functions and these relationships, but these are bounded by them and subject to restrictions flowing from them.[87] So it is the goal of relational autonomy to build up relationships that enhance our lives, rather than seeking to maximize freedom and thereby enhancing our lives.

C. Health

Ethics of Care has much to say about the understanding of health. Health is typically seen as the absence of disease and impairment. The standard approach is based on an image of a normal or perfect body and departures from this norm are characterized as disease or ill health. The role of medicine is to challenge these. Ethics of care provides a powerful challenge to these assumptions.[88] It would emphasize that vulnerability, leakiness, and dependence on others is a normal part of the human condition and is hardly a sign of ill health. We should recognize the need for assistance for others and our bodies changing and our minds failing as a normal part of human life. Our society has built up a wide range of structures and forms of assistance which disguise our mutual dependence. Indeed, we are forced by a wide range of societal pressures to disguise or mitigate our vulnerability so that we can behave in an acceptable way in the public realm. Elsewhere, I have argued:

> essential to the nature of human beings, and therefore to the concept of health is that we are vulnerable, interdependent and relational beings. The image of the capacitous, autonomous, self-sufficient adult is not, in fact the image most people either aspire to or want, even if they were capable of achieving it. The characteristics most people seek out in friends are not marked by such characteristics: they look for gentleness, openness, fun, a sense of the ridiculous. Characteristics as often found in those labelled ill or disabled, as much at the healthy. It is recognising that we in our nature vulnerable; that caring relationships are core to our being human; and that we need each other; that we might begin to find true health. We must never seek to hide from or be embarrassed by our precarious, leaky, interdependent bodies. True health is found not in the scalpel of the surgeon or the pill of the pharmacist; but in the touch of a lover; the smile of a child; and the wind in the hair.[89]

D. Best Interests

When a person is unable to make a decision for themselves, the standard approach in medical law is to make a decision based on an assessment of their best interests. English courts have recommended drawing up a list of the pros and cons of the alternative decisions available for the patient (P) and determining which will produce the best outcome for P. The court should focus on P's best interests and not take into account the interests of others or the wider community. However, an ethic of care approach would be sceptical of such an

[87] B Clough. 'What about Us? A Case for Legal Recognition of Interdependence in Informal Care Relationships' (2014) 36 Journal of Social Welfare and Family Law 129.
[88] J Herring, 'Health as Vulnerability; Interdependence and Relationality' (2016) 22 The New Bioethics 18.
[89] Ibid 22.

endeavour.[90] It assumes that we can determine what is best for P, without looking at the interests of those in caring relationships with P. An ethic of care would argue that we need to assess the interests of P in the context of and as constituted by the relationships which P is in. This involves looking at the history of the relationships. It is only in understanding where the relationship has travelled that we can understand what responsibilities might have arisen as a result. It also involves looking forward to what is likely to be undertaken during the course of the relationship in the future and asks why a decision now will (1) be a fair aspect of the relationship and (2) provide the best foundation of an ongoing caring relationship. We must focus on the particular caring relationships P is in rather than general rules about assessment. As Jo Bridgeman, writing about children, powerfully argues:

> unless consideration is given to the individual child, to the person they are, their personality, character, feelings of pleasure and pain, and relational interests (relationships with those upon whom they depend), determination about the best interests of the child are reached according to current ideas about the child and according to adult memories of childhood.[91]

VI. Other Feminist Approaches

Care ethics has certainly played a central role in contemporary feminist approaches to bioethics. Anne Donchin and Jackie Scully refer to the 'two distinct and distinctive areas of contribution to theory by feminist bioethics',[92] being care ethics and relational autonomy, which are closely linked.[93] Relational autonomy ideas have been explored in section V.B (above). Catriona Mackenzie and Natalie Stoljar explain that at the heart of relational autonomy is the claim that 'agents' identities are formed within the context of social relationships and shaped by a complex of intersecting social determinants, such as race, class, gender, and ethnicity'.[94]

It flows from this that the image of the independent, free, self-sufficient, self-defined person upon which traditional models of autonomy are based is a fiction. Our deeply relational nature means that the formation, communication, implementation, and conception of our plans for our lives are intertwined with others. We must be alert to the powerful influences that can impact on people's choices which can mean they are not fully their own. Further, we must also be aware that the promotion of autonomy is not about isolating people and giving them the information they need to make their decisions. It is about supporting and encouraging cooperative decision making and solution finding.

Most feminist writing has focused on particular issues, rather than seeking grand theories.[95] Indeed, as the discussion of care ethics has shown, much feminist analysis is

[90] For a detailed discussion, see C Foster and J Herring, *Welfare, Altruism and the Law* (Springer, 2016).

[91] Bridgeman, *Parental Responsibility* (n 1) 9.

[92] A Donchin and J Scully, 'Feminist Bioethics' in *Stanford Encyclopedia of Philosophy* (University of Stanford, 2014).

[93] For an attempted integration, see Herring, *Law and the Relational Self* (n 1).

[94] C Mackenzie and N Stoljar, *Relational Autonomy: Feminist Perspectives on Autonomy, Agency, and the Social Self* (Oxford University Press, 2000), 4.

[95] See eg: D Dickenson, *Property in the Body; Feminist Perspectives* (Cambridge University Press, 2007); K Hall, *Feminist Disability Studies* (Indiana University Press, 2011).

sceptical of using 'grand theories', rather than finding solutions to particular cases involving particular relationships. Plenty of examples can be found in the second half of this book.

VII. Conclusion

This chapter has sought to set out the main themes adopted by an ethic of care approach. It has also indicated some practical consequences of adopting such an approach. As with all overarching theories, it is not claimed that all supporters of an ethic of care will reach the same conclusions, but I hope I have successfully identified at least the questions they will ask.

I will now summarize some of the main themes. Under an ethic of care, the practices of caring would become highly valued in our society. Indeed, meeting needs through caring would be an essential activity for society. It would be a key role of the state to enable, encourage, and support caring to take place; to ensure a fair division of caring responsibility; and to protect people from relationships which were abusive, rather than caring.

Work would need to be done to ensure that the burden of caring did not fall on the few, but was shared across the community. On a broader scale internationally, a caring world would be one in which the essential needs of citizens around the world would be met. We should be seeking not only caring individuals, but caring institutions and governments.[96] Virginia Held calls for international practices of 'cultivating relations of trust, listening to the concerns of others, fostering international cooperation, and valuing interdependence'.[97]

Our legal structure would not be based on individualist models prioritizing autonomy and independence. It would recognize that we are typically weak, incapacitated, vulnerable people. The law should be based on a norm of enabling a cooperative and relational approach. Never should it be a matter of assessing a person in isolation; rather, each person's needs and rights would have to be considered in the context of their relationships.

An ethic of care, therefore, offers a radical alternative to mainstream ethical approaches. It elevates caring relationships as the focus of attention and requires a shift away from abstract principles and individualism, towards tailoring a response to ethical dilemmas which promotes love, care, and mutual flourishing.

[96] J Tronto, 'Creating Caring Institutions: Politics, Plurality, and Purpose' (2010) 4 Ethics and Social Welfare 158.
[97] Held (n 1) 48.

3

The Natural Law Foundations of Medical Law

Robert P George and Christopher O Tollefsen

I. Introduction

Natural law theorists hold that the foundations of morality are in the well-being and fulfilment of human persons, individually, and in the communities they form. When natural law theorists turn, therefore, to questions of medical practice and medical law, they seek to reveal the foundations of that practice and law precisely in prescriptions about well-being and human fulfilment, for both individuals and their communities. The effort is normative: no practice, and no body of law, is entirely as it should be; but the effort is also explanatory, demonstrating that certain features of law and practice are as they are, or were as they were, because of the insights into human well-being and fulfilment, and the moral principles specifying its integral directiveness, that explicitly or implicitly guided the development of medicine and medical law.

This chapter seeks to identify: first, the basic human goods that are the foundational principles of the natural law; second, a derived set of moral norms that emerge from consideration of the integral directiveness or prescriptivity of those foundational principles; and, third, the implications of these norms for medical practice and medical law, specifically as regards four questions. First, how should medical practice and medical law be structured with respect to the intentional taking of human life by members of the medical profession? As we will see, a sound answer to this question requires consideration of the so-called Principle of Double Effect. Second, who, in the clinical setting, has authority for medical decision making, and what standards should guide their decisions? Third, what standards should govern the distribution of health-care resources in society, and do those standards give reasons for thinking, from the natural law standpoint, that there is a 'right to health care'? Fourth, what concern should be shown in medical practice and medical law for the rights of 'physician conscience'?

II. Foundations of the Natural Law

To reiterate: the foundations of the natural law are basic goods that are constitutive aspects of the well-being and fulfilment of human persons, individually and in community, and specifically the principles that direct human persons to realize or participate in those goods—goods that are intrinsically as well as instrumentally constitutive of the well-being of human persons. In being constitutive of our fulfilment as human persons, those principles provide

Robert P George and Christopher O Tollefsen, *The Natural Law Foundations of Medical Law* In: *Philosophical Foundations of Medical Law*. Edited by: Andelka M Phillips, Thana C de Campos, and Jonathan Herring, Oxford University Press (2019). © Andelka M Phillips, Thana C de Campos, and Jonathan Herring
DOI: 10.1093/oso/9780198796558.003.0004

more-than-merely-instrumental reasons for actions:[1] they are indeed principles of human *reason*. It is because reason is 'natural' to human persons—human beings are beings whose nature is a rational nature—that the principles of human reason may be called principles or precepts of 'natural' law. (It is not, as is often wrongly supposed, because of any presumed 'derivation' of the moral 'ought' from the 'is' of nature.) Moreover, these principles of human reason are prescriptive: they emerge from reason when it is functioning *practically*, namely, in a mode that is directive towards human action: they are principles of practical reasons.[2] Thus, the most basic principles of natural law direct us (by appealing to our intellects and not merely to sentient aspects of our selves) towards basic human goods, the variegated aspects of human well-being that provide our most fundamental reasons for action.

Basic human goods include human life and health, which are, of course, the most important of human goods for our topic. Threats to, or compromises of, these goods bring medical professionals and patients together in an effort to stave off disease, disability, and death. Few would deny that human life and health are good in some sense; but most natural law theorists agree further that this complex and multifaceted good is basic and intrinsic, rather than merely instrumental. Theories that deny this are committed to some form of self-body dualism, a separation of the human 'person' (considered as the psyche, mind, or spirit) from the human animal (the biological organism). According to natural law theorists, however, that animal organism *is* the person (though it is not all that there is to the person) and not merely a vehicle in which the person rides or an extrinsic instrument of the person considered as the conscious and desiring aspect of the self.[3]

Life and health are not the only basic human goods, and this claim too will be shown to be important in the context of medicine and medical practice. The other constitutive aspects of human fulfilment include knowledge, aesthetic experience, work and play (as skilful performances), friendship, marriage, integrity, and religion (understood as the quest for harmony with the ultimate source or sources of meaning and value). Each such good provides its own distinct category of opportunity for human fulfilment, distinct from and incommensurable with the others. There is no natural hierarchy of goods of a sort that would require one kind of good always to give way before another.

Similarly, the options for morally significant choosing provided by the basic human goods are also incommensurable. Options thus may not be measured by a common standard of goodness so as to find, as the utilitarian account in Chapter 4 claims, the 'greatest good' (or 'greatest good of the greatest number', or 'net best proportion of benefit to harm overall and in the long run') in some option for choice. Options may be generated by different basic goods, such as the choice to become a doctor or a philosopher or professional athlete or rabbi or insurance salesman; or by the same good, such as the choice between pursuit of a medical intervention promising greater mobility, but with an increased risk of mortality, or an increased life expectancy, but with diminished mobility.

[1] For a recent account of the foundational principles of natural law ethics, see C Tollefsen, 'Natural Law, Basic Goods, and Practical Reason' in G Duke and RP George (eds), *The Cambridge Companion to Natural Law Jurisprudence* (Cambridge University Press, 2017), 133–58.

[2] For discussion of the prescriptive nature of the first principles of the natural law, see G Grisez, 'The First Principle of Practical Reason: A Commentary on the *Summa Theologiae*, 1–2, Question 94, Article 2' (1965) 10 Natural Law Forum 168–201.

[3] See P Lee and RP George, *Body-Self Dualism in Contemporary Ethics and Politics* (Cambridge University Press, 2008), responding to dualist theories such as those in D Parfit, *Reasons and Persons* (Oxford University Press, 1989) and J McMahan, *The Ethics of Killing* (Oxford University Press, 2003).

Were such options fully commensurable in terms of their goodness, as the utilitarian claims, no choice would be needed, or even possible: the agent would select what offered the greatest good. Any other selection would be irrational, unthinkable. So, where there is full commensurability, there are not, in fact, genuine options. But when the options are genuine, each option offers benefits, and typically burdens, different from the competing options; thus a choice is necessary, and something will be lost or forgone in the option passed over; the option chosen will not have in it everything of value available in the alternative option plus some more.

How can a choice between incommensurable options be guided if not by a consideration of which option promises the greatest good? A key claim of the tradition of natural law thought is that the standard for upright choice in natural law is provided by right reason. And reason, faced with a multiplicity of incommensurable goods, directs rightly when it directs *integrally*, that is, in a way that is open to the fullness of all the goods for all the persons for whom they are good, and is not deflected by sub-rational factors, such as emotions or other preferences that are not themselves guided by reason.[4] The first (in the sense of most abstract) principle of morality may thus be articulated as: 'Always will and choose in ways that are compatible with a will to integral human fulfillment.' The immediate implications of this principle will be the subject of the next section; we then turn to the further implications for medical practice and law.

III. Intermediate Principles of Morality

In this section, we identify three norms that are implications of the first principle of morality and that, as we will show below, are of central importance to medical morality and law.[5] These norms concern the intentional destruction of basic goods, the need for fairness between persons, and the necessity of accepting one's personal vocation. These norms are essential for addressing the morality of abortion; physician-assisted suicide and euthanasia; the location of the decision-making authority in the clinical setting; the right to health care; and, ultimately, the role of physician conscience in medicine.

A. No Intentional Damage or Destruction of Basic Goods

The first norm bears upon unreasonable damage or destruction of basic human goods. This occurs when we act directly against one good for the sake of another: for example, we deliberately inflict harm on one person for the sake of benefiting another, or damage one instance of a basic good for the sake of another. Such action could only be fully reasonable, and compatible with a will to integral human fulfilment, if goods and good options were in fact commensurable and therefore 'weighable' for purposes of comparing value. It would

[4] For discussion of the first principle of morality, see J Boyle, 'On the Most Fundamental Principle of Morality' in J Keown and RP George (eds), *Reason, Morality, and Law: The Philosophy of John Finnis* (Oxford University Press, 2013), 56–72.

[5] For a more in-depth treatment of the derivation of such intermediate norms, see G Grisez, *The Way of the Lord Jesus*, vol 1: *Christian Moral Principles* (Franciscan Herald Press, 1983), ch 8.

make sense to harm or destroy this instance of a basic good—this person's life, say—for the sake of some other good only if that other good were a *greater* good.

Yet, as we have seen, the notion of 'greater good' is out of place in speaking of *basic* goods. And so a norm that emerges from consideration of the rational requirement of openness to (in the sense of having a will favourably disposed to) all the basic aspects of human well-being and fulfilment (the human good integrally conceived) is this: never directly damage or destroy one instance of a basic good for the sake of some other or putatively 'greater' good: such choices can never be fully reasonable, or in line with full openness to basic goods and persons. Of course, one would also be unreasonable in choosing directly to damage or destroy an instance of a basic good out of hostility. So, the norm can be expanded: never directly damage or destroy an instance of a basic good.

This norm clearly has implications for questions of killing, since killing clearly damages, and indeed destroys, and instance of the basic good of human life. Thus, the norm rules out direct killing. What is the sense of 'directly' in this norm? The natural law tradition converges on the claim that the form of damage that is never permissible is *intended* damage: damage pursued as a means or as an end. It is thus not the case that every form of damage to a basic good that would be impermissible *if intended* would be impermissible *if brought about as a side effect* (though, similarly, not every form of damage that is not intended is therefore permissible). We will return to this in our discussion of Double Effect. Distinguishing between intended killing and death accepted as a side effect will be important for the discussion of abortion, assisted suicide and euthanasia, and the refusal of medical interventions.

B. Fairness and the Golden Rule

A second norm that is implied by the first principle of morality relates to fairness and the so-called Golden Rule. Consider the way our lives are shaped by particular attachments to those near to us, like us, or in some other way specially connected to us. This can be entirely reasonable: we are attached to our children or spouse, or parents; we have neighbourhood, religious, cultural, or national attachments as well. These are important, and can play a significant role in our moral deliberations. But sometimes we privilege such persons (or ourselves) in ways that are arbitrary and unfair. We are deflected from full practical reasonableness by emotions that are not guided by reason. We allow our child to take a greater share of some common stock than the other children simply because she is ours, for example. How can we test for this kind of arbitrary privileging of what is near and dear to us? One traditional test for such arbitrary privileging of persons is the Golden Rule, which in a negative formulation says: Do not do to others as *you* would not have them do to you.

Thus, when our privileging of some comes at the expense of others in such a way that *we* would reasonably object to such privileging were we on the receiving end, then we have reason to think that our privileging is unreasonable, arbitrary, *unfair*. So, a norm of fairness emerges from the requirements of reason, integrally considering all the goods for all persons; we should never let mere emotion blind us to the goodness of the goods for others in ways that unfairly benefit some and harm others. Parents who help their children cheat to get ahead in school, for example, act unfairly as regards other people's children.

There are times when our commitments do require that we give some people special treatment: physicians' commitments to their patients, for example, entitle them to carve out a special space in their lives for those patients and their needs. But this is clearly fair: everyone has reason to accept the possibility of special commitments like this, for without them, there could be no medical profession, no doctor–patient *relationships*, none of the benefits that come from a doctor's special knowledge and even friendship with his or her patients. So, while the doctor gives privileged treatment to her patients, that treatment is not for that reason unfair.

Although not the whole of justice, which involves what is owed to others, fairness is a necessary condition for ensuring justice within any community. A community, for our purposes, involves persons engaged in cooperative and shared action for the sake of some common good or goods.[6] In natural law thought, the concept of 'common good' is far ranging; in its most generic use, it simply refers to any good which is the object of a shared pursuit among multiple persons. But in different communities, the common good is specified in more determinate ways. For doctors and patients, the common good is the patient's health; for families, it is the overall welfare of the family members individually and as a unit; for a political society, it is the totality of conditions necessary for citizens to pursue upright and flourishing lives, individually, and in community (communities) with one another. Fairness ought normatively to structure all of these cooperative pursuits so that the distribution of benefits and burdens, understood ultimately by reference to the basic human goods, does not arbitrarily favour some at the expense of others. Failures in this respect will result in injustices in the relevant communities; success will protect opportunities for genuine human flourishing. The norm of fairness will be essential to the discussion of beginning and end-of-life ethics below (much, though not all, killing is unfair); and to the discussion of the right to health care in a political community.

C. Vocation

The third norm implied by the first principle of morality relates to the idea of vocation. It is clear that a person's life must be ordered in his or her pursuit of human goods. A life in which goods are pursued in a merely serial or unreflective manner, without prudent discernment and organization or structure, would inevitably be both shallow and chaotic in ways detrimental to human flourishing. Consider, for example, the following sorts of difficulties.

First, such a life would and could involve no true achievement of excellence at anything: no excellence of scholarship, medicine, or virtue. Second, such a life could involve no commitments to other persons; life in community, even the simplest community of friendship, is impossible if it is not deliberately ordered towards the goods of others and towards cooperation with those others. And, third, such a life would be chaotic; life without an overarching ordering structure would easily lead to conflict when the demands of one desired good conflicted with the demands of another.

Accordingly, human persons require something like a rational life plan if our actions and lives are to be reasonably oriented to goods and persons. This line of thought, congenial to many outside the natural law tradition, such as John Rawls, is enhanced within the natural law tradition by reflection on the relationship between the natural law and God's eternal law,

6 See J Finnis, *Natural Law and Natural Rights* (2nd edn, Oxford University Press, 2011), ch VI.

which, inter alia, directs human persons to their good for their own sake, while orienting and ordering their actions for the service of others and God. God is the source of all order, not just in general, but for each particular person. Thus, human beings naturally and reasonably seek to identify the upright, virtuous, and flourishing lives to which they have been called by God. This calling is their personal vocation, and natural law reflection encourages each person to consider his or her life vocationally. Persons must ask to what they are being called, and how they may respond to that call in such a way as to cooperate with the Divine One who is calling. Responding to this invitation to cooperate in one's vocation is understood by many people as a central feature of their pursuit of the good of religion, and likewise as essential to the good of personal integrity. We will see later the implications of this for questions of physician conscience. The idea of personal vocation is also important for understanding the nature and limits of patient decision-making authority, which we will discuss below.[7]

IV. Medical Practice and Law

We now turn to four disputed areas of medical practice and medical law. For a considerable period in the history of the West, natural law reflections such as those we will provide have guided both medical practice and law, even if at times only implicitly or inchoately and imperfectly. Of late, by contrast, there is strong and often explicit opposition to the principles, norms, and conclusions we will discuss. This is especially evident where questions at the beginning and end of human life are concerned.

A. Killing at the Beginning and End of Life

Should physicians ever be engaged in the intentional taking of life, whether at its beginning or at its end? Widespread toleration of the practice of abortion suggests an affirmative answer as regards the beginning of life; rapidly increasing toleration of the practice of assisted suicide and voluntary euthanasia suggests a similarly affirmative answer at the end of life. The natural law tradition, by contrast, offers negative answers in both cases.

1. Abortion

Natural law thought approaches the question of abortion from a moral, a medical-professional, and a political-legal standpoint. The three-fold approach is necessary; for example, to demonstrate that a practice ought to be prohibited by law, it is not sufficient (though it is usually necessary) to show that the practice is morally impermissible. It is additionally necessary to show that the wrong in question is, or threatens, a serious wrong against persons, and is thus unjust; and that a restrictive, rather than a permissive, legal regime is a more reasonable way to prevent and educate about the wrong. Professional practice also might be more or less concordant with the demands of law and morality. Here, it is necessary to show that the human goods served by the practice will be best served by

[7] For further discussion of the concept of vocation and its importance, see G Grisez, *The Way of The Lord Jesus*, vol 2: *Living a Christian Life* (Franciscan Press, 1993), 77–130.

considerations that are essentially moral, and not merely legal. Thus, that abortion or euthanasia (or capital punishment) are permitted at law may not be sufficient to show that these practices are compatible with medicine's vocational commitments.

As regards the moral question of abortion, natural law theory offers the following considerations in defence of the inviolability of human life, that is, for the clam that it is not to be violated, damaged, or destroyed intentionally (whether as an end-in-itself or as a means to some other end).[8]

What is the nature of the being whose life is ended in abortion? Is it a living human being, or is it some living thing which is not (or not yet) a human being, something perhaps merely in transit towards being human?[9] Natural law thinkers urge that the question must be addressed by the most up-to-date science, notably embryology and developmental biology. That science does indicate the nature of the being whose life is ended in abortion: the entity destroyed in abortion is a human being, a living member of the species *homo sapiens*, genetically and functionally distinct from his or her biological parents, and possessed of the genetic and epigenetic primordia necessary to be the agent of its own growth and development to the next stage(s) of human life. Apart from disagreements at the very earliest stages of human life, when the human embryo is capable of twinning, most philosophers and virtually all human embryologists recognize that the early embryo and foetus is an identifiable human being.[10]

Moreover, even objections concerning the earliest stages of human life are weak; that the very early embryo is capable of dividing into twins (or perhaps budding to generate a second embryo) hardly shows that the embryo which does not twin, or even the embryo that will twin, is not a single unified whole organism. Individual organisms such as single-celled amoebae or multi-celled flatworms can be capable of division without this is any way jeopardizing their organic unity and determinateness. Thus, the possibility of twinning gives us no reason to doubt the unity and determinateness of the embryo.[11]

The answer to the question on the nature of the being whose life is ended in abortion is this: the unborn entities destroyed in abortion are human beings. Should the norm against intentional damage to a basic good—human life—be considered applicable where unborn human beings are concerned? Unborn human beings are *human beings*, precisely the class of beings for whom basic *human* goods are good. There are compelling reasons to protect the good of life and health in and for all human beings, including unborn human beings. So, the norm against intentional damage to a human life is applicable to unborn human beings, too.

[8] For a recent and thorough treatment of inviolability and medical law, see J Keown, *The Law and Ethics of Medicine: Essays on the Inviolability of Human Life* (Oxford University Press, 2012).

[9] For an extended and more detailed discussion on this point, see RP George and C Tollefsen, *Embryo: A Defense of Human Life* (2nd edn, Witherspoon, 2011). For a thorough discussion of the moral arguments surrounding abortion, see also C Kaczor, *The Ethics of Abortion: Women's Rights, Human Life, and the Question of Justice* (2nd edn, Routledge, 2015).

[10] On the question of the scientific consensus, see C Tollefsen, P Lee, and RP George, 'Marco Rubio Was Right: The Life of a New Human Being Begins at Conception', *The Public Discourse* (15 August 2015), http://www.thepublicdiscourse.com/2015/08/15520/ accessed 15 July 2019; an extensive list of quotations from the relevant authorities is available online: http://clinicquotes.com/list-of-quotes-from-medical-textbooksscientists-proving-life-begins-at-conception/ accessed 15 July 2019.

[11] For helpful discussion of this issue, with references, see A Gomez-Lobo, *Bioethics and the Human Goods: An Introduction to Natural Law Bioethics* (Georgetown University Press, 2015); see also, for critical engagement with a biologist who denies the humanity of the early embryo, P Lee, C Tollefsen, and RP George, 'The Ontological Status of Embryos: A Reply to Jason Morris' (2014) 39 Journal of Medicine and Philosophy 483–504.

Moreover, every attempt to deny basic moral protections to *all* human beings inevitably relies upon a contingently (and ultimately arbitrarily) drawn boundary between some human beings and others: that *these* human beings have achieved consciousness, or can now reason, or engage in self-conscious thought, for example, while *those* cannot. None of these boundaries divides one essential kind of thing from another; but the boundaries dividing what are human beings from what are not do divide entities in a morally non-arbitrary way.

What is the source of the inviolability of human persons? Human beings are thought to be worthy of respect, and thus entitled to immunity from intentional killing, enslavement, torture, and the like, because of their intrinsic *dignity*: because they are *persons*, possessed of the capacities for freedom and reason. But those capacities are possessed in root, or radical form, by *every* member of the species, including human beings at the zygotic and foetal stages. Thus, those very young members of the species *homo sapiens* are also possessed of human dignity, and are persons from the moment of fertilization, and they share with all other members of the species the grounds for said inviolability.

Is abortion intentional killing? The answer requires some nuance. Most abortion is surely intentional killing: whenever motivated by the desire 'not to be a mother', for example, a desire that is satisfied only by the destruction of the entity whose existence makes one a mother. Judith Jarvis Thomson has argued, in effect, that some abortions might only include an intention to expel, which she believes is justified in the absence of a special duty to provide aid.[12] Natural law thinkers have argued extensively against Thomson that there are natural obligations, some based in biological–familial relatedness, which mothers owe to their unborn children; and that the choice to expel in the absence of very serious reasons, such as the need to save the mother's life, is inevitably unfair and thus unjust.[13] A reasonable natural law position on abortion would first identify abortion as the intentional *or unjust* expelling—namely, killing—of an unborn human being; and then conclude that abortion as so defined is always morally impermissible.[14]

Should medical *practice* allow the killing of unborn human beings, in spite of the moral impermissibility of such killing? It should not. Any upright practice, and thus any profession established on the basis of an upright practice, is constituted by its orientation to some basic good or goods. Practices are professionalized when there are good reasons to ensure widespread distribution of the benefits of the practice, to ensure that appropriate standards of education and behaviour are transmitted to all practitioners, and to provide the external goods necessary for the practice to flourish. Medical practice is fundamentally guided by a vocational commitment to human life and health; as such, it would be contradictory and disastrous for the profession were its practitioners to include the privation of this good as among their purposes. Abortion as defined above (ie as the intentional *or unjust* killing of an unborn human being) seems entirely contrary to the appropriate professional ethos of physicians, who are committed to healing, rather than killing. This recognition was crucial to the physicians' movement of the nineteenth century to eradicate abortion.[15]

[12] JJ Thomson, 'A Defense of Abortion' (1971) 1 Philosophy and Public Affairs 47–66.

[13] On natural obligations founded on biological relatedness, see M Moschella, *To Whom Do Children Belong? Parental Rights, Civic Education, and Children's Autonomy* (Cambridge University Press, 2016); for the argument of unfairness, see P Lee and RP George, 'The Wrong of Abortion' in AI Cohen and CH Wellman (eds), *Contemporary Debates in Applied Ethics* (Blackwell, 2005), 13–26.

[14] See C Tollefsen, 'Double Effect and Two Hard Cases in Medical Ethics' (2015) 89 American Catholic Philosophical Quarterly 407–20.

[15] The history of the nineteenth-century physicians' crusade against abortion is related in FN Dyer, *The Physician's Crusade against Abortion* (Science History Publications, 2005).

Should medical *law* also hew closely to the moral judgment that abortion is always an offence against an innocent human life? It should; abortion is not only contrary to the good of life, but an offence against that good in particular persons, without—ever—their consent. Abortion is thus always unjust, and is concerned with a grave violation of a basic good (ie human life); it is precisely the sort of matter over which legal guidance is necessary. For the law even to remain 'neutral' on this matter is for the law to permit attacks on innocent human life. This does not mean that natural lawyers favour criminal sanctions against women who seek or obtain abortions. Recognizing in some cases diminished responsibility, and other mitigating factors, natural lawyers generally recommend that it be illegal for doctors or others to perform abortions; criminal or regulatory penalties should thus fall on those who carry out, rather than those who undergo, abortions.[16]

2. Physician-Assisted Suicide and Euthanasia

When we turn to the question of so-called 'medical assistance in dying,' the situation is somewhat more complicated. Here, the most plausible proposals to allow, or perhaps require, physicians to aid their patients in ending their lives require that those patients give their informed consent in the form of a request; these proposals also argue that patients be assisted in ending their lives as a way to forestall or end human suffering. So, there are significant differences from the abortion case: unlike in abortion, the one killed, or helped to kill him- or herself, consents; and the killing is done for the benefit of the one killed.

Natural law's assessment of assistance in self-killing starts from a moral standpoint, and here the judgment is straightforward. If every intentional killing of an innocent live is morally impermissible, then so is self-killing, assisting in self-killing, and killing at the request of another.[17] It is true that the natural law tradition has held, going back to Aristotle, that it is impossible for a man to do injustice to himself, or to suffer injustice willingly.[18] So, self-killing, or assistance in self-killing, might not be unjust towards the one killed. But not every moral wrong is an injustice, and the moral demands of the natural law prescription against intentional killing go beyond the demands of justice.

Should the medical profession take this moral standard as its own? Where abortion was concerned, the answer seemed straightforward: killing is contrary to the medical profession's ethos of healing. That judgment may seem complicated here by the presence of consent and suffering; doctors are to honour patient consent; and they are thought by many to have the relief of suffering as among their primary purposes. But proposals for a 'right' to physician assistance in dying do not ask physicians to honour consent, but go beyond that in requiring physicians to acquiesce in all patient demands. And suffering, unlike disease or impairment, is in part a function of a patient's awareness of and response to the deficiencies in her own life and health. While the physician's task is surely to respond to some of those *deficiencies*, when possible, it is not clear that the good physician is charged with ending

[16] See R Lu, 'Why Pro-Lifers Don't Support Punishing Women for Abortion', *The Federalist* (5 April 2016), http://thefederalist.com/2016/04/05/why-pro-lifers-dont-support-punishing-women-for-abortion/ accessed 15 July 2019.

[17] Joseph Boyle explores these implications of the natural law idea of sanctity or inviolability of life in 'Sanctity of Life and Suicide: Tensions and Developments within Common Morality' in BA Brody (ed), *Suicide and Euthanasia* (Kluwer, 1989), 221–50.

[18] For further discussion of justice in the natural law tradition, see Finnis (n 6) ch VII; as Finnis points out at 161–3, justice 'embraces three elements' in the natural law tradition: it is other directed, it designates what is owed, and it involves some form of equality.

patient *suffering* at all costs, including where the means of achieving that goal is killing the patient or helping the patient to kill himself.

There are additional reasons for resisting the turn to physician assistance in dying, and some of these considerations will carry over to the discussion of medical law as well. Medical professionals, especially, but not only, those who care for patients at the end of life, are charged with caring for persons who are in a radically dependent and vulnerable state.[19] The vulnerability of the patient requires a professional ethos that cultivates trustworthy physicians, and makes possible reasonable trust by patients. It is difficult to see how the necessary trust can be maintained, however, when doctors constitute an exception to the general and indefeasible norm against intentional killing of innocent human beings. Rather than knowing and trusting that a physician will never abandon the patient in her vulnerability, the patient will know that killing (ie the taking of her life in her vulnerability) is always an option. The nature of the doctor–patient relationship will fundamentally change, and medical professionals, in recognizing this, are right to worry about it.[20]

The revision to the exception against the intentional killing of an innocent requires great care on the part of the medical profession to produce and enforce protocols that ensure that persons will not be killed against their will, or coerced, even subtly, to end their lives; moreover, these same protocols must ensure that the will of the patient requesting death should not be compromised by depression or other psychological impairment. These are all issues of justice, of what is *owed* to others, and the introduction of a practice of assisted death into the medical profession threatens pervasive injustice to those who are poor, depressed, or at the mercy of uncharitable (or greedy, or impatient) family members or others if exacting protocols are not developed and then rigorously enforced.[21]

Many medical professionals not committed to the inviolability of human life as are natural law theorists nonetheless have recognized the undesirability and perhaps impossibility of the medical profession developing protocols of this sort. They are further concerned that the availability of assisted death will detract from the efforts and resources necessary to care for dying patients. Thus, Ezekiel Emanuel writes:

> Instead of attempting to legalize physician-assisted suicide, we should focus our energies on what really matters: improving care for the dying—ensuring that all patients can openly talk with their physicians and families about their wishes and have access to high-quality palliative or hospice care before they suffer needless medical procedures. The appeal of physician-assisted suicide is based on a fantasy.[22]

[19] See RM Zaner, *A Critical Examination of Ethics in Health Care and Biomedical Research: Voices and Visions* (Springer, 2015) for recapitulation of his important work demonstrating the importance of patient vulnerability for an understanding of the doctor–patient relationship.

[20] See J Finnis, 'Euthanasia and the Law' in *Human Rights and Common Good, Collected Essays* (Oxford University Press, 2011), vol III, 251–70 for discussion of these and related points.

[21] An important body of literature now exists arguing that current laws permitting physician assistance in dying notably fail as regards both the content and the enforcement of such protocols. See eg J Keown, 'Euthanasia in the Netherlands: Sliding down the Slippery Slope?' (1995) 9 Notre Dame Journal of Law, Ethics & Public Policy 407–48; NM Gorsuch, *The Future of Assisted Suicide and Euthanasia* (Princeton University Press, 2006).

[22] E Emanuel, 'Four Myths about Doctor Assisted Suicide', *The New York Times* (27 October 2012), https://opinionator.blogs.nytimes.com/2012/10/27/four-myths-about-doctor-assisted-suicide/?smid=tw-share accessed 15 July 2019.

There is an additional difficulty. Two main justifications are typically given, as noted above, for a right to assistance in dying: that consent has been given autonomously, and that the patient is suffering. Both justifications, if followed to their logical conclusions, justify far more, however, than a right to assistance in dying *for those who are dying*. Rather, both autonomy and suffering seem capable of justifying a right to die, and to receive assistance in dying, for many non-terminal patients, who might nevertheless be suffering greatly, and autonomously desire death. Such patients might include those whose suffering is existential or moral (eg an alcoholic who cannot quit the bottle), or whose 'life narratives' lead them to desire an entirely controlled resolution to their story at the time of their choosing.[23]

For all these reasons, medicine should *not* admit the practice of assisted dying into its practice. But for the same reasons, neither should the law contemplate such. Recall that the common good of political society is the totality of conditions necessary for citizens to pursue upright and flourishing lives, individually, and in community (communities) with one another. Those conditions include, pre-eminently, and a central task of the law is thus establishing and maintaining, just social conditions between citizens. But justice is threatened for the most vulnerable by a regime of assisted death. Moreover, the practice of assisted death threatens to erode the possibilities for upright self-constitution for members of the medical community, by encouraging them to abandon their commitment to heal and never to harm. The general and stringent legal restriction against intentional killing of the innocent should thus not be loosened for doctors treating patients at the end of life.[24]

B. Double Effect

An objection raised to those who oppose assistance in dying, however, leads to important further issues. How is it possible to refuse a permission on self-killing and assistance in self-killing, yet countenance current medical practice and law as regards refusal or withdrawal of forms of life-sustaining or life-saving treatment? Patients who refuse consent are not treated against their will, and some die as a result of their refusal. Similarly, life-sustaining technologies are withdrawn from some patients at the end of life, with death as the consequence. What principled line can be drawn between these practices and the practice of assisted death?

In this section, we address the question of the principled distinction, which hinges on the notion of intention; in the next section, we address the related question of patient autonomy and patient authority.

The natural law tradition is distinguished, among the variety of approaches to ethics, by its claim that there are some acts that are never to be done. Norms concerned with such acts may be called 'moral absolutes': they do not mandate a single course of action for all agents in all circumstances; rather, they identify an action type which is never to be engaged in by an agent.[25] Such absolutes most typically flow from the general norm identified above: that

[23] John Keown pursues these implications in vol III of *The Law and Ethics of Medicine: Essays on the Inviolability of Human Life* (Oxford University Press, 2012), vol III.

[24] For further discussion, see R Anderson, 'Always Care, Never Kill: How Physician-Assisted Suicide Endangers the Weak, Corrupts Medicine, Compromises the Family, and Violates Human Dignity and Equality', Report of the Heritage Foundation (24 March 2015), http://www.heritage.org/health-care-reform/report/always-care-never-kill-how-physician-assisted-suicide-endangers-the-weak accessed 15 July 2019.

[25] See J Finnis, *Moral Absolutes: Tradition, Revision, and Truth* (Catholic University of America Press, 1991).

basic goods are never to be directly (that is, *intentionally*—as an end or means) damaged or destroyed, whether out of hostility, or for the sake of some further good. That norm makes sense, recall, given the incommensurability of the basic goods and the options for morally significant choosing generated by those goods.

That norm is clearly violated in suicide or euthanasia, for in both, death is brought about as a means to a further benefit, such as the relief of suffering. Consider, by contrast, a case in which treatment options are framed as packages in which one set of health benefits is linked to a set of health burdens and compared to a different set of health benefits linked to another set of health burdens. The options are exclusive. So, for example, if one chooses the chemotherapy course in response to one's cancer, one may experience an increase in life expectancy, but accompanied by significant health burdens. Those burdens—nausea, hair loss, fatigue, sores, blood disorders, and others—are side effects: they are not, obviously, pursued as an end of the medical treatment; but neither are they chosen as a means to the desired health outcome—increased life expectancy. They are thus not *intended*. But similarly, if one refuses the chemotherapy *because* one desires to avoid the health burdens associated with that treatment, and thus to live one's fewer remaining days in a less health-compromised state, then one likewise does not intend the shortening of one's life. It too is a side effect of the choice to avoid burdens.

But it is thus clear that whatever choice one will make (for the chemotherapy or for its refusal) will have negative consequences for the good of life and health: such negative consequences are unavoidable and foreseeable. So, the absolute norm against intentional damage or destruction to a basic good could not be extended to include damage or destruction that occurs as a side effect (ie an unavoidable, yet foreseeable, negative consequence). That is, there could be no norm of the form 'You ought never to cause harm as a side effect', for ought implies can, and it is impossible *always* to avoid causing harm as a side effect.[26]

There thus emerges, in the course of the natural law tradition, the *Principle of Double Effect*.[27] Put simply, an effect that would always be wrong to intend (eg harming the basic goods of life and health) can sometimes (though not always: more on that in a moment) be permissible if brought about as a side effect if there is a proportionate reason for permitting it. More traditional formulations articulate four parts to the rule: that the act be permissible in itself; that the evil effect not be intended; that the good effect not come about through the evil effect; and that there be a proportionate reason for accepting the bad effect in pursuit of the good.[28]

What is a proportionate reason? This can be answered in one way by returning to the case of abortion. In cases of vital conflict, where both the mother's and the child's life are at stake, natural law theorists have considered it permissible to remove the child (eg in a hysterectomy of a cancerous uterus) to save the mother. The child's death is not intended: it is

[26] For further articulation of this position, see J Boyle, 'Who Is Entitled to Double Effect?' (1991) 16 Journal of Medicine and Philosophy 475–94; and 'Intention, Permissibility, and the Structure of Agency' (2015) 89 American Catholic Philosophical Quarterly 461–78.

[27] The origins of the Principle are standardly traced back to St Thomas Aquinas's discussion of killing in self-defence, in his *Summa Theologica* (hereafter, *ST*) II-II, q 64, Art 7; for further commentary, see J Boyle, '*Praeter intentionem* in Aquinas' (1978) 42 Thomist 649–65.

[28] For such a formulation, see Gomez-Lobo (n 11) 59–60. Our simpler formulation captures parts 2 and 3 in the requirement that the bad effect not be intended, by which we mean 'intended as an end or as a means'. But an act in which the bad effect is intended just is one that is impermissible in itself, so part 1 is encompassed in our simple formulation as well. Both formulations share the requirement that there be a proportionate reason, that is, that bad side effects be proportionate to the good sought.

neither an end nor a means. It is rather an accepted side effect. That side effect is considered proportionate because it is *fairly* accepted: it passes the test of the Golden Rule. By contrast, even if we assume, with Judith Jarvis Thomson, that there exist abortions that are merely expellings, with death as a side effect, that side effect will typically be disproportionate—unfair—if done for reasons less grave than preservation of the mother's life.

An account must likewise be given in end-of-life cases of the norms governing proportionate acceptance of bad, including lethal, side effects when life-sustaining or saving treatment is refused; we will provide that account in the next section. Here, it is important to note that the distinction between what is intended and what is a side effect is one with important legal weight. US Supreme Court Chief Justice William Rehnquist in *Vacco v Quill*, a case in which a right to assistance in death was claimed, detailed the importance that the distinction between intending death and permitting death as a side effect has had in a long line of precedents, and concluded that while a right to refuse treatment was constitutionally well-grounded, no such claim could be made for a right to hasten or bring about death.

Of course, some patients do refuse treatment in order to die; their refusals are, strictly speaking, suicidal. But, in general, the law correctly grants the right to refuse treatment to patients in order to protect them from unwanted interventions, with the side effect that this right might be abused; and the law straightforwardly prohibits the always impermissible act of intentionally taking life. The erosion of the distinction between intending and hastening death, on the one hand, and accepting death as a side effect, on the other, in recent law governing assistance in dying, as in Canada, some jurisdictions in the United States, and several European countries, obscures what the Rehnquist court, in its unanimous decision in *Quill*, saw clearly: while a right to refuse treatment is constitutionally well-grounded, no such claim could be made for a right to hasten or bring about death; this is a key moral distinction.[29]

C. Authority in Health Care

We can say something more about the justification for the patient's right to refuse treatment, and indeed this is necessary in order to stave off a line of argument for assisted death that begins from false claims about the patient's autonomy. Patients are granted, in law, a broad right of refusal of medical treatment, even when the consequences for the patient are lethal, and even when the motivations of the patient are obscure to many. Thus, Jehovah's Witnesses are not to be given blood transfusions against their will, even when the transfusion is necessary to save their life, and when it seems *obvious* to all non-Witnesses that the transfusion is reasonable and right.

Typically, bioethicists see the importance of consent as rooted in the value of *autonomy*: to act contrary to a patient's wishes is to violate that autonomy, and to fail to respect the patient as a person.[30] And many bioethicists track the rise of their discipline to the rise of awareness of the importance of autonomy by contrast to an era in which physicians are thought

[29] *Vacco v Quill* (1997) 521 US 793. Gorsuch (n 21) ch 4 defends the importance of the intend-foresee distinction for end-of-life issues.

[30] See eg TL Beauchamp and R Childress, *Principles of Biomedical Ethics* (7th edn, Oxford University Press, 2013).

to have exercised an overly paternalistic approach to patients, failing to provide them with adequate information and treating them for their own good without seeking consent.[31] The extent to which this description accurately characterizes medicine prior to the second half of the twentieth century need not concern us here; what is important is that 'respect for autonomy' has increasingly become the source not just of negative side constraints—do not treat without informed consent—but also of positive obligations: do what the patient autonomously requests, provided that it is legal. We will return to this in our discussion of physician conscience in the final section. For now, we will provide an alternative account of the side constraint on treating patients without consent.

The alternative account focuses less on patient autonomy than on patient *authority*. Medical decisions are, like many other decisions, made in a social space that includes the patient, the patient's family and friends, the medical professionals involved, and often others (eg institutional decision-makers, insurance providers, clergy). But all decisions involving more than one party face a similar problem: given that the various persons involved will have different reasons for acting, and different conceptions of the reasons available to be acted on, how is a final decision to be reached?

There are, as John Finnis has argued, only two possible ways when it comes to the decision-making process: either there must be unanimity, or authority.[32] There are no further options, for *every* way of making a decision short of unanimity involves some form of authority. Even a vote in which the majority wins substitutes the authority of the majority for the decision of all. It is not a third way. So, who is to have authority in the context of medical decision making?

With rare exceptions, the authority is to be exercised by the patient. The reason for this can be seen by recalling that the goods of human life are variegated, whereas the goods of medicine are, for the most part, singular (though complex). Medicine is concerned for human life and health, and physicians have expertise precisely with regard to techniques, medicines, and other interventions that offer health-related benefits. But life and health are not the only good for patients. Rather, the chief good for patients in some particular decision is usually a function of their commitments, obligations, and circumstances as regards a number of goods, and how those goods are ordered in the patients' lives with their families, communities, and neighbours. That ordering with regard to goods and persons, brought about by the agent's commitments, is itself the patient's life plan, or personal vocation. And this provides the rational standard by which the variety of options presented by the physician, in light of the physician's health-care expertise, are to be evaluated: which option fits best (and is otherwise morally reasonable) with the patient's overall vocation, with the ordering of his or her life as regards goods and persons.

A competent patient is clearly the person best placed to make that assessment. The idea of personal vocation thus plays two roles here: (1) it provides the justification for patient authority, an authority that is to be honoured by the medical profession and protected legally; and (2) it provides the standard for patients themselves to bring to bear on their health-care choices. In those choices, each option will bring about competing sets of benefits and

[31] See the discussion of two 'models', one paternalistic, one autonomy focused and consumerist; in M Siegler, 'Searching for Moral Certainty in Medicine: A Proposal for a New Model of the Doctor-Patient Encounter' (1981) 57 Bulletin of the New York Academy of Medicine 56–69.

[32] See Finnis (n 6) ch IX.

burdens that are incommensurable with one another; there can, therefore, be no 'weighing up' to see which option is 'the best'. Yet, the natural law tradition has embraced the idea that burdens may be rejected, and benefits foregone, if those burdens are not 'proportionate' to the promised benefits. The idea of patient vocation provides an interpretation for this claim: if it is unreasonable, in light of one's vocation, to accept some burden in the pursuit of the promised benefit, then that burden is not proportionate. If it is reasonable, in light on one's vocation, to accept some burden, then that burden is proportionate.[33] Thus, for example, a treatment option might be judged to be not proportionate if it offered some chance of extended life at the cost of rendering a patient unable to fulfil his or her familial responsibilities. It is important to note, of course, that when such a patient refuses a life-extending intervention, the shortening of life is not intended, but a reasonably accepted side effect.

This conception of patient authority overlaps considerably, but not entirely, with the notion of patient autonomy. The overlap extends to converging claims on both accounts that competent patients have a nearly absolute veto on proposed medical interventions. But it differs in at least the following two ways. First, it is commonplace that authority is always limited, and a patient's decision-making authority is likewise limited: it is primarily an authority to accept some offers made by physicians and to reject others. It is *not* of itself an authority to demand some particular intervention independently of the physician's best medical judgment. The idea of patient authority thus does not bring with it an internal nisus towards the idea of a patient entitlement to, for example, assistance in ending her life.

A second difference is this: autonomous acts increasingly are thought to be self-ratifying: if the decision is autonomously made, then it is correct. But a decision may be legitimately authoritative, while also being *wrong*. Authority can be exercised legitimately, but foolishly, and even immorally, without eroding the reasons those under authority have for obedience. Thus, patients can and sometimes will make imprudent and even immoral choices to refuse care; that the decisions are their own does not render these decisions correct. But that the patient has authority does create a strong, though sometimes defeasible, obligation on the part of physicians and others to honour the patient's exercise of authority. The law, again, rightly recognizes this, and does not require physicians or others to subject a patient's refusals to a judgment of overall moral propriety in order to comply.

D. Allocation of Resources and the Right to Health Care

We turn now to a rather different domain of medical law and public policy: that concerned with the allocation of health-care resources; and to the question of whether persons may be said to have a right to health care. Whereas questions concerning the refusal or withdrawal of medical care, particularly, though not exclusively, at the end of life, are questions that require essentially *personal* considerations, such as considerations of personal vocation, questions of the political distribution of resources, and establishment of political or legal entitlements, require more impersonal considerations, and are governed especially by norms of fairness.

[33] For further elaboration of this claim, see Grisez (n 7).

The questions of this section are complicated and controversial, even among natural law thinkers, to a much greater extent than any of the other issues addressed in this chapter. Nevertheless, natural law thinkers in general start from a shared set of claims, which we will articulate here; working out the implications of these claims is beyond the scope of this chapter.

The foundational claims concern the natural law justification for private property; the nature of interpersonal obligations of charity;[34] and the nature and role of political authority. As regards the natural law approach to private property, theorists recognize a 'natural' but not *original* right to private property. The goods of the world do not come with particular persons' names affixed to them, nor are they collectively owned. But ownership of the world's goods is a reasonable way of dividing up and caring for those resources which by their nature exist, all of them, for the benefit of all human persons. Private ownership is thought to foster the common good for a number of pragmatic reasons, such as facilitating the development and use of resources in ways that advance the common good, and avoiding quarrels; and because it promises greater personal discretion in the discerning and carrying out of individuals' personal vocations.[35]

Nevertheless, most natural law thinkers hold with St Thomas, and contrary to, for example, certain libertarians, that the 'universal destination of the world's goods' remains a limiting principle on the authority that individuals have over their property. That which is not used for grave needs, of the person and those to whom he or she owes duties of care, and for the carrying out of personal vocation, is considered *superflua*, and is *owed* to those in need.[36] Of course, making decisions as to how to meet those needs with one's *superflua* is itself a self-constituting act and part of many persons' personal vocations, so there is value in persons making those decisions for themselves.

Under certain conditions, however, thinkers in the natural law tradition have held that political authority may be permitted or required to ensure that the grave needs of some are met, and that the significant obligations of charity of those with *superflua* are not left unfulfilled.[37] The role of the state is, again, to ensure that the totality of conditions necessary for citizens to pursue upright and flourishing lives, individually, and in community (communities) with one another, is satisfied; this set of conditions is the political common good. It is also the source of political authority, for that authority is necessary and hence justified to ensure the successful realization of those conditions for flourishing that individuals and the many forms of civil society are incapable of providing for themselves.

Thus, where grave individual needs will go unmet despite individual and societal initiatives, *and* resources exist to meet those needs, then the state can, and sometimes ought to, ensure that those needs are in fact met. Indeed, even where needs can be met without the exercise of political authority, if those needs can be met more successfully or efficiently with the aid of political authority, then again, the exercise of that authority is called for.

[34] By 'obligations of charity', we mean simply obligations to give; such obligations are obligations in justice. No contrast between charity and justice is supposed here.

[35] For recent natural law accounts of private property, see Finnis (n 6) 169; and A MacLeod, *Property and Practical Reason* (Cambridge University Press, 2015). Both accounts are indebted to that of Aquinas in *ST* II-II, q 66, Art 1.

[36] For a nuanced account of Aquinas's concept of *superflua*, see J Finnis, *Aquinas: Moral, Political and Legal Theory* (Oxford University Press, 1998), 191–6.

[37] See J Boyle, 'Fairness in Holdings: A Natural Law Account of Property and Welfare Rights' (2001) 18 Social Philosophy and Policy 206–26.

(By the same token, when those needs may be more efficiently met *without* the use of that authority, they should be.) So, certain welfare rights or entitlements will be justified if: (1) there are grave unmet needs; (2) there are adequate resources for meeting those needs; (3) the state can more efficiently help ensure those needs are met than can other agents; and (4) it can do so without seriously eroding the capacity of those with resources from being self-constituting agents, or doing other harms.

One important feature of health care suggests that political authority in developed nations can and will need to be exercised with regard to its distribution.[38] This is the already deeply social nature of health care. Health-care services in developed nations are distributed across many agents, including patients, physicians, nurses, administrators, and others; and across many institutions, such as physician practices and networks, hospitals, drug companies, insurance companies, and others. This situation marks a significant change from health care in times past. Is it the case that such a widely distributed set of agents, practices, technologies, and institutions, with their competing interests, problems, and challenges, will be adequately efficient, upright, and cooperative to ensure that health care is fairly provided, paid for, and consumed? It seems unlikely.

Accordingly, at a minimum, political authority seems needed for regulatory and coordination purposes. Without such regulation and coordination, or with only poor regulation and coordination, access to health care is likely to be impaired for some persons and this is an injustice.[39]

A second feature of health care is also relevant: all persons have an abiding and significant need for health care, yet not all will be adequately cared for in the absence of political authority, and not merely because some agents default on their responsibilities. Rather, as the cost of health care and health technology rises, it is increasingly difficult or impossible for the health-care needs of the poor to be met using their own resources, or to be met by charitable individuals or organizations, without assistance by the state (though it is desirable, to the extent possible, to rely on institutions of civil society than on the state). So, not only must the state engage in some regulation of health care to ensure fairness, it must also create and maintain some political entitlements to health care for those unable to provide it for themselves.

It is in light of these considerations that a 'right to health care' must be understood: that right will pertain in the minimum case to individuals who are unable to provide adequate health care for themselves, living in societies and states sufficiently developed that they can effectively provide, or coordinate the provision of, health care to those individuals. In any given society, however, this right must then be much more concretely specified than we have done here: who precisely has that right; what precisely are they entitled to; how precisely are those entitlements to be funded and delivered; and so on.[40]

How far beyond this minimum does natural law carry us? That is a matter of controversy. Some, sensitive to natural law's demand that citizens not be taxed beyond their power to

[38] In some undeveloped countries, it will make little sense to speak of the right to health care of the citizens against their own state. We prescind here from the question of what health-related rights such states might have as regards more developed countries; that issue is addressed from a natural law perspective in TC de Campos, *The Global Health Crisis: Ethical Responsibilities* (Cambridge University Press, 2017).

[39] See G Grisez, 'Health Care Technology and Justice' in C Tollefsen (ed), *Bioethics with Liberty and Justice: Themes in the Work of Joseph M. Boyle* (Springer, 2011), 221–41.

[40] See the discussion in J Boyle, 'Limiting Access to Healthcare: A Traditional Roman Catholic Analysis' in HT Engelhardt and MJ Cherry (eds), *Allocating Scarce Medical Resources* (Georgetown University Press, 2002), 89–91.

exercise their own self-determination and fulfil their obligations of charity themselves, advocate lesser state involvement, and perhaps more market-based solutions to meeting the broader health-care needs of citizens. Others, impressed with the difficulties of achieving transparent market conditions, and with the pervasive injustices found in much health-care provision and funding, argue for a more extensive use of political authority in addressing these issues. These disagreements do not admit of resolution here.[41]

There is also, inevitably, a natural degree of indeterminacy in how a particular political society can or should work out the details of its scheme of health-care entitlements and regulations. This indeterminacy results from different answers that can be given that arise from within the domain of health care: different societies, for example, will make different judgments about what resources to direct to preventative, basic, or intensive care, as a result of differences in need, resources, and priorities. Other indeterminacies will result from the fact that resources spent on health care could also be spent elsewhere, for the sake of other equally important basic goods. What amount of resources should be directed to health care instead of education is a question that has no determinate answer, and that will be reasonably answered in different ways by different societies.[42]

For these reasons, natural law theorists have not provided, and to some extent cannot provide, determinate answers to all questions about health-care distribution and rights. Settling such questions requires prudence and in many cases determinations of the law: decisions that things will be thus and so, even though they could reasonably have been determined to be otherwise.

E. Conscience

We turn now to the final area in which natural law reflection generates sound norms for medical practice and law, the questions surrounding 'physician rights of conscience'. Such questions arise as a result of an erosion of agreement on the norms that should govern critical areas of health care, prominent among them being the areas we have discussed above, such as abortion and euthanasia. Western societies almost universally enforce, legally, extensive rights to abortion, and they increasingly enforce considerable rights to assistance in ending one's life. At the same time, a significant part of the population, and many members of the health-care profession, continue to recognize the truth of the norms we have here articulated concerning, especially, the protection of innocent human life, the difference between intention and side effect, and the limited authority of patients. They recognize, as well other norms, which we have not addressed, but which follow from the principles we have identified, in particular the principle that the organic functioning and unity of a human person are not to be damaged save for the sake of the overall organic functioning and unity of that same person. Human health is to be considered integrally, and the removal of a diseased limb, for example, is not seen by natural law theorists as intentional damage to health for the sake of health, but rather action for the patient's health, integrally understood. By

[41] For instances and discussion of the controversies, see the contributions by C Lustig and J Boyle to C Tollefsen (ed), *Bioethics with Liberty and Justice: Themes in the Work of Joseph M. Boyle* (Springer, 2011).

[42] See the discussion in KW Wildes, 'Creating Critical Care Resources: Implications for Distributive Justice' in HT Engelhardt and MJ Cherry (eds), *Allocating Scarce Medical Resources* (Georgetown University Press, 2002), 200–11.

contrast, surgeries meant to reassign the biological sex of a human being are characteristically seen by natural law theorists as a form of mutilation, as are surgeries to eliminate an agent's reproductive capacity for non-medical reasons; they are thus ruled out by the natural law prescription against intentional *damage* to the basic good of health.

Many physicians who adhere to these norms of the natural law are conflicted because the requirements of natural law and of the positive law (and increasingly the norms of their profession) point to different directions. This creates a situation of conflict among physicians and their patients, their profession, and the broader society. When physicians refuse to provide certain services (eg abortion, euthanasia, gender reassignment surgery, or sterilization), patient expectations are thwarted; increasingly rigid professional norms are violated; and there is a default on a perceived social contract, ratified by the laws that give physicians a monopoly on certain rights (such as the right to perform surgery) in exchange for their willing provision of services.[43]

Natural law thought raises two considerations in response to this situation that provide guidance for law and professional policy. First, it is to be stressed that the gap in current law and professional practice between physicians who adhere to norms against intentional killing and mutilation, and to consistently health-and-life-oriented practices, on the one hand, and laws and practices permissive of intentional killing, mutilation, and non-health-related expectations of medical professionals, on the other, is a failure on the part of the law and the medical profession, and *not* those physicians with both good moral judgment and practical integrity. The *first* form of advice to be given in such circumstances is that better laws and professional standards need to be (re)developed that consistently respect the vocational commitment of medicine to heal and never to harm.

The *second* form of advice is that, in the current deficient state of affairs in which law and the medical ethos remain permissive of practices that are at odds with the good of life and health, natural lawyers point to two important goods that will be served by accommodating physicians who accept the more traditional health-and-life-oriented norms—namely, integrity and religion. Integrity is the good of having an integrated practical character, in which judgment, choice, action, and emotion are all coherently unified. To some extent, that unity can be achieved in an evil person whose character is entirely oriented to what is bad. Nevertheless, like all basic goods, the good of integrity is realized more fully when it is realized in morally upright ways. But integrity is a basic good that is to be protected not just in oneself, but in others.

Thus, laws and practices that require acts of persons that are contrary to their integrity do a wrong to those persons if there is not adequate reason for requiring those acts.[44] *Of course*, persons may be thwarted from pursuing wicked plans even if they pursue them with integrity; but when possible human persons are to be given the practical possibility of living out their lives without significant threats to the integrity of their practical character.

The same is true of the good of religion. Agents who see their lives and character as shaped by religious commitments and concerns are, when possible, to be given the practical space necessary for them to be able to do so: this fosters a basic good. *Of course*, human sacrificers

[43] See, for articulation of such criticisms, J Savulescu and U Schuklenk, 'Doctors Have No Right to Refuse Assistance in Dying, Abortion, or Contraception' (2016) 31 Bioethics 162–70.

[44] See the discussion by Anderson and Girgis in J Corvino, R Anderson, and S Girgis, *Debating Religious Liberty and Discrimination* (Oxford University Press, 2017).

and suicide bombers are to be thwarted, even when they act for religious reasons, in order to safeguard the lives and health of innocent persons. But many other circumstances can be envisaged when the stakes are not so high that agents *must* be stopped from acting on the basis of religious convictions.[45] Thus, for example, many states have exemptions from otherwise general drug laws providing exemptions if certain drugs, such as peyote, are used in religious ceremonies.

Both the good of integrity and the good of religion are obviously implicated in the decisions of many 'dissenting' physicians and other health-care professionals who refuse to participate in abortions or a patient's suicide; or who refuse to aid in the mutilation of healthy bodies; or to prescribe medications whose purposes are, they believe, contrary to good health and morality. The integrity and religious commitments of such health-care practitioners ought to be protected to the extent possible, barring serious reasons not to. Can opponents of accommodating physician conscience in these situations offer such reasons?

In these cases, they cannot. The question is not to be settled simply by identifying what the law permits or what patients expect, since the question is primarily normative. Nor can doctors who refuse to perform these services be convicted of acting unfairly or in a discriminatory manner: they are acting from sincere and intelligently formed conscience in refusing to perform or cooperate with certain kinds of *acts* that harm the goods of life and health. Their refusals are thus unlike the refusals of racist doctors in times past to serve classes of *persons*. Is, then, the medical profession and its values put at risk by such dissenting physicians' actions? If it were, this too would be a good reason to refuse them accommodation. But it is not: such physicians in fact act from considered convictions about the importance of the very good on which the medical profession is based and towards which, in principle, its existence is ordered: the good of life and health (this again differentiates them from racist physicians). There is no real medical profession absent this conviction, merely a set of technical skills that can be put at the service of whatever desires it is legally permitted to satisfy. Accordingly, we suggest, the medical profession is itself best served by accommodating those professionals whose conscientious refusals are governed by the considerations that reflect the authentic ethos of the profession, the authentic concerns of law, and the true and practically reasonable deliverances of the natural law.

V. Conclusion

Natural law theorists approach the task of moral theory by enquiring into the foundational reasons for human action. Such reasons are found in basic human goods that are constitutive of human flourishing. Natural law theorists then ask what norms are prescribed by practical reason as protecting those goods and what forms of authority, including legal authority, are likewise needed to protect those goods. Such an approach bears fruit in the domain of medical ethics and law, where an especially vulnerable good, life and health, is at stake. The natural law approach to medicine, both in ethics and in law, thus serves to protect and promote human flourishing in this important domain.

[45] See C Tollefsen, 'Conscience, Religion, and State' (2009) 54 American Journal of Jurisprudence 93–116.

Bibliography

Anderson, R, 'Always Care, Never Kill: How Physician-Assisted Suicide Endangers the Weak, Corrupts Medicine, Compromises the Family, and Violates Human Dignity and Equality', Report of the Heritage Foundation (24 March 2015), http://www.heritage.org/health-care-reform/report/always-care-never-kill-how-physician-assisted-suicide-endangers-the-weak accessed 15 July 2019.

Aquinas, St T, *Summa Theologica* (Benziger Bros, 1947).

Beauchamp, TL and Childress, R, *Principles of Biomedical Ethics* (7th edn, Oxford University Press, 2013).

Boyle, J, '*Praeter intentionem* in Aquinas' (1978) 42 Thomist 649.

Boyle, J, 'Sanctity of Life and Suicide: Tensions and Developments within Common Morality' in BA Brody (ed), *Suicide and Euthanasia* (Kluwer, 1989), 221–50.

Boyle, J, 'Who Is Entitled to Double Effect?' (1991) 16 Journal of Medicine and Philosophy 475.

Boyle, J, 'Fairness in Holdings: A Natural Law Account of Property and Welfare Rights' (2001) 18 Social Philosophy and Policy 206.

Boyle, J, 'Limiting Access to Healthcare: A Traditional Roman Catholic Analysis' in HT Engelhardt and MJ Cherry (eds), *Allocating Scarce Medical Resources* (Georgetown University Press, 2002), 77–95.

Boyle, J, 'An Appreciative Response' in C Tollefsen (ed), *Bioethics with Liberty and Justice: Themes in the Work of Joseph M. Boyle* (Springer, 2011), 243–58.

Boyle, J, 'On the Most Fundamental Principle of Morality' in J Keown and RP George (eds), *Reason, Morality, and Law: The Philosophy of John Finnis* (Oxford University Press, 2013), 56–72.

Boyle, J, 'Intention, Permissibility, and the Structure of Agency' (2015) 89 American Catholic Philosophical Quarterly 461.

Cherry, MJ, 'Social Justice, Charity, and Tax Evasion: A Critical Inquiry' in C Tollefsen (ed), *Bioethics with Liberty and Justice: Themes in the Work of Joseph M. Boyle* (Springer, 2011), 185–204.

Corvino, J, Anderson, R, and Girgis, S, *Debating Religious Liberty and Discrimination* (Oxford University Press, 2017).

De Campos, TC, *The Global Health Crisis: Ethical Responsibilities* (Cambridge University Press, 2017).

Dyer, FN, *The Physician's Crusade against Abortion* (Science History Publications, 2005).

Emanuel, E, 'Four Myths about Doctor Assisted Suicide', *The New York Times* (27 October 2012), https://opinionator.blogs.nytimes.com/2012/10/27/four-myths-about-doctor-assisted-suicide/?smid=tw-share accessed 15 July 2019.

Finnis, J, *Moral Absolutes: Tradition, Revision, and Truth* (Catholic University of America Press, 1991).

Finnis, J, *Aquinas: Moral, Political and Legal Theory* (Oxford University Press, 1998).

Finnis, J, 'Euthanasia and the Law' in *Human Rights and Common Good, Collected Essays* (Oxford University Press, 2011), vol III, 251–70.

Finnis, J, *Natural Law and Natural Rights* (2nd edn, Oxford University Press, 2011).

George, RP and Lee, P, 'The Wrong of Abortion' in AI Cohen and C Wellman (eds), *Contemporary Debates in Applied Ethics* (Blackwell Publishers, 2005).

George, RP and Tollefsen, C, *Embryo: A Defense of Human Life* (2nd edn, Witherspoon, 2011).

Gomez-Lobo, A, *Bioethics and the Human Goods: An Introduction to Natural Law Bioethics* (Georgetown University Press, 2015).

Gorsuch, NM, *The Future of Assisted Suicide and Euthanasia* (Princeton University Press, 2006).

Grisez, G, 'The First Principle of Practical Reason: A Commentary on the *Summa Theologiae*, 1–2, Question 94, Article 2' (1965) 10 Natural Law Forum 168.

Grisez, G, *The Way of the Lord Jesus*, vol 1: *Christian Moral Principles* (Franciscan Herald Press, 1983).

Grisez, G, *The Way of The Lord Jesus*, vol 2: *Living a Christian Life* (Franciscan Press, 1993).

Grisez, G, 'Health Care Technology and Justice' in C Tollefsen (ed), *Bioethics with Liberty and Justice: Themes in the Work of Joseph M. Boyle* (Springer, 2011), 221–41.

Kaczor, C, *The Ethics of Abortion: Women's Rights, Human Life, and the Question of Justice* (2nd edn, Routledge, 2015).

Kass, L, 'Neither for Love Nor Money: Why Doctors Must Not Kill' (1989) 94 Public Interest 25.

Keown, J, 'Euthanasia in the Netherlands: Sliding down the Slippery Slope?' (1995) 9 Notre Dame Journal of Law, Ethics & Public Policy 407.

Keown, J, *The Law and Ethics of Medicine: Essays on the Inviolability of Human Life* (Oxford University Press, 2012).

Lee, P and George, RP, *Body-Self Dualism in Contemporary Ethics and Politics* (Cambridge University Press, 2008).

Lee, P, Tollefsen, C, and George, RP, 'The Ontological Status of Embryos: A Reply to Jason Morris' (2014) 39 Journal of Medicine and Philosophy 483.

Lu, R, 'Why Pro-Lifers Don't Support Punishing Women for Abortion', *The Federalist* (5 April 2016), http://thefederalist.com/2016/04/05/why-pro-lifers-dont-support-punishing-women-for-abortion/ accessed 15 July 2019.

Lustig, A, 'Natural Law, Property, and Welfare Rights' in C Tollefsen (ed), *Bioethics with Liberty and Justice: Themes in the Work of Joseph M. Boyle* (Springer, 2011), 205–20.

MacLeod, A, *Property and Practical Reason* (Cambridge University Press, 2015).

McMahan, J, *The Ethics of Killing* (Oxford University Press, 2003).

Moschella, M, *To Whom Do Children Belong? Parental Rights, Civic Education, and Children's Autonomy* (Cambridge University Press, 2016).

Parfit, D, *Reasons and Persons* (Oxford University Press, 1989).

Savulescu, J and Schuklenk, U, 'Doctors Have No Right to Refuse Assistance in Dying, Abortion, or Contraception' (2016) 31 Bioethics 162.

Siegler, M, 'Searching for Moral Certainty in Medicine: A Proposal for a New Model of the Doctor-Patient Encounter' (1981) 57 Bulletin of the New York Academy of Medicine 56.

Thomson, JJ, 'A Defense of Abortion' (1971) 1 Philosophy and Public Affairs 47.

Tollefsen, C, 'Conscience, Religion, and State' (2009) 54 American Journal of Jurisprudence 93.

Tollefsen, C (ed), *Bioethics with Liberty and Justice: Themes in the Work of Joseph M. Boyle* (Springer, 2011).

Tollefsen, C, 'Double Effect and Two Hard Cases in Medical Ethics' (2015) 89 American Catholic Philosophical Quarterly 407.

Tollefsen, C, 'Natural Law, Basic Goods, and Practical Reason' in G Duke and RP George (eds), *The Cambridge Companion to Natural Law Jurisprudence* (Cambridge University Press, 2017), 133–58.

Tollefsen, C, Lee, P, and George, RP, 'Marco Rubio Was Right: The Life of a New Human Being Begins at Conception', *The Public Discourse* (15 August 2015), http://www.thepublicdiscourse.com/2015/08/15520/ accessed 15 July 2019.

Wildes, KW, 'Creating Critical Care Resources: Implications for Distributive Justice' in HT Engelhardt and MJ Cherry (eds), *Allocating Scarce Medical Resources* (Georgetown University Press, 2002), 200–11.

Zaner, RM, *A Critical Examination of Ethics in Health Care and Biomedical Research: Voices and Visions* (Springer, 2015).

4

Consequentialism and the Law in Medicine

Julian Savulescu and Dominic Wilkinson

I. Overview

There are two broad schools of ethical theory: consequentialism and non-consequentialism.

According to consequentialism, the right act is that act which has the best consequences. According to non-consequentialism, the rightness of an action is not solely determined by its consequences (although most versions of non-consequentialism allow some ethical relevance of consequences). The most famous version of non-consequentialism is deontology, which holds that one has an absolute duty to obey certain rules. 'Never kill an innocent person' or 'never lie' are examples of such rules. Christianity is one form of deontology and the Ten Commandments represent one set of rules.

Medical law exists at the intersection between consequentialism and deontology. Much of medical law is consequentialist in nature. However, having evolved from a set of Christian values and principles, it retains certain deontological characteristics. In particular, it retains a commitment in many jurisdictions to the Sanctity of Life Doctrine, though this is being shed or modified as assisted dying becomes legalized.

In this chapter, we will begin by defining consequentialism, and contrasting it with deontology. We will describe some examples of the influence of consequentialism over current medical law. We will close by outlining the areas where consequentialism is at odds with current medical law and how medical law should evolve according to consequentialism.

II. Elements of Consequentialism

Consequentialism is a theory of right action. It instructs the agent to outline all the possible actions, including doing nothing at all. One must then assign a value to the possible outcomes of each action, and a probability for each of these outcomes occurring. The expected value of each action is the sum of the value of the outcomes of each action, where each value is multiplied by the probability of it eventuating. The agent should choose that act with the greatest expected value.

There are two key components to consequentialism:

(1) The *probability* of outcomes occurring. These should be based on the best evidence available. Thus, consequentialism sits naturally with scientific approaches to medicine and evidence-based medicine.
(2) The *value* of the outcomes. This is a distinctively ethical evaluation of the good.

Julian Savulescu and Dominic Wilkinson, *Consequentialism and the Law in Medicine* In: *Philosophical Foundations of Medical Law*. Edited by: Andelka M Phillips, Thana C de Campos, and Jonathan Herring, Oxford University Press (2019).
DOI: 10.1093/oso/9780198796558.003.0005

Consequentialism is a broad school of ethical theory. There are many different forms of consequentialism depending on how one values outcomes. For example, welfare consequentialism, or welfarism, maintains that all that matters or is good is welfare, or well-being. The right act is the act which maximizes well-being.

Utilitarianism is a version of welfare consequentialism. It instructs the agent to choose the action which maximizes utility. Utility has traditionally been defined in terms of either happiness or preference satisfaction (though there are other versions).

According to Hedonistic Utilitarianism, the right act is the act which maximizes happiness or pleasure. According to Preference Utilitarianism, the right act is the one which maximizes preference satisfaction.

The goal of medicine has traditionally been the promotion of health. The goals of medicine are thus consequentialist: maximizing health. But this has evolved over the last decades to include well-being. The goal of medicine is to promote the best interests of the patient. For example, in a recent judgment, Justice Francis said: 'The term "best interests" encompasses medical, emotional, and all other welfare issues.'[1]

The 'best interests' principle of medicine is essentially a part of welfare consequentialism. And when it comes to groups of patients—resource allocation or public health—medicine is explicitly welfare consequentialist. It aims to bring about the greatest improvement in well-being for the whole population, as we shall see.

A. Act and Rule Consequentialism

There are two different ways of evaluating consequences. According to act consequentialism, the right act is the act which produces the best consequences. According to rule consequentialism, the right rule is the rule which produces the best consequences. The law is in many instances an instantiation of rule consequentialism: laws are chosen because they bring about the best consequences. When governments are contemplating whether or not to change the law, evidence about the potential impact of the law (in terms of risks and harms) is highly important. This is clearly consequentialist.

These versions of consequentialism can come apart. Sometimes an act will clearly have better consequences, or no adverse consequences, but a rule proscribes that act. As an example, in 2017, a transplant surgeon was found guilty of 'assault by beating' for using an argon beam laser to draw his initials in two cases on the under-surface of a liver that he was transplanting.[2] In this case, there was clear evidence that marking the initials had no medical effect on the patients whatsoever. The surgeon's actions had not caused any harm to the patients concerned. Nevertheless, there may be good reasons to, in general, prohibit doctors from taking advantage of their patients while unconscious to make personal markings on the inside of their bodies. That could lead to harm in other cases, or could lead to patients losing trust in health professionals.

Principles or laws around non-discrimination are other examples. For example, one example would be not considering social worth criteria (eg whether someone is a criminal,

[1] *Re A (Medical Treatment: Male Sterilisation)* [2000] 1 FLR 549, (2000) 1 FCR 193.

[2] C Dyer, '"Arrogant" Surgeon Fined for Writing his Initials on Patients' Livers' (2018) 360 British Medical Journal k200, https://www.bmj.com/content/360/bmj.k200 accessed 15 July 2019.

or has dependents, etc) in the allocation of resources, including doctors' time. Some have argued, for example, that in a disaster setting, victims of a terrorist attack should be prioritized over the perpetrators.[3] It might be clear that in a particular case, deprioritizing a terrorist in the emergency room will maximize short-term utility, but such a practice may well lead to worse consequences in the long term (see slippery-slope arguments).

B. Two-Level Consequentialism

The two different schools of consequentialism can be combined. Famous utilitarian Richard Hare described a two-level approach.[4] Hare argued that moral thinking occurs at two levels: intuitive and critical. At the intuitive level, we have many rough rules of thumb that can be rapidly deployed without protracted and demanding reflection: don't kill, don't steal, be honest, etc; these enable us to act efficiently in everyday life.

However, at times, these conflicts or situations are more complex and we must rise to the more reflective and deliberative critical level and ask what kinds of rules or principles we should endorse. What really is the right answer? Here, he argues, we should employ act utilitarianism (this corresponds to system 1 and 2 thinking in psychology[5]).

If medical law were to adopt this approach, that might allow a more coherent response to exceptional cases—see, for example, the case of Jodie and Mary below.

C. Autonomy

Besides aiming to promote the best interests of the patient (maximizing welfare or well-being), modern medicine aims to respect the autonomy of the patient. This is encapsulated in the need to obtain valid consent for any medical procedure. In the precedent-setting case of *Schloendorff v New York Hospital*,[6] Justice Cardozo observed that: 'Every human being of adult years and sound mind has a right to determine what shall be done with his own body.'[7]

This might appear to be a deontological, non-consequentialist element to the law. The very strong emphasis on the importance of consent seems to conflict with welfare consequentialism. For example, occasionally during an operation a surgeon may find something unrelated to the procedure, perhaps a tumour or a blood vessel aneurysm. In those circumstances, there may be good reason to think that it would be best for the patient to address the incidental finding (eg by biopsying a tumour or clipping an aneurysm); this would be in the patient's best interests. It would save the patient having to have a separate operation. However, if the surgeon hasn't discussed this possibility with the patient beforehand (and if it isn't urgent to intervene), additional procedures would appear to be

[3] A Gold and RD Straus, 'Second Thoughts about Who Is First: The Medical Triage of Violent Perpetrators and Their Victims' (2016) 43(5) Journal of Medical Ethics 293–300.

[4] RM Hare, *Moral Thinking: Its Levels, Method and Point* (Clarendon Press, 1981).

[5] D Kahneman, *Thinking Fast and Slow* (Farrar, Straus & Giroux, 2011).

[6] *Schloendorff v. New York Hospital* [1914] 211 NY 125.

[7] Ibid [129]–[130].

a breach of patient autonomy. In other situations, patients refuse medical treatment that would be in their best interests. A patient might, for example, refuse a blood transfusion because they have a fear of needles, or refuse antibiotics because they believe in the power of prayer to heal them. Doctors are legally obliged to respect those decisions, as long as the patient has capacity, even if withholding treatment would lead to serious harm, even the death of the patient.

A rule consequentialist might endorse patient autonomy for epistemic reasons. In general, people know their own circumstances better than others do. It might be thought that the patient is better placed than the doctor to know what would be best for them. However, there are going to be situations (eg those described above) where there is good reason to believe that the patient is mistaken about their own interests. Surely, the consequentialist should then believe that the patient's decision should not be respected?

Perhaps surprisingly, respect for patient autonomy in medical law sits very comfortably with the arguments of one famous utilitarian, John Stuart Mill. Mill was a hedonistic utilitarian. Mill claimed that 'pleasure, and freedom from pain, are the only things desirable as ends'.[8] However, Mill accorded great importance to individuality and originality:

> He who lets the world, or his own portion of it, choose his plan of life for him, has no need of any other faculty than the ape-like one of imitation. He who chooses his plan for himself, employs all his faculties. He must use observation to see, reasoning and judgement to foresee, activity to gather materials for decision, discrimination to decide, and when he has decided, firmness and self-control to hold to his deliberate decision … It is possible that he might be guided in some good path, and kept out of harm's way, without any of these things. But what will be his comparative worth as a human being? It really is of importance, not only what men do, but what manner of men they are that do it. Among the works of man, which human life is rightly employed in perfecting and beautifying, the first in importance is surely man himself.[9]
>
> … individuality is the same thing with development, and … it is only the cultivation of individuality which produces, or can produce, well-developed humans …[10]

This quote comes from the chapter from *On Liberty* entitled, 'Of Individuality, as One of the Elements of Well-Being'. Mill clearly believes that individuality is one of the goods of life. The value of individuality for Mill is intrinsic. For although a person may 'be guided in some good path', that is, achieve good, something very important will be lacking: that life will not be his own.

> If a person possesses any tolerable amount of common sense and experience, his own mode of laying out his existence is the best, not because it is the best in itself, but because it is his own mode.[11]

[8] JS Mill, *On Liberty* (JM Dent and Sons, 1910), 6.
[9] Ibid 117.
[10] Ibid 121.
[11] Ibid 125.

Mill calls 'individuality' what we call 'autonomy'. He attaches such importance to it that he believes it ought only to be obstructed in a few very special circumstances (when it results in harm to others—harm to self is not sufficient).

While Mill did not write on either medical law or ethics, it would seem that giving priority to autonomy in promoting well-being would be entirely consistent with his influential approach to utilitarianism.

Such an approach also supports modern changes to the doctor–patient relationship. While the old paternalistic model involved doctors imposing their value judgment of what is in the best interests of the patient, modern conceptions such as shared decision making or liberal rationalism take seriously the patient's own values in arriving at what is best for the patient.

The law has gradually come to adopt this Millian perspective. In recent years, medical law has moved away from the paternalistic Bolam standard,[12] which involved disclosing risks to patients according to what a reasonable body of medical practitioners would disclose, to a more person-centred approach. The Supreme Court in the United Kingdom in its 'Montgomery' judgment[13] ruled that clinicians must enter into 'dialogue' with their patient to achieve sufficient understanding of the advantages and disadvantages of the options available to make a choice that 'take(s) into account her own values'.[14] This follows similar decisions in Australia[15]

This Millian approach, which might be called liberal welfarist consequentialism, has two values or two factors: liberty and well-being. It is important to enable the patient to both make their own decision and promote their well-being. It is consistent with the strong emphasis on the principles of autonomy and beneficence in medical ethics. (The principle of distributive justice, which also features in the oft-cited 'four principles' of medical ethics,[16] might be partly understood to incorporate Mill's concept of harm to others as limiting individual freedom to choose.)

Importantly, sometimes there might be large discrepancies in the values of liberty and well-being. For example, some intervention may minimally promote well-being, but significantly promote freedom and autonomy. Some cases of sterilization, contraception, or abortion may fit this category (though clearly in many cases such procedures do promote the interests of the patient). They would still be justified on a liberal welfarist consequentialist approach.[17]

In some cases, freedom or autonomy are not significantly at issue—such as when patients have impaired decision-making capacity. In those cases, the patient's best interests (welfare) should purely be promoted. However, courts in recent decisions have emphasized that the patient's prior wishes should be given considerable weight in a best-interests determination.[18]

[12] *Bolam v Friern Hospital Management Committee* [1957] 1 WLR 583.

[13] *Montgomery v Lanarkshire Health Board* [2015] UKSC 11.

[14] Ibid 115.

[15] *Rogers v Whitaker* [1992] HCA 58; 175 CLR 479.

[16] T Beachamp and J Childress, *Principles of Biomedical Ethics* (Oxford University Press, 1979).

[17] J Savulescu, 'Autonomy, the Good Life, and Controversial Choices' in R Rhodes, LP Francis, and A Silvers (eds), *The Blackwell Guide to Medical Ethics* (Blackwell Publishing, 2007), 17–37.

[18] *Briggs v Briggs* [2016] EWCOP 48.

D. Acts and Omissions

Consequentialists care only about the consequences, not how they were brought about. This is often caricatured by the following phrase: 'The end justifies the means.'

Importantly, consequentialists see no morally relevant differences between acting and omitting to act, if that would result in the same outcome. James Rachels famously provided the case of Smith and Jones:

> Smith stands to inherit a lot of money if his four-year-old cousin dies. He sneaks into the bathroom of his cousin and drowns him, arranging things so that it will look like an accident.

Jones also stands to gain a similar large inheritance from the death of his four-year-old cousin. Like Smith, Jones sneaks into the bathroom with the intention of drowning his cousin. The cousin, however, accidentally slips and knocks his head. He falls face down into the bath, struggles but drowns all by himself in the bath. Jones could easily have saved his cousin, but far from trying to save him, he stands ready to push the child's head back under if this becomes necessary. However, it is not necessary.[19]

Smith acted; Jones omitted to act. From a moral point of view, Rachels argues that Smith and Jones are equally blameworthy. From a consequentialist point of view, their act or omission is equally wrong. However, the law would not necessarily see it that way.

In medicine, the difference between acts and omissions appears to have strong relevance to decisions about either withholding (not starting) or withdrawing (stopping) treatment. Doctors frequently believe there is a moral difference between withholding and withdrawing life-prolonging medical treatment.[20] Withholding is seen as an omission, while withdrawing is more of an action. It is seen by doctors and by some families to be more acceptable to withhold than to withdraw. This has the consequence that trials of treatment are not started and sometimes patients are not given a chance to benefit, when the chances are small. It also means that sometimes treatment is prolonged for a long period of time, because once started, it cannot be stopped.

Consequentialists reject any distinction between withholding and withdrawing treatment. If it would be ethical to withhold treatment, all other things being equal it must be ethical to withdraw treatment (if that treatment had already been started). Conversely, if it would be wrong to withdraw treatment, it would be equally wrong to withhold that treatment.

Here, medical law has adopted an approach that sometimes appears compatible with consequentialism, and in some ways incompatible. The courts have explicitly endorsed the idea that withholding and withdrawing are equivalent. In the case of Tony Bland, where the court debated whether it was acceptable to withdraw artificial feeding from a man in a persistent vegetative state, Lord Goff noted that 'discontinuation of life support is, for present purposes, no different from not initiating life support in the first place.'[21] However, the

[19] J Rachels, 'Active and Passive Euthanasia' (1975) 292 New England Journal of Medicine 78–80.

[20] D Wilkinson and J Savulescu, 'A Costly Separation between Withdrawing and Withholding Treatment in Intensive Care' (2014) 28 Bioethics 127–37.

[21] *Airedale NHS Trust v Bland* [1993] AC 789.

judges in that case were not supporting the wider consequentialist view that actions and omissions are equivalent. Lord Mustill stated that: 'For the time being all are agreed that the distinction between acts exists, and we must give effect to it.' Rather, they appeared (perhaps implausibly) to accept the view that since withholding treatment is obviously an omission, and withholding and withdrawing were equivalent, then withdrawing life-sustaining treatment should also be categorized as an omission. (The law lords mentioned, but dismissed, the counter-argument that if, in a parallel case, an interloper had crept into a hospital and disconnected a mechanical ventilator, or pulled out a feeding tube, that no one would have any doubt that the interloper had 'acted'.)

E. Intention-Foresight and Doctrine of Double Effect

In deontological ethics and law, intentions play a significant role. For example, murder is distinguished from manslaughter on the basis of whether killing was intentional. This distinction also plays a role in medical law—it is legal to administer potentially life-shortening doses or types of medication (such as large doses of morphine) in the care of a terminal patient provided that the intention is to relieve pain and not to shorten life. One is permitted to foresee that the action might shorten life, but provided it is not intentional, it can be permissible.

The doctrine of double effect captures this: it is permissible to act in a way which brings about harm (that would ordinarily be impermissible, such as leading to the death of an innocent person) provided that one merely foresees the harm and does not intend it, that the positive effects of the act do not occur via the negative effects, and that the benefits of the act outweigh the harm.

Consequentialists reject any distinction between intended and foreseen effects. What matters is the predicted outcome of an action, and whether that is justified, not the intent. Accordingly, consequentialists are typically sceptical of the doctrine of double effect.

In some situations, medical law does take a more consequentialist approach. In the case of Tony Bland, the judges rejected the significance of intention. Lord Browne-Wilkinson stated that 'there can be no doubt that … the whole purpose of stopping artificial feeding is to bring about the death of Anthony Bland', while Lord Lowry stated that 'even though the intention to bring about the patient's death is there, there is no proposed guilty act'.[22] It seems that intentions are not deemed to be relevant to omissions—rather, the issue is whether the doctor has a duty to act.

F. Applications of Consequentialism: Cases

1.. Killing and Conjoined Twins: Jodie and Mary

In 2000, Rina Attard gave birth to conjoined twins known as Jodie and Mary.[23] They were joined at the pelvis and spine. Lord Justice Ward described their plight in this way:

[22] Ibid.

[23] J Savulescu, 'Abortion, Infanticide and Allowing Babies to Die, 40 Years on' (2013) 39 Journal of Medical Ethics 257–9.

> Jodie and Mary are conjoined twins. They each have their own brain, heart and lungs and other vital organs and they each have arms and legs. They are joined at the lower abdomen ... [T]hey can be successfully separated. But the operation will kill the weaker twin, Mary. That is because her lungs and heart are too deficient to oxygenate and pump blood through her body. Had she been born a singleton, she would not have been viable and resuscitation would have been abandoned. She would have died shortly after her birth. She is alive only because a common artery enables her sister, who is stronger, to circulate life sustaining oxygenated blood for both of them. Separation would require the clamping and then the severing of that common artery. Within minutes of doing so Mary will die. Yet if the operation does not take place, both will die within three to six months, or perhaps a little longer, because Jodie's heart will eventually fail.[24]

The High Court authorized surgical separation, knowing it would kill Mary.

> Mary may have a right to life, but she has little right to be alive. She is alive because and only because, to put it bluntly, but nonetheless accurately, she sucks the lifeblood of Jodie and she sucks the lifeblood out of Jodie. She will survive only so long as Jodie survives. Jodie will not survive long because constitutionally she will not be able to cope. Mary's parasitic living will be the cause of Jodie's ceasing to live. If Jodie could speak, she would surely protest, 'Stop it, Mary, you're killing me'. Mary would have no answer to that. Into my scales of fairness and justice between the children goes the fact that nobody but the doctors can help Jodie. Mary is beyond help.
>
> Hence I am in no doubt at all that the scales come down heavily in Jodie's favour. The best interests of the twins is to give the chance of life to the child whose actual bodily condition is capable of accepting the chance to her advantage even if that has to be at the cost of the sacrifice of the life which is so unnaturally supported. I am wholly satisfied that the least detrimental choice, balancing the interests of Mary against Jodie and Jodie against Mary, is to permit the operation to be performed.[25]

This was a consequentialist decision. There were two courses of action: do nothing, and both would die. Or, 'separate', which would kill Mary, and Jodie would survive.

In this case, the judges were unable to pretend that the surgical procedure to separate the twins was an omission. It was, moreover, a fiction to describe Mary as a parasite and to couch this in terms of justifiable self-defence. Mary and Jodie arose from the same original embryo. Neither had a greater claim to shared body parts. It is not accurate to describe Mary as killing Jodie. They were both dying because their body could not support both of their lives. The common artery was the property as much of Mary as it was of Jodie. Mary was killed to save Jodie.

The ethics of separating conjoined twins are complex.[26] From a consequentialist point of view, one must consider the length and quality of life, and probability of achieving these, with and without separation for both twins. Importantly, when separation risks death, and

[24] *In Re A (Children) (Conjoined Twins: Surgical Separation)* [2001] Fam 147, 155.

[25] Ibid 147, 197.

[26] J Savulescu and I Persson, 'Conjoined Twins—Philosophical Problems and Ethical Challenges' (2016) 41(1) Journal of Medical Philosophy 41–55; I Persson and J Savulescu, 'Conjoined Twins' in H LaFollette (ed), *International Encyclopedia of Ethics* (2nd print edn, Wiley, forthcoming).

continued existence is possible without separation, one must carefully evaluate the quality of life with and without separation. The improvement in quality of life with separation may not be sufficient to justify the risks of separation from a consequentialist perspective. In contrast, those who hold a deontological view about the value of normality may be prepared to accept much higher risks of surgery.

There is no question that the court made the right decision in the case of Jodie and Mary. However, their attempt to reconcile that decision with the existing deontological framework of the law appears incoherent.

2. The Case of Charlie Gard

In 2017, the courts heard the case of Charlie Gard.[27] This was a young infant with a rare severe mitochondrial disorder—infantile onset encephalomyopathic mitochondrial DNA depletion syndrome (MDDS). This resulted in failure of mitochondria to make DNA necessary for energy supply to all cells. The result was that all cells were being starved of energy. There were only a handful of patients who had ever been described with Charlie's illness. He was profoundly weak, unable to move or breathe, and experienced seizures.

In December 2016, Charlie's parents identified an experimental treatment after contacting other parents on the internet. This had been used in a related but less severe form of MDDS. The clinicians treating Charlie had become convinced that treatment, both continued intensive care and the nucleoside therapy, would be futile. In contrast, a US expert offered to provide the nucleoside replacement therapy if Charlie were transferred to the United States. The parents began crowd-sourcing funds to take Charlie overseas.

However, doctors in the United Kingdom applied to the Family Division of the High Court on 28 February for permission to withdraw life support and to provide palliative care. On 11 April, Justice Francis ruled in favour of the hospital. A series of legal appeals were unsuccessful, and after a further court hearing, and new tests, his parents accepted that further treatment could not help him. He died after withdrawal of life support.

This case illustrates the strengths and challenges of consequentialism. It was clearly a welfare consequentialist decision. As Charlie's own wishes were unknown, the decision was reached on the basis of consideration of his best interests. Justice Francis concluded:

> It is with the heaviest of hearts, but with complete conviction for Charlie's best interests, that I find it is in Charlie's best interests that I accede to these applications and rule that GOSH may lawfully withdraw all treatment save for palliative care to permit Charlie to die with dignity.[28]

The gesture to dignity is not an essential part of the judgment. Indeed, consequentialists typically eschew discussions of dignity (which are rarely cashed out or operationalizable) except where this is defined as either a subjective or an objective value to be considered in the consequentialist calculus.

One of the challenges of consequentialism is that it is heavily dependent on the facts to decide what has best consequences. In medicine, there is often great uncertainty as to what the effects of medical interventions will be. Because of that uncertainty, assessment of the

[27] Material for this section on Charlie Gard is drawn from D Wilkinson and J Savulescu, *Ethics, Conflict and Medical Treatment for Children: From Disagreement to Dissensus* (Elsevier, 2018).

[28] *Great Ormond Street Hospital v Yates, Gard and Gard* [2017] EWHC 972 (Fam) 23.

consequences may be heavily influenced by an individual's prior beliefs as well as by their values. This is nowhere more apparent than in judgments of medical futility.

The most common argument that further treatment is not in the interests of the patient is on grounds of 'futility'.[29] This can be for two reasons.

1. Treatment Itself Has No Relevant Biological Activity

One early consideration in Gard was whether nucleoside replacement would cross the blood–brain barrier. If it didn't, it would be futile. However, it was accepted later in the case that it would cross.

The dominant ground for a judgment of futility in the High Court Decision was that there was no direct evidence that such therapy would have any effect in Charlie's condition because it had never been tried in humans or animal models.

The only evidence produced by the US expert (Dr Hirano) was from patients with a related disorder. These studies were small with modest results, and no blinded controlled trials had been conducted. However, there was a physiological rationale and the US expert stated the chances of improvement in Charlie's condition were 'low, but not zero'.[30] Despite this, Judge Francis concluded that 'that there is no scientific evidence of any prospect of any improvement in a human with RRM2B strain of MDDS'.[31]

It is a value judgment whether there was any evidence of any prospect of improvement. According to some, Hirano did present such (albeit weak and indirect) evidence.

In the late stages of the case, several experts wrote with scientific evidence for the experimental treatment in laboratory models. They urged reconsideration of scientific plausibility. It supported the US doctor's claim earlier that the chances of it working were non-zero and thus it was not futile.

2. Irreversible Damage

Indeed, argument shifted after this to the second ground for futility. Although an agent might have biological utility, features about this particular patient mean it will not work. In particular, it was the alleged fact that Charlie had suffered irreversible brain damage that led the court to find that treatment would be futile.

However, the assessment that someone's condition is irreversible implies that it cannot be reversed (ie that there is no chance of this outcome occurring). Yet, this is an extremely difficult conclusion to reach for a condition that is rare or unique, and for a treatment that has never been tried. (Absence of evidence is not the same thing as 'evidence of absence'.)

The crux of the matter for consequentialists was how reversible was Charlie's brain damage. His initial brain scans did not appear to show loss of actual brain tissue. Recordings of electrical brain activity showed seizures; however, even if it was thought unlikely that nucleoside treatment would improve these, that could not be known with certainty unless it was tried.

Consequentialism thus faces at least three challenges:

[29] D Wilkinson and J Savulescu, 'Knowing When to Stop: Futility in the Intensive Care Unit' (2011) 24(2) Current Opinion in Anesthesiology 160–5.

[30] *Great Ormond Street Hospital* (n 28) 104.

[31] Ibid 106.

(1) to define what is of value;
(2) to determine what the probability is of various outcomes occurring; and
(3) to compare the expected value of different courses of action.

This requires the most up-to-date science, but also normative interpretation of that science.

The second version of the interests argument is that the chance, although non-zero, of improvement was too low to justify the suffering which would occur in trying to realize a beneficial outcome. At the very least, a three-month trial of intensive care seemed necessary, with the painful procedures and suffering associated with that.

But what is too low? One per cent, or a one in a thousand chance? The harms of intensive care are also debatable. Some patients with severe brain damage may be so severely affected that they are unaware of everything, even pain. Some of the evidence in Charlie's case appeared to indicate that professionals believed that this applied to him,[32] in which case he would not suffer if subjected to a trial. Alternatively, if he was capable of experiencing pain, this could, in theory, be controlled with careful analgesia and sedation.[33]

This argument is ethical, necessarily involving value judgments about probability and value, and what risks are worth taking. The challenge for the consequentialist is epistemic: how to evaluate the probability of different harms (or benefits) and how much value to place on them.

The third way in which the treatment could be against Charlie's interests is that, even if it were 'successful', the best outcome that could be achieved is still not one worth aiming for either in terms of length or quality of life. This brings us to the hardest challenge of consequentialism: deciding what constitutes well-being and a life worth living.

The parents' own medical expert elaborated on the quality of life that Charlie would face (assuming no improvement):

> The nature of Charlie's condition means that he is likely to continue to deteriorate, that he is likely to remain immobile, that he will exhibit severe cognitive impairment, that he will remain dependent on ventilatory support to maintain respiration, will continue to need to be tube fed and that he will always be dependent on mechanical ventilation to maintain life.[34]

Elsewhere, it was said that Charlie was deaf.[35]

If the argument is that Charlie's life should not be prolonged in such a state, it must be based on a view that life with severe cognitive impairment, paralysis, deafness, and dependent on artificial nutrition and ventilation is a life not worth living.

There are three challenges for this welfarist account of the worth of life based on dependency and disability. First, it seems to suggest that at some point disability makes life not worth living. The severely disabled would be better off dead, from their own perspective. Disability groups may well disagree. Some people who are quadriplegic on a ventilator

[32] J Savulescu, 'Is It in Charlie Gard's Best Interest to Die?' (2017) 389 Lancet 1868–9.

[33] RD Truog, 'The United Kingdom Sets Limits on Experimental Treatments: The Case of Charlie Gard' (2017) 318 Journal of the American Medical Association 1001–2; J Savulescu and P Singer, 'Charlie Gard: Why Donald Trump and the Pope are Right', *ABC Online* (14 July 2017), http://www.abc.net.au/news/2017-07-13/charlie-gard-donald-trump-and-the-pope-are-right/8706390 accessed 15 July 2019.

[34] *Great Ormond Street Hospital* (n 28) 91.

[35] Ibid 58.

with spinal muscular atrophy find their lives worth living. Many severely disabled people find their own lives worth living.[36] It runs the risk of being accused of being 'ableist', discriminating against those with disability. Perhaps for this reason, where the line lies on this account has been left fuzzy.

Second, disability is instrumentally bad: it is not, in itself, what matters. Rather, as Judge Francis acknowledged, it is well-being or welfare that is intrinsically good. As one of us has argued elsewhere,[37] whether deafness or paralysis reduces well-being is context dependent. How bad functional disabilities are will depend on the social context and state of technology.

Indeed, Justice Hedley, in another case of Charlotte Wyatt cited as the basis of the Gard decision, said that '[b]est interests must be given a generous interpretation',[38] but although he referred to the broader concept of best interests as including non-medical interests, he did not go further, saying simply that: 'The infinite variety of the human condition never ceases to surprise and it is that fact that defeats any attempt to be more precise in a definition of best interests.'[39]

Third, the bar of a life worth living has elsewhere been set very low—even at minimal consciousness as the case of M illustrates.

M was an adult who contracted viral encephalitis, leaving her in a minimally conscious state over a period of many years. Her family petitioned a court to remove artificial nutrition and hydration on the basis of her previously expressed wishes. However, the judge, using the 'balance sheet' approach used in Gard and other cases, came up with the view:

> M does experience pain and discomfort, and her disability severely restricts what she can do. Having considered all the evidence, however, I find that she does have some positive experiences and importantly that there is a reasonable prospect that those experiences can be extended by a planned programme of increased stimulation.[40]

M was profoundly disabled. Despite her family's evidence that she would not want to live in such a state, the judge decided that it was in her best interests to live with such profound disability.

Consequentialism needs to tether the line of a life more closely to well-being, and specify more what constitutes well-being, rather than the vague, open-ended accounts employed so far in law. Philosophers Derek Parfit and James Griffin describe three theories of well-being: Hedonistic, Desire Fulfilment, and Objective List theories.[41] According to Hedonistic Theories, what makes life go well is pleasure and happiness, and what makes life go badly is pain and unhappiness. According to Desire Fulfilment Theories, what makes life go well is being able to satisfy desires, and what makes it go badly are frustrated desires.

Parfit explains Objective List Theories in the following way:

> certain things are good or bad for people, whether or not these people want to have the good things or avoid the bad things. The good things might include moral goodness, rational

[36] 'Not Dead Yet', http://notdeadyetuk.org/about/ accessed 15 July 2019; Y Newbold, 'Why Severely Disabled Lives Matter Too', World Health Innovation Summit (26 July 2016), http://www.worldhealthinnovationsummit.com/blog/2016/07/26/health-why-severely-disabled-lives-matter-too/ accessed 15 July 2019.

[37] J Savulescu and G Kahane, 'Disability: A Welfarist Approach' (2011) 6 Clinical Ethics 45–51.

[38] *Wyatt v Portsmouth NHS Trust* [2006] 1 FLR 554.

[39] Ibid 87.

[40] *W v M and Others* [2011] EWHC 2443 (Fam) 8.

[41] D Parfit, *Reasons and Persons* (Oxford University Press, 1984); J Griffin, *Well-Being: Its Meaning, Measurement, and Moral Importance* (Clarendon Press, 1986).

> activity, the development of one's abilities, having children and being a good parent, knowledge and the awareness of true beauty. The bad things might include being betrayed, manipulated, slandered, deceived, being deprived of liberty and dignity, and enjoying either sadistic pleasure, or aesthetic pleasure in what is in fact ugly.[42]

Objective list theories can be extended.[43] Other items might include love, deep and varied personal relationships, originality, creativity, autonomy, engagement with nature, sex, etc.

Each of the three accounts of well-being—Hedonistic, Desire-Fulfilment, and Objective List theories—has some plausibility. Parfit concludes that an adequate account of well-being must accord weight to all valuable mental states, desire-satisfaction, and objectively valuable activity.[44] It may be best not only to engage in activities that possess objective value, but also to want to engage in such activities, and to derive pleasure from them.

Given the wide disagreement about what constitutes a good life and a life worth living, the least controversial account of a life not worth living is one which is not worth living on all three accounts:

(1) balance of pain over pleasure;
(2) greater desire frustration than fulfilment; and
(3) lack of any objective goods or objectively valuable activity in life.

Disability will be relevant to these three criteria, but we cannot say what its precise effect will be on welfare or well-being, out of the specific context, and especially the social and technological context. A life with loving and devoted parents may tip the balance of pleasure over pain.

The pervading presence of pain in such an account is important. It is on the basis of unrelenting pain that some people believe life with severe dystrophic epidermolysis bullosa (where the skin peels off and death occurs very early in life) and Lesch-Nyhan disease (characterized by intellectual disability and painful self-mutilation) are lives which are not worth living.

So, whether Charlie Gard's life could have been worth living is dependent on the substantive account of the value of life which one holds. On the most conservative view, it is dependent on happiness, desire satisfaction, and ability to engage in objectively valuable activity. A judgment of the value of life will be heavily influenced by pain and suffering. The degree to which Charlie Gard was suffering from pain was the subject of considerable disagreement and unclarity.[45]

Although the central question in the Gard case can be understood to be consequentialist, there are several features of the case that were not part of the legal decision, but which would be relevant from the perspective of consequentialism.

In the Gard case, and other cases relating to medical treatment for children, decisions focus almost exclusively on the interests of the child. However, that might be unjustified.

In cases like this, where parents have very strong desires for treatment to be provided, but that treatment is (potentially) not in the child's interests, there is a potential clash. It may

[42] Parfit, ibid.

[43] M Nussbaum, *Creating Capabilities: The Human Development Approach* (Harvard University Press, 2011), 33–4.

[44] Parfit (n 43) 502.

[45] Wilkinson and Savulescu (n 27).

be better for the parents to provide the desired treatment (that may mitigate their grief and distress if they know that experimental treatment has been tried). A consequentialist would potentially need to weigh up the parents' interests against those of the child. Even if treatment were contrary to the child's interests, if the harm were slight, it might be that the best outcome overall would be to provide it.

Second, faced with a situation of conflict, the consequentialist would need to take into account not simply which treatment would be best, but also which way of resolving a dispute would be best. In the Gard case (and in the subsequent Alfie Evans case), the high-profile court cases (with multiple subsequent legal appeals) were costly, and involved investments of huge amounts of time by the health professionals and legal teams. They led to extremely negative publicity for the health system and for the hospitals involved. It might have been better overall, in retrospect, to have allowed the parents' request rather than embarking on a potentially prolonged, painful, and costly legal dispute.

Third, in the Gard case, the judge specifically set aside the question of the cost of treatment (in part because Charlie's parents had raised funds to pay for it). However, concern about the impact of providing treatment is a crucial consequentialist consideration.

3. Resource Allocation and Distributive Justice: Jaymee Bowen

In 1995, Cambridge Health Authority was taken to court. The Authority had refused to make NHS money available for a second bone marrow transplant, following an unsuccessful bone marrow transplant for a 10-year-old girl ('Child B' or Jaymee Bowen) suffering from leukaemia. The estimated cost of the treatment was £75,000. In the view of the Health Authority, the treatment had little chance of success. This view was based on her own doctor's opinion backed up by specialists from the Royal Marsden Hospital in London. The initial justification was that treatment was not in the child's best interests. Her doctor said, 'it would not be right to subject her to all this trauma'.[46] The Health Authority wrote to B's parents that the decision was taken with 'B's best interests in mind' and not 'on financial grounds'.[47]

However, a specialist from the Hammersmith Hospital in London believed that a further course of treatment was worth attempting. The chances of inducing a remission were put at 5 per cent, and the chance of cure less. Her father objected to the Trust's decision. He believed that a 5 per cent chance was worth taking. Cambridge Health Authority refused to fund the treatment.

When the case came to court, the Health Authority changed its tune. It said that treatment would not be 'an effective use of resources', that its funds were 'not limitless', and that it had to consider the interests 'of other patients'.[48] On the basis of guidance from the Department of Health in relation to funding unproven treatment, the Authority decided: 'the substantial expenditure on treatment with such small prospect of success would not be an effective use of resources'.[49]

When the case was heard in the High Court, the judge (Laws) said that Child B's fundamental right to life required that the Health Authority show compelling objective reasons

[46] *R v Cambridge Health Authority, ex p B* [1995] 2 All ER 129, 133 (CA).
[47] Ibid.
[48] Ibid.
[49] Ibid.

for giving other patients priority over her. He said that it was not sufficient to state merely that resources were limited. He said, 'the responsible authority ... must do more than toll the bell of tight resources'.[50]

However, this viewpoint was not upheld in the Court of Appeal. Sir Thomas Bingham, Master of the Rolls, said: 'Difficult and agonizing judgments have to be made as to how a limited budget is best allocated to the maximum advantage of the maximum number of patients. That is not a judgment the court can make.'[51]

Jaymee Bowen was denied a second transplant by the court. However, she did end up receiving one after support from a private donor. The transplant was not prevented in her best interests.

4. QALYs

Health economists have attempted to combine all these factors into the QALY (quality adjusted life year) approach to allocating health resources. A QALY is a year of life adjusted by its quality.

> The essence of a QALY is that it takes a year of healthy life expectancy to be worth 1, but regards a year of unhealthy life expectancy as worth less than 1. Its precise value is lower the worse the quality of life of the unhealthy person (which is what the quality adjusted bit is all about).[52]

Cost-effectiveness requires assigning a Cost/QALY for each drug or medical procedure. There is currently a threshold of about £20,000/QALY for new drugs, though more expensive drugs can be approved in special circumstances.

Cost-effectiveness is a form of consequentialism, aiming to maximize the health outcomes of medical interventions. One of the challenges of consequentialism is to apply this approach consistently across medicine. While it is uniformly used in the approval of pharmaceuticals, it is not uniformly used when evaluating procedures, including surgery, or complex interventions, such as the provision of intensive care. We have attempted elsewhere to show how it could be more widely applied.[53]

III. Strengths of Consequentialism

A. Well-Being

The sole focus of welfare consequentialism is promoting well-being. If anything matters in ethics, how well people's lives go matters. Well-being is a common currency of all ethical theories.

Well-being is also clearly a centrally important consideration for the law. One of the prime functions of the law is to safeguard the well-being of citizens.

50 Ibid.

51 Ibid.

52 A Williams, 'The Value of QALYs' (1985) 94 Health and Social Service Journal 3–5.

53 D Wilkinson, S Petrou, and J Savulescu, 'Expensive Care? Resource-Based Thresholds for Potentially Inappropriate Treatment in Intensive Care' (2018) 35 Monash Bioethics Review 2–23, https://doi.org/10.1007/s40592-017-0075-5 accessed 15 July 2019.

Consequentialism is a good place to start in ethical deliberation. If the consequentialist course of action is not adopted, that implies that somebody is suffering or their life is not going as well as it could go for the sake of some rule, principle, or moral. It is important to ask: is it worth this person's life going worse for the sake of this rule or moral? In many cases, it is hard to justify. In some cases, for example, a commitment to some non-consequentialist theory of distributive justice (for instance, priority to the worst off), it might be worth it.

B. Impartiality and Equality

According to consequentialism, everyone's health gains or well-being matters equally. Utilitarianism was a revolutionary philosophy in the 1700s because the pauper's happiness mattered as much as the prince's.

This egalitarian ethos is shared with the law. The law is committed to strict impartiality.

C. Clear Link to Moral Responsibility

For consequentialists, moral responsibility is a function of the foreseeability and avoidability of outcomes. If one has knowledge and control, one is responsible, whether or not one acted or omitted to act. Consequentialists are not primarily concerned with intentions, or virtue, but with consequences and the goodness or badness of those. If one chooses a course of action foreseeing it is likely to have worse consequences, one is morally responsible or blameworthy.

D. Consistency

Consequentialism is a highly consistent theory. It treats acts and omissions, treatment withholding and withdrawal, active and passive euthanasia, intentions and foresight the same, where these would have the same consequences.

Again, the fundamental desire for consistency is shared with the law.

E. Demanding

Consequentialism, at least utilitarianism, is a highly demanding theory. Provided that the benefit to one is greater than the harm to another, consequentialism demands action.

IV. Challenges

We have already discussed the challenge of defining well-being, gathering evidence relevant to the probabilities of different outcomes, and comparing the expected utility of different options. There are other challenges.

A. Distribution and Separateness of persons

John Rawls famously objected that utilitarianism fails to recognize the separateness of persons.[54] By this, he means that consequentialism generally doesn't take account of where or how well-being is distributed, just that it is maximized. One instantiation of this problem in health care is that consequentialism (and health economics and QALYs) potentially favours providing a very small good to a very large number of people, rather than one very large good to a single person. Thus, consequentialism favours public health (and very small reductions in risk across a whole population) rather than life-saving interventions for smaller, discrete populations.

B. Discrimination

Another problem with consequentialism is that it is said to discriminate against the old, those with a disability, and those with a poorer prognosis.[55] It does give lower priority to potentially life-saving treatment, such as transplants, to those who will derive less benefit, either because it will prolong their life less, or their life will be a lower quality or the chances of success are smaller. For this reason, heart transplants have sometimes not been offered to children with significant disabilities, such as Down's syndrome or Trisomy 18.[56]

V. A Consequentialist Manifesto for the Evolution of Medical Law

If the medical law were to fully embrace consequentialism, at least fourteen potential changes would be warranted.

A. Legalize Active Euthanasia

Consequentialists have been the most ardent proponents of active euthanasia,[57] arguing for a quality of life ethic. However, if there were evidence of worse outcome overall in countries that have legalized assisted dying, that would potentially lead the welfare consequentialist to support restricting access to this option. For example, 'slippery slope' type objections are often rejected by consequentialists because of lack of evidence that the feared negative outcomes of legal change would necessarily (or probably) eventuate. Yet, if such evidence emerged, consequentialists would potentially change their minds about policy. Consequentialists would support scientific evaluations of the impact of different legislative options.

[54] Rawls, John. 1999. *A theory of justice*. Rev. ed. Oxford: Oxford University Press.

[55] J Harris, 'What Is the Good of Health Care?' (1996) 10 Bioethics 262–91.

[56] J Savulescu, 'Resources, Down Syndrome and Cardiac Surgery' (2001) 322 British Medical Journal 875–6.

[57] J Rachels, 'Active and Passive Euthanasia' (1975) 292 New England Journal of Medicine 78–80; P Singer, *Rethinking Life and Death* (Oxford University Press, 1995); H Kuhse and P Singer, *Should the Baby Live?: Problem of Handicapped Infants* (Oxford University Press, 1985).

B. Limit Costly and Ineffective Treatment on the Basis of Distributive Justice

Within public health-care systems, providing highly expensive treatment for little benefit may harm other patients (by consuming limited resources). A consistent consequentialist application of the law would find it justified to withhold (or withdraw) such treatment, even if that treatment is desired by the patient (or family) and would be in their best interests.[58]

C. Reject the Right to Conscientious Objection

Many consequentialists are against a right to conscientiously object (usually on religious grounds) to medical interventions which are legal, in the patient's interests, desired by the patient, and consistent with distributive justice.[59] Examples include assisted dying, contraception, sterilization, assisted reproduction, and abortion.[60]

D. Human Enhancement

Consequentialists are generally in favour of biological interventions to enable people to have better lives, not merely healthier lives.[61] So, consequentialists are in favour of genetic selection to choose children who will have greater abilities and dispositions associated with higher well-being[62] and the use of gene editing and other biological interventions to increase well-being.

E. Autonomy

Liberal welfarist consequentialists like Mill place great weight on autonomy and favour interventions which promote autonomy.[63] Thus, interventions like gender reassignment or body modification (such as the amputation of a healthy limb in Body Identity Integrity Disorder) could be provided on grounds of respect for autonomy, even if there were minimal effects on well-being.

[58] Wilkinson and Savulescu (n 29); D Wilkinson, S Petrou, and J Savulescu, 'Rationing Potentially Inappropriate Treatment in Newborn Intensive Care in Developed Countries' (2017) 23(1) Seminars in Fetal and Neonatal Medicine 52–8.

[59] J Savulescu, 'Conscientious Objection in Medicine' (2006) 332 British Medical Journal 294–7.

[60] J Savulescu and U Schuklenk, 'Doctors Have No Right to Refuse Medical Assistance in Dying, Abortion or Contraception' (2017) 31 Bioethics, 162–70.

[61] J Savulescu, 'Genetic Interventions and the Ethics of Enhancement of Human Beings' in B Steinbock (ed), *The Oxford Handbook of Bioethics* (Oxford University Press, 2007), 516–35.

[62] J Savulescu, 'Procreative Beneficence: Why We Should Select the Best Children' (2001) 15(5) Bioethics 413–26.

[63] J Savulescu, 'Autonomy, the Good Life, and Controversial Choices' in R Rhodes, LP Francis, and A Silvers (eds), *The Blackwell Guide to Medical Ethics* (Blackwell Publishing, 2007), 17–37.

F. Sale of Body Parts

Consequentialists often favour allowing people to sell organs, such as kidneys, and tissues.[64] They might support different legal approaches in different countries (eg prohibition of organ sales might be justified in countries where abuse or exploitation is more likely).

G. Organ Procurement

Consequentialists generally favour opt-out systems for organ donation[65] to increase supply or organ conscription, or even organ donation euthanasia.[66]

H. Risk

Research ethics places significant limits on the risk to which human participants can be exposed in research. Consequentialism places no absolute limits on risk either in research or in innovation. Thus, consequentialists may support challenge studies and the use of experimental treatments.

I. Animals

Consequentialists draw no moral distinctions between humans and other animals. The belief is that suffering matters equally, whether it is in a human or a non-human animal. They are thus against the use of animals in research unless it is clear that consequences justify it.

J. Harm Reduction

Consequentialists favour harm-reduction strategies over preservation of moral fabric, principles, or rules. Thus, they are in favour of legalization of drugs and prostitution, together with harm-reduction strategies. While it may be preferable for people not to consume nicotine, nicotine replacement therapy might produce less harm overall than efforts to avoid tobacco and nicotine completely.

[64] J Radcliffe Richards, *The Ethics of Transplants* (Oxford University Press, 2012).

[65] W Isdale and J Savulescu, 'Three Proposals to Increase Australia's Organ Supply' (2015) 33(2–3) Monash Bioethics Review 91–101.

[66] D Wilkinson and J Savulescu, 'Should We Allow Organ Donation Euthanasia? Alternatives for Maximizing the Number and Quality of Organs for Transplantation' (2012) 26(1) Bioethics 32–48.

K. Artificial Reproduction

Consequentialists may permit cloning,[67] same sex reproduction (eg by using pluripotent stem-cell-derived gametes),[68] creation of saviour siblings,[69] surrogacy, and any alternative form of reproduction provided it has good consequences.

They usually do not believe that early human life has moral status and that destruction of early human embryos for research or reproduction is wrong.

L. Disability

Some consequentialists have advanced a welfarist account of disability that holds that any state of biology or psychology which tends to reduce well-being in a given social or environmental circumstance is a disability.[70] This view encompasses many human characteristics and is consistent with a widespread programme of human enhancement.

M. Natural vs Non-Natural

Consequentialists do not see any moral relevance in the natural versus non-natural distinction. What matters is well-being and nature should be modified to improve well-being.

N. Playing God

Consequentialists typically deny that there is any divine order to the world and subscribe to a Darwinian view of humans as the product of evolution. Thus, they believe there is great imperfection and natural inequality that science and medicine can improve or correct.

Consequentialism is a fundamental element of common-sense morality, while attention to the consequences of decisions appears to be an element of any plausible moral theory. Consequentialism is already incorporated into the law in many places; however, in others, current medical law appears to retain deontological prohibitions or norms that appear overall to lead to worse outcomes. There is a strong case for carefully and rigorously evaluating the outcomes of any legislative change that can help to identify the consequences of policy. This evidence would be compelling for the consequentialist. However, it can also be important in helping to establish what price our societies are willing to pay for retaining or endorsing the non-consequentialist features of the law.

[67] M Tooley, 'The Moral Status of the Cloning of Humans' in JM Humber and RF Almeder (eds), *Human Cloning; Biomedical Ethics Reviews* (Humana Press, 1998), 65–101.

[68] T Douglas, C Harding, H Bourne, et al, 'Stem Cell Research and Same Sex Reproduction' in M Quigley, S Chan, and J Harris (eds), *Stem Cells: New Frontiers in Science and Ethics* (World Scientific Press, 2011).

[69] RJ Boyle and J Savulescu, 'Ethics of Using Preimplantation Genetic Diagnosis to Select a Stem Cell Donor for an Existing Person' (2001) 323 British Medical Journal 1240–3.

[70] G Kahane and J Savulescu, 'The Welfarist Account of Disability' in A Cureton and K Brownlee (eds), *Disability and Disadvantage* (Oxford University Press, 2009), 14–53.

5

Justice and Responsibility

A Deontological Approach to Medical Law

*Thana C de Campos**

> The notion of obligations comes before that of rights, which is subordinate and relative to the former. A right is not effectual by itself, but only in relation to the obligation to which it corresponds, the effective exercise of a right springing not from the individual who possesses it, but from other men who consider themselves as being under a certain obligation towards him.
>
> Simone Weil, *The Need For Roots* (Routledge, 1952), 3

I. Introduction

Deontological ethics is typically traced back to Immanuel Kant and is for this reason also called Kantian ethics.[1] Deontology (from Greek *deon*, meaning 'duty') falls within the domain of moral theories that guide choices of what is morally required (*leges praeceptiva*), forbidden (*leges prohibitivae*), or permitted (*leges permissivae*),[2] as a matter of duty, obligation, or responsibility (I use these words interchangeably here). Deontological or Kantian ethics guides choices and defines actions based on the rightness or wrongness of the action in and of itself, rather than defining the rightness or wrongness of an action based on the consequences of said action.[3]

What distinguishes deontology from other moral theories? To understand deontology thoroughly, one should contrast it with other prominent moral theories, especially the consequentialism (see Chapter 4 in this volume), virtue ethics (see Chapter 1), and natural law (see Chapter 3). First, the consequentialist approach, the most contrarian theory to the deontological approach, guides choices primarily based on the outcomes of such choices (eg the utilitarian calculation of benefits and costs related to a particular state of affairs). For deontology, however, the decision to act should rest not on the consequence of the action,

* I am grateful to Trevor Stammers, Fernando Contreras, and Andelka Phillips for their comments on earlier drafts of this chapter. Special thanks are due to Mary Clare Enright for her research assistance, proofreading, and critical feedback.

[1] Kant's discussions of ethics are found mainly in his *Groundwork for the Metaphysics of Morals* (Cambridge University Press, 1997), but also in *The Metaphysics of Morals* (Cambridge University Press, 1991), *The Critique of Practical Reason and Other Works on Theory of Ethics* (Longman, Green & Co, 1909), and *Practical Philosophy* (Cambridge University Press, 1996).

[2] See I Kant, 'Towards Perpetual Peace' in *Practical Philosophy* (Cambridge University Press, 1996), 8:348, 321.

[3] For Kant's discussion of ethics, see I Kant, *Groundwork for the Metaphysics of Morals* (Cambridge University Press, 1997); *The Metaphysics of Morals* (Cambridge University Press, 1991); *The Critique of Practical Reason and Other Works on Theory of Ethics* (Longman, Green & Co, 1909); *Practical Philosophy* (Cambridge University Press, 1996).

Thana C de Campos, *Justice and Responsibility* In: *Philosophical Foundations of Medical Law*. Edited by: Andelka M Phillips, Thana C de Campos, and Jonathan Herring, Oxford University Press (2019). © Andelka M Phillips, Thana C de Campos, and Jonathan Herring
DOI: 10.1093/oso/9780198796558.003.0006

but rather on the responsibility of an agent to act in a particular way. Second, virtue ethics focuses on the definition of goodness, the idea of the human person, and the choices one needs to make to become a good, virtuous person. Deontological ethics, on the other hand, focuses mainly on the idea of duties. More specifically, deontology yields normative practical principles of what the person ought to do as a matter of duty. Third, since natural law builds on the virtue ethics tradition, it is also predicated on the idea of the human person. In this respect, natural law differs from deontology's exclusive focus on the actions called for by responsibility.[4] However, both deontology and natural law share in common an emphasis on reasons and certain universal moral absolutes (eg a human being is always an end in itself and never a mere means to one's end).[5]

What can deontological ethics offer to contemporary medical law and bioethics? The current discussions in contemporary medical law and bioethical debates have been almost exclusively concerned with and framed around the autonomy of patients and their individual rights.[6] This chapter demonstrates how a deontological approach to debates in this field can create a more balanced and inclusive discussion, which is less individualistic and more focused on relational duties. A less individualistic approach to medical law is practically as well as theoretically relevant. At the practical level, when one over-values autonomy, particularly in the context of biomedical ethics, one forgets that when individuals are ill and vulnerable, they necessarily experience a reduction in their capacity for individual autonomy, along with an increased dependence and need for caring relationships.[7] At the theoretical level, the modern emphasis on individual autonomy[8] in the fields of health law and clinical ethics has resulted in a neglect of the relational principles of biomedical ethics, including the principles of non-maleficence, beneficence, and particularly the principle of justice.[9] Above all, this modern emphasis on autonomy and individual rights has distorted the meaning of the principle of justice, originally relational in its nature. In reducing the understanding of justice to the realm of individual rights—particularly the individual right to autonomous choices[10]—the modern emphasis on individual autonomy

[4] For the differences between deontology and a natural law perspective, see J Finnis, *Fundamentals of Ethics* (Georgetown University Press, 1983), ch 5.

[5] For Kant's emphasis on reason, see CM Korsgaard, *Creating the Kingdom of Ends* (Cambridge University Press, 1996), chs 10, 11. For Kant's conception of morality as universal, see her chs 3, 4

[6] O O'Neill, 'Public Health or Clinical Ethics: Thinking beyond Borders' (2002) 16(2) Ethics and International Affairs 35–45; O O'Neill, *Bounds of Justice* (Cambridge University Press, 2000), ch 6.

[7] O'Neill, 'Public Health or Clinical Ethics' (n 6) 2, 35–45, 36.

[8] There is Feminist critique of the concept of 'individual autonomy', but I will not engage it in this chapter. Feminist theorists argue for the idea of 'relational autonomy', which is compatible with this critique of 'individual autonomy'.
Responding to this modern emphasis on individual autonomy, feminist theorists seek to re-conceptualize autonomy by questioning individual independency and self-sufficiency, and coining the term 'relational autonomy', which emphasizes relationships of care and interdependency. They argue that autonomy is compatible with relationships of care and interdependency, and autonomy cannot be adequately conceptualized outside of the context of relationships. See eg: C Mackenzie and N Stoljar, *Relational Autonomy Feminist Perspectives on Autonomy, Agency, and the Social Self* (Oxford University Press, 2000); DT Meyers, 'Personal Autonomy and the Paradox of Feminine Socialization' (1987) 84(11) Journal of Philosophy 619–28; P Besson, 'Feminist Second Thoughts about Free Agency' (1990) 3 Hypatia 47–64; M Friedman, 'Autonomy and Social Relationships: Rethinking the Feminist Critique' in DT Meyers (ed), *Feminists Rethink the Self* (Westview, 1997), 40–61; M Friedman, *Autonomy, Gender, Politics* (Oxford University Press, 2003).

[9] For the four primary principles of bioethics, see TL Beauchamp and JE Childress, *Principles of Biomedical Ethics* (Oxford University Press, 2001).

[10] See eg: J Tasioulas, 'Justice, Equality, and Rights' in R Crisp (ed), *The Oxford Handbook of the History of Ethics* (Oxford University Press, 2013); MA Glendon, *Rights Talk: The Impoverishment of Political Discourse* (The Free Press, 1991), chs 4, 5.

in the fields of health law and clinical ethics fails to understand and implement justice fully. The intellectual traditions of deontology, virtue ethics, and natural law have always defined justice as a relational idea between rights-holders and duty-bearers. However, the modern emphasis on rights-holders and the language of rights (ie individual autonomy) overshadows duty-bearers and the language of duties (ie the relational responsibilities one owes to rights-holders).[11] The upshot of this overshadowing has been a proliferation of individual rights—in particular, the individual right to autonomous choices in contemporary medical law and bioethics. Although a multitude of autonomous choices by patients are claimed as rights, they often cannot be realized because they cannot be attributable to specific duty-bearers.[12]

In order to argue that deontology's emphasis on responsibilities can restore the lost balance between rights and duties (and the lost relationship between rights-holders and duty-bearers), this chapter is structured thus: section II discusses the problems of the current state of affairs, where the modern conception of justice (and human rights) has reduced the idea of justice—particularly in the field of medical law—to unconstrained rights to choose autonomously according to one's individual preferences. This modern conception of justice, reduced to autonomy rights, is, as I will show, weak, or at the very least not the only conception available. Section III presents the deontological approach as an alternative to this modern conception of justice by outlining the deontological approach to justice, especially as it relates to the human right to health. More specifically, I look at O'Neill's deontological conception of justice and human rights, which establishes the connection between justice and human rights, on the one hand, and responsibilities, on the other. This section then juxtaposes O'Neill against Tasioulas to clarify 'the minimum core obligations' that correspond to the right to health. Finally, section IV applies the theoretical discussions of sections II and III to typical debates of medical law and bioethics, in the context of the minimum core obligations. This section first examines possible interpretations of the idea of minimum core obligations according to the modern conception of justice. It then contrasts the modern conception of justice interpretation against an interpretation based on the deontic conception of justice. I use this contrast to justify a deontic interpretation of the list of minimum core obligations correlated to the human right to health, and to argue that this list would more clearly determine priorities when allocating scarce health-care resources than the list provided by the modern conception.

II. The Problems of the Current State of Affairs: Justice as Unconstrained Individual Rights to Choose Autonomously According to the Patients' Preferences

To understand the problems of the current state of affairs, one must understand the academic theories that supposedly purport justice as unconstrained individual rights to choose

[11] O'Neill, *Bounds of Justice* (n 6) ch 6, 97, 100.

[12] Ibid. A similar point is also made by Glendon (n 10). See also: M Sandel, *Democracy's Discontent: America in Search of a Public Philosophy* (Harvard University Press, 1996); J Raz, 'Human Rights without Foundations' in S Besson and J Tasioulas, *The Philosophy of International Law* (Oxford University Press, 2010).

(eg Rational Choice Theory) and the theories that challenge such a view of justice (eg Onora O'Neill). Social sciences in general and medical law and bioethics in particular still live in the age of the *homo economicus:* the ideal of the rational man who makes rational choices autonomously according to his individual preferences.[13] This model emphasizes rationality, autonomy, and individual preferences. The origin of this model relates to the intellectual tradition of Rational Choice Theory, which introduced empiricist conceptions of human action to most disciplines in social sciences. The '*homo economicus*' stands as 'the ideal citizen of the liberal state':[14] he models the right course of action for Liberals in political economy, Contractualists in political philosophy, and Utilitarians in law, ethics, and public policy. Modern empiricist theories of human action—ranging from theories of justice that focus on individual self-sufficient states (eg Rawls's theory of justice) to theories of medical ethics that focus on individual self-sufficient patients (eg Beauchamp and Childress's Principlism)—have the *homo economicus* archetype as their background.

These modern theories link individual self-sufficient actions and individual preferences through rationality.[15] Rational actions are self-sufficient actions based on individual preferences. In other words, rational actions are autonomous actions. In praising rationality, these modern theories elevate autonomy as a supreme value: the rational agent (ie the *homo economicus*) is first and foremost autonomous (ie self-sufficient), and he chooses autonomously by following his individual preferences—namely his desires, motivations, and inclinations—free from undue paternalistic interference from others.

This modern conception of autonomy as unconstrained rights to choose autonomously according to one's preferences is commonly—though mistakenly—attributable to Kant, whose theory emphasized rationality in decision making.[16] In this connection, modern empiricist theories of human action are purportedly called 'Kantian theories'. Take, for example, Rawls's theory of justice. Rawls's theory is perhaps the most influential theory of justice in modernity—having also influenced debates on health law and bioethics, including notably Beauchamp and Childress's discussion of the principle of justice as it applies to the context of biomedical ethics.[17] Rawls's theory is typically considered a Kantian account of justice as it adopts 'the concept of rationality standard in social theory'.[18] However, Onora O'Neill—a leading Kantian philosopher whose deontological perspective of justice has greatly advanced the field of medical law and bioethics—challenges the Kantian grounds of modern empiricist theories of human action, in general, and of Rawls's conception of justice, in particular. As she puts it: 'Kant's conception of action differs from the broadly

[13] T de Campos, 'MAiD in Canada and the *Homo Economicus* View of Dignity: Inclusive Enough?' (2019) 22(3) Journal of Disability, Religion, and Health 246–65. See also: E Anderson, 'Beyond Homo Economicus: New Developments in Theories of Social Norms' (2000) 29(2) Philosophy and Public Affairs 170–200; MS Archer, '*Homo Economicus, Homo Sociologicus* and *Homo sentiens*' in MS Archer and JQ Tritter (eds), *Rational Choice Theory: Resisting Colonization* (Routledge, 2001), 36–56; IM Young, *Justice and the Politics of Difference* (Princeton University Press, 1990), 126. The white male archetype described by Young correlates to the *homo economicus* model.

[14] I Murdoch, *The Sovereignty of The Good* (Routledge & Kegan Paul, 1970), 80.

[15] O'Neill, *Bounds of Justice* (n 6) 32–3.

[16] I put this argument forth in 'The Well-Being Conception of Health and the Conflation Problem' (2016) 22(1) New Bioethics 71–81. See also O'Neill, *Bounds of Justice* (n 6) 40.

[17] See n 9. For another example of a Rawlsian account of health care and justice, see N Daniels, *Just Health: Meeting Health Needs Fairly* (Cambridge University Press, 2008).

[18] J Rawls, *A Theory of Justice* (Harvard University Press, 1971), 143.

empiricist conceptions of action, in which so many have tried to embed a conception of autonomy.'[19]

O'Neill goes on to say that this modern conception of autonomy leads to an alarming 'over-valuing of mere independence and (supposedly) independent lives'.[20] And the trouble with an over-valuing of autonomy, particularly in the context of biomedical ethics, is that 'all of us when we are feeling ill and frail have reduced or no capacity for individual autonomy'.[21] This may be a strong indication that the *homo economicus* archetype does not work well as a model in real-life situations of ill health and death, where vulnerabilities are greater and mutual dependence, rather than individual independence, is the norm.

Yet, the centre of biomedical ethics *is* autonomy. Autonomy dominates contemporary discourses as scholars extoll the idea as the supreme principle of bioethics.[22] Autonomy in contemporary bioethics translates to patients' unconstrained rights to access and choose medical treatments autonomously according to their preferences and without undue paternalistic restraints from health-care professionals.[23] Accordingly, while justice in contemporary bioethics would require equal access to medical treatments, it would also require the safeguard of patients' autonomous medical choices regarding their therapeutic and prophylactic preferences from the dangers of medical paternalism.[24] As O'Neill remarks, this conception of justice in contemporary bioethics takes the standpoint of patients as 'recipients, who are *entitled to* or *have a claim to* action or forbearance by others'.[25]

This standpoint, according to O'Neill, creates a social division between the 'victims' and the 'oppressors'. It exacerbates a victimization mentality in rights-holders (in this case, patients) while magnifying a culture of blaming the 'oppressor' (in this case, health-care professionals or others who might limit the autonomous choices of patients).[26] For O'Neill, the modern rhetoric on justice and human rights has become an 'ideology for the oppressed'.[27] Such rhetoric aspires to create empowerment by giving voice to the oppressed. However, in actuality, it perpetuates, she argues, the mentality of passive recipients of rights, who blame the oppressor and the complaint about their rights violations, in the hopes of receiving what they claim and desire. [28] In short, the modern conception justice is all about claiming and receiving rights—human rights in particular.[29]

[19] O'Neill, *Bounds of Justice* (n 6) 41.

[20] Ibid 49.

[21] O'Neill, 'Public Health or Clinical Ethics' (n 6) 36.

[22] See CE Scheneider, *The Practice of Autonomy: Patients, Doctors, and Medical Decisions* (Oxford University Press, 1998), 226–31; T Stammers, 'The Evolution of Autonomy' (2015) 21(2) New Bioethics 155–63; O'Neill, 'Public Health or Clinical Ethics' (n 6) 35; NPG Austriaco, *Biomedicine and Beatitudes: An Introduction to Catholic Bioethics* (Catholic University of America Press, 2010), 255–6; PR Wolpe, 'The Triumph of Autonomy in American Medical Ethics: A Sociological View' in R DeVries and J Subedi (eds), *Bioethics and Society: Constructing the Ethical Enterprise* (Prentice Hall, 1998), 38–59; GM Stirrat and R Gill, 'Autonomy in Medical Ethics after O'Neill' (2005) 35(3) Journal of Medical Ethics 127–30.

[23] de Campos (n 16); see also T Saad, 'Mistakes and Missed Opportunities Regarding Cosmetic Surgery and Conscientious Objection' [2017] 44 Journal of Medical Ethics 649–650, where Saad argues against what he calls 'Patient Preference Absolutism'.

[24] For a conception of justice and autonomy in contemporary bioethics, see (n 9) 246, 58. For a critique, see eg de Campos (n 16).

[25] O O'Neill, 'The Dark Side of Human Rights' (2005) 81(2) International Affairs 427–39, 430.

[26] Ibid 439.

[27] Ibid.

[28] Ibid, 438.

[29] O'Neill, *Bounds of Justice* (n 6) ch 6, 97. See also: Glendon (n 10); Sandel (n 12); Raz (n 12).

This schema translates justice into a rights-based approach mainly focused on claim-rights that give entitlements to the rights-holder, irrespective of considerations regarding duty-bearers. Because numerous manifestos (eg charters and declarations) around the world have formally promulgated claim-rights, claim-rights are now synonymous with 'manifesto-rights'. For O'Neill, despite the formal affirmation of 'manifesto-rights' on paper, they remain mostly empty in substance and content. Phrases such as 'right to health', 'right to equal access', and 'women's rights'[30] identify 'what right holders are entitled to', but fail, she argues, to identify the duty-bearers and the cost of fulfilling such rights. In doing so, these phrases actually prevent the full realization of 'manifesto-rights' due to their ambiguity in language.[31] In other words, for O'Neill, the overshadowing of both duty-bearers and the language of duties prevents the realization of rights in practice.[32]

In failing to use the language of duties and to recognize duty-bearers, the modern conception of justice distinguishes itself from the original conception of justice. No longer does the modern definition of justice include a relationship between rights-holders and duty-bearers as seen in deontology, virtue ethics, and natural law traditions. Justice is no longer relational. Rights-holders can now claim rights independent of the existence of duty-bearers. Justice now is therefore equated to the unconstrained right to choose autonomously according to one's individual preferences.

How could one restore the lost balance of duties and rights described here in section II? Section III will explore how the deontological emphasis on duty, obligation, or responsibility can be particularly valuable in restoring this balance, as well as the lost relationship between rights-holders and duty-bearers. Further detail of O'Neill's deontological approach to justice in general and the human right to health in particular will appear in section III.

One may not agree that the deontological approach to justice is the best one. This is a fair claim. The purpose of this chapter, however, is not to show that the deontological approach to justice is the only available one, let alone the best one for all endeavours. The purpose of this chapter (and of its section III in particular) is merely to contend that deontology is especially promising for restoring balance in contemporary medical law and bioethical debate, making it more inclusive and relational.

III. The Deontological Approach to Justice as an Alternative

While contemporary and modern discourses of justice and human rights focus on the perspective of rights-holders, deontology emphasizes the importance of responsibilities (and not rights alone) when conceptualizing justice.[33] Responsibilities are the starting point of a deontological account of justice, so duties of justice have a special prominence in Kant's theory of justice. Kant calls certain duties of justice 'universal principles of obligations'. [34] Because universal principles of obligations serve

[30] O'Neill, 'Public Health or Clinical Ethics' (n 6) 42. O'Neill, *Bounds of Justice* (n 6) ch 7, 126.
[31] O'Neill, *Bounds of Justice* (n 6) ch 6, 97, 100.
[32] Ibid. A similar point is also made by Glendon (n 10). See also: Sandel (n 12); Raz (n 12).
[33] O O'Neill, *Towards Justice and Virtue: A Constructive Account of Practical Reasoning* (Cambridge University Press, 1996), ch 5, 128.
[34] O'Neill, *Bounds of Justice* (n 6) ch 7, 136.

the purpose of guiding actions and choices, they are therefore principles of practical reasoning.[35]

Universal principles of obligations have three main features: they are 'universal', 'fundamental', and 'abstract' principles. First, they are 'universal' because these duties of justice can be held and adopted by all. Second, they are 'fundamental' because they structure institutions (the most relevant for our purpose being human rights). In structuring institutions, universal principles of obligations can guide actions and choices in the realms of laws and policies: universal principles of obligations structure legal and political institutions, and then such institutions later structure their laws and policies, where rights are specified and corresponding duties are allocated. Third, universal principles of obligations are also 'abstract' because they are general enough to allow the structure of an institution to specify their laws and policies later and not be so rigid as to require highly specified or uniform actions and choices from all. Universal principles of obligations are meant to guide the actions and choices taken by institutions loosely, which will, in turn, enforce specific rights and allocate specific duties. In short, the quality of being 'abstract' enables principles of obligations to be 'universal' and 'fundamental'. Because universal principles of obligations are general (ie abstract), rather than highly specific, all institutions can hold and adopt such principles (ie universal) as well as structure themselves by such principles (ie fundamental).[36]

Deontological justice, therefore, requires universal principles of obligations and institutions to be structured in such a way that public officials can practically (or feasibly) enforce rights by allocating corresponding responsibilities to specific duty-bearers. Accordingly, deontological justice requires the *institutionalization* of rights: only after the specification of duty-bearers and the allocation of obligations can rights-holders claim those rights and exercise the specified claim-right in concrete reality. Without enforcing institutions that allocate responsibilities, O'Neill argues that rights are mere empty rhetoric—and this is especially the case, she argues, when it comes to welfare rights (ie universal rights to goods and services, such as a universal right to health).[37]

O'Neill continues her discussion of the *institutionalization* of rights by examining the asymmetry between liberty rights (ie rights that require permission, but not allocation) and welfare rights (ie rights that require both permission and allocation, such as the universal right to health). Because liberty rights ground negative duties while welfare rights ground both negative and positive duties,[38] individuals can claim liberty rights without institutions, while they can only claim welfare rights through institutions.[39] She further explains this asymmetry by comparing the universal welfare right to food, to two universal liberty rights, namely the right not to be killed and the right to speak freely. While the latter 'are matched by and require universal obligations not to kill or not to obstruct free speech',[40] the former 'cannot simply be matched by a universal obligation to provide an aliquot morsel of food'.[41]

[35] Kantian justice is first and foremost predicated on reason, which is universal as well as practical. Reason is universal because its principles can be held and adopted by all. It is also practical because its principles guide concrete actions and choices. For Kant, the 'Supreme Principle of Practical Reason' is the 'Categorical Imperative' (O O'Neill, 'Bounded and Cosmopolitan Justice' (2000) 26(5) Review of International Studies 45–60, 52, 56.).

[36] O'Neill, *Bounds of Justice* (n 6) ch 7, 137.

[37] O'Neill (n 33) ch 5, 129–33.

[38] O'Neill (n 25) 429.

[39] Ibid 131.

[40] O'Neill, *Bounds of Justice* (n 6) ch 7, 135.

[41] Ibid.

In stretching O'Neill's argument, one would conclude that the universal right to health would analogously not simply be matched by a universal obligation to provide an easily commensurable quantity of health-care goods and services. The universal right to health, as a welfare right, can only be claimed if it is institutionalized: enforcing institutions have to specify and allocate the corresponding negative and positive duties, and only then can the universal right to health be claimed and enforced.

IV. O'Neill vs Tasioulas: The Corresponding Duties to the Human Right to Health

This asymmetry between liberty rights and welfare rights has spurred protracted debates both in philosophical theories and in human rights practice. While I have explored elsewhere the divergences and the common ground among these schools of thought regarding the universal right to health and its corresponding duties, here I will only discuss the most recent remarks by the legal theorist John Tasioulas.[42] His philosophical disagreements with O'Neill help to clarify the corresponding duties to the human right to health, according to the deontological tradition.

Tasioulas does not radically disagree with O'Neill's deontic emphasis on responsibilities.[43] The main division between the two philosophers stems from O'Neill's conception of justice (in the context of human rights) in terms of the institutional enforceability and the claimability of human-rights-related duties, and Tasioulas's belief that enforceability and claimability are not necessary conditions to speak of the existence of rights in any relevant sense. Examining Tasioulas clarifies some distinctions that O'Neill conflates when she speaks about existence, institutionalization, specification, allocation, claimability, enforcement, and feasibility. For O'Neill, these are all inter-linked. For Tasioulas, these are not. He separates (1) the *existence* of a given right (and its correlated obligations) from (2) the process of *institutionalization* of said rights and duties (ie the specification of duty-bearers and the allocation of specific duties to them, which then allows for claimability and enforceability), and (3) the *feasibility* of such rights (ie the determination of what is possible and not unduly burdensome for duty-bearers). For Tasioulas, the *existence* of rights (and their correlated duties) is independent of their *institutionalization* and their *feasibility*. The existence of a right is a primary question, while the *institutionalization* of a right (including its specification, allocation, claimability, and enforceability) and the *feasibility* of said right are distinct and further questions.[44]

Tasioulas's distinctions are crucial to help clarify a key point of O'Neill's deontological approach to justice in the context of the human right to health. His remarks on the *existence* of a right and the indeterminacy of its correlated duties as separate from their

[42] TC de Campos, *The Global Health Crisis: Ethical Responsibilities* (Cambridge University Press, 2017), ch 2.

[43] In discussing O'Neill's approach to justice, Tasioulas puts it in his partial agreement with her deontological approach in the following way: 'it is clear that obligations are conceptually prior to rights ... A right can only be elucidated by reference to the notion of obligation, since rights are defined as grounds for the duties that are correlative to them' (J Tasioulas, 'The Moral Reality of Human Rights' in T Pogge (ed), *Freedom for Poverty and a Human Right* (Oxford University Press, 2007), ch 3, 99).

[44] As Tasioulas puts it: 'the allocation and specification of duties arising from the rights ... [are] further questions ... Once we have separated out claimability as a further question, we can admit that a right may exist even though the allocation and specification of its correlative duties remain indeterminate' (Tasioulas (n 43) ch 3, 93).

institutionalization and *feasibility* are relevant. As discussed above, for Kant, principles of obligations are universal, fundamental, and abstract.[45] The fact that they are abstract (ie indeterminate) enables them to be universal and fundamental, because principles of obligations need to be general enough to allow institutions to be structured in a way that allows them to later allocate and specify laws and policies, in accordance with the specific context of a given community. Even though O'Neill's deontic approach to justice is clearly predicated on abstract (ie indeterminate) duties—which do not (and shall not) require highly specified, let alone uniform, actions and choices from all—when she talks about existence, institutionalization, specification, allocation, claimability, enforcement, and feasibility, she relates all of these. And in doing so, as Tasioulas points out, O'Neill's account inevitably requires duties of justice to be too specific in order to exist and be enforceable.[46] But if duties of justice need to be that specific in order to exist and be enforceable, then they will inevitably be unfeasible. How does Tasioulas solve this feasibility problem? He does so by introducing (1) the idea of 'duties of progressive realization' as well as (2) the doctrine of 'the minimum core obligations'. Both allow for the flexibility that duties of justice need in order to exist and be enforced in a feasible manner.

A. The Idea of 'Duties of Progressive Realization'

The asymmetry between liberty and welfare rights highlighted by O'Neill manifests itself in the duties correlated respectively to these two classes of rights. While liberty rights, such as those enshrined in the 1966 International Covenant on Civil and Political Rights, are generally interpreted as requiring duties of immediate effect, welfare rights, such as those enshrined in the 1966 International Covenant on Economic, Social, and Cultural Rights (ICESCR), which includes the human right to health, are generally interpreted as requiring duties of progressive realization.[47] The concept of duties of progressive realization is defined in article 2(1) of the ICESCR, and then further explained in paragraph 9 of General Comment 3 ('The Nature of State Parties' Obligations') by the UN Committee on Economic, Social and Cultural Rights, thus:

> The principal obligation of result reflected in article 2(1) is to take steps 'with a view to achieving progressively the full realization of the rights recognized' in the Covenant. The term 'progressive realization' is often used to describe the intent of this phrase. The concept of progressive realization constitutes a recognition of the fact that full realization of all

[45] O'Neill, *Bounds of Justice* (n 6) ch 7, 137.

[46] Although Tasioulas explicitly disagrees with certain aspects of O'Neill's deontological approach, Tasioulas's Razian/interest-based account of human rights is predicated on the correlation between rights and duties. As he puts it, his interest-based approach 'can allow for knowledge of the existence of rights (hence of the justification of duties corresponding to those rights) without the duties being precisely specified or allocated to particular agents. Instead, the allocation and specification is a further question, not one that needs to be answered in order to establish the existence of the right' (Tasioulas (n 43) ch 3, 92).

In arguing against some aspects of O'Neill's Kantian approach to justice, Tasioulas puts forth his own pluralistic account of human rights, which is both indeterminate and context-sensitive. In his pluralistic account, 'the indeterminacy of a right's deontic implications' is complemented by the 'dynamic character' of rights, viz., 'the duties that a right generates are not comprehensively specifiable once and for all; instead, they can vary with changes in the nature of the agents, institutions, and social contexts in question' (Tasioulas (n 43) ch 3, 94).

[47] See eg J Tasioulas, *Minimum Core Obligations: Human Rights in the Here and Now* (World Bank, 2017), v.

> economic, social and cultural rights will generally not be able to be achieved in a short period of time. In this sense the obligation differs significantly from that contained in article 2 of the International Covenant on Civil and Political Rights which embodies an immediate obligation to respect and ensure all of the relevant rights. Nevertheless, the fact that realization over time, or in other words progressively, is foreseen under the Covenant should not be misinterpreted as depriving the obligation of all meaningful content. It is on the one hand a necessary flexibility device, reflecting the realities of the real world and the difficulties involved for any country in ensuring full realization of economic, social and cultural rights. On the other hand, the phrase must be read in the light of the overall objective, indeed the raison d'être, of the Covenant which is to establish clear obligations for States parties in respect of the full realization of the rights in question.[48]

As stated in General Comment 3, the progressive realization of certain duties does not deplete them of their content and force. On the contrary, their progressive character permits certain flexibility necessary for and conducive to the feasibility and full realization of those duties in the future. In other words, even though the full realization of those duties is somehow delayed in time, their full realization is still required. The justification for the delay comes from resources constraints and other practical contingencies that impede the immediate full realization of all duties correlated to welfare rights, such as the right to health. Parties cannot, however, indefinitely delay the full realization of rights.

Duties of progressive realization, as defined in General Comment 3, mirror Kant's definition of permissions (*leges permissivae*). First, Kant's idea of permission emphasizes the transitory and progressive nature of *leges permissivae*. As he puts it: 'the permission is directed to the present … in the transition from the state of nature to the civil condition'.[49] Second, Kant explains what permissions are by contrasting permissions (*leges permissivae*) and prohibitions (*leges prohibitivae*). There are two kinds of prohibitions: *leges strictae* and *leges latae*. The former are prohibitions strictly speaking: they are absolute prohibitions and accommodate no exemption. The latter are in actuality permissions: they are prohibitions that allow certain flexibility, 'taking into consideration the circumstances in which they are to be applied'.[50] Even though the prohibition is fully valid, the effects of the prohibition are somehow delayed in time. Such delay is only justified because of 'the practical contingency of certain actions'[51] that impede the immediate full realization of the prohibitions in question. Their full realization shall not be indefinitely delayed. While it is acceptable 'to *postpone* putting these laws into effect',[52] one 'may not postpone [them] to a non-existent (*ad calendas graecas*, as Augustus used to promise); for any delay is permitted only as a means of avoiding a premature implementation which might frustrate the whole purpose'[53] of the prohibition.

[48] UN Committee on Economic, Social and Cultural Rights, General Comment 3—'The Nature of State Parties' Obligations', 14 December 1990 (UN Doc E/1991/23).

[49] In 'Towards Perpetual Peace', Kant reflects on what justice morally requires, permits, and forbids in states' interaction with one another, so that the international order may transition from a state of nature to a civil condition of peace (see n 2).

[50] Kant, 'Towards Perpetual Peace' (n 2).

[51] Ibid 321.

[52] Ibid 320–1 (emphasis added).

[53] Ibid.

Although welfare rights, including the human right to health, typically correlate to these duties of progressive realization, which, according to its deontic justifications, have a transitional and progressive nature that implies delays, General Comment 3 also emphasizes the existence of certain duties of immediate effect correlated to welfare rights. Although scholars typically interpret liberty rights as duties of immediate effect, and welfare rights (like the human rights to health) as duties of progressive realization,[54] this typical interpretation does not preclude welfare rights from also having duties of immediate effect. These duties of immediate effect are called the 'minimum core obligations'.[55]

B. The Doctrine of 'the Minimum Core Obligations'

Paragraph 10 of General Comment 3 establishes a test that would help determine if a state cannot feasibly meet the minimum core requirement. This test involves the state '[demonstrating] that every effort has been made to use all resources that are at its disposition in an effort to satisfy, *as a matter of priority*, those minimum obligations'.[56] The theoretical purpose of minimum core obligations is to establish the minimum essentials of what constitutes each welfare right (such as the human right to health). In the specific case of the human right to health, General Comment 3 defines that its minimum core obligations are 'essential primary health care'.[57] The practical purpose of distinguishing minimum core obligations from the remaining duties of progressive realization is to attain feasibility. The doctrine of the minimum core obligation aims at feasibility by helping to define priorities in the allocation of scarce resources, which, together with other practical contingencies, impede the immediate full realization of all duties correlated to welfare rights. The theoretical and practical purposes of distinguishing minimum core obligations from the remaining duties of progressive realization is therefore particularly crucial in the context of the human right to health, given that health-care resources are especially scarce and other practical

[54] See Tasioulas (n 47).

[55] John Tasioulas defines the minimum core obligations as 'the sub-set of obligations associated with socio-economic rights that must be immediately complied with in full (obligations of "immediate effect") and hence to which the doctrine of progressive realization is inapplicable'. See J Tasioulas, *The Minimum Core of the Right to Health* (World Bank, 2017), 1.

Tasioulas identifies three elements of minimum core obligations: '(a) *immediacy*: they demand immediate compliance, (b) *completeness*: they must be fully complied with at any given time, and (c) *universality*: they bind all states (presumably all state parties to the Convention) irrespective of variations in wealth and other resources'. See Tasioulas (n 47) 12.

Paul Hunt, the former Special Rapporteur on the right to health, echoes Tasioulas's definition in his latest report: 'the right to health imposes overlapping obligations of *immediate* effect on States. They include ... the core obligation to ensure the minimum essential levels of the right. Immediate obligations are outside the ambit of the article 2(1) of the International Covenant on Economic, Social and Cultural Rights. Core obligations are the minimum essential level of a right and are not progressively realized' (P Hunt, 'The Right of Everyone to the Enjoyment of the Highest Attainable Standard of Health', 11 August 2014 (UN Doc A/69/150), para 10 (emphasis added)).

Audrey Chapman also highlights the *immediacy* component of minimum core obligations. She argues that the minimum core obligations should be primarily interpreted as obligations of conduct (to be immediately implemented), rather than obligations of results (AR Chapman, 'Core Obligations Related to the Right to Health' in AR Chapman and S Russell (eds), *Core Obligations: Building a Framework for Economic, Social and Cultural Rights* (Intersentia, 2002), 185–215.

[56] UN Committee (n 57) para 10 (emphasis added).

[57] Ibid.

contingencies (such as the lack of sufficiently available, accessible, acceptable, and appropriate medical treatments worldwide)[58] apply.

General Comment 14 (on 'The Right to the Highest Attainable Standard of Health') supposedly specifies in its paragraphs 43 and 44 the concept of the minimum core of the human right to health. One would expect these paragraphs to define the core obligations that would explain a feasible provision of 'essential primary health care', as first mentioned in General Comment 3.[59] However, instead of explaining the content of the core duties and their duty-bearers, paragraphs 43 and 44 merely repeat some possible items or components of a right to essential primary health care. Paragraph 43 reinforces the '*right* of access to health facilities, goods and services on a non-discriminatory basis'.[60] Paragraph 44 then goes on to list further items of 'comparable priority'[61] of a right to essential primary health care, including, for example: 'reproductive, maternal (pre-natal as well as postnatal) and child health care ... immunizations against major infectious diseases ... measures to prevent, treat and control epidemic and endemic diseases ... education and access to information'.[62]

If 'obligations have to specify not only what is to be accorded, but which obligation-bearers are going to have to do what for whom and at what cost',[63] and if the lists provided in paragraphs 43 and 44 at best catalogue some of the items or components of a right to essential primary health care, then these lists say very little (if anything) about right-to-health-related minimum core obligations, as well as their conditions of immediate enforceability and feasibility. Although paragraphs 43 and 44 are under the title right-to-health's 'Core Obligations' in General Comment 14, the focus of these paragraphs is not on obligations and their feasibility. Instead, their focus is actually on rights—more specifically on the *claims* that a right to essential primary health care allegedly entails and on the *entitlements* that victims of the violations of said right are supposed to receive. The feasibility problem is not addressed. In short, the fact that paragraphs 43 and 44 (which were supposed to explain (1) what is to be accorded as 'Core Obligations' and (2) which duty-bearers should do what for whom and for what cost) merely provide a list of claims to be demanded and of entitlements to be received, irrespective of their feasibility, corroborates O'Neill's critique on 'empty manifestos-rights'.

As discussed in section II, the contemporary rhetoric of manifesto-rights puts forth an understanding of justice where responsibilities and duty-bearers are neglected and

[58] OHCHR and WHO, 'The Right to Health—Fact Sheet No. 31', 4, https://www.ohchr.org/Documents/Publications/Factsheet31.pdf accessed 15 July 2019.

[59] The literature on the minimum core obligations of the human right to health is generally critical. Tasioulas provides the most thorough critical analysis, emphasizing, eg, the lack of conceptual clarity as well as the unfeasible and overly burdensome requirements that General Comment 14 demands of all states. On the content of the obligations enumerated in paragraph 43 as minimum core or of 'comparable priority' in paragraph 44, he says: 'These seem overly demanding to be feasibly conceived as obligations of immediate effect incumbent on all states, especially on an invariant reading of the Minimum Core Doctrine' (see J Tasioulas, *The Minimum Core of the Right to Health* (World Bank, 2017), 8).

In a similar vein, John Tobin argues that 'the vision of the minimum core obligations of states under the right to health, as advanced by the ESC Committee, is dissociated from the capacity of states to realize this vision. It simply does not offer a principled, practical, or coherent rationale with is sufficiently sensitive to the context in which the right to health must be operationalized' (J Tobin, *The Right to Health in International Law* (Oxford University Press, 2012), 340).

[60] UN Committee on Economic, Social and Cultural Rights, General Comment 14—'The Right to the Highest Attainable Standard of Health', 11 August 2000 (UN Doc E/C.12/200/4), para 43(a)–(e) (emphasis added).

[61] Ibid para 44.

[62] Ibid para 44(a)–(d).

[63] O'Neill, *Bounds of Justice* (n 6) 97, 100.

overshadowed by an excessive preoccupation about rights and rights-holders.[64] As a result, rights-holders have become mere passive recipients, 'who are entitled to or have a claim to action or forbearance by others'.[65] Instead of explaining which duty-bearers should do what for whom and for what cost when it comes to realizing the human right to health, and by focusing on merely listing health-related claims that individuals can demand and health-related entitlements they can receive, General Comment 14 perpetuates this mentality of 'passive recipients of rights' to which O'Neill has alluded. These 'passive recipients of rights' typically, as O'Neill has argued, can do nothing but blame the 'oppressor' and complain about the supposed violation of their human right to health. In this vein, their health-related individual rights in general and their health-related autonomy rights in particular are purportedly violated when 'oppressors' deprive right-to-health holders of the opportunity to freely choose any medical treatments as they would have wished to choose for their health and well-being.

In a nutshell, paragraphs 43 and 44 of General Comment 14, which should supposedly explain 'Core Obligations' and address the feasibility of the human right to health merely validates the 'manifesto rights' mentality, namely patients' unconstrained rights to access and choose medical treatments autonomously according to their preferences and without undue paternalistic restraints from health-care professionals or other people.[66] This renders the human right to health in general and its core obligations in particular unfeasible. In failing to define the core obligations of 'essential primary health care' that would have to be met immediately, General Comment 14's paragraphs 43 and 44 therefore fail to respond to General Comment 3's call to the feasibility and priority of minimum core obligations.[67]

To recap: in section II, this chapter showed how the concepts of justice and human rights, particularly in the context of medical law and bioethics, have been distorted to become now tantamount to unconstrained rights to access and choose medical treatments autonomously and according to patients' preferences. Here, section III suggested an alternative conception of justice and human rights: the deontological approach, where individuals can claim rights only when such rights are correlated to establishable duties. The deontological approach to justice and human rights is, as I contended, promising in the context of medical law and bioethics because it can re-establish responsibilities and duty-bearers as key components of justice alongside rights and rights-holders.

Section III discussed and examined in greater detail what the deontological understanding of the human right to health and its correlated core duties would require. Specifically, the section introduced (1) the idea of 'duties of progressive realization' and

[64] Ibid.

[65] O'Neill (n 25) 430.

[66] See de Campos (n 16) 71–81; Saad (n 23).

[67] The literature on the minimum core obligations of the human right to health is generally critical. Tasioulas provides the most thorough critical analysis, emphasizing, eg, the lack of conceptual clarity as well as the unfeasible and overly burdensome requirements that General Comment 14 demands of all states. On the content of the obligations enumerated in paragraph 43 as minimum core or of 'comparable priority' in paragraph 44, he says: 'These seem overly demanding to be feasibly conceived as obligations of immediate effect incumbent on all states, especially on an invariant reading of the Minimum Core Doctrine' (J Tasioulas, *The Minimum Core of the Right to Health* (World Bank, 2017), 8).

In a similar vein, John Tobin argues that 'the vision of the minimum core obligations of states under the right to health, as advanced by the ESC Committee, is dissociated from the capacity of states to realize this vision. It simply does not offer a principled, practical, or coherent rationale with is sufficiently sensitive to the context in which the right to health must be operationalized' (J Tobin, *The Right to Health in International Law* (Oxford University Press, 2012), 340).

(2) the doctrine of 'the minimum core obligations' of the human right to health, as well as its central importance to the feasibility of said right. Section IV will further examine the doctrine of the 'minimum core obligations'. It will assess how the minimum core duties of the human right to health would be interpreted according to the modern conception of justice (reduced to the language of rights—in particular, the right to autonomous choices, as discussed in section II), and then contrast it to how it would be interpreted according to the deontic conception of justice (defined in terms of both rights and corresponding institutionalized duties, as discussed here in section III).

IV. The Minimum Core Obligations of the Human Right to Health: Two Possible Interpretations

As mentioned above, in General Comment 3, the minimum core obligations of the human right to health include 'essential primary health care'. General Comment 14 tries to specify what 'essential primary health care' means in its paragraph 43. Among the items listed by paragraph 43, some are not exclusive components of the right to health. In other words, they are components of other human rights as well. For example, paragraph 43 includes as components of 'essential primary health care': 'access to food', a component of the right to adequate nutrition, and 'access to shelter', a component of the right to adequate housing. However, two items listed in paragraph 43 are exclusive components of the right to health. These are: 'access to health care facilities, goods, and services' and 'access to essential medicine'. In fact, the latter can be interpreted as being part of the former, as essential medicine is a type of health-care good. 'Access to health care facilities, goods, and services' is, therefore, the least contentious item included in paragraph 43 of what a right-health-related minimum core obligation would look like. Few people would deny that 'access to health care facilities, goods, and services' (including 'access to essential medicines') would not qualify as an element of the minimum core duties correlated to the human right to health, because without 'access to health care facilities, goods, and services', no human right to health can ever be realizable. Controversy will certainly arise on trying to specify what kinds of health-care facilities, goods, and services the minimum core obligations should (and should not) encompass. However, stakeholders share the common ground of understanding the minimum core obligations as requiring priority access to *basic* health-care facilities, goods, and services.[68]

How can one interpret access to *basic* health-care facilities, goods, and services? The purpose of analysing how one interprets access to *basic* health-care facilities, goods, and services is to examine how one can better understand the minimum core duties of the human right to health. The precise question to ask here is this: which duty-bearers should do what, for whom, and for what cost, to secure access to *basic* health-care facilities, goods, and services? Answering this question will require analysing two different scenarios. Scenario 1 analyses

[68] 'Basic' means essential or indispensable for the realization of other (non-basic) components of the right to health. In other words, the health-care facilities, goods, and services that are *basic* are the components without which a *basic* human right to health cannot be minimally realized; they are the condition *sine qua non* of the right to health. On the definition of basic and its comparison to non-basic, see also TC de Campos, *The Global Health Crisis: Ethical Responsibilities* (Cambridge University Press, 2017), ch 1.

how the modern conception of justice interprets access to basic health-care facilities, goods, and services. Scenario 2 analyses how the deontic conception of justice interprets it.

A. Scenario 1

The modern conception of justice (as discussed in section II) is expressed chiefly by the language of rights—in particular, the individual right to autonomous choices. If justice in this scenario is equated to unconstrained rights to choose autonomously according to the patients' preferences, then *basic* health-care facilities, goods, and services will here be interpreted and identified as those facilities, goods, and services patients autonomously choose to suit their preferences without constraints or interferences from others. This conception of justice requires governments and health-care providers (duty-bearers) to respect (ie negative duty of non-interference) patients' self-sufficiency and to protect and fulfil (ie positive duties) their individual autonomy by providing the facilities, goods, and services chosen and preferred. Patients, in turn, are entitled to claim and receive their preferred choice, as they demand.

There are numerous examples of facilities, goods, and services that one could define as 'basic' in the first scenario, since 'basic' here could encompass any medical treatment that patients feel inclined to prefer, desire, and choose. We could include here less contentious examples, which are more clearly urgent and directly related to one's survival, such as access to essential medicines, emergency clinics, intensive care units, maternal care, and palliative care. We could also include more contentious and specific examples within the categories of maternal care and palliative care, such as access to abortion clinics and euthanasia/physician-assisted suicide units, debatably less urgent or perhaps not so evidently related to survival according to some, but certainly defended as the preferred choices of many patients.

All of these examples could legitimately fall within the interpretation of 'basic health care' envisioned by scenario 1 because they could all express patients' autonomous choice according to their most desired preferences. If justice here would require governments and health-care providers—as duty-bearers—to provide this wide range of facilities, goods, and services, then governments (and society in general) bear the obligation to afford financially these desired choices and preferences. Also, health-care providers bear the obligation to inescapably provide patients' most desired requests, even if certain health-care providers view the choice as unethical or not in the patients' best interests. In the modern conception of justice, patients' autonomy rights would trump health-care providers' rights to conscientious objections to certain health-care facilities, goods, and services. The modern understanding of justice requires (not only from health-care professionals and government, but also from all members in the society) the duties to respect, protect, and fulfil patients' autonomous medical choices, and to safeguard those choices from the dangers of medical paternalism, with the goal of upholding the autonomy (ie self-sufficiency) of patients at all times. This is the minimum requirement of duty-bearers in the context of the human right to health according to scenario 1's understanding of justice (as unconstrained rights to choose autonomously according to patients' preferences). Would a different conception of justice justify different requirements?

B. Scenario 2

The deontic conception of justice (as described in section III) includes both rights and corresponding institutionalized duties. As described above, deontic justice entails universal, fundamental, and abstract obligations. First, the deontic understanding of justice will not require obligations that cannot be upheld by all, as they would not be universalizable. Second, the deontic understanding of justice will not require obligations inconsistent with the fundamental values of the institutions they structure (eg human rights). Inconsistency at such a fundamental level would prevent the institutions from practically structuring their actions and choices, and then later specifying their laws and policies adequately. Third, the deontic understanding of justice would not require highly specified obligations because this would impede structuring of an institution in a more general way and allow them to more freely specify their laws and policies in accordance with their universalizable and fundamental values. So, if justice here in scenario 2 demands obligations that are universal, fundamental, and abstract, then *basic* health-care facilities, goods, and services would here be interpreted in a universal, fundamental, and abstract way as well. This means that duty-bears would not be obligated to adhere to a highly specified set of facilities, goods, and services that could contain contentious items and that not all duty-bearers could universally uphold. Also, patients, as rights-holders, could not claim a particular or contentious list of facilities, goods, and services that does not take into consideration the fundamental moral values of the institutions providing them.

If the focus of the deontic conception of justice is on institutionalized duties as counterparts of rights, then a deontic conception of justice would simply emphasize the allocation of certain responsibilities (ie universalizable, fundamental, and abstract) to certain duty-bearers (eg governments and health-care professions), and then be institutionalized, specified, allocated, claimed, and enforced in accordance with the universal and fundamental moral values held by the institution. Now, what are the duties that could be fundamental and abstract enough to be able to be universalizable and agreeable to all duty-bearers in the context of the human right to health?

The answer to this question is key because it will point to what deontic justice minimally requires of duty-bearers (eg governments and health-care professionals or even society in general). Deontic justice would interpret the minimum core obligations of the right to health—and therefore *basic* health-care facilities, goods, and services—as those health-care facilities, goods, and services that are more clearly and less contentiously viewed as indispensable to one's survival, such as access to essential medicines, emergency clinics, intensive care units, maternal care, and palliative care. Most people would agree (or at least not oppose the idea) that these are evident examples of urgent matters related to subsistence. Most people would also agree that these should take prima facie priority over other remaining (non-urgent or non-survival-related) matters, other things being equal.[69] However, deontic justice would not include within the minimum core obligations of the right to health those health-care facilities, goods, and services that cannot be universally accepted as essential or indispensable to survival, including those more contentious matters like access to abortion clinics and euthanasia/physician-assisted suicide units (which scenario 1 legitimately

[69] de Campos (n 16) 71–81.

includes). They would not qualify as *basic* health-care facilities, goods, and services here in scenario 2 because they are not morally fundamental and abstract enough to be universalizable and agreeable to all duty-bearers in the context of the human right to health.

The deontic interpretation of the minimum core is therefore much less extensive than the interpretation provided by the modern idea of justice. Deontic justice would not charge governments (and society in general) with the obligation to afford a myriad of health-care facilities, goods, and services, even if patients deeply desire such choices. Nor would deontic justice charge health-care providers with the obligation to fulfil every inclination and request of patients simply based on the patient's rights to choose autonomously according to his or her preference. Under the Kantian reasoning, such preferences could be reasonably denied when health-care providers do not morally uphold preferences. Said denial would be predicated on health-care providers', governments' and society's duty to assess their moral conscience regarding the patients' best interests.[70] A deontic conception of justice would therefore not only allow for the right, but also require the duty of health-care providers, governments, and society in general to conscientiously object[71] to morally contentious health-care facilities, goods, and services, such as those that involve the intentional ending of human life,[72] on the basis that these cannot be morally upheld by all (ie they are not universalizable, fundamental, and abstract enough).

Deontic justice would nevertheless not be overly abstract and underspecified: it would charge certain duty-bearers (ie governments and health-care providers) with the obligation to provide certain health care facilities, goods, and services considered universally indispensable for survival and that therefore qualify as 'basic'. This universal obligation would fall on all governments and health-care providers. Yet, this would also require a context-sensitive obligation because its specifications would certainly depend on the specificities of local institutions. In this sense, deontic justice would charge local governments (and society in general) with the obligation to specify the institutions that would have to enforce and financially afford those basic health-care facilities, services, and goods. What would this mean in more concrete terms?

As discussed above, access to essential medicines, emergency clinics, intensive care units, maternal care, and palliative care are examples of what Kantian justice would interpret as

[70] Individuals and institutions are moral agents with conscience rights and duties. As Sulmasy puts it: 'Conscience is a fundamental moral commitment on the part of a moral agent to moral integrity, involving a commitment to uphold fundamental moral precepts and moral identity and, based upon these fundamental moral commitments, to make use of reason, emotion, and will to arrive at proper moral judgments and to act on these judgments. Health care institutions seem fully capable of this' (D Sulmasy, 'Institutional Conscience and Moral Pluralism in Health Care' (1997) 10(4) New Theology Review 5–21). See also K Wildes, 'Institutional Identity, Integrity and Conscience' (1993) 7(4) Kennedy Institute of Ethics Journal 413–19. On conscience rights and duties more generally applied to the context of health-care provision, see C Lamb, 'Conscientious Objection—Understanding the Right to Conscience in Health and Healthcare Practice' (2016) 22(1) New Bioethics 33–44.

[71] As Kant puts it: 'every human being, as a moral being, has a conscience within him originally. To be under the obligation to have a conscience would be tantamount to having a duty to recognize duties. Conscience is practical reason holding the human being's duty before him for his acquittal or condemnation in every case that comes under a law' (I Kant, 'The Metaphysics of Morals' in *Practical Philosophy* (Cambridge University Press, 1996), 6:400, 529).

[72] As Kant puts it: 'Willfully killing oneself can be called murdering oneself . . . only if it can be proved that it is in general a crime committed either against one's own person or also, through one's killing oneself, against another (as when a pregnant person takes her life). Killing of oneself is a crime (murder). It can be regarded as a violation of one's duty to other people (the duty of spouses to each other, of parents to their children . . . A human being cannot renounce his personality as long as he is a subject of duty, hence as long as he lives; and it is a contradiction that he should be authorizes to withdraw from all obligation' (Kant, ibid, 422–3, 546–7).

basic health-care facilities, goods, and services that integrate the minimum core obligations of the right to health. Take access to essential medicines. Because access to essential medicine is a *basic* health good that grounds a universal obligation, all governments (and possibly societies in general) are required to secure it. However, a deontic justice would not require, for example, a highly specified list of essential medications because this would impede the structuring of local institutions in a general way that allows them to later and more freely specify their medical laws and policies, in accordance with their universalizable and fundamental values. A highly specific list of the exact medications that qualify as essential in one jurisdiction or another is context-sensitive, according to the epidemiological reality and the particular health needs of each population. It is therefore the responsibility of local governments and local medical institutions to elaborate a suitable list of essential medicines, adequate to their local population, according to their own health needs and medical priorities.

Now, take the example of maternal health care and palliative care. All health-care providers, governments, and societies are required, as a matter of justice, to provide adequate and good prenatal, post-natal, new-born, and child health care, as well as adequate and good palliative care for the dying and those facing terminal illness. These are universal obligations, required of all health-care providers, governments, and societies. Yet, the specifics of the provision would be defined at a later stage by each local government better-situated and better-acquainted with local needs, priorities, and customs.

Again, these examples are certainly not meant to offer a list of items patients can claim and receive: this would not be consistent with a deontic approach to justice. Instead, these examples merely offer an illustration of the kinds of *basic* prophylactic and therapeutic facilities, goods, and services that any human being objectively and universally speaking needs prima facie to ensure his or her survival, avoid a premature death, and allow for a well-managed natural death, other things being equal.[73]

V. Conclusion

This chapter demonstrated that the deontological approach to justice and human rights can be particularly valuable in contemporary medical law and bioethics debates. Current discussions in these fields have been almost exclusively concerned with and framed around the autonomy of patients and their individual rights—particularly the individual right to patients' autonomous choices.[74] Although a multitude of autonomous choices by patients are claimed as rights, they often cannot be realized because they cannot be attributable to specific duty-bearers.[75] The chapter argued that a deontological approach to medical law could not only create a less individualistic and more inclusive/relational discussion, but also increase the probability of the realization of rights—particularly the human right to health.

[73] de Campos (n 16) 75.

[74] See Scheneider (n 22); Stammers (n 22); O'Neill, 'Public Health or Clinical Ethics' (n 6) 35; Austriaco (n 22); Wolpe (n 22); Stirrat and Gill (n 22).

[75] O'Neill, *Bounds of Justice* (n 6) ch 6, 97, 100. A similar point is also made by Glendon (n 10). See also: M Sandel, *Democracy's Discontent: America in Search of a Public Philosophy* (Harvard University Press, 1996) and J Raz, 'Human Rights without Foundations' in S Besson and J Tasioulas (eds), *The Philosophy of International Law* (Oxford University Press, 2010).

The chapter argued that deontology's emphasis on responsibilities could potentially restore the lost balance between rights and duties, as well as the lost relationship between rights-holders and duty-bearers. It put this argument forth in the following manner:

Section II discussed the problems of the current state of affairs, namely the modern conception of justice, where justice and human rights have become tantamount to unconstrained rights to choose autonomously according to one's individual preferences. This conception is weak and contested by the many different theories of justice. Section III presents one alternative, which I consider helpful and promising in the context of medical law and bioethics: the deontological approach to justice, where the claim of rights rests on the establishment of correlated duties.

Section III discusses the Kantian understanding of justice and human rights, and examines in greater detail the deontological understanding of the human right to health (and its correlated minimum core obligations), given the prominence of this specific human right in the fields of medical law and bioethics. More specifically, section III looked at O'Neill's deontological conception of justice and human rights, which establishes the connection between justice and human rights, on the one hand, and responsibilities, on the other. This section then juxtaposed O'Neill against Tasioulas to clarify what the right-to-health-corresponding minimum core obligations are.

Finally, section IV applied the theoretical discussions of sections II and III to typical debates of medical law and bioethics, in the particular context of the minimum core obligations that spur from the human right to health. Section IV first examined how the modern conception of justice (discussed in section II) would interpret the doctrine of minimum core obligations correlated to the human right to health (reduced to the language of rights—in particular, the right to autonomous choices). It then contrasted this interpretation based on the modern conception of justice against an interpretation based on the deontic conception of justice (defined by both right and corresponding duties, as discussed in section III). Contrasting these two different interpretations proved helpful for practical purposes: each interpretation justifies a different list of minimum core obligations correlated to the human right to health that should arguably be given priority when allocating scarce health-care resources.

6

Abortion, Feminism, and 'Traditional' Moral Philosophy

*Kate Greasley**

I. Introduction

A certain strain of feminist ethical thinking has long been critical of the way many moral philosophers do things when it comes to abortion. The criticism often voiced from such quarters is, briefly put, that traditional philosophical approaches to the abortion problem suffer from a flawed methodology. That flaw, it is suggested, has certain unfortunate implications. In particular, it is responsible for a perennial failure to apprehend some of the most salient features of the abortion situation and their significance for the moral evaluation of abortion practice.

This allegation levelled at 'traditional' or non-feminist abortion ethics implicates a wider dispute about the correct methodology for approaching complex ethical problems in general. 'Traditional' ethics, it is broadly claimed, is greatly impoverished by its preoccupation with abstract, general principles of morality, and its resultant failure to acknowledge the ethical significance of 'context' in moral thinking. In such critiques, traditional philosophical analysis is then juxtaposed with feminist ethics in terms of its methodological orientation. Scholars who castigate conventional philosophical approaches for paying inadequate attention to context take feminist ethics to be, by contrast, largely defined by its greater interest in the contextual details of the problems with which it concerns itself—details that are awarded higher value in its moral accounting.

It is, of course, hardly correct to speak of 'feminism' as if it denotes a unified theory. There is no single feminist theory, but rather many kinds of feminisms, loosely bound together. Still, assuming that there is some common thread which links all feminisms to one another, it is sensible to ask what that thread is. Janet Halley has attempted to capture it by offering two essential components of feminist thought.[1] The first is the descriptive claim that makes some distinction between M and F (whether this be 'man' and 'woman', 'male' and 'female', or 'masculine' and 'feminine') and posits that F is disadvantaged relative to, and subordinated by, M. The second is the evaluative claim that F's subordination is unjust and ought to be resisted. 'Feminism is feminism because', she says, 'as between M and F, it carries a brief for F'.[2] As far as feminism is identified only with these two core claims, the complaint against traditional moral philosophy cannot be ascribed to all feminists. However, since

* I would like to thank Jeff McMahan, Barbara Havelková, Meghan Campbell, Maggie O'Brien, and Denise Réume for providing extremely useful comments on earlier drafts of this chapter.

[1] J Halley, '"Taking a Break from Feminism", in Cossman et al, "Gender, Sexuality and Power: Is Feminist Theory Enough?"' (2003) 12 Columbia Journal of Gender and Law 604.

[2] Ibid.

Kate Greasley, *Abortion, Feminism, and 'Traditional' Moral Philosophy* In: *Philosophical Foundations of Medical Law*. Edited by: Andelka M Phillips, Thana C de Campos, and Jonathan Herring, Oxford University Press (2019). © Andelka M Phillips, Thana C de Campos, and Jonathan Herring
DOI: 10.1093/oso/9780198796558.003.0007

those levelling the complaint regard it as distinctive of feminist ethics, I will, for the purposes of this discussion, describe it as the 'feminist ethics' position.

In what follows here, I offer a basic defence of the nature and methods of traditional abortion ethics against the feminist ethics challenge about flawed methodology. This, of course, means first getting a handle on exactly what proponents of the methodologically based criticisms believe most moral philosophers are doing wrong in their exchanges on abortion, and why. In addition to (hopefully) getting clearer about this, I seek to show how those fielding such complaints have misunderstood or misjudged the practice and merits of conventional moral theorizing about abortion ethics and that, in spite of such contentions, the methodological disagreement between the two approaches is, in fact, largely illusory.

II. The Challenge to 'Traditional' Abortion Ethics

A chief proponent of the feminist ethics challenge under consideration is Susan Sherwin. Sherwin's scholarship about abortion ethics has insightfully and significantly exposited the numerous ways in which women's interests in equality and sexual autonomy are deeply implicated in the question of reproductive control. Along with some other feminist scholars, her contributions to these claims have been invaluable and undoubtedly correct. Characterizing the feminist ethics approach more broadly, however, Sherwin describes what she takes to be the prevalent attitude among feminist ethical scholars working on problems such as abortion. This is, in her words,

> [a] sense of frustration with the level of abstraction and generality that characterises traditional philosophic work in ethics and a common commitment to including contextual details and allowing room for the personal aspects of relationships in ethical analysis.[3]

Unlike 'traditional philosophic work', feminist ethics analysis is, Sherwin says, 'interested in developing the sort of analysis that can offer meaningful guidance in the morally troubling situations of real life'.[4] Conversely, the abstraction and generality which characterize traditional ethics

> speak of the limitations of restricting ethical analysis to the level of general principles, and ... demonstrate the need to focus quite explicitly on the contextual details of life situations that are problematic for morally concerned persons.[5]

For anyone engaged in what Sherwin understands to be 'traditional' moral philosophy, the suggestion that they are not interested in unearthing guidance for 'real-life' situations will be fairly dismaying, for this is precisely what work in normative and applied ethics sees itself as doing. The fact that imaginary or supposed cases are often considered in the process of ethical argument should not create any confusion on this point. In the course of ethical

[3] S Sherwin, 'Feminist and Medical Ethics: Two Different Approaches to Contextual Ethics' in HB Holmes and LM Purdy (eds), *Feminist Perspectives in Medical Ethics* (Indiana University Press, 1992), 17.
[4] Ibid.
[5] Ibid.

debate about abortion, a discussant may pose a question such as: is it morally permissible to abort a foetus of twenty-eight weeks' gestation because the pregnant woman has suffered a breakdown of her spousal relationship? Or perhaps she may ask whether it is more or less ethical for a pregnant woman to abort a foetus of twenty-eight weeks' gestation because it is discovered to have a cleft lip palate, and what is the relevant moral difference between the two cases, if there is one. She may ask what difference it would make to our answers in *both* cases if the foetus were not twenty-eight weeks gestated, but twelve weeks, or if the woman concerned were extraordinarily rich, or particularly poor. These test cases are only 'abstract' in the sense that they do not have particular, real-life referents. There are no names, dates, or medical records produced. But the ethical questions are absolutely intended to refer to 'real-life' situations bearing out the characteristics described, and to shed moral light on those cases and, by extrapolation, on others.

At times, moral philosophers do argue about abortion using truly imaginary cases that are not expected to have real-life incarnations. One prevalent example is Judith Jarvis Thomson's 'violinist analogy' argument, which asks you, the reader, to imagine a scenario in which you are kidnapped by a musical society that forcibly connects your kidneys to the body of an ailing, unconscious, famous violinist, who requires the use of them for nine months in order to survive.[6] Thomson poses the question of whether, in that scenario, you would be permitted to unplug the violinist from your body before the nine months is up, resulting in his certain death. Assuming that your answer will be 'yes', she then analogizes unplugging the violinist to aborting a pregnancy. If it is permissible for you to unplug the violinist, knowing that he will die, why cannot a pregnant woman abort a pregnancy to be free of the foetus's bodily imposition?

Thought-experiments such as these *are* meant to be purely imaginary. It is not as if Thomson believes this exact moral quandary is ever likely to arise. But their use is no less oriented towards understanding what we should do in the 'real-life' abortion scenario. The point of Thomson's violinist analogy is to demonstrate that abortion is morally permissible in almost all cases, even if the foetus is a fully rights-holding 'person', because continued pregnancy is really an act of Good Samaritanism, and, hence, is not morally obligatory. The use of the violinist analogy is just to make this Good Samaritan argument. If you think it is permissible to unplug the violinist, then you must agree it is permissible to abort a pregnancy, Thomson argues, since a similar relationship of bodily intertwinement holds in both, and the stakes are the same: the death of the dependent person or the months-long bodily imposition upon the host. The analogy is indeed aimed at demonstrating a principle at a certain level of generality. The principle is that one is permitted to end the burdensome and parasitic dependence of another person upon one's body, even if that results in the dependent party's death. But the same principle is meant to give us a concrete answer to the 'real-life' abortion case as well. Abortion is permissible because, like unplugging the violinist, it only ends non-obligatory bodily assistance. The violinist argument tells us that we do, in fact, accept that principle, and the principle is meant to tell us what to think about abortion.

So, 'traditional' moral philosophy, whatever its methods, is certainly directed at determining what right action amounts to in real abortion cases. But there is clearly more to the

[6] J Thomson, 'A Defense of Abortion' (1971) 1(1) Philosophy and Public Affairs 47.

feminist ethics charge than the suggestion that it is not. For Sherwin, as well as for others, it might well be the very use of general principles to reach conclusions in specific cases that is the problem. As Mary Mahowald writes:

> Feminists argue that this type of deductive analysis cannot absolutely attend to the complexity and uniqueness of real cases and issues. To rectify the inadequacy, attention to context is essential.[7]

According to this view, the deduction of principles might be *aimed* at discovering the moral truth about real-life cases, but the method is not fit for purpose. In particular, it is suggested, the centrality of principles in traditional philosophy is antagonistic to an appreciation of 'context'. Since principles (putatively) preclude considering context, arguing by way of them is likely to obscure many of the salient moral considerations which context throws up.

This naturally raises the question as to what exactly feminist ethicists mean when they speak of inattention to 'context' here. We will surely want to know exactly which aspects of the abortion context traditional moral argument, by appeal to principles, cannot avoid missing. The various discernible answers to this question demonstrate the multidimensional nature of the 'context' complaint. One important aspect is the idea that mainstream ethical theory, carried out in what Sherwin calls 'the masculine voice', crowds out a more quintessentially feminine approach to ethical dilemmas, which looks to the unique features of each case and the possibilities for interpersonal resolution. On this point, Sherwin refers to the well-known work by the psychologist Carol Gilligan, who conducted experiments to observe the different tendencies of women as compared with men when reasoning about ethical problems.[8] In Gilligan's experiments, separate groups of female and male subjects were presented with identical ethical dilemmas, being asked, for example, whether it would be morally permissible for an impoverished person to steal medicine from a chemist to save the life of her sick child. Gilligan found that whereas the men argued with one another about abstract principles such as the immorality of theft and the sanctity of human life, the women tended to ask further questions about the particular scenario, such as: 'Why doesn't the parent just ask the chemist to give her the medicine she needs?' Gilligan's conclusions, in Sherwin's words, were that:

> female subjects tried to preserve relationships and to find new options through better communication and a presumption of co-operation; they tended to respond by seeking more information, or by trying to reconceive the terms set by the example.[9]

While the women were especially interested in the 'particular narrative details' and 'specific human dynamics' of a situation, the men were, instead, 'preoccupied with developing comprehensive, generalizable, abstract ethical systems which are based on rights'.[10]

[7] M Mahowald, 'As If There Were Fetuses without Women: A Remedial Essay' in J Callahan (ed), *Reproduction, Ethics, and the Law: Feminist Perspectives* (Indiana University Press, 1995), 200.
[8] C Gilligan, *In a Different Voice: Psychological Theory and Women's Development* (Harvard University Press, 1982).
[9] Sherwin (n 3) 18.
[10] Ibid.

By invoking the Gilligan experiments, Sherwin gives added texture to her claim that mainstream ethical analysis is restricted by its abstractness, helping to explicate what in particular it is thought to leave out. The failure to attend to all of the concrete details of a morally contentious situation is likely to result in the neglect of important ethical considerations, specifically, the moral relevance of the relationships that exist among the parties involved. As she elaborates: 'an ethics of action is incomplete when evaluation is done in abstraction from the relationships holding between the participants performing them and those affected by them'.[11] Quite significantly, the *unequal* power relations that can hold between parties underscores, for Sherwin, 'the importance of evaluating behaviour in terms of its effect on the quality of relationships'.[12]

In abortion ethics specifically, inattention to the importance of relationships—especially the relationship holding between a pregnant woman and her foetus—and of the typically 'feminine' ethical concern with caring values are seen to be major vices of the traditional philosophic approach. Mary Mahowald has written that 'traditional ethics emphasizes the rights of individuals, neglecting the realm of relationships'.[13] Hence, when it comes to abortion:

> through its assumption that impartiality is a requirement of ethically justifiable judgments, traditional ethics eschews considerations based on particular relationships such as occur between pregnant women and their fetuses.[14]

In Mahowald's view, ethical discussions in which abortion ends up being opposed or supported 'solely on the grounds of the moral status of the fetus' bear out this myopia. In contrast, feminist approaches care far more about 'the essential role that relationships play in moral decision making'.[15] One hugely important aspect of the foetus–woman relationship that Mahowald believes is woefully underappreciated by traditional ethicists is the dependence of foetuses on women for their very existence—the fact that, in her words, 'fetuses do not exist apart from women, who are inevitably affected by decisions about fetuses'.[16] Mahowald accuses non-feminist theorists of being unmindful of this special relationship, which results in their *ignoring* the 'interests and preferences of pregnant women', which may well conflict with the interests of their foetuses.[17]

III. Principles and Context

There is much that can be said in response to all of this. In short, I believe the suggestion by Sherwin and Mahowald that 'traditional' ethics does not account for the moral significance of context, and that this omission blights abortion discussion in particular, is both unfair and wrong-headed.

11 Ibid 21.
12 Ibid.
13 Mahowald (n 7) 200.
14 Ibid.
15 Ibid 201.
16 Ibid 199.
17 Ibid 201.

Let us start with Mahowald's suggestion that features of the 'context' of pregnancy which traditional abortion argument *ignores* include the interests and preferences of pregnant women and the fact that the foetus cannot exist (at least until viability) without depending on the body of the woman. This charge is simply false. First, the weight of a pregnant woman's possible interests in obtaining abortion is accounted for by pretty well every ethical appraisal of abortion, whatever is concluded about abortion's moral defensibility. Mostly, this is because the existence of those interests and their strength are seen as axiomatic. The fact that women's stakes in abortion access do not appear to occupy centre stage in most traditional philosophic enquiries can be explained by the fact that almost all discussants readily acknowledge them. Even those who conclude that abortion is almost always morally impermissible tend to be in agreement with others regarding the significant interest women have in abortion access and the profoundly negative consequences they may face when abortion is unavailable. Their disagreement is about how this interest stacks up against the foetus's interest in remaining alive, which in most cases rests heavily upon what level of moral status the various discussants accord the foetus. Philosophical disagreements about abortion therefore do not usually *turn* on the 'women's interest' issue, which explains why it does not take up more space in the literature. This is not the same as its being *ignored*. The interest is factored into the moral calculations of all engaged in the abortion argument (though they may, of course, disagree on its exact strength). But depending on how those calculations proceed, it may not end up being dispositive.

Mahowald is wrong in a different way when she accuses traditional ethics of neglecting the 'foetus–woman' relationship, since many philosophers are in fact deeply engaged in determining the normative implications for abortion of the foetus and the woman's positioning relative to each other. This is the entire angle of thought-experiments such as Thomson's, which seek to draw out the moral meaningfulness of the foetus's bodily dependence on the woman. To complain that this enquiry should not proceed by analysing cases which resemble pregnancy in some respects but are *not* pregnancy would be unfair, since the only way to determine the ethical significance of one detail of a case is to isolate it by importing it into a different case. The violinist thought-experiment, for example, enables us to ask whether the fact of one human being's bodily dependence upon another for a certain length of time entitles the 'host' to end that support even if it means ending the dependent's life.

Mahowald seeks to bolster her own conclusions about abortion by pointing out the fact that foetuses *as such* do not exist apart from women, since they are defined by their location in the womb (a foetus outside the womb is not a foetus, but a baby). But this argument is somewhat vague and tautological. It is a conceptual truth that 'foetuses' do not exist without women (though the *thing* that is a foetus at one stage and a baby later possibly can, depending on one's view of the conditions for numerical identity). But we cannot derive a substantive moral point about abortion from a conceptual truth about foetuses. The mere fact that foetuses are defined by their location in the womb does not tell us anything about the morality of abortion. Reaching any moral conclusions would require further, moral argument about the significance of the foetus's dependence upon the woman, which is precisely what contributions like Thomson's attempt to provide.

One may, of course, argue that the violinist scenario is disanalogous to pregnancy in some morally relevant ways, meaning that our conclusions in that case (whatever they are) do not carry over to the pregnancy context. Someone might object, for instance, that the biological relation which holds between a pregnant woman and her foetus but not between the violinist and his host changes the ethical answer in the abortion case. If this were true, it would tell us something useful: that the 'bodily dependence' relation is not the only ethically salient feature of pregnancy and abortion. We might then test the importance of the *biological* relation by considering a case of conjoined twins and asking whether one twin, whose vital organs support the other, may have the other killed to be free of the imposition. Again, the feminist ethicist (as Sherwin defines her) may object that conjoined twins reflect some of the features of pregnancy, but not *all* of its features. But this would be to miss the point. The analogous cases are not *meant* to resemble pregnancy in all respects, but to isolate certain features whose ethical significance we are testing—here, the combined effect of bodily interdependence and biological relation. If the feminist ethicist thinks that other features of pregnancy not captured by the conjoined twins case are also ethically salient to abortion (perhaps the fact that the foetus is entirely enclosed within the woman), then she will have to explain what they are and why they are morally meaningful. But in doing so, she will be doing the day-to-day work of 'traditional' moral philosophy.

It warrants saying something particular about the claim that traditional ethics, with its fixation on abstract principles and the 'impartial point of view', is uninterested in the ethical significance of personal relationships. This again is plainly false, as the great volume of work on the value and importance of personal attachments and projects—including for ethical decision making—suggests. Just how and why relationships can be relevant to the rightness or wrongness of an action depends, of course, on context. Is it more permitted to kill strangers for no good reason than to kill my family members? No. If a man comes across two people drowning and one of them is his wife, is he permitted to save *her* because she is his wife? Some would say that he is. Perhaps breaking promises to friends and loved ones is more of a moral infraction than breaking promises to business associates. One could certainly make the case.

Insofar, then, as the question 'What is right to do?' must take account of all morally relevant considerations, the existence and nature of personal relationships cannot be ruled out. But the precise significance those relationships have for any moral question will depend entirely on what is being asked, and on all other morally relevant considerations. One cannot show that a personal relationship is relevant to a decision about what one ought to do without explaining why this is so. If the feminist ethicist claim is that personal relationships are *always* determinative of what one should do, then it is they, not their interlocutors, who are abstracting from context. Of course, many moral questions will have nothing whatsoever to do with personal relationships, such as whether one should be a vegetarian.

In the case of abortion, it is not always entirely clear what discussants have in mind when they say that traditional philosophy is not sufficiently sensitive to the 'feminine' concern with valuing and preserving relationships. As we saw, Mahowald's suggestion was that only feminists 'insist on the moral relevance of relationships', but since no moral philosopher would exclude the potential relevance of a relationship to moral questions (it just cannot be relevant to *all* moral questions), one is left asking how they view 'relationships' as affecting abortion morality in particular. One answer that seems broadly expressive of what has come to be known as the 'relational view' of abortion is that the nature of a woman's relationship with her foetus is the sole or determinative consideration for abortion's moral permissibility. If a woman lacks a relationship with her foetus, abortion is morally permissible, since its value in the context of a relationship with the woman is the only value the foetus possesses.

I am deeply sceptical about the notion that a foetus and a pregnant woman can be in a relationship of any kind, once we take reciprocity to be a condition of a relationship, which I think we should.[18] The foetus cannot relate *back* in any way. Hence, the 'relationship' captured by the relational view of abortion is simply the strength of connection or positive emotion a woman feels with regard to her foetus, the claim being that this is the only morally relevant feature of abortion. Proponents of the relational view do not suggest, however, that a woman who has strong positive feelings towards her foetus cannot permissibly abort, even where she judges, all things considered, that this would be the best thing for her to do. That is to say, the relational view does not produce any moral imperatives either way; it is only a permissive principle that a woman may do what she wants with her own pregnancy, regardless of how she 'relates' to the foetus. Once this is appreciated, it is difficult to see just what moral work the relational value is really doing in relational theories of abortion ethics. The argument boils down to the claim that women are morally permitted to abort their pregnancies if they wish to do so, based on a justification that must surely invoke something *other* than the value of a woman's emotional attitude towards her foetus.

As I have noted, a related aspect of the feminist ethics challenge claims that ethics carried out in the characteristic 'feminine voice' tends to put greater emphasis on caring values in particular. But it is not always made clear what ramifications the 'ethics of care' would have for abortion. At least at first glance, terminating the life of one's foetus is not a clear instance of exercising caring values, a problem that has not gone entirely unnoticed.[19] We surely want to know how, exactly, a permissive attitude to abortion (the conclusion reached by almost all feminist ethicists) better exemplifies an ethics of care than the alternative.

In the Gilligan study cited above, it is difficult to see why relational values are relevant at all. The would-be thief has no stated relationship with the chemist, making it unclear as to how the value of 'preserving relationships' holds any moral weight. It might be thought that by responding to the moral problem set by asking questions such as why the woman did not ask for the medication, the women in the experiment were simply evading the real question, which is whether she is morally permitted to steal the medication if there is no other way to save her child. Perhaps, however, the point being made by the example is the broader one that the more particular features of an ethical dilemma of which one is cognizant, the more likely one is to reach the morally correct conclusions. From this perspective, the women's disposition to ask further questions about the concrete details of the case better positioned them to pick up on morally salient features which those preoccupied with abstract theorizing might be liable to overlook.

But sound moral philosophizing in the analytic tradition *also* requires attention to any potentially morally relevant feature of a problem. In fact, it quite fundamentally requires it. Moral philosophy must take account of all *morally relevant* features of a problem. Discussants may well argue with one another about which facts are indeed morally relevant, and this is where analogies and thought-experiments can prove useful as control tests.

[18] To be sure, non-reciprocal *relations* of various kinds may hold between two individuals, such as biological relations, or the relation of unrequited love. But the relational view distorts the nature of the connection between foetus and woman by describing it as a relationship, rather than as a kind of relation.

[19] See eg C Wolf-Devine, 'Abortion and the "Feminine Voice"' (1989) 3 Public Affairs Quarterly 81..

But to the extent that feminist ethicists charge any argument about abortion morality with missing out on an ethically pertinent feature or miscalculating the implications of that feature, they will be fully partaking in that same method.

Inasmuch, then, as the women in the Gilligan experiments were adverting to more and more potentially significant facts about the moral problems presented, one might just think that they were doing traditional philosophy better than the men. By asking the further questions, perhaps they only revealed their scepticism that any moral principle taking the form 'Do not steal, no matter what' can be correct. By wanting to know whether all other options (like asking for the medicine) were exhausted, we might instead take them to be considering a different principle, such as 'Do not steal unless it is absolutely necessary'. This might not suggest any resistance to the use of principles, but only the rejection of the *particular* principle: Never steal, no matter what.

The ethical relevance of any fact or feature will always need to be explained and defended, however. This is simply what is required in the process of moral reasoning. It would not have been enough for some of the women in the group to enquire whether the protagonist thief has the opportunity of asking for the medicine, unless they also explained by reference to which moral standards—or principles—they thought that mattered. This is because it cannot contribute to one's moral appraisal of any problem to point out that there are additional, 'unique' or 'concrete' features of a case, and to leave it at that. It may be a concrete feature of an abortion scenario that the pregnant woman is wearing blue shoes, but this does not establish that the fact is morally relevant. Judgements will always have to be made about which real-life features of an ethical dilemma, of all the infinite facts that are available, are potentially morally relevant, and these judgements cannot be made, nor their normative implications argued for, other than by reference to more general moral claims, the correctness of which can only be tested by abstracting them from the case at hand.

The upshot of all of this is the following. When feminist ethics advocates accuse traditional abortion ethicists of employing a method that is bound to overlook key moral features of the abortion situation, yet fail to provide concrete examples of relevant features that are overlooked, it will again be they who are the more guilty of abstractness, by omitting to explain how the supposed superiority of their way of doing things actually works. To make their own claim at anything more than an abstract level, what is needed is a comparison which underscores precisely what is missed when abortion ethics is carried out in the traditional method, and why that method cannot be trusted to reach plausible conclusions. But as soon as the discussant attempts to formulate such an explanation, she will invariably find herself doing the normal work of mainstream philosophy. (To wit: 'The bodily dependence of the foetus matters because we do not have duties to sustain the lives of those imposing on us in such a way. But is that true? Let us attend to the case of the violinist.' And so on.) Sherwin is wrong, therefore, to set up principled moral thinking in opposition to contextual moral thinking. Picking the relevant features out of the entire context of an ethical problem and drawing moral conclusions from those features *is* the process of conventional moral reasoning, and feminist ethicists are no less engaged in this enterprise than is anyone else.

It may be wondered what kind of relationship holds between the feminist ethics claim that argument by way of principles is liable to induce moral mistakes and the view termed 'moral particularism' in normative ethics. In its less radical form, moral particularism claims, in Jonathan Dancy's words, that 'moral principles are at best crutches that a morally sensitive person would not require, and indeed the use of such crutches might even lead us into moral error'.[20] In its stronger form, it claims that there simply *are* no defensible moral principles and that sound moral thinking cannot therefore proceed by appeal to them. Appraising the merits of the moral particularist thesis is well beyond the scope of this chapter. But if the feminist ethics claim about the hazardousness of principles, is, in essence, the moral particularist claim, we might wonder if there is anything distinctively feminist about it. Moreover, like moral particularism, it will stand or fall on the plausibility of the view that moral principles do not exist or that they ought not to be relied upon when making individual moral assessments.

IV. Sex Equality

If the quarrel that feminist ethics has with mainstream philosophical treatments of abortion is not methodological, perhaps it is, instead, a substantive one. Perhaps feminist ethicists tend to attribute a degree of ethical significance to particular features of the abortion problem which other accounts do not (which is not at all to say that they ignore or neglect them). Reflecting on this possibility might better elucidate the tension between characteristically 'feminist' approaches to abortion and those which Sherwin would define as 'non-feminist'.

One obvious candidate is the relative importance placed by both kinds of analyses on the relationship between reproductive control and sex equality. Sherwin writes that 'in doing feminist ethics, we must appeal to contextual details, and the context cited should involve the broad political context of reproduction in a given society'.[21] Whereas medical ethics, she argues, tends to keep debate focused on the moral status of the foetus, feminists distinguish themselves by the importance they place on 'the implications for women's overall freedom and relative power' if this or that abortion policy is adopted.[22] The difference that freedom to abort makes to 'all women's lives' is, for them, a fundamental part of the equation.

Here, then, is a good indication that the disagreement, if there is one, is not between the general and abstract versus the contextual and concrete, but has more to do with the discrete moral significance of one specific consideration: the effect of abortion policy on sex equality. The sex equality interest in reproductive autonomy is right at the forefront of feminist analysis of the abortion problem and constitutes its distinctive contribution to abortion debate. This account stresses that unwanted pregnancy only happens to women. Hence, the suggestion might be, mainstream philosophical discussions are led astray when underestimating the importance of this fact.

The myriad ways in which abortion prohibitions damage equality between the sexes is not, I believe, very much in doubt, and hardly needs much elaboration here. Sherwin aptly summarizes the implications of mandated pregnancy for women's equality with men when she writes:

[20] J Dancy, 'Moral Particularism' entry in Stanford Encyclopaedia of Philosophy (2013), http://plato.stanford.edu/entries/moral-particularism/ accessed 15 July 2019.

[21] Sherwin (n 3) 26.

[22] Ibid.

> In many circumstances, having a child will exacerbate the social and economic forces already stacked against her by virtue of her sex (and her race, class, age, sexual orientation, or the effects of some disability, etc). Access to abortion is a necessary option for many women if they are to escape the oppressive conditions of poverty.[23]

Sherwin and other feminist scholars have ably expounded the connections between control of reproduction and women's social disadvantage, subordination to men, and sexual autonomy. Pregnancy and child-rearing can aggravate a woman's condition of poverty, reduce her chances of a good education, retard her career prospects, and keep her dependent on men, perhaps in a situation of abuse. For feminists like Sherwin, these are key contextual features which must not be abstracted from abortion analysis. Abortion cannot be considered in isolation from the fact that mandated pregnancy exacerbates women's powerlessness especially when conditions of inequality between the sexes already persist with or without abortion rights. She continues:

> Since we live in a patriarchal society, it is especially important to ensure that women have the authority to control their own reproduction . . . virtually all feminists seem to agree that women must gain full control of their own reproductive lives if they are to free themselves from male dominance.[24]

Sherwin claims that feminist analysis, unlike non-feminist analysis, 'regards the effects of unwanted pregnancies on the lives of women individually and collectively as a central element in the moral evaluation of abortion'.[25] Feminist ethics, she says, 'demands that the effects on the oppression of women be a principal consideration when evaluating abortion policies'.[26] Perhaps, then, the distinctive feature of non-feminist philosophy is not resistance to the idea that abortion rights are intimately bound up with sex equality, but where and how this consideration is positioned in the overall argument. For feminist ethicists, it is really *the* principal consideration; for non-feminists, it is just one piece of a larger puzzle.

As I have already suggested, none of the important observations about the relationship between abortion policy and sex equality can seriously be doubted. And, in the main, they are not. Traditional philosophic approaches to abortion ethics (especially of the liberal persuasion) do not dismiss or reject these findings. The disagreement between such accounts and feminist abortion ethics does not therefore have to do with the veracity of claims about reproductive control and sex equality. Rather, as Sherwin indicates, what disagreement exists concerns the correct moral weight to be assigned to the sex equality interest. In Sherwin's view, this feature of abortion ought to be central, whereas in traditional philosophic accounts it is not, often playing second fiddle (if that) to protracted debates about the moral status of the foetus. This is because on many such views the sex equality interest in abortion's availability, while real, is not ethically dispositive. That is, it is not thought to be determinative for the morality of abortion rights *however* one answers

23 S Sherwin, 'Abortion through a Feminist Ethics Lens' (1991) 30 Dialogue 327, 329.
24 Ibid 330.
25 Ibid.
26 Ibid.

the more philosophically contentious question about the independent moral value of the foetus—or, put differently, whether the foetus is a creature with as strong a right to life as you or I possess.

If this is indeed a disagreement between self-proclaimed 'feminist' and traditional moral theorizing about abortion, then it is a real one. But if *this* is the nature of the disagreement, then I believe the traditionalists are in the right. Catherine MacKinnon asserts that because 'fetal rights as such are in direct tension with sex equality rights', they cannot be tolerated.[27] But the sex equality interest is not sufficient for a philosophical defence of abortion if it is meant to establish abortion's permissibility regardless of the moral status of the foetus. This is because to claim that abortion rights are defensible because they are integral to sex equality *even* if the foetus is a fully rights-holding person commits one to a principle I think is plainly unreasonable to accept.

This can be shown by the following consideration. MacKinnon and Sherwin correctly point out that it is not chiefly pregnancy but more so *child-rearing* which threatens to socially disadvantage women and curtail their independence from men. Thus, laws which prohibit infanticide of born children up to any age at which they are still significantly dependent *also* impede sex equality, if women would otherwise choose to liberate themselves that way. Thus, we can imagine a scenario in which women could secure better equality with men if they could choose to have their born children exterminated at any time. But it is unthinkable that the sex equality interest could ever be strong enough to justify such killings. This thought-experiment tells us that we do not think the furthering of sex equality is a justification for homicide. Consequently, if the foetus is presumed to be a person, the sex equality interest is not sufficient to show that abortion is morally justified. Such a claim would rely on the argument that conduct otherwise amounting to murder is transformed into justified homicide if it is needed to combat sex inequality. But any further thinking shows that we cannot embrace this principle.

In sum, inasmuch as there is a substantive disagreement about the moral implications of sex equality considerations in the abortion debate, I think the traditionalists are right. Still, that disagreement will not yield different ultimate conclusions for philosophical defenders of abortion that do *not* accord the foetus a high moral status. Moreover, on such accounts, the meaning of abortion prohibitions for women's social disadvantage is still hugely important, since it explains, along with other things (including the right to bodily autonomy and the value of procreative control), why abortion rights are essential as a matter of justice, albeit on the proviso that the foetus lacks full moral status.

V. Physical Enmeshment and Moral Status

As a last rejoinder, the feminist ethics scholar might reply that it is the very idea of considering foetal moral status independently from its embedded context—in particular, its complete physical dependence upon another—which she considers to be so wrong-headed.

As was seen, Mary Mahowald underscores the fact that foetuses cannot exist in isolation from pregnant women (though we would have to reconsider in what way this would still be

[27] CA MacKinnon, 'Feminism, Marxism, Method, and the State: Toward Feminist Jurisprudence' (1983) 8(4) Signs 635–58.

true if medical advancements made artificial wombs a reality). Sherwin argues that 'because of a fetus's unique physical status—*within* and dependent on a particular woman—the responsibility and privilege of determining its specific social status must rest with the woman carrying it'.[28] Sherwin also points out that, unlike born human beings, foetuses are characteristically limited regarding the relationships in which they can participate. It is simply impossible for them to fulfil the kinds of relational roles which it is possible to fulfil after birth. Hence, although foetuses are, in her view, morally significant, their status is 'relational not absolute', meaning, I take it, that their moral status can only be dictated by the pregnant women in whose bodies they reside.

These comments could be taken to suggest that it is not so much their concern with foetal moral status which mars mainstream accounts, but their failure to properly appreciate the importance of complete physical enmeshment with another for a creature's moral status. Understood this way, the disagreement here would be about which qualities are relevant to moral status, and how much weighting bodily interdependence has. These are indeed arguments about foetal moral status, and they are also arguments about moral status as such. The claims are that complete bodily dependence or lack of access to certain social goods, like relationships, preclude a human organism like the foetus from possessing full moral status.

These arguments may be correct or they may be wrong. There is no denying that moral philosophers spend a good deal of time debating their veracity—and accordingly, questions about the relevance of physical enmeshment for moral status are at the heart of many accounts in traditional abortion ethics. As we should know by now, Thomson's famous 'violinist' analogy *is* an argument that complete bodily dependence on another human being alters the moral status of the dependent being (for her, it alters it in such a way that the dependent being has no right not to be killed by the host being or her agents). In a different vein, Frances Kamm has argued at length that the pregnant woman's role in bringing a foetus into being and sustaining its life through bodily support means that she renders the foetus 'no worse off' by having it aborted.[29] The fact that the foetus is not, to begin with, entitled to this bodily support and could never have survived without it entails that it is not harmed relative to its baseline condition by being terminated, she argues.

These are doubtless contentious claims, but they both open up potentially promising ways of understanding the relevance of physical enmeshment for moral status. Both examine possible reasons why moral status might be altered by a condition of bodily dependence, provide arguments which show that we are indeed committed to that view of moral status, and consider obvious and less obvious objections. For all this, Thomson and Kamm may still be wrong (it is my view that they are). But it would be a strange thing for Sherwin to impugn someone like Thomson for focusing too much argumentative energy on the moral status of the foetus given that Thomson, we see, is only making the same claim—that bodily dependence alters moral status—only by means of a more elaborate argument.

For Sherwin's 'relational' view of the foetus *is* an argument about the conditions for moral status, or 'personhood'. By attacking traditional philosophical accounts of abortion which focus on the moral status of the foetus, Sherwin might be seen to be denigrating

[28] Sherwin (n 23) 10.

[29] See generally F Kamm, *Creation and Abortion: An Essay in Moral and Legal Philosophy* (Oxford University Press, 1992).

accounts which make the same claims about foetal status as she does, and on much the same ground: that thoroughgoing physical dependence colours moral status. One must ask, on this view, what theorists such as Thomson and Kamm can be said to be doing wrong. The only difference I can see is that such accounts rely on further arguments about harm and obligation to substantiate the same claim about moral status which Sherwin herself endorses. Indeed, feminist ethics claims about 'relational' moral status rest on wider principles too, though they may go unstated. Sherwin and other feminist ethicists are not really moral particularists. Sherwin believes that the foetus's 'unique physical status' of dependence makes it *generally* true that only the woman carrying it can determine its moral status, not that the permissibility of every abortion decision is entirely individual. And she seems to think this is, in part, because the foetus's unique situation prevents it from entering into relationships. There is very much a general principle at work here, then: the principle that opportunities to enter into relationships condition moral status.

Just as they have done so regarding the issue of bodily dependence, some philosophers may want to look more closely at the idea that the inability to partake in relationships strips a being of moral status. They may ask whether it can really be correct that moral status depends on the relationships one forms, or is able to form, with others—what about the misanthropic, the perpetually isolated, the person stranded alone on a desert island? These doubts may lead in turn to larger questions about what sort of access to human fellowship is needed for moral status (actual or only hypothetical?), if indeed it is. It is at this point that some feminist ethicists might again complain that there is too much talk of foetal moral status and not enough talk about the effects of unwanted pregnancy on women. But since claims about foetal moral status also inform their own accounts and, as we see, must do so, this will not amount to much more than a demand to go 'thus far and no further' in one's thinking about moral status. We should understand if moral philosophers feel that resisting this demand is part of their job description.

7

How the Philosophy Gets In

Jesse Wall

We sometimes talk about 'gaps' in the law. We sometimes also talk of 'discretion' in legal reasoning and talk of how the law requires 'interpretation'. We talk of gaps, discretion, and interpretation when we encounter particular cases or questions that cannot be addressed or answered by the content of the existing law. Since the content of the existing law cannot answer all the practical questions that are asked of it, the process of legal reasoning must therefore draw upon resources beyond the existing legal standards. It follows that the process of legal reasoning is not hermetically sealed; somehow foreign objects get in. The purpose of this chapter is to explain how philosophy gets in and then consider a 'deflationary' account of the role of philosophy in legal reasoning. The account suggests that when foreign objects get into the law, they are refashioned in light of the distinctly legal task that the foreign objects are used to perform, rendering the foreign objects 'no longer foreign'. This critique calls for an explanation of how philosophical materials can be incorporated into an enquiry that is methodologically distinct from philosophy itself. It also requires us to consider what we can expect from interdisciplinary work, such as *Philosophical Foundations of Medical Law*.

I will begin this chapter with a brief outline of some of the philosophical foundations of the medical law. I will then outline two ways in which philosophy gets into the law. First, and more obviously, philosophy gets in through our reasoning *about* the law; it gets in through our explanations, criticisms, and recommended reforms of the law. Second, philosophy gets into our reasoning *according* to the law; it gets in when we ascribe meaning to a legal standard, substantiate its content, and qualify its scope. I will then consider the suggestion that, in all these instances, it is not philosophy that gets into the law, but it is the law borrowing philosophical materials to put to its own distinct use. Finally, I will attempt to reconcile my account of legal reasoning with this deflationary account of theory.

I. Philosophy

As the preceding chapters in this collection illustrate, a major fault line in the philosophical foundations of medical law concerns the properties that constitute moral norms. Some philosophers disagree as to whether moral properties depend upon the consequences of an action, the conformity of the action with duties, the exercise of a virtue in performing the action, or the realization of a prior good. This disagreement is complicated by the lack of consensus within these camps as to what types of consequences and what set of duties, virtues, or goods are relevant to the constitution of moral norms. Moreover, we may need to revise our understanding of these moral norms if our contemporary ethics depreciates

Jesse Wall, *How the Philosophy Gets In* In: *Philosophical Foundations of Medical Law*. Edited by: Andelka M Phillips, Thana C de Campos, and Jonathan Herring, Oxford University Press (2019).
DOI: 10.1093/oso/9780198796558.003.0008

the moral experience of women,[1] or any other undervalued group (such as caregivers).[2] In light of this disagreement as to the constitution of moral norms, other philosophers embrace the irreducible conflict between different moral properties. For instance, it may be that we ought to identify what is a morally right action by allocating the appropriate weight between a set of heterogeneous principles[3] or by assessing whether an action promotes a set of incommensurate aspects of human flourishing.[4]

The philosophical foundations of medical law also include contestable metaphysical assumptions within any given normative account. It is one thing for the law to assign certain legal rights (on the basis of certain moral properties). However, it is another thing for the law to identify the rights-holders (with a particular metaphysical status) who benefit from certain legal rights. Hence, even if we agree on a set of relevant moral norms, we may disagree as to what entities have the relevant metaphysical status. An entity could have this status on the basis that they possess (sophisticated or rudimentary) cognitive capacities, the capacity to develop these capacities, belonging to a species that has these capacities.[5] Alternatively, an entity could have the necessary metaphysical status because we have a special relationship with them or because others do. We may also disagree as to how we ought to identify a rights-holder across a period of time. We could, for instance, identify rights-holders with reference to overlapping chains of psychological states, their biological continuity, or some other conception of personal identity.[6] Moreover, given the potential primacy of mental, psychological, or cognitive states in our normative analysis, further metaphysical questions remain as to whether our mental states and processes are reducible to, run parallel with, or have a casual influence on our physical existence.[7] It therefore remains unclear how we ought to understand the relationship between a person's metaphysical properties (that establish an entity as a rights-holder) and a person's physical properties (to which the rights themselves pertain).

When we consider the philosophical foundations of medical law, we encounter ethical fractions, revisionary arguments, meta-ethical divides, and metaphysical disagreement (and the above is in no way an exhaustive taxonomy). As I will explain here, analysing and applying medical law 'draws upon' these debates. This explains the agonizing complexity and the intellectual lure of medical law. But note that these debates are philosophical debates. In particular, they are debates that adhere to a specific methodology; they adhere to a set of assumptions about what is important, interesting, or relevant. Put simply, philosophers undertake abstracted enquiries about the world (or our experience of it), break a statement down into its irreducible parts, translate the statement to display its logical form, and seek an explanation of the statement that has a general or universal application. This is not what lawyers do. Not even well-rounded medical lawyers. As we shall see, although it is

[1] AM Jaggar, 'Feminist Ethics: Projects, Problems, Prospects' in C Card (ed), *Feminist Ethics* (University Press of Kansas, 1991); AM Jaggar, 'Feminist Ethics' in *Encyclopedia of Ethics* (Routlegde, 2nd edn, 2001), vol 1, 528.

[2] V Held, *The Ethics of Care: Personal, Political, and Global* (Oxford University Press, 2006); J Herring, *Caring and the Law* (Hart Publishing, 2013).

[3] See TL Beauchamp and JF Childress, *Principles of Bioethics* (7th edn, Oxford University Press, 2013).

[4] MC Nussbaum, 'Human Functioning and Social Justice: In Defense of Aristotelian Essentialism' (1992) 20 Political Theory 202; A Sen, 'Capability and Well-Being' in MC Nussbaum and A Sen (eds), *The Quality of Life* (Clarendon Press, 1993).

[5] MA Warren, *Moral Status: Obligations to Persons and Other Living Things* (Clarendon Press, 1997); A Jaworska, 'Caring and Full Moral Standing' (2007) 117 Ethics 460.

[6] D Shoemaker, *Personal Identity and Ethics: A Brief Introduction* (Broadview Press, 2008).

[7] DM Armstrong, *The Mind-Body Problem: An Opinionated Introduction* (Westview Press, 1999).

one thing for medical law to 'draw upon' these debates, it may be entirely another thing for medical law to 'engage' in these debates.

II. Reasoning about the Law

There is little disagreement (if any) that once we have identified the content of the existing law, there is a range of questions that we may ask about the law.[8] The first question we might ask is: why? That is, we might ask why the law protects a particular right, prohibits a particular wrong, or permits a particular activity. While historical accounts may explain that the law protects *this* right because the Court of Chancery did *that* and sociological accounts may explain that the law protects *this* because the empowered sectors of society value *that*, a philosophical explanation will explain that the legal norm permits *this* because it aligns with *this* philosophical norm. It is not that the relevant law-maker had the philosophical norm in mind when formulating the legal norm, but rather the philosophical account is that the best available explanation of the rule is that it aligns with a set of moral norms (or metaphysical concepts). In other words, to understand a legal rule is to understand that it takes a set of philosophical assumptions to be sound assumptions.

Let us start with a relatively straightforward legal rule: every 'mentally competent patient has an absolute right to refuse to consent to medical treatment for any reason ... even where that decision may lead to his or her own death'.[9] Butler-Sloss LJ has explained that the right reflects a principle of self-determination, which takes priority over the principle of sanctity of human life and a doctor's duty to act in the best interests of his or her patient.[10] Moreover, the right to refuse medical treatment applies regardless of whether the patient refuses consent for rational reasons, irrational reasons, or no reason at all, since '[t]he weight which an individual chooses to give competing factors is an essential part of the decision-making process'.[11] There are a number of ways to explain this legal rule. For example, we may be under a duty to respect the deliberative process of every patient. To do otherwise and provide treatment without consent is to deny the patient's autonomy and therefore breach a moral duty. Alternatively, or in addition, morality may require us to promote some good, such as well-being, utility, or preference satisfaction. With regard to consent to medical treatment, we may consider the patient themselves to be best able to determine what is in his or her interests.[12] Both philosophical accounts can explain why the law protects the right to refuse medical treatment. Moreover, this convergence of predominant moral theory (while noting that other theories may want to offer a diverging account) can also explain why the legal rule is an absolute rule.

[8] J Gardner, 'Legal Positivism: 5½ Myths' (2001) 46 American Journal of Jurisprudence 199, 224: 'But, in fact, once one has tackled the question of whether a certain law is valid there remain many relatively independent questions to address concerning its meaning, its fidelity to law's purposes, its role in sound legal reasoning, its legal effects, and its social functions, to name but a few. To study the nature of law one needs to turn one's mind to the philosophical aspects of these further questions too.'

[9] *Re MB (medical treatment)* [1997] 8 Med LR 217 (CA) 221.

[10] *Ms B v An NHS Hospital Trust* [2002] EWHC 429 (Fam); [2002] 2 All ER 449, [22]–[27].

[11] *Ms B* (n 10) [78].

[12] MM Dempsey, 'Victimless Conduct and the *Volenti* Maxim: How Consent Works' (2013) 7 Criminal Law and Philosophy 11, 20: 'This is B's decision. He's an adult and can decide for himself whether he thinks the risk is worth it. In considering what to do, I will assume that his decision is the right one for him. After all, he is in a better position than I to judge his own well-being.'

The next question we might ask is: *should* the law protect a particular right, prohibit particular a wrong, or permit a particular activity? There may be a range of reasons why a law should not protect a particular right. Some may be practical; it may be difficult to enforce such laws or doing so may cause perverse incentives or other unintended consequences. Other reasons may follow from philosophical commitments about the law (in general), such as its appropriate role in encouraging or coercing particular behaviours.[13] One further way of determining whether a law should protect a particular right is to assess whether its philosophical foundations are sound. That is, we can assess whether the moral (or metaphysical) assumptions that explain the law are sound assumptions. If our best theoretical justification for a legal norm is that it is predicated on a philosophical norm, any reasons that we have for holding the philosophical norm to be either valid or invalid also apply to the legal norm.

Consider, for example, how the law protects posthumous interests in a deceased person's body. In order for the law to be philosophically defensible, the posthumous interests ought to be philosophically recognizable interests. Some argue that they are not. According to John Harris, our moral obligations to others are on respect for another's autonomy and concern for another's welfare.[14] These are, according to Harris, moral properties that are absent in deceased persons; since the dead 'have no will, no preferences, wants nor desires, [they] cannot be autonomous and so cannot have their autonomy violated'.[15] Posthumous rights in the body are, according to this view, without philosophical foundations.

If we consider that the best available philosophical explanation of a legal norm is that it is predicated on a set of philosophical assumptions and we consider these assumptions to be unsound assumptions, a constructive way of reasoning about the law is to provide sound philosophical foundations upon which to construct a preferable and defensible legal norm. For example, we may take the best explanation of the anticipatory refusals of consent ('advance directives') to be premised upon respect for a patient's 'values, commitments, convictions' that is greater than our concern for their presently felt experiences.[16] We may alternatively consider this explanation to be philosophically unsound and seek to reform the law on advance directives. For instance, if advance directives only have moral force when there is a 'sufficiently close relationship of psychological connectedness and continuity between past and present selves',[17] then they will not apply to patients suffering from forms of neurological degeneration. In addition, if consent only has moral force when it is sufficiently informed, the advance directives ought not to apply to circumstances that could not have been anticipated by the patient.[18] Further, if there is no good reason why critical interests should have priority over experiential interests, then the best interests of the patient should determine his or her treatment instead of an advance directive.[19] Hence, reconfiguring the philosophical foundations of the law puts us in a better position to argue that the law itself should be reformed.

[13] See, for instance, J Raz, *The Morality of Freedom* (Clarendon Press, 1986), ch 15.
[14] J Harris, 'Law and Regulation of Retained Organs: The Ethical Issues' (2002) 22 Legal Studies 527, 531.
[15] Ibid.
[16] R Dworkin, *Life's Dominion: An Argument about Abortion and Euthanasia* (HarperCollins, 1993), 224.
[17] AR Maclean, 'Advance Directives, Future Selves and Decision-Making' (2006) 14 Medical Law Review 291, 298.
[18] D Shaw, 'A Direct Advance on Advance Directives' (2012) 26 Bioethics 267.
[19] R Dresser, 'Life, Death, and Incompetent Patients: Conceptual Infirmities and Hidden Values in the Law' (1986) 28 Arizona Law Review 373.

The philosophical foundations of medical law inform our reasoning *about* medical law. They provide the resources with which we can explain, justify, criticize, and reform the law. This has become bread and butter for academic lawyers, and it is a somewhat obvious way in which philosophy is relevant to medical law. The question that we will consider below is whether commentators, who reason about the law in this philosophical way, are engaged at all in a philosophical task.

III. Reasoning According to the Law

How philosophy informs our reasoning *according* to the law is much less obvious. It is not even obvious where, in theoretical terms, 'reasoning according to the law' fits in the cascade of judicial tasks of (1) identifying the law, (2) doing what the law requires, and (3) doing what ought to be done, all things considered.[20] It may seem obvious that the adjudicative task of 'reasoning according to the law' fits squarely into category (2). It may seem this way since (1) the task of identifying a legal standard is distinct from (2) using the standard to determine what ought to be done in relation to a given issue, and (3) reasoning according to the law is distinct still from (3) reasoning according to considerations beyond the relevant legal standard. This simple tripartition, as useful as it is, is complicated by two factors. First, it may be that (2) reasoning about how a particular case ought to be resolved in accordance with legal reasons amounts to (1) identifying the content of existing law, since 'interpreting' the law straddles the divide between (1) and (2). Second, it may be that (2) reasoning about how a legal standard applies invites (3) reasoning according to considerations beyond the relevant legal standard. Again, 'interpreting' the law straddles the divide between (2) and (3).

We ultimately need not be troubled by whether the simple tripartition is a decisive framework or a helpful fiction. It is sufficient for our purposes that to 'reason according to the law' is to find 'rational support for legal conclusions ... as to what is to be done' according to the authoritative legal standard.[21] Whether we take 'interpretation' to be a distinctly (2)-type activity or an activity that straddles the divide between (1) and (2) and (2) and (3), the observation remains that the process of using the content of the existing law to determine what ought to be done in a particular instance is a process that involves 'interpreting' the law.

Moreover, broadly speaking, 'interpretation' is how philosophy gets into our legal reasoning. However, 'interpretation' has become the label for a range of distinct exercises that form part of the legal reasoning process.[22] In what follows, I will explain how legal reasoning consists of three main exercises that all draw upon philosophy as a resource. These exercises are ascribing meaning to the authoritative standard (interpretation *proper*), specifying the

[20] See J Dickson, 'Interpretation and Coherence in Legal Reasoning', *The Stanford Encyclopaedia of Philosophy* (winter edn, 2016), https://plato.stanford.edu/entries/legal-reas-interpret accessed 15 July 2019: 'There are thus three things (at least, there may be others) which legal theorists could mean by legal reasoning: (a) reasoning to establish the existing content of the law on a given issue, (b) reasoning from the existing content of the law to the decision which a court should reach in a case involving that issue which comes before it, and (c) reasoning about the decision which a court should reach in a case, all things considered.'

[21] T Endicott, 'Legal Interpretation' in A Marmor (ed), *Routledge Companion to Philosophy of Law* (Routledge, 2012), 110.

[22] Endicott (n 21) 109–10: '... it is easy and attractive to think of legal reasoning generally as a matter of interpretation. This mistake means forgetting just how extravagantly the law may leave matters for decision by the parties to a transaction, or by an institution that must resolve a dispute'.

requirements of an authoritative standard (specification), and determining the scope of the legal requirement (qualification). It is through these components that philosophy gets into our reasoning according to the law.[23]

A. Interpretation *Proper*

When we consider the task of 'reasoning according to the law', we encounter a number of distinct components to this task. One component is the exercise of 'legal interpretation' in the narrow sense. As Timothy Endicott explains, 'legal interpretation is the activity of identifying legal reasons that support a conclusion as to the meaning that is to be ascribed to a legal communication'.[24] Legal interpretation—the exercise of ascribing meaning—forms only one component of the task of 'finding rational support for legal conclusions … as to what is to be done according to law'.[25] This is because there are circumstances (considered below) where, although the meaning of a legal standard may be indisputably clear, there remains a gap between the content of the law and what ought to be done 'according to the law'.

If legal interpretation is the process of identifying legal reasons that argue towards a particular meaning, then the task—if performed well—will identify *good* reasons in favour of a particular meaning. Hence, if we want to be able to say that the interpretative exercise was performed well, or poorly, we must be able to differentiate between good and bad reasons in favour of a particular meaning. When we attempt to interpret the law, we assume some kind of theory of interpretation: some set of resources that can substantiate our assertion that a reason for a particular meaning is a good or bad reason. We may consider aspects of the legal standard itself, we may turn to the broader law, and we may draw upon philosophical norms, to inform our reasons in favour of a particular meaning.

For example, the term 'suicide' in a criminal code that prohibits assisting suicide may require interpretation. One possible meaning is where 'a person intentionally causes his or her own death'.[26] An alternative meaning is that suicide is where 'a person intentionally causes his or own death as a result of irrational or impaired thinking'.[27] To interpret criminal provisions concerning suicide, we must search for reasons in favour of one of these possible meanings. We may look to the legal provisions themselves and infer that the decriminalization of suicide was not intended to prioritize personal autonomy over the sanctity of human life, even where the suicide is the result of rational thinking.[28] We may also look to the broader law and identify that '[t]he only legitimate aim which has been advanced for [the prohibition on assisting suicide] is the protection of vulnerable people'[29] who may be

[23] See Endicott (n 21) 110–11: '… each of the following aspects of legal reasoning need not involve interpretation: 1. Resolving indeterminacies as to the content of the law'; '2. Working out the requirements of abstract legal provisions'; '3. Deciding what is just'; '4. Equitable interference with legal duties or powers or rights'; '5. Understanding the law'.

[24] T Endicott, 'Interpretation and Indeterminacy: Comments on Andrei Marmor's *Philosophy of Law*' (2014) 10 Jerusalem Review of Legal Studies 46, 48.

[25] Ibid.

[26] Sir J Stephen, *A History of the Criminal Law of England* (McMillan, 1883), vol 3, 104–5; *Seales v AG* [2015] NZHC 1239; [2015] 3 NZLR 556, [117].

[27] *Seales*, ibid, [134]–[135].

[28] *R (Pretty) v DPP* [2001] UKHL 61; [2002] 1 AC 800, [35] (Lord Bingham), [106] (Lord Hope); *R (Nicklinson) v Ministry of Justice* [2014] UKSC 38; [2015] 1 AC 657, [212] (Lord Sumption JSC); *Seales* (n 26) [132].

[29] *Nicklinson* (n 28) [311] as cited (incorrectly) in *Seales* (n 26) [125].

'induced to commit suicide at a time of weakness'.[30] And we may consider whether there are any sound philosophical reasons for narrowing what the law means by suicide to exclude rational decisions by non-vulnerable people.[31]

Theories of interpretation place varying degrees of confidence in features of the authoritative standard itself, and the wider law, as providing sufficient guidance in the interpretative process. Let us briefly consider three views. We could view the wider law as being 'infused with irresolvably opposed principles and ideals'[32] that render it unable to guide the interpretative process on the basis that 'different sets of principles fit past decisions well enough to count as eligible interpretations of them'.[33] In which case, an interpreter must draw upon moral and political norms that are relevant to the particular circumstances (the 'relevant normative context') in order to generate reasons that favour a particular meaning to be ascribed to a legal standard. Such an interpreter 'should always do the best they can for the future, in the circumstances, unchecked by any need to respect or secure consistency in principle with what other officials have done or will do'.[34]

In comparison, we could maintain our scepticism over whether the wider law is sufficiently coherent to guide the interpretative process on the basis that the law 'reflects the vagaries of pragmatic compromises, of changing fortunes of political forces',[35] while relying on the authoritative standard itself to inform our interpretive exercise. Conventions of interpretation provide 'established ways … for interpreting [law-making actions]' that 'ensure that the law-makers' intentions become law'.[36] However, the intended meaning of an authoritative standard cannot be interpreted in isolation. According to this view, the interpreter may therefore draw upon two sets of 'interwoven' resources: 'the content of authoritatively endorsed legal standards' and the 'moral considerations which bear on the issue'.[37] Whenever a legal standard is to be interpreted, it should be interpreted 'in a way which retrieves its intended meaning', while also being interpreted in light of the relevant normative context.[38]

Alternatively, we could be more sanguine with regard to the role of the wider law in the interpretative exercise. We could 'assume, so far as this is possible, that the law is structured by a coherent set of principles'.[39] Given that the law may have 'conflicting inspirations',[40] moral and political norms are required to make sense of the existing legal materials in a way that 'impose[s] order over doctrine' (rather than seeking 'to discover order in the forces that created it').[41] A properly constructed combination of the wider law, the values that best

[30] *Carter v Canada (AG)*, 2015 SCC 5; [2015] 1 SCR 331, [78], as cited in *Seales* (n 26) [127]. See also *Pretty v United Kingdom*, App No 2346/02, 29 April 2002, [74].

[31] *Seales* (n 26) [136] (citations omitted): 'The appropriateness of the ordinary meaning of suicide in all cases where the deceased takes his or her own life has been called into question by a number of philosophers, such as Emile Durkheim and Manuel Velasqueiz.'

[32] A Altman, 'Legal Realism, Critical Legal Studies, and Dworkin' (1986) 15 Philosophy & Public Affairs 205, 217.

[33] R Dworkin, *Law's Empire* (Belknap Press, 1986), 266.

[34] Ibid 161.

[35] J Raz, 'The Relevance of Coherence' (1992) 72 Boston University Law Review 273, 294.

[36] J Raz, 'On the Nature of Law' (1996) 82 Archives for Philosophy of Law and Social Philosophy 1, 22.

[37] Ibid.

[38] Ibid.

[39] Dworkin (n 33) 243.

[40] J Waldron, 'Did Dworkin Ever Answer the Crits?' in S Hershovitz (ed), *Exploring Law's Empire: The Jurisprudence of Ronald Dworkin* (Oxford University Press, 2006), 169.

[41] Dworkin (n 33) 273.

justify the law, and the relevant normative context provide sufficient resources to guide our interpretation of a particular legal standard.

The common thread that runs through these three distinct theories of interpretation is that ascribing meaning to a legal standard draws on the 'relevant normative context'. We have seen three different accounts of how it does this: by acting as the only resource available to the interpreter, by providing a context for applying an intended meaning to particular circumstances, and by helping to construct a coherent set of legal principles that determine the meaning of the particular standard. It is through the interpretative process that philosophical norms form part of our reasoning about the law.

B. Specification

We sometimes encounter general legal standards that need to be applied to particular circumstances. Even once we have ascertained the meaning that ought to be attributed to a legal standard, that meaning itself does not determine what ought to be done in any particular case. Even if the meaning of the standard is clear, what is required from the standard can be indeterminate, vague, or abstract. As Endicott argues: 'Determining the undetermined is one of the standard functions of adjudication, and it is not an interpretive function.'[42] It is a standard adjudicative function, since 'lawmakers are not in a position to be specific'. It therefore falls to the courts 'to give substance to abstract categorizations'.[43] This process of specification is often described as interpretation, since judges and advocates prefer to explain what they are doing as 'interpreting what others have decided' instead of 'claiming authority to invent a resolution to a dispute'.[44] To describe this process of specification as 'interpretation' is nonetheless a convenient fiction. It is a fiction because ascertaining the particular demands of a general requirement (specification) follows once we have ascertained the meaning that is to be ascribed to the general requirement (interpretation). Hence, part of the process of reasoning according to the law is to specify how (clear but) general legal standards apply to particular circumstances. It is in this exercise of specification that philosophy, again, gets into the law.

One example of an abstract category in medical law is the 'best interest' test that is applied when a patient lacks capacity to consent to treatment. The test involves 'a welfare appraisal in the widest sense, taking into account, where appropriate, a wide range of ethical, social, moral, emotional and welfare considerations'.[45] Since the legal standard needs to be applied to a range of circumstances, it provides an abstract standard, the particular implications of which are specified on a case-by-case basis. A broad assessment of a patient's best interests imports normative philosophy into the process of specifying the implications of general legal standards.

Human rights standards also start out as abstract norms. Article 2 of the European Convention on Human Rights guarantees that '[e]veryone's right to life shall be protected

[42] Endicott (n 21) 112.
[43] Ibid 114.
[44] Ibid 110.
[45] *Re MM (an adult)* [2007] EWHC 2003 (Fam); [2009] 1 FLR 443, [99].

by law'.[46] However, we must specify what this provision means in order to determine the duties that an NHS trust must discharge when considering the withdrawal of artificial nutrition and hydration from patients in a persistent vegetative state.[47] Normative philosophy forms part of this process, insofar as the court needs to determine whether the right to life represents a strict sanctity of life requirement or whether the right protects life to the extent that this has value as an instrument for the realization of more fundamental moral values.[48] Similarly, article 3 of the Convention prohibits 'inhuman or degrading treatment'.[49] Whether non-consensual medical treatment that is not a therapeutic necessity but is in the patient's bests interests amounts to 'degrading treatment' is a question of specifying the normative implications of 'dignity'.[50]

This process of specification may colour legal reasoning as a discretionary exercise. There are at least two factors that narrow the scope of discretion in legal reasoning that are worth highlighting. First, the process of specifying the particular implications of a general legal standard is itself a 'gap-closing' exercise. Once an authority has identified some of these implications, there will be less indeterminacy in the standard. Legal standards that are, at face value, indeterminate, vague, or abstract, can become precise and determinative legal standards through the process of judicial specification. Second, if to have 'discretion is to be given power to make a decision, without being bound to decide on a particular outcome',[51] then even if the general legal standard does not indicate a particular outcome that ought to follow from the application of the standard, the relevant normative context might. As Endicott explains, while 'a legal requirement to apply moral considerations does give courts discretion', the courts have discretion only when 'moral considerations are vague'.[52]

C. Qualification

We sometimes talk of a 'purposive interpretation' of the law.[53] We sometimes 'interpret' the law in order to avoid applying a standard to a set of circumstances that would result in an absurd, unjust, or unconscionable outcome. The 'interpretation' is purposive in the sense that we infer that applying the law in this way would be contrary to its purpose. It is part of the adjudicative function to qualify legal standards in order to ensure that they are not applied inequitably. While this process of qualification is often described as 'interpretation', the act of carving out an exception to a rule has nothing to do with ascertaining the meaning of the rule. Rather, it is because the meaning of the rule is clear that we can appreciate how

[46] European Convention on Human Rights (formerly the Convention for the Protection of Human Rights and Fundamental Freedoms) (signed 4 November 1950, entered into force 3 September 1953) 213 UNTS 221 art 2 (hereafter, ECHR).

[47] *NHS Trust A v M; NHS Trust B v H* [2001] Fam 348; [2001] 2 WLR 942.

[48] E Wicks, *Human Rights and Healthcare* (Hart Publishing, 2007), 247.

[49] ECHR (n 46) art 3.

[50] *Herczegfalvy v Austria*, App No 10533/83, 24 September 1992. cf *Re MM* (n 45).

[51] TAO Endicott, 'Raz on Gaps—the Surprising Part' in LH Meyer, SL Paulson, and TW Pogge (eds), *Rights, Culture and the Law: Themes from the Legal and Political Philosophy of Joseph Raz* (Oxford University Press, 2003), 110 (emphasis omitted).

[52] Ibid 100.

[53] Endicott (n 21) 119–20: 'English and American lawyers used to speak of "equitable interpretation" of legislation, equity being a jurisdiction in a court to dispense with the enforcement of legal rights and duties on grounds of conscience … The phrase may have passed out of vogue because of the hint that it involves departing from the legislation; these days, judges and lawyers speak of "purposive" interpretation instead.'

absurd its application is to these facts. Each legal doctrine engineers its own set of bases upon which the application of a rule can be qualified. The story of doctrines of equity is a familiar one. Less familiar are the malleability of common law rules or the techniques for 'purposive' statutory construction. This process of qualifying the scope of a legal standard is a component of legal reasoning, and, again, it is an entry point for philosophy to get into our reasoning according to the law. The process of qualification draws upon philosophical resources as the means with which to determine the absurd, unjust, and unconscionable. Of course, qualification is only half of the story. It is just as much part of the adjudicative task to expand the scope of application of a legal standard as it is to qualify the scope.

For example, a court may find that a patient can claim general damages for the pain, suffering, and inconvenience of pregnancy and childbirth following negligent contraceptive treatment.[54] However, the court may not find that the patient can recover the costs of raising the child. It may consider that there is no morally acceptable reason for redistributing the burdens of raising a healthy child beyond the parents themselves; it may consider that relieving the parents of the financial burden went beyond a reasonable correction or restitution of the wrong that was inflicted upon them.[55] If the court were to make these findings, the scope of recoverable damages for an action in negligence would be qualified to exclude the costs of raising a healthy child motivated by (contestable) normative assumptions.

In a similar way, in the context of physically assisted suicide, a court may consider expanding the scope of the common law defence of necessity.[56] It is arguable that the common law should configure a physician's 'duty to preserve life' to be subject to their 'duty to respect patient autonomy'[57] and allow the physician to act in order to prevent 'the continuation of [a patient's] unbearable suffering'.[58] The priority of one duty over the other is, in this context, a question that is informed by normative philosophy. Both the possible expansion of the defence of necessity and the qualification of recoverable damages in negligence are manoeuvres in judicial reasoning motivated by arguments based in normative philosophy. Hence, even when the task is to reason according to the law, the law itself allows the import of normative philosophy to expand or contract the scope of legal standards.

IV. It Is Not Philosophy that Gets In

I have so far briefly identified how philosophy informs our reasoning about the law: when we explain, justify, criticize, and reform the law. I have also identified how philosophy informs our reasoning according to the law: through the tasks of interpretation, specification, and qualification. All this implies that legal reasoning is somehow interdisciplinary; that we—as commentator or adjudicator—must engage in normative philosophy in our reasoning process. In this section, I consider a critical response to this implication: that as commentators or adjudicators, we can only ever appropriate and refashion the materials of normative

54 *McFarlane v Tayside Health Board* [2000] 2 AC 59 (HL).

55 See S Todd, 'Wrongful Conception, Wrongful Birth, and Wrongful Life' (2005) 27 Sydney Law Review 525, 528.

56 *R (Nicklinson) v Ministry of Justice* [2012] EWHC 2381 (Admin).

57 S Michalowski, 'Relying on Common Law Defences to Legalise Assisted Dying: Problems and Possibilities' (2013) 21 Medical Law Review 337, 347.

58 *Nicklinson v Ministry of Justice* [2012] EWHC 304 (QB); [2012] HRLR 16, [11(i)].

philosophy. We can only 'draw upon' the materials of normative philosophy without ever 'engaging' in normative philosophy itself. It follows that it may not be philosophy (itself) that gets into the law, but rather it is the law appropriating philosophical materials.

If we are interested in the philosophical foundations of medical law, this is most likely because we assume that there is something productive about viewing medical law in light of normative philosophy. The hope is that we can better understand and perform the practice of medical law if we draw upon the underlying and corresponding philosophical debates. This hope rests upon a commonplace assumption about philosophy (or, more broadly, about theory). The assumption is that:

> whatever the surface configurations of our actions, *at bottom* we are guided by principles of the kind that philosophy takes as its special province. Thus it is to philosophy we should look to get a perspective on those principles and on the actions we perform in everyday life.[59]

Our interest in the philosophical foundations of medical law is most likely motivated by the optimistic belief that *underneath it all* there are philosophical principles that can inform and guide our reasoning about the law and our reasoning according to the law. After all, the first half of this chapter appears (at least) to have said as much. Here, with the help of Stanley Fish's deflationary account of theory, I aim to apply some critical pressure to this optimism.

Philosophy is its own discipline. The same is true for law, sociology, economics, and so on. 'Those who do philosophy', Michael Robertson explains, 'are embedded within a particular academic discipline, with its own distinctive history, projects, revered authorities, modes of reasoning, values, institutional structures etc'.[60] As I have mentioned earlier, normative philosophy has its own distinctive range of enquiries, including the following questions. What properties of an action make it a right action? Are moral properties pluralistic or monistic? What metaphysical status is a morally relevant one? Philosophy also has its own distinctive methodology; it takes statements about the world (including how we experience it), breaks these statements into irreducible parts, translates these parts into a logical form, and identifies a way to explain the original statement that provides some general insight into the world. These enquiries and methods have been shaped by certain figures, puzzles, and institutions—all of which is fitting since philosophy is a theoretical practice that, like all other practices, has its own purpose, tasks, and mode of reasoning.

However, in one way, law and other practices are different from philosophy, because they do not represent purely theoretical enquiries. Determining how the law should be applied is ultimately a practical matter; legal standards are concerned with preventing, protecting, or promoting some type of human behaviour or activity, and the law is situated in the context of a dispute or some other practical question. In addition, the object of the enquiry—the law itself—is a social phenomenon. Particular legal standards originate (entirely or in part) from social sources, and each legal system has institutionally defined techniques for applying the law. When we determine how to apply a legal standard, we must account for tests

[59] S Fish, *Doing What Comes Naturally: Change, Rhetoric, and the Practice of Theory in Literary and Legal Studies* (Duke University Press, 1989), 333. See also S Fish, 'Truth But No Consequences: Why Philosophy Doesn't Matter' (2003) 29 Critical Inquiry 389.

[60] M Robertson, *Stanley Fish on Philosophy, Politics and Law: How Fish Works* (Cambridge University Press, 2014), 57–8.

of legal validity, law-specific tools of problem solving, and other features of the law. We must therefore employ a mode of reasoning that engages with these features as well as what the standard itself aims to achieve.

Beyond being its own discipline, philosophy also presumes for itself a certain type of privilege. It claims to be 'the master art underlying all the other arts'.[61] Because philosophy is concerned with the general and irreducible, it appears to sit behind all other enquires. According to this privilege, philosophical findings can then inform and guide other, more particular and practical enquiries. However, in order to claim this privilege and provide general and irreducible explanations about the world, the philosophical method must be a method of abstraction. It sheds away facts about the world (or our experience of it) that are inessential to the irreducible components or logical structure of the object or concept that it seeks to explain. However, it has the consequence of 'abstracting away from particular situations and stripping from them the specificity and detail that come along with situatedness'.[62] Curiously, philosophy 'is a kind of theory that has deliberately distanced itself from everyday contexts',[63] yet somehow presumes to be able to offer guidance to the enquires concerned with the everyday context.

According to this deflationary account of theory, philosophy can either offer detached and abstract normative mantras (which offer no guidance) or it can engage the everyday context (that it had supposedly risen above). For example, when confronted by a normative problem, we might ask: '"Which is most responsive to the imperative of fairness?" or "which most conduces to the achievement of equality?" or "which will promote the greatest diversity?"'[64] The problem is that we are unable to answer these questions 'without fleshing out [our] favorite abstraction with some set of the particulars it supposedly transcends'.[65] Our abstract, ethereal, and philosophical answer to our normative problem becomes substantive, granular, and contextual, as Fish explains:

> If you are determined to go with the alternative that is fairest, you will first have to decide whether by 'fairness' you mean fairness to everyone independently of his or her achievements, failures, crimes, citizenship, gender, sexual orientation, or fairness inflected by at least some of the considerations in my non-exhaustive list. If 'equality' is your lodestar, then you will have to decide whether you mean equality of access (a strongly procedural notion) or equality of opportunity (which will take into substantive account the current situation and past history of those on whom equality is to be conferred). And, if 'diversity' is your watchword, you will have to decide whether under its umbrella you wish to include pedophiles and Neo-Nazis; if you do not, you will have to think of reasons—and those reasons will inevitably be particular and historical—for excluding them.[66]

Alternatively, our enquiry could remain abstract and refuse to substantiate what we mean by fairness, equality, or diversity. In which case, an interlocutor will

61 S Fish, *There's No Such Thing as Free Speech . . . and It's a Good Thing, Too* (Oxford University Press, 1994), 228.
62 S Fish, *The Trouble with Principle* (Harvard University Press, 1999), 286.
63 Robertson (n 60) 56.
64 S Fish, 'Theory Minimalism' (2000) 37 San Diego Law Review 761, 762.
65 Ibid.
66 Ibid.

> rightly complain that you have given him no direction, that if the abstraction is not thickened and provided with content, there is no way to get from it to the real-world dilemma he faces, or—it is the same thing—there are so many ways that the choosing of any one them will be arbitrary.[67]

Either our philosophical enquiry remains detached and abstract, in fidelity to its own task and modes of reasoning, but as a result, philosophy remains unable to guide other practices. Or our philosophical enquiry becomes contextual and granular, departing from its own discipline-specific methodology, in order to engage in the everyday context.

Interdisciplinary methodology might appear to offer a way out of this dilemma by combining the general and irreducible nature of philosophy with more contextual and practical disciplines. But while it is possible to construct new modes of reasoning out of the methodologies of specific disciplines, it is a mistake to think that an interdisciplinary method 'provides a metaphysically superior perspective in light of which any or all things can be better viewed'.[68] An interdisciplinary method cannot claim this privilege any more than the philosophical method can. Each discipline is constrained by its own distinctive aims and modes of reasoning, and no particular discipline or methodology can offer a privileged perspective.

All of this is not to imply that philosophy represents a 'hermetically sealed silo' from which philosophical norms and concepts cannot escape.[69] As I hope the previous discussion has demonstrated, philosophy somehow finds its way into our reasoning about the law and our reasoning according to the law. Rather, when the law (or any other discipline) acquires philosophical norms and concepts, it uses them for a different purpose from their original (philosophical) purpose. While there is an exchange of ideas between disciplines, there is nonetheless a figurative 'stamping whatever is imported or appropriated with a proprietary imprint'.[70] Since law and philosophy are methodologically distinct, the law can appropriate philosophical materials, put them to use for its own purposes, engraft them into a distinct mode of reasoning, *and, as a result*, convert a philosophical norm or concept into a legal one. Once philosophical materials form part of a legal reasoning process, rather than part of a philosophical enquiry, they become legal norms and concepts. The key point is that while the legal reasoning '*requires* the incorporation of foreign elements', once these foreign elements are appropriated—'seen in light of the discipline's underlying point or purpose'—the elements are 'no longer foreign'.[71]

Fish's own examples of the law appropriating foreign objects include the law borrowing insanity from medicine and borrowing oath-taking from religion. When lawyers invoke the notion of insanity, Fish explains, 'they turn it into something that links up with legal categories'.[72] Insanity in law is used to assess 'an inability to tell right from wrong', which is 'not a definition that would recommend itself to the medical community'.[73] Similarly, the practice of oath-taking in law is underwritten by legal penalties for dishonesty, which, again, is

[67] Fish (n 64) 762.
[68] S Fish, *Professional Correctness: Literary Studies and Political Change* (Harvard University Press, 1999), 80.
[69] Robertson (n 60) 71.
[70] Fish (n 61) 22.
[71] Ibid.
[72] S Fish, 'Empathy and the Law', *New York Times Opinionator* (24 May 2009), https://opinionator.blogs.nytimes.com/2009/05/24/empathy-and-the-law accessed 15 July 2019.
[73] Ibid.

distinct from how oaths are understood in religious practices. When the law appropriates these concepts, they are 'emptied of their empirical content and given the content the law's internal imperatives require'.[74]

If Fish is right, then it is not philosophy that gets in when we draw upon the philosophical foundations of medical law, but rather medical law is refashioning philosophical materials into legal tools. Even if we are not entirely convinced by this deflationary account of the role of philosophy, there is nonetheless a case to answer; what happens to philosophical materials when they are incorporated into an enquiry that is methodologically distinct from philosophy itself? We must be able to answer this question in order to properly use the philosophical foundations of medical law.

V. Interdisciplinary Analysis

It may be unclear at this stage whether I have come here to bury the philosophical foundations of medical law or to praise them. There is, I believe, much promise in exploring and developing philosophical foundations. But we need to be clear as to what we can, and cannot, expect from this type of interdisciplinary analysis. In this section, I aim to reconcile my account of legal reasoning (reasoning about and according to the law) with the above deflationary account of theory in order to explain what we can expect from the philosophical foundations of medical law.

As I have described above, using philosophical material is common in our reasoning about the law. Legal commentators offer explanations, criticisms, justifications, and reforms of the law and premise these analyses on philosophical norms and concepts. Such analyses are 'interdisciplinary', but only in the following sense: there are theoretical practices and modes of reasoning that have developed with the aim of providing explanations and justifications of the law. We may, for instance, take some legal phenomenon as the object of enquiry. We may then identify the necessary and sufficient features of the legal phenomenon and explain its logical structure. Or we may audit all of our observations and experiences of the law and abstract them into a theoretical concept of the phenomenon. Or we may locate the legal phenomenon 'in a complex network of cultural, social and political influences'.[75] These are established modes of reasoning in legal theory, and they are *similar* to the modes of reasoning in philosophy.

However, the modes of reasoning in legal theory are not the *same* as those in philosophy; legal theory aims to resolve practical problems within the law, and the law is a social phenomenon that fits into a wider structure of norms. Legal theory carries the burden of explaining something about *the law*, which has its own internal structure and contingent features that nonetheless require explanation. This adds a series of constraints to the mode of reasoning. Legal theory is interdisciplinary in the sense that its methods have been developed out of other disciplines; it adopts modes of reasoning from both philosophy and the law.

[74] Ibid.

[75] M Davies, 'Method in Legal Theory' in P Cane and J Conaghan (eds), *The New Oxford Companion to Law* (Oxford University Press, 2008), 783.

Using philosophical material in the process of reasoning *according* to the law is interdisciplinary in a difference sense. When we use normative philosophy in our reasoning according to the law, we are borrowing from another discipline. When a philosophical norm or concept is used to generate a reason in favour of a particular interpretation of a legal standard used to specify the implications of a general legal standard or qualify the scope of a legal standard, the philosophical norm is being used to perform a particular, situated, and contextual task. That is, it is used to perform a practical task (ascribe meaning, specify implications, or avoid absurdity), in a particular context (of the dispute or practical problem), while being situated in the social phenomenon of the law itself. What the norm or concept requires, in the context of the dispute, and in the context a wider web of legal standards, is a non-philosophical question. It is a legal question. Philosophy may loan the raw materials—the abstract norms and values—but these materials are used in a distinctly legal enquiry.

Exploring and developing the philosophical foundations of medical law is therefore interdisciplinary in two ways. First, our theoretical reasoning about medical law follows an interdisciplinary methodology that has adopted modes of reasoning from both law and philosophy. Second, our reasoning according to medical law requires us to borrow materials from other disciplines, such as normative philosophy, in order to determine how the law should be applied. The above deflationary account of theory has no objection to these types of interdisciplinary analysis.

Instead, the deflationary account of theory objects to a further interdisciplinary optimism. That is, 'the hope that by moving from field to field and back again you can enlarge the boundaries of your consciousness and become a more clear-sighted human being'.[76] In other words, the deflationary account of theory objects to any privilege that theoretical (and interdisciplinary) enquiries may claim for themselves. The claim that one can, through a theoretical or interdisciplinary methodology, 'see through the limitations of one's professional practice and come to engage in it without being confined within its imperatives'.[77] Once privileged with this clarity and depth of insight, we can then claim further that theoretical or interdisciplinary answers can guide other practices. The deflationary account of theory argues that this form of interdisciplinary analysis is not possible.

Since theory cannot guide other practices, this may leave the impression that good theoretical analysis will be of no consequence. I do not consider that to be an implication of the deflationary account of theory. The legal reasoning is not hermetically sealed; it needs to borrow from other disciplines. If theoretical analysis is performed well, it will become predominant in our reasoning about the law and will be appropriated by the process of legal reasoning itself. Philosophy, after all, still gets into the law. It only ceases to be philosophy when it does.

Finally, allow me to summarize this contention by way of a metaphor. A language has a vocabulary and its own set of grammatical rules. The contemporary languages that we speak have developed out of historical ones. For example, English is a West Germanic language, shaped by lexical borrowing and grammatical changes influenced by Northern Germanic, Scandinavian, and Norman languages, as well as Latin and Classical Greek. English has developed out of different languages into a distinct language with its own vocabulary and rules of grammar. Moreover, languages continue to evolve. The English language continues to

[76] Fish (n 61) 23.
[77] Ibid.

appropriate the vocabulary of other languages. Often, it does so in order to fill a gap in its own vocabulary. Hence, English borrows *kindergarten*, *zeitgeist*, and *schadenfreude* from German.

However, there is no master language. Old English or Latin do not *guide* or inform how we ought to speak contemporary English. Nor does the appropriation of foreign vocabulary into the English language necessarily affect the grammatical rules of the language. Hence, readers of Latin do not have the privilege to determine whether, according to the English language, the plural of stadium is 'stadia' or 'stadiums'. While speaking a second language can be enriching in many ways, it does not liberate the speaker from the constraints of any particular language. To speak German is to be constrained by a set of grammatical rules and a recognized vocabulary. As is the case with all languages.

We would probably object to a bilingual person claiming for him- or herself a special privilege to guide the practice of speaking English (by virtue of being bilingual). In the same way, we should reject any claim that interdisciplinary theory can guide the practice of a particular discipline (by virtue of being interdisciplinary). So, as multi-disciplinary scholars, we can build new methodologies out of the old ones, and we can lend theoretical materials to practical enquiries, but we cannot expect our theories to guide practice nor ascend above the differences between theory and practice.

VI. Conclusion

There is a role for normative philosophy to play in medical law. We draw upon philosophical norms when we explain, criticize, justify, and reform medical law. We also draw upon philosophical norms when we interpret, substantiate, qualify, and expand legal standards. What this chapter calls into question is whether the role of normative philosophy in medical law is a *foundational* role. According to Fish's deflationary account of theory considered here, normative philosophy has a contingent role in medical law.[78] A commentator or adjudicator may (or may not) borrow materials from normative philosophy and put them to their own distinctive use. I have argued that this phenomenon of interdisciplinary borrowing is a commonplace phenomenon in our reasoning about and according to the law. It does not follow from this interaction between normative philosophy and medical law that normative philosophy has a foundational role to play in medical law. Normative philosophy does not 'guide and reform' medical law 'from a superior position of oversight'.[79] Instead, normative philosophy 'occupies a subordinate position' of 'being used as a tool' for reasoning about and according to the law.[80] In the chapters that follow in this collection, we can expect an interdisciplinary methodology that has borrowed modes of reasoning from philosophy in order to enquire into something about the law, and we can expect philosophical materials to be used as tools in the task of reasoning according to the law. We ought not, however, to expect philosophy to be used as a means of providing a privileged, superior, or 'foundational' insight into medical law.

[78] Robertson (n 60) 70–8.
[79] Ibid 77.
[80] Ibid.

PART B
APPLICATIONS OF THEORIES

8

Virtue Theory and the Lawfulness of Withholding or Withdrawing Treatment or Care

David Albert Jones

I. Virtue Theory and Withholding or Withdrawing Treatment

A. The Opposite Vices of Overtreatment and Undertreatment

The ethics of offering, withholding, or withdrawing medical treatment falls very naturally into the virtue ethics scheme of finding a middle way between extremes.[1]

Medicine is clearly a goal-directed practice which aims to cure or alleviate suffering due to sickness and hence to promote health and prolong life.[2] The ethos of medicine includes, among other things, the imperative to save life where this is within the power of the physician. It might therefore seem that medical intervention is always a good where intervention is possible and that the virtue of offering beneficial treatment has only one opposite vice, the vice of neglect or undertreatment. Neglect may occur where the life or health of the patient is not regarded as worth saving—for example, because of prejudice against certain groups, or because of stereotyping and underestimation of the value of life with mental or physical disability.

On the other hand, people in hospital may suffer not from the lack of an intervention, but from an inappropriate intervention. Medical treatments and surgical interventions typically place a burden on the patient and many carry significant risks. Where an intervention is unlikely to produce benefit, the imposing of such burdens and risks may be unjustifiable. The imperative to rescue irrespective of the burdens and risks of treatment leads to overtreatment. Overtreatment (eg over prescription of antibiotics in general practice, or overuse of sedatives in end-of-life care) is a real problem in modern health care and may exist side by side in the same hospital with undertreatment. Indeed, both problems reflect a failure to attend appropriately to the needs of the patient.

[1] Aristotle, *Nichomachean Ethics* (C Rowe (tr), Oxford University Press, 2002), II.4 1106a26–b28; JO Urmson, 'Aristotle's Doctrine of the Mean' (1973) 10(3) American Philosophical Quarterly 223–30.

[2] LR Kass, 'The Pursuit of Health' (1975) 40 Public Interest 11–44; ED Pellegrino, 'The Internal Morality of Clinical Medicine: A Paradigm for the Ethics of the Helping and Healing Professions' (2001) 26(6) Journal of Medicine and Philosophy 559–79; L Gormally, 'The Good of Health and the Ends of Medicine' in H Zaborowski (ed), *Natural Moral Law in Contemporary Society* (Catholic University of America Press, 2010), 264–284.

David Albert Jones, *Virtue Theory and the Lawfulness of Withholding or Withdrawing Treatment or Care* In: *Philosophical Foundations of Medical Law.* Edited by: Andelka M Phillips, Thana C de Campos, and Jonathan Herring, Oxford University Press (2019).

DOI: 10.1093/oso/9780198796558.003.0009

B. Virtue Theory Applied to Offering, Withholding, or Withdrawing Treatment

In a virtue ethics framework, the pursuit of health and life in health care, if it is ethical, will achieve a golden mean between the opposite vices of overtreatment and undertreatment. The discernment of that mean will consider the potential benefits, burdens, and risks of the intervention not only in relation to the good of health, but also to the other goods of a person's life. For example, someone may wish to receive risky treatment, which could provide only a few more months of life, in the hope of seeing the birth of their grandchild. Or again, a person may forego treatment that has some clinical benefits because it requires staying in hospital and away from home and loved ones. The integration of the goods of health and life with other goods is the responsibility of each person. It is for this reason that, in general and for the most part, patients should have the final say in accepting or refusing treatment offered, not because they are necessarily the best judge of what is good for them, but because taking responsibility for one's health and life is a part of the work (*ergon*)[3] of a human being and is an occasion to exercise those virtues that constitute human flourishing (*eudaimonia*).[4]

The role of the doctor, while secondary to and supportive of the decision making of the patient, is not simply the provision of information and technical skill (*techne*).[5] The physician is an advocate for health and offers treatments insofar as, in his or her best prudential judgment (*phronesis*),[6] these would be of overall benefit to the patient. Patients may underestimate the importance of health or the impact on health of their life choices. Where patients refuse treatments that the doctor thinks would be beneficial or where patients seek treatments that the doctor does not think would be beneficial, the doctor should try to understand why the patient has come to this decision. It may be that the doctor should revise his or her estimate of what is in the best interest of the patient. The fact that the doctor is ultimately constrained, practically, ethically, and legally, by what the patient will accept does not mean that the doctor should be an indifferent spectator. Rather, the role of the doctor is both a skilled and an ethical one: helping the competent patient to come to a good decision on which the doctor can act.

While virtue seeks the mean between vices, it also excludes some actions altogether as incompatible with the goods of a worthwhile practice.[7] Since the time of the Hippocratic Oath, doctors have rejected some actions as incompatible with the aims of medicine. Significant among these is the deliberate ending of human life. Lethal force and capital punishment may or may not have a place in the realm of policing or criminal justice, but, in a Hippocratic understanding, they are incompatible with the role of the doctor. The

[3] Aristotle (n 1) I.7, 1097b25–8; SH Baker, 'The Concept of *Ergon*: Towards an Achievement Interpretation of Aristotle's "Function Argument"' (2015) 48 Oxford Studies in Ancient Philosophy 227–66.

[4] Aristotle (n 1) I.4, 1095a15–20; JL Ackrill, 'Aristotle on *Eudaimonia* (Book I. 1–5 [1–3] and 7–8 [5–6]' in *Aristotle's Nicomachean Ethics* (Brill, 2010), 33–52.

[5] Aristotle (n 1) VI.4, 11.40a1–23; T Angier, *Techné in Aristotle's ethics: Crafting the Moral Life* (Bloomsbury Publishing, 2010).

[6] Aristotle (n 1) VI.4, 1140a24–6. K Kristjansson, '*Phronesis* as an Ideal in Professional Medical Ethics: Some Preliminary Positionings and Problematics' (2015) 36(5) Theoretical Medicine and Bioethics 299–320.

[7] Aristotle (n 1) II.6 1107a9–27; ED Pellegrino, 'Some Things Ought Never Be Done: Moral Absolutes in Clinical Ethics' (2005) 26(6) Theoretical Medicine and Bioethics 469–86; E Harcourt, 'The Place of Psychoanalysis in the History of Ethics' (2015) 12(5) Journal of Moral Philosophy 598–618, n 27.

Hippocratic Oath prohibits the physician from giving a deadly drug, even if asked.[8] It is not that the doctor is always bound to extend the life of a patient. Nor is it the case that the doctor should avoid taking risks. The form of courage special to the doctor will include the willingness to take risks for which the doctor may be blamed. A doctor has a duty to explain the risks to the patient, but should be willing at times to offer risky treatments. What is excluded absolutely is very specifically the use of medical knowledge or skill with the intention of bringing about the death of the patient. It is not the aim of this chapter to defend the exclusion of intentional killing from a Hippocratic conception of medicine, only to show how this exclusion can be accommodated by virtue theory.[9]

If actions that intentionally bring about death are excluded from Hippocratic medicine, what of omissions that have the same effect? Omissions are not always or generally equivalent to actions. If someone is doing something, then typically it makes sense to ask why he or she is doing it.[10] 'What are you doing that for?' In contrast, there are always an indefinitely large number of possible actions that someone is *not* doing, and generally the fact that someone is not doing something does not call for an explanation. If someone is asked, out of the blue, 'why are you not in Australia?' or 'why did you not become a teacher?', there may be no reason to give. Only if there is some expectation that the person might have gone to Australia or might have considered a teaching profession does the question make sense. Nevertheless, there are circumstances where action is not only expected, in the sense of predictable, but is also expected in the sense of being a prima facie duty of someone in that situation. Then an omission will require explanation. 'Why were you not at work today?', 'Why have you not paid your bill?' These omissions, where unjustified, may be blameworthy even if they are inadvertent or unintended. Furthermore, when omissions are intentional, they can fall under the same criteria of virtue or vice as intentional actions. The withdrawal of treatment with the intention of ending life is equivalent to an action that intentionally ends life (eg administering poison) and both are inherently contrary to the virtues of Hippocratic medicine.

II. Medical Law on Withholding and Withdrawing Treatment

A. Acts, Omissions, Negligence, and Defensive Medicine

English law distinguishes between acts and omissions. A person is generally liable for harm resulting from an action, but is liable for harm resulting from an omission only if he or she was under a duty to act. A doctor is, however, under a duty of care in respect of anyone he or she accepts as a patient.[11]

In circumstances where omissions, like actions, demand justification, they can be contrary to virtue by excess or by defect. Negligence is an instance of erring by defect. It is a

[8] WHS, Jones *The Doctor's Oath* (Cambridge University Press, 1924); LR Kass, 'Is There a Medical Ethic? The Hippocratic Oath and the Sources of Ethical Medicine' in LR Kass (ed), *Toward a More Natural Science: Biology and Human Affairs* (Free Press, 1985).

[9] For an extended defence of the exclusion of killing from medicine, see L Kass, *Life, Liberty and the Defense of Dignity: The Challenge for Bioethics* (Encounter Books, 2002).

[10] GEM Anscombe, *Intention* (Basil Blackwell, 1957).

[11] D Bryden and I Storey, 'Duty of Care and Medical Negligence' (2011) 11 Continuing Education in Anaesthesia Critical Care & Pain 124–7.

lack of due care, a carelessness which might be shown in acting thoughtlessly or in omitting to act where action was called for. In this way, the law on medical negligence accords well with a virtue-related conception of ethics. Nevertheless, despite legal sanctions and an extensive body of regulation and professional guidance, there have been repeated large-scale failures of care within the National Health Service.[12] For the most part, these are not due to a lack of rules (or to bad rules), nor do they necessarily imply a lack of desire on the part of health-care professionals to benefit patients. They are wholly or at least partly systemic failures: failures of leadership, management, institutional structures, and/or working practices.[13] Greater attention to the fact that medical practice is shaped by the character and dispositions of practitioners, and that these require a supportive institutional context, can help identify the roots of institutional failures of care.

While neither the law of negligence nor the creation of statutory duties is sufficient to address the causes of systemic negligence, the law can nevertheless act as a spur to action. However, as stated above, virtue typically exists as a mean between two vices, one of defect and one of excess. This raises the question of whether the law of negligence may also have negative effects, not because of its insufficiency, but because it can induce the opposite vice.

As a general rule, the more litigious the social context, the more the doctors will err in the direction of overtreatment.[14] This may also be seen in the amount of information provided by doctors prior to seeking consent. The greater the fear of litigation, the more information will be provided about any and every possible risk or side effect even though information overload undermines informed consent. The offering of treatments and diagnostic tests of marginal benefit and the provision of excess information are examples of 'defensive medicine'.[15]

B. Homicide by Omission, *Bland*, and the Loss of Legal Consistency

The Hippocratic tradition has identified any intentional ending of life, by action or omission, as inherently contrary to the virtues of medicine. The exclusion of intentional acts of killing is reflected in the law, both in the common law and in the Homicide Act 1957. Where the law is less clear is in relation to deliberate omissions. Case law clearly shows that where someone has a duty of care and intentionally causes death by failing to discharge that duty, that person may be liable to a charge of homicide.[16] In principle, the same should apply to

[12] Age Concern, *Hungry to be Heard: The Scandal of Malnourished Older People in Hospital* (Age Concern, 2006); R Francis, *Report of the Mid Staffordshire NHS Foundation Trust Public Inquiry* (HM Stationery Office, 2013); Independent Review of the Liverpool Care Pathway, *More Care, Less Pathway: A Review of the Liverpool Care Pathway* (Department of Health, 2013); Gosport War Memorial Hospital, *The Report of the Gosport Independent Panel* (HMSO, 2018).

[13] eg: 'The underlying reason . . . was a failure of the leadership to give sufficient explicit priority to the protection of patients and to ensuring that patient safety and quality standards were being observed there. In common with the system as a whole at the time, the focus was unduly directed at financial and organizational issues and an over reliance on assurances given by others, while losing sight of the central purpose of the service it was seeking to support' (Francis Report, ibid, 1.43).

[14] With the qualification that, as mentioned earlier, a failure of medical courage can also lead to undertreatment due to the avoidance of risky procedures.

[15] DM Studdert, MM Mello, WM Sage et al, 'Defensive Medicine among High-Risk Specialist Physicians in a Volatile Malpractice Environment' (2005) 293 Journal of the American Medical Association 2609–17; A Antoci, AF Maccioni, and P Russu, 'The Ecology of Defensive Medicine and Malpractice Litigation' (2016) 11 PLoS One e0150523.

[16] *R v Gibbins & Proctor* (1918) 13 Cr App Rep 134.

a physician who deliberately withholds medical treatment. However, as medical treatment typically imposes risks and burdens, and may provide limited benefits, there is a strong presumption that doctors are withholding or withdrawing treatment on the basis of weighing up the benefits of treatment and not with intent to cause death.

It has been said that, in the past, courts have been excessively deferential to the medical profession.[17] Certainly, in dealing with suspected homicide by doctors in the course of their medical practice, whether by action or omission, judges have sometimes either directed juries to acquit or have imposed a lenient sentence.[18] Nevertheless, this does not necessarily imply a fault in the law. From a Hippocratic virtue ethics perspective, more problematic than the lack of convictions for medical homicide by omission is the decision in *Airedale NHS Trust v Bland*.[19] It that case, it was held that the withdrawal of artificial nutrition and hydration (ANH) from an incompetent patient was lawful even though, in the view of a majority of the Law Lords, it was done with the intention of bringing about the patient's death.[20]

The circumstances of this case were unusual. The patient, Tony Bland, had for more than three years been in what doctors described as a 'persistent vegetative state' (PVS).[21] This diagnosis, which was not disputed, implied that Bland lacked all awareness of his environment and that there was no prospect of his recovering consciousness. The family and the doctors did not regard it as being in Bland's best interests to continue to sustain his life in this state. The case was also remarkable because of the origin of Bland's condition, which had resulted from injuries sustained in the Hillsborough disaster of 1989. This led his family, and wider public opinion, to see Bland as another victim of a tragedy which had already claimed the lives of ninety-five people and for which no one had to that date been held legally responsible.[22] In these circumstances, there was an understandable (albeit misguided) impetus to regard the cause of Bland's death as that disaster rather than the withdrawal of his tube-feeding.

If the *Bland* case did establish the lawfulness of intentional killing by omission, albeit for a narrowly defined group of patients, it undoubtedly left the law 'both morally and intellectually misshapen': prohibiting intentional killing by an act, but permitting intentional killing by deliberate omission.[23] Several of the judges in this case showed awareness of the problematic nature of their ruling and drew attention to the exceptional circumstances of the case. They indicated that, as a matter of good practice, ANH should not be withdrawn from someone in PVS without first seeking a judicial declaration.[24]

[17] H Woolf, 'Are the Courts Excessively Deferential to the Medical Profession?' (2001) 9 Medical Law Review 1–16.

[18] *R v Dr Bodkins Adams* [1957] Crim LR 365; *R v Arthur* [1981] 12 BMLR 1; *R v Cox* [1992] 12 BMLR 38; the conviction and sentencing of Dr Harold Shipman being a notable exception.

[19] [1993] AC 789, House of Lords; [1993] 1 All ER 821.

[20] [1993] 1 All ER 821, 876–7: 'Even though the intention to bring about the patient's death is there, there is no proposed guilty act because ... it is not in the interests of an insentient patient to continue the life-supporting care and treatment.'

[21] B Jennett and F Plum, 'Persistent Vegetative State after Brain Damage: A Syndrome in Search of a Name' (1972) 299 Lancet 734–7.

[22] R Heywood, 'Hillsborough: Legal Culpability in the Aftermath of the Findings of the Independent Panel' (2014) 65 Northern Ireland Legal Quarterly 101–19.

[23] Lord Mustill in *Bland* (n 19) [1993] 1 All ER 821, 885, cited by J Keown, 'Restoring Moral and Intellectual Shape to the Law after *Bland*' (1997) 113 Law Quarterly Review 481–503, 503. See also JM Finnis, 'Bland: Crossing the Rubicon?' (1993) 109 Law Quarterly Review 329–37.

[24] [1993] 1 All ER 821, 833, 842, 862, 872.

C. Best Interests, Incapacity, and the Mental Capacity Act 2005

In the course of the *Bland* judgment, Lord Keith made reference to the legal status of advance refusals of treatment. He stated that the right to refuse treatment 'extends to the situation where the person, in anticipation of his, through one cause or another, entering into a condition such as PVS, gives clear instructions that in such event he is not to be given medical care, including artificial feeding, designed to keep him alive'.[25]

In England and Wales,[26] the Mental Capacity Act 2005 placed advance directives on a statutory footing.[27] It also provided the means to appoint a health and welfare attorney to act on one's behalf.[28] The Act clarified that a health-care professional or an attorney should make a decision on the basis of the 'best interests' of the patient, not only on the basis of clinical considerations.

The explicit acknowledgement that assessment of best interests needs to take account of the views and situation of the patient accords with the virtue ethics approach sketched out here. The golden mean between undertreatment and overtreatment takes into account the potential benefits, burdens, and risks of the intervention not only in relation to the good of health, but also to the other goods of a person's life. It is a prudential (*phronesis*) judgment, not only a clinical (*techne*) judgment.

In the attempt to include a range of factors that might be important to the person, however, the Mental Capacity Act failed even to mention the goods of physical health and length of life. It mentioned only 'the person's past and present wishes and feelings (and, in particular, any relevant written statement made by him when he had capacity), the beliefs and values that would be likely to influence his decision if he had capacity, and the other factors that he would be likely to consider if he were able to do so'.[29] The Act failed to acknowledge the essential role of clinical life- and health-related goods in the practice of medicine. It may be that the Act presupposed the clinical duties of a doctor and presupposed the presumption of the law in favour of saving, sustaining, or prolonging life. However, the Act's failure to mention these elements served to give priority to speculations about what the patient might have wanted, which are by their nature counterfactual and open to projection, while marginalizing consideration of evident clinical benefit.

More generally, the Mental Capacity Act did not fully acknowledge that, when someone no longer has the capacity to make a decision, he or she is simply unable to exercise an authentically autonomous choice. Decisions made previously were not made in precisely *these* circumstances and, unlike contemporaneous decisions, cannot be explored or challenged by discussion or by new information. Furthermore, people can adapt to their new circumstances in a way they may not previously have anticipated.[30] Decisions made by a

[25] Ibid 860.

[26] In Scotland, similar provisions were included in the Adults with Incapacity (Scotland) Act 2000, but for simplicity this chapter focuses on the legislation in England and Wales.

[27] Mental Capacity Act 2005, ss 24–26.

[28] Ibid ss 9–14.

[29] Ibid s 4(6).

[30] Someone with a prolonged disorder of consciousness, *ex hypothesi* has no ability to revise his or her view when in the situation, but it should be noted that, in the case of quadriplegia, a state that induces a similar 'visceral horror', 90 per cent report that they are glad to be alive. See K Fitzpatrick and DA Jones, 'A Life Worth Living? Disabled People and Euthanasia in Belgium' in DA Jones, C MacKellar, and C Gastmans, *Assisted Suicide and Euthanasia: Lessons from Belgium* (Cambridge University Press, 2017), 42, citing I Basnett, 'Health Care Professionals and Their Attitudes toward Decisions Affecting Disabled People' in GL Albrecht, K Seelman, and M Bury (eds), *Handbook of Disability Studies* (Sage Publications, 2001), 450–67.

designated proxy can be explored and challenged, but such decisions are ultimately made by the proxy, not by the person who appointed him or her. This is acknowledged, implicitly, in the stipulation of the Mental Capacity Act that advance refusals of treatment and the powers of health and welfare attorneys only have application where a person cannot make a decision for him- or herself.[31]

Such legal instruments are a poor second best to the exercise of autonomy in an informed contemporaneous decision. Even leaving aside problems of drafting and interpretation, as these instruments are not rationally or ethically equivalent to a contemporaneous autonomous decision, it seems unreasonable to make them legally binding, especially in situations where they could seriously prejudice the patient's life or health.[32]

D. *Burke* and the GMC Guidance—the Duty to Feed

The attempt to make autonomy not only an important consideration, but the ruling principle, even in circumstances where autonomy is compromised or is absent, comes at the expense of considerations of beneficence. The concern that leads to the promotion of proxy and advance decision making is a concern to avoid unwanted overtreatment, but it carries with it the real risk of undertreatment. It leads to a default where beneficial treatments are not provided to patients who lack capacity.

An overemphasis on avoiding overtreatment was evident not only in the Mental Capacity Act, but also in the professional guidance on withholding and withdrawing treatment produced by the General Medical Council (GMC) in 2002.[33] This Guidance was challenged by Mr Leslie Burke, who complained that it allowed him to refuse ANH, but gave him no assurance that, if he lost capacity, doctors would respect his wish always to receive nutrition and hydration, by artificial means if necessary. He feared that, on the basis of prejudiced assumptions about his quality of life, doctors would withdraw or withhold ANH such that he would die of starvation or dehydration. He therefore sought a declaration that the GMC Guidance was unlawful.

Mr Burke prevailed in the High Court,[34] but not in the Court of Appeal.[35] Lord Philips, delivering the judgment of the court, stated that 'it is our view that Mr Burke's fears are addressed by the law as it currently stands and that declaratory relief, particularly in so far as it declares parts of the Guidance unlawful, is both unnecessary for Mr Burke's protection and inappropriate as far as the Guidance itself is concerned'.[36]

In relation to 'the law as it currently stands', Lord Philips helpfully made it explicit that a doctor's duty of care extends to steps that are reasonable to keep the patient alive, including the provision of ANH:

31 MCA, ss 25(3), 11(7)(a).

32 J Keown and L Gormally, 'Human Dignity, Autonomy and Mentally Incapacitated Patients: A Critique of *Who Decides*?' (1999) Web Journal of Current Legal Issues 4, http://www.bailii.org/uk/other/journals/WebJCLI/1999/issue4/keown4.html accessed 15 July 2019.

33 General Medical Council. *Withholding and Withdrawing: Guidance for Doctors* (GMC, 2002).

34 *R (on the Application of Burke) v General Medical Council* [2004] EWHC 1879 (Admin).

35 *Burke, R (on the application of) v General Medical Council and Others* [2005] EWCA Civ 1003 (28 July 2005).

36 *Burke* (n 33) [23].

> A fundamental aspect of this positive duty of care is a duty to take such steps as are reasonable to keep the patient alive. Where ANH is necessary to keep the patient alive, the duty of care will normally require the doctors to supply ANH. This duty will not, however, override the competent patient's wish not to receive ANH. Where the competent patient makes it plain that he or she wishes to be kept alive by ANH, this will not be the source of the duty to provide it. The patient's wish will merely underscore that duty.[37]

Mr Burke was therefore unsuccessful in his efforts to have the GMC Guidance declared unlawful. However, he was at least partially successful in that, acknowledging the concerns that had been expressed in the course of this case, the GMC undertook a revision of their Guidance. This revision did not represent any fundamental change at the level of ethical or legal principle, but the GMC did make explicit some elements of 'the law as it currently stands' that previously had been implicit.

In particular, the new Guidance more clearly acknowledged the presumption in favour of prolonging life and the right of patients to receive, and thus the duty on doctors to offer, treatment and care that is clinically indicated. In relation to nutrition and hydration, the Guidance begins with this right.

> All patients are entitled to food and drink of adequate quantity and quality and to the help they need to eat and drink…
>
> If you are concerned that a patient is not receiving adequate nutrition or hydration by mouth, even with support, *you must* carry out an assessment of their condition and their individual requirements. *You must* assess their needs for nutrition and hydration separately and consider what forms of clinically assisted nutrition or hydration [CANH] may be required to meet their needs.[38]

E. Homicide by Omission Revisited, the Mental Capacity Act, and the *Y* Case

Lord Philips made it clear in *Burke* that the withholding or withdrawing of CANH, in circumstances where it was both indicated and had not been refused by the patient, could constitute intentional homicide: 'for a doctor deliberately to interrupt life-prolonging treatment in the face of a competent patient's expressed wish to be kept alive, *with the intention of thereby terminating the patient's life*, would leave the doctor with no answer to a charge of murder'.[39]

This statement of the law is broadly in conformity with the Hippocratic tradition of virtue ethics, which excludes both actions and deliberate omissions made with the intention of thereby terminating the patient's life. Similarly, the Mental Capacity Act 2005

[37] Ibid [32].

[38] General Medical Council, *Treatment and Care towards the End of Life: Good Practice in Decision Making* (GMC, 2010), paras 109, 111 (emphases added). It should be noticed that, within the Guidance, the phrase 'you must' is used for 'an overriding duty or principle' (ibid p 4) and that 'serious or persistent failure to follow this guidance will put your registration at risk' (ibid).

[39] *Burke* (n 33) [34] (emphasis added).

excludes omissions that are 'motivated by a desire to bring about [the patient's] death'.[40] The language of the Mental Capacity Act 2005 is taken up in the GMC Guidance, which states that: 'Following established ethical and legal (including human rights) principles, decisions concerning potentially life-prolonging treatment must not be motivated by a desire to bring about the patient's death, and must start from a presumption in favour of prolonging life.'[41]

From the perspective of virtue ethics, the GMC Guidance touches on an important distinction. Actions or omissions where the patient's death is intended (which are motivated by death as the desired outcome, even if reluctantly) are prohibited because they are inherently incompatible with aims of medicine, as understood in the Hippocratic tradition. In contrast, the duty to prolong life is not an absolute, but is a matter of more or less. It seeks a golden mean between undertreatment and overtreatment. Hence, the GMC Guidance goes on to say: 'This presumption will normally require you to take all reasonable steps to prolong a patient's life. However, there is no absolute obligation to prolong life irrespective of the consequences for the patient, and irrespective of the patient's views, if they are known or can be found out.'[42]

From the perspective of a Hippocratic virtue-based approach to ethics, the comments of Lord Philips in *Burke*, the relevant section of the Mental Capacity Act 2005, and the wording of the revised GMC Guidance restore a consistency that was compromised in *Bland*. At the same time, if patients in PVS are treated just the same as other patients from whom treatment or care may be withheld or withdrawn, it becomes less clear why *every* case of withdrawal of CANH from a PVS patient needs to go to court.

In *An NHS Trust v Y*,[43] the Supreme Court, following the reasoning of Lord Philips in *Burke*,[44] held there is no legal obligation to seek a judicial declaration before withdrawing CANH from a person with a prolonged disorder of consciousness where the patient's doctor and family agree that withdrawal is in the patient's best interests. There was no such obligation at common law and the Law Lords in Bland held that cases involving patients in PVS be brought to court only as a matter of good practice.

The decision of the Supreme Court in *Y* is regrettable. In the case of persons with a prolonged disorder of consciousness, and especially in the case of patients in PVS, CANH will not be experienced as burdensome by the patient. Given the effectiveness of CANH in keeping the patient alive, and the strong (though not irrebuttable) legal presumption in favour of preserving life, why is there not a strong prima facie ethical and legal obligation to provide CANH in such cases? In the absence of a clear advanced statement by the patient refusing such interventions, it would seem in their best interests to continue to receive CANH, just as it would be in their best interests to spoon feed such patients if this were feasible.[45] Taking this category of case to court allows the rationale for withdrawing CANH to

40 MCA 2005, s 4(5).
41 GMC (n 38) para 10.
42 Ibid.
43 *An NHS Trust and Others (Respondents) v Y (by his litigation friend, the Official Solicitor) and another (Appellants)* [2018] UKSC 46.
44 *Burke* (n 33) [71].
45 A distinction is sometimes made in medical law and ethics between medical treatment and basic care (such that, after *Bland*, CANH is categorized as medical treatment in English law, but some ethicists assert that it should be regarded as basic care). Nevertheless, abstracting from this dispute, while CANH has clinical aspects, a key question is whether it provides clinical benefits and whether it imposes undue harms. The duty to provide spoon feeding for someone in a minimally conscious state who is capable of swallowing helpfully illustrates the need for nutrition and hydration (ie the health benefit of providing nutrition and the harm of not doing so).

be scrutinized and tested against the duty of doctors to take all reasonable steps to provide patients with the treatment and care they need to live.

The basis for the decision not to provide nutrition and hydration to an unconscious or minimally conscious patient, even where this is clinically effective and not unduly burdensome, seems often to reflect one of two confusions in relation to best-interests decisions.

In the first place, there is a confusion between a patient's right or freedom to refuse treatment and the patient's best interests. A doctor is generally constrained, ethically and legally, by the refusal of a patient to receive treatment or care. This does not imply that such treatment or care would thereby not be in the patient's best interests. The refusal might well be unwise and contrary to a person's best interests. The refusal has force because invasive treatment of a competent patient generally requires consent. Refusal of consent trumps best-interests considerations. To treat despite a competent refusal, without specific legal authorization (such as that provided by the Mental Health Act 1983), would be battery. It is also the case that, where a person can neither give nor refuse consent, the person's previous wishes and feelings are relevant to the assessment of best interests. However, in these circumstances, subjective wishes and feelings are not determinative. Previous feelings inform rather than trump a best-interests decision.

The second confusion is between assessing the worthwhileness of a particular treatment or care plan and assessing the worthwhileness of life with disability. The former kind of assessment is specific to an intervention and is relevant to the prudential decision (an exercise of the virtue of *phronesis*) about whether to provide, maintain, or withdraw that intervention. The focus of the latter is not on the specifics of the intervention, but invites a value judgment on the person's continued existence. A decision based on a negative judgment of the person's very existence is either a decision 'motivated by a desire to bring about death', and thus contrary to the Mental Capacity Act, or a decision to abandon the patient.

There is no suggestion in the Supreme Court judgment in *Y* that omissions with the intention to end life are lawful, nor is it implied that the *Bland* decision declared such omissions lawful. Indeed, contrasting the act of euthanasia with the withdrawal of CANH from an unconscious patient, Lady Black stated that there is 'a critical distinction' between 'an act which constitutes the intentional taking of life and therapeutic abstention from treatment'.[46] The word 'therapeutic' here implies assessment of specific interventions in relation to their benefits and burdens, in contrast to decisions that aim to bring about death.

On the other hand, the judgment in *Y* could and should have been much clearer in stating that omissions with the intention to bring about death are unlawful. While the judgment reiterated the requirement that a best-interests decision must not be 'motivated by a desire to bring about death', the court failed to highlight the danger that just such a desire could well be engaged if relatives were invited to ask whether the 'quality of life' of someone in this condition would have been acceptable to the patient. In general, the reasoning in *Y* has reinforced the regrettable shift of focus seen in the Mental Capacity Act away from evident clinical benefit and towards speculation about subjective aspects of benefit. This has

46 *An NHS Trust v Y* (n 43) 114.

rendered best-interests decisions very vulnerable to the influence of societal prejudice, particularly against those with mental disabilities.

It is an irony that the *Bland* decision, while it introduced a serious moral error into the law, provided a practical mechanism—referral to the court as a matter of good practice—which, at least to some extent, helped protect many hundreds of patients with prolonged disorders of consciousness. As a result of the decision in *Y* that referral is in general no longer required as a matter of good practice, and where doctors and relatives agree, it is likely that people will die from dehydration who would not otherwise have done so.

III. Conclusion

In contrast to the clear and applicable principles of autonomy and utility, the concept of virtue is often presented offering little practical guidance in making ethical decisions. The promotion of such generic virtues as courage, temperateness, and prudence seems unobjectionable, but by the same token it adds little to the discussion of specific ethical or legal questions. Furthermore, the internal subjective focus of virtue theory is often thought to offer no contribution to discussion of the external objective requirements of professional ethics and law. This chapter has shown how virtue theory can do practical ethical work. Framing the decision to withdraw treatment in relation to virtue prompts the asking of key ethical questions. What are the dangers of excess and defect in this context? Are there actions or intentions that should be excluded from practice before seeking a prudent middle course? What institutional factors support or inhibit the expression of virtuous behaviour?

A Hippocratic conception of virtues ethics excludes intentional ending of life by act or omission and then seeks the mean between overtreatment and undertreatment. There are thus two ways that an omission may be unethical. It may be inherently wrong because of its intention or it may be wrong because it is a form of undertreatment. This approach to medical ethics provides a critical perspective on medical law in relation to withholding and withdrawing treatment.

The *Bland* case apparently endorsed the withdrawal of tube-feeding even with intent to end life.[47] The *Burke* decision, the subsequent GMC Guidelines, and the Mental Capacity Act largely rectified that error. Unfortunately, the *Y* decision has reinforced another error,[48]

[47] Keown (n 23); Finnis (n 23); see also DA Jones, 'Judgment 2—*Airedale NHS Trust v Bland* [1993] AC 789' in S Smith, J Miola, C Hobson, et al (eds), *Ethical Judgments: Re-writing Medical Law* (Hart, 2016).

[48] The same dangerous error is seen in the cases of Charlie Gard (*Yates and Another v Great Ormond Street Hospital for Children NHS Foundation Trust and Another* [2017] EWCA Civ 410) and Alfie Evans (*E (A Child)* [2018] EWCA Civ 550), neither of which explicitly declare intentional homicide by omission to be lawful, but both of which go beyond judgments about the worthwhileness of treatment and make negative judgments about the worthwhileness of prolonging the life of a disabled person. Both cases cite with approval the guidance of the Royal College of Paediatrics and Child Health (in the Alfie Evans case more extensively). Life-sustaining treatment is said not to be in the best interests of a child where 'the severity of the child's condition is such that it is difficult or *impossible* for them to derive benefit from continued life ... Examples include children in Persistent Vegetative State (PVS), Minimally Conscious State, or those with such severe cognitive impairment that they lack demonstrable or recorded awareness of themselves or their surroundings ... Even in the absence of demonstrable pain or suffering, continuation of LST [life sustaining treatment] may not be in their best interests because it *cannot* provide overall benefit to them'. *E (A Child)*, ibid, 46, citing V Larcher, F Craig, K Bhogal, et al, 'Making Decisions to Limit Treatment in Life-Limiting and Life-Threatening Conditions in Children: A Framework for Practice' (2015) 100(Suppl 2) Archives of Disease in Childhood s1–s23, s14 (emphases added).

which in effect undermines the lives of vulnerable people with severe mental disabilities. This is not, at least overtly, an error in relation to intrinsically wrongful intentions, but it is an error in relation to the more-or-less aspect of virtue. It offers less than the person reasonably needs to live.

9

Dignity in Medical Law

Charles Foster

I. Introduction

The notion of dignity occupies a curious place in modern medical law. It is often invoked and often derided. When it is invoked, it is often not clear how it is defined. When it is derided, the derision is often strangely strident.

But whatever one's view of dignity, dignity cannot be ignored by medical lawyers. The word 'dignity' appears frequently in international and national conventions, declarations, and laws; it is apparently determinative of many judicial decisions. Turning a blind eye to dignity is not a respectable option.

II. A (Western) Historical Perspective

In the ancient Mediterranean world, dignity was a rare commodity. It was an attribute of gods and an occasional gift of gods. Mesopotamian and Egyptian monarchs had dignity because they were gods. The hoi polloi on the streets of Babylon and Thebes were not divine, and hence had no dignity. Homeric heroes had dignity because their sponsoring god or goddess chose to give them dignity: the rank and file Achaeans and Trojans, having no champions on Olympus, had no dignity.

The consequences of not having dignity were clear: ordinary people were cattle, chattels, and cannon-fodder.

The Jewish (and later Christian) notion of the *Imago Dei* erupted dramatically into this world. *All* humans were made in the image of God, and since God had dignity, so did everyone. This sowed the seeds of many principles which today we see as foundational, such as democracy, equal treatment under the law, and the intrinsic value of human life. Indeed it might be said to be the root of basic moral obligation: If X is made in the image of God, and God is good, then X should behave in a good way. That will entail treating Y in a way that acknowledges the God-image in her: to behave otherwise would be a sort of blasphemy.

The Stoics too were revolutionary—but their revolution was more modest and more easily neutralized. All men had dignity, they held, because of their intrinsic rationality. There were two corollaries: first, that all had a duty to act in accordance with this rational nature. And second (and often unstated but implicit), that to act in a way deemed non-rational was to lose the status (and hence the protection) conferred by dignity.

This Stoical version has survived and flourished in the West. It is not surprising. It is politically useful to be able to grant or withhold dignity (like those Olympians did) on the basis of one's own definition of rationality. This account of dignity was unlikely to, and did

Charles Foster, *Dignity in Medical Law* In: *Philosophical Foundations of Medical Law*. Edited by: Andelka M Phillips, Thana C de Campos, and Jonathan Herring, Oxford University Press (2019). © Andelka M Phillips, Thana C de Campos, and Jonathan Herring
DOI: 10.1093/oso/9780198796558.003.0010

not, give the protection to the ordinary citizen implicit in the Judaeo-Christian version (although rarely enacted in notionally Judaeo-Christian societies).

Stoic dignity, while never quite disappearing, was rediscovered at the Renaissance. It chimed well with the general rationalist pretensions of the age. It was in the Renaissance that a crucial and repercussive move was made: reason was equated with self-determination/autonomy, and hence autonomy was equated with dignity. That equation persists: it is arguably the governing principle of mainstream modern discourse about dignity.

Then there was Kant. He is cited reverentially in most discussions of dignity. This deference is unjustified. The architecture of his dignity-thinking is essentially Stoic. He insists, along with the mainstream autonomists of the Renaissance and the Enlightenment, that to have dignity is to be 'free'. That formulation, in Kant's cold hands, is less laissez-faire than it sounds. Freedom, for him, is to act in accordance with the 'Universal Law'. Just as their account was for the Stoics, so this view of Kant's is a tyrant's charter. If one doesn't agree with Kant about the content of the Universal Law (which for him was, more or less, a Teutonic conception of Christian morality), one will not agree with him about what it is to be free—and hence to have dignity. The Book of Common Prayer talks about God 'whose service is perfect freedom'. Kantian ethics can, to a first degree of approximation, be summarized as an appeal to: 'The Universal Law, whose service is perfect freedom . . .'. If a government, or the *zeitgeist*, differs from your conception of the demands of the Universal Law, beware: they will regard you as un-free, and will consider that they have a moral and/or ethical duty, in your own interests, to compel you into the concordance with their conception of the law that will enable you to be truly free.

Even if this overstates the danger of Kantian ethics, Kant's preconditions for freedom are so restrictive that those ethics will be of very limited use in medical contexts. For him, like his Stoic ancestors, dignity was a creature of reason. If one is incapable of discoursing rationally with oneself (for instance, if one is in a permanent vegetative state, or is a young child, or is under anaesthesia), then, presumably, the label 'dignified' (with all the empowerment and protection it entails) cannot be applied. Kant allows the dignity of professional philosophers (assuming that they agree with him about the content of the Universal Law: it would seem that too much rational speculation might disqualify you from being deemed rational and thus dignified): he disallows a claim of dignity on behalf of many of the subjects of bioethical and medico-legal discourse.

For Kant, then, humans are quintessentially brains on sticks. A human will be dignified if the brain comes to a conclusion, arbitrarily designated as acceptable, using coldly logical algorithms. Many consider that humans are more than that. Adam Schulman puts it well: 'Kant denies any moral significance to other aspects of our humanity—including family life, loves, loyalties and other emotions—as well as the way we came into the world and all other merely biological facts about us.'[1]

To come to a workable conclusion about the nature of human dignity, one should, surely, take into account all the available evidence about humans. To turn a wilfully blind eye to most of that evidence is a fatal indictment of a theory. The Stoics, the main dignity theorists of the Renaissance and the Enlightenment, and, most importantly, Kant, come to philosophically unsustainable conclusions because they are talking not about the dignity

[1] A Schulman, 'Bioethics and the Question of Human Dignity' in ED Pellegrino, TW Merrill, and A Schulman (eds), *Human Dignity and Bioethics* (University of Notre Dame Press, 2009).

of real breathing, weeping, dependent, contradictory humans, but about the dignity of pure abstractions.

The eighteenth and nineteenth centuries saw dignity increasingly used in slogans—notably in the French Revolution and in the rhetoric of American constitutional theory. Rarely were there detailed philosophical footnotes.

Whatever dignity is, it was violated on a tectonic scale at Auschwitz, and it was Auschwitz, more than anything else, that resulted in dignity being ubiquitous in post-war declarations and laws. Again, dignity was rarely defined: the word appeared, and remains there, as a placeholder.

III. Dignity Today: An Overview

So far as the modern consideration of dignity by philosophers is concerned, Richard Ashcroft has identified four camps.[2] First: those who say that all talk about dignity is necessarily incoherent. They, says Ashcroft, dominate English-speaking bioethics. Second: those who admit that it can be useful to talk about dignity, but who assert (expressly or impliedly) that dignity is essentially autonomy. Third: pluralists, who admit the usefulness of dignity, but who see it as one principle among many—not having any priority among principles, let alone being in any way the foundational principle from which the other bioethical principles spring. And fourth: those (representing the mainstream in European bioethics, says Ashcroft) who see dignity as a metaphysical property possessed by all humans, and possessed only by humans. This is a direct bequest from the notion of the *Imago Dei*.

This is a useful taxonomic scheme, but runs the risk, inherent in all neat schemes, of suggesting that the divisions are less porous than they are. I nonetheless adopt it below.

IV. 'Dignity Is Incoherent'

Ruth Macklin speaks for many proponents of this view. Having noted that '[a]ppeals to human dignity populate the landscape of medical ethics', she asks: 'Is dignity a useful concept for an ethical analysis of medical activities?' Her own answer is much cited: 'A close inspection of leading examples shows that appeals to dignity are either vague restatements of other, more precise notions, or mere slogans that add nothing to an understanding of the topic.'[3]

She is not the first to come to this conclusion. In 1837, Schopenhauer, fulminating (understandably) against Kant, denounced not only Kant, but the whole idea of dignity.

> This expression 'Human Dignity', once it was uttered by Kant, became the shibboleth of all perplexed and empty-headed moralists. For behind that imposing formula they concealed their lack, not to say, of a real ethical basis, but of any basis at all which was possessed of an

[2] R Ashcroft, 'Making Sense of Dignity' (2005) 31 Journal of Medical Ethics 679.
[3] R Macklin, 'Dignity Is a Useless Concept' (2003) 327 British Medical Journal 1419.

> intelligible meaning; supposing cleverly enough that their readers would be so pleased to see themselves invested with such a 'dignity' that they would be quite satisfied.[4]

Peter Singer sees the invocation of dignity as a way of avoiding proper, hard thinking, correctly observing that '[p]hilosophers frequently introduce ideas of dignity, respect and worth at the point at which reasons appear to be lacking, but this is hardly good enough'.[5] And John Harris, while noting that '[a]ppeals to human dignity are, of course, universally attractive', considers that 'they are also comprehensively vague'.[6]

Bagaric and Allen argue that:

> the concept of dignity is itself vacuous. As a legal or philosophical concept, it is without bounds and ultimately is one incapable of explaining or justifying any narrower interests; it cannot do the work non-consequentialist rights adherents demand of it. Instead, it is a notion that is used by academics, judges and legislators when rational justifications have been exhausted.[7]

Many of these criticisms are just. The dignity-deniers are often strident. While they rightly point out that dignity is often used imprecisely, as a slogan, they are often guilty of meeting slogan with slogan; imprecision with imprecision; rant with rant. And when they do choose to analyse rather than declaim, their analyses are often problematic. Three examples will make the point.

First: When criticizing the notion of dignity, these authors seldom specify which account of dignity they are indicting.

Partly, of course, this is the fault of the dignity-invokers for failing to make it clear. A US Presidential Commission in 1983 noted that 'Phrases like ... "death with dignity" ... have been used in such conflicting ways that their meanings, if they ever were clear, have become hopelessly blurred'.[8] Quite right. But one should be cautious about concluding *too* much from these conflicts—and certainly it is wrong to conclude from them that there is *no* account of dignity that could generate internally consistent and more broadly correct ethical answers. The conflicts often indicate only that different accounts are being used. I, for instance, have noted elsewhere that Aquinas thought that 'a man who sins deviates from the rational order, and so loses his human dignity',[9] while Pope John Paul II declared that '[n]ot even a murderer loses his personal dignity'[10] and wrongly took this as an example of an *Imago Dei*-based dignity theory generating two different answers.[11] It was wrong because, on a closer look (and although Aquinas and the Pope were both Catholics of supposedly canonical orthodoxy), it is clear that Aquinas is being straightforwardly Stoic: had he derived his answer directly from the *Imago Dei*, his answer would have been the same as the Pope's.

[4] AB Bullock (tr and intro) in A Schopenhauer, *The Basis of Morality* (S Sonnenschein, 1903), Pt II, *Critique of Kant's Basis of Ethics*.

[5] P Singer, *Applied Ethics* (Oxford University Press, 1986), 228.

[6] J Harris, 'Cloning and Human Dignity' (1998) 7 Cambridge Quarterly of Healthcare Ethics 163.

[7] M Bagaric and J Allan, 'The Vacuous Concept of Dignity' (2006) 5 Journal of Human Rights 257, 260.

[8] President's Commission for the Study of Ethical Problems in Medicine and Biomedical and Behavioral Research, *Deciding to Forego Life-Sustaining Treatment* (US Government Printing Office, 1983).

[9] *Summa Theologiae*, IIaIIae, q 64, a 2, ad 3.

[10] Encyclical *Evangelium Vitae*, 1995.

[11] C Foster, *Human Dignity in Bioethics and Law* (Hart, 2011), 29.

Second: They often denounce dignity without suggesting another account that would do the necessary intellectual work better. It is easy to knock down: it is harder to build up. Sometimes a decision is needed: discussion is not enough. And while (and particularly where life, death, and health are at stake) one should be very cautious about adopting an account which has the sole virtue of producing *an* answer—as opposed to the demonstrably *right* answer—there will be situations in which an account which can produce *a* practical answer to a bioethical conundrum when one is needed is preferable to one that does not even purport to do so.

Third: those who criticize dignity on the ground that it is (for instance) too amorphous to be useful and who do propose alternative paradigms often advocate alternatives that are even more problematic than dignity itself. The best example is Ruth Macklin. Remember that one of her criticisms of dignity was that appeals to dignity were often 'vague restatements of other, more precise notions'. What are those 'more precise notions'? The subtitle of her article is '[Dignity] Means No More than Respect for Persons or Their Autonomy'. She reiterates that contention in the body of the text.[12] She is clearly saying that 'respect for persons or their autonomy' are more precise notions. This is a difficult contention to sustain. There are many objections, but the most fundamental are, first, that it is not at all clear, absent recourse to a principle that looks very like dignity, *why* one should respect persons or their autonomy (as opposed to respecting, for instance, a stone, or the autonomy of a rabbit); and second, that without dignity, it is wholly unclear what 'respect' would entail. 'Respect' appears to be a second or third-order principle, parasitic on something deeper. The same is true of the components of other ethical schemes that set themselves up to do the job that dignity's proponents claim that only dignity can do. The most obvious examples are the famous Four Principles identified by Beauchamp and Childress:[13] autonomy, non-maleficence, beneficence, and justice.

We have glanced already at autonomy: what justification can be given, other than something that looks like dignity, for a moral or legal obligation to respect autonomy?

As to non-maleficence: to give this idea meaning one has to describe the harm which there is an obligation to avoid. Sometimes this will be easy: a harm has been caused when a surgeon cuts off the healthy left leg when he intended to cut off the diseased right leg. But often it is not easy at all. Two examples will make the point.

First: suppose an unconscious patient is left naked on a hospital trolley, in full sight of the admiringly lustful teenagers in the waiting room. She knows nothing about it, and will never know anything. It is wrong: the wrongness cannot be described except by reference to some notion of human dignity. It is fanciful to try to find harm in some supposed corruption of the teenagers.

Second: suppose that schoolchildren use a human head, disinterred from a mediaeval cemetery, as a football. There are no living relatives of the deceased to be outraged. It is true that one might say that harm accrues to the children: they might be dangerously calloused by treating a human head like that. But that is not the real reason for our disquiet: we all feel, rightly, that human heads should not be treated that way because it is contrary to human dignity (whatever that means). Even if, in articulating the relevant harm, we do rely on the effect on the children, we need to ask why it should have that effect. It only has that effect

12 Ibid 1420.
13 TL Beauchamp and JF Childress, *Principles of Biomedical Ethics* (Oxford University Press, 2001).

because to behave in a way contrary to human dignity callouses. And note, too, if the effect on the children is our main concern, that the harm about which we are concerned is future violation of human dignity by calloused children.

As to beneficence: we encounter the same difficulties in giving an account of what constitutes the good as we did in trying to define harm. Some might assert that 'good' means 'respecting autonomy': that Beauchamp and Childress should have identified just three principles, not four. But we have seen already that violation of autonomy does not capture all our moral outrage.

And as to justice. In the context of medical law this principle is usually understood as being about an obligation to ensure a level playing field: about treating like cases in a like way; about avoiding inequity in resource allocation and other decisions relating to medical treatment. This understanding is so deeply engrained in our intuition that we rarely enquire into its origins. But the origin is surely in that Judaeo-Christian notion that kings and peasants are of equal value—a notion so thoroughly secularized into egalitarianism and democracy that its inevitable dependence on dignity is sometimes hard to recognize.

Thus those who contend that dignity is incoherent are right to call to account those who use the notion of dignity too loosely, without defining their terms. But they have failed to demonstrate that ethics can be done without dignity. They depend, for their ethical building blocks, on second-order principles, necessarily dependent on dignity. Often, those second-order principles give satisfactory answers. But sometimes they do not. When they do not, it is necessary to call in the parent principle to give the answer. And even when the children can give a reasonably satisfactory answer, one will always get a more nuanced, less question-begging answer if one goes to the parent.

V. 'Dignity Is Autonomy'

Beyleveld and Brownsword, in a highly influential text,[14] contend (as summarized by Dwyer, and adopting Gewirth's neo-Kantian Principle of Generic Consistency[15]):

> (1) that we possess rights by virtue of our rationality, and must similarly respect the rights of other rational agents; (2) that human dignity is the basis of these agency rights; (3) that legal reasoning increasingly recognizes this agency-derived concept of dignity; (4) that bio-law decisions are best informed by bioethical decisions made in this paradigm.[16]

For them, 'being subject to existential anxiety is central to what constitutes possessing dignity as the basis for generic rights'.[17] Then, following Kant and the Stoics:

> Dignified conduct may be said to reflect a dignified character, which may be viewed as the personality to which reason requires human agents to aspire. With this in mind, we might view a dignified character simply as a personality disposed to respect the moral law.

[14] D Beyleveld and R Brownsword, *Human Dignity in Bioethics and Biolaw* (Oxford University Press, 2004).
[15] A Gewirth, *Reason and Morality* (University of Chicago Press, 1978).
[16] D Dwyer, 'Beyond Autonomy: The Role of Dignity in "Biolaw"' (2003) Oxford Journal of Legal Studies 23(2), 319, 320.
[17] Ibid 134.

> Relative to this, dignified conduct is action in accordance with the moral law performed out of commitment to obey the moral law.[18]

It follows from this that 'displaying fortitude in the face of adversity is to be considered virtuous'.[19] Rights, for Beyleveld and Brownsword, depend on the possession of dignity.[20]

This is a sophisticated plea for respect for autonomy as the ground of morality. Sophisticated though it is, it does not answer the objection, voiced above, that respect for autonomy does not adequately account for many obvious moral imperatives. Its reliance on Kant's idea of the Universal Law is troubling: what is the content of the Universal Law? Does not the idea of dignity itself dictate the content of any Universal Law that can coherently be identified? And what if one is cognitively (or for any other reason) unable to aspire to a 'dignified' character, or not 'disposed to respect the moral law'? Does a person in PVS not have any dignity?

Martha Nussbaum similarly equates or conflates autonomy and dignity. In discussing whether or not dangerous sports should be allowed, she observes that:

> respecting human dignity requires informing people about their choices, restricting dangerous choices for children, but permitting adults to make a full range of choices, including unhealthy ones—with the proviso that competitive sports need to set reasonable safety conditions so that unwilling participants are not dragooned into taking a health risk that they don't want to take.[21]

That seems an undemanding formulation: to treat you with dignity I just have to let you go your own way. Does that reflect adequately the mystery of agency? Does it account for the complexity of human beings and the porosity of the boundaries between individuals and the societies which determine the shape of humans?

Nussbaum bravely grasps the Kantian nettle: 'We would not accord equal dignity to a person in a persistent vegetative state, or an anencephalic child, since it would appear that there is no striving there, no reaching out for functioning.'[22] She seeks to broker a marriage between Kant and Aristotle, reaching back to the idea of the Good Life to argue that we are all entitled to a threshold level of ten core capabilities or opportunities to function. All are 'necessary conditions of a life worthy of human dignity'.[23] This list makes it clear what she thinks is entailed in an autonomous life, capable of 'striving'. The list is: 'life, bodily health, bodily integrity, senses/imagination/thought, emotions, practical reason (being able to form a conception of the good and to engage in critical reflection about the planning of one's life), affiliation, concern for and relation to other species, play, control over one's environment (political and material)'.[24] It is rather terrifying: you don't have to be in PVS to lack one of the necessary conditions of a life worthy of dignity. If you are blind, deaf, immobile, or socially isolated—beware. The list is revealing: Nussbaum is no doubt right to say that all

[18] Ibid 138.
[19] Ibid 141.
[20] Ibid 134.
[21] M Nussbaum, 'Human Dignity and Political Entitlements' in Pellegrino et al (n 1) 372.
[22] Ibid 374.
[23] Ibid 351.
[24] Ibid 377–8.

the faculties on the list are necessary for complete autonomy. Has any of us ever met anyone who, for any extended period, satisfies all Nussbaum's criteria for autonomy—and hence dignity? I doubt it. That shows, if demonstration is necessary, that autonomy is a synthetic notion, unfitted for the governance of real humans. Dignity, though, in the sense that we identified when thinking about the undraped woman on the hospital trolley and the mediaeval head being kicked around in the street, seems, whatever else you say about it, to be so profoundly natural that (however much we try to educate our intuitions out of reliance upon it) we simply can't stop it being secreted by our ethical reason.

VI. The Pluralists

These are those who consider that dignity is one of many tools in the bioethical or medicolegal toolbox—along with, for instance, autonomy, non-maleficence, and beneficence—but that it has no special, foundational status. According to their view one should use whatever tool or combination of tools is necessary to do the job in hand.

This view is rarely expressed so straightforwardly, but is implicit in the way that dignity is often used.

It is problematic, for it is a view that dignity itself does not appear to allow. Whatever dignity is, dignity claims supremacy. That claim is expressed in various ways: sometimes, as we have seen, it claims the right to trump claims made by other principles on the grounds that its imperatives are in some way more important. Sometimes it claims that other principles should give way because they are its children—that they are secondary, derivative principles that are ultimately dependent on and derived from dignity. But however the claim of supremacy is put, it *is* always put. Dignity is too jealous a principle to share a toolbox.

VII. Dignity and the *Imago Dei*

This was discussed above in the context of the history of dignity. Despite the secularizing of Western society, it continues to have rhetorical force and intuitive appeal. Its appeal is to the intuition that humans are special (a fairly easy argument to make to a human audience).

If the *Imago Dei*, secularized, does have that meaning, a possible objection is the implication that non-humans are not special, or are less special. This objection (speciesism—a type of colonialism) is loudly voiced, but inconsistently applied. The proponents of the *Imago Dei* might respond in various ways. They might say that the assertion that humans are made in the image of God does not mean that non-humans are not—and that the *Imago Dei* is principally a vehicle for imposing on humans a specific set of obligations, rather than a device for conferring on humans a peculiar status. They might suggest that it is unlikely that *any* creature does not bear to some degree the image of its creator—just as a pot is a reflection of the mind of the potter. But many proponents would attempt no such defence—thinking it blasphemy to do so.

VIII. Two Types of Dignity?

This brief survey has shown that, very broadly, there are two senses in which dignity is understood: first, an intrinsic, inalienable sense—a status which one possesses in consequence of what one is (whether that is a human, or a creature made in the image of God, or something else); and, second, an 'aspirational' sense,[25] which, according to Suzie Killmister, contains 'both comportment dignity and meritorious dignity... [which] are states to which individuals aspire... This means that aspirational dignity can be lost, or we can be stripped of it, either through our own actions, the actions of others, or the circumstances in which we find ourselves...'.[26]

These two aspects of dignity map onto, or are identical with, respectively, the rival notions of dignity as constraining (one should be inhibited from doing something to a person because, whatever they do, they possess intrinsic dignity), and dignity as empowering (because to possess some of the dignity qualities to which one can aspire entitles one to a certain regard or entitlement).

The problem for those who seek to use dignity in practical ethics or law is that these two ways of talking about dignity might seem to mean that two wholly different concepts are being used. If that is the case, to invoke 'dignity' itself is hopelessly ambiguous.[27] For Bagaric and Allan, this is a fatal objection:

> What is clear, at least to us, is that the concept of human dignity is easily able to be used as some sort of empowering notion, one that confers rights and entitlements and protects interests. Here is the world of Dworkin and Beyleveld and Brownsword. Yet the same concept of dignity is equally able to be used as a sort of constraint on action, in the Kantian and Linacre Centre sense. Worse, nothing within the concept of dignity itself provides any obvious criteria for adjudicating between these two conceptions even though they lead to polar opposite results. The dispute appears insoluble because of the amorphous nature of the concept being used to try to resolve it. Hence, it is tempting to agree that 'an argumentative device capable of justifying anything is capable of justifying nothing'.[28]

This is a powerful challenge. It draws force from the fact that dignity is often recruited by (for instance) both the proponents and the opponents of euthanasia, and the proponents and opponents of abortion.

Can both of these two ways of talking about dignity be shown to be two sides of the same coin?

I have previously suggested that it can. The argument is as follows:

> The error [of assuming that inalienable status dignity and dignity as a quality evinced by dignified people—the 'aspirational dignity' of Killmister] arises because the attributes associated with dignity (fortitude, patience, consideration for others, and so on) are wrongly seen as akin to chattels that we might possess and then lose; as something

[25] S Killmister, 'Dignity: Not Such a Useless Concept' (2010) 36 Journal of Medical Ethics 160, 161.

[26] Ibid.

[27] D Schroeder, 'Dignity: Two Riddles and Four Concepts' (2008) 17 Cambridge Quarterly of Healthcare Ethics 230, 236.

[28] M Bagaric and J Allan, 'The Vacuous Concept of Dignity' (2006) 5 Journal of Human Rights 257, 265.

> separate from us; as instruments that we use in order to do life. In fact they are a way of *being*, not of *doing* life. The 'mind-less' cases are human (if they're alive) or were human (if they're dead).The dead human is still alive in the minds of many people. Why should the PVS patient not be subjected to unnecessary rectal examinations? One important reason is ... because being human [in the sense demonstrated by a clearly dignified terminal cancer patient whose principle concern is for her carers] ... means that one should not be treated that way.[29]

We are all embarked on the enterprise of being human. Being human doesn't *necessarily* entail *doing* anything, or having done, or even having the potential to do anything. It need not (as demonstrated by the cases in which our intuitions insist that one treat the parts of dead human bodies with dignity) even involve having a beating heart. Doing the right thing, as prescribed by dignity-thinking, entails 'facilitating the full humanness of each person: of encouraging flourishing. The fact that someone doesn't have the neuronal hardware necessary to appreciate that their own flourishing is being maximized is neither here nor there. Flourishing is primarily about *being*, and only secondarily [and not necessarily] about *doing* ....'[30]

If this attempt is successful: good. But if not, it does not mean that all the philosophical and legal work done on dignity has been wasted. Both of the senses in which dignity is described have something to bring to law and ethics that other principles cannot.

IX. The Legal Inescapability of Dignity

The word 'dignity' appears in many national constitutions, international declarations, and international conventions.[31] These include (in relation specifically to health care): the Convention for the Protection of Human Rights and Dignity of the Human Being with Regard to the Application of Biology and Medicine: Convention on Human Rights and Biomedicine (the Oviedo Convention); the Additional Protocols to the Oviedo Convention (concerning Biomedical Research, the Prohibition of Cloning Human Beings, on Transplantation of Organs and Tissues of Human Origin, and on Genetic Testing for Health Purposes); the UNESCO Universal Declaration on Bioethics and Human Rights; the UNESCO Universal Declaration on the Human Genome and Human Rights; and the World Medical Association Declaration of Helsinki: Ethical Principles for Medical Research involving Human Subjects.

Although the European Convention on Human Rights, unusually among statements of fundamental principles of human rights, does not refer explicitly to dignity, the Strasbourg court has said that 'the very essence of the Convention is respect for human dignity and human freedom'.[32] Catherine Dupre rightly asserts that '[t]here is general agreement that dignity is both the foundation and the ultimate aim of human rights systems'.[33]

[29] Foster (n 11) 5.

[30] Ibid 6.

[31] C McCrudden, 'Human Dignity and Judicial Interpretation of Human Rights' (2008) 19 European Journal of International Law 655.

[32] *Pretty v United Kingdom* (1997) 35 EHRR 423, [65].

[33] C Dupre, 'Unlocking Human Dignity: Towards a Theory for the 21st Century' (2009) 2 European Human Rights Law Review 190, 201.

McCrudden, summarizing the way in which 'dignity' is regarded in such instruments, notes that:

> some jurisdictions use dignity as the basis for (or another way of expressing) a comprehensive moral viewpoint, a 'whole moral world view', which seems distinctly different from region to region. In this sense, to speak of human dignity is a shorthand way of summing up how a complex, multi-faceted set of relationships involving Man is, or should be, governed: relationships between man and man, man and God, man and animals, man and the natural environment, man and the universe.[34]

This is a very general formulation indeed. There are few conceptions of dignity that are not captured by a net spread so wide. So McCrudden tries to do rather better. He succeeds.

> [W]e can, perhaps, see the outlines of a basic minimum content of 'human dignity' that all who use the term historically and all those who include it in human rights texts appear to agree is the core, whether they approve of it or disapprove of it. This basic minimum content seems to have at least three elements. The first is that every human being possesses an intrinsic worth, merely by being human. The second is that this intrinsic worth should be recognized and respected by others, and some forms of treatment by others are inconsistent with, or required by, respect for this intrinsic worth. The first element is what might be called the 'ontological' claim; the second might be called the 'relational' claim. This minimum core of the meaning of human dignity seems to be confirmed both by our discussion of the historical roots of dignity, and by the ways in which it has been incorporated into the human rights texts we have considered. The human rights texts have gone further and supplemented the relational element of the minimum core by supplying a third element regarding the relationship between the state and the individual. This is the claim that recognizing the intrinsic worth of the individual requires that the state should be seen to exist for the sake of the individual human being, and not vice versa (the limited-state claim).[35]

Whether McCrudden is right or wrong in identifying the basic minimum content of human dignity as it is seen by lawyers, what is indisputable is that, however suspicious they may be of the legal usefulness of dignity, lawyers will have to work with it. It is ubiquitous not only in international and national instruments, but also in professional codes (which can mould private law obligations—for instance, via the medium of the *Bolam* test in England).

Where dignity does appear expressly in instruments which courts have had to construe, it has done work that other notions could not, or could not comfortably do. Dignity outlawed the practice of dwarf-tossing in France[36] and discrimination against homosexuals in South Africa,[37] conferred a right to have one's gravestone inscribed in the language of one's choice in Israel,[38] and plainly has a vitally important future in medical law.

[34] Ibid 674.
[35] Ibid 679.
[36] *Re Manuel Wackenheim*: Conseil d'Etat decision, http://www.bayefsky.com/html/france_t5_iccpr_854_1999.php accessed 15 July 2019.
[37] *National Coalition for Gay and Lesbian Equality and Another v Minister of Justice and Others* [1998] 2 ZACC 15.
[38] *Jerusalem Community Burial Society v Kestenbaum*, (1991) CA 294/91, 46(2); *Shavit v Rishon Le-Zion Jewish Burial and Charitable Society*, [1999] IsSC 53(3) 600.

10

The Beginning and Ending of Life

Medical Law and Ethical Incoherence

John Keown

A chapter identifying several respects in which medical law in England and Wales suffers (and may soon suffer further) from a lack of ethical coherence in relation to its protection of human life will not be out of place in a volume dedicated to the philosophy of medical law.

English law has historically been informed by the principle of the 'sanctity' or 'inviolability' of human life.[1] To the extent that the law has over the last half century departed from that principle by accommodating utilitarian thinking as well as a 'dualistic' understanding of who is to count as a subject of justice (thereby excluding certain human beings from its protection),[2] the lines it has drawn are both arbitrary and liable to further erosion.[3]

This chapter is divided into three sections. Section I contends that it is philosophically incoherent for the law to calibrate its protection of human life according to arbitrary stages of human development such as birth, viability, the fourteenth day after fertilization, and implantation. Section II contends that to the extent that the law permits life-sustaining treatment to be withheld or withdrawn from incompetent patients on the ground that their 'quality of life' is insufficient, and even with an intent to hasten death, this again displays ethical incoherence. Section III maintains that, were the law to endorse intentionally assisting suicidal refusals of treatment or food and water, or to permit physician-assisted suicide for the 'terminally ill', its ethical incoherence would be aggravated.

I. Before Birth

It is clear law that a physician who administers a lethal injection with intent to end the life of a child who has been completely born alive commits murder.[4] Yet, the law's protection of the child before she reaches that geographical point has been seriously compromised over

[1] For an account and defence of that principle, see generally NM Gorsuch, *The Future of Assisted Suicide and Euthanasia* (Princeton University Press, 2006), esp chs 9 and 10; J Keown, *The Law and Ethics of Medicine: Essays on the Inviolability of Human Life* (Oxford University Press, 2012), esp ch 1.

[2] On the difference between 'dualist' and 'monist' understandings of personhood see A Gómez-Lobo and J Keown, *Bioethics and the Human Goods* (Georgetown University Press, 2015) ch 4; Keown (n 1) 332–3.

[3] The law in England and Wales is not, of course, alone in having compromised its adherence to the principle. Several of the key criticisms made in this chapter could equally be levelled at the law in other common law (and civil law) jurisdictions.

[4] 'The meaning of birth is taken in the English cases to mean complete extrusion from the body of the mother. The umbilical cord need not have been severed, but no part of the child must remain within the parts of the mother if it is to be regarded as born' (G Williams, *The Sanctity of Life and the Criminal Law* (Alfred A Knopf, 1957), 5). If a child is wholly born and is alive, it is homicide to kill it even if it has not breathed (ibid 7–8). For a critique of Williams's book, see J Keown and D Jones, 'Surveying the Foundations of Medical Law: A Reassessment of Glanville Williams's *The Sanctity of Life and the Criminal Law*' (2008) 16(1) Medical Law Review 85.

John Keown, *The Beginning and Ending of Life* In: *Philosophical Foundations of Medical Law*. Edited by: Andelka M Phillips, Thana C de Campos, and Jonathan Herring, Oxford University Press (2019). © Andelka M Phillips, Thana C de Campos, and Jonathan Herring
DOI: 10.1093/oso/9780198796558.003.0011

the last fifty years, mainly as a result of legislation, but partly as a result of judicial decision. The lines drawn by the law to calibrate its protection lack ethical coherence.

A. Complete Live Birth

While the law prohibits the intentional destruction of a child after she has been completely born alive it sometimes permits her to be intentionally killed during birth. In 1929, the Infant Life (Preservation) Act was passed to protect children during delivery, who fell into a gap between the crime of using means with intent to procure miscarriage contrary to section 58 of the Offences against the Person Act 1861 and the crime of homicide. The 1929 Act made it an offence intentionally to destroy a child 'capable of being born alive' before it had an existence independent of its mother (unless its destruction was for the purpose only of preserving the life of the mother).[5] However, the Abortion Act 1967 as amended by the Human Fertilisation and Embryology Act 1990 provides that when a registered medical practitioner terminates a pregnancy in accordance with the Abortion Act, no offence is committed against the 1929 Act.[6] Consequently, provided an abortion is performed in accordance with the Abortion Act, a physician commits no crime by intentionally destroying a child who emerges alive, even if capable of survival, before complete live birth.

There is broad agreement among bioethicists that there is no significant ethical distinction between abortion and infanticide. The consensus embraces philosophers who oppose both, such as Christopher Kaczor,[7] and those who endorse both, such as John Harris. As the latter has observed, it is not plausible to think that any moral change occurs during the journey down the birth canal and: 'The geographical location of the developing human, whether it is inside the womb or not, is not the sort of thing that can make a moral difference.'[8]

Achas Burin has, by contrast, attempted to defend what she calls the 'bright line' drawn by the law at birth. She has argued that 'expressing sentience in the world is essential for the attainment of personhood'.[9] She writes that legal personhood begins when a child sees the light of day and that this kind of sensory experience is 'integral to attainment of personhood'.[10] Expressing sentience in the world is, we are told, central to legal concepts of personhood.[11] Her ambitious argument invites many questions. For example, just how 'bright' a line is birth?[12] What if only the baby's head emerges, but she sees the light of day? What of babies removed from the womb for surgery who are then replaced? Are non-human creatures which express their sentience after birth persons?[13] Is it not murder intentionally

[5] This crime of 'child destruction' went further than plugging the gap as it protected children 'capable of being born alive' even prior to the onset of delivery. See, generally, Keown (n 1) ch 7.

[6] Abortion Act 1967, s 5(1).

[7] C Kaczor, *The Ethics of Abortion: Women's Rights, Human Life, and the Question of Justice* (2nd edn, Routledge, 2015), ch 3. See also Gómez-Lobo and Keown (n 2) esp chs 4 and 6. More recently, Kaczor has co-authored C Kaczor and K Greasley, *Abortion Rights: For and Against* (Cambridge University Press, 2017).

[8] 'Adviser Sparks Infanticide Debate', *BBC News* (26 January 2004), https://bbc.in/2G9VCZ5 accessed 15 July 2019.

[9] AK Burin, 'Beyond Pragmatism: Defending the "Bright Line" of Birth' (2014) 22(4) Medical Law Reviews 494.

[10] Ibid 499.

[11] Ibid 505.

[12] See ibid 498–9.

[13] We are told 'the young of other species . . . closely resemble adults at birth' (ibid 503).

to kill a living child who has been delivered even if she is unconscious? Burin claims the *actus reus* of murder applies only postnatally,[14] but (even leaving aside the law of homicide's 'live-birth murder' rule) what about foetal homicide statutes?[15] Moreover, why should it be thought necessary to 'express' one's sentience to qualify as a person? What if a newborn child (or indeed an adult with a condition like 'locked-in' syndrome) is incapable of any expression?[16] What if a baby's sensory experience and expression after birth is, perhaps due to brain damage during birth, less than it was before birth? What if a baby were born into an environment, such as an opaque incubator, in which she received either no stimuli or fewer than she did in the womb, where she regularly heard her mother singing lullabies to her? Burin writes that 'the womb is more akin to a cupboard'[17] (a peculiar way to describe an organ of the pregnant woman, not least because it elides her from the mother-child relationship), but if the child were delivered and placed in a cupboard, would it not be a person? If adults were placed in an environment with no stimuli, or plugged into Nozick's 'experience machine' (which Burin incorporates into her argument[18]), would they lose their personhood? This machine, and the womb, we are told, are 'controlled environments'.[19] What about children or adults living in other controlled environments, perhaps for reasons of health or punishment? If 'interaction with the world is the key to personhood',[20] do such humans lack personhood? Further, what *degree* of sensory experience (and of *which* sensory experience(s)) is essential to personhood, and do those with lesser degrees of sensory experience (such as those born deaf-blind) enjoy lesser degrees of personhood? Finally, Burin writes, 'it is impossible to be a person when contained entirely within the person of another'.[21] If you were somehow shrunken in size and placed into someone else's body (like in the movie *Fantastic Voyage*), would you lose your personhood? Burin's entire argument is as implausible as it is unpersuasive.

The law, then, by attaching crucial significance to complete live birth, draws an ethically incoherent line. It regards the physician who kills a child before complete live birth as meriting payment, but the physician who kills the child seconds later as meriting prison (in England, a mandatory life sentence, no less). In the United States, abortionist Dr Kermit Gosnell was given three consecutive life sentences for murdering three children, who had survived abortion, by severing their spinal cords.[22] The Philadelphia District Attorney commented that he had witnessed much senseless violence and cruelty, but that this case was arguably 'the most gruesome, the most vile'.[23] Had Gosnell killed the babies during birth he would not have been liable for homicide, but would his actions have been any less gruesome and vile?[24]

[14] Ibid.

[15] And historically the law has severely punished the intentional destruction of the child throughout pregnancy, and does so still absent compliance with the Abortion Act 1967.

[16] Burin writes (ibid 517 n 172) that she does not imply that those with 'locked-in' syndrome are dead, but does she think they are persons?

[17] Ibid 514.

[18] Ibid 505–8.

[19] Ibid 507.

[20] Ibid 517.

[21] Ibid 525.

[22] V Lattanzio, '"House of Horrors" Trial', *NBC10 News* (15 May 2013), http://bit.ly/2GtbwRC accessed 15 July 2019.

[23] Ibid.

[24] Reflecting on the case, Kate Greasley asked, but did not answer, whether birth represents a morally relevant boundary: K Greasley, 'The Pearl of the "Pro-Life" Movement: Reflections on the Kermit Gosnell Controversy' (2014) 40(6) Journal of Medical Ethics 419, 422. She argued that opponents of abortion who hold that all abortion

Finally, when a pregnancy is terminated under the Abortion Act, the child may lawfully be killed, before or during birth, even if she is capable of survival. The law allows the termination not only of unwanted *pregnancies*, but of unwanted *children*, even if those children are desperately wanted by scores of prospective adoptive parents. Even on a utilitarian calculus, why does the happiness of the prospective parents and of the child not outweigh the wish of the mother that her viable child be put to death?

B. Viability

The grounds for abortion under the Abortion Act 1967 as amended are very extensive for the first twenty-four weeks of pregnancy[25] (permitting virtual abortion on request[26]), but less extensive thereafter. Abortion after the twenty-fourth week is permitted when two registered medical practitioners believe in good faith that abortion is necessary to prevent grave permanent injury to the physical or mental health of the pregnant woman; or that the continuance of the pregnancy would involve risk to the life of the pregnant woman greater than if the pregnancy were terminated, or that there is a substantial risk that if the child were born it would suffer from such physical or mental abnormalities as to be seriously handicapped.[27] Precisely how restrictive these limitations are will turn on the courts' interpretation of unclear terms like 'substantial risk' of 'serious handicap' (which some abortionists think, remarkably, includes such relatively minor and largely remediable conditions as harelip and cleft palate[28]). The line was drawn at twenty-four weeks to distinguish unborn children who are capable of survival if born from those who are not.[29]

What is the moral distinction between an unborn child who is, and one who is not, capable of survival if delivered? The law prohibits the intentional killing of infants after birth whether or not they are viable. As Glanville Williams observed: 'If an aborted fetus is alive it is a person, no matter how short the period of gestation.'[30] Similarly, at the other end of life, the law prohibits the intentional killing of those who may have only hours or minutes to live. Why, then, does it distinguish between killing unborn children who are viable and those who are not? The question gains added traction when we recall a point made above, that if a child emerges alive from an abortion performed in accordance with the Abortion Act 1967, the law allows her deliberate destruction before complete live birth, even if she is viable. Where, then, is any supposed higher moral status attaching to viability?

involves the killing of a person are disingenuous if they exhibit amplified moral horror at Gosnell's killings, and that their use of the case is 'a contradiction of their most fundamental premise: that inviolable human life begins at conception' (ibid). Not so. There is nothing contradictory in holding that all intentional killings are seriously wrong, but that some are worse than others; that it is, eg, wrong to kill a sleeping person painlessly, but worse to torture someone to death. See also DP Lang, 'The Sea of the Pro-Life Movement: A Brief Response to "Reflections on the Kermit Gosnell Controversy"' (2014) 40 Journal of Medical Ethics 424.

---

[25] Abortion Act, s 1(1)(a).

[26] The Act's sponsor observed in the early 1980s that abortion was being used 'as a contraceptive' (P Bartram, *David Steel: His Life and Politics* (A STAR book, 1982), 85).

[27] Abortion Act , s 1(1)(b), (c), (d) respectively.

[28] See J Finnis, 'We Warned Them; They Mocked Us, Now We've Been Proved Right', *The Daily Telegraph* (7 December 2003).

[29] Viability also explains the twenty-eight-week evidential presumption of capacity for life birth in s 1(2) of the Infant Life (Preservation) Act 1929. See Keown (n 1) ch 7.

[30] G Williams, *Textbook of Criminal Law* (1st edn, Steven & Sons, 1978), 263 n 8.

The lines drawn at complete live birth and at viability, which made some sense when they were aspects of a panoply of overlapping protections for human life from fertilization to live birth, ceased to make sense when that panoply was ruptured by the Abortion Act 1967 and the Human Fertilisation and Embryology Act 1990.

C. Fourteen Days

A third line of legal demarcation for which sound ethical support is lacking concerns the time limit for destructive research on human embryos in vitro. The Human Fertilisation and Embryology Act 1990 permits such research, subject to specified regulatory approval, up to the appearance of the 'primitive streak', the 'longitudinal groove that develops in the gastrula during the development of bird and mammal embryos'.[31] This streak, the Act provides, is to be taken to have appeared no later than the end of the fourteenth day after the process of creating the embryo began.[32]

A central moral argument in favour of distinguishing between embryos before and after the development of the primitive streak is the argument from 'twinning'. It is argued that the possibility, before the formation of the primitive streak, that the embryo may split into twins means that it is not a human individual. As some members of the US President's Council on Bioethics argued, only after fourteen days or the formation of the primitive streak can the being in question be anything other than a single being.[33] As other members of the Council countered, however:

> There is the obvious rejoinder that if one locus of moral status can become two, its moral standing does not thereby diminish but rather increases. More specifically, the possibility of twinning does not rebut the individuality of the early embryo from its beginning. The fact that where 'John' alone once was there are now both 'John' and 'Jim' does not call into question the presence of 'John' at the outset.[34]

Two other arguments often adduced to support the fourteen-day limit[35] are that the incidence of natural abortion is high and that the limit marks the end of the implantation stage. However, one cannot sensibly reason from the fact that a particular proportion of human beings die at a certain stage of their lives to the ethical conclusion that their lives lack value and we are therefore justified in ending them.[36] Nature is not a moral agent, but we are. Would a high incidence of infant mortality justify infanticide? As for fourteen days marking the end of the implantation stage, why is this thought to be morally relevant, especially when the embryos subjected to research are never going to be implanted anyway?

[31] 'Primitive Streak' in *Oxford Reference*, http://bit.ly/2H4gYZk accessed 15 July 2019.

[32] Human Fertilisation and Embryology Act 1990, ss 3(3)(a), (4), as amended by the Human Fertilisation and Embryology Act 2008, s 3(4).

[33] President's Council on Bioethics, *Human Cloning and Human Dignity* (2002), ch 6, III, B 1 (a)(i).

[34] Ibid IV A.

[35] For a discussion of the arguments for and against, see ibid ch 6.

[36] For a paper questioning the scientific basis on which claims about a very high incidence of spontaneous abortion have been based, see GE Jarvis, 'Estimating Limits for Natural Human Embryo Mortality' (2016), http://bit.ly/2GvC3e6 accessed 15 July 2019.

The end of the fourteenth day, a line drawn for utilitarian reasons to facilitate research on human embryos,[37] is a marker that is as unstable as it is arbitrary. If the pursuit of improvements in scientific knowledge about early human development, human diseases, and the treatment of infertility justify research up to the end of the fourteenth day, they justify research beyond that time. Indeed, the utilitarian case for breaching the barrier has already been made. John Harris has argued that the overwhelming consensus of scientific opinion holds that much of considerable scientific and therapeutic importance could be gained by extending the fourteen-day limit (with its 'bizarre origins') to twenty-one days, and he underscores the incoherence of the fourteen-day limit by noting that the law freely allows abortion up to the twenty-fourth week.[38] Recognition of the arbitrariness of the fourteen-day limit does not, of course, mean the limit should be extended. One could equally argue that the arbitrariness should be resolved by prohibiting the intentional destruction of any embryonic human being (whether in vitro or in vivo).[39]

D. Implantation

Yet another legal distinction lacking any cogent ethical basis is that between destruction of the human embryo before and after implantation in the womb. In *Smeaton*,[40] Munby J (as he then was) held that sections 58 and 59 of the Offences against the Person Act 1861, which respectively prohibit the use of, and procurement or supply of, means with intent to procure miscarriage, did not bite before implantation. The judgment has been subjected to extensive criticism elsewhere.[41] Suffice it here to ask what principled justification there could be for drawing a legal line at implantation.

When Parliament enacted those sections, its purpose was undoubtedly to protect human life from fertilization. It was well known by 1861 that human life began at fertilization and medical and medico-legal experts had long been pressing legislators to enact stricter laws to protect the unborn from that point.[42] It was also well known that attempts to procure abortion were risky to women. Are we seriously to believe that the legislature intended to protect the unborn, and women, only after implantation? Are we to suppose that Parliament wished, as Victor Tunkel vividly put it, to grant a 'free for all moratorium of a week or more after intercourse during which every sort of abortionist could ply his craft with impunity'?[43] Yet, *Smeaton* effectively amends the 1861 Act to render lawful the modern practice of doctors and pharmacists, without complying with the Abortion Act, using or supplying means

[37] M Warnock, *A Question of Life: The Warnock Report on Human Fertilisation and Embryology* (Basil Blackwell, 1985), xv, 64.

[38] J Harris, 'It's Time to Extend the 14 Day Limit for Embryo Research', *The Guardian* (6 May 2016).

[39] See Keown (n 1) ch 8.

[40] *R (Smeaton) v Secretary of State for Health* [2002] EWHC 610 (Admin).

[41] See Keown (n 1) ch 6; J Keown, '"Morning after" Pills, "Miscarriage" and Muddle' (2005) 2 Legal Studies 296.

[42] Keown (n 1) 147–50. Sheldon, acknowledging the Act's purpose 'of preventing or condemning the intentional destruction of fetal life', has observed that 'the search for a good contemporary reason for according implantation such profound significance is ... elusive' (S Sheldon, 'The Regulatory Cliff Edge between Contraception and Abortion: The Legal and Moral Significance of Implantation' (2015) 41 Journal of Medical Ethics 762, 764).

[43] V Tunkel, 'Modern Anti-Pregnancy Techniques and the Criminal Law' [1974] Criminal Law Review 461, 465. See also Keown (n 1) 160.

to prevent implantation. As Sally Sheldon has observed, the legal line drawn at implantation falls 'woefully short' of what clear moral reasoning requires.[44]

In short, the law's protection of early human life is philosophically unsound. The lines it draws at implantation, fourteen days, viability, and birth seem grounded on little more than utilitarian pragmatism, combined with philosophical dualism, to facilitate the destruction of preborn human life. Whether one thinks such destruction ethical or not is (for the purposes of this chapter) beside the point. The point is that the law permitting it is, plainly, ethically incoherent.

II. After Birth

A. Non-Treatment of Infants

Although the law continues to prohibit as murder the intentional administration of a lethal injection to kill a child after she has been completely born alive, a series of judicial decisions has undermined that principle by holding that it can be in the 'best interests' of a child for life-prolonging treatment to be withheld or withdrawn on the ground that the child's 'quality of life' is not worthwhile.[45] For example, in the *Charlie Gard* case, Francis J, having cited a previous case in which the judge had found that the lives of the patients in question had 'some value' and were 'worth preserving', held that, by contrast, Charlie's 'quality of life'[46] was not one that should be sustained.[47] The Court of Appeal endorsed the judge's finding that the treatment proposed by his parents would simply prolong Charlie's 'awful existence'.[48]

Is it not ethically incoherent for the courts to hold that it is unlawful intentionally to hasten the child's death by an act, but lawful to withhold or withdraw life-prolonging treatment on the ground that continued life is no longer in the child's best interests (especially if the intention is to hasten the child's death)?

B. Non-Treatment of Incompetent Adults

A similar question arises in relation to withholding or withdrawing of treatment (and tube-feeding) from mentally incapacitated adults. While it remains unlawful to administer a

[44] Sheldon (n 42) 765. Her ensuing comment (ibid)—that the distinction is 'determined' by the phrase with intent to procure 'miscarriage' in an Act passed by a parliament in which women had no voice and in a world very different from the modern world in matters sexual, is wayward. The distinction resulted from a modern judicial misinterpretation of the phrase. Moreover, given that early feminists were opposed to abortion, it should not be assumed that any female MPs would have opposed ss 58 and 59.

[45] See J Keown, *Euthanasia, Ethics and Public Policy* (Cambridge University Press, 2002), 230–2.

[46] On two inconsistent meanings of 'quality of life', which judges (with rare exceptions) fail to distinguish, see ibid 43–51.

[47] *Great Ormond Street Hospital v Yates and Gard* [2017] EWHC (Admin) 972 (Fam), [126].

[48] *In the Matter of Charles Gard* [2017] EWCA Civ 410, [97]. Counsel for the hospital, which favoured withdrawal of Charlie's ventilation, reportedly told the Court of Appeal that the parents' wishes would result in significant harm to Charlie, namely, a 'condition of existence which is offering the child no benefit' and that it was 'inhuman to permit that condition to continue'. Why wasn't this equally an argument for giving Charlie a lethal injection? 'Who is Charlie Gard, What Is the Disease He Suffered from and What Happened in the Court Case?' *The Daily Telegraph* (31 July 2017).

lethal injection to such patients, it is lawful to withhold or withdraw treatment, including tube-feeding, on the ground that continued life is no longer in their 'best interests'. In *Bland*, the Law Lords held that tube-feeding could lawfully be withdrawn from a patient in a 'persistent vegetative state'.[49] Three of their Lordships thought that the intention in stopping the tube-feeding would be to kill the patient. If they were right, and if the case held that, notwithstanding such an intent, the tube-feeding could nevertheless lawfully be withheld, then it clearly left the law ethically confused. Lord Mustill famously and aptly observed that the case left the law in a 'morally and intellectually misshapen' state.[50] The incoherence may have been largely resolved by the Mental Capacity Act 2005. Section 4(5) of the Act provides that where the determination of the best interests of a mentally incapacitated adult relates to life-sustaining treatment, the person making the determination 'must not, in considering whether the treatment is in the best interests of the person concerned, be motivated by a desire to bring about his death'.[51] If that Act does rule out the withdrawal of treatment with intent to kill, ethical incoherence nevertheless remains, tracking that in relation to the determination of the 'best interests' of infants. There would appear to be nothing in the definition of 'best interests' in section 4 of the Act to prevent carers or courts from judging that continued life is no longer in the incompetent adult's 'best interests' and that he or she would be 'better off dead'. Indeed, section 4 is phrased in such subjective terms—as to the wishes, feelings, and values of the person and of others as to what is in the person's 'best interests'—that it appears to accommodate, if not invite, such judgments.

III. Future Incoherence?

A. Physician-Assisted Suicide by Refusing Treatment or Food and Water

In a number of cases, the courts have observed not only that competent patients have a right to refuse treatment (which is largely uncontroversial), but also that this right is 'absolute' (which is highly controversial). If the right to refuse treatment were truly absolute, then it would include a right to refuse treatment precisely in order to end one's life. It would appear that suicide may have been the intention of the patient in *Re B*, whose request that her life-prolonging ventilation be withdrawn was upheld.[52] If, however, patients have a right to end their lives by refusing treatment and if doctors have a duty to assist them (or at least if doctors act lawfully by intentionally assisting them), then the law against assisting suicide is undermined. How can the law sensibly prohibit physicians from intentionally assisting their patients from ending their lives by an act, but permit them (if not require them) to do precisely the same thing by deliberate omission, especially when the line between act and omission may be negligible, as in disconnecting a ventilator?

[49] *Airedale NHS Trust v Bland* [1993] AC 789.
[50] Ibid 887. See, generally, Keown (n 1) ch 12.
[51] See J Finnis, 'The Mental Capacity Act 2005: Some Ethical and Legal Issues' in H Watt (ed), *Incapacity and Care* (The Linacre Centre, 2009), 95.
[52] J Keown, 'The Case of Ms B: Suicide's Slippery Slope?' (2002) 28 Journal of Medical Ethics 238.

Despite their incautiously sweeping dicta, however, it is far from clear that the courts have held either that patients have an absolute right to refuse treatment[53] that includes a right to end their lives by refusing treatment or that doctors may intentionally assist them to hasten their end. In *Re B*, the judgment does not address the issue.[54] Moreover, there is authority that there is a duty to prevent suicide in certain circumstances.[55] It may well be that if a patient's refusal is clearly suicidal, as it would be if the patient refused food and water to hasten their death,[56] a doctor could lawfully act with the sole intention of palliating the patient's suffering while he or she dehydrated to death. An intention to palliate should not be confused (by the law or by the doctor) with an intention to assist suicide.[57]

B. Physician-Assisted Suicide for the Terminally Ill?

Over the past quarter of a century, the campaign for voluntary, active euthanasia (VAE) has rebranded itself as a campaign for 'death with dignity' which seeks (for now) physician-assisted suicide (PAS) for the 'terminally ill'. Oregon-style bills have been introduced in Parliament on several occasions and attempts have been made to persuade the courts that there is a right to assisted suicide under the European Convention on Human Rights or under a (peculiar) parallel English version of those rights.[58] The latest attempt was rebuffed in June 2018 by the Court of Appeal.[59]

If such a bill or such a case were to succeed, it would inflict further ethical incoherence on the law. If there is a 'right to die', how can it sensibly be limited to those who are 'terminally ill' and those who can end their lives with the help of a physician? If the principles of autonomy and beneficence justify PAS, they justify VAE, especially for those unable to end their own lives even with physician assistance. If those principles justify a hastened death for the 'terminally ill', they justify a hastened death for the chronically ill, who may have years of suffering to endure. The narrower focus of the contemporary campaign seems little more than a clever ploy to get a 'foot in the door'. It has proved effective in several US states, but not, as yet, in the United Kingdom. UK law may, then, continue to resist the invitation to admit yet another ethically incoherent guest.

[53] The right cannot be absolute. If, eg, a patient's refusal to have a deadly disease like smallpox or Ebola treated endangered the community, it would surely be lawful to detain and treat the patient.

[54] See Keown (n 52). For a lucid discussion of relevant cases in England and the United States, see Gorsuch (n 1) 181–91.

[55] See Keown (n 45) 227–30.

[56] See RJ Jox, I Black, GD Borasio, et al, 'Voluntary Stopping of Eating and Drinking: Is Medical Support Ethically Justified?' (2017) 15 BMC Medicine 186. Mistakenly, Dutch medical and nursing guidance on assisting such refusals does not regard them as suicidal. See J Keown, *Euthanasia, Ethics and Public Policy* (2nd edn, Cambridge University Press, 2018), ch 16.

[57] See Gorsuch (n 1) 65–9, 166.

[58] *R (Nicklinson) v Ministry of Justice* [2014] UKSC 38. See J Finnis, 'A British "Convention Right" to Assistance in Suicide?' (2015) 131 Law Quarterly Review 1.

[59] *R (Conway) v The Secretary of State for Justice* [2018] EWCA Civ 1431.

C. Voluntary Euthanasia?

If the law were to allow such a guest to cross its threshold, however, the law would not only logically commit itself to permit VAE and for the chronically ill. It would also commit itself to permitting non-voluntary, active euthanasia (NVAE). This 'logical' slippery slope argument has been explained and defended elsewhere.[60] Suffice it to say that the ethical case for VAE rests not only on the principle of autonomy, but also on the principle of beneficence, and that the absence of autonomy does not cancel the duty of beneficence. The few attempts to refute this logical argument have proved wanting.[61]

IV. Conclusions

This chapter has suggested that the law in relation to the protection of human life at its beginning and end exhibits profound ethical incoherence. It has also suggested that if legislators or judges were to make it lawful for physicians intentionally to assist suicidal refusals of treatment, or to endorse a right to PAS for the 'terminally ill', the law's ethical incoherence would be seriously aggravated.

Could it not be argued that the law regularly draws arbitrary lines and that this does not amount to ethical incoherence? The counter-argument is that some lines are necessarily determined by prudential and pragmatic considerations, such as whether the speed limit should be 60 or 70, and involve a certain degree of arbitrariness. By contrast, the determination of who is a subject of justice and whose basic rights, not least the right not to be intentionally killed, are entitled to the protection of the law is a question of fundamental principle, not a matter for arbitrary judgment.[62]

If, as the principle of the inviolability of life holds, all human beings share an intrinsic equality in dignity and enjoy a right not to be intentionally killed, there is no room for arbitrary distinctions between human beings so as to deny them that right, whether on the basis of sex, race, ethnicity, sexual orientation, nationality, religion, physical or mental disability, age, or stage of development.

[60] See Keown (n 56) ch 6.

[61] See eg J Keown, 'Debating Euthanasia: A Reply to Emily Jackson' in M Heneghan and J Wall (eds), *Law, Ethics and Medicine: Essays in Honour of Peter Skegg* (Thomson Reuters, 2016), 65.

[62] Sheldon rightly notes that we need to be able to determine when someone acquires the full human rights that accompany legal personhood and that it is important to ensure that they are grounded in 'careful consideration, informed by clear moral reasoning and a solid medical evidence base' (Sheldon (n 42) 765). Unfortunately, her article gets off on the wrong foot by quoting (ibid 762) Glanville Williams's misleading statement that '[a]bstract human life does not "begin"; it just keeps going'. While the life of the human species continues, the lives of individual human beings (like Glanville Williams) begin, and end.

11

Proportionality in Medical Law

*Francisco J Urbina**

The idea of proportionality is present in most areas of law.[1] Medical law is no exception. Yet, proportionality is an elusive idea. It is not always clear what proportionality entails, and the requirements associated with it can change from context to context. Here, I will attempt to shed some light on the idea of proportionality as it applies to medical law. In particular, I intend to analyse the specific requirements entailed by proportionality, and to suggest some jurisprudential, moral, and institutional questions raised by its application.

Because here we are interested in the philosophical foundations of medical law, my main aim is not to provide a doctrinal study of what proportionality requires in a specific jurisdiction. Although I will rely on some examples (primarily from the United Kingdom, the European Court of Human Rights (ECtHR), and Canada) to ground my analysis of proportionality, there is, I believe, nothing exotic about these examples. They are representative of the main features of proportionality reasoning, of the variety of ways it allows of addressing a case, and of the kinds of questions raised by its application.

I will focus on one prominent way in which proportionality reasoning is applied in the domain of medical law, by exploring how proportionality features in cases concerning euthanasia and assisted suicide. These cases are especially useful in illustrating both how proportionality operates and the range of issues it raises. But there are other ways in which the idea of proportionality can be instantiated in medical law. In the final section of this chapter, I illustrate how proportionality could be applied and evaluated in contexts different from those involving fundamental rights by exploring the use of proportionality in medical research involving human subjects.

I. Proportionality, Medical Law, and Human Rights

Human or constitutional rights[2] are understood to permeate the whole of the legal system. They relate to basic requirements of justice that ought to be respected in all domains of social life. The domain of affairs regulated by medical law is no exception, and thus, human rights—together with the principles in accordance to which human rights are interpreted, specified, and adjudicated—apply to medical law as well. The principle of proportionality is said to be a 'staple of adjudication on fundamental rights in international and domestic

* I wish to thank the editors for valuable comments, and the Conicyt Fondecyt Iniciación grant no 11150872, awarded by the Chilean Ministry of Education, for its contribution in funding my research leading to this chapter.

[1] See FJ Urbina, *A Critique of Proportionality and Balancing* (Cambridge University Press, 2017), 4 n 6.

[2] Here, I refer to 'human' or 'constitutional' rights indistinctly. Although I am aware that these terms may refer to different legal regimes, the differences between the two are not relevant here.

Francisco J Urbina, *Proportionality in Medical Law* In: *Philosophical Foundations of Medical Law*. Edited by: Andelka M Phillips, Thana C de Campos, and Jonathan Herring, Oxford University Press (2019). © Andelka M Phillips, Thana C de Campos, and Jonathan Herring
DOI: 10.1093/oso/9780198796558.003.0012

courts',[3] as its usage extends to constitutional and human rights courts all around the world.[4] Proportionality is an important, often defining, element in human rights cases that bear on issues of medical law. This is one of the ways in which proportionality becomes a crucial principle of the law regulating medical affairs.

Proportionality features in cases regarding a limitation or interference with a human right. In such cases, courts commonly address the issue in two steps. In step one, courts enquire whether there has been an interference with a human right. Because at this stage the scope of the right is commonly taken to be very broad, this step is not very demanding and courts usually find that there has been an interference with a right. In step two, courts evaluate whether this limitation is justified. To determine this, they apply the principle of proportionality or proportionality test. This test is usually formulated as comprising the following four sub-tests:

(1) legitimate aim—the measure interfering with the right has to have an objective of sufficient importance;
(2) suitability—the measure interfering with the right has to be rationally connected to the legitimate aim;
(3) necessity—the measure should impair as little as possible the right in question;
(4) proportionality *stricto sensu*—there must be a proportionality between the *effects* of the measures which are responsible for limiting the right, and the objective which has been identified as of sufficient importance.[5]

Other formulations of the different sub-tests are possible, but the ones just provided are typical.[6] The last prong is also often formulated as the following question: 'do [the measures in question] strike a fair balance between the rights of the individual and the interests of the community?'[7] As Lord Reed puts it in his oft-quoted exposition of the principle of proportionality in *Bank Mellat*: 'In essence, the question at step four is whether the impact of the rights infringement is disproportionate to the likely benefit of the impugned measure.'[8] For the measure to be justified, it must pass all the sub-tests.

Perhaps the more significant human rights cases that apply proportionality in the domain of medical law are those dealing with euthanasia and assisted suicide. These cases provide a useful illustration of both the use of proportionality in the domain of medical law and human rights, and some of the problems and tensions involved in proportionality analysis.

[3] G Verdirame, 'Rescuing Human Rights from Proportionality' in R Cruft, SM Liao, and M Renzo (eds), *Philosophical Foundations of Human Rights* (Oxford University Press, 2015), 341.

[4] A Barak, *Proportionality: Constitutional Rights and Their Limitations* (Cambridge University Press, 2012) ch 7 B–L.

[5] This formulation of the proportionality test is that of the Canadian *Oakes* test, which has been especially influential. See *R v Oakes* [1986] 1 SCR 103, [69]–[70]; and T Endicott, *Administrative Law* (3rd edn, Oxford University Press, 2015), 96–7.

[6] There are other formulations of the proportionality test, some of which divide it into three sub-tests. For a survey of such alternative formulations, see Urbina (n 1) ch 1.2. It seems to me that the four-part formulation of the test is the clearest and most explicit as to the requirements imposed by the test, and thus here I will use that formulation.

[7] This is Lord Wilson's oft-quoted formulation of the test in *R (Aguilar Quila) v The Secretary of State for the Home Department* [2012] 1 AC 621, [45]. See also *R (Nicklinson) v Ministry of Justice* [2014] UKSC 38; [2014] 3 WLR 200, [80], [120], [310], [337]; and *R (Conway) v Secretary State for Justice* [2017] EWHC 2447 (Admin), [78].

[8] *Bank Mellat v HM Treasury* [2013] UKSC 39; [2013] 3 WLR 179, [74].

The ECtHR, in addressing these issues, deploys the two-step analysis explained above.[9] The court has consistently viewed cases involving euthanasia and assisted suicide as concerning mostly the right to private life.[10] This right, as other rights in the European Convention on Human Rights, is formulated in relatively general terms, followed by a limitation clause. The limitation clause refers to the values for the sake of which the right may be limited, as well as other conditions for such limitation to be justified under the Convention. In the court's characteristic way of conceiving rights,[11] a great range of interests are understood to fall under 'private and family life', and thus to be within the scope of article 8. This includes the kinds of interests involved in the decision to terminate one's life. Thus, for example, in *Pretty v United Kingdom*, the ECtHR, after examining its extensive jurisprudence on the broadness of the concept of 'private life' in article 8,[12] concluded that:

> The applicant in this case is prevented by law from exercising her choice to avoid what she considers will be an undignified and distressing end to her life. The Court is not prepared to exclude that this constitutes an interference with her right to respect for private life as guaranteed under Article 8 § 1 of the Convention. It considers below whether this interference conforms with the requirements of the second paragraph of Article 8.[13]

The statement that the applicant's right for private life has been interfered with raises the question of whether this 'interference with the right', as the court puts it, can be justified on the terms of the limitation clause contained in article 8(2). The question then is whether an interference with 'private life' is in accordance with the law, and, crucially, 'necessary

[9] Which follows more or less from the drafting of the provision that is of most relevance to these cases: article 8 of the European Convention on Human Rights. Article 8 reads as follows:

> 1. Everyone has the right to respect for his private and family life, his home and his correspondence.
> 2. There shall be no interference by a public authority with the exercise of this right except such as is in accordance with the law and is necessary in a democratic society in the interests of national security, public safety or the economic well-being of the country, for the prevention of disorder or crime, for the protection of health or morals, or for the protection of the rights and freedoms of others.

[10] Other rights are commonly discussed in these types of cases. Lord Neuberger, eg, affirms in *Nicklinson* that: 'The two most central rights contained in the Convention for the purposes of the present appeals are in articles 2 and 8. Article 2, in summary form, guarantees the right to life, and, unsurprisingly, it is an unqualified right. Article 8.1 entitles everyone to "respect for his private … life". This right is qualified' (*Nicklinson* [27]). Yet, while UK courts and the ECtHR have come to see art 8 as being interfered with by restrictions on euthanasia or assisted suicide, they have understood the right to life in more restricted terms, as not stretching to the point where it could include a right to terminate one's life or to receive assistance in doing so. See, eg, *Nicklinson* [58], [60] (Lord Neuberger, presenting the 'issues raised by the appeals' exclusively in terms of art 8), and *Pretty v United Kingdom* (2002) 35 EHRR 1, [39]–[42].

[11] According to Tsakyrakis, the court applies what he calls the 'principle of definitional generosity', which consists in assuming 'a broad definition of what can conceivably count as an instance of the exercise of a certain right'. S Tsakyrakis, 'Proportionality: An Assault on Human Rights?' (2009) 7 International Journal of Constitutional Law 468, 481.

[12] 'The concept of "private life" is a broad term not susceptible of exhaustive definition.' See *Pretty* [61]. After providing several examples of diverse interests protected by art 8, the court concludes: 'Although no previous case has established as such any right to self-determination as being contained in Article 8 of the Convention, the Court considers that the notion of personal autonomy is an important principle underlying the interpretation of its guarantees' (ibid).

[13] *Pretty* [67]. In *Haas v Switzerland* (2011) 53 EHRR 33, [51], the court was more emphatic, affirming that

> an individual's right to decide by what means and at what point his or her life will end, provided he or she is capable of freely reaching a decision on this question and acting in consequence, is one of the aspects of the right to respect for private life within the meaning of article 8 of the Convention.

The same statement is repeated in subsequent decisions involving end-of-life debates. See, eg, *Koch v Germany* (2013) 56 EHRR 6, [52].

in a democratic society' for the pursuit of one of the values mentioned in the limitation clause. The ECtHR has consistently understood that the latter entails a requirement of proportionality.[14]

UK courts have adopted a similar approach in deciding whether legislation and prosecutorial policy contravene human rights in cases involving euthanasia and assisted suicide, since those cases are brought under the Human Rights Act 1998, which gives internal legal effect to most rights of the European Convention. Thus, although the House of Lords in *Pretty* did not find that the right to private life was engaged, it addressed the question of whether the measure would have been justified nevertheless.[15] Subsequent cases have adopted the framework of the ECtHR, namely, have assumed that legal prohibitions of euthanasia and assisted suicide constitute an interference with a human right,[16] and have proceeded to address whether this interference can be regarded as unjustified.[17] In establishing this, UK courts will use the four-part proportionality test.[18] Similarly, the Canadian Supreme Court is known for using proportionality to adjudicate cases involving so-called limitations or interferences with rights,[19] and cases related to euthanasia and assisted suicide constitute no exception to this.[20]

II. Legitimate Aim, Rational Connection, and Necessity

As is often the case with proportionality analysis, it is not difficult for the challenged measures to pass the first of proportionality's sub-tests. Thus, laws and other government

[14] 'According to the Court's established case-law, the notion of necessity implies that the interference corresponds to a pressing social need and, in particular, that it is proportionate to the legitimate aim pursued' (*Pretty* [70]).

[15] *R (Pretty) v Director of Public Prosecutions* [2001] UKHL 61; [2002] 1 AC 800, [26]–[30]. The Lords did not rely explicitly on the four-part proportionality test, which at the time had not been as clearly received in UK human rights law as it later was. See below n 18.

[16] With the caveat that there is some discussion in *Nicklinson* regarding how rights and their limitations are conceptualized. Lord Mance offered an alternative interpretation of the scope and force of the right in art 8: 'article 8.1 is, on the authority of *Pretty v United Kingdom*, engaged in this area. But it does not by itself create a right. A right only exists (at least in any coherent sense) if and when it is concluded under article 8.2 that there is no justification for a ban or restriction' (*Nicklinson* [159]). See also ibid [263] (Lord Hughes). Lord Sumption also challenges the idea that art 8.1 entails a right to certain end-of-life decisions as expressed by the ECtHR, suggesting that rather it contains 'an immunity from interference by the state' (though it is unclear why this immunity could not be aptly termed a 'right'). Confront with Lord Wilson's treatment of the same question, referring to 'a positive legal *right* to commit suicide' (*Nicklinson* [200] (emphasis in the original)). Yet, the kind of analysis deployed in this decision seems to be unaffected by whether one reserves or not the word 'right' for after the process of justification under art 8.2. Some academic commentators have argued for a narrower understanding of rights à la Lord Mance, coupled with a rejection of proportionality reasoning, which entails a generous prima facie protection of the interests referred to by bills of rights at some initial point of the analysis. See G Webber, *The Negotiable Constitution: On the Limitation of Rights* (Cambridge University Press, 2009) ch 4; and Urbina (n 1) ch 9.

[17] Lord Neuberger's presentation of the issue in *Nicklinson* is characteristic of this approach: 'Section 2 interferes with the article 8 right of Applicants (as I have called them) to determine how and when they should die. Accordingly, it can only be a valid interference if it satisfies the requirements of article 8.2, i.e. if it is "necessary in a democratic society" for one or more of the purposes specified in that article' (*Nicklinson* [79] (Lord Neuberger)).

[18] Thus, eg, in *Nicklinson*, immediately after presenting the issue as involving determining whether the requirements established in art 8.2 are met (see n 17), Lord Neuberger asserts that: 'When considering whether legislative measures satisfy those requirements, "four questions generally arise", as Lord Wilson explained in *R (Aguilar Quila) v The Secretary of State for the Home Department* [2012] 1 AC 621, para 45' (referring to the four sub-tests of the proportionality test mentioned in text attached to n 7 above). *Nicklinson* [80].

[19] See VC Jackson, 'Constitutional Law in an Age of Proportionality' (2015) 124 Yale Law Journal 3094, 3111–20.

[20] See *Rodriguez v Canada (Attorney General)* [1993] 3 SCR 519; and *Carter v Canada (Attorney General)*, 2015 SCC 5, [2015] 1 SCR 331.

measures that may restrict or forbid assisted suicide or euthanasia are found to pursue a legitimate aim of sufficient importance: preventing abuse and, in particular, 'the perceived risk to the lives of other, vulnerable individuals who might feel themselves a burden to their family, friends or society and might, if assisted suicide were permitted, be persuaded or convince themselves that they should undertake it, when they would not otherwise do so'.[21] As the ECtHR notes, 'doubtless the condition of terminally ill individuals will vary. But many will be vulnerable and it is the vulnerability of the class which provides the rationale for the law in question'.[22] The protection of a social ecology where the value of life is upheld, as well as the promotion of trust between doctors and patients, have also been considered legitimate aims of norms that forbid euthanasia and assisted suicide.[23]

The second sub-test is also not a difficult one to pass. Restrictions on euthanasia and assisted suicide, particularly in the form of a blanket ban of these practices, are often seen as rationally connected to the aim of protecting vulnerable individuals.[24]

The third sub-test, however, can be more challenging. On the one hand, the necessity and balancing sub-tests (third and fourth sub-tests) are sometimes addressed together, without analytically distinguishing the different requirements imposed by each of the tests.[25] Kai Möller is right in this regard in observing that often a measure that is less detrimental to rights either realizes to a lesser degree its legitimate aim or does so at a greater cost. When this occurs, enquiry into less restrictive means can quickly lead into analysis of whether the increased realization of the aim or the lesser cost justify the additional interference with the right—the kind of analysis to be undertaken at the balancing stage.[26] On the other hand, the necessity sub-test raises difficult empirical questions, which in turn give rise to institutional questions concerning deference and restraint. True, the second sub-test also involves a factual assessment, but because its demands are easier to meet, difficult questions relating to the assessment of facts tend to be addressed more in relation to the two final sub-tests. Is the judicial branch capable of addressing the empirical evidence (if there is such evidence) necessary for determining whether an alternative scheme would be possible, viable, and not more detrimental to the affected rights while capable of delivering the relevant legitimate aim?[27] Is the judiciary better placed than the primary decision-maker in this regard (parliament and/or the executive)?[28] Is the primary decision-maker entitled to make a decision based on its judgment and independent assessment of the facts, even in the face of

[21] *Nicklinson* [171].

[22] *Pretty* [74]. See also *Carter* [78].

[23] *Conway* [91]–[94].

[24] In *Nicklinson*, this was accepted by both parties (see [82]). Lord Kerr was the only justice to argue that the measure lacked rational connection to the aim. See ibid [349]–[351]. Even in *Carter*, which held that the ban on medically assisted death was contrary to the Charter, it was accepted that the measure passed the rational connection test. See *Carter* [100]–[101].

[25] See D Grimm, 'Proportionality in Canadian and German Constitutional Jurisprudence' (2007) 57(2) University of Toronto Law Journal 383, 394–5.

[26] See K Möller, 'Proportionality: Challenging the Critics' (2012) 10(3) International Journal of Constitutional Law 709, 714.

[27] For a comprehensive study of the institutional capacities of courts for assessing empirical evidence in the context of cases involving fundamental rights (arriving at the conclusion that courts often lack the required capacities), see P Yowell, *Constitutional Rights and Constitutional Design: Moral and Empirical Reasoning in Judicial Review* (Hart Publishing, 2018).

[28] For a comparative analysis of epistemic capacities of courts and legislatures in relation to constitutional issues, see A Vermeule, *Law and the Limits of Reason* (Oxford University Press, 2008) (arguing against the claim that courts possess superior epistemic capacities).

inconclusive empirical evidence or lack of it?[29] If so, can courts revise that judgment, and on what grounds? Would they have the required legitimacy to do this?[30] And how strict should the assessment of the judiciary be, taking into account that 'as Blackmun J once observed, a judge would be unimaginative indeed if he could not come up with something a little less drastic or a little less restrictive in almost any situation ... especially, one might add, if he is unaware of the relevant practicalities and indifferent to considerations of cost'[31] and that a more lax approach would be in order 'if there is to be any real prospect of a limitation on rights being justified'?[32]

Medical law is a realm of difficult factual and normative questions, which sometimes concern the deeply held convictions of many people. This is particularly true of euthanasia and assisted suicide. Thus, the epistemic capacities and the legitimacy of decision-makers matter greatly. The ECtHR grants states an important margin of appreciation in deciding these matters.[33] In *Nicklinson*, most of the UK Supreme Court judges found strong institutional reasons for being especially deferential to other branches of government (crucially, parliament) and restrained in engaging with the difficult moral and factual questions arising from the case in a matter in which there is no social consensus. They also found reasons for deference in the case involving issuing complex directives the judicial body is ill-suited to produce and implement.[34] This affects the application of the proportionality test. As Lord Mance put it:

> It is in my view a mistake to approach proportionality as a test under the Human Rights Act which is insensitive to considerations of institutional competence and legitimacy... [S]ome judgments on issues such as the comparative acceptability of differing disadvantages, risks and benefits have to be and are made by those other branches of the state in the performance of their everyday roles, and ... courts cannot and should not act, and do not have the competence to act, as a primary decision-maker in every situation. Proportionality should in this respect be seen as a flexible doctrine.[35]

[29] See *Nicklinson* [232] (Lord Sumption) (referring, among others, to *Bank Mellat* [93]–[94] (Lord Reed)); and *Nicklinson* [348] (Lord Kerr), pointing to the fact that some matters 'may not be susceptible of categorical proof', particularly 'in the realm of social policy', which may 'call for a less exacting examination' of the measure reviewed.

[30] On the issue of legitimacy, see FJ Urbina, 'How Legislation Aids Human Rights Adjudication' in G Webber, P Yowell, R Ekins, et al, *Legislated Rights: Securing Human Rights Through Legislation* (Cambridge University Press, 2018), 166–7, 177–80.

[31] *Bank Mellat* [75] (Lord Reed).

[32] Ibid.

[33] *Pretty* [70]–[71], [87]; *Haas* [55]; *Koch* [70].

[34] The majority of the Supreme Court in *Nicklinson* offered institutional considerations against a declaration of incompatibility in this case. Partly because of this sort of consideration, Lords Neuberger, Mance, Wilson, and Reed thought that it would be inappropriate to issue a declaration of incompatibility and that the views of Parliament should be given considerable weight. See *Nicklinson* [113]–[118] (Lord Neuberger); [164]–[170], [188]–[190] (Lord Mance); [197](c), (d) (Lord Wilson); and [296]–[298] (Lord Reed). Lord Sumption was joined by Lord Hughes in thinking that not only institutional considerations militate against a declaration of incompatibility in this case, but that the end-of-life questions posed by the case are 'a classic example of the kind of issue that should be decided by Parliament' (ibid [230]). See also [231]–[235] (Lord Sumption) and [259], [267] (Lord Hughes). Lord Clarke struck a somewhat intermediate position between the two previous groups, but relied explicitly on institutional considerations expressed by Lords Mance and Sumption. See ibid [293]. For some of the justices, the fact that 'the appellants' primary case has become not to "invite the Supreme Court to embark upon a close study of the evidence that is now available of the relative risks and advantages of relaxing the prohibitions on assisted suicide" but instead to submit that the Supreme Court "can strike the necessary balance without such a forensic exercise"' (ibid [178] (Lord Mance)) also played a role in determining the degree of judicial deference appropriate in this case. See ibid and [126]–[127] (Lord Neuberger), [201]–[202] (Lord Wilson). But confront this with ibid [234] (Lord Sumption).

[35] *Nicklinson* [166] (Lord Mance).

The approach of the UK Supreme Court in *Nicklinson* contrasts with that of the Canadian Supreme Court in *Carter*.[36] In *Carter*, the Supreme Court of Canada (SCC) found that a blanket ban on assisted suicide and euthanasia was unconstitutional on account of it entailing a violation of section 7 of the Canadian Charter of Rights and Freedoms (right to life, liberty, and to the security of the person) that was not justifiable under section 1 of the Charter. In determining whether the law justifiably interfered with the rights of the applicants, the court applies the proportionality test. In *Carter*, the trial judge had determined that the challenged legal provisions failed the necessity sub-test: 'After reviewing the evidence, she concluded that a permissive regime with properly designed and administered safeguards was capable of protecting vulnerable people from abuse and error.'[37] The Supreme Court relied on the conclusions on the facts established at the trial stage and, thus, concurred with the trial judge in finding that the measures in question failed the necessity sub-test.[38]

There is little discussion of institutional considerations in *Carter*. The court acknowledges that 'courts must accord the legislature a measure of deference', and that 'proportionality does not require perfection', but rather that limits imposed by legislation on rights be 'reasonable', recalling previous case law, where the court 'emphasized that there may be a number of possible solutions to a particular social problem, and suggested that a "complex regulatory response" to a social ill will garner a high degree of deference'.[39] The court agrees with the trial judge, who noted that 'physician-assisted death involves complex issues of social policy and a number of competing societal values', and that 'Parliament faces a difficult task in addressing this issue', concluding that 'it follows that a high degree of deference is owed to Parliament's decision to impose an absolute prohibition on assisted death'. Yet, '[o]n the other hand … the absolute prohibition could not be described as a "complex regulatory response". The degree of deference owed to Parliament, while high, is accordingly reduced'.[40]

These are rather vague statements which point in different directions, leaving matters notoriously unsettled. They could play the role of preliminary remarks, to be further specified as they are applied to the case. Yet, the remarks on institutional considerations just reproduced have no bearing in the proportionality reasoning of the court and, crucially, in establishing that the measure fails the necessity sub-test. For the court, it is 'the task of the trial judge to determine whether a regime less restrictive of life, liberty and security of the person could address the risks associated with physician-assisted dying'.[41] There may be good legal-procedural reasons for this, yet this leaves open the question of whether courts have appropriate institutional capacities to address such crucial and factually complex matters, and whether these can be best addressed at the level of the single trial judge rather than parliament or the executive. The court side-lines these questions by adopting the factual

[36] In other respects, the approaches are not opposed. Part of the reasons of some of the judges in *Nicklinson* relate to the fact that the court (as the lower courts and the Secretary of State) did not have the opportunity to assess evidence as to whether 'there was a physically and administratively feasible and robust system whereby Applicants could be assisted to kill themselves' (*Nicklinson* [120]); in *Carter*, the point of the SCC is that the lower court did have the opportunity to assess the relevant evidence.

[37] *Carter* [105].

[38] Ibid [102]–[109].

[39] Ibid [97].

[40] Ibid [98] (citation omitted).

[41] Ibid [103].

conclusions of the trial judge[42] and by granting to these a high level of deference,[43] without sustained discussion of who is better placed to make the decisions involved in the case.

It is in this respect that there is a strong contrast between *Nicklinson* and *Carter*. And the contrast favours the former. It is surely relevant in this case whether courts have the capacity for processing such complex factual information, whether they have the legitimacy for making controversial moral and political decisions, and how said capacities and legitimacy compare to those of other bodies, particularly to those of the legislature. The factual element (especially in addressing the third sub-test, but also in relation to the second and fourth sub-tests) in proportionality, as we saw above, gives rise to some of these questions, and it is best to tackle them directly. Both the minority or the majority of the judges in *Nicklinson* displayed an awareness of the institutional question that is largely absent in *Carter*.

III. Balancing or Proportionality *Stricto Sensu*

The last sub-test (balancing or *proportionality stricto sensu*) is often referred to as the most characteristic and 'important of proportionality's tests'.[44] It is at this stage where the costs that the measure under review would entail for a right are compared to its potential benefits to a public good or other rights. The point of this comparison is often formulated in terms that are tautological: the measure would fail the *proportionality stricto sensu* sub-test if the costs of the measure to a right are *disproportionate* to the benefits of the measure (the achievement of its legitimate aim).[45] This leaves room for different accounts of proportionality.[46] Yet, in further expressing the demands both of the proportionality test and of its fourth sub-test, courts often signal that what would be ultimately required is a quantitative comparison (a comparison in terms such as 'more', 'less', or 'equal') of the costs of the measure for the affected right and the benefits in terms of its legitimate aim, such that the benefits must at least be equal to the costs, or, as a leading commentator puts it, it must be the case that 'the gain to the public interest at least balances out the cost to the right'.[47] Thus, in the seminal and oft-quoted Canadian *Oakes* case, shortly after characterizing the last sub-test in terms of demanding that there is 'a proportionality' between the costs to the engaged right and the benefits of the measure, the Supreme Court of Canada explains that what the balancing sub-test requires is that 'the more severe the deleterious effects of a measure, the more important the objective must be'.[48]

[42] Ibid [102]–[121].

[43] Ibid [109].

[44] Barak (n 4) 340. For similar statements, see, eg, M Klatt and M Meister, *The Constitutional Structure of Proportionality* (Oxford University Press, 2012), 6; R Ekins, 'Legislating Proportionately' in G Huscroft, B Miller, and G Webber (eds), *Proportionality and the Rule of Law: Rights, Justification, Reasoning* (Cambridge University Press, 2014), 343.

[45] For examples of such formulations, see above, nn 5 and 8. See also Case C-112/00, *Schmidberger Internationale Transporte und Planzüge v Austria* [2003] ECR I-5659, [81], [90].

[46] See Urbina (n 1) 9–12.

[47] J Rivers, 'Proportionality and Variable Intensity of Review' (2006) 65 Cambridge Law Journal 174, 177. Rivers also characterizes the balancing sub-test as involving the more demanding requirement that the measure 'represent[s] a net gain, when the reduction in enjoyment of rights is weighed against the level of realisation of the aim' (ibid 181). Yet, the nature of the comparison (a quantitative comparison of costs and benefits) is the same.

[48] *Oakes* [71].

Cases involving euthanasia and assisted suicide convey a similar understanding of the balancing sub-test. In *Pretty v UK*, for example, the ECtHR said that 'the more serious the harm involved the more heavily will weigh in the balance considerations of public health and safety against the countervailing principle of personal autonomy'.[49] And in *Conway*, a recent decision of the UK High Court that is exceptional in the clarity and ingenuity with which it performs the proportionality analysis, the ban on assisted suicide and euthanasia is said to pass the balancing stage on the grounds of a comparison with previous judicial decisions that also upheld the ban. Thus, the High Court notes that 'Mr. Conway is expected to die soon and the evidence about the palliative care available to him indicates that that Mr Conway's interests are less badly affected by the interference with his Article 8 rights . . . than was the case in relation to Mr Nicklinson, Mr Lamb, and Mr Martin [the plaintiffs in previous cases]'. Therefore, 'the same public interest . . . is present in this case, but the price to be imposed on Mr Conway and people in his position to secure that interest is lower'.[50]

This way of addressing the issue entails a comparison between costs and benefits, demanding that there is at least no net loss. An interference with a right is justified *by reference to* a benefit to a public good or other right. The benefit must be greater or at least of the same magnitude than the cost.[51] Establishing this requires the comparison of the relative weights of benefits and costs at the balancing sub-test.

All this is problematic as an approach to human or constitutional rights, for three reasons. First, it is unclear that the costs and benefits can be compared in this way. How do we establish that the burden on the interests of the applicants is sufficiently matched by some gain for other persons? For example, how does one establish whether a specific level of deterrence in forced marriages is more or equal to the burden imposed on the family life of the set of married couples affected by a measure whereby a foreign spouse is denied permission to enter or remain in the country?[52] This is the incommensurability objection that has been levelled against balancing.[53]

Second, and more important, the balancing approach entails a form of addressing the conflict that does away with rights. Determining the intensity and extension of the interests on the different sides of the equation is different from determining what is each person's due—what is it that the parties are entitled to as a matter of their rights? As a result, the special normative force that is often attributed to rights in moral and legal discourse and practice is also lost: the interests purportedly protected by human rights can be legitimately interfered with, as long as there are corresponding benefits deriving from that interference. They can also feature as mere legitimate aims of state action—again, as aims that can be freely traded-off against other interests interfered with by the measure.[54]

[49] *Pretty* [74].

[50] *Conway* [117]. Another related reason to find the measure proportionate is that the blanket ban on assisted suicide had been confirmed as compatible with the rights scheduled to the Human Rights Act 1998 and in the European Convention, in cases involving patients suffering from the same condition as Mr Conway, both by the House of Lords and by the ECtHR. See *Conway* [115].

[51] For a further elaboration of this point, see Urbina (n 1) 35–8.

[52] See ibid 53 and *Quila*.

[53] See Webber (n 16) 89–100; and Urbina (n 1) ch 3. For a related critique of proportionality, but drawing on Ruth Chang's theory of 'parity' rather than on incommensurability, see C Caviedes, 'Chang's Parity: An Alternative Way to Challenge Balancing' (2017) 62(2) American Journal of Jurisprudence 165–95. The most elaborate and influential defence of proportionality against this objection remains V Afonso da Silva, 'Comparing the Incommensurable: Constitutional Principles, Balancing and Rational Decision' (2011) 31 Oxford Journal of Legal Studies 273.

[54] For the rights-based critique of proportionality, see Urbina (n 1) ch 5. See also Tsakyrakis (n 11).

Now, if the reasons for and against euthanasia and assisted suicide were purely about consequences, then there would be nothing troublesome in the balancing framing of the issue. If rights are not at stake, then there is no deficiency in not taking rights into account—though there would be a deficiency in conveying the misleading impression that these are (human) *rights* cases. But many arguments in the euthanasia debate, and perhaps the more influential ones on both sides of the debate, are not consequentialists. Some focus on the inalienability of the right to life,[55] or on the strength and scope of a right to 'make momentous personal decisions'.[56] Others are deontological in structure, pointing to our duties not to perform certain types of actions, such that it would be always wrong to intentionally kill another human being and thus there can be no right to euthanasia or assisted suicide (and, rather, there is a right to be protected from intentional harm to one's life).[57] This does not mean that consequences do not matter at all, but that rights—an especially strong kind of reason—play a role, and methods for deciding on medically assisted dying need to be sensitive to them. Yet, from the perspective of this challenge to proportionality, the test would do away with rights by treating claims of rights merely as standing for interests, values, or principles to be maximized and traded-off against opposing interests, values, or principles, rather than as the particularly strong reasons that rights are supposed to be.

Third, it can be asked whether proportionality is an apt legal tool, suitable for judicial use. At the crucial balancing stage, it provides no guidance as to how to perform this complex exercise. As a result, judicial determinations of balancing are accused of being often impressionistic[58] and opaque.[59] Note, in this respect, how the balancing exercise in the *Conway* case mentioned above is exceptionally clear by virtue of deploying a specifically legal form of reasoning, which is only accidentally related to proportionality. In *Conway*, the UK High Court was confronted with the case of 'a person with a serious wasting disease who wishes to commit suicide'.[60] The court notes that *Conway* 'follows a line of cases that have addressed that or similar issues', including *Nicklinson* and *R (Pretty) v Director of Public Prosecutions*. The court concludes that the measure passes the proportionality assessment. In particular, the balancing stage favours the measure under review on the grounds that said measure had both been found acceptable in previous decisions of a superior court and, in relation to those previous cases, the situation of the applicants was better (thus his interests were less burdened), while the public benefit was the same.[61] This decision solves the difficult problem of determining when the benefits are sufficient to justify the costs of the measure—when are they not 'outweighed' by the costs or in 'disproportion' to them—by finding a secure point of departure in an authoritative settlement of the question (in the precedent

[55] See, eg, J Feinberg, 'Voluntary Euthanasia and the Inalienable Right to Life' (1978) 7(2) Philosophy and Public Affairs 93–123.

[56] R Dworkin, T Nagel, R Nozick, et al, 'Assisted Suicide: The Philosopher's Brief', *The New York Review of Books* (27 March 1997), http://www.nybooks.com/articles/1997/03/27/assisted-suicide-the-philosophers-brief/ accessed 15 July 2019.

[57] See, eg, J Keown, *Euthanasia, Ethics, and Public Policy: An Argument against Legalisation* (Cambridge University Press, 2002), 40.

[58] Tsakyrakis (n 11) 482. See also J Finnis, 'Human Rights and Their Enforcement' in *Human Rights and the Common Good: Collected Essays of John Finnis* (Oxford University Press, 2011), vol III, 44–5; and J Finnis, 'Endorsing Discrimination between Faiths: A Case of Extreme Speech?' in I Hare and J Weinstein (eds), *Extreme Speech and Democracy* (Oxford University Press, 2009), 430, 433.

[59] T Endicott, 'Proportionality and Incommensurability' in G Huscroft, B Miller, and G Webber (eds), *Proportionality and the Rule of Law: Rights, Justification, Reasoning* (Cambridge University Press, 2014), 311–28.

[60] *Conway* [2].

[61] Ibid [116]–[118].

provided by previous decisions), establishing a proportion of benefits and costs deemed acceptable. After this is undertaken, the question is mainly one of analogy, establishing that this case falls under the same type as the case already settled, and of applying the legal consequence determined by the previous cases. Both these operations are specifically legal and different from the substantive assessment of costs and benefits, or of the 'weights' of rights and public goods, required by the balancing sub-test.

Yet, balancing is still problematic. It is problematic for the original decision on which subsequent decisions may rely, and also on account of the fact that, by inviting ad hoc weighing based on the circumstances, balancing renders unstable this use of precedent. In *Conway*, the circumstances had changed in a way that allowed for its efficacious use of precedents in performing the balancing exercise. But this was a very specific situation (though not necessarily a rare one), characterized by the conjunction of two circumstances: the applicants were in a more favourable position than those in the previous cases, and in the previous cases the challenged measure had been upheld. Had it been different, this is, had either the applicants in *Conway* been in a worse situation than those in the previous cases, or had the public benefit been achieved to a lesser degree than in those cases, or had the previous decisions not upheld uniformly the measure under review, for example, the High Court would not have been able to rely so strongly on precedents and would have had to engage in substantive balancing reasoning.

Of course, it could be argued that the flexibility of proportionality is one of its advantages. But the claim here is not that proportionality is too flexible, but rather that it entails a form of addressing conflicts that is unsuitable for legal reasoning and unhelpful on account of its vagueness. If its flexibility were an advantage, it would be an advantage that would come at a price.[62]

IV. Proportionality in Medical Law and Ethics—Beyond Balancing

It is useful to remember that the idea of proportionality can be instantiated in different ways. Perhaps the most prominent today is the four-pronged test used in human rights disputes. Yet, proportionality can mean other things and apply in other contexts. Depending on the context to which it is applied, some version of proportionality and some form of balancing can raise less institutional and moral concerns than the proportionality tests applied in human or constitutional rights judicial review. In certain contexts, proportionality can be adequate (in giving expression to a morally relevant requirement that bears on a given choice in that context, without leaving out other relevant considerations) and useful (in aiding decision making in conforming to such a morally relevant requirement, in circumstances where, if proportionality were not adopted, the requirement would go unfulfilled or would be fulfilled to a lesser degree).

In the domain of medical law and ethics, medical research involving human subjects provides a useful contrast to the use of proportionality in human rights law. The World Medical Association produced the Declaration of Helsinki (1964, though regularly

[62] For a more detailed account of the kinds of deficiencies of open-ended balancing reasoning, see Urbina (n 1) chs 7, 8.

revised and last amended in 2013). Although the Declaration is not hard law, in some places, as in the United Kingdom, 'it has become the benchmark against which current ... research projects are measured'.[63] Articles 17 and 18 establish duties of physicians and researchers to carefully monitor and assess the risks, burdens, and benefits of research, and to contain and manage the risks. Article 16 states: 'Medical research involving human subjects may only be conducted if the importance of the objective outweighs the risks and burdens to the research subjects.' This is sometimes characterized as a proportionality requirement.[64]

This use of the idea of proportionality is less controversial. Above, I presented four challenges to proportionality: institutional considerations, inaptness for judicial reasoning, incommensurability, and lack of attention to rights. Of the four, only incommensurability may continue to present a challenge, and in an attenuated form.

The first two problems can be addressed together here. The proportionality reasoning demanded by the Declaration is not inapt for the kind of ethical deliberation in which physicians and researchers need to engage. It requires that their deliberation on choices regarding medical experimentation addresses matters they are well (probably uniquely well) positioned to evaluate, matters which they are habituated to evaluate as consubstantial to any medical decision, such as the impact of a given treatment, its risks and burdens for the patient/subject, and its potential health benefits. Proportionality here does not constitute, nor aims to replace, specific medical knowledge, which will factor into the process in determining the specific benefits, burdens, and risks of the experimental treatment. Thus, questions arising from epistemic capacities such as those relating to the factual element of the four-part proportionality test are not present. Physicians and medical researchers (those primarily tasked with evaluating the research project involving human subjects and thus engaging in the balancing exercise required by the Declaration) are well suited to engage with the issues regulated by the Declaration.[65]

The balancing required by the Declaration does not raise a question of rights, but of the well-being of the patient, as the balancing that is required entails weighing the importance of the objective against the risks and burdens of the research 'to the research subjects' (article 16). The question of rights appears in thinking whose interests should have priority in a case of a conflict of interests of different persons. If, for example, subjecting a patient to a given experimental treatment would entail more risks and burdens than benefits for that patient, yet other persons would stand to win from the knowledge acquired through such course of action, there would be a question as to whose interests should prevail. But *this* question is removed from the balancing process by the Declaration, which rightly focuses its proportionality requirement on the assessment of advantages and disadvantages for one person: the patient.[66] The question of rights, thus, is resolved in favour of the patient, whose

[63] S Mclean, *Medical Law and Ethics* (Ashgate, 2002), 607, quoted in J Herring, *Medical Law and Ethics* (6th edn, Oxford University Press, 2016), 616.

[64] See Herring (n 63) 616; and RV Carlson, KM Boyd, and DJ Webb, 'The Revision of the Declaration of Helsinki' (2004) 57(6) British Journal of Clinical Pharmacology 695, 709.

[65] Though there may be still a problem of motivation, this is, of willing to adopt the right course of action, since the researcher may have conflicting interests (an interest in preserving the health of the patient which could be opposed to an interest in pursuing the research project, and in advancing the career of the researcher). This motivational problem also raises institutional considerations, but the problem is not tied specifically to balancing reasoning (in the way institutional issues *are* associated to balancing in the context of human rights) and would be present whatever the method for establishing the moral or legal acceptability of experimental research.

[66] This kind of 'balancing' reasoning is at least pertinent when what is balanced is referred to one single subject, one locus of value and respect. When there are more individuals at stake, the primary question becomes not one of

'best interests' are to be the physician's 'first consideration' (article 3), while the goal of 'generating new knowledge ... can never take precedence over the rights and interests of individual research subjects' (article 8).

In many choice situations concerning medical experimentation, there may not be incommensurability, as it is possible that they concern similar aspects of health, which could be ranked as more severe or important, or less. Yet, in some cases, there may be incommensurability (as when possible outcomes of the trial are a healthier life and/or a potentially shorter one for the patient). Yet, incommensurability does not preclude choice, not even rational choice. Incommensurability only entails that some choices *may* be reasonably underdetermined. If the alternatives appear as neither better nor worse nor equal on the grounds of incommensurability, and there is value in choosing any of the alternatives, then it is reasonable to choose an alternative—the value of the alternative justifying that particular choice even if it does not preclude another choice, which would also have been reasonable.[67] Incommensurability, it must be remembered, grounds an objection to a form of *reviewing* certain choices, on the ground that such a form of reviewing choices presupposes that the primary decision-maker could have *balanced* wrongly, when attention to incommensurability precludes that possibility.[68] Such is a contingent feature of the institutional context and of the specific way in which proportionality is applied in certain settings. It could be that in applying the Declaration an ethical panel reviewing a medical choice treats it as if it had acted on the wrong balance of benefits, risks, and burdens, when in sound moral reasoning incommensurability should have been acknowledged as entailing a greater level of indeterminacy of the choice, and thus as allowing discretion in judgment. But this is not a necessary feature of the balancing required by the Declaration, which is 'addressed primarily to physicians' (article 2), which are, at least typically, primary decision-makers.

V. Conclusion

Proportionality features in several areas of law and morality. Medical law and ethics are no exception. From a normative point of view, proportionality requirements may or may not be adequate and useful. In medical law, proportionality features prominently in cases commonly involving human rights in a medical context. Here, the use of proportionality receives the same evaluation than it receives in human rights in general. Despite its prevalence in human rights adjudication worldwide, proportionality is open to important challenges. Yet, less controversial uses of proportionality are possible, particularly in the medical domain. The use of proportionality in medical research involving human subjects provides one illustration of this.

weighing costs and benefits, but of establishing right relations between individuals. I offer a more detailed explanation of this in *A Critique of Proportionality and Balancing* (n 1) ch 5.4.

67 See ibid 45–6.
68 See ibid 73–4.

12

Priority Setting, Judicial Review, and Procedural Justice

Daniel Wang and Benedict Rumbold

I. Introduction

Priority setting, as it is understood here, describes the allocation of resources directed to health and health care across different population groups by some designated decision-maker(s). This is taken to include: 'macro'-level allocations such as the decision about the size of the national budget for health care; 'meso'-level allocations at local level between, say, different services and treatments across medical specialities; and 'micro'-level allocations between, say, individual patients within a clinical setting (sometimes referred to as 'bed-side rationing'). Although one might think of each of these levels as independent, decision-makers at each level are routinely constrained by decisions made at the levels above.

Priority setting might be seen as a function of three conditions common to all health-care systems: a scarcity of available resources; a demand for health care that outstrips supply; and a funding system that assigns authority for allocating resources across population groups to some decision-maker or set of decision-makers (referred to here as 'priority setters').[1] If there is a ubiquitous need to set priorities, then the question of how to meet health needs fairly when we cannot meet them all becomes of central importance for health systems, including the best-funded ones.[2] This imperative to set priorities fairly is partly moral: where resource constraints entail that the decision to fund interventions benefiting one population group will necessarily come at the cost of others, the affected parties are entitled to know the decision was justified.[3] However, the requirement can also be a legal one. For example, the right to health, as expressed in the International Covenant on Economic, Social and Cultural Rights, engenders an obligation that states make every possible effort, within available resources, to guarantee the right of everyone to the enjoyment of the highest attainable standard of physical and mental health.[4] As made clear in General Comment 14, arguably an authoritative interpretation of the human right to health, this requires that trade-offs between ensuring effective interventions—including between health-care services, public health policies, and tackling the social determinants of health—are made fairly.[5]

[1] World Health Organization, 'Making Fair Choices on the Path to Universal Health Coverage' (2014), http://apps.who.int/iris/bitstream/10665/112671/1/9789241507158_eng.pdf?ua=1 accessed 15 July 2019.

[2] N Daniels, *Just Health: Meeting Health Needs Fairly* (Cambridge University Press, 2008).

[3] B Rumbold, A Weale, A Rid et al, 'Public Reasoning and Health Care Priority Setting: The Case of NICE' (2017) 27(1) Kennedy Institute for Ethics Journal 107–34; cf Daniels (n 2) 109.

[4] UN General Assembly, International Covenant on Economic, Social and Cultural Rights (16 December 1966), http://www.ohchr.org/EN/ProfessionalInterest/Pages/CESCR.aspx accessed 15 July 2019.

[5] UN Committee on Economic, Social and Cultural Rights, General Comment 14—'The Right to the Highest Attainable Standard of Health' (art 12 of the Covenant), 11 August 2000 (UN Doc E/C.12/2000/4), para 19, http://www.refworld.org/docid/4538838d0.html accessed 15 July 2019; B Rumbold, R Baker, O Ferraz, et al,

Daniel Wang and Benedict Rumbold, *Priority Setting, Judicial Review, and Procedural Justice* In: *Philosophical Foundations of Medical Law*. Edited by: Andelka M Phillips, Thana C de Campos, and Jonathan Herring, Oxford University Press (2019).

DOI: 10.1093/oso/9780198796558.003.0013

Needless to say, what constitutes a fair allocation of resources continues to be a subject of extensive controversy. Two broad kinds of approaches dominate this discussion: *substantive* and *procedural*. Substantive approaches look first to the outcome of an allocation. On this approach, what is important from the perspective of justice is the extent to which the outcome of a given allocation adheres to some substantive principle of distributive justice—for example, utilitarianism (maximizing total benefits), prioritarianism (favouring the worst-off), or egalitarianism (treating people equally).[6] Procedural approaches, by contrast, look instead to the way in which any given allocation is made. On this approach, what is important from the perspective of justice is not necessarily the outcome of an allocation, but the procedure by which the allocation was arrived at. The most influential procedural approach to fair allocation in health care is probably Daniels and Sabin's 'Accountability for Reasonableness', which will be discussed later in this chapter.

This is the background against which this chapter discusses the judicial accountability of priority-setting decisions made in the English National Health Service (NHS). In section II, we show how English courts see their role in the control of priority-setting decisions primarily as directed towards matters of procedure rather than matters of substance. Using arguments from the philosophical literature, in section III, we then explain how such an approach to judicial accountability might be justified, drawing in particular on arguments around priority setting's 'procedural turn' and the idea that we might ensure just priority setting through just processes—'Accountability for Reasonableness' being one possible example. In section IV, we temper this analysis by arguing that courts' reliance upon the substance/procedure distinction will also attract to judicial review another set of problems that have been raised in the philosophical literature with regard to the idea of securing just priority setting through procedural means. We conclude in section V that, although the courts' procedural approach to judicial accountability with regard to priority-setting decisions will find support in the philosophical literature's 'procedural turn', much argumentative work remains if we are to offer a robust justification of the courts' approach in England.

II. Priority Setting and Legal Accountability in England

In England, courts enforce priority setters' legal accountability in various ways: in the interrogation of discretionary allocative decisions; in the interpretation and enforcement of statutory law; and in the determination of the legal duties that health professionals owe to their patients. In this section, we consider how English courts have conceived priority setters' legal accountability for discretionary allocative choices and, in particular, how they have understood their role in holding priority setters accountable for the fairness of their decisions.

As with judicial challenges to allocative decisions in social policy more generally, courts adjudicating in this area routinely find themselves caught in the dilemma between

'Viewpoint: Universal Health Coverage, Priority Setting and the Human Right to Health' (2017) 390 Lancet 712–14.

[6] Daniels (n 2); G Persad, A Wertheimer, and E Emanuel, 'Principles for Allocation of Scarce Medical Interventions' (2009) 373 Lancet 423–31.

'usurpation' (substituting their own policy preferences for the prevailing political or administrative views) and 'abdication' (ceding to political and executive bodies a *carte blanche* to decide about the provision of services).[7] The boundaries of what constitutes a case of 'usurpation' or 'abdication' are obviously debatable, and are largely determined by one's views as to the domains within which courts possess the requisite institutional competence and constitutional legitimacy. With regard to priority-setting decisions in the NHS, English courts have tried to avoid both accusations by drawing a distinction between matters of substance *versus* matter of procedure. Thus, what we see in the jurisprudence around priority-setting decisions is a marked reluctance for the courts to adjudicate on the merits of the outcome of a particular decision, or the substantive principles upon which it was decided, while they will hold decision-makers to account with regard to the fairness of their decision-making procedure.

In explicating the English system, perhaps the first thing to note is that English courts, as opposed to the Judiciary in some other jurisdictions,[8] have never recognized a patient's enforceable right to a particular level of care from the NHS or an unqualified right to the funding of specific treatments.[9] English courts have accepted that the provision of care can be legally denied for reasons of health professionals' clinical judgment[10] and that courts should not interfere with matters of expert clinical judgment if a decision is properly taken and adequate reasons are given, even when there is scope for different views.[11] Moreover, even when professionals are willing to administer a treatment to which a patient consents and to certificate that there is a potential benefit for the patient, this does not create a duty for the NHS to fund it.[12] Rather, courts have accepted that health authorities can deny or restrict the funding of treatments on the grounds of scarcity of resources and the need to set priorities. As stated by the Court of Appeal in *Child B*:

> They [health authorities] cannot pay their nurses as much as they would like, they cannot provide all the treatments they would like; they cannot purchase all the extremely expensive medical equipment they would like; they cannot carry out all the research they would like; they cannot build all the hospitals and specialist units they would like. Difficult and agonizing judgements have to be made as to how a limited budget is best allocated to the maximum advantage of the maximum number of patients.[13]

As well as recognizing that priorities have to be set, courts have also held that they are not in the best position to make priority-setting decisions.[14] In several judgments, the courts have

[7] F Michelman, 'The Constitution, Social Rights, and Liberal Political Justification' (2003) 1(1) International Journal of Constitutional Law 13–34, 16.

[8] A Yamin and S Gloppen (eds), *Litigating Health Rights* (Harvard University Press, 2011); D Wang, 'Right to Health Litigation in Brazil: The Problem and the Institutional Responses' (2015) 15(4) Human Rights Law Review 617–41.

[9] *R (Dyer) v The Welsh Ministers and Others* [2015] EWHC 3712 (Admin), 17.

[10] In *Burke, R (on the application of) v General Medical Council and Others* [2005] EWCA Civ 1003, the Court of Appeal ruled that a doctor does not have the legal obligation to provide a treatment demanded by the patient if the professional considers it not to be clinically indicated.

[11] *SB, R (on the application of) v NHS England* [2017] EWHC 2000 (Admin), 28.

[12] The only exception are the drugs approved by NICE. According to the NHS Constitution: 'You have the right to drugs and treatments that have been recommended by NICE for use in the NHS, if your doctor says they are clinically appropriate for you.'

[13] *R v Cambridge Health Authority, ex p B* [1995] 2 All ER 129; [1995] 1 WLR 898.

[14] Ibid; *R v National Institute for Health and Clinical Excellence and Another, ex p Servier Laboratories Ltd* [2010] EWCA Civ 346.

made it clear that they lack the constitutional legitimacy and the institutional capacity to allocate scarce health-care resources. This position was reiterated in the judgment of *National Aids Trust*[15]—a case involving statutory interpretation about the extension of the commissioning powers of NHS England, but with important implications for the funding of an anti-retroviral treatment. Courts have also been reluctant to interfere in choices they consider to be political. For instance, in *A and B*,[16] no illegality was found in the Secretary of State for Health's decision not to exercise his power to require abortion services to be provided free of charge in England to women from Northern Ireland who could not have abortions in their own country due to the more restrictive legislation there. The issue of the affordability of a treatment for the public health system, as in *Pfizer*,[17] was also considered a political decision that should not be reviewed by courts. The courts have also avoided second-guessing the substantive rationales for priority-setting decisions. In *Condliff*,[18] the health authority's decision to exclude social or non-clinical factors when making decisions about the funding of treatment was upheld by the Judiciary. Similarly, in *AC*,[19] the courts decided not to interfere with the 'clinical and ethical' judgment of the health authority that refused funding for breast augmentation surgery to a patient with gender identity disorder—an intervention that was given low funding priority because the authority considered it as merely cosmetic.

However, while courts have maintained that they lack the necessary legitimacy and institutional capacity to adjudicate on matters of substance, courts have controlled how authorities exercise their discretion by evaluating the fairness and quality of the procedures they have followed. At local level, not only have courts required authorities to provide clear and rational reasons for general policies, but also that a policy needs to take into account individual and exceptional circumstances. Courts have controlled how the concept of exceptionality has been defined by authorities and applied to individual circumstances,[20] they have engaged with the scientific evidence presented by authorities to confer whether they support a certain policy decision,[21] and they have requested health authorities and Clinical Commissioning Groups (local bodies charged with purchasing health services for citizens within a designated area) to give clear and rational reasons for not complying with national guidance, even when it is not binding,[22] and also for overriding a patient's legitimate expectation.[23]

Courts have also focused on the fairness of the procedure by which the relevant decision was made in cases challenging NICE decisions. Courts have looked into the issue of whether the refusal to release a fully executable version of the economic model NICE used to calculate cost-effectiveness of a technology would prevent interested parties from

[15] *R (National Aids Trust & Local Government Association) v NHS Commissioning Board* [2016] EWCA Civ 1100.

[16] *A (A Child) and Another, R (on the Application of) v Secretary of State for Health* [2015] EWCA Civ 771.

[17] *R v Secretary of State for Health, ex p Pfizer* [2002] EWCA Civ 1566.

[18] *R v North Staffordshire Primary Care Trust, ex p Condliff* [2011] EWCA Civ 910.

[19] *R v Berkshire West PCT, ex p AC* [2011] EWCA Civ 247.

[20] *R v Swindon NHS Primary Care Trust, Secretary of State for Health, ex p Rogers* [2006] EWCA Civ 392; *R v Bromley NHS Primary Care Trust, ex p Gordon* [2006] EWCA Civ 392; *R v Barking & Dagenham NHS PCT, ex p Otley* [2007] EWHC 1927 (Admin); *R v West Sussex Primary Care Trust, ex p Ross* [2008] EWHC B15 (Admin); *R v Salford Primary Care Trust, ex p Murphy* [2008] EWHC 1908 (Admin); *SB* (n 11).

[21] *R v North West Lancashire Health Authority, ex p A, D and G* [1999] All ER (D) 911; *Otley* (n 20); *Ross* (n 20).

[22] *R v North Derbyshire Health Authority, ex p Fisher* [1997] 8 Med LR 327; *Rose, R (on the application of) v Thanet Clinical Commissioning Group* [2014] EWHC 1182 (Admin).

[23] *R v North and. East Devon Health Authority, ex p Coughlan* [2001] QB 213.

challenging the analyses made by the institution,[24] and whether the fact that members of the group entrusted to develop the guidelines for the treatment of a disease had previously expressed views about it would create a bias and predetermine the result of the process.[25] In *Servier*,[26] the court judged that NICE should make a fresh decision because the reasoning provided was considered 'inadequately explained' and did not go into details about the scientific reasoning underpinning it.

Issues of procedural fairness, in particular the statutory duty to involve and consult the public in service reconfiguration decisions, have also been central in cases involving services reconfiguration. Courts have reiterated that they are 'neither required nor qualified to comment on the merits or otherwise of the proposals concerning of reconfiguration decisions'[27] and that the lawfulness does not depend on whether or not a person agrees with the merits or substance of a decision.[28] However, courts have found several consultation processes unlawful on procedural grounds, which includes the authorities' failure to disclose the relevant information to allow consultees to make intelligent and informed responses, to take into account relevant considerations,[29] and to engage with relevant stakeholders.[30] But even in these cases where there were flaws in the procedure, courts have been reluctant to undo the reconfiguration that has already been carried out due to the concerns of how this would affect the provision of care to patients.[31]

In sum, courts have been insisting on the transparency, justification, consistency, and involvement in decisions about priority setting in health care. Courts do not see it as their job to ensure that decision-makers make the *right* decision about which services are funded, but rather to ensure that the process by which decision-makers made the relevant decision was a fair one. And even if illegality is found, instead of substituting a different conclusion and ordering the provision of a treatment or the reallocation of resources, courts tend to, by way of remedy, quash the decision and remit the issue back to the health authority for a fresh decision in light of the court's finding.[32] This reinforces the substance/procedure contrast: as the illegality does not result from a state of affairs or from the non-provision of a service or benefit per se, the outcome of the corrected procedure may in principle still be the same.

[24] *R v National Institute for Health and Clinical Excellence, ex p Elsai Ltd* [2007] EWHC 1941 (Admin); *R v National Institute for Health and Clinical Excellence, ex p Bristol-Myers Squibb Pharmaceuticals Ltd* [2009] EWHC 2722; *Servier* (n 14).

[25] *R v National Institute for Health and Clinical Excellence and Another, ex p Fraser and Another* [2009] EWHC 452 (Admin).

[26] See n 14.

[27] *London Borough of Lewisham and Another, R (on the application of) v Secretary of State for Health and Others* [2013] EWHC 2381 (Admin) (31 July 2013); [2013] EWCA Civ 1409.

[28] *Copson, R (on the application of) v Dorset Healthcare University NHS Foundation Trust* [2013] EWHC 732 (Admin) (28 March 2013); *Flatley, R (on the application of) v Hywel DDA University Local Health Board and Another* (Rev 1) [2014] EWHC 2258 (Admin); *Enfield v Secretary of State & PCTs* [2013] EWHC 3496 (Admin); *Royal Brompton & Harefield NHS Foundation Trust v Joint Committee of Primary Care Trusts and Another* [2012] EWCA Civ 472, [118].

[29] *R (on the Application of Save Our Surgery Ltd) v Joint Committee of Primary Care Trusts* [2013] EWHC 439 (Admin); *Royal Brompton & Harefield* (n 28).

[30] *London Borough of Lewisham* (n 27).

[31] *Enfield* (n 28) [38]; *Morris, R (on the application of) v Trafford Healthcare NHS Trust* [2006] EWHC 2334 (Admin).

[32] *Gordon* (n 20) can be considered an exception as the High Court required the PCT to fund a cancer drug treatment to the claimant for a determined period.

III. Judicial Accountability and the Priority-Setting's 'Procedural Turn'

As intimated in the previous section, one way in which courts have sought to defend their approach to priority setters' legal accountability is by distinguishing between matters of substance and matters of procedure. The thought here, then, is that in order to avoid criticisms of 'usurpation', courts are restricting themselves to questions of procedural fairness by virtue of the fact that they arguably possess neither the expertise nor democratic mandate to adjudicate on the outcome of allocative choices.[33]

To a certain extent, arguments from the philosophical literature around priority setting provide good grounds for this position. That is, since around the mid-1990s, it has become increasingly recognized in philosophical circles that we are unlikely to reach consensus on what substantive principles we ought to appeal to in order to resolve priority-setting dilemmas any time soon. As Daniels explains, the problem here is that in 'setting limits' as to who gets what with regard to health services, we are faced with two intractable issues: 'First ... they all rest on value judgements *about which reasonable people may disagree*. Second, general principles of justice do not resolve many of these controversies.'[34]

To illustrate this point, Daniels refers to three 'unsolved' rationing problems: (1) how to balance our efforts to give priority to the worst off with efforts to produce the greatest net benefit; (2) when we should allow an aggregation of modest benefits to large numbers of people to offset more significant benefits to fewer people; and (3) how much we should favour producing the best outcome with our limited resources as opposed to giving people a fair chance of deriving some benefit from them.[35] In all these cases, Daniels argues, we either lack substantive principles sufficiently fine-grained to resolve the relevant problem, or we lack 'prior consensus' on principles fine-grained enough to provide any such guidance.[36]

Faced with this dilemma, an increasing number of philosophers—led by Daniels—have argued that the best way to ensure justice in priority-setting decisions is by procedural means; that is, by looking not to the extent to which the outcome of a given allocation adheres to some substantive principle of distributive justice, but rather the procedure by which an allocation was settled. Within the literature, this is commonly referred to as priority setting's 'procedural turn'.[37]

The notion that decision-makers might ensure fair decisions by adopting a fair decision-making procedure builds on a rich tradition within philosophical thinking about justice, the most famous articulation of this argument, perhaps, being by John Rawls. On Rawls's account, insofar as a given decision-making procedure meets the standards of what he terms 'pure procedural justice', this alone suffices to ensure the justice of the outcome, whatever outcome that may be. One example of pure procedural justice, then, might be when

[33] This assumption has been challenged by, eg, D Bilchitz, *Poverty and Human Rights: The Justification and Enforcement of Socio-Economic Rights* (Oxford University Press, 2007); M Langford, 'The Justiciability of Social Rights: From Practice to Theory' in M Langford (ed), *Social Rights Jurisprudence* (Cambridge University Press, 2008).

[34] Daniels (n 2) 105 (emphasis in original).

[35] Ibid 105–7.

[36] Ibid 108.

[37] S Holm, 'Goodbye to the Simple Solutions: The Second Phase of Priority Setting in Health Care' (1998) 317 British Medical Journal 1000–2; R Ashcroft, 'Fair Process and the Redundancy of Bioethics: A Polemic' (2008) 1(1) Public Health Ethics 3–9.

people play tennis. Assuming they do so voluntarily and the rules are followed, the result is always just. Those who lose have no grounds for complaining. Those who win are entitled to any winnings.[38]

Rawls also describes two further possible systems of procedural justice which he takes to be just simply in the sense that they generate substantively just outcomes. Systems of *perfect* procedural justice, then, are just insofar as they automatically produce results that meet some standard of substantive justice (Rawls gives an example of one person dividing a cake and letting all others choose their slice first).[39] Similarly, systems of *imperfect* procedural justice are just insofar as they minimize the possibility of injustice, even if they fail to always produce entirely just results (here, Rawls suggests a jury trial).[40]

It is to these Rawlsian arguments that Daniels turns in defending his own, hugely influential model of procedural justice in priority setting: the Accountability for Reasonableness (AfR) framework.[41] Working under the assumption that there will always be reasonable disagreement about the substantive principles to determine the fairness of resource allocation, AfR looks to offer a pragmatic solution of procedural justice through the application of four conditions, each of which may be said to speak to principles of procedural fairness:

(1) Publicity: Decisions and supporting rationales must be transparently stated.
(2) Relevance: Rationales for priority-setting decisions should aim to provide a reasonable explanation of how the organization seeks to provide 'value for money' in meeting the varied health needs of a defined population. And a rationale will be reasonable if it appeals to evidence, reasons, and principles that stakeholders can accept as relevant.
(3) Revision and appeals: Mechanisms must be in place to challenge decisions.
(4) Regulation: There must be uniform enforcement of the other three conditions.[42]

Daniels's thought, then, is that insofar as we abide by the four conditions set out in the AfR framework, we can be confident that the decisions we make will at least be fair and legitimate.

Within this context, then, one defence one might offer of the *courts'* approach to judicial accountability over priority-setting problems in England is that (either consciously or not) they are reflecting precisely these phenomena. First, since there is no established consensus on what would make the outcome of a priority-setting decision substantially fair, it is reasonable for courts to avoid adjudicating on matters of substance for such judgments would involve them 'usurping' the role of other institutions that, at least in principle, have either

[38] W Nelson, 'The Very Idea of Pure Procedural Justice' (1980) 90 Ethics 502–11.
[39] cf J Rawls, *A Theory of Justice* (rev edn, Harvard University Press, 1999), 85.
[40] cf ibid.
[41] As well as being popular internationally, this framework has been picked up by several bodies in the United Kingdom, including now called National Institute for Health and Care Excellence—NICE (indeed, Daniels refers to NICE as one exemplar of his account). For international influence, see N Daniels and JE Sabin, 'Accountability for Reasonableness: An Update' (2008) 337 British Medical Journal a1850; MR Moosa, JD Maree, MT Chirehwa, et al, 'Use of the "Accountability for Reasonableness" Approach to Improve Fairness in Accessing Dialysis in a Middle-Income Country' (2016) 11(10) PLoS One e0164201. For NICE, seeM Rawlins, 'Playing Fair on Treatments' (2012) 122(6315) Health Service Journal 18; *Social Values Judgements: Principles for Development of NICE Guidance* [Internet]. Version 2. London: National Institute for Health and Care Excellence (NICE); (2008) Jul 31; and Daniels (n 2) 295–6.
[42] Daniels (n 2) 113–17.

(or both) the requisite democratic and constitutional legitimacy or the scientific, technical, and managerial expertise to consider the trade-offs and political choices involved. In other words, it is reasonable for judges to recuse themselves from adjudicating between competing legitimate claims for public funds, or to thinking prospectively about the implications of fulfilling an individual need on the health service, given any appeal to substantive principles is likely to be highly contentious.

Second, by demanding and scrutinizing the reasons for a decision and by examining the fairness of the procedures through which decisions are made, courts are enforcing the other conditions for procedural fairness. They are, in effect, fulfilling the 'regulation' principle within Daniels's framework to enforce that the other conditions for AfR are met. Some, including Daniels himself, would argue that this is the role of judicial accountability in issues of resource allocation in health care.[43] This is arguably a role that is best performed by an institution, such as courts, that have a certain degree of independence and have expertise in controlling the fairness of procedures. Therefore, not exercising this role would be a form of 'abdication' on the part of the Judiciary.

IV. Judicial Accountability and the Limits to Procedural Justice

One way, therefore, in which one might defend English courts' approach to the oversight of priority setters—that is, one restricted primarily to questions of procedure—is by appeal to the same kinds of considerations that have motivated the 'procedural turn' in the literature on justice in health. However, before expecting that the courts' procedural approach will help ensure priority-setting decisions are *just*, morally speaking, one needs to be aware of many of the concerns philosophers have raised more widely about the idea that one can secure just outcomes through just procedures.

A. What Constitutes a Fair Procedure?

First, although it was precisely the continued disagreements about what constituted a substantially just outcome that led many philosophers to turn instead to matters of procedure, it is worth stressing that there may be reasonable disagreement as to what kinds of properties render any given procedure just. For example, there are those who have argued that Daniels's AfR framework does not capture all the principles of procedural fairness necessary to ensure a fair procedure. One principle it might be argued to miss, for example, is a 'participation' condition, that is, one which ensures that those about whom decisions are made may actively participate in the decision-making process itself.[44]

Applying this same thought to courts, it is not always clear whether existing positions adopted by courts as to what extent a fair decision-making process necessarily reflect the requirements of procedural fairness. As discussed in the section above, to date courts have

[43] See N Daniels, S Charvel, AH Gelphi et al, 'Role of the Courts in the Progressive Realization of the Right to Health: Between the Threat and the Promise of Judicialization in Mexico' (2015) 1(3) Health Systems & Reform 229–234. See also K Syrett, 'Health Technology Appraisal and the Courts: Accountability for Reasonableness and the Judicial Model of Procedural Justice' (2011) 6 Health, Economics, Policy and Law 469–88.

[44] A Friedman, 'Beyond Accountability for Reasonableness' (2008) 22 Bioethics 101–12.

had to adjudicate on contentious issues of procedural fairness, such as the necessary level of transparency, justification, participation, and decision-makers' independence for a priority-setting decision to be lawful. Yet, all these questions look open to what Daniels might describe as 'reasonable disagreement'.

Once one recognizes that *both* the principles governing substantive justice and those governing procedural justice remain contested, it becomes less clear why courts have deemed the former as outside their remit and the latter as a domain in which they may legitimately exercise their authority. Perhaps there is a compelling justification courts may offer on this score. They might argue, for example, that matters of procedural fairness attract greater consensus, or are less complex, or simply that this is the role they have been traditionally assigned. However, at present, the capacity and legitimacy of courts to determine the fairness of a procedure to decide on the allocation of health-care resources can seem assumed, rather than clearly articulated and justified.

B. Distinguishing between Substance and Procedure

The courts' approach to judicial accountability over priority setting is also premised on their being able to draw a firm distinction between matters of procedure and matters of substance. However, as has also been long-recognized in the legal scholarship, this distinction is not always clear.[45] For example, providing reasons is an essential element in the control of rule-making because it permits courts to retrace the authority's reasoning process to make sure the decision was not arbitrarily, capriciously, or unreasonably made. However, depending on the intensity of the scrutiny, the thin line that separates scrutinizing the quality of the reasons for a decision and second-guessing its merits can be easily blurred.[46] Rid registers this as one of the problems with AfR. That is, although Daniels claims that one of the great virtues of AfR lies in the fact that it enables us to escape having to resolve disputes about matters of substantive justice, AfR's 'relevance condition' may be seen as placing significant *substantive* constraints on making limit-setting decisions.[47]

A case can highlight the difficulties here. In *R v Northwest Lancashire Health Authority*, the court decided to quash a health authority decision not to fund gender reassignment surgery for three patients who suffered from 'gender identity dysphoria'.[48] One of the grounds for this judgment was that the authority's decision to give gender identity dysphoria low priority for funding was not rationally based upon a proper consideration of the facts: this condition was not regarded a serious psychiatric pathology for which the requested treatment could be effective. This case could be framed as one in which authorities failed to meet the relevance condition in AfR, but it could also be seen as courts, based on competing

[45] See C Harlow and R Rawlings, *Law and Administration* (Cambridge University Press, 2009), 124, 631; M Shapiro, 'The Giving Reasons Requirement' (1992) 8 University of Chicago Legal Forum 179–220; S Rose-Ackerman, S Egidy, and J Fowkes, *Due Process of Lawmaking: The United States, South Africa, Germany and European Union* (Cambridge University Press, 2015).

[46] See J Mashaw, 'Public Reason and Administrative Legitimacy' in J Bell, M Elliott, JNE Varuhas, et al (eds), *Common Law Systems: Process and Substance* (Hart, 2015). On the difficulty of distinguishing between substance and procedure, but also on the importance of maintaining this distinction to avoid 'over-intrusive' judicial review, see Rose-Ackerman et al (n 45).

[47] A Rid, 'Justice and Procedure: How Does "Accountability for Reasonableness" Result in Fair Limit-Setting Decisions?' (2009) 35 Journal of Medical Ethics 12–16.

[48] See n 21.

evidence, disagreeing with the authorities' evaluation of the relevance of the medical condition and the quality of the treatment.

C. Securing Just Outcomes through Just Procedures

The courts' endorsement of certain kinds of procedures also raises a set of questions about the extent to which they see such procedures as securing just outcomes. They might argue here that such procedures, if followed, generate a fair outcome. This would be to see such procedures as exemplars of pure procedural justice. Another would be to say that such procedures simply make it more likely that the priority-setting process will generate a just outcome, which can be verified by some independent criterion. This would be to see the procedures they endorse as exemplars of either perfect or imperfect procedural justice.

However, both these responses raise further questions. First—as is well noted in the philosophical literature—one might question the extent to which a fair process is sufficient to ensure a fair outcome. Earlier, for example, we suggested that a game of tennis might be one example of what Rawls would describe as a case of pure procedural justice. However, as Nelson points out, the mere fact that a game or process has a certain kind of property does not appear sufficient to secure a just outcome. After all, 'no matter how fair the game, the winners would not be entitled to their winnings if the losers had stolen them'![49]

Courts might instead argue that they do not assume the procedure alone ensures the outcome is just; rather, it only makes it more likely that a just outcome will be reached. However, to make this argument, courts would be expressing a view as to what constitutes a fair outcome and thus bring in all the debate around substantive notions of justice they wanted to avoid. If those determining the fairness of a procedure are trying to promote a just outcome, then one can raise questions about the risk of courts reverse-engineering an outcome to determine the procedure that will make it more likely.

For instance, one of the problems with distinguishing between procedure and substantive outcomes is that it is possible to control the procedure in a way that will increase the probability of a certain policy result, for instance, if procedural requirements are so demanding that it may reduce the range of discretion to an extent that practically predetermines the outcome of the policy. Harlow and Rawlins argue that this is what the English Court of Appeal did in *Rogers*.[50] According to them, the court obliged the health authority to reconstruct the decision about the funding of a then new cancer drug to a patient in a way that 'made an answer favourable to the appellant virtually inevitable'.[51] Another example is *Murphy*,[52] where the authority decided not to fund a treatment to a patient because it was not ordinarily available on the NHS and none of the seven factors brought by the patient could make her case exceptional according to its policy. The High Court accepted that priority setting is necessary, that this treatment was indeed too expensive to be justified in the ordinary course of cases, and that none of the factors brought by the patient to advocate for her exceptional case would make her case exceptional when looked at separately.

49 Nelson (n 38) 507.
50 See n 20.
51 Harlow and Rawlings (n 45) 124.
52 See n 20.

Nonetheless, the health authority's decision was still quashed on the basis that it had evaluated each of the seven factors separately, rather than looking at them 'in the round'. This case may be read as an example of courts increasing the number of items in the checklist of what would constitute a fair procedure until the preferred outcome becomes likely.

D. Problems of Repeated Application

It can also be questioned what we are to do when procedures that are arguably fair with regard to deciding what treatments ought to be funded for a single individual simultaneously generate results that are arguably *unfair* from a service provision perspective. One good example, discussed by Amy Ford, is the insistence by English courts that the NHS needs to consider individual 'exceptional circumstances' in priority-setting decisions as there cannot be any blanket bans for a treatment. Since the concept of exceptionality is taken very broadly, and decisions are made on a case-by-case basis, this procedural requirement can create situations in which individuals with very similar clinical conditions will have different decisions about the funding of their care.[53] In this way, then, it may be that there are some procedures that we recognize as just, and that would appear to produce just outcomes when viewed on a case-by-case basis, and yet may still have the potential to bring about unjust outcomes when applied repeatedly, generating either vast inequalities or inconsistent policy outcomes.

There is a parallel here, perhaps, to Rawls's criticism of Nozick's Entitlement Theory of Justice. Namely, that 'the accumulated results of many separate and seemingly fair agreements entered into by individuals and associations are likely over an extended period to undermine the background conditions required for free and fair agreements'.[54]

It is beyond the scope of this chapter to offer a normative argument about how courts in general, or English courts in particular, should decide claims challenging priority-setting decisions. This section is rather showing that the substance/procedure contrast that guides judicial accountability in England, although offering a solid normative justification for the role of courts in the control of priority-setting decisions in the NHS, will also raise a set of unresolved questions. There is still extensive work that needs to be done in justifying courts' interpretation of what constitutes a 'just' procedure; clarifying the distinction between issues of procedure and those of substance; and deciding whether (or to which extent) concerns about unfair outcomes should inform their decisions about what a fair procedure entails, which may involve courts in discussions about substantive justice that they have been seeking to avoid.

V. Conclusion

In this chapter, we have sought to analyse and critically assess courts' understanding of priority setters' legal accountability and, in particular, their accountability for the fairness of their decisions—drawing on examples from England and the English NHS. We have

[53] A Ford, 'The Concept of Exceptionality: A Legal Farce?' (2012) 20 Medical Law Review 304–36.
[54] J Rawls, *Justice as Fairness* (Belknap Press, 2001), 53.

shown that courts' approach in this domain is best understood as premised upon a distinction between substantive policy decisions and matters of procedural fairness, with courts themselves perceiving their role as restricted primarily to normative assessments of the procedure by which priority-setting decisions are made. Arguments from the philosophical literature provide important grounds for justifying courts' restricted approach on issues of substance and their high scrutiny on matters of procedure. However, as discussed in the latter stages of the chapter, the substance/procedure distinction offers only a partial solution to the 'usurpation'/'abdication' dilemma and there are a number of areas in which further justification is required.

13

Philosophy and Restrictions on Access to Assisted Reproductive Technologies

Imogen Goold

I. Introduction

The term 'Assisted Reproductive Technologies' (ARTs) covers an array of methods to help people conceive children, including standard in vitro fertilization (IVF), artificial insemination (AI), and intra-cytoplasmic sperm injection (ICSI). It can also encompass egg and sperm freezing and the preservation and use of ovarian tissue. These technologies are deployed in an increasingly broad range of situations to enable the conception of children that would not previously have been possible. This includes the fairly common use of IVF by a heterosexual couple to conceive and carry their own genetically related embryo, through same-sex couples using IVF to create embryos related to one partner (carried by one partner or by a surrogate), to posthumous use of sperm or ovarian tissue, carried by the remaining partner or even a family member. In addition to *enabling* the conception of children, ART, via prenatal diagnosis techniques and the ever-increasing understanding of the genetic causes of disease and other traits, also afford prospective parents much greater control over the *kind* of children they will conceive.

At first blush, then, ART use might seem to be an obviously good thing and hence something to be promoted. ART access enables the infertile to have children, whether via IVF, use of donor gametes, full surrogacy, or a combination of these. Reproduction is demonstrably a highly important aspect of the human experience for the majority of people, and having children brings great emotional, social, and psychological benefits to many of those who choose to do so. As Harry Brighouse and Adam Swift argue, raising children is a uniquely valuable and non-substitutable value for many people.[1] There is also research to suggest that infertile women 'have significantly higher levels of depressive symptoms, and twice the prevalence of depressive symptoms relative to fertile women', and this may stem in part from beliefs '[a]cross many cultures' that childlessness is 'a sign of diminished status, defectiveness, and reduced competence'.[2] This would seem to speak prima facie in favour of offering very wide access to the technology.

ARTs can also address childlessness that arises from non-medical causes, such as single woman and lesbian couples who need donor sperm to achieve pregnancy, and homosexual couples via surrogacy (including where a donor egg is used). In this way, ARTs can enable a

[1] H Brighouse and A Swift, *Family Values: The Ethics of Parent–Child Relationships* (Princeton University Press, 2016).

[2] T Cousineau and A Domar, 'Psychological Impact of Infertility' (2007) 21 Best Practice & Research Clinical Obstetrics & Gynaecology 293, 295–6.

Imogen Goold, *Philosophy and Restrictions on Access to Assisted Reproductive Technologies* In: *Philosophical Foundations of Medical Law.* Edited by: Andelka M Phillips, Thana C de Campos, and Jonathan Herring, Oxford University Press (2019).
DOI: 10.1093/oso/9780198796558.003.0014

wider group of people to fulfil their reproductive goals, and can also facilitate the creation of new familial forms.

ARTs, specifically IVF, also enable embryo selection. This entails a morphological assessment of embryos with a view to selecting the embryo(s) with maximum implantation potential. Prenatal genetic diagnosis (PGD) can be undertaken prior to implantation to make a diagnosis of any suspected genetic conditions. It involves removing cells from the embryo to obtain genetic material. It is generally carried out to avoid selection of an embryo that carries a disease-causing genetic mutation, preventing the creation of a child who will suffer that condition. The assumed benefit is the avoidance of a life affected by that condition. Embryo selection also allows for embryos to be selected *for* rather than against, when there is a desire to create a child who can act as a tissue donor for another child and must be a match. Such children are referred to as 'saviour siblings'. Embryos undergo 'tissue typing' to determine which is a match for the prospective recipient.

But with these uses come concerns. The expansion in both the possibilities and our desires about how to deploy these technologies raises questions about how far we should restrict the use of ARTs. They press us to consider head-on the question of whether just because we *can* do something, we *should* do it? Under this broad concern sit questions about *who* should be permitted to use ARTs and to *what ends*? To answer these questions, we must consider difficult questions about the ambit of reproductive liberty and whether the right approach is to facilitate choice, or merely to permit people to reproduce as they wish, but without actively enabling the full range of options they could have. Should we prohibit certain uses or certain *users*? Given that many techniques are expensive, the further question of how far we should help people to access technologies arises, and whether conversely to merely permit but not assist access is unreasonably discriminatory. These particular issues about funding and access bring the relationship between law and ethics into sharp focus, for a purely liberty-based approach will have differential impacts and hence we cannot avoid questions about the role of the state in enabling access to ART and the most defensible policy position on funding that access.

This raft of questions and difficult matrix of issues therefore gives rise to a multitude of philosophical questions, some of which go to the very heart of issues around autonomy. This chapter explores these questions by engaging with what we mean by reproductive liberty and autonomy, and considers whether, if at all, constraints on either can be justified. It necessarily examines these questions from both an ethical and a legal perspective, as well as touching on policy arguments related to reproductive choices.

II. Reproductive Liberty versus Reproductive Autonomy

At the very heart of the question of restricting ART access is the question of what limits, if any, should be placed on autonomy. Given the benefits of ARTs and the general commitment in most legal systems to individual choice, and the personal nature of reproduction, we might think that ART access should be relatively unrestricted. Reproductive choice falls within the protection of private and family life under article 8 of the European Convention on Human Rights (ECHR), which recognizes the deeply personal nature of decisions about becoming a parent (and, indeed, the choice *not* to become a parent as held in *Evans v UK* to include the right to choose *not* to be a parent).[3] But before we can really consider reasons to restrict access, we need to unpack what we mean by 'autonomy' in the context of reproduction. Autonomy here breaks down into two foundational concepts: reproductive liberty and reproductive autonomy. These sit within the notion of 'private and family life' as enshrined in article 8.

'Reproductive liberty' is the view that people should be free to make their own, unfettered choices about reproduction insofar as these do not have unreasonable harmful impacts on others (which they largely do not). This includes choosing to have children and choosing to avoid doing so.[4] Reproductive liberty is important, MM Peterson suggests, because:

> It is a valid interpretation to suggest that denial of procreative choice equates to denial of basic personal respect and dignity. Individuals or couples that experience infertility often experience guilt, low self-esteem, disappointment, depression, increased rates of relationship conflict, and sexual dysfunction.[5]

This is buttressed by the practical difficulties entailed by any attempt to restrict many reproductive decisions, which can be achieved only via very grave violations of personal privacy or of invasions of bodily integrity. For those who do not need any assistance to procreate, protecting their reproductive liberty will largely be sufficient to enable them to achieve their reproductive goals.

For those who cannot achieve those goals without assistance, the picture is rather more complex. Those afflicted by infertility or inherited conditions, those who wish to create a saviour sibling, and those who prefer to use a surrogate (for full surrogacy) cannot do so without ARTs. Simply leaving them to their own devices to choose as they wish may not be sufficient. If there is a lack of choices, or those choices are restricted (such as by restricting access to ARTs), then they may not be able to achieve their goals. The concept of 'reproductive autonomy' comes into play at this point.

'Reproductive autonomy' goes beyond the notion of merely permitting choice and demands more—that people's choices about reproduction are facilitated. The bounds of this autonomy might be very wide, demanding that all that can be done to fulfil everyone's desires about reproduction is done, and done to the full. Or it might be narrower, requiring the provision of reasonable choices and affording people, in some sense, sufficient capacity to pursue their reproductive goals. For example, fairly limited reproductive autonomy might entail offering some cycles of IVF to those who cannot afford it, or PGD in certain cases, while very broad reproductive autonomy might demand that PGD be permitted for any reason (or no reason at all).

The extent to which restrictions on ART access can be regarded as permissible necessarily rests on whether we are committed only to affording people reproductive liberty, or consider actively facilitating choices more appropriate. If the latter, we can be committed to a greater or lesser degree. We will explore the impact of this distinction in relation to the various grounds on which ART access might be restricted.

[3] *Evans v United Kingdom* (App No 6339/05, 2007), [71].

[4] See eg J Robertson, *Children of Choice: Freedom and the New Reproductive Technologies* (Princeton University Press, 1994).

[5] MM Peterson, 'Assisted Reproductive Technologies and Equity of Access Issues' (2005) 31 Journal of Medical Ethics 280, 281.

Harm and limits on reproductive liberty or autonomy also come into play when consideration is taken of the outcomes of people's reproductive choices. While some uses of ARTs will produce benefits to both parents and resulting children, others potentially will not. So, even though we need to frame questions about restricting access through the lens of liberty, autonomy, and private and family life, it is important to think in terms of benefits and harms as well. The following sections delve into these issues more deeply.

III. Reasons for Limiting Access

A. Does Access Promote Autonomy?

It seems counter-intuitive, but arguably the choices offered by ARTs to enable people to conceive may, in fact, reduce autonomy. Infertility is no longer infertility as it once was. When people cannot conceive naturally, the availability of ARTs means that they have the option to use ARTs to try to conceive. They must almost choose *not* to use ARTs, such is the prevalence of their use in infertility cases, that not to use them seems in need of an explanation. This, in itself, places pressure on people to go through a process that is at times painful, exhausting, and stressful, as well as emotionally draining.

This ubiquity and expectation also reinforces the notion that having children is the norm, and those who choose not to follow this norm have behaved aberrantly. Feminist scholars have raised concerns about the pro-natalist impact of ART access.[6]

B. Harm to Future Children

1. Welfare Concerns

One of the key bases on which access to ARTs might be restricted is to prevent a child being born into a harmful situation or a state of harm. This very broad basis could cover a situation in which the parents may not be able to provide adequate care, or there is a risk they will harm the child. This is the welfare concern reflected in restrictions on ART access in place in some jurisdictions, such as the United Kingdom, where ART use is contingent on account being taken of the welfare of any child born as a result.[7] In making a determination on welfare, account must be taken of the need of that child for 'supportive parenting' (previously 'for a father'), which is defined as 'a commitment to the health, well-being and development of the child'. It is presumed under the Human Fertilisation and Embryology Authority (HFEA) Guidelines that such parenting is available unless there is evidence to indicate the contrary.[8] Welfare concerns will arise if there are indications that the resulting child will be at risk, and clinics can take account of: previous convictions in relation to harming a child; child protection measures in relation to existing children; violence in the family; drug or alcohol abuse; and any mental or physical conditions that may mean the

[6] A Smajdor, 'Between Fecklessness and Selfishness: Is There a Biologically Optimal Time for Motherhood?' in F Simonstein (ed), *Reprogen-Ethics and the Future of Gender* (Springer, 2009); R Chadwick, *Ethics, Reproduction and Genetic Control* (Routledge, 1992), xvi.

[7] Human Fertilisation and Embryology Act 1990 (as amended in 2008), s 13.

[8] Human Fertilisation and Embryology Authority, 'Code of Practice: 8th Edition' (HFEA, 2009), 8.11.

parents will be unable to care for the child.[9] These factors all centre on the parents and the likelihood that the child will be born into a potentially harmful situation. In addition, the HFEA also provides that IVF may be restricted on child welfare grounds if there is a parental medical history that suggests that the child may be born with a serious medical condition.[10] Here, then, the concern is about welfare harms that derive from the resulting child's own potential disability, which is quite a different kind of concern.

What, however, is the threshold for a sufficient welfare concern? Is it a mere risk of harm based on past behaviour? Lack of ability to provide sufficient care? Insufficient income? An unstable parental relationship? Past behaviour of members of the wider family who are likely to come into contact with the child? And what of the concerns sometimes raised about older parents, particularly older mothers, that they are likely to die before the child reaches adulthood?[11]

2. Disability and Welfare

It could also encompass a child being born with a health condition or disability that leads to (arguably) a lesser quality of life compared with unaffected children. It might seem odd to think that such a restriction might need to be contemplated, but in fact there have been a number of cases of couples wishing to use ARTs to create a child that could (on some definitions) be regarded as disabled. Perhaps the most high profile was that of Sharon Duchesneau and Candy McCullough, who, in 2002, used sperm donated by a friend with a background of familial deafness in the hopes that this would help them conceive a deaf child.[12] For some critics, this was problematic as it sought to create a child who was in some sense disabled, or who at least lacked a capacity that many consider an integral and valuable part of being human. Julian Savulescu sums up these concerns:

> Many would see deliberately creating deaf babies as the most perverse manifestation of creating designer babies. Deafness, they would say, is a disability. Deaf people are denied the world of sound, music, and the most fundamental form of human communication. People who claim that deafness represents a unique culture that can be fostered only by being deaf are mistaken. Hearing children of deaf parents can learn to sign, just as children of English parents can learn to speak Chinese as well as English. It is better to speak two languages rather than one, to understand two cultures rather than one.[13]

For the couple, deafness was not a disability, but a difference, and brought with it the benefits associated with being part of the close-knit deaf community. Rosalind McDougall explains that they regarded deafness as 'a minority cultural identity rather than a disability'

[9] Ibid 8.10a–b.

[10] Ibid 8.10iii.

[11] Some jurisdictions, such as Indonesia and the UAE, restrict based on sexuality, banning same-sex couples from using ARTs to conceive. By contrast, others such as the United Kingdom explicitly reject such restrictions, with Part 2 of the HFEA 2008 making clear that any individual regardless of sexual orientation or marital status is permitted to seek IVF. Some countries, like Germany and Spain, allow only female same-sex couples access. Both the UAE and Indonesia also prevent the use of ARTs by singles, unlike many other jurisdictions, while Germany and Spain limit access to single women.

[12] M Spriggs, 'Lesbian Couple Create a Child Who Is Deaf Like Them' (2002) 28 Journal of Medical Ethics 283.

[13] J Savulescu, 'Deaf Lesbians, "Designer Disability," and the Future of Medicine' (2002) 325 British Medical Journal 771.

and that they 'sought to have a child who shared this cultural identity. They wanted a child "who is the same as us", and believed they could be better parents to a deaf child'.[14]

The case was challenging because it was far from clear whether trying to create a deaf child was, in effect, an attempt to create a child who was suffering harm to such an extent that bringing him or her into existence was itself wrong. It seems intuitive that we should not bring into the world people who are likely to suffer from a disability, and certainly not those who will face a life of pain and suffering. This is the argument that has been mounted, at various different times, by John Harris and Julian Savulescu in accordance with Savulescu's Principle of Procreative Beneficence.[15] However, for the child in question, the choice being made about them is whether to bring them into existence at all, so therefore logically unless existence is worse than non-existence, it cannot be wrong to choose them even though they will experience the (arguable) detriments of a disability. This response to the Principle of Procreative Beneficence has been outlined by Bennett, who argues that, logically, the non-refutation of Parfitt's Non-Identity Problem necessarily entails the refutation of the Principle of Procreative Beneficence.[16] According to Bennett, while Harris and Savulescu might be able to show that *intuitively* we feel wrongness attaches to bringing to birth an impaired child, that intuition fails to find a basis in any stronger moral claim.

3. Saviour Siblings

While saviour siblings may in some cases experience benefits—the value of altruistically helping a sibling[17]—they face the possibility of substantial disbenefits. Donation may be painful, as in the case of bone marrow. They may feel parental pressure to donate when they would prefer not to (because of the pain or for other reasons). As most saviour-sibling children lack capacity, they may be subject to bodily invasions for the benefit only of someone else, which might be considered wrong.[18] Some may believe (correctly or otherwise) that they are wanted only or largely as a means to save another child, and this may have a negative impact on their sense of self-worth and their relationship with their parents. It may also be harming to be brought into existence for the sake of another child who is ill if the parents direct the majority of their attention towards the unwell child at the expense of the saviour. Not all donations are risk-free, too, and some, such as organ donation, carry permanent bodily changes. Such donations might be difficult to justify if they pose too great a risk to the donor child largely to benefit only the recipient sibling.

[14] R McDougall, 'Parental Virtue: A New Way of Thinking about the Morality of Reproductive Actions' (2007) 21 Bioethics 181, 187–8.

[15] J Harris, *The Value of Life: An Introduction to Medical Ethics* (Routledge, 1985), 146–9; J Savulescu, 'Procreative Beneficence: Why Should We Select the Best Children?' (2001) Bioethics 413.

[16] R Bennett, 'When Intuition Is Not Enough. Why the Principle of Procreative Beneficence Must Work Much Harder to Justify Its Eugenic Vision' (2014) Bioethics 447; D Parfit, *Reasons and Persons* (Clarendon Press, 1987).

[17] J Herring and C Foster, 'Welfare Means Relationality, Virtue and Altruism' (2012) 32 Legal Studies 3, 480.

[18] However, see points made by Merle Spriggs in support of the view that saviour siblings are not harmed and hence parental consent on the child's behalf for the bodily invasion and donation is not morally objectionable: M Spriggs, 'Is Conceiving a Child to Benefit Another against the Interests of the New Child?' (2005) Journal of Medical Ethics 31, 341.

C. Harm to the Embryo

The use of many ARTs leads to embryos being discarded. For those who consider the embryo to have the same or similar moral status as a person, this raises sanctity of life concerns. As Guido Pennings and Guido de Wert explain, 'the sanctity of human life argument states that an embryo should be respected as a human person' and they note that 'this position focuses on the potentiality of the embryo'. In their view, there is a range of difficulties with this perspective, and it is '[i]n fact, at odds with various accepted practices, such as the use of intrauterine devices, in vitro fertilization (IVF), and PD. During IVF, embryos are routinely discarded in the attempt to obtain a pregnancy'.[19] Many people are unconcerned by this, but for some who regard the embryo as having important moral status, they may choose to create only as many embryos as they intend to implant to avoid this outcome.

D. Public Harms

As the world's population continues to balloon, it is sometimes suggested that using expensive technology to help the infertile to reproduce is irrational or wrong. Better, it is suggested, to let nature take its course than exacerbate an existing problem.[20] A related point is that it is simply a poor use of scarce health resources to help people reproduce, and that these would be better spent on other, more obviously health-related needs. Some go the further step and argue that this is particularly appropriate because infertility is not (they argue) a disease and therefore treating it is not a therapeutic intervention of the kind that should be offered as health care.[21]

E. Rationing

Offering cycles of IVF on the NHS is a good example of a context in which the liberty/autonomy distinction bites. If we felt it appropriate only to support choice, but not facilitate it, we would permit people to pay for IVF, but would not regard it as something the state ought to provide to ensure everyone is able to act on their desire to have children. If, however, we felt it important to actively help people achieve their reproductive goal of having a child, we would see it as a state responsibility to offer IVF. But there might be limits to how far we ought to divert resources to offering IVF, particularly when they could be used for other purposes.

Generally, when we consider what the resource limits should be, this is necessarily a case of weighing the importance of helping people have children (and hence the importance of

[19] G Pennings and G de Wert, 'Preimplantation Genetic Diagnosis' in *Encyclopedia of Applied Ethics* (2nd edn, Academic Press, 2012), vol 3, 577.

[20] Lori Andrews and Nanette Elster note this as one of the major early objections to IVF, in which it was often argued that 'maintaining the couple's infertility might further other social goals by reducing overpopulation': L Andrews and N Elster, 'Regulating Reproductive Technologies' (2000) 21 Journal of Legal Medicine 35, 36–8.

[21] Leon Kass has made this argument in LR Kass, '"Making Babies" Revisited' (1979) 54 Public Interest 32; 'Babies by Means of In Vitro Fertilization: Unethical Experiments on the Unborn?' (1971) 285 New England Journal of Medicine 1174; and 'Making Babies—the New Biology and the "Old" Morality' (1972) 26 Public Interest 18.

reproduction to people) against other social goals, particularly health care. How is that balance to be struck? On the one hand, it has regularly been pointed out that having children is deeply important to many people, and therefore facilitating that is an important way to promote human flourishing.[22] However, promoting health, providing social care, and the like also promote flourishing, and so this might tip the balance towards other goals. Some also suggest that the fact that people can bring children into their lives via adoption speaks against too many resources being diverted to facilitate reproduction,[23] but a response to this might be that this gives insufficient weight to the importance of a genetic link between parents and child, and to the value of experiencing pregnancy for some women. A further issue is that if people are not offered IVF by the state and must enter the market to access it, the poor will be effectively excluded from achieving their reproductive goals, while the wealthy are not.

Thinking about the limits of facilitating choice in this way is necessarily a discussion about benefits versus harms, because it involves scarce resources and diverting those to one person takes them away from another, harming them. So, in this sense, limiting ART access may prevent harm to others even though it also limits a person's reproductive autonomy, which itself is arguably harming. The core issue, then, is how serious a harm is the inability to have children. This is inherently subjective, but given that most people have children (usually by choice), we should not too easily dismiss the potential harm of limiting access for rationing reasons.

F. Harms to Adult Participants

Sometimes, it is considered right for the law to prevent people from doing things that will cause them to suffer harm. Such restrictions are, of course, paternalistic and in line with John Stewart Mill's harm principle, and are often, therefore, thought to be limits that should be resisted.[24] However, as is the case with many similar legal restrictions, good justifications for the law restricting the behaviour of citizens for their own benefit can be found. The question in this context is whether this is the case with ARTs, and if so, to what extent and relation to which uses or contexts.

There is a range of harms that might be suffered by adults who use ARTs, with the majority being shouldered by women. Pregnancy and birth are not entirely safe undertakings. Hundreds of thousands of women die each year during birth or as a result of pregnancy complications.[25] But these risks are not limited to ART pregnancies, and so it would be discriminatory as well as paternalistic to prevent women becoming pregnant generally by restricting ART access. That said, mortality rates increase with age, and where certain

[22] eg, as Lord Robert Winston has commented: 'Chief among the core human impulses is the desire to have children. Nothing will alter the fact that the most important thing that most people do in their lives is to bring a child into the world. It changes our lives completely, and it reaffirms the cycle of life and our place in it.' Professor R Winston, *The IVF Revolution* (1st edn, Vermilion, 1999), viii.

[23] See eg E Bartholet, *Family Bonds* (2nd edn, Beacon Press, 1999), 35–7. Bartholet argues that it 'makes no sense for a society that thinks of itself as sane and humane to be driving people in the direction of child production rather than adoption' when many children 'will grow up without homes unless they are adopted'.

[24] JS Mill, *On Liberty* (2nd edn, London JW Parker & Son, 1860), 20–1.

[25] There is a rise in maternal mortality rates as age increases, with a sharp increase after age 30—data from A Blanc, W Winfrey, and J Ross, 'New Findings for Maternal Mortality Age Patterns: Aggregated Results for 38 Countries' (2013) 8 PLoS One e59864.

conditions such as diabetes are present.[26] Some women may be more prone to complications or post-natal depression. Some may have pre-existing conditions that might be exacerbated by pregnancy or birth, and in fact one in four maternal deaths is a result of pre-existing conditions such as diabetes, HIV, and malaria, the health implications of which can all be aggravated by pregnancy.[27] These risks might, in some cases, be considered sufficient to restrict such women from becoming pregnant by preventing access to ARTs. But again, given a woman's competence to evaluate these risks, as well as being highly discriminatory, this would seem rather a baseless reason to restrict access to ARTs. There are, however, some contexts in which more convincing concerns based on harm to the woman have been raised.

1. Egg Freezing and Fertility Extension

There has been resistance by both professional bodies and some academics to permitting women to use egg freezing technology to prolong their reproductive life. John A Robertson, for example, has warned of the harms women may suffer if their desire for children is thwarted by relying on egg freezing as an insurance policy that fails to pay out.[28] The American Society for Reproductive Medicine has also expressed reservations about women being sold egg freezing as a viable means to extend their fertility on the basis that the technology is still too unreliable, and so women may fail to try for children during their fertile life and then find that their frozen eggs do not enable them to become pregnant later.[29] To these concerns, one can respond that as long as women have information about the risks and costs, then as with other life decisions, they should be permitted to run those risks as they choose, even if they may suffer harm as a result.[30]

2. Surrogacy

ARTs have facilitated more appealing forms of surrogacy, as they enable couples or single people to have a child that is entirely related to them (via sperm donation and IVF using gametes from the commissioning couple). For many, this has brought considerable joy and satisfaction into their lives. However, surrogacy arrangements are not always successful, and can precipitate harms to the parties involved.[31]

[26] Diabetes—on the maternal side, morbidity and mortality rates are also higher among pregnant women with diabetes. Rates of pre-eclampsia (12.7 per cent), Caesarean section (44.3 per cent), and maternal mortality (0.6 per cent) found among women with type 1 diabetes are considerably higher than in the background population: C Negrato, R Mattar, and M Gomes, 'Adverse Pregnancy Outcomes in Women with Diabetes' (2012) 4 Diabetology & Metabolic Syndrome 41.

[27] L Say, D Chou, A Gemmill, et al, 'Global Causes of Maternal Death: A WHO Systematic Analysis' (2014) 2 Lancet Global Health e323. Pregnant women infected with malaria usually have more severe symptoms and outcomes, with higher rates of miscarriage, intrauterine demise, premature delivery, low-birth-weight neonates, and neonatal death. They are also at a higher risk for severe anaemia and maternal death. J Schantz-Dunn and N Nour, 'Malaria and Pregnancy: A Global Health Perspective' (2009) 2 Reviews in Obstetrics and Gynecology 186.

[28] JA Robertson, 'Egg Freezing and Egg Banking: Empowerment and Alienation in Assisted Reproduction' (2014) Journal of Law and the Biosciences 113, 120–2.

[29] C Schubert, 'Egg Freezing Enters Clinical Mainstream', *Nature Blogs* (23 October 2012), http://blogs.nature.com/news/2012/10/egg-freezing-enters-clinical-mainstream.html accessed 15 July 2019.

[30] I Goold, 'Trust Women to Choose: A Response to John a Robertson's "Egg Freezing and Egg Banking: Empowerment and Alienation in Assisted Reproduction"' (2017) 4 Journal of Law and the Biosciences 3, 507; I Goold and J Savulescu, 'In Favour of Freezing Eggs for Non-Medical Reasons' (2009) 23 Bioethics 47.

[31] Surrogacy is in fact prohibited in many jurisdictions: Spain, Austria, Italy, Germany, Indonesia, and China all bar the use of ARTs for this purpose. Others prohibit surrogacy agreements being enforced—this is the case in the United Kingdom (see Surrogacy Arrangements Act 1985).

Most obvious is the surrogate mother herself who may, after carrying the foetus, feel so bonded to it that she cannot bear to give it up at birth. This applies to both partial surrogacy (where the surrogate provides her own egg) and full surrogacy where her link to the foetus is not genetic, but is often still strong from the experience of gestating it.[32] If the surrogate is required to give up the child, this may have profoundly harming impacts, but at the same time, the commissioning couple are very likely to be emotionally invested in the child and they, too, will be harmed if the surrogate is permitted to keep the child she had considered her own. Conversely, where the commissioning parents reject the child, as the legal mother, the surrogate will be burdened with the responsibility of a child she did not want. In such situations, it is hard to see how, in the face of dispute, any solution will not cause harm to one of the parties. These potential harms, coupled with the risks of harm to the child, might be considered sufficiently likely and sufficiently severe to be ground for avoiding their possibility altogether by restricting (or at least controlling) ART use.[33] For example, following the high-profile case of Baby Gammy and concerns about trafficking women to be surrogates, the Thai government imposed restrictions on IVF access (it banned egg donation) as part of steps to ban commercial surrogacy.[34]

3. Donors

Both men and women donate gametes that are used by others to conceive children via ARTs. Sometimes, donation is to a stranger, but in some cases family members or friends will donate to a loved one. Sperm donation has been a fairly well-known process for some time, but egg donation is a more recent practice precipitated by the development of IVF in the 1970s. Improvements in freezing techniques have increased the capacity of women to freeze and transfer their eggs, leading some to posit that a market for eggs may emerge in the same way that a market for sperm already exists in some countries.[35]

How might a donor be harmed? And will those harms be great enough to justify restricting ART access on this basis? Some people might underestimate how knowing that a child created from their genetic material is living in the world will affect them. Those who are contacted by children born in this way may find the interaction distressing; others may find it fulfilling.[36] We do know that some people find donating gametes a rewarding experience, and rejoice in being able to help others to have children.[37] Robertson has suggested that women, particularly, might find alienation from their gametes in this way problematic,[38] but the evidence suggests that both men and women may experience harms, as well as benefits, from donation.[39] So, this is not self-evidently harming. The only convincing

[32] V Jadva, C Murray, E Lycett, et al, 'Surrogacy: The Experiences of Surrogate Mothers' (2003) Human Reproduction 2196.

[33] B Steinbock, 'Surrogate Motherhood as Prenatal Adoption' (1988) Law, Medicine and Healthcare 44, 47–50; LS Cahill, 'The Ethics of Surrogate Motherhood: Biology, Freedom and Moral Obligation' (1988) Law, Medicine and Healthcare 65, 71.

[34] A Whittaker, 'From "Mung Ming" to "Baby Gammy": A Local History of Assisted Reproduction in Thailand' (2016) 2 RBMOnline 71, 76.

[35] Robertson (n 28) 124–35.

[36] See further on the trend towards legislating against donor anonymity: G Cohen, T Coan, M Ottey, et al, 'Sperm Donor Anonymity and Compensation: An Experiment with American Sperm Donors' (2016) 23 Journal of Law and the Biosciences 468.

[37] V Jadva et al, 'Sperm and Oocyte Donors' Experiences of Anonymous Donation and Subsequent Contact with their Donor Offspring' (2010) 26 Human Reproduction 638, doi: https://doi.org/10.1093/humrep/deq364.

[38] Robertson (n 28).

[39] Goold (n 30).

concern is that some *may* experience harm, and so the question is whether they should be protected from such a risk. Respect for autonomy suggests that adults are probably capable of evaluating such risks for themselves well enough to speak against restriction on this basis.

4. Disputes between Partners

Once an embryo is created, a new entity comprised of the gametic material of two people exists. In many cases, it will have been created with the joint, agreed purpose of creating a child. But sometimes, that joint purpose will evaporate before the embryo is implanted and, in such cases, disputes can arise over the fate of stored embryos. The Natalie Evans case is a good example of such a situation. After Evans was diagnosed with ovarian cancer, she and her then-partner, Howard Johnston, decided to create embryos using their sperm and ova to enable them to have children once her cancer was treated. Six embryos were produced and stored. Evans's ovaries were subsequently removed as part of her treatment, rendering her infertile. The couple split before Evans was well enough to have the embryos implanted, and Johnston requested the embryos be destroyed in accordance with his rights under the Human Fertilisation and Embryology Act 1990 (UK). Evans challenged this request, but was ultimately unsuccessful.

One of the key issues in the case was whether Johnston's right to have the embryos destroyed could be overridden by Evans's right to private and family life protected under article 8 of the ECHR. The European Court of Human Rights found that it could not. A particular issue in such cases is that where couples cannot agree over the fate of embryos, there will be harm to at least one party—either one will be unable to have children (or have *those* children that would be born from those embryos), or the other will lose control over their genetic material and become a parent when they do not wish to be.

5. Deceased Partners

IVF has enabled a wholly unique innovation in the creation of children—the ability to conceive a child using gametes from those who have died. Perhaps the least controversial situation is the use of embryos created by the couple prior to the person's death with the intention of creating a child.[40] Less clear-cut are cases where the deceased person had their gametes preserved, and so might have been intending to create a child, possibly with their current partner. Most problematic are the often high-profile cases of gametes (generally sperm) being removed from the body of a recently deceased person to create a child posthumously.[41]

In some cases of this kind, it will be possible to know what the deceased would have wanted to happen. They may have stored gametes knowing they would die and consenting to their partner using them after their death, or they may have expressed wishes about posthumous conception. Usually, however, this will not be the case and respecting their autonomy becomes highly complex. Many such cases involve an attempt to extrapolate what the deceased person would have wanted. This reflects the desire to respect autonomy even post-death, evidencing the deep commitment the law and the community feel to such a

[40] For an example of a recent case approving the implantation of frozen embryos following the father's death, see *Jefferies v BMI Healthcare* [2016] EWHC 2493 (Fam).

[41] In the case of posthumous sperm use, see: *R v Human Fertilization and Embryology Authority, ex p Blood* [1997] 2 All ER 687; and J Keown, 'Life after Death' (1997) 56 Cambridge Law Journal 270.

cause. But we might ask why we should be so concerned, given that the person cannot (it is often argued) be harmed once they have died. John Harris, for example, has argued strongly that the dead cannot have interests, and so cannot be harmed by the choices made by the living once they are gone.[42] Others, such as Margaret Brazier, have countered this view, with some exploring the idea of a narrative conception of life, where our 'story' continues after we die.[43]

If we think the dead have interests after they die, then it may be that we should restrict the use of ARTs to produce posthumous children from the gametes of those we know would have objected, or even more stringently, where we are unsure of their wishes either way. Autonomy concerns are not, however, necessarily the sole determinant of the issue, as a child conceived posthumously might suffer harms—from the knowledge of how they were conceived, as well as the absence of a parent. Given, however, that such children would otherwise not exist at all, we might question whether these harms are sufficient to deny them existence. If existence suffering such potentially quite minor harms is not worse than non-existence, then following Parfit, these harms alone would be insufficient to justify restriction on the harm to the child basis alone.[44]

IV. Restrictions on Selection

Restricting access to ART use encompasses both complete restriction on use and restrictions on *how* it might be used. The primary concerns about the latter relate to using ARTs to determine the characteristics of the child who will result. This encompasses selecting an embryo based on sex (sex selection) or traits (with the goal of producing the 'best' child), and also selecting *against* disability.

A. Sex Selection

Sex selection can be achieved via PGD, and people have varied reasons for wanting a child of a particular sex. For some, it is a matter of family balancing; for others, they may simply prefer a child of one sex because they feel more affinity for male or female children. In such situations, using ARTs to choose the sex of the child will usually be a fairly anodyne decision in terms of impact on others and the community generally. Where there is no cultural preference for a particular sex, one would expect that the gender balance would remain unchanged, and it is not clear that such preferences are likely to harm the child. In context where this is true, prohibition sex selection might then be harming because people are prevented from achieving their reproductive goals without sufficient justification.

However, there is clear evidence that in some cultures there is a gender preference, and this had led to skewed gender ratios. This may have widely harming impacts, as well as

[42] J Harris, 'Law and Regulation of Retained Organs: The Ethical Issues' (2002) 22 Legal Studies 527; J Harris, 'Organ Procurement: Dead Interests, Living Needs' (2003) 29 Journal of Medical Ethics 130.
[43] S McGuiness and M Brazier, 'Respecting the Living Means Respecting the Dead Too' (2008) 28(2) Oxford Journal of Legal Studies 297–316, doi: https://doi.org/10.1093/ojls/gqn005.
[44] Referring back to the Non-Identity Problem mentioned earlier, see D Parfit, *Reasons and Persons* (Clarendon Press, 1987).

reinforcing the legitimacy of preferring one gender over another. However, prohibition of a choice that individuals strongly wish to make can itself have deleterious consequences.[45] In China, while the One-Child policy was still in place, the discarding of female infants was in large part a result of the prohibition on sex selection. The gender imbalance in China suggests that many were managing to find ways to detect the sex of their child,[46] in addition to the well-known phenomenon of female children being left to die.[47]

This makes the restriction of ART use for sex selection complex, as it suggests that the wider cultural context should determine whether individuals can make their own choices about reproduction. It also means that those who happen to bear a child of the desired sex naturally benefit, while others who are not so lucky are denied an outcome they wanted and could otherwise have achieved had they been permitted to use technology to do so. Given the responses to the banning of sex selection we see in India and China, we might also wonder whether the harms of a gender imbalance produced by collective sex selection for the same sex are worse than the harm of female children being abandoned.

B. Trait Selection

This concern has less relevance to the use of ARTs to enable the *choice* of children's traits or which embryo will be implanted, as such choices can only really be effected via ARTs. Even via careful partner choice, the traits of the resulting child for almost all traits and conditions cannot be chosen, although some traits or conditions could be avoided by choosing not to reproduce with a particular person, such as where one or both potential parents are aware that they carry a disease-causing genetic mutation.

Once ARTs can be used to select for or against particular traits beyond disease, these signalling concerns will have greater bite. At present, ARTs cannot really be used to choose a child's traits beyond those disease conditions that are tested for, but it is not too remote a possibility that this will be feasible in the future. Some traits are demonstrably preferred in some communities—beauty (in various forms), intellect, and sporting prowess all seem to be characteristics that many value in their children.[48] If ARTs could be used to select for these traits, we might rightly worry that this would reinforce them as desirable traits. This would be a problem if such reinforcement created a harmful reduction in diversity. It might also be a concern if the selection of these traits led to a more disease-susceptible population or the diversion of resources into the creation of these traits at the expense of others.[49] By

[45] Very few jurisdictions permit sex selection aside from the United States, and in some jurisdictions where there is a clear cultural gender preference, quite stringent controls are in place to prevent illegal sex-selective practices. In India, pre-conception and post-conception sex selection is prohibited by the Pre-Conception and Pre-Natal Diagnostic Techniques (PCPNDT) Act 1994 (India). In China, the Ministry of Health outlawed the practice in 1989, see: Ministry of Health, 'Urgent Notice on Strictly Forbidding the Use of Medical Technology to Perform Prenatal Sex Determination' (1989) (China).

[46] CL Chan, PS Yip, EH Ng, et al, 'Gender Selection in China: Its Meanings and Implications' (2002) 19 Journal of Assisted Reproduction and Genetics 426, 428–9.

[47] D Tabutin and M Willems, 'Excess Female Mortality in the Developing World During the 1970s and 1980s' (1995) 39 Population Bulletin of the United Nations 45; K Johnson, 'The Politics of the Revival of Infant Abandonment in China, with Special Reference to Hunan' (1996) 22 Population and Development Review 77.

[48] D Alwin, 'Changes in Qualities Valued in Children in the United States, 1964 to 1984' (1989) 18 Social Science Research 195.

[49] I am grateful to Charlotte Elves for these points.

contrast, if there was a shift towards selecting for a trait that is *relationally* valuable (that is, valuable if one has it and others do not), this may simply undermine its value. For example, being tall confers a relative advantage, but this might be eradicated if genetic markers for height were always selected for, creating a uniformly tall population with very little variation in height. Alternatively, such selection might simply shift the bell-curve for height variation sideways and redefine what constitutes being 'tall'.

Finally, an oft-cited harm of ART use is the so-called 'commodification' of children that is thought will result if parents actively select the traits of their children. Some suggest this will lead to parents regarding children as commodities rather than valuing them for themselves. For example, Heather Widdows has commented that using technology to choose traits has the potential to 'transform our expectations of the parenting relationship from one of "gift" to one of "contract" and thus potentially encourage a more commodified view of children'.[50]

What would this mean? Well, it might be the case that the parental relationship is damaged in some way, because arguably part of the importance of that relationship is the 'you get what you're given' dimension—parents give children unconditional love regardless of their traits, which is vitally important to a child's sense of self-worth.[51] A variant of this concern is that selecting the traits of children will reduce their capacity for an open future. As Dena Davis writes in relation to sex selection, such choices about a child's traits can limit their right to an open future because:

> it promotes gender role stereotyping and encourages parents to invest heavily in having certain types of children. This combination of investment and stereotyping makes it more difficult for the child to grow and develop in ways that are different than, perhaps even in conflict with, parental expectations.[52]

It may also lead them to face negative parental pressure and adversely affect their sense of self if they cannot or do not wish to fulfil the expectations of their parents' choices about their traits.

3. Disability

After the treatment of infertility, one of the main uses of ARTs is to avoid the creation of a child who will suffer from a serious disability or condition.[53] The definition of 'serious'

[50] H Widdows, 'Persons and Their Parts: New Reproductive Technologies and Risks of Commodification' (2009) 17 Health Care Analysis 36, 38.

[51] For further exploration of this point, see Michael Sandel on 'accepting love' and 'transformational love': M Sandel, 'The Case against Perfection' (2004) 293 Atlantic Monthly 51–62.

[52] D Davis, 'Genetic Dilemmas and the Child's Right to an Open Future' (1997) 28 Rutgers Law Journal 549, 591.

[53] Using ARTs to *select* embryos is controlled in most jurisdictions. In the United Kingdom, eg, PGD is permitted only where there is a particular risk that the embryo may have a genetic condition that will lead to a serious mental or physical disability. Where the condition is sex-linked (and only where this is so), PGD may be used to establish the embryo's sex. Implicitly, then, PGD cannot be used to select against minor conditions, nor (when possible) to select *for* desired traits. The HFEA also permits tissue-typing of embryos to enable the creation of so-called 'saviour siblings', who will be able to provide donor tissue such as bone marrow for an existing child. The HFEA's decision to permit tissue typing for the creation of 'saviour siblings' was approved by the House of Lords in *Quintavalle (on behalf of the Comment on Reproductive Ethics) v Human Fertilisation and Embryology Authority* [2005] UKHL 28.

varies, but tends to encompass conditions with high mortality rates, severe disability, and those which may cause substantial pain and suffering (or a combination of these). Conditions that meet this threshold in many jurisdictions include Fragile X syndrome, cystic fibrosis, beta-thalassemia, and Duchenne muscular dystrophy.[54] Different jurisdictions have adopted various approaches to the use of PGD. In the United Kingdom, a list of conditions for which PGD can be used is proscribed by the HFEA.[55] In France, the decisions regarding the use of PGD are taken on a case-by-case basis by the Multidisciplinary Centre for Pregnancy Diagnosis, and, in Italy, no list of conditions nor formal mechanism for decision making exists.[56]

It is sometimes argued in relation to some disabilities that selection against them sends a signal to those living with disability (particularly the same disability) that their lives are less valuable than those of able-bodied persons. Tom Shakespeare has commented that: 'It may be claimed that prenatal diagnosis discriminates against disabled children and adults, because it sends the message that it would have been better if they, too, had not been born.'[57]

He goes on to explain that upon hearing the ways in which avoiding disability is spoken about and the language used: 'A person with a congenital impairment immediately imagines whether their own parents would have taken advantage of the technology. It brings up fears about rejection and not being wanted by one's own family or society.'[58]

This argument has often been made in response to Julian Savulescu's Principle of Procreative Beneficence, which holds that where the choice is available, all other things being equal, parents should choose to implant the 'best' embryo, that is, the one who will have (as far as we can tell with the information at hand) the greatest well-being.[59] Savulescu's argument is made in relation to embryo selection and he is referring to genetic traits as the information we can access to make predictions about well-being, as such traits can contribute to (as well as reduce) well-being.

Savulescu responds that even if the disability discrimination concerns voiced by the like of Shakespeare are not without basis, to inflict upon a couple a higher risk of having a child with a disability in favour of social equality is an undesirable step.[60] While this may be the case, it does not entirely address the concern that a clear indication is made at the community level that some lives are to be prevented, while others are to be promoted, and for those who experience their disability as an integral aspect of their life, then the message that theirs is not a wanted life remains. The issue is whether this causes harm to such people, and even if it does, whether the harm of knowing that others would avoid their life is a sufficient reason to continue to bring into existence people whose lives will be attended by disability.

[54] See eg Reproductive Technology Council of Australia, 'Policy on Approval of Diagnostic Procedures Involving Embryos' (April 2017), http://www.rtc.org.au/wp-content/uploads/2016/11/V2-PGD-Policy-on-approval-of-Diagnostic-Procedures-Involving-Embryos-Mar-2008-2017_03_30-web.pdf accessed 15 July 2019.

[55] Human Fertilisation and Embryology Agency, 'PGD Conditions Licensed by the HFEA,' https://www.hfea.gov.uk/pgd-conditions/ accessed 15 July 2019.

[56] For a comparative analysis of PGD policy and law, see MJ Bayefsky, 'Comparative Preimplantation Genetic Diagnosis Policy in Europe and the USA and Its Implications for Reproductive Tourism' (2017) 3 Reproductive BioMedicine and Society Online 41–7, doi: https://doi.org/10.1016/j.rbms.2017.01.001; Loi No 94-654 du 29 juillet 1994 relative au don et à l'utilisation des éléments et produits du corps humain, à l'assistance médicale à la procréation et au diagnostic prénatal (France); L 40/2004 (Italy).

[57] T Shakespeare, *Disability Rights and Wrongs Revisited* (2nd edn, Routledge, 2014), 118–19.

[58] Ibid.

[59] Savulescu (n 13).

[60] Ibid 423.

A blanket position on this point is difficult to take because the impact of disability on a person's life varies by the condition, the context, the support they receive, and their own personal reaction to that condition. The issue is far more contentious in relation to conditions that seemingly lead to less harm, whereas (as in the legislation in many jurisdictions) there is at least legally widespread agreement that it is right to prevent ARTs from being used to bring into the world children who will experience substantial pain or suffering.

These restrictions stand in some contrast to the concerns about the welfare of the child. While access to ART might be entirely denied on the basis of the *possibility* that the parents will harm the child (based on past actions), or the *risk* of an inherited condition, PGD can only be used to avoid creating a child who will suffer harm if that harm is very serious. Conversely, ARTs are not restricted when used to create children who may suffer in the course of providing tissue for a sibling. This suffering might include pain and anxiety, medical complications, and possibly parental approbation if they refuse to comply (attended by emotional and psychological impacts). Such a child might also struggle with their own sense of identity and self-knowing that they were created not for their own sake perhaps, but for that of someone else. There is a degree of incoherence in this approach to welfare as a basis for restricting access.

V. Discrimination Concerns

Amel Alghrani and John Harris have rightly pointed out that using access to ARTs to restrict the reproductive decisions of those who need them to have children is a form of discrimination. They argue that: 'The very fact the law insists that only those individuals who require assistance in founding a family are screened for their potential as prospective parents is not only inconsistent and unjustifiable, but is a clear violation of reproductive liberty.'[61]

One response to this is that where those choices are likely to be harming to the child who will result, then this outweighs the harm of discrimination. Arguably, limiting some harmful choices is better than limiting none for the sake of avoiding discrimination where those choices are likely to lead to a child experiencing real suffering. We could avoid discrimination and prevent harm by restricting all people who might cause harm to their future child from procreating, but to do so would entail policing people's sexual habits or infringing their bodily integrity to enforce contraception upon them, both of which are such substantial infringements on liberty. It is likely that such an invasion could not be tolerated even to prevent harm to a future child, because of this impact on bodily integrity. By contrast, the mere restriction of access to ART carries no such harm and so such restrictions seem less problematic and the discrimination objection might pale against the desire to save at least some future children from problems.

[61] A Alghrani and J Harris, 'Reproductive Liberty: Should the Foundation of Families Be Regulated?' (2006) 18 Child and Family Law Quarterly 191, 197.

F. Conclusion

The questions of whether and how we restrict access to ARTs are ethically challenging because they involve the welfare and autonomy of one or more existing people, and the interests of a person who may one day come to exist. They demand that we think about the highly vexed question of the moral status of the embryo, and how much importance we place on facilitating people's choices about reproduction. Into this mix comes the question of resource allocation, as well as difficult issues around our attitudes towards and understanding of disability. It is not surprising that these questions continue to challenge us, and with ongoing advances in reproductive technology, no doubt they will continue to do so.

14
Abortion on the Basis of a Risk of Disability
The Parents' Interests and Shared Interests

Heloise Robinson

I. Introduction

The morality of abortion is a particularly contentious issue, and the morality of abortion on the basis of a risk of disability is no less so—in fact, it raises all the same moral issues as abortion generally, as well as concerns specifically relating to the use of disability to justify abortion. Interestingly, however, in the literature there is no agreement as to whether the risk of disability should make any difference as to the permissibility of abortion on the ground of disability, as compared to abortion for other reasons. Further, for those who believe that the risk of disability should make a difference, there is significant support in the literature both for the perspective that abortion for this reason is *less* morally objectionable, and for the view that it is *more* morally objectionable.

The aim of this chapter is to briefly review these different ethical perspectives on the morality of abortion on the basis of a risk of disability, and to examine the extent to which arguments made in this area are strongly linked to the interests of certain relevant persons or groups—especially to the interests of the parents, the foetus, and others such as disabled people living with the same condition which can be detected prenatally. Although the moral status of the foetus is, of course, a crucial question to determining the morality of abortion on the basis of a risk of disability, I will not argue for or against foetal personhood, but will instead focus on examining the extent of the apparent conflict between the interests of various stakeholders—in particular, between the interests of the parents and those of others. Although at first it appears as though the interests of the parents in having the choice to avoid the perceived additional burdens which come from caring for a disabled child are strongly opposed to the interests of many others, in particular to those of the foetus and of disabled people, I will argue that the parents' interests are often only superficially understood. When the nature of the parents' choice is analysed more fully, and when the consequences and costs of choice are taken into consideration, the parents' interests become more aligned with the interests of others than they may at first appear to be.

II. Abortion and the Relevance of the Disability Ground

The morality of abortion on the basis of disability is not always considered to raise significantly different questions from the morality of abortion generally. According to a 'pro-life' view which contends that abortion is generally morally unacceptable, abortion on the basis of disability could be considered to be equally morally unacceptable as abortion for other

Heloise Robinson, *Abortion on the Basis of a Risk of Disability* In: *Philosophical Foundations of Medical Law*. Edited by: Andelka M Phillips, Thana C de Campos, and Jonathan Herring, Oxford University Press (2019).
DOI: 10.1093/oso/9780198796558.003.0015

reasons. If the foetus should be given the same consideration as other human beings from the time of conception (or at the time of the abortion), he or she should not be killed any more than a born infant or adult who is disabled should be killed;[1] the fact that the foetus is disabled does not have an impact on its moral status.[2]

Similarly, the morality of abortion on the basis of disability does not necessarily raise significantly different moral issues from abortion generally for some people with a 'pro-choice' view. Whereas the belief that the foetus has full moral status can lead to the condemnation of abortion, whether or not there is a risk of disability, the view that the foetus lacks moral status can lead to the permissibility of abortion, whether or not there is a risk of disability. In particular, the argument that women should have access to abortion on the basis of reproductive freedom can be similarly used in the case of abortion where there is a risk of disability. John Robertson, for example, has stated that having access to prenatal testing and abortion is essential to procreative freedom, since women are 'deprived of procreative freedom if the state bans use of prenatal screening techniques because of objections to abortion'.[3] According to this author:

> If a woman has a moral right to end an unwanted pregnancy when the fetus is healthy, she would also have a right to terminate a pregnancy when the fetus has a genetic defect. Freedom to abort a normal pregnancy implies an equal freedom to avoid the special burdens of having a handicapped child.[4]

Despite the fact that a very 'pro-life' view and a very 'pro-choice' view surprisingly share an important point in common—that abortion on the basis of disability need not be considered morally different from abortion generally[5]—there is considerable support in the

[1] John Finnis, eg, states that 'the foetus from conception has human rights, i.e. should be given the same consideration as other human beings': J Finnis, 'The Rights and Wrongs of Abortion: A Reply to Judith Thomas' (1973) 2 Philosophy and Public Affairs 117, reprinted in RM Dworkin (ed), *The Philosophy of Law* (Oxford University Press, 1977), 129. This work is also found in J Finnis, *Human Rights and Common Good: Collected Essays* (Oxford University Press, 2011), vol III, 282–306. Other authors who consider that embryos and foetuses are persons with a right to life include, eg: C Wolf-Devine and PE Devine, 'Abortion: A Communitarian Pro-Life Perspective' in M Tooley et al, *Abortion: Three Perspectives* (Oxford University Press, 2009), 87. See also RP George and C Tollefsen, *Embryo: A Defense of Human Life* (1st edn, Doubleday, 2008) and (2nd edn, Witherspoon Institute, 2011); P Lee, C Tollefsen, and RP George, 'The Ontological Status of Embryos: A Reply to Jason Morris' (2014) 39 Journal of Medicine and Philosophy 483; P Lee, CO Tollefsen, and RP George, 'Marco Rubio Is Right: The Life of a New Human Being Begins at Conception', *The Public Discourse* (2015), http://www.thepublicdiscourse.com/2015/08/15520 accessed 15 July 2019. See also J Finnis, 'Capacity, Harm and Experience in the Life of Persons as Equals' (2013) 39 Journal of Medical Ethics 281, 282: what matters is the capacity for self-consciousness, which is shared by all humans, 'even when its exercise is prevented by sleep, illness, disability, immaturity or decay'.

[2] I am grateful to Jonathan Herring for his remark that there might conceivably be a case where the disability is so severe that the foetus could be considered to be already dead, or to never have been a person, perhaps, eg, in the case where the foetus has no brain at all. I am also grateful to him for drawing my attention here to the fact that in relation to sentencing in murder cases, distinctions can be drawn with regard to the seriousness of the offence, which may suggest that the law does seem to accept that some murders are worse than others. The seriousness of the offence can be considered to be particularly or exceptionally high, eg, if it involves the murder of a police officer, or the murder of a child involving the abduction of the child or sexual or sadistic motivation (see, eg, Sch 21 of the Criminal Justice Act 2003).

[3] JA Robertson, *Children of Choice: Freedom and the New Reproductive Technologies* (Princeton University Press, 1994), 157.

[4] Ibid 158–9.

[5] This interesting point of agreement between two divided sides of the debate is noted in S Sheldon and S Wilkinson, 'Termination of Pregnancy for Reason of Foetal Disability: Are There Grounds for a Special Exception in Law?' (2001) 9 Medical Law Review 85.

literature for the view that the morality of abortion for this reason should be evaluated differently, and this appears to be supported by the current position in the law.

III. The Parents' Interests and the Law

The Abortion Act of 1967 appears to reflect the view that abortion on the basis of a risk of disability is *less* morally objectionable than abortion for most other reasons.[6] Section 1(1)(d) of the Act provides that a pregnancy may be terminated if there is a 'substantial risk that if the child were born it would suffer from such physical or mental abnormalities as to be seriously handicapped'. This provision, together with the other three grounds under section 1(1), provides an exception to the law on abortion which normally makes abortion a crime, in particular under the Offences against the Person Act 1861.[7] However, whereas the vast majority of terminations in England and Wales take place under section 1(1)(a), which is a ground available only up to twenty-four weeks' gestation, section 1(1)(d) allows termination until birth.[8] Section 1(1)(a) allows termination based on a risk of injury to the woman's physical or mental health, and 97.7 per cent of abortions take place under this ground, according to the latest statistics from 2018.[9] Sections 1(1)(b) and 1(1)(c), which are very rarely used—they comprised 0.07 per cent of cases in 2018[10]—also provide grounds for abortion at any stage of pregnancy; section 1(1)(b) may be used if the termination is necessary to prevent 'grave permanent injury' to the physical or mental health of the pregnant woman, and section 1(1)(c) may be used if there is a risk to the pregnant woman's life.

Due to the fact that abortion is a crime unless it falls under one of the exceptions under the Abortion Act, the law on abortion reflects the view that abortion is generally undesirable, but that it can be allowed in certain exceptional circumstances.[11] The law also appears to suggest that abortion on the basis of disability is less morally objectionable than most other abortions, given that this ground can be invoked until birth. It is true that the absence of a time limit under section 1(1)(d) might reflect the fact that a substantial risk of disability can only in some cases be discovered after twenty-four weeks. However, a risk to the pregnant woman's physical or mental health, which could legally justify termination for only the first twenty-four weeks under section 1(1)(a), may also be only discoverable after twenty-four weeks. For example, the pregnant woman could develop a health condition which is a risk to her health only after twenty-four weeks, but that is nevertheless not serious enough to cause her grave permanent injury.

Recently, some authors have examined what arguments could justify a special exception in the law based on the risk of disability.[12] Sheldon and Wilkinson, for example, argue that

[6] Abortion Act 1967 (as amended).

[7] Sections 58 and 59. See also the Infant (Life) Preservation Act 1929.

[8] Department of Health and Social Care, 'Abortion Statistics, England and Wales: 2018', Department of Health and Social Care (June 2019), https://www.gov.uk/government/statistics/abortion-statistics-for-england-and-wales-2018 accessed 6 September 2019.

[9] Ibid. Section 1(1)(a) can also be used where there is a risk of injury to any existing children of the family, although this reason is far more rarely invoked: ibid. In cases relying only on the risk to the woman's physical or mental health, 99.9 per cent of abortions were reported as being performed due to a risk to the woman's mental health (ibid).

[10] Ibid.

[11] See Sheldon and Wilkinson (n 5) 99.

[12] In addition, a number of speakers, including John Finnis, recently examined some of the issues raised by abortion on the ground of disability at a conference organized by the Anscombe Bioethics Centre, 'Abortion,

the only acceptable explanation—and only then it would be merely a partial justification—is the Parental Interests Argument: that the parents have an interest in being able to choose to avoid the additional strain of caring for a disabled child.[13] The authors insist, however, that much of the strain may result from social discrimination and lack of support, rather than from the impairment itself. It would only be the strain caused by the impairment itself, according to the authors, which could provide a justification for the disability ground.

Sheldon and Wilkinson also examine two other arguments which could potentially justify section 1(1)(d), but they reject them both. The first of these is based on the foetus's interests, the 'Foetal Interests Argument'; this argument cannot succeed, say the authors, because in most cases the child will have a life worth living and therefore it cannot be in the foetus's interests to die rather than to live life as a disabled person. The second argument, which they call the 'Replacement Argument', is that the disabled foetus should be killed for utilitarian reasons, in order to increase overall welfare; if the disabled foetus is killed, it is thought that another child would be conceived instead, who, if healthy, would increase the overall level of welfare in the world. However, Sheldon and Wilkinson note that this argument is based on the foetus having a very low status, and that proponents of the Replacement Argument would not normally be in favour of killing adults with disabilities in order to replace them with non-disabled adults. Furthermore, the authors explain that the replacement argument would in fact call for a much more permissive abortion law generally, which would allow all sorts of utilitarian considerations to justify abortion, including, for example, if the parents wished to replace an average foetus with an enhanced one, or to have an abortion in order to address world overpopulation. Thus, according to Sheldon and Wilkinson, the Replacement Argument does not explain why the disabled foetus should be singled out, and cannot provide a justification for section 1(1)(d) specifically.

Sheldon and Wilkinson are not alone in stressing the importance of the parents' interests in avoiding the perceived additional burdens of caring for a disabled child, and this consideration features frequently in the literature. Although the same considerations can apply to rearing children without disabilities, many authors nevertheless point to the perceived unending work for the parents, and especially for mothers, in caring for a disabled child, to the sacrifice of their career and interests, to the loss of time available for other family members, and to the increased financial strain.[14] Furthermore, despite the studies which show that many families of disabled children report that their disabled child enriched their lives,[15] there is also a common assumption, found in much of the medical, social science, and bioethics literature, that raising a disabled child offers no benefit in return for all the parents'

Disability and the Law', which took place on 18 February 2017. The podcasts are available at http://www.bioethics.org.uk/page/resources/multimedia accessed 15 July 2019.

13 Sheldon and Wilkinson (n 5).

14 See eg DC Wertz and JC Fletcher, 'A Critique of Some Feminist Challenges to Prenatal Diagnosis' (1993) 2 Journal of Women's Health 173. For a critique of the negative assumptions about disability, see A Asch, 'Prenatal Diagnosis and Selective Abortion: A Challenge to Practice and Policy' (1999) 89 American Journal of Public Health 1649.

15 See eg with regard to trisomy 13 and 18: A Janvier, B Farlow, and BS Wilfond, 'The Experience of Families with Children with Trisomy 13 and 18 in Social Networks' (2012) 130 Pediatrics 293. See also, eg, with regard to parents of children with Down's syndrome, BG Skotko, SP Levine, and R Goldstein, 'Having a Son or Daughter with Down Syndrome: Perspectives from Mothers and Fathers' (2011) 155 American Journal of Medical Genetics Part A 2335.

sacrifice, on the basis that disabled children cannot bring the same rewards as non-disabled children.[16]

However, an argument based on the parents' interests is also logically deficient. If burdens to parents are a reason to justify abortion up until birth, it is not clear why only the alleged burdens of raising a disabled child provide a justification, and not burdens arising from other causes. For example, a parent losing a job, the death of the child's father, or a sudden illness in the family that would involve significant caring responsibilities might also materially increase the parents' (or mother's) perceived burdens in raising the child after he or she is born, even if the child is not disabled.

IV. The Interests of Others: The Disabled Child and Disabled People

As seen above, for many authors, the parents' interests can be seen as a reason to view abortion on the basis of disability as less morally objectionable than abortion for most other reasons. I have examined some reasons for which the parents' interests appear to be an insufficient consideration to justify the disability ground. Moreover, even if it were in the parents' interests to have the choice to abort their disabled child, these interests would be in conflict with the interests of other key constituencies—in particular, those of the disabled foetus or child and of disabled people generally.

As mentioned above, abortion on the basis of disability can be said to harm the child's own interests, who would be better off alive. Indeed, although some say that it is in the child's interests not to be born if it would have a very low quality of life, and even that the parents may have a duty to avoid the birth of such a child,[17] it is doubtful that there are many, if any, conditions that would mean that it is in the child's own interests not to be born. Very often, reference is made to only a few serious conditions, in particular Tay-Sachs and Lesch-Nyhan syndrome.[18] However, if it is thought that the disabled child will have a good or even a reasonable quality of life once he or she is born, it cannot be said that it is not in his or her interests to be born.[19] Current data on the quality of life of disabled people indicate that disability does not prevent a satisfying life.[20] In fact, while non-disabled people

[16] This assumption is discussed and criticized in Asch (n 14) 1653. It is important to note here that this assumption can be expressed by those who are not raising disabled children, and many of those who are do not agree.

[17] J Glover, *Choosing Children: Genes, Disability and Design* (Clarendon Press, 2006), 58.

[18] See eg R Scott, *Choosing between Possible Lives: Law and Ethics of Prenatal and Preimplantation Genetic Diagnosis* (Hart Publishing, 2007), 29–30; T Shakespeare, *Disability Rights and Wrongs Revisited* (2nd edn, Routledge, 2014), 123–4.

[19] See R Scott, 'Interpreting the Disability Ground of the Abortion Act' (2005) 64 Cambridge Law Journal 388, 398. I am also grateful to Jonathan Herring for pointing out here a different argument with regard to the child's interests, based on the view that it is in the child's interests to be virtuous; according to this argument, there may be a case where the burdens to the parents are sufficiently great, and the value of the child's life is considered to be sufficiently limited, that it may be argued that it is in the child's *own* interests to spare the parents the burden of caring for him or her, based on the child's wish to deny detriment to his or her loved ones. This type of case may, however, never arise in practice, and, of course, there are a number of risks in taking this approach, including in particular from the act of judging the value of the child's life, and from the fact that the parents are in a much more powerful position than disabled unborn children, whose interests are wholly determined by others and who cannot speak for themselves. For more on the virtue idea of well-being, see eg J Herring and C Foster, 'Welfare Means Relationality, Virtue and Altruism' (2012) 32 Legal Studies 480.

[20] See eg Asch (n 14); J Wyatt, 'End of Life Decisions, Quality of Life and the Newborn' (2007) 96 Acta Paediatrica 790; CV Bellieni and G Buonocore, 'Flaws in the Assessment of the Best Interests of the Newborn' (2009) 98 Acta Paediatrica 613.

generally consider that disabled people appear to live an undesirable existence, many disabled people themselves consider that they have a good or excellent quality of life.[21] Further, the quality of life of patients with severe medical disorders is often underestimated by other people, including healthy individuals, caregivers, and health-care professionals.[22] Indeed, listening to the views of disabled people and their families may well be our best guide to assess the experience of disability.[23]

Further, and as noted earlier, many of the challenges faced by disabled people and their families are not due to the impairment itself, but from discrimination and a lack of social support. The view that disability is an individual medical problem, resulting merely from the impairment itself, is supported by the medical conception of disability.[24] However, proponents of the social conception of disability argue that there is not necessarily a causal link between impairment and disability; while the existence of impairment is not denied, it is not considered to be the cause of disabled people's economic and social disadvantage.[25] A number of the challenges facing disabled people and their families can be overcome by environmental, architectural, societal, and cultural changes.

In addition to the harm directed to the children themselves from not being born, many have claimed that prenatal testing expresses discriminatory or hurtful views about disabled people living with the same traits—this has been called the expressivist argument.[26] Thus, disabled people may say that prenatal screening for the same condition which they have devalues their lives, and sends the message that they would be better off dead. In prenatal testing, parents and others are also focusing on only one of the child's traits—the potential disability—and are not considering the child as a whole person. Adrienne Asch explains that prenatal testing leads to a single trait standing in for the whole (potential) person, and gives the message that 'people are reducible to a single, perceived-to-be-undesirable trait'.[27] Similarly, genetic determinism—the idea that our identity or behaviour is merely a result of our genes—reduces the complexity of human identity. People should not be defined by a single trait, whether that be sex, hair colour or blindness, or musical ability or intellectual impairment, and it is dehumanizing—not only for the disabled foetus, but also for disabled people living with the same trait, and indeed for all of us—to ignore that we are complex beings with many facets to our identity. An inclusive and tolerant society must therefore not only accept people with a wide range of different traits, but must also see beyond these traits and consider the whole person.

[21] GL Albrecht and PJ Devlieger, 'The Disability Paradox: High Quality of Life against All Odds' (1999) 48 Social Science & Medicine 977.

[22] Z Simmons, 'Patient-Perceived Outcomes and Quality of Life in ALS' (2015) 12 Neurotherapeutics 394.

[23] On the importance of listening to the parents of children with Down's syndrome, see eg C Kaposy, *Choosing Down Syndrome: Ethics and New Prenatal Testing Technologies* (MIT Press, 2018).

[24] C Barnes, 'Understanding the Social Model of Disability: Past, Present and Future' in N Watson, A Roulstone, and C Thomas (eds), *Routledge Handbook of Disability Studies* (Routledge, 2012), 12.

[25] M Oliver and C Barnes, *The New Politics of Disablement* (Palgrave Macmillan, 2012), 22.

[26] See eg E Parens and A Asch, 'The Disability Rights Critique of Prenatal Genetic Testing: Reflections and Recommendations' (1999) 29(5) Hastings Center Report S1, S2.

[27] Ibid: this view is specifically attributed to one of the authors, Adrienne Asch. To give just one example of termination as a result of one trait/disability, in 2013, 90 per cent of women had a termination following a prenatal diagnosis of Down's syndrome in England and Wales: JK Morris and A Springett, 'The National Down Syndrome Cytogenetic Register for England and Wales 2013 Annual Report', Queen Mary University of London, Barts and The London School of Medicine and Dentistry (December 2014), https://www.qmul.ac.uk/wolfson/research-projects/current-projects/projects/national-down-syndrome-cytogenetic-register-ndscr.html accessed 6 September 2019.

The expressivist argument may be understood from the point of view of the woman's decision, so that the woman's choice to have an abortion on the grounds of disability expresses the view that it is better for a disabled child not to be born. However, as Jonathan Herring explains, a stronger version of the expressivist argument is that it is the legislation which expresses a negative message about disability, and that singling out disability as one of the few grounds for which abortion is lawful after twenty-four weeks expresses the view of the state that disability alone is a good enough reason for an abortion.[28]

The interests of disabled people, then, can be seen as a reason for which abortion on the basis of disability, and in particular legislation allowing abortion specifically on the basis of disability, may be *more* morally objectionable than abortion (or legislation permitting abortion) for most other reasons, or at least, for which abortion on the basis of disability raises additional moral considerations.

V. The Parents' Interests and Shared Interests

As mentioned above, and despite the numerous limitations to the argument, it is commonly considered that it is in the parents' interests to have the choice (although not the obligation) to use prenatal testing and to abort, in the case of a substantial risk of serious disability, on the basis that caring for a disabled child will involve considerable additional strain. However, an analysis of the parents' interests cannot be complete without examining two additional considerations: first, whether the parents of disabled children do in fact have a free choice; and, second, even assuming that their choice is free, whether there are also significant costs to their choice which work against their own interests. When these considerations are also taken into account, the parents' interests may appear to be more aligned with those of others than they first appear to be—and these others include not only the disabled foetus or child and disabled people generally, but also society as a whole.

A. A Free Choice?

There is an important body of literature supporting the view that, in many cases, the parents' choice to abort a disabled child is not in fact fully free.[29] In fact, for some, this leads to a fear that prenatal testing constitutes a form of eugenics. Given that eugenics is usually considered to constitute efforts to improve the human gene pool and to involve state coercion, individual and autonomous parental decisions to abort a disabled child are not morally problematic for some authors, as they are not a deliberate attempt to improve human hereditary qualities on a large scale, nor do they result from coercion.[30] However, even in the absence of coercion, a form of eugenics may be involved if the parents' choices are constrained, and if the parents are pressured or encouraged to abort their disabled child due to the perceived disadvantages associated with disability. If this is the case, the parents would

[28] J Herring, 'Re B (A Minor) (Wardship: Medical Treatment) [1981]: "The Child Must Live": Disability, Parents and the Law' in J Herring and J Wall (eds), *Landmark Cases in Medical Law* (Hart Publishing, 2015), 80.

[29] See the rest of the discussion on this point in this section; relevant references can be found in nn 32–47.

[30] See eg Shakespeare (n 18) 115–16; S Wilkinson, *Choosing Tomorrow's Children: The Ethics of Selective Reproduction* (Oxford University Press, 2010), 155.

not necessarily be acting freely, and they may be pressured into acting in a way that conforms to societal expectations. Even if it is accepted that they have an interest in having a choice, their interest is not protected if the choice is merely illusory as they were pressured into making it.[31]

Thus, as mentioned earlier, and as those who support the social conception of disability will argue, many of the disadvantages associated with disability can be overcome with proper social support and funding. If the cost of screening and abortion is provided through public funding, but society does not provide adequate assistance to disabled children, there is not in fact a real choice, or at least, there is only a choice between difficult or impossible options,[32] which does not in fact allow for autonomy. The fact that merely having choices is not sufficient to allow for autonomy is illustrated, for example, by Joseph Raz in his well-known example of the man in the pit.[33] Raz describes an imaginary case where a man falls down a pit and stays there for the rest of his life. He has just enough food to allow him to survive, but he cannot do much, and can hardly move. As Raz states: 'His choices are confined to whether to eat now or a little later, whether to sleep now or a little later, whether to scratch his left ear or not.'[34] In this case, the man does not lead an autonomous life, because his range of options is extremely limited. One need not (nor could have) full control over every choice, explains Raz, but in order to be autonomous, one needs an adequate range of options.[35]

Another reason why the parents' choice is not fully free is that it is often based on misinformation, including overly negative information about disability.[36] Indeed, the very act of offering prenatal screening is not neutral; it implies that screening is a recommendation, that the trait in question is undesirable, and that a positive diagnosis should lead to termination.[37] Numerous authors point to the fact that so-called non-directive genetic counselling is not in fact neutral.[38] There is also considerable support from research that families of disabled people do not in fact experience more stress than other families.[39] For a choice to be more fully informed as well as more fully free, it is not sufficient for it to be based only on a description of the impairment. There could also be, for example, a list of the legal rights and services available to disabled people, as well as financial assistance, information from disabled people and their families themselves, and the offer of a visit with both a child and family and an adult living with the disability in question.[40] Of course, although this

[31] Making a constrained choice is not the same, however, as not having the capacity to make the decision; see s 2(1) of the Mental Capacity Act 2005: 'a person lacks capacity in relation to a matter if at the material time he is unable to make a decision for himself in relation to the matter because of an impairment of, or a disturbance in the functioning of, the mind or brain'. My discussion of choice here does not relate to capacity.

[32] See A Lippman, 'Choice as a Risk to Women's Health' (1999) 1 Health, Risk & Society 281; T Shakespeare, 'Choices and Rights: Eugenics, Genetics and Disability Equality' (1998) 13 Disability & Society 665.

[33] J Raz, *The Morality of Freedom* (Clarendon Press, 1986), 373–4.

[34] Ibid 374.

[35] Ibid 373. See also *R v Kirk* [2008] EWCA Crim 434: there was no genuine consent to sexual intercourse in this case, where an adolescent girl had run away from home, had nowhere to go, and was very hungry. In return for sex, she was paid £3.25, with which she bought food.

[36] On the relationship between disclosure and informed consent, see *Montgomery v Lanarkshire Health Board* [2015] UKSC 11.

[37] Shakespeare (n 32), 676. See also C Williams, P Alderson, and B Farsides, 'Too Many Choices? Hospital and Community Staff Reflect on the Future of Prenatal Screening' (2002) 55 Social Science & Medicine 743.

[38] See eg A Kerr, S Cunningham-Burley, and A Amos, 'Eugenics and the New Genetics in Britain: Examining Contemporary Professionals' Accounts' (1998) 23 Science, Technology, & Human Values 175.

[39] Asch (n 14).

[40] Ibid 1655.

information would provide a more balanced view of the choice in question, it would still be impossible for parents ever to have all the information which could be relevant to their decision, given the infinite amount of potentially relevant facts.[41] It is also uncertain that the parents would have the time to confidently assimilate a significant amount of information within a short period of time, especially if they are emotionally vulnerable and in a state of shock. However, in the absence of credible efforts to provide a more balanced and nuanced approach (one that reviews not only the challenges, but also the opportunities for families with disabled children), the parents' choice cannot be understood as a truly free one.

A further constraint on the choice of parents results from the risk of blaming the pregnant woman if she refuses to undergo prenatal screening and then has a disabled child with the condition in question.[42] Elisabeth Beck-Gernstein, for example, writes how good health is now seen as a responsibility and an obligation, but that with responsibility comes blame; women who choose not to undergo prenatal testing 'are seen as ignorant, stupid or egoistic'.[43] In addition, Abby Lippman writes how choice can leave women worse off, as it is difficult to refuse prenatal diagnosis without being made to feel culpable if a baby with Down's syndrome is born.[44] David Pfeiffer explains how an inaccurate assumption about disabled people is the 'myth of sin': 'Frequently, people in society attempt to locate the blame or reason for everything perceived as "bad". When nothing else can be blamed, sin is the obvious alternative explanation.'[45] Thus, 'the cause of a disability must be someone's sin or wrong doing'.[46] Similarly, Jonathan Herring writes how we like to think of disabled people as the 'other' in order to mask our fear, and convince ourselves (mistakenly) that their vulnerability and dependence are not features which we in fact all share: 'Illness is too powerful a reminder of our finality and precarious nature. We are "other" than these things.'[47] Thus, if we believe that having a disabled child is not something that can happen to any of us, but only to those 'others' who are in some way at fault, we may believe that we can distance ourselves from what feels like an uncomfortable reality. This, in turn, also risks making us less likely to promote tolerance and inclusion, which are values that are generally highly regarded in society.[48]

B. Choice and Costs

The above constraint on a truly free choice—that it is accompanied by blame and distancing—shows that choice does not come without its own additional costs. Indeed, even

[41] See C Foster, *Choosing Life, Choosing Death: The Tyranny of Autonomy in Medical Ethics and Law* (Hart Publishing, 2009), 13. Of course, this impossibility in obtaining all potentially relevant facts applies to all decisions, not just to the decision to abort or not a foetus feared to be disabled.

[42] See Williams et al (n 37); E Beck-Gernstein, 'Health and Responsibility: From Social Change to Technological Change and Vice Versa' in B Adam, U Beck, and J Loon (eds), *The Risk Society and Beyond: Critical Issues for Social Theory* (Sage Publications, 2000); Lippman (n 32).

[43] Beck-Gerstein, ibid, 131. See also G Dworkin, *The Theory and Practice of Autonomy* (Cambridge University Press, 1988), 67–8.

[44] Lippman (n 32) 287.

[45] D Pfeiffer, 'Eugenics and Disability Discrimination' (1994) 9 Disability & Society 481, 487–8.

[46] Ibid.

[47] J Herring, 'Health as Vulnerability; Interdependence and Relationality' (2016) 22 New Bioethics 18, 21.

[48] On some of the positive sides of raising disabled children, see also J Herring, 'Parental Responsibility, Hyper-Parenting and the Role of Technology' in R Brownsword, E Scotford, and K Yeung (eds), *The Oxford Handbook of Law, Regulation and Technology* (Oxford University Press, 2017), 404–23.

if there were a completely free choice in prenatal screening, it is well recognized that having more choice is not necessarily better. There are a number of cases where more choice is not necessarily desirable: these include, for example, cases where a proliferation of choices means that we need to take more time and effort in making a choice, where there may be a psychic cost because we worry afterwards about whether we have made the right decision, and where the pressure to conform may put pressure on us to make a decision we may not otherwise necessarily want to make.[49] With regard to prenatal testing, many who believe in the moral permissibility of abortion on the ground of disability may think that it is worth spending time and effort over making a decision with such significant consequences; however, it is easy to imagine how having the choice increases the chance of second-guessing the decision, leading to long-term regret and anxiety.[50] It is also not difficult to understand how, the more parents use the technology to avoid having disabled children, the more there will be pressure on other parents to do the same, thus making the choice more constrained, and society less tolerant and inclusive of disabled people.[51]

With regard to regret, it is also worth noting that many parents with disabled children are very grateful for their children, even while admitting that they would have done anything to avoid having them.[52] As Andrew Solomon writes, many parents of disabled children conclude that while they thought they were being held back by a catastrophic loss of hope, 'they were in fact falling in love with someone they didn't yet know enough to want. As such parents look back, they see how every stage of loving their child has enriched them in ways they never would have conceived, ways that are incalculably precious'.[53] Parents of disabled children often come to realize how much their children can contribute to the diversity and richness of society, and appreciate the special traits and skills that their disabilities can produce.[54]

Recent findings from hedonic psychology, a new field of research in social psychology, also support the view that more choice does not necessarily lead to greater happiness. According to the process of hedonic adaptation, large changes in hedonic states—such as extreme happiness or sadness—do not last very long, and are soon followed by a return to the previous levels of happiness. Thus, a lottery winner will experience a temporary heightened state of happiness, and a person becoming paraplegic will experience a temporary loss of happiness, but both will eventually find their happiness levels revert to their previous state.[55] We can therefore understand why parents of disabled children, once they have overcome the shock of having a child with an unexpected disability, might report similar levels of happiness to parents of non-disabled children. This also suggests that we may be very bad judges of our own future happiness. However, according to Ron Amundson, who describes the process of hedonic adaptation, there is a crucial condition for the process to

[49] See Dworkin (n 43) ch 5. For a further discussion of whether more choice is necessarily better than less, see also JS Taylor, *Practical Autonomy and Bioethics* (Routledge, 2009).

[50] Of course, with any decision we make in life, there is a risk of regretting the decision. However, it is nevertheless important to acknowledge the fact that the risk of regret is a risk that results from having a choice, and that a parent who later regrets an abortion may experience strong feelings of regret.

[51] For a discussion of this pressure in the context of genetic engineering, see P Singer and D Wells, *The Reproduction Revolution: New Ways of Making Babies* (Oxford University Press, 1984), 187.

[52] See A Solomon, *Far from the Tree: Parents, Children and the Search for Identity* (Vintage Books, 2014), 47.

[53] Ibid 47.

[54] See eg Solomon (n 52).

[55] R Amundson, 'Quality of Life, Disability, and Hedonic Psychology' (2010) 40 Journal for the Theory of Social Behaviour 374.

work: the change must be accepted as permanent, and the belief that the change is temporary may delay or even eliminate the process of hedonic adaptation.[56] Thus, this may help to explain why many people who were averse to having a disabled child but nevertheless become parents of one are typically glad, in retrospect, to have that child.[57] After the birth, the situation is permanent, and its acceptance brings greater happiness.

We should not be surprised by the fact that choice can delay or diminish our acceptance, and love, of disabled children. In general, people are more committed to relationships they do not choose—in particular, those with their immediate families.[58] In the case of relationships between spouses, while spouses typically choose each other in Western society, the commitment of marriage often makes the choice feel irreversible, or at least difficult to reverse.[59]

There is a further consideration in the argument that more choice is not necessarily better than less, and this is that increased choice does not simply add additional options, but may affect the existence and nature of the original choice, by changing the nature of the parent–child relationship.[60] By allowing the possibility of rejection based on the child's characteristics, the parents' relationship with their child is no longer based on unconditional love and acceptance. For some authors, this is not necessary; Stephen Wilkinson, for example, writes that a child with severe mental impairment may lack the kinds of personal characteristics according to which people are generally loved.[61] However, a different view is that parents who unconditionally love their child, and especially where their child does not have the characteristics expected or desired by the parents, are acting as more virtuous parents. As Alasdair MacIntyre writes, parents must be committed to care for their child even if the child does not turn out to have the characteristics desired by the parents, and indeed parents of seriously disabled children may have the opportunity to rise to the occasion and become examples for other parents: '. . . it is the parents of the seriously disabled who are the paradigms of good motherhood and fatherhood as such, who provide the model for and the key to the work of all parents'.[62]

Similarly, Michael Sandel describes the special role that the absence of choice can have in the parent–child relationship: 'That we care deeply about our children, and yet cannot choose the kind we want, teaches parents to be open to the unbidden.'[63] This openness, in turn, as Sandel writes, can lead to greater humility, and solidarity with those less fortunate in the genetic lottery.[64] Thus, parents who love and accept their child unconditionally are

[56] Ibid.

[57] See J McMahan, 'Preventing the Existence of People with Disabilities' in D Wasserman, J Bickenbach, and R Wachbroit (eds), *Quality of Life and Human Difference: Genetic Testing, Health Care, and Disability* (Cambridge University Press, 2005). However, according to McMahan, the parents' retrospective gladness does not mean that having the disabled child was in fact objectively better for them.

[58] We cannot choose our parents, or our siblings. Some people may object on the basis that we can choose to have children. However, this is not entirely true; we can only choose to try to have them, and we cannot choose their individual characteristics (although it might be said that this is changing, in the case of certain genetic engineering techniques which could make it possible to choose certain characteristics; the full effect of these changes remains to be seen).

[59] Dworkin notes how the possibility of dissolving marriage alters the expectations brought to the marriage, the ability to tolerate imperfections, and the sense of commitment: Dworkin (n 43) 72. See also Raz (n 33) 393.

[60] See Dworkin (n 43) ch 5; Raz (n 33) 394.

[61] Wilkinson (n 30) 24.

[62] A MacIntyre, *Dependent Rational Animals: Why Human Beings Need the Virtues* (Duckworth, 1999), 91.

[63] MJ Sandel, *The Case against Perfection: Ethics in the Age of Genetic Engineering* (Belknap Press, 2007), 86. Sandel is quoting theologian William F May in his call for an 'openness to the unbidden': ibid 45.

[64] Ibid ch 5.

not only showing the traits of better parents, but of better human beings. They may be more willing to support others who need assistance, and less likely to blame parents for having a disabled child. They are more likely to accept that we are all as human beings vulnerable and dependent.[65] This openness to others is not only in the parents' interests, but in the interests of us all.

VI. Conclusion

Depending on whose interests are considered to be most important, some authors have appeared to imply that abortion on the basis of a risk of disability is less, or more, morally objectionable than abortion for most other reasons. However, whereas the parents' interests are frequently considered to be a central reason why abortion for this reason could be more acceptable, these interests are often described as simply avoiding the perceived additional strain of caring for a disabled child. I have argued that the parents' interests cannot be construed so narrowly. First, if it is in the parents' interest to have a choice, the choice is merely illusory if it is not free, but rather based on misinformation, pressure, and a lack of true options. Second, even if the parents did have a free choice, it is important to consider the important costs which result from having additional options, and which may go against the parents' own interests. One of the most important costs is the change in the nature of the parent–child relationship, moving away from one of unconditional love and acceptance.

It is hard to measure the full effect of this cost, but it is undeniable that it will affect not only family relations, but also relations more broadly in society. Choice dupes us into thinking that there is a way out of our vulnerable character, our propensity to illness and fragility, and perhaps even our mortality. It is grossly insufficient to consider that the parents' interests are merely to avoid the perceived additional burdens involved in caring for a disabled child. The parents' interests are far wider and more complex. When they are more comprehensively understood, the parents' interests become far more in line with the interests of others than they may at first appear to be.

Bibliography

Albrecht, GL and Devlieger, PJ, 'The Disability Paradox: High Quality of Life against All Odds' (1999) 48 Social Science & Medicine 977.

Amundson, R, 'Quality of Life, Disability, and Hedonic Psychology' (2010) 40 Journal for the Theory of Social Behaviour 374.

Anscombe Bioethics Centre, 'Abortion, Disability and the Law', conference (18 February 2017), podcasts available at http://www.bioethics.org.uk/page/resources/multimedia accessed 15 July 2019.

Asch, A, 'Prenatal Diagnosis and Selective Abortion: A Challenge to Practice and Policy' (1999) 89 American Journal of Public Health 1649.

Barnes, C, 'Understanding the Social Model of Disability: Past, Present and Future' in N Watson, A Roulstone, and C Thomas (eds), *Routledge Handbook of Disability Studies* (Routledge, 2012).

[65] See: Herring (n 17); C Foster and J Herring, 'What Is Health' in M Freeman, S Hawkes, and B Bennett (eds), *Law and Global Health: Current Legal Issues* (Oxford University Press, 2014), vol 16.

Beck-Gernstein, E, 'Health and Responsibility: From Social Change to Technological Change and Vice Versa' in B Adam, U Beck, and J Loon (eds), *The Risk Society and Beyond: Critical Issues for Social Theory* (Sage Publications, 2000).

Bellieni, CV and Buonocore, G, 'Flaws in the Assessment of the Best Interests of the Newborn' (2009) 98 Acta Paediatrica 613.

Department of Health and Social Care, 'Abortion Statistics, England and Wales: 2018', Department of Health and Social Care (June 2019), https://www.gov.uk/government/statistics/abortion-statistics-for-england-and-wales-2018 accessed 6 September 2019.

Dworkin, G, *The Theory and Practice of Autonomy* (Cambridge University Press, 1988).

Finnis, J, 'The Rights and Wrongs of Abortion: A Reply to Judith Thomas' (1973) 2 Philosophy and Public Affairs 117, reprinted in RM Dworkin (ed), *The Philosophy of Law* (Oxford University Press, 1977) and J Finnis, *Human Rights and Common Good: Collected Essays* (Oxford University Press, 2011), vol III, 282–306.

Finnis, J, 'Capacity, Harm and Experience in the Life of Persons as Equals' (2013) 39 Journal of Medical Ethics 281.

Foster, C, *Choosing Life, Choosing Death: The Tyranny of Autonomy in Medical Ethics and Law* (Hart Publishing, 2009).

Foster, C and Herring, J, 'What Is Health' in M Freeman, S Hawkes, and B Bennett (eds), *Law and Global Health: Current Legal Issues* (Oxford University Press, 2014), vol 16.

George, RP and Tollefsen, C, *Embryo: A Defense of Human Life* (1st edn, Doubleday, 2008) and (2nd edn, Witherspoon Institute, 2011).

Glover, J, *Choosing Children: Genes, Disability and Design* (Clarendon Press, 2006).

Herring, J, 'Re B (A Minor) (Wardship: Medical Treatment) [1981]: "The Child Must Live": Disability, Parents and the Law' in J Herring and J Wall (eds), *Landmark Cases in Medical Law* (Hart Publishing, 2015).

Herring, J, 'Health as Vulnerability; Interdependence and Relationality' (2016) 22 New Bioethics 18.

Herring, J, 'Parental Responsibility, Hyper-Parenting and the Role of Technology' in R Brownsword, E Scotford, and K Yeung (eds), *The Oxford Handbook of Law, Regulation and Technology* (Oxford University Press, 2017).

Herring, J and Foster, C, 'Welfare Means Relationality, Virtue and Altruism' (2012) 32 Legal Studies 480.

Janvier, A, Farlow, B, and Wilfond, BS, 'The Experience of Families with Children with Trisomy 13 and 18 in Social Networks' (2012) 130 Pediatrics 293.

Kaposy, C, *Choosing Down Syndrome: Ethics and New Prenatal Testing Technologies* (MIT Press, 2018).

Kerr, A, Cunningham-Burley, S, and Amos, A, 'Eugenics and the New Genetics in Britain: Examining Contemporary Professionals' Accounts' (1998) 23 Science, Technology, & Human Values 175.

Lee, P, Tollefsen, C, and George, RP, 'The Ontological Status of Embryos: A Reply to Jason Morris' (2014) 39 Journal of Medicine and Philosophy 483.

Lee, P, Tollefsen, CO, and George, RP, 'Marco Rubio Is Right: The Life of a New Human Being Begins at Conception', *The Public Discourse* (2015), http://www.thepublicdiscourse.com/2015/08/15520 accessed 15 July 2019.

Lippman, A, 'Choice as a Risk to Women's Health' (1999) 1 Health, Risk & Society 281.

MacIntyre, A, *Dependent Rational Animals: Why Human Beings Need the Virtues* (Duckworth, 1999).

McMahan, J, 'Preventing the Existence of People with Disabilities' in D Wasserman, J Bickenbach, and R Wachbroit (eds), *Quality of Life and Human Difference: Genetic Testing, Health Care, and Disability* (Cambridge University Press, 2005).

Morris, JK and Springett, A, 'The National Down Syndrome Cytogenetic Register for England and Wales 2013 Annual Report', Queen Mary University of London, Barts and The London School of Medicine and Dentistry (December 2014), https://www.qmul.ac.uk/wolfson/research-projects/current-projects/projects/national-down-syndrome-cytogenetic-register-ndscr.html accessed 6 September 2019.

Oliver, M and Barnes, C, *The New Politics of Disablement* (Palgrave Macmillan, 2012).

Parens, E and Asch, A, 'The Disability Rights Critique of Prenatal Genetic Testing: Reflections and Recommendations' (1999) 29(5) Hastings Center Report S1.

Pfeiffer, D, 'Eugenics and Disability Discrimination' (1994) 9 Disability & Society 481.
Raz, J, *The Morality of Freedom* (Clarendon Press, 1986).
Robertson, JA, *Children of Choice: Freedom and the New Reproductive Technologies* (Princeton University Press, 1994).
Sandel, MJ, *The Case against Perfection: Ethics in the Age of Genetic Engineering* (Belknap Press, 2007).
Scotko, BG, Levine, SP, and Goldstein, R, 'Having a Son or Daughter with Down Syndrome: Perspectives from Mothers and Fathers' (2011) 155 American Journal of Medical Genetics Part A 2335.
Scott, R, 'Interpreting the Disability Ground of the Abortion Act' (2005) 64 Cambridge Law Journal 388.
Scott, R, *Choosing between Possible Lives: Law and Ethics of Prenatal and Preimplantation Genetic Diagnosis* (Hart Publishing, 2007).
Shakespeare, T, 'Choices and Rights: Eugenics, Genetics and Disability Equality' (1998) 13 Disability & Society 665.
Shakespeare, T, *Disability Rights and Wrongs Revisited* (2nd edn, Routledge, 2014).
Sheldon, S and Wilkinson, S, 'Termination of Pregnancy for Reason of Foetal Disability: Are There Grounds for a Special Exception in Law?' (2001) 9 Medical Law Review 85.
Simmons, Z, 'Patient-Perceived Outcomes and Quality of Life in ALS' (2015) 12 Neurotherapeutics 394.
Singer, P and Wells, D, *The Reproduction Revolution: New Ways of Making Babies* (Oxford University Press, 1984).
Solomon, A, *Far from the Tree: Parents, Children and the Search for Identity* (Vintage Books, 2014).
Taylor, JS, *Practical Autonomy and Bioethics* (Routledge, 2009).
Wertz, DC and Fletcher, JC, 'A Critique of Some Feminist Challenges to Prenatal Diagnosis' (1993) 2 Journal of Women's Health 173.
Wilkinson, S, *Choosing Tomorrow's Children: The Ethics of Selective Reproduction* (Oxford University Press, 2010).
Williams, C, Alderson, P, and Farsides, B, 'Too Many Choices? Hospital and Community Staff Reflect on the Future of Prenatal Screening' (2002) 55 Social Science & Medicine 743.
Wolf-Devine, C and Devine, PE, 'Abortion: A Communitarian Pro-Life Perspective' in M Tooley, C Wolf-Devine, PE Devine, and AM Jaggar, *Abortion: Three Perspectives* (Oxford University Press, 2009).
Wyatt, J, 'End of Life Decisions, Quality of Life and the Newborn' (2007) 96 Acta Paediatrica 790.

15
Property in the Body and Medical Law

Donna Dickenson

Most people probably think that they own their bodies, but they would be wrong. In the best-known example proving the popular view incorrect, a patient was held to have no further rights in a cell line developed from his tissue.[1] The case concerned John Moore, a man diagnosed with leukaemia who underwent a splenectomy for therapeutic purposes. He was subsequently asked to return to the hospital several times to donate further tissue samples unrelated to the spleen. It transpired that his unusually active immune cells had been used to produce an immortal cell line with an estimated commercial value of US $3 million. Moore mounted an action in conversion, but failed to establish proprietary rights in the cell line created from his tissue.

In common law, the traditional rule has been that there is no property in excised human tissue. Behind this position lay both practical and philosophical reasons. In this chapter, I will argue that the practical reasons are increasingly outdated and the philosophical grounds are paradoxical. After a brief summary of some empirical reasons for thinking that the no-property rule ignores the reality of modern biotechnology, I will be concentrating primarily on the philosophical foundations.

Tangible rights in human tissue and intangible rights in the human genome have been said to be the subject of a new enclosure movement by researchers, biotechnology corporations, and governments.[2] As in the old agricultural enclosure movement, 'things that were formerly thought to be uncommodifiable, essentially common or outside the market altogether are being turned into private possessions under a new kind of property regime'.[3] Commodification of the body, broadly construed to include private property rights by third parties in tissue, DNA samples, umbilical cord blood, and other substances derived from individuals' bodies, has caused great if sometimes belated outrage among patients' rights organizations, academic commentators, journalists, and the general public.[4]

As in Moore's case, human biomaterials extracted from the body now enter into research and commerce as commodified objects, increasingly on a global level. 'The twentieth century brings the production process *inside* the body and puts organs, blood, and cell lines into circulation *outside* the body, scrambling the classical Marxist distinction between

[1] *Moore v Regents of the University of California*, 51 Cal 3rd 120, 793 P 2d, 271 Cal Rptr 146 (1990).
[2] J Boyle, 'The Second Enclosure Movement and the Construction of the Public Domain' (2003) 66 Law and Contemporary Problems 33.
[3] Ibid 37.
[4] In a large literature, see: D Dickenson, *Property in the Body: Feminist Perspectives* (2nd edn, Cambridge University Press, 2017); D Dickenson, *Body Shopping: Converting Body Parts to Profit* (Oneworld, 2009); D Satz, *Why Some Things Should Not Be for Sale* (Oxford University Press, 2010); M Cooper, *Life as Surplus: Biotechnology and Capitalism in the Neoliberal Era* (Washington University Press, 2008); MJ Radin, *Contested Commodities: The Trouble with Trade in Sex, Children, Body Parts and Other Things* (Harvard University Press, 1996).

Donna Dickenson, *Property in the Body and Medical Law* In: *Philosophical Foundations of Medical Law*. Edited by: Andelka M Phillips, Thana C de Campos, and Jonathan Herring, Oxford University Press (2019). © Andelka M Phillips, Thana C de Campos, and Jonathan Herring
DOI: 10.1093/oso/9780198796558.003.0016

the living and the dead.'[5] So far in the twenty-first century, this process has continued to gather pace, in such unexpected areas as the global trade in umbilical cord blood units, donated altruistically by women in labour to public banks, which may sell them in the global 'immunitary bioeconomy'.[6] An even more active and highly differentiated market exists in human eggs:[7] 'desirable' phenotypes—usually defined in terms of intelligence test scores and physical appearance—can fetch $50,000 per egg cycle or even more.[8] A recent class action lawsuit by egg 'donors'—really sellers—overturned American Society of Reproductive Medicine guidelines limiting payment to $10,000, branding them as a 'price cap' that violated federal antitrust legislation.[9]

Real-world evidence makes it increasingly impossible to maintain that there simply *is* no property in human tissue. Whether there *should be* is another matter. Here, we enter the realm of the philosophical foundations to the no-property rule. The practical reasons for that rule used to be self-evident: before modern biomedicine, tissue extracted from the body was typically diseased, so that the donor's only interest lay in having it removed. The examples given so far should suffice to illustrate that this is no longer true.

Indeed, English law is beginning to recognize this reality, in such decisions as *Yearworth and Others v North Bristol NHS Trust*,[10] which upheld a claim from several men for negligent damage to the semen that they had stored prior to operations for testicular cancer. The court recognized that the samples could be considered sufficiently as property for purposes of the men's claim.[11] But rather than taking a piecemeal approach as cases arise, should we systematically rethink the philosophical foundations of the no-property rule?

Once tissue is separated from the living body, the common law has generally assumed either that it has been abandoned by its original 'owner', or that it is and always was *res nullius*: no one's thing, belonging to no one when removed.[12] Civil law systems such as that of France typically view the body as *une chose hors commerce* or *res extra commercium*: a thing not subject to contract or exchange.[13] Similarly, under French law, tissue removed during a procedure is considered to be abandoned, *res derelictae*. In both common and civil

[5] M Cooper, 'The Living and the Dead: Variations on De Anima' (2002) 7 Angelaki: Journal of the Theoretical Humanities 81.

[6] Dickenson (n 4) ch 4; N Brown, L Machin, and D McLeod, 'The Immunitary Bioeconomy: The Economisation of Life in the International Cord Blood Market' (2011) 30 Social Science and Medicine 1; N Brown, 'Contradictions of Value—between Use and Exchange in the Cord Blood Bioeconomy' (2013) 35 Sociology of Health and Illness 97.

[7] R Almeling, *Sex Cells: The Medical Market in Eggs and Sperm* (University of California Press, 2011).

[8] AD Levine, 'Self-Regulation, Compensation, and the Ethical Recruitment of Oocyte Donors' (2010) 40(2) Hastings Center Report 27.

[9] *Kamakahi v American Society for Reproductive Medicine and Society for Assisted Reproductive Technologies*, summarized in SH Johnson, 'A Buyer's Market: Fixing the Price for Human Ova for Assisted Reproduction' (2015) 45 Hastings Center Report 9.

[10] [2009] EWCA Civ 37; [2010] QB 1.

[11] For analysis of the *Yearworth* case, see, inter alia: M Quigley, 'Property: The Future of Human Tissue?' (2009) 17 Medical Law Review 457; J Lee, 'The Fertile Imagination of the Common Law: *Yearworth v North Bristol NHS Trust*' (2009) 17 Torts Law Journal 130; and SHE Harmon and G Laurie, '*Yearworth v North Bristol NHS Trust*: Property, Principles and Paradigms' (2010) 69 Cambridge Law Journal 476.

[12] J McHale, 'Waste, Ownership and Bodily Products' (2000) 8(2) Health Care Analysis 123.

[13] Eg an influential and determinative early report of the French Comité Consultatif National d'Ethique (CCNE) (French National Consultative Ethics Committee) states: 'Il faut dresser une digue contre cette merchandisation de la personne, et il n'en est pas d'autre que le principe intangible selon lequel le corps humain est hors commerce' ('We must set up a bulwark against such commodification of the person, and the most fitting is the intangible principle according to which the human body is beyond commerce'). See CCNE, *Recherche biomédicale et respect de la personne humaine* (DF, 1987), cited in A Fagot-Largeault, 'Ownership of the Human Body: Judicial and Legislative Responses in France' in H ten Have and J Welie (eds), *Ownership of the Human Body: Philosophical Considerations on the Use of the Human Body and Its Parts in Healthcare* (Kluwer, 1998), 130.

law systems, contracts in bodily tissue and materials are difficult or impossible to enforce, although for different reasons. In both systems, patients traditionally have had no further property rights in their tissue once informed consent to its extraction or donation has been given.[14] Many scholars have argued cogently for giving tissue donors some property rights because of the dearth of protections offered by other forms of law,[15] but these recommendations have not yet had a major impact on the governance of biomaterials.[16]

The common law also posits that something can be either a person or an object—but not both—and that only objects can be regulated by property-holding. This core distinction between persons and things is as much philosophical as legal. As Kant writes:

> Man cannot dispose over himself because he is not a thing; he is not his own property; to say that he is would be self-contradictory; for insofar as he is a person he is a Subject in whom the ownership of things can be vested, and if he were his own property he would be a thing over which he could have ownership. But a person cannot be a property and so cannot be a thing which can be owned, for it is impossible to be a person and a thing, the proprietor and the property.[17]

The implication is clear: to the extent that persons' body parts can be regulated by property-holding, those body parts are objects or things. Since we are embodied persons, then to some extent we become objects too. The question is to what extent. Human tissue and human genetic material typically fall between the two stools, containing elements of both person and thing, subject and object.

Of course, some commentators argue that our rights as moral agents and human subjects actually require us to have the free right of disposal over our bodies.[18] Because we are embodied agents, however, it is paradoxical to assert that we should have entirely free right of disposal over our bodies. The *reductio ad absurdum* of this claim would be to assert that I have the free right to dispose of my body by selling myself into slavery. Selling oneself into slavery is legally and philosophically invalid, because the ongoing autonomy of the agent is

[14] In France, the CCNE *Avis* (Opinion) on products derived from human materials (no 9, February 1987) stipulates that products of commercial benefit derived from donated tissues should be sold at a market price which only reflects the researchers' and manufacturers' labour, with no additional profit, and that the patient should have no right to any financial benefits. See Fagot-Largeault (n 13) 131.

[15] See eg: Quigley (n 11); H Widdows, 'Persons and Their Parts: New Reproductive Technologies and Risks of Commodification' (2009) 17 Health Care Analysis 36–46; JK Mason and GT Laurie, *Law and Medical Ethics* (8th edn, Oxford University Press, 2011), ch 14; I Goold and M Quigley, 'The Case for a Property Approach' in I Goold, K Greasley, J Herring, et al (eds), *Persons, Parts and Property: How Should We Regulate Human Tissue in the 21st Century?* (Hart, 2014), 231.

[16] A partial exception can be made for the charitable trust model, which has been incorporated into the governance mechanism of a state infant heel prick blood biobank in the United States. See D Chrysler, H McGee, J Bach, et al, 'The Michigan BioTrust for Health: Using Dried Blood Samples for Research to Benefit the Community while Respecting the Individual' (2011) 39 Journal of Law, Medicine and Ethics 98; DE Winickoff and LB Neumann, 'Towards a Social Contract for Genomics: Property and the Public in the "Biotrust" Model' (2005) 1(3) Genomics, Society and Policy 8.

[17] I Kant, *Lectures on Ethics* (Bobbs-Merrill, 1963), 4, cited in GA Cohen, *Self-Ownership, Freedom and Equality* (Cambridge University Press, 1995), 211.

[18] For arguments in favour of removing or modifying legal prohibitions on commodification of human tissue, see DB Resnik, 'The Commercialization of Human Stem Cells: Ethical and Policy Issues' (2002) 10 Health Care Analysis 127; S Wilkinson, 'Commodification Arguments for the Legal Prohibition of Organ Sale' (2000) 8 Health Care Analysis 189; M Goodwin, *Black Markets: The Supply and Demand of Body Parts* (Cambridge University Press, 2006).

negated when the agent becomes a slave. Yet any supposed right to sell oneself into slavery would have to rest on respect for the agent's autonomy.

It is entirely consistent in philosophical and legal terms to bar such forms of alienation of the entire body by sale or other means. The more difficult cases concern disposing of parts of the body that do not threaten the continued autonomous existence of the subject. Is it permissible to sell eggs, for example? Although the procedure by which eggs are extracted carries insufficiently documented but potentially serious risks,[19] they can be separated from a woman's body. But is separability the sole criterion?

While Kant clearly states that we are not authorized to sell any part of our bodies, he seems to make exceptions for separable and non-vital elements such as hair. But he is uneasy even about that, because I am not entitled to use my body merely as a tool. That would violate a form of the Categorical Imperative: it would entail treating a human subject—myself in this case, rather than another person—as a mere means, rather than as a member of the Kingdom of Ends.

In other situations, for example in the permissible amputation of a diseased foot, Kant does appear to draw a dualistic distinction between body as object and moral person as subject, so that we are entitled to 'use' the body in such a way as to preserve the life of the person. (I have put 'use' in inverted commas because amputating a diseased foot does not seem to be using the body as a tool in the same way as selling a part of the body, even selling a body part in order to keep body and soul together.) That would still rule out egg sale, since the egg donor's life is not saved—indeed, risk is imposed. Nor is anyone else's life saved by egg donation and sale.

What about tissue extractions that *do* save another person's life and that pose little or no risk to the donor? For example, there is little or no minimal risk involved in giving a DNA swab or a blood sample to a research biobank, but potentially, at least, lives might be saved if beneficial cures are developed from that donation. Kantian ethics does not allow that kind of balancing calculation; we would have to look to a version of utilitarianism, although a subtle one that does take into account the actual probability of a cure being found—rather than simply assuming that science will benefit. It is by no means clear that an unregulated approach to property in the body will necessarily help science to progress. Indeed, research has been hampered rather than helped by a light-touch approach to granting genetic patents, as was argued by the plaintiffs in the *Myriad Genetics* case.[20]

Liberal political theory, rather than either Kantianism or utilitarianism, is generally thought to be most sympathetic to the idea that we can own our bodies. However, that is

[19] For further detail, see D Bodri, JJ Guillen, A Polo, et al, 'Complications Resulting from Oocyte Stimulation and Oocyte Retrieval in 4,052 Oocyte Donor Cycles' (2008) 17(2) Reproductive Biomedicine Online 237; J Schneider, 'Fatal Colon Cancer in a Young Egg Donor: A Physician Mother's Call for Follow-Up and Research on the Long-Term Risks of Ovarian Stimulation' (2008) 90(5) Fertility and Sterility 2016e–e5; W Kramer, J Schneider, and N Schultz, 'US Oocyte Donors: A Retrospective Study of Medical and Psychosocial Issues' (2009) 24(12) Human Reproduction 3144; L Giudice, E Santa, and R Pool, 'Assessing the Medical Risks of Human Oocyte Donation for Stem Cell Research', Institute of Medicine and National Research Council of the National Academies Workshop Report (2007); R Calderon-Margalit, Y Friedlander, R Yanetz, et al, 'Cancer Risk after Exposure to Treatments for Ovulation Induction' (2009) 169 American Journal of Epidemiology 365.

[20] *Association for Molecular Pathology v Myriad Genetics, Inc*, 133 S Ct 2107 [2013]. Although the rationale for patents is that they encourage research by offering secure protection for inventions, legal restrictions on patented genes have actually *reduced* product development by 20–30 per cent, when compared with diagnostic products resulting from freely available genetic sequences. See HL Williams, 'Intellectual Property Rights and Innovation: Evidence from the Human Genome' (2013) 121 Journal of Political Economy 1.

a misinterpretation of Lockean liberalism.[21] There is no justification in liberal theory for a generalized notion of property in the body, as is widely assumed.[22] Because we do not create our bodies, the claim that we *cannot* own our bodies is actually more consistent with Locke's position. Self-ownership in the sense of ownership of the physical body is not the crux of Locke's argument: rather, what is central to Locke is the claim that I own my actions, and therefore the resources or wealth produced by my actions. It is not necessary to assert that I own my physical body in order to stake a claim in the results produced by my agency.

We do not have a property in that which we have not laboured to create. We do not own our bodies merely because 'we' inhabit them (whoever that disembodied 'we' may be). In Locke's view, we do not own our bodies at all: God does, because He alone created them. But whether or not one shares Locke's belief in God, the logic is the same: we do not own our bodies because we have not worked to make them.

Rather, we have a property in our moral *persons* as agents. Locke is careful to distinguish between persons and bodies, and between the labour of our bodies and our bodies themselves, when he says: 'Every man has a property in his own person; this nobody has any right to but himself. The labour of his body and the work of his hands we may say are properly his.'[23] We have a title to that with which we have 'mixed our labour' because our labour is the expression of our agency and status as persons, but not a property in our bodies as such.

In the case of women's labour in producing tissue such as ova for clinical and research purposes, however, there is a strong Lockean basis for thinking that women should have certain property rights because these extracted tissues are separate from the body, and because they have put effort, intentionality, and agency into the laborious and risky procedure by which the tissues are extracted.[24] Such property entitlements could help us resist the 'new enclosures' by which women's tissue, in particular, is simply assumed to be available for use in research, without any recognition of women's labour in producing it: the phenomenon that I have called 'the lady vanishes'.[25] That problem arose in the large-scale use of women's eggs for some stem cell research and has continued to mar debates on other forms of biomedicine, most recently concerning 'mitochondrial transfer' or three-parent IVF.[26] Likewise, but to a lesser degree, a Lockean labour-desert argument might justify a limited form of property for donors in biobanks and patents (which could perhaps be administered collectively by a form of charitable trust on their behalf).

We would probably not want to give people who have merely donated a cheek swab for genetic analysis equal property rights with women who have put hours of risk-laden effort into donating eggs. It seems appropriate to differentiate property rights in tissue by criteria

[21] J Waldron, *The Right to Private Property* (Clarendon Press, 1988); A Phillips, 'It's My Body and I'll Do What I Like with It: Bodies as Objects' (2011) 39(6) Political Theory 724.

[22] D Resnik, 'Regulating the Market for Human Eggs' (2001) 15(1) Bioethics 1; R Arneson, 'Commodification and Commercial Surrogacy' (1992) 21(2) Philosophy and Public Affairs 132; M Cherry, *Kidney for Sale by Owner: Human Organs, Transplantation and the Market* (Georgetown University Press, 2005).

[23] J Locke, *The Second Treatise on Civil Government* (D. Van Nostrand, 1689), 1047, cited in GA Cohen, *Self-Ownership, Freedom and Equality* (Cambridge University Press, 1995), 209. See also my further elaboration of the claim that Locke distinguishes between property in the person and property in objects in D Dickenson, *Property, Women and Politics: Subjects or Objects?* (Polity Press, 1997), 78.

[24] I first made this argument in my *Property, Women and Politics* (n 23) and have developed it further in subsequent work, including the second edition of my *Property in the Body* (n 4).

[25] D Dickenson, 'The Lady Vanishes: What's Missing from the Stem Cell Debate' (2006) 3 Journal of Bioethical Inquiry 43.

[26] D Dickenson, 'The Commercialization of Human Eggs in Mitochondrial Replacement Research' (2013) 19(1) New Bioethics 18.

such as agency, intentionality, labour, and risk-taking.[27] We can envision a spectrum of property rights for tissue donors, based on these criteria, all of which relate to the concept of labour as deserving reward or 'desert', and thus as conferring property rights.[28]

Some forms of tissue donation, such as voluntarily offering one's ova for research, will fall near the higher end of the spectrum. So, they will merit either more of the rights in the bundle or stronger forms of those rights. '[T]he appropriate choice of a bundle of rights may differ for different types of biological material',[29] not because of any inherent characteristics of the tissues, but because of the characteristics of the donor's action and agency in producing them. Many of the difficulties associated with reversing the no-property rule can be avoided if we do not view property as a unitary concept, instead using the differentiated 'bundle' concept of property.[30]

We do not have to allow research subjects the right to profit from their tissue, for example—an objection raised in *Moore*. Profit is only one of several possible 'sticks' in the property 'bundle', and we can distinguish between these various entitlements. Moore himself was not primarily motivated by profit: he was only advised to mount an action in conversion because it seemed the likeliest way to assert the management rights and transparency that he sought. Reversing the no-property rule will not necessarily entail full-blown markets in tissues between donors and researchers. It would not simply be a matter of untrammelled commodification. Properly and philosophically understood, reversing the no-property rule could actually have the reverse effect, because it could share out property rights among a variety of holders and prevent any one party from having monopoly rights.

Honoré's classic list of entitlements and duties involved in the property relationship[31] demonstrates the variety of entitlements and duties into which the concept of property can be disaggregated. The owner of object X may have some or all of the following:

(1) a right to the physical possession of X;
(2) a right to its use;
(3) a right to its management, that is, to determine the ways in which others can use it;
(4) a right to the income that can be derived from its use by others;
(5) a right to its capital value;
(6) a right to security against its being taken by others;
(7) a right to transmit or alienate it to others by gift or bequest;
(8) a right to transmit or alienate it to others by sale;
(9) a permanent right to these other rights, without any limit or term;
(10) a duty to refrain from using X in a way that harms others, that is, liability for harm caused by X.

Moore was primarily concerned with rights 3 (management) and 6 (security against unauthorized taking). However, the court seems to have feared that if Moore benefited from rights 4, 5, and 8 (to income, capital value, and sale proceeds), there would be no incentive

[27] Dickenson, *Property in the Body* (n 4) 118.
[28] Here, I am using the terminology adopted by S Munzer in *A Theory of Property* (Cambridge University Press, 1990).
[29] B Bjorkmann and BO Hansson, 'Bodily Rights and Property Rights' (2006) 32 Journal of Medical Ethics 214.
[30] AM Honoré, 'Ownership' in *Making Law Bind: Essays Legal and Philosophical* (Clarendon Press, 1987), 161.
[31] Honoré (n 30).

for research sponsors or firms to develop the cell line for their own commercial purposes, as well as for the benefit of society. Further, it was thought inequitable to allow Moore the enjoyment of income or capital value from his T-cells, when it was only by good fortune that he happened to possess a particularly effective immune system. This last argument from justice has its compelling merits, but it need not be determinative if we disaggregate the rights to income and capital (rights 4 and 5) from the rights to determine the management of the tissue's use (3) and to enjoy protection from taking by others (8).

However, the bundle concept is not immune from criticism within jurisprudence. As James Penner argues, the core meaning of property is simple: 'Keep Off'. The bundle, in this view, gives us both too much and too little: too much, because what we are really concerned with are the rights proclaiming 'No Trespass';[32] too little, because there is little separate content to the bundle other than already pre-existing rights under other headings than 'property'. Similarly, if the concept of property is so disaggregated as to mean nothing more than a set of relationships, does it retain any core meaning? Is there any whole that is more than the sum of the parts?[33] If the idea of property in law has no independent existence, this argument runs, its applicability will be lessened. But why should that be true? If anything, the idea's applicability will be greater, because it will be much more flexible.

The flexibility of the 'bundle' concept has been illustrated in practical applications, such as developing a bundle of 'traditional resource rights' for indigenous communities, drawing on concepts already recognized in international and national law, but with the addition of new 'sticks' allowing more effective protections.[34] The 'bundle' also afforded protections in the *Havasupai* case.[35] Here, members of an Arizona tribe objected to what they viewed as stigmatizing schizophrenia research, which had been performed without their fully informed consent on samples originally taken for diabetes studies. In 2004, some forty tribe members filed a $50 million lawsuit against Arizona State University researchers for fraud, breach of fiduciary duty, negligence, and trespass. Although the case was settled out of court, the implication of the university's apology and willingness to settle was evident, as was the implicit utility of the 'bundle'. Even if the tribe lacked full ownership rights in tissue that they had donated for research, they did have sufficient ongoing proprietary rights of management to determine which uses of their tissue were unacceptable.

One pair of distinctions in the property 'bundle' needs particular care: the right to transmit by gift (7) versus the right to transmit by sale (8). It is sometimes argued that because we have a right to give our blood, for example, there is no reason why we should not have the right to sell it. That argument is clearly specious, because it fails to distinguish between these two separate sticks in the property 'bundle'. It may be permissible to transmit some objects of property by either sale or gift, others by gift but not sale, and others by

[32] J Penner, *The Idea of Property in Law* (Clarendon, 1987), 73: 'The general injunction to "keep off" or "leave alone" the property that is not one's own defines the practice of property much better than a series of specific duties which work to facilitate particular uses of others' property.' See also JL Schroeder, 'Chix Nix Bundle-o-Stix: A Feminist Critique of the Disaggregation of Property' (1994) 83 Michigan Law Review 239.

[33] T Grey, '"The Disintegration of Property' in JP Pennock and J Chapman (eds), *Nomo XXII: Property* (New York University Press, 1980), 69.

[34] D Posey and G Dutfield, *Beyond Intellectual Property: Towards Traditional Resource Rights for Indigenous Peoples and Local Communities* (International Development Research Centre, 1996).

[35] *Tilousi v Arizona State University Board of Regents*, 2007 WL 4934760 (Ariz App Div 1). See also K Van Assche, S Gutwirth, and S Sterckx, 'Protecting Dignitary Interests of Biobank Research Participants: Lessons from *Havasupai Tribe v Arizona Board of Regents*' (2015) 5(1) Law, Innovation and Technology 55.

neither means. To the extent that my vote is my property, for example, I am not allowed to either sell it or give it away.

Some *objects* may be inappropriate for either sale or gift, but all *persons* are: persons may be neither sold nor given away, because persons cannot rightfully be property. If that sounds self-evident, it has certainly not been so in the debates over surrogacy. 'Altruistic' or unpaid surrogacy seems more acceptable than paid surrogacy to some commentators,[36] but babies are persons, and persons should be neither sold nor given away.[37]

In terms of Calabresi and Melamed's influential framework,[38] we can think of the struggles over surrogacy as disputes between those who want to maintain pure property rules, in which gift and sale are both permitted; advocates of market-inalienability, which would permit gift but not sale; and complete inalienability, meaning that babies should neither be sold nor given away. In my view, babies should be subject to a complete inalienability regime, ruling out either altruistic or paid surrogacy. Although that may sound utopian, it is actually becoming the dominant position in the Third World countries that had previously been the focus of 'reproductive tourism'.[39]

Nevertheless, as Melinda Cooper and Catherine Waldby have argued powerfully, a feminized model of 'clinical labour' predominates in the global bioeconomy—extending beyond areas that only affect women, such as commercial surrogacy and egg sale, to the vulnerable status of male and female labour alike, in such areas as commercialized clinical trials in the pharmaceutical industry.[40] Although bioindustry valorizes the intellectual labour of the researcher, it views the bodily contribution of tissue providers and human research subjects 'as an already available biological resource, as *res nullius*, matter in the public domain'.[41]

The no-property rule has been construed so as to deprive tissue providers of ongoing rights, whereas researchers, universities, and biotechnology companies are prone to assume that once they acquire any proprietary rights, those rights are complete and undifferentiated. That position can and should be remedied, drawing on a more sophisticated and nuanced philosophical understanding of property as a bundle of rights. Those rights that we most need in order to protect ourselves from the enclosure of the body are only partial. Just as our ancestors merely demanded rights of use over the commons, rather than powers of complete alienation such as gift or sale, so too can we comfortably make do with a limited number of sticks from the bundle, primarily those to do with control and management.

True, some commentators prefer a statute approach to regulation of human bodily materials, rather than a property law model.[42] While it is good to see the need for regulation

[36] See eg MJ Radin, *Contested Commodities: The Trouble with Trade in Sex, Children, Body Parts, and Other Things* (Harvard University Press, 1996).

[37] For further development of this argument, see Dickenson, *Property in the Body* (n 4) ch 4; and M Brazier, 'Can You Buy Children?' (1999) 8 Contemporary Reviews in Obstetrics and Gynaecology 50.

[38] G Calabresi and AD Melamed, 'Property Rules, Liability Rules and Inalienability: One View of the Cathedral' (1972) 85 Harvard Law Review 1089.

[39] D Dickenson, 'The End of Cross-Border Surrogacy?', Project Syndicate (25 February 2016), https://www.project-syndicate.org/commentary/crackdown-on-international-surrogacy-trade-by-donna-dickenson-2016-02 accessed 15 July 2019.

[40] M Cooper and C Waldby, *Clinical Labor: Tissue Donors and Research Subjects in the Global Bioeconomy* (Duke University Press, 2014). See also C Elliott, *White Coat, Black Hat: Adventures on the Dark Side of Medicine* (Beacon Press, 2010).

[41] Cooper and Waldby (n 40) 9.

[42] See eg: J Herring, 'Why We Need a Statute Regime to Regulate Bodily Material' in Goold et al (n 15) 215; L Skene, 'Raising Issues with a Property Law Approach' in ibid 263.

recognized by advocates of a statutory regime, however, there is no inherent reason why we must choose one route over the other. If the law is to have any hope of shedding its frequently criticized tardiness in keeping up with new developments in biotechnology and the global bioeconomy, we need to pursue both a statute and a case-law approach to limiting commodification of the body through the 'new enclosures'.

And we do need to pursue reform. To the extent that we remain property-less in our own bodies, through the conventional no-property doctrine, we are vulnerable to the 'new enclosures'. Personal rights such as informed consent are necessary but not sufficient to rectify that position. Indeed, the doctrine of informed consent, if interpreted as blanket consent to all further uses, may simply be a cover for one-way altruism: from individual donor to tissue banks, research team, or corporate entity.[43] Consent needs to be supplemented with property rights in the body, although it will be a large task to delineate which rights those should be.

Although the 'new enclosures' metaphor is powerful, it likens the body to land, but the body is not a thing in the same sense as land. True, land carries some of the same sense of agency and personality as the body, particularly for indigenous peoples.[44] Ultimately, however, persons can exist without land, but not without their bodies. The body is not just a thing like any other, because it is the only 'thing' without which we cannot exist. Treating the body merely as an object among objects fails to capture the strangeness, strength, and depth of the ways in which the body does or does not constitute a mere thing. As Maurice Merleau-Ponty argued, 'if the body is a thing among things, it is so in a stronger and deeper sense than they'.[45]

The idea that the body has a fixed character, separate from its surroundings, is also increasingly untenable when external objects such as pacemakers can be incorporated into the body and bodily tissues can become external objects such as biobank samples.

When genes are patented, ova are 'harvested', or cord blood is 'banked', that strangeness and that depth are ignored. This process of commodification has strengthened in some areas, with biocapital manifesting new and unexpected developments such as the international trade in cord blood units. In other areas, however, it has been defeated: for example, the regulation or banning of cross-border commercial surrogacy in the Third World and the substantial limitations imposed on gene patenting in the *Myriad Genetics* case. Commodification of the body through modern biotechnology is not triumphantly inevitable, but only when we understand the full extent of the process and the philosophical assumptions on which it rests can we successfully regulate and resist it.

[43] This contention is illustrated by the decision in *Washington University v William J Catalona*, 437 F Supp 2d; ESCD Ed Mo 2006. Although the men who donated their samples for Catalona's research wanted the tissue to transfer with him to his new university, they were held to have no right to contest the biobank's remaining with his previous employer. Effectively, their permission was held to be blanket consent, on the grounds that gifts *inter vivos* are final.

[44] See eg: N Simmonds, 'Transformative Maternities: Indigenous Stories as Resistance and Reclamation in Aotearoa New Zealand' in M Robertson and P Tsang (eds), *Everyday Knowledge, Education and Sustainable Futures. Education in the Asia-Pacific Region: Issues, Concerns and Prospects* (Springer, 2016), 71; M Henare, 'Tapu, Mana, Mauri, Hau, Wairua: A Maori Philosophy of Vitalism and Cosmos' in JA Grim (ed), *Indigenous Traditions and Ecology: The Interbeing of Cosmology and Community* (Harvard University Press, 2001), 197.

[45] M Merleau-Ponty, *The Visible and the Invisible* (Northwestern University Press, 1968), 137.

16

Trafficking, Tourism, and Trading

A Dark Convergence in Transplantation?

Trevor Stammers

I. Introduction

Organ transplantation is undoubtedly one of the greatest medical success stories of the twentieth century. From the first successful kidney transplant in 1954,[1] organ transplantation has become a routine part of medical practice worldwide. In 2008, the World Health Organization (WHO) estimated that around 100,800 solid organ transplants were performed globally, more than two-thirds being kidney transplants.[2] This had risen to almost 126,670 in 2015, equating to over fourteen transplants every hour.[3]

Transplantation has, however, arguably become a victim of its own success as patients in need of organs continue to vastly outstrip supply. The only country in the world where there is no waiting list for a kidney transplant is Iran. In the United Kingdom, 466 patients died while on the active waiting list for a transplant during 2016 and a further 881 were removed from the list because their condition deteriorated, many of whom would have died shortly afterwards.[4]

Shortage of any commodity always opens up the possibility of illegal markets developing and organ shortage is no exception. People trafficking is a reality[5] that took a long time to be acknowledged,[6] but herever people are trafficked, organ trafficking is likely to form a part of it,[7] though organ trafficking also takes other forms, such as transplant tourism.[8]

[1] JP Merrill, JE Murray, JH Harrison, et al, 'Successful Homotransplantations of Human Kidneys between Identical Twins' (1956) 160 Journal of the American Medical Association 277–82.

[2] World Health Organization, http://www.who.int/transplantation/gkt/statistics/en/ accessed 15 July 2019.

[3] Global Observatory on Organ Donation and Transplantation, http://www.transplant-observatory.org/ accessed 15 July 2019.

[4] NHS Blood and Transplant, 'Highest Number of Organ Transplants Ever across UK, But Many Families Still Say No to Donation' (1 September 2016), https://www.organdonation.nhs.uk/news-and-campaigns/news/highest-number-of-organ-transplants-ever-across-uk-but-many-families-still-say-no-to-donation/ accessed 15 July 2019.

[5] Two top stories on UK news-sites on the day of writing this chapter illustrate this reality: F Perraudin, 'Eighteen People Found Guilty over Newcastle Sex Grooming Network', *The Guardian* (9 August 2017), https://www.theguardian.com/uk-news/2017/aug/09/newcastle-sex-grooming-network-operation-shelter accessed 15 July 2019; 'Syrian People Traffickers Jailed in Germany', *BBC News* (11 August 2017), http://www.bbc.co.uk/news/world-europe-40899132 accessed 15 July 2019.

[6] Some still minimize its extent even now. A 2015 US article refers to it as 'less a clear-cut crime and more a call to moral panic'. See N Berlatsky, '"Human Trafficking" Has Become a Meaningless Term', *The New Republic* (30 October 2015), https://newrepublic.com/article/123302/human-trafficking-has-become-meaningless-term accessed 15 July 2019.

[7] M Delgado, 'Boy of 12 Smuggled into UK for Gang to Sell His Body Parts', *Daily Mail* (8 March 2015), http://www.dailymail.co.uk/news/article-2984489/The-organ-snatchers-Boy-12-smuggled-UK-gang-sell-body-parts-black-market.html accessed 15 July 2019.

[8] R Evans, 'Pakistani Police Rescue 24 from Organ Trafficking Gang', *BBC News* (24 January 2017), http://www.bbc.co.uk/news/health-38722052 accessed 15 July 2019.

Trevor Stammers, *Trafficking, Tourism, and Trading* In: *Philosophical Foundations of Medical Law*. Edited by: Andelka M Phillips, Thana C de Campos, and Jonathan Herring, Oxford University Press (2019).
DOI: 10.1093/oso/9780198796558.003.0017

Supporters of regulated organ markets are understandably keen to distance themselves from organ trafficking and transplant tourism and indeed most argue that such markets would reduce the incidence of both. However, this chapter argues that harm to vendors is involved in all three.

II. Organ Trafficking, Tourism, and Trading

People trafficking, though practised since antiquity, is a term which gained popular attention since the 2000 UN General Assembly adopted its Convention against Transnational Organized Crime together with three supplementary protocols, particularly the Protocol to Prevent, Suppress and Punish Trafficking in Persons, Especially Women and Children, now widely known as the 'Palermo Protocol'.

Article 2 of the protocol defines 'trafficking in persons' as:

> the recruitment, transportation, transfer, harbouring or receipt of persons, by means of threat or use of force or other forms of coercion, of abduction, of fraud, of deception, of the abuse of power or of a position of vulnerability or of the giving or receiving of payments or benefits to achieve the consent of a person having control over another person, for the purpose of exploitation. Exploitation shall include, at a minimum, the exploitation of the prostitution of others or other forms of sexual exploitation, forced labour or services, slavery or practices similar to slavery, servitude or the removal, manipulation or implantation of organs . . .[9]

However, at the end of the listed forms of exploitation, organ trafficking is included within the definition of human trafficking. Lee categorizes the pattern of human trafficking into three categories: sex trafficking, labour trafficking, and trafficking body parts.[10]

The first reports of the selling of human organs began to emerge from South Asia in the late 1970s, mainly relating to kidneys being sold by the poor for transplantation into Middle Eastern men.[11] In 1994, India passed the Transplantation of Human Organs and Tissues Act, which states:

> Any person who renders his services to or at any hospital and who, for purposes of transplantation, conducts, associates with, or helps in any manner in, the removal of any human organ without authority, shall be punishable with imprisonment . . .[12]

Following the Indian Act, Pakistan and the Philippines gradually became the foci in the region for illegal transplants, largely in the form of 'transplant tourism'. This term may be contentious though, 'as it disregards the patients' desperate motives and fails to reflect ethical

[9] United Nations, Protocol to Prevent, Suppress and Punish Trafficking in Persons Especially Women and Children, supplementing the United Nations Convention against Transnational Organized Crime (adopted and opened for signature, ratification, and accession by General Assembly resolution 55/25 of 15 November 2000), http://www.ohchr.org/EN/ProfessionalInterest/Pages/ProtocolTraffickingInPersons.aspx accessed 15 July 2019.

[10] M Lee, *Trafficking and Global Crime Control* (Sage Publications, 2017), 37–43.

[11] N Scheper-Hughes, 'Organ Trafficking: A Protected Crime', *Al Jazeera Magazine* (5 November 2003), 1–14.

[12] The Transplantation of Human Organs and Tissues Act 1994 (India), section 18, https://indiankanoon.org/doc/71680523 accessed 15 July 2019.

issues. However, it is used … in international health policy discussion to refer to overseas transplantation when a patient obtains an organ through the organ trade or other means that contravene the regulatory frameworks of their countries of origin.'[13]

By 2007, *The Lancet* was reporting organ tourism and trafficking in many parts of the world.[14] According to the WHO's Dr Luc Noel, at least 10 per cent of kidneys transplanted globally each year were trafficked, with an illegally acquired organ transplanted every hour.[15]

Such concerns prompted the WHO to commission a study of the global status of organ transplantation to update their Guiding Principles on Human Organ Transplantation[16] unchanged since adoption in 1991. The resulting 2010 guidance[17] urged member states

> to promote the development of systems for the altruistic voluntary non-remunerated donation … and increase public awareness and understanding of the benefits as a result of the voluntary non-remunerated provision of cells, tissues and organs as such from deceased and living donors, in contrast to the physical, psychological and social risks to individuals and communities caused by trafficking in material of human origin and transplant tourism …

and

> to oppose the seeking of financial gain or comparable advantage in transactions involving human body parts, organ trafficking and transplant tourism, including by encouraging healthcare professionals to notify relevant authorities when they become aware of such practices …

Following the WHO's lead, both the Transplantation Society and the International Society of Nephrology subsequently began examining global transplantation practices. This culminated in a summit on the topic in Istanbul in 2008, which resulted in the Declaration of Istanbul,[18] and a Declaration of Istanbul Custodian Group (DICG) was set up to promote the Declaration and see it upheld.[19] The DICG met in Doha in April 2013 and the resulting Doha Communiqué[20] resolved

[13] Y Shimazono, 'The State of the International Organ Trade: A Provisional Picture Based on Integration of Available Information' (2007) 85(12) Bulletin of the WHO 955–62, http://www.who.int/bulletin/volumes/85/12/06-039370/en/ accessed 15 July 2019.

[14] 'Legal and Illegal Organ Donation' (2007) 369 Lancet 1901–72.

[15] Cited in D Campbell and N Davison, 'Illegal Kidney Trade Booms as New Organs "Sold Every Hour"', *The Guardian* (27 May 2012), https://www.theguardian.com/world/2012/may/27/kidney-trade-illegal-operations-who accessed 15 July 2019.

[16] World Health Organization, 'WHO Guiding Principles on Human Cell, Tissue and Organ Transplantation 1991' (May 2010), http://www.who.int/transplantation/Guiding_PrinciplesTransplantation_WHA63.22en.pdf?ua=1 accessed 15 July 2019.

[17] World Health Organization, 'Human Tissue and Organ Transplantation', Sixty-Third World Health Assembly, WHA63.22 (21 May 2010), http://apps.who.int/gb/ebwha/pdf_files/WHA63/A63_R22-en.pdf?ua=1 accessed 15 July 2019.

[18] International Summit on Transplant Tourism and Organ Trafficking, 'The Declaration of Istanbul on Organ Trafficking and Transplant Tourism' (2008) 86(8) Transplantation 1013–18.

[19] The Declaration of Istanbul on Organ Trafficking and Transplant Tourism, http://www.declarationofistanbul.org/governance/dicg accessed 15 July 2019.

[20] Doha Communiqué of the Declaration of Istanbul Custodian Group (14 April 2013), http://cofs.org/home/wp-content/uploads/2012/06/Doha-Communique.pdf accessed 15 July 2019.

> [t]o develop and recommend implementation of systematic ways for physicians to identify and report to appropriate registries (in a quantifiable but non-judgmental manner) patients returning with a donor organ from an 'unverifiable source' or manifesting other indications of a vended organ.

With so much global condemnation of organ tourism, trafficking, and indeed of organ vending altogether, it is essential to consider the perpetuating factors and ideologies which nevertheless continue to support these practices.

III. Why Do Organ Sales Continue?

Danovich et al, in their Doha DICG report, clearly view organ sales, transplant tourism, and organ trafficking as points along a single spectrum:

> the sale of human organs ... metamorphosed from a hidden and limited activity in the back streets of a handful of developing countries to a widespread, and sometimes brazen, activity that involved potential recipients traveling to clinics around the world to receive a kidney from poor, and poorly paid, 'donors.' Trafficking in organs and the persons from whom they were removed in India, Pakistan, Egypt, the Philippines, and Eastern Europe or executed prisoners in China came to have a pervasive, malign influence on transplant activities in many parts of the world.[21]

They list three particular groups of people (aside from the grassroots vendors, brokers, and buyers) who provide the rationale and means for sustaining organ markets:

> [(a)] philosophers who think that 'donors' should be allowed to exercise their autonomy by selling their organs; (b) believers in neoclassic economics, who think that treating organs as a market commodity will increase the supply; and (c) nephrologists and surgeons whose eagerness to serve their patients' needs have led them to flirt with 'regulated markets' in kidneys and other organs[22].

Each of these groups and their involvement are further considered in turn below.

A. Philosophers' Justifications

Philosophers who have argued the case for organ markets include Mark Cherry,[23] Gerald Dworkin,[24] and James Stacey Taylor.[25] However, Janet Radciffe-Richards, author of one of

[21] GM Danovitch, J Chapman, AM Capron, et al, 'Organ Trafficking and Transplant Tourism: The Role of Global Professional Ethical Standards—the 2008 Declaration of Istanbul' (2013) 95 Transplantation 1306–12.
[22] Ibid.
[23] M Cherry, *Kidney for Sale by Owner* (Georgetown University Press, 2005).
[24] G Dworkin, 'Markets and Morals: The Case for Organ Sales' in G Dworkin (ed), *Morality, Harm and the Law* (Taylor & Francis, 1994), 155–61.
[25] JS Taylor, *Stakes and Kidneys: Why Markets in Human Body Parts Are Morally Imperative* (Ashgate, 2005).

the most influential early papers advocating markets for organs,[26] will be my focus here as she is singled out for criticism by Nancy Scheper-Hughes,[27] arguably the world's foremost researcher into organ trafficking..

In her book, *Careless Thought Costs Lives*, Radcliffe-Richards argues for organ markets starting from the premise of presumption against any policy which restricts organ availability for transplantation. She suggests:

> we should start by acknowledging that there are costs to our being protected against begin killed or captured for our organs. As the idea of the Survival Lottery[28] shows, we could all increase our statistical life expectancy if we allowed the killing of one individual whenever we needed a set of organs to save several others. We are already familiar with the idea of defences which make deliberate killing not count as murder so ... we should consider extending such a defence to surgeons who send out hit squads whenever they have accumulated half a dozen patients who could be saved by the organs of a single victim.[29]

She does, however, later retract from advocating such proposals[30] on the grounds that most people won't buy into them and bioethicists merely appear irrelevant if their ideas are too remote from what most people want.

After expressing incredulity at the passing of the WHO instruments and the Declaration of Istanbul, Radcliffe-Richards explains why she views objections to organ-selling as being without substance. To her starting presumption in favour of increasing the availability of organs, she adds two further presumptions:

(1) allowing the vendor to achieve any potential benefit; and
(2) protecting both vendor and recipient from harm.

She then suggests that arguments in favour of prohibition of organ markets need to outweigh all three of these presumptions.

Radcliffe-Richards identifies the strongest case for prohibition as the argument that respect for vendor autonomy in practice is inevitably compromised by coercion through poverty, an unrefusable offer, or exploitation. She maintains that such fears regarding vendor autonomy are spurious and, in terms of abstract logic, her rebuttal of prohibition on these grounds at first appears convincing.

Radcliffe-Richards maintains that prohibition does *not* remove the coercion of poverty, but rather makes it worse by adding the coercion of a supposed 'protector' who

[26] J Radcliffe-Richards, AS Daar, RD Guttmann, et al for the International Forum on Transplant Ethics, 'The Case for Allowing Kidney Sales' (1998) 351 Lancet 1950–2.

[27] N Scheper-Hughes, 'Parts Unknown: Undercover Ethnography of the Organs-Trafficking Underworld' (2004) 5 Ethnography 29–73.

[28] The Survival Lottery is a thought experiment proposed by John Harris in which hypothetically everyone is assigned a number and if drawn out of a lottery when a donation is needed, is expected to give up their life to allow two or more people to live. The incentive is that statistically any individual is more likely to be a recipient than a donor. See J Harris, 'The Survival Lottery' (1975) 50 Philosophy 81–7.

[29] J Radcliffe-Richards, *Careless Thought Costs Lives: The Ethics of Transplants* (Oxford University Press, 2012), 33.

[30] Ibid 35.

takes away what the vendors consider as the best option they have left of selling an organ. As for the concept of 'the unrefusable offer', she does not view this as coercion at all, as it simply increases rather than decreases the options for the vendor who still has a free choice to accept or reject the offer. All the money is doing is merely making something not wanted per se (ie losing a kidney) into part of a wider package the vendor does want, such as having enough money to pay for their child's schooling. Finally, 'exploitation', which Radcliffe-Richards mischievously refers to as 'suspiciously like free market capitalism',[31] is reckoned to work by inducement. For her, the unethical element in exploitation is in offering the *minimal* inducement that can be got away with. However, she argues that complete prohibition of sales removes *all* inducements, including those which the vendor, all things considered, would have chosen over nothing at all since they would have viewed that inducement as far more than 'minimal', which is a relative concept.

However, Radcliffe-Richards later remarks that 'so called pragmatic judgments involve *both* empirical claims about the way the world works *and* moral claims about which values we should use to compare different possible arrangements'.[32] This is of course true, but conversely it is also true that so-called *philosophical* judgments also often involve both empirical and moral claims. The 'Survival Lottery' to which Radcliffe-Richards alludes only has traction because one life sacrificed can save two or more lives and not the other way around. However, those with first-hand practical experience of vendors in the real world of organ trafficking see the concept of vendors' autonomy very differently from Radcliffe-Richards.

The very discourse of personal autonomy of the individual vendor versus the basic human right to bodily integrity[33] leaves 'the foundation of those arguing for an organ trade unquestioned. The ethical argument assumes that the body parts of the poor are assets in a world of globalized capitalism; it also assumes that the poor are autonomous in the same way as those who are not economically constrained'.[34]

While philosophers advocating organ markets blithely assume that '[p]eople would be free to negotiate a bargain in which both parties win: on the one side a life is saved, on the other a family is lifted from poverty',[35] Cohen argues that:

> The problem with an ethical argument of this sort is the unrelenting presumption that ethics can be reduced to a primary transaction ... But in fact the primary transaction is constituted out of the very second order phenomena that the analyst would defer: everyday

[31] Ibid 71.

[32] Ibid 96.

[33] Article 3—'Right to of the Person' of the European Union Charter of Fundamental Rights states:
Everyone has the right to respect for his or her physical and mental integrity. In the fields of medicine and biology, the following must be respected in particular:

- the free and informed consent of the person concerned, according to the procedures laid down by law,
- the prohibition of eugenic practices, in particular those aiming at the selection of persons,
- *the prohibition on making the human body and its parts as such a source of financial gain,*
- the prohibition of the reproductive cloning of human beings.

See http://fra.europa.eu/en/charterpedia/article/3-right-integrity-person accessed 15 July 2019 (my emphasis).

[34] G Pleasants, 'Problematising Organ Sales' (2006), archived material available at https://web.archive.org/web/20170121101406/http://www.bc.edu/clubs/mendel/ethos/archives/2006/pleasants.shtml accessed 15 July 2019.

[35] M Cherry, 'Put Donor Organs on the Open Market' (2005) 187(2512) New Scientist 20, https://www.newscientist.com/article/mg18725125-700-put-donor-organs-on-the-open-market/ accessed 15 July 2019.

> indebtedness and extraordinary debt bondage in which money passes from the patient through the donor and to the moneylender and other creditors.[36]

Cohen concludes that decisions to sell organs are usually to pay off high-interest debts to local money-lenders rather than to achieve specific goals. Consequently, vendors are usually back in debt within a few years. Radcliffe-Richard's exasperated plea that if use of the term 'exploitation' 'is supposed to have content—to express some aspect of organ selling as such that supports the inference that it should be prohibited—we need to be able to be told what it is in order to assess it',[37] is surely answered by Cohen's findings in Chennai.[38] He vividly describes there what 'organ selling as such' actually is. If there is also empirical evidence that 'organ selling as such' is working in accordance with the more utopian vision of Western philosophers like Radcliffe-Richards, it is surely incumbent upon them to produce it as well?

This is important because, as mentioned earlier, advocates of organ markets are keen to maintain as much clear water as they can between organ trafficking and trading. Radcliffe-Richards, for example, criticizes the Declaration of Istanbul because it rules out 'transplant tourism' and 'transplant commercialism' alongside trafficking, while she maintains that there is no necessary connection between trafficking and the other two.[39] Furthermore, she suggests that since payment for organs is now so widely illegal, this makes organ trading *ipso facto* akin to trafficking, whereas it need not be so in a world of widespread legalized markets. However, as Cohen makes clear, exploitation of the poor to sell their organs to clear their debts was taking place in India well before the 1994 Act prohibiting organ sales was passed.[40]

The Istanbul Declaration's stance that 'transplant commercialism ... leads inexorably to inequity and injustice'[41] is dismissed by Radcliffe-Richards as merely 'another piece of rhetoric'[42] on the ground that no empirical evidence is produced for the claim. Ironically, this is followed by a repetition of her own claim, also without any supporting evidence, that everyone would benefit from 'a properly controlled, legal paid donation'.[43]

B. Economists' Justifications

Philosopher Mark Cherry states: 'If an organ market would best utilize the available organ resources or would best maximize benefits for persons, *these factors would be sufficient to make a market morally acceptable*.'[44] This comment illustrates well Roscoe's observation of

[36] L Cohen, 'Where It Hurts: Indian Material for an Ethics of Organ Transplantation' (1999) 128(4) Daedalus 135–65, 148.
[37] Radcliffe-Richards (n 28) 74.
[38] Cohen (n 35) 135–65.
[39] Radcliffe-Richards (n 28) 84–5.
[40] Cohen (n 35) 137.
[41] International Summit (n 18).
[42] Radcliffe-Richards (n 28) 86.
[43] Ibid. I suspect that the sort of 'proper control' that Radcliffe-Richard has in mind is not that exerted in Iran (see Iran: A Model Market? Pages 249–251 of this chapter).
[44] M Cherry, *Kidney for Sale by Owner: Human Organs, Transplantation, and the Market* (Georgetown University Press, 2015), 70.

how 'the common intellectual ancestry of autonomist moral philosophy and neoliberal economics allows the narrative of one to segue neatly into the other'.[45]

Economist Walter Bock puts the economic case for organ markets concisely in terms of supply and demand. If a market-clearing price were legal, then supply and demand would intersect at a price at which there would be no shortage of organs. Where sales are illegal, the government-mandated price is zero and demand then vastly outstrips supply, '*hence* the shortage is brought about by unwise state policy'.[46] Notice the knight's move from economic modelling to imputing moral blame on the state for the shortage. This illustrates another point raised by Roscoe, that economic modelling has a tendency towards implying an 'ought' from a 'might be',[47] in a similar way to the logical fallacy that Hume warned against about implying an 'ought' from an 'is'.[48]

> Demonstrating that a functioning market might have certain beneficial effects *in principle* carries a strong normative claim that such a market should be enacted *in practice*. Economic analysis moves seamlessly into social commentary. In fact ... the economic literature on markets for transplants is rich in explicitly normative content.[49]

Inshort, economic modelling frequently morphs into morality. Clay and Bock's paper is full of examples of this, sometimes one after another: 'We conclude that the case for repealing all laws that interfere with a free market in bodily organs is a strong one. That *it* **(emphasis added)** will save numerous lives is a foregone conclusion. That present violations of this law [against organ markets] are "victimless crimes," and ought to be Iegalized, is also suggested by our analysis.'[50]

As Roth notes, 'when confronted with repugnance towards a market transaction, economists often respond as if a sufficiently clear argument focused on welfare gains due to trade will overcome that repugnance'.[51] However, the 'facts' often used in economic argument are often artefacts created by economic modelling and 'the offspring of the models cut loose from their origins and travel unquestioned into subsequent models and debates'.[52]

Both autonomy and the free market are frequently invoked as key factors in maximizing people's choice.[53] Recently, however, within moral philosophy, the 'tyranny of autonomy'

[45] P Roscoe, 'On the Possibility of Organ Markets and the Performativity of Economics' (2013) 6 Journal of Cultural Economy 386–401, 389.

[46] M Clay and W Bock, 'A Free Market for Human Organs' (2002) 27 Journal of Social, Political and Economic Studies 227–36, 228 (emphasis added).

[47] Roscoe (n 44) 387.

[48] The eighteenth-century Scottish philosopher, David Hume, insisted that you cannot draw moral conclusions from non-moral premises. 'In every system of morality ... I am surpriz'd to find, that instead of the usual copulations of propositions, *is*, and *is not*, I meet with no proposition that is not connected with an *ought*, or an *ought not*. This change is imperceptible; but is, however, of the last consequence. For as this *ought*, or *ought not*, expresses some new relation or affirmation, 'tis necessary that it shou'd be observ'd and explain'd; and at the same time that a reason should be given, for what seems altogether inconceivable, how this new relation can be a deduction from others, which are entirely different from it' (D Hume, *Treatise of Human Nature* (1739), section 3.1.1.27, http://www.davidhume.org/texts/thn.html accessed 15 July 2019).

[49] Roscoe (n 44) 389.

[50] Clay and Bock (n 45) 227–36, 231.

[51] A Roth, 'Repugnance as a Constraint on Markets' (2007) 21 Journal of Economic Perspectives 7–58, 49.

[52] Roscoe (n 44) 386–401, 388.

[53] See eg: T Burchardt, M Evans, and H Holder, *Public Policy and Inequalities of Choice and Autonomy* (Centre for Analysis of Social Exclusion, London School of Economics, 2013), CASE/174, http://eprints.lse.ac.uk/51267/1/__Libfile_repository_Content_Burchardt,%20T_Burchardt_Public_%20policy_inequalities_2013.pdf accessed

has increasingly been criticized.[54] In 2007, Waldfogel's *The Tyranny of the Market*[55] similarly challenged the myth that, as with autonomy, markets will deliver all you want. However, despite the tyrannical tendencies of both of these concepts, neither of them could actually deliver a market in organs without the cooperation of clinicians in preparing patients for transplantation and performing the surgery required.

C. Clinicians' Justifications

The almost universal opposition of twentieth-century transplant health-care workers to organ sales is gradually breaking down and 'has slowly been replaced by an open debate of plans that offer financial rewards to persons willing to donate their organs or the organs of their deceased kin'.[56] One prominent clinician advocating regulated organ markets in that debate is the US nephrologist Benjamin Hippen, who believes:

> A morally defensible version of a regulated market in organs, which treats human beings as embodied moral agents, need not be synonymous with a corrosive dehumanization. And in a nation that grants individuals a considerable amount of freedom in the body, prohibiting the sale of organs is an unnecessary and unwise limitation on the basic right of self-determination.[57]

For Hippen, the primary question is not whether organ shortages imply a moral imperative to increase organ supplies, but is rather one of the proper limits of respect for individual autonomy and 'under what conditions the state is or is not justified in legally proscribing free individuals from actualizing their moral commitments in market relationships, whether by participation in or abstention from the buying and selling of organs'.[58]

The striking things about Hippen's case for organ markets is that it rests on political and ideological grounds rather than on any specifically medical reasoning. He states: 'In a free society, a hallmark of which is an irreducible moral pluralism … the burden of proof [is on] those who insist on maintaining the current legal proscription on a regulated market in organs.'[59] He claims, in contrast to the 'insufficiency' of the recommendations of the US Institute of Medicine's report, 'Organ Donation: Opportunities for Action',[60] that the

XXXX; D King, *The New Right: Politics, Markets and Citizenship* (Macmillan, 1987). However, the idea of increased choice let alone maximized choice resulting from introducing free markets has been increasingly challenged: see eg K Dowding, 'Choice: Its Increase and Its Value' (1992) 22 British Journal of Political Science 301–14.

[54] C Foster, *Choosing Life, Choosing Death: The Tyranny of Autonomy in Medicine Ethics and Law* (Hart Publishing, 2009); T Stammers, 'The Evolution of Autonomy' (2015) 21 New Bioethics 155–63.

[55] J Waldfogel, *The Tyranny of the Market: Why You Can't Always Get What You Want* (Harvard University Press, 2007).

[56] D Joralemon, 'Shifting Ethics: Debating the Incentive Question in Organ Transplantation' (2001) 27 Journal of Medical Ethics 30–5, 30.

[57] B Hippen, 'The Case for Kidney Markets', *The New Atlantis* (Fall 2006), 14, 47–61, http://www.thenewatlantis.com/publications/the-case-for-kidney-markets accessed 15 July 2019.

[58] Ibid 47–61.

[59] Ibid.

[60] Institute of Medicine, *Organ Donation: Opportunities for Action* (National Academies Press, 2006).

advantages of a regulated organ market are 'many and varied'.[61] His subsequent list of nine purported such 'advantages', however, can actually be reduced to just three:[62]

(1) a large-scale increase in organs is made available, enabling higher quality organs to be transplanted pre-emptively, before dialysis is even needed, to a wider pool of patients and with less likelihood of rejection and greater survival times;
(2) more time for vendor screening, with selection of lowest-risk vendors and more respect for vendors' moral agency; and
(3) guaranteed reduction and possible elimination of organ trafficking and unregulated organ sales.

Each element of these claims is, however, highly contestable and Hippen presents them without any supporting evidence. Nevertheless, two influential reports to which US transplant physicians and surgeons made a significant contribution have found no ethical justification for a total ban or organ sales[63] and also recommended that the debate on the introduction of legal organ markets should be reopened.[64]

These reports are keen to stress the wide gulf between a strictly regulated market and the negative connotations involved in organ trafficking, and hence they 'limit discussion to issues concerning a regulated system in the industrialized Western world'.[65] So, what features of such a regulated market do its advocates consider might ensure it remains free from exploitation and injustice?

IV. An Ideal Regulated Market in Organs

Any effective regulated market of organs would need to be safe, just and transparent. Nearly all discussion about such a market is restricted to kidneys, as the risks for the vendor are usually very low. Matas gives a comprehensive list of the issues that would need to be determined in implementing such a market for kidneys, which forms the basis of the following discussion.[66]

[61] Hippen (n 56) 47–61.
[62] I discount completely Hippen's view that the 'opportunity for truly altruistic donors to donate' is an advantage of the introduction of markets. The opportunity to donate exists prior to the introduction of markets and there is evidence that the introduction of markets actually reduces altruistic donations.
[63] D Rothman, E Rose, B Awaya, et al, 'Bellagio Task Force Report on Transplantation, Body Integrity, and the International Traffic in Organs' (1997) 29 Transplantation Proceedings 2739–45.
[64] Radcliffe-Richards et al (n 25) 1950–2.
[65] A Matas, 'The Case for Kidney Sales: Rationale, Objections and Concerns' (2004) 4 American Journal of Transplantation 2007–17.
[66] Ibid.

A. Criteria for Vendors and Provision for Their Assessment, Ongoing Health Care, and Follow-Up

The age and origin of vendors would need to be clearly prescribed. Organs donated from children and young people are especially valuable for transplantation and a minimum age for legal organ sales would be essential to agree upon. As with blood donation, an upper age limit would also be required.

The origin of vendors would also need to be delineated. It would almost certainly be necessary to stipulate a geographical regional marketplace in order to prevent poorer people coming to richer countries just to sell their organs.[67]

Screening costs for suitability for donation of potential vendors would need to be covered. Although the risks of kidney donation are low, they are not zero. Countries such as the United Kingdom with a National Health Service would arguably provide free ongoing care, but payments for health insurance cover would need to be made in those countries without free universal heath cover.

B. Logistics of Both Payment and Organizational Practice

The price of a kidney would need to be determined in any government-regulated market and would need regular periodic adjustment. Decisions would need to be made about the taxation and benefit status of such payments. Bearing in mind that, as far back as 2004, one US cost-analysis estimate[68] arrived at a sum of $100,000 for a kidney, questions of timing and status of such a payment today are not inconsequential to either the vendor or the treasury.[69] There is also the question of whether a fixed price per organ is fair when kidneys from younger vendors offer potentially better outcomes than those from older ones.

Since Iran is the only country which actually operates such a state-regulated market in kidneys, it is essential to consider what is happening there.

V. Iran: A Model Market?

In the midst of rather conflicting data and opinions about the Iranian kidney market, several clear background facts can be identified.

(1) Iran is the world's only official Shi'a Islamic country and its approach to biomedicine 'is dramatically different from that in most Islamic countries',[70] let alone the rest of the world.

[67] J Harris and C Erin, 'An Ethically Defensible Market in Organs' (2002) 325 British Medical Journal 114–15.

[68] A Matas and M Schnitzler, 'Payment for Living Donor (Vendor) Kidneys: A Cost-Effectiveness Analysis' (2004) 4(2) American Journal of Transplantation 216–21.

[69] However, Alexander Berger, a *New York Times* commentator in December 2011, quotes the market price of a kidney at $50,000: see A Berger, 'Why Selling Kidneys Should Be Legal', *New York Times* (5 December 2011), http://www.nytimes.com/2011/12/06/opinion/why-selling-kidneys-should-be-legal.html?_r=0 accessed 15 July 2019. This should be compared with the cost of a kidney in Iran in 2007 of $1,100: see MH Nourbala, B Einollahi, B Kardavani, et al, 'The Cost of Kidney Transplantation in Iran' (2007) 39(4) Transplant Proceedings 927.

[70] D Tober, 'Kidneys and Controversies in the Islamic Republic of Iran: The Case of Organ Sales' (2007) 13 Body and Society 151–70, 151.

(2) The Iranian system has significantly evolved over thirty years. Although some government compensation to 'donors'[71] began in 1988,[72] it was not until 1995 that the practice was formalized 'to provide donors with a million tomans ... to cover donation related expenses, one year of health insurance, and exemption from military service'.[73]

(3) The payment for the kidney itself is negotiated between the donor and the recipient through the Iranian Patients' Kidney Foundation, with which both must be registered.

(4) The national scheme has considerable regional variation. In Shiraz province, for example, payment beyond that set by the national compensation scheme is prohibited.[74]

What is also certain within a disputed picture in Iran is the fact that the kidney transplant waiting list was totally eliminated in 1999.[75] However, while most supporters of organ markets highlight this fact,[76] far fewer consider the evidence about the fate of the paid donors.

Over 80 per cent of recipients of a transplanted kidney from the Iranian living unrelated donor (LURD) scheme had a potential living related donor, but they were not used. Most LURDs are men in their 30s or late 20s.[77] All LURDS are from low or middle classes, 84 per cent being poor in one study (though 50.4 per cent of the recipients were also poor).[78]

A recent study concluded that 'there are major deficiencies in the health evaluation of donors in the Iranian model'.[79] Only 40 per cent of the donors had been informed about the risks of donation; 11 per cent had not had a full physical examination; 5 per cent had not even had their blood pressure taken; and 50 per cent did not have any follow-up after kidney removal. The authors lament that if only 10 per cent of the 20,000 Iranians who die from traffic accidents each year were used for organ donation, there would be no need for living donors; however, there were no active measures in Iran to implement using organs from brain-dead donors. They attribute this inertia to the 'availability of deliberate unlimited living donors'[80]—donors whom they conclude are 'stupendously neglected'. There are,

[71] 'Donors' is the officially used term for vendors in Iran and which will therefore be used exclusively in this section.

[72] M Mahdavi-Mazdeh, 'The Iranian Model of Living Renal Transplantation' (2012) 82 Kidney International 627–34.

[73] S Fry-Revere, 'The Truth about Iran' (2014) 14 American Journal of Bioethics 37–8, 38.

[74] Ibid.

[75] A Ghods, 'Renal Transplantation in Iran' (2002) 17 Nephology Dialysis and Transplantation 222–8.

[76] In a fifty-five-page article arguing for legal organ sales in the United States, the only reference to Iran is: 'Offering monetary compensation for organs will likely increase the number of organ donors in the United States and thus narrow the gap between the number of organs needed and the number of organs available. Iran has successfully eliminated its waiting list for kidney recipients since legalizing the sale of organs from living donors': KL Williams, M Finley, and J Rohack, 'Just Say No to NOTA: Why the Prohibition of Compensation for Human Transplant Organs in NOTA Should Be Repealed and a Regulated Market for Cadaver Organs Instituted' (2014) 40 American Journal of Law & Medicine 275–329, 302.

[77] B Larjani, F Zahedi, and E Taheri, 'Ethical and Legal Aspects of Organ Transplantation in Iran' (2004) 36 Transplantation Proceedings 1241–4.

[78] A Ghods, S Ossarch, and P Khosravani, 'Comparison of Some Socioeconomic Characteristics of Donors and Recipients in a Controlled Living Related Donor Renal Transplantation Program' (2001) 33 Transplantation Proceedings 2626–7.

[79] M Khatami, N Nikravan, and F Alimohammadi, 'Quality and Quantity of Health Evaluation and the Follow-Up of Iranian Living Donor' (2015) 47 Transplantation Proceedings 1092–5.

[80] Ibid 1094.

however, many other religious, cultural, and logistical barriers in Iran to donation from deceased donors diagnosed as brain dead. A recent study concludes that 'denial of brain death was the most important cause of disagreement with organ donation'.[81]

Several other studies[82] have also concluded that the poor quality of life of many Iranian donors means the Iranian system needs considerable change before being 'presented as a successful model to the rest of the world'.[83] Even Fry-Revere, who considers the Iranian system is 'though flawed, remarkably successful', notes the conflicting evidence concerning Iranian vendor outcomes and acknowledges that 'in Iran, many regions could do a better job of providing more detailed disclosures regarding risks and benefits for both donors and recipients'.[84]

VI. Conclusions

There is universal condemnation of organ trafficking and widespread unease about transplant tourism among both supporters and opponents of regulated organ sales as currently practised in Iran, as a solution to global organ shortage. There is a marked difference, however, in how the two sides of the debate view the relationship between legalized organ markets and transplant tourism and organ trafficking: while supporters of organ markets view them as the solution to transplant trafficking and tourism, opponents tend to view all three as transplantation practices inimical to the ends of medicine.[85]

Although elements of the organ markets debate, such as their possible effects on altruistic donation and human dignity, are outside the scope of this chapter, it is the fate of organ vendors in particular which appears to consistently link organ trading, tourism, and trafficking, whether in international declarations or academic research. Although this link may be dismissed by detractors as mere rhetoric or moral panic, neither of these is likely to account for the fact that a recent multidisciplinary work on organ trafficking[86] has only four chapters on trafficking *per se* and nine on the pros and cons of organ markets!

My assessment of the evidence to date indicates that the poor and vulnerable are certainly worse off in illegal organ markets, but are likely to still be worse off even if legal organ markets are introduced. Supporters of organ markets generally do acknowledge vendor vulnerability, even in Iran. However, such concerns seem to be outweighed more by utilitarian ideology and extrapolations from economic models than by sound philosophical reasoning or the empirical evidence on vendor outcomes.

[81] A Bahrami, E Khaleghi, AK Vakilzadeh, et al, 'Process and Barriers to Organ Donation and Causes of Brain Death in Northeast of Iran' (2017) 2 Electronic Physician 3797.

[82] See eg M Fallahzadeh, L Jafari, J Roozbeh, et al, 'Comparison of Health Status and Quality of Life of Related versus Paid Unrelated Living Kidney Donors' (2013) 13 American Journal of Transplantation 3210–14.

[83] FL Delmonico, 'The Alternative Iranian Model of Living Renal Transplantation' (2012) 82 Kidney International 625–6, 626.

[84] AH Jahromi, S Fry-Revere, and B Bastani, 'A Revised Iranian Model of Organ Donation as an Answer to the Current Organ Shortage Crisis' (2015) 9(5) Iranian Journal of Kidney Diseases 354–60, 355.

[85] See eg FD Davis and SJ Crowe, 'Organ Markets and the Ends of Medicine' (2009) 34 Journal of Medicine and Philosophy 586–605.

[86] L Territo and R Matteson, *The International Trafficking of Human Organs: A Multidisciplinary Perspective* (CRC Press, 2011).

Bibliography

Bahrami, A, Khaleghi, E, Vakilzadeh, AK, and Afzalaghaee, M, 'Process and Barriers to Organ Donation and Causes of Brain Death in Northeast of Iran' (2017) 2 Electronic Physician 3797, https://www.ncbi.nlm.nih.gov/pmc/articles/PMC5410908/ accessed 15 July 2019.

Berlatsky, N, '"Human Trafficking" Has Become a Meaningless Term', *New Republic* (30 October 2015), https://newrepublic.com/article/123302/human-trafficking-has-become-meaningless-term accessed 15 July 2019.

Burchardt, T, Evans, M, and Holder, H, 'Public Policy and Inequalities of Choice and Autonomy', Centre for Analysis of Social Exclusion, London School of Economics (2013), CASE/174, http://eprints.lse.ac.uk/51267/1/__Libfile_repository_Content_Burchardt,%20T_Burchardt_Public_%20policy_inequalities_2013.pdf accessed 15 July 2019.

Campbell, D and Davison, N, 'Illegal Kidney Trade Booms as New Organs "Sold Every Hour"', *The Guardian* (27 May 2012), https://www.theguardian.com/world/2012/may/27/kidney-trade-illegal-operations-who accessed 15 July 2019.

Cherry, M, *Kidney for Sale by Owner* (Georgetown University Press, 2005).

Cherry, M, 'Put Donor Organs on the Open Market' (2005) 187(2512) New Scientist 20, https://www.newscientist.com/article/mg18725125-700-put-donor-organs-on-the-open-market/ accessed 15 July 2019.

Clay, M and Bock, W, 'A Free Market for Human Organs' (2002) 27 Journal of Social, Political and Economic Studies 227.

Cohen, L, 'Where It Hurts: Indian Material for an Ethics of Organ Transplantation' (1999) 128(4) Daedalus 135.

Danovitch, GM, Chapman, J, Capron, AM, et al, 'Organ Trafficking and Transplant Tourism: The Role of Global Professional Ethical Standards—the 2008 Declaration of Istanbul' (2013) 95(11) Transplantation 1306.

Davis, FD and Crowe, SJ, 'Organ Markets and the Ends of Medicine' (2009) 34 Journal of Medicine and Philosophy 586.

Delgado, M, 'The Organ Snatchers: Boy of 12 Smuggled into UK ... for Gang to Sell His Body Parts on Black Market', *Daily Mail* (8 March 2015), http://www.dailymail.co.uk/news/article-2984489/The-organ-snatchers-Boy-12-smuggled-UK-gang-sell-body-parts-black-market.html accessed 15 July 2019.

Delmonico, FL, 'The Alternative Iranian Model of Living Renal Transplantation' (2012) 82 Kidney International 625.

Doha Communiqué of the Declaration of Istanbul Custodian Group (14 April 2013), http://cofs.org/home/wp-content/uploads/2012/06/Doha-Communique.pdf accessed 15 July 2019.

Dowding, K, 'Choice: Its Increase and Its Value' (1992) 22 British Journal of Political Science 301.

Dworkin, G, Markets and Morals: The Case for Organ Sales' in G Dworkin (ed), *Morality, Harm and the Law* (Taylor & Francis, 1994), 155–61.

European Agency for Fundamental Human Rights, EU Charter of Fundamental Rights, http://fra.europa.eu/en/charterpedia/article/3-right-integrity-person accessed 15 July 2019.

Evans, R, 'Pakistani Police Rescue 24 from Organ Trafficking Gang', *BBC News* (24 January 2017), http://www.bbc.co.uk/news/health-38722052 accessed 15 July 2019.

Fallahzadeh, MK, Jafari, L, and Roozbeh, J, et al, 'Comparison of Health Status and Quality of Life of Related versus Paid Unrelated Living Kidney Donors' (2013) 13 American Journal of Transplantation 3210.

Foster, C, *Choosing Life, Choosing Death: The Tyranny of Autonomy in Medicine Ethics and Law* (Hart Publishing, 2009).

Fry-Revere, S, 'The Truth about Iran' (2014) 14 American Journal of Bioethics 37.

Ghods, AJ, 'Renal Transplantation in Iran' (2002) 17 Nephology Dialysis and Transplantation 222.

Ghods, AJ, Ossarch, S, and Khosravani, P, 'Comparison of Some Socioeconomic Characteristics of Donors and Recipients in a Controlled Living Related Donor Renal Transplantation Program' (2001) 33 Transplantation Proceedings 2626.

Harris, J, 'The Survival Lottery' (1975) 50 Philosophy 81.

Harris, J and Erin, C, 'An Ethically Defensible Market in Organs' (2002) 325 British Medical Journal 114.
Hippen, B, 'The Case for Kidney Markets', *The New Atlantis* (Fall 2006), http://www.thenewatlantis.com/publications/the-case-for-kidney-markets accessed 15 July 2019.
Hume, D, *Treatise of Human Nature* (1739–40), section 3.1.1.27, http://www.davidhume.org/texts/thn.html accessed 15 July 2019.
Institute of Medicine, *Organ Donation: Opportunities for Action* (National Academies Press, 2006).
International Summit on Transplant Tourism and Organ Trafficking, 'The Declaration of Istanbul on Organ Trafficking and Transplant Tourism' (2008) 86(8) Transplantation 1013.
Jahromi, AH, Fry-Revere, S, and Bastani, B, 'A Revised Iranian Model of Organ Donation as an Answer to the Current Organ Shortage Crisis' (2015) 9(5) Iranian Journal of Kidney Diseases 354.
Joralemon, D, 'Shifting Ethics: Debating the Incentive Question in Organ Transplantation' (2001) 27 Journal of Medical Ethics 30.
King, D, *The New Right: Politics, Markets and Citizenship* (Macmillan, 1987).
Larjani, B, Zahedi, F, and Taheri, E, 'Ethical and Legal Aspects of Organ Transplantation in Iran' (2004) 36 Transplantation Proceedings 1241.
Lee, M, *Trafficking and Global Crime Control* (Sage Publications, 2017).
Mahdavi-Mazdeh, M, 'The Iranian Model of Living Renal Transplantation' (2012) 82 Kidney International 627.
Matas, A, 'The Case for Kidney Sales: Rationale, Objections and Concerns' (2004) 4 American Journal of Transplantation 2007.
Matas, A and Schnitzler, M, 'Payment for Living Donor (Vendor) Kidneys: A Cost-Effectiveness Analysis' (2004) 4(2) American Journal of Transplantation 216.
Merrill, JP, Murray, JE, Harrison, JH, and Guild, WR, 'Successful Homotransplantations of Human Kidneys between Identical Twins' (1956) 160 Journal of the American Medical Association 277.
Pleasants, G, 'Problematising Organ Sales' (2006), archived material available at https://web.archive.org/web/20170121101406/http://www.bc.edu/clubs/mendel/ethos/archives/2006/pleasants.shtml accessed 15 July 2019.
Radcliffe-Richards, J, 'The Case for Allowing Kidney Sales' (1998) 351 Lancet 1950.
Radcliffe-Richards, J, *Careless Thought Costs Lives: The Ethics of Transplants* (Oxford University Press, 2012).
Roscoe, P, 'On the Possibility of Organ Markets and the Performativity of Economics' (2013) 6 Journal of Cultural Economy 386.
Roth, A, 'Repugnance as a Constraint on Markets' (2007) 21 Journal of Economic Perspectives 7.
Rothman, D, Rose, E, Awaya, B, et al, 'Bellagio Task Force Report on Transplantation, Body Integrity, and the International Traffic in Organs' (1997) 29 Transplantation Proceedings 2739.
Scheper-Hughes, N, 'Organ Trafficking: A Protected Crime', *Al Jazeera Magazine* (5 November 2003), 1.
Scheper-Hughes, N, 'Parts Unknown: Undercover Ethnography of the Organs-Trafficking Underworld' (2004) 5 Ethnography 29.
Shimazono, Y, 'The State of the International Organ Trade: A Provisional Picture Based on Integration of Available Information' (2007) 85(12) Bulletin of the WHO 955, http://www.who.int/bulletin/volumes/85/12/06-039370/en/ accessed 15 July 2019.
Stammers, T, 'The Evolution of Autonomy' (2015) 21 New Bioethics 155.
Taylor, JS, *Stakes and Kidneys: Why Markets in Human Body Parts are Morally Imperative* (Ashgate, 2005).
Territo, L and Matteson, R, *The International Trafficking of Human Organs: A Multidisciplinary Perspective* (CRC Press, 2011).
Tober, DM, 'Kidneys and Controversies in the Islamic Republic of Iran: The Case of Organ Sales' (2007) 13 Body and Society 151.
Waldfogel, J, *The Tyranny of the Market: Why You Can't Always Get What You Want* (Harvard University Press, 2007).

Williams, KL, Finley, M, and Rohack, J, 'Just Say No to NOTA: Why the Prohibition of Compensation for Human Transplant Organs in NOTA Should Be Repealed and a Regulated Market for Cadaver Organs Instituted' (2014) 40 American Journal of Law and Medicine 275.

World Health Organization, 'Human Tissue and Organ Transplantation', Sixty-Third World Health Assembly, WHA63.22 (21 May 2010), http://apps.who.int/gb/ebwha/pdf_files/WHA63/A63_R22-en.pdf?ua=1 accessed 15 July 2019.

World Health Organization, 'WHO Guiding Principles on Human Cell, Tissue and Organ Transplantation 1991' (May 2010), http://www.who.int/transplantation/Guiding_PrinciplesTransplantation_WHA63.22en.pdf?ua=1 accessed 15 July 2019.

United Nations, Protocol to Prevent, Suppress and Punish Trafficking in Persons Especially Women and Children, supplementing the United Nations Convention against Transnational Organized Crime (adopted and opened for signature, ratification, and accession by General Assembly resolution 55/25 of 15 November 2000), http://www.ohchr.org/EN/ProfessionalInterest/Pages/ProtocolTraffickingInPersons.aspx accessed 15 July 2019.

17

How Can a Reformed Surrogacy Law Reflect Pragmatism and Respect Ethics?

Kirsty Horsey

I. Introduction

AAccording to recently published guidance from the Department of Health and Social Care, surrogacy 'is when a woman carries a child for someone who is unable to conceive or carry a child for themselves'.[1] It can take two forms: 'traditional surrogacy' or 'full surrogacy'. In traditional surrogacy, the surrogate uses her own egg (either retrieved in a clinic and fertilized with sperm outside of the body before being replaced, or via insemination of sperm either in a clinic or at home) and thus is also an egg donor. Full surrogacy requires in vitro fertilization (IVF), as an already-created embryo is transferred into the surrogate in the hope of implantation. The recipients, commonly known as the intended parents, may both have provided the genetic material to create the embryo (if in a heterosexual relationship), or part of the genetic material might come from either an egg or a sperm donor. It is unusual for neither of the intended parents to provide genetic material, but there may be situations where the fertility problems faced by a couple are complex, and donor embryos are required, as well as surrogacy.

Surrogacy, therefore, enables people who would otherwise be childless to have children, without recourse to adoption. Given the importance of reproduction to the overall human experience, this would appear to make surrogacy socially valuable and suggest that we should protect the practice. This is further emphasized when we consider that infertility is understood to be a disease,[2] and we know that not being able to have children can have devastating emotional and psychological consequences on those affected.[3] It is worth remembering that many intended parents come to surrogacy as a 'last resort', having tried and failed to have children using other assisted reproductive technologies, presumably at great emotional cost, and often at huge financial expense. Alternatively, surrogacy may be the *only* option to have children for some people and couples. Women born without a uterus, or who lose their uterus to cancer, for example, know—often from an early age—that they will

[1] Department of Health and Social Care, 'Care in Surrogacy: Guidance for the Care of Surrogates and Intended Parents in Surrogate Births in England and Wales' (28 February 2018).

[2] Infertility is defined as 'a disease of the reproductive system defined by the failure to achieve a clinical pregnancy after 12 months or more of regular unprotected sexual intercourse' by the International Committee for Monitoring Assisted Reproductive Technology (ICMART) and the World Health Organization (WHO) in the *Revised Glossary on ART Terminology* (2009). Other definitions (as collated by the WHO) suggest that infertility is a disability; thus, there are potential issues regarding equality and discrimination.

[3] T Cousineau and A Domar, 'Psychological Impact of Infertility' (2007) 21(2) Best Practice & Research: Clinical Obstetrics & Gynaecology 293.

Kirsty Horsey, *How Can a Reformed Surrogacy Law Reflect Pragmatism and Respect Ethics?* In: *Philosophical Foundations of Medical Law*. Edited by: Andelka M Phillips, Thana C de Campos, and Jonathan Herring, Oxford University Press (2019).
DOI: 10.1093/oso/9780198796558.003.0018

not be able to carry a child.[4] Similarly, for same-sex male couples planning to have a family, surrogacy is really the only possibility to have a child with any biological relationship to either parent. Surrogacy thus facilitates both traditional and new family forms, and increased social acceptance of it as a means of assisted reproduction is a reflection of changed social attitudes to both alternative types of family and different parenting norms.

Some might suggest that people who find themselves in situations where they are unable to have children should consider adoption—and that is, of course, an alternative. However, notwithstanding what we know about the difficulties in pursuing adoption,[5] it seems cruel and discriminatory to deny people the opportunity to have their own child based on their biological problems or sexuality, when there is another option that can be tried to enable them to do so. Curtailing reproductive liberty and autonomy in this way would seem to fly in the face of ideas about equality and fairness.[6]

In addition, since the emergence of surrogacy as a 'new' reproductive technology in the late 1970s, as well as with the developments in IVF technology since that time, an initial distrust of surrogacy seems for the most part to have evaporated.[7] Social, medical, judicial, media, and even governmental attitudes towards surrogacy have become more positive. Indeed, the recently issued Department of Health and Social Care guidance clearly states that the '[g]overnment supports surrogacy as part of the range of assisted conception options'[8] and a statement from the Law Commission of England and Wales in the report on its thirteenth programme of law reform, presented to Parliament in December 2017, acknowledges that the law on surrogacy 'has fallen behind changing social attitudes and the increasing prevalence of surrogacy, including surrogacy arrangements with international aspects'.[9] As with other areas of medicine, including reproductive donation and other

[4] Although womb transplantation may one day be more than a mere possibility, and has generated a few successes, as yet the techniques are not developed enough to suggest a real and viable alternative to surrogacy. There are also ethical considerations attached to the procedure (see J Robertson, 'Other Women's Wombs: Uterus Transplants and Gestational Surrogacy' (2016) 68 Journal of Law and the Biosciences 68–9).

[5] See J Doughty, 'Adoption' in R Lamont (ed), *Family Law* (Oxford University Press, 2018).

[6] That said, there are of course critics of surrogacy, as a practice, and in particular in relation to cross-border surrogacy as a manifestation of global capitalism, neo-liberalism, and pronatalism (as well as race and class). For a good overview of some of these arguments, see FW Twine, *Outsourcing the Womb: Race, Class and Gestational Surrogacy in a Global Market* (Taylor & Francis, 2015). Also see E Luik, 'Cross-Border Surrogacy: Exploiting Low Income Women as Biological Resources?', *The Guardian* (28 March 2017). This chapter focuses on UK-based surrogacy, acknowledging that some 'outsourced' surrogacy arrangements may be problematic, thus adding to the imperative to design a 'domestic' law that is both pragmatic and ethical.

[7] There are some feminist arguments against surrogacy, some extending to the practice per se, not only the commercial model. Many of these focus on issues of commodification or exploitation of women's labour and bodies. See eg: G Corea, *The Mother Machine: Reproductive Technologies from Artificial Insemination to Artificial Wombs* (Harper Collins, 1985); ES Anderson, 'Is Women's Labor a Commodity?' (1990) 19(1) Philosophy and Public Affairs 71; D Satz, 'Markets in Women's Reproductive Labor' (1992) 21(2) Philosophy and Public Affairs 107; A Wertheimer, 'Two Questions about Surrogacy and Exploitation' (1992) 21(3) Philosophy and Public Affairs 213; A Van Niekerk and L Van Zyl, 'The Ethics of Surrogacy: Women's Reproductive Labour' (1995) 21 Journal of Medical Ethics 345; SG Berkhout, 'Buns in the Oven: Objectification, Surrogacy, and Women's Autonomy' (2008) 34(1) Social Theory and Practice 95; K Sloan, 'Trading on the Female Body: Surrogacy, Exploitation, and Collusion by the US Government' (2017) Public Discourse, https://www.thepublicdiscourse.com/2017/04/19109/ accessed 6 September 2019.

[8] See n 1, above.

[9] Since then, after consultation, the Law Commission announced that it would include surrogacy in its thirteenth programme of law reform (Law Commission, Thirteenth Programme of Law Reform (Law Com No 377), December 2017). Its work—in tandem with the Scottish Law Commission—commenced in 2018, after Department of Health funding was secured (see Law Commission, 'Surrogacy Laws Set for Reform as Law Commissions Get Government Backing' (4 May 2018), https://www.lawcom.gov.uk/surrogacy-laws-set-for-reform-as-law-commissions-get-government-backing/ accessed 15 July 2019). A period of public consultation began on 6 June 2019 and closed on 11 October 2019, and recommendations for new surrogacy laws are expected to follow (see https://www.lawcom.gov.uk/project/surrogacy/).

services, the availability of cross-border arrangements has increased for British people seeking surrogacy.

Given the fact that it seems that surrogacy is here to stay, and because there will continue to be some (if only few) hard cases, re-regulation of surrogacy is clearly necessary. The law, currently, does not serve the interests of those involved to the extent it should, including intended parents, surrogates, and—importantly—children. Partly, this is because of its age—the bulk of the law was enacted in the 1980s, when many aspects of family law and policy were very different. Also, it was always intended that the tone of the law should permit but discourage surrogacy. It can be argued that a direct result of this, in conjunction with other developments in information technology and travel, for example, has led to the increase in intended parents seeking surrogacy overseas, which potentially raises more ethical questions. In reforming the law, however, we must think carefully and pragmatically about the message we need to send—to maximize its utilitarian potential and minimize ethical concern.[10] There may be some questions about the regulatory limits we place on surrogacy in order to carefully balance the ideals of reproductive liberty and autonomy, and the welfare interests of children and surrogates in particular.

II. How Can Law Balance Pragmatism and Ethical Issues in Surrogacy?

In the United Kingdom, surrogacy is already permitted by law, but the law contains a number of disincentives introduced deliberately or otherwise to both prevent certain kinds of surrogacy arrangement occurring and to discourage all surrogacy. The late Lady Mary Warnock, the moral philosopher and later member of the House of Lords, whose 1984 Inquiry Report underpins the law,[11] admitted that she hoped the way her report and the subsequent law that was based on its recommendations was framed would mean that surrogacy would 'wither on the vine', though also that she 'may have got it wrong' in respect of her opinion on surrogacy.[12] Writing in 2016, she said that her perspective on surrogacy had changed, and she recognized its value as a form of family-forming and respected the altruism of surrogates.[13] However, though it may have been the intention to discourage surrogacy, in reality the law has not stopped the growth of surrogacy as a means of people having their families, and the internet age has made doing so much easier, with greater access to information, as well as cheap and easy international travel.[14]

Much of the way in which the law is framed can be understood as existing to prevent the exploitation of surrogates and the commodification of women's reproductive capacities and of children. The Warnock Report was written in the midst of a moral concern about surrogacy stemming from one or two very public examples of commercial surrogacy arrangements.[15] As a result, the law prohibits third parties like agencies or brokers from

[10] On utilitarianism, see Dominic Wilkinson and Julian Savalescu, 'Consequentialism and the Law in Medicine' in AM Phillips, Thana C de Campos, and J Herring (3ds), Philosophical Foundations of Medical Law (OUP 2019), chapter 4.

[11] Report of the Committee of Inquiry into Human Fertilisation and Embryology, Cm 9314, HMSO (July 1984).

[12] M Warnock, 'Foreword: The Need for Full Reform of the Law on Surrogacy' (2016) 4 Journal of Medical Law and Ethics 155.

[13] Ibid.

[14] K Horsey, 'Not Withered on the Vine: The Need for Surrogacy Law Reform' (2016) 4 Journal of Medical Law and Ethics 181.

[15] See eg the 'Baby Cotton' case (*Re C (a minor)* [1985] FLR 846): Kim Cotton, often thought of as the United Kingdom's 'first' surrogate, gave birth to a baby girl for a foreign couple for £6,500, following an arrangement

profiting from surrogacy—thus, commercial surrogacy of the kind that operates in some jurisdictions, including numerous US states (where regulation of surrogacy is state-based), Canada, Russia, Georgia, the Ukraine, Kenya, and others, is prohibited.[16] However, despite a commonly held belief that it is otherwise, the law does not prohibit payments for surrogacy.[17] Neither an intended parent who pays nor a surrogacy who accepts payment commits an offence. This is another legacy of Warnock, who did not want the individual parties and, most importantly, children, to have a 'taint of criminality'. In respect of payments to surrogates, which are also not illegal,[18] the law introduces a further disincentive, in that a 'parental order' (the mechanism by which legal parenthood is transferred to the intended parents after birth) could in theory be denied where there are payments above what the court considers to be 'reasonable expenses'. Further limitations are placed on the acquisition of legal parenthood by the intended parents, all in the interests of protecting the surrogate from the supposed harm of relinquishment and the broader risk of exploitation of either surrogates or children.

It can be seen, then, that surrogacy raises interesting and difficult ethical and philosophical issues. The reproductive liberty of the intended parents is obviously at stake, especially in the context of constraints placed on their reproductive choices. Provided that they harm no one else in exercising this liberty, so the argument goes, they should be able to exercise their choice to have children and by what means.[19] Ronald Dworkin suggested that 'procreative autonomy' is the 'right of people to control their own role in reproduction unless the state has a compelling reason for denying them that control'.[20] However, this is more difficult to protect for infertile people who need assistance to be able to achieve their choices. Their reproductive (or procreative) autonomy is at stake, as to allow them to be able to exercise this right requires their choices to be facilitated rather than hindered. As Goold explains,[21] this might occur in a 'wide' or 'narrow' sense.

Surrogacy also raises questions about the surrogate's own agency and autonomy—her freedom to decide for herself how to use her own body, and respect for the choices she

brokered by an American agency. The baby girl—whom Kim Cotton was happy to relinquish—was initially made a ward of court, and Ms Cotton was investigated by Scotland Yard.

[16] In the majority of jurisdictions where surrogacy is formally regulated *and* permitted (it is banned in many countries), surrogacy is operated on a commercial basis. The exception to the rule (as well as the United Kingdom) is Greece, where surrogacy is regulated by a detailed piece of legislation, but only altruistic surrogacy is permitted, and only in cases of medical need (defined so as to exclude same-sex male couples): see K Horsey and K Neofytou, 'The Fertility Treatment Time Forgot: What Should Be Done about Surrogacy in the UK?' in K Horsey (ed), *Revisiting the Regulation of Human Fertilisation and Embryology* (Routledge, 2015). For an idea of what form of surrogacy is allowed where, see the website of the organization Growing Families: https://www.growingfamilies.org/surrogacy-by-country/ accessed 6 September 2019.

[17] This was found to be one of many pervasive 'surrogacy myths' in a survey conducted by the Surrogacy UK Working Group on Surrogacy Law Reform in 2015 (K Horsey, 'Surrogacy in the UK: Myth Busting and Reform', Report of the Surrogacy UK Working Group on Surrogacy Law Reform (November 2015).

[18] They are only supposed to cover a surrogate's 'reasonable expenses' (Human Fertilisation and Embryology Act 2008, s 54), but what is 'reasonable' is obviously subjective and, in any case, judges can (and must) retrospectively authorize any payment made in connection with surrogacy (including commercial) if it would be in the child's best interests to do so. The child's interests are the courts' paramount concern: The Human Fertilisation and Embryology (Parental Orders) Regulations 2010.

[19] J Robertson, *Children of Choice: Freedom and the New Reproductive Technologies* (Princeton University Press, 1994).

[20] R Dworkin, *Life's Dominion* (Harper Collins, 1993), 48.

[21] See Chapter 13, this volume.

makes.[22] On the other hand, there are questions about exploitation of women—both of their reproductive capacity and potentially their economic or social position.[23] Over and above the situations of individual women, however, surrogacy raises questions about how we view and treat women more generally. Additionally, surrogacy induces notions of commodification of children, childbirth, and reproduction, which need to be explored. In a traditional Kantian view of autonomy, where one is free to act in relation to others as long as doing so involves treating others as ends in themselves and not a means to an end (see Chapter 5), surrogacy inevitably raises some questions. Although this is true, some scholars also contend that autonomy can be facilitated by the provision of truly informed consent, again relevant in the surrogacy context,[24] and the existence of the conditions in which true, meaningful choice is able to be exercised.[25]

If we were looking to update the law, which seems to be necessary given the changes in society that have occurred since current surrogacy law was first enacted, then what should be our priorities in doing so? What limits, if any, should we place on any of the parties' reproductive and personal autonomy? The answer to this in any context depends on how we weigh autonomy against potential harms,[26] thus any harms that might arise from surrogacy arrangements should be investigated. If the actual or potential harm outweighs the good that may come from exercising autonomy, only then would there be reason to curtail autonomy.

III. Reasons for Limiting Access to Surrogacy

A. Potential Harm to the Surrogate

1. Relinquishment and Informed Consent

The argument here is that surrogacy is not ethical, and therefore should not be facilitated by law, because it is not possible for the surrogate's consent to handing over a child to whom she gives birth to be fully informed. Reasons for this include the unpredictability of her emotional state and her feelings towards the baby, to whom she may have bonded during pregnancy, and may therefore no longer want to relinquish.[27]

However, not allowing someone to exercise an autonomous choice because they may not know how they will feel in the future seems to set a very high standard for all people entering any kind of agreement. In fact, constraining any right to autonomy because of putative emotions (which are fleeting) rather than reasons is unjustifiable and unreasonable. Although a surrogacy arrangement is a very different kind of agreement from many others entered into in life, as long as a woman enters it having been given accurate and impartial information,

[22] See eg LB Andrews, 'Surrogate Motherhood: The Challenge for Feminists' in L Gostin (ed), *Surrogate Motherhood: Politics and Privacy* (Indiana University Press, 1990), 168. The arguments are explored more broadly in E Nelson, *Law, Policy and Reproductive Autonomy* (Hart Publishing, 2014).

[23] See nn 6 and 7, above.

[24] TL Beauchamp and JF Childress, *Principles of Biomedical Ethics* (6th edn, Oxford University Press, 2009); O O'Neill, *Autonomy and Trust in Bioethics* (Cambridge University Press, 2002); S Wilkinson, *Bodies for Sale: Ethics and Exploitation in the Human Body Trade* (Routledge, 2003), 134–81. See also Thana C de Campos, 'Justice and Responsibility A Deontological Approach to Medical Law' in AM Phillips, Thana C de Campos, and J Herring (3ds), Philosophical Foundations of Medical Law (OUP 2019), chapter 5, this volume.

[25] Nelson (n 22) 50.

[26] As identified by JS Mill in *On Liberty* (John W. Parker and Son, 1859).

[27] J Oakley, 'Altruistic Surrogacy and Informed Consent' (1992) 6(4) Bioethics 269.

and without coercion, she should be able to do so. What this suggests is that for any surrogacy law to be effective, it must have the capacity to reflect the surrogate's autonomy by facilitating her acquisition of information and, perhaps, counselling. As it currently stands, existing law on surrogacy does not do this (though if the surrogacy involves treatment in a licensed clinic, it is likely that all parties would be recommended or even mandated to have counselling). Built into the law is the unwavering constant that the woman who gives birth to a child is always to be regarded as its mother.[28] In practical terms, this means that the surrogate (and her partner in many cases) must formally register the child as her own to avoid breaking the law on birth registration. Although there is a formal legal mechanism for the transfer of legal parenthood in the form of the bespoke 'parental order',[29] a surrogate is required to give her consent to the making of such an order, but is deemed not to be able to give this consent until the child is at least six weeks old. This reflects a paternalistic or protectionist view, because it takes little heed of the surrogate's capacity for autonomous decision making. It also helps to perpetuate the idea that surrogacy is about women giving away 'their' babies when, in fact, the majority of surrogates do not view themselves as 'mothers' of the children they carry for others.[30]

In addition, the law does little to help women acquire good information from reputable sources about surrogacy, what it entails, how she might feel, and so on. Largely, this is because of the historical distaste for surrogacy, and the idea that tight regulation, particularly of the commercial aspects of surrogacy, might cause the practice to gradually disappear.[31] Thus, surrogacy undertaken in the United Kingdom is largely facilitated by non-profit groups run by volunteers—who may well have first-hand experience of surrogacy and can offer professional-style support, but can only do so much. Alternatively, those interested in either becoming a surrogate or having a child through surrogacy may seek out information online or through social media, leading many into believing any of a number of surrogacy myths:[32] surrogacy is not legal, thus must be done clandestinely; payments are not legal in this country, thus the only way to 'guarantee' a child is to travel overseas and pay for surrogacy; and various other permutations of those ideas. Given the prevalence of myths and the lack of understanding of how a version of altruistic surrogacy can be practised legally, it is perhaps true that fully informed consent is unlikely.[33]

However, assuming a lack of truly informed consent because of a lack of access to reputable information does a disservice to both women who act as or consider acting as surrogates, and reflects a very paternalistic view of their knowledge of their own bodies and minds and their ability to make autonomous decisions. In addition, such an assumption

[28] Section 33 of the Human Fertilisation and Embryology Act 2008 says that the woman who gives birth, 'and no other woman', is to be regarded as the mother, despite what the surrogate (and future parents) intend. Legal parenthood can only be transferred (for those who are eligible) by a parental order authorized by the court, or by adoption.

[29] Human Fertilisation and Embryology Act 2008, s 54.

[30] Horsey (n 17) illustrates that only 3.6 per cent of the surrogates who responded to a survey in 2015 thought that they should be recognized as the legal mother at birth (ibid 21). See also M Rose, 'Surrogate Mother Calls for 'Old-Fashioned' Laws on Births to Be Changed', *The Guardian* (18 January 2018).

[31] Horsey (n 14); A Alghrani and D Griffiths, 'The Regulation of Surrogacy in the United Kingdom: The Case for Reform' (2017) 29 Child and Family Law Quarterly 165.

[32] Horsey (n 17) above.

[33] This is one of the reasons why the 2015 'myth busting' report mentioned above recommended centralized surrogacy information (as recently published by the DHSC (n 1)), either via a surrogacy regulator or one of the agencies that currently collects some parts of the information held on surrogacy.

does disservice to the non-profit groups who work with surrogacy, as what they bring is experience and knowledge and, importantly, the sharing of experiences and support throughout arrangements. Therefore, the argument can be made that, to truly prioritize the informed nature of the consent that a woman must give to become a surrogate, such organizations should be recognized as welcome additions and partners in the surrogacy world. This would be a better alternative than acting alone or without assistance, or with little support or information.[34] Thus, the government guidance on surrogacy arrangements is to be welcomed, not least because it points potential surrogacy participants to the reputable non-profit organizations and, it is hoped, this will also be reflected in any proposed new surrogacy law that may arise following the Law Commissions' review.

Further, any law that seeks to restrict the exercise of personal choice should be underpinned by evidence. Although much of the available evidence to date has been anecdotal, as indicated above, there is emerging empirical evidence that UK-based surrogates do not view themselves as the mothers of the children they carry, do view their role as altruistic, and are often driven by empathy for other women and couples, based on their own love of children or motherhood, or own experiences of fertility difficulties.[35] What is true is that in the forty years of UK case law on surrogacy that we have, there are very few examples of surrogates having changed their mind about relinquishing the child and, of these, not all of these doubts about relinquishment were because the surrogate wanted to keep the baby she had given birth to.[36] This was also indicated in studies of surrogates at or around the turn of the century, as well as in a more recent study of surrogates and their own families.[37]

2. Commercial Surrogacy Arrangements

In true commercial surrogacy arrangements, the surrogate receives not only her expenses, but a fee, often construed as payment for the service she has provided. Strangely, despite the paternalism of the existing law, to pay a surrogate is not illegal. Many overseas surrogacy arrangements are entered into on a commercial basis by intended parents from the United Kingdom. Commercial agencies and brokers of surrogacy arrangements are criminalized in the United Kingdom, but not the participants in arrangements themselves, and agencies and brokers operating overseas cannot be covered by our laws. What does exist in law is a disincentive to enter into commercial agreements either at home or abroad, because supposedly doing so affects whether or not a parental order can be granted to the intended parents.[38] However, this provision has been routinely circumvented by the courts, whose paramount responsibility in deciding cases is the consideration of the lifelong welfare of

[34] There are examples of cases where surrogates have unfortunately found themselves in less than ideal circumstances when they have not had the kind of support or information referred to here. A good example is *Z (surrogacy agreements: Child arrangement orders)* [2016] EWFC 34 (see A Blackburn-Starza, 'Judge Condemns Surrogacy "Market" and Allows Surrogate to Keep Baby', *BioNews* (4 July 2016), 858).

[35] See n 29, above.

[36] See eg: O van den Akker, 'Genetic and Gestational Surrogate Mothers' Experience of Surrogacy' (2003) 21 Journal of Reproductive and Infant Psychology 145; T Appleton, 'Emotional Aspects: Effective Counselling and Support' in R Cook, S Sclater, and F Kaganas (eds), *Surrogate Motherhood: International Perspectives* (Hart Publishing, 2003).

[37] V Jadva, S Imrie, and S Golombok, 'Surrogate Mothers 10 Years on: A Longitudinal Study of Psychological Wellbeing and Relationships with the Parents and Child' (2015) 30(2) Human Reproduction 373.

[38] K Horsey and S Sheldon, 'Still Hazy after All These Years: The Law Regulating Surrogacy' (2012) 20 Medical Law Review 67.

the child concerned. Thus, it is not uncommon for large payments, including those made in overseas arrangements, to be retrospectively authorized.

As we have seen earlier in the chapter, it has been claimed that commercial surrogacy harms the surrogate, and renders the consent of a woman entering a commercial arrangement invalid. This is because money is viewed as a form of coercion, and there is an assumption that a woman would not agree to be a surrogate without payment. The extension of this is that certain women, particularly the poor or the vulnerable, will be most negatively affected. However, an interesting counter-argument is made by Wilkinson in the context of the (then flourishing) Indian commercial surrogacy industry, where the true consent of the surrogates might reasonably be thought to have been flawed. For Wilkinson, this is *outweighed* by the harm that banning (international) surrogacy would do to the interests of surrogates and prospective parents (and by extension, wider society), as well as the observation that some children who would otherwise have been born and lead worthwhile lives would not be born.[39] In any case, outside of situations of coercion, it is at least arguable that even paid surrogates are driven by a degree of altruism, which is not negated by the fact that they receive money.[40]

3. Risks to Bodily and Personal Autonomy

Surrogacy agreements may contain clauses that require the surrogate to adhere to certain behaviour during the period of time conception is being attempted and/or throughout the pregnancy. They may also require her to submit to certain medical tests and procedures in the course of the pregnancy, even to the extent of requiring her to undergo amniocentesis, selective foetal reduction in the case of multiple pregnancies, or even termination of the pregnancy in certain situations. While it is hard to imagine how such terms would be easily policed, such clauses doubtlessly attempt to curtail the surrogate's exercise of bodily autonomy (should she adhere to them). Also, although these terms are perhaps more likely to be found in commercial arrangements, they should not ease our concern as many international surrogacy agreements entered into are commercial.

For our own law in the United Kingdom, we could legislate to prevent the use of such terms, or restrict their effectiveness. The law already deems all aspects of surrogacy arrangements to be wholly unenforceable, which would seem to capture this problem. Even if we might want, in the future, to make the main aspect of the agreement (who gets the baby) enforceable in either 'hard' (requiring the surrogate to hand over the child at the end of the agreement) or 'soft' (reversing the presumption of motherhood) form, it could be written into law that the surrogate retains full bodily autonomy (subject to capacity) at all times until the agreement is complete.[41]

In terms of what might be called 'extended' personal autonomy, a law that holds the surrogate to be the legal mother, as ours does, potentially curtails women's personal autonomy, despite that being the opposite of its intention. For instance, if the intended parent(s) reneged on the agreement and did not take the baby—either because they changed their mind, or their own situation had changed—the surrogate (and usually her partner) would

[39] S Wilkinson, 'Exploitation in International Paid Surrogacy Arrangements' (2016) 33 Journal of Applied Philosophy 125, 137.

[40] An argument originally made by Helene Ragoné, 'The Gift of Life: Surrogate Motherhood, Gamete Donation and Constructions of Altruism' in Cook et al (n 36).

[41] As is the situation in Greek law, detailed in Horsey and Neofytou (n 16).

be legally responsible for the baby,[42] thus curtailing her/their personal autonomy, since she (and her partner) would then be forced to care for a child they did not want. Of course, the surrogate would be free to give the baby up for adoption—but should she ever be able to be left in such an invidious position? Given that we know that very few arrangements go wrong (in the sense that the surrogate decides to keep the baby), coupled with the fact that we should respect women's autonomous choices to act as a surrogate, as well as the fact that surrogates do not view themselves as 'mother' of the child they carry, this supports the argument for reversing the presumption of legal parenthood that currently exists. In that case, legal responsibility for the child would rest solely with the intended parents from birth onwards, preserving the surrogate's personal autonomy.

B. Potential Harm to Women in General

Any pregnant woman exposes herself to general medical and emotional risks, but in relation to surrogacy, the question arises whether a woman should expose herself to those kinds of potential harms for someone else. This obviously has links to questions of autonomy and consent, but additionally raises the question about expectations of women more generally in society. Is surrogacy then a manifestation of a normative view of women and motherhood?

Arguments have been made that surrogacy perpetuates a normative ideal of women as child-bearers and vessels and thus objectifies and exploits women,[43] as well as treating them as a means to an end, rather than an end in themselves. Thus, surrogacy would devalue all women in the eyes of society. By extension, for some, surrogacy promotes a patriarchal view of womanhood and reproduction.[44] This argument informed the Warnock Report and thus formed part of the notion that surrogacy is distasteful and to be discouraged, as part of a more conservative understanding of what families and mothers are.[45] However, there has been no empirical or other proof that surrogacy harms women in this way and, in fact, what empirical evidence there is suggests that women can feel empowered by being surrogates and that many do it more than once, especially in the non-commercial context.[46]

C. Commodification of Children

To be a commodity, understood in the usual sense, means to be something that is an object or service that is for sale, to be bought, sold, and passed on to an ultimate consumer. When people criticize surrogacy as a manifestation of the commodification of children, they mean this in a moral sense, in that children are wrongly used as goods, which can be bargained for and traded. Really, this argument can only apply to commercial surrogacy and, specifically,

[42] Or perhaps because they either did not want *that* child, or only wanted one of a set of twins or triplets—see eg the controversial 'Baby Gammy' Thai surrogacy case.

[43] See eg Corea and others cited in n 7, above.

[44] Ibid.

[45] See J Lewis and F Cannell, 'The Politics of Motherhood in the 1980s: Warnock, Gillick and Feminists' (1986) 13(3) Journal of Law and Society 321.

[46] See eg: H Ragone, *Surrogate Motherhood: Conception in the Heart* (Westview Press, 1994); van den Akker (n 36); K Busby and D Vun, 'Revisiting the Handmaid's Tale: Feminist Theory Meets Empirical Research on Surrogate Mothers' (2010) 26 Canadian Journal of Family Law 13; Horsey (n 17).

to particular kinds of commercial surrogacy operations where the surrogate is unvalued and treated as a means to an end, thus the baby she carries is the commodity. Arguably, few of these models of surrogacy exist anywhere worldwide, though there may have been some instances of these in the past, or risks of them—for example, certain aspects of Indian commercial surrogacy.[47] Thus, this suggests that even in a global commercial surrogacy market, there is a degree of self-regulation and insight into perceptions of the type of surrogacy offered and how people might view it.[48] In any case, if the potential commodification of children is one of our concerns,[49] then we must put in place ways that minimize the risk of this occurring, or our being complicit in it. Thus, again the argument pertains that good domestic regulation of surrogacy is essential, while also we seek to highlight any 'bad practice' elsewhere (and perhaps in 'underground' channels at home).

IV. Conclusion

Although there are some concerns about surrogacy, many of these relate not to surrogacy per se, but to specific aspects of the way in which it is practised and in particular in relation to commercial surrogacy arrangements entered into overseas. Such concerns, however, should lead us to reflect on our own law, what messages it sends, and what can be done to minimize the potential for harm. As regards international surrogacy, which is almost entirely commercial in nature, the troublesome aspects are related to the commerciality and to the question of autonomy. International surrogacy raises the question of whether women who agree to be surrogates (or are subject to either explicit or situational coercion, such as poverty, to do so) are exercising free, autonomous consent.

Coupled with a changed social understanding of surrogacy, which has evolved over time, this suggests that surrogacy ought to continue to be regulated, in such a way as to encourage people to enter 'domestic' arrangements rather than international ones. Not only would this save some of the financial costs associated with overseas surrogacy, but it may also help to evade the problematic issues that arise with commercialization in a global marketplace. Although we do not already ban payments to surrogates, the evidence suggests that surrogacy in the United Kingdom is undertaken on an altruistic basis, with altruistic taken to include the reimbursement of agreed expenses, and even including reasonable gifts. Despite the written law seeming to suggest that intended parents may put their parental order in

[47] See eg: A Pande, 'Commercial Surrogacy in India: Manufacturing a Perfect Mother-Worker' (2010) 35 Signs 969; A Pande, *Wombs in Labor: Transnational Commercial Surrogacy in India* (Columbia University Press, 2014); F Baylis, 'Transnational Commercial Contract Pregnancy in India' in F Baylis and C McLeod (eds), *Family-Making: Contemporary Ethical Challenges* (Oxford University Press, 2014); S Saravanan, 'A Feminist Discourse on the Global Indian Surrogacy Bazaar' (2018) 8(1) Feminists@Law.

[48] A question emerges about the potential for global regulation of surrogacy, similar to the model for intercountry adoption. However, in surrogacy, it is less likely—probably because it is a form of reproduction, rather than a method of caring for already existing children—that there would be any global consensus, due to the wide disparity of laws (including absence of laws) in different jurisdictions (and in fact the closeness the content of laws often has to the dominant religious and cultural beliefs within a country). Since 2011, the Hague Conference on Private International Law has been considering how a global convention on international surrogacy could be implemented, as yet producing no definitive suggestions (see details on the Parentage/Surrogacy Project, available at https://www.hcch.net/en/projects/legislative-projects/parentage-surrogacy accessed 15 July 2019).

[49] It should be noted that the commodification argument has also been applied to women (surrogates), wombs, and pregnancy/reproduction in general, in similar terms. Due to constraints of space and not wishing to repeat the arguments, I focus only on children here.

danger if they pay for surrogacy, as indicated above, the 'agreed reasonable expenses' practice, broadly interpreted, is now clearly endorsed by government.[50] So, what is it that drives some people overseas for surrogacy, when it is clear that *despite* the current law a good model exists in the United Kingdom?

I would contend that the primary drivers for overseas surrogacy are some of the myths about surrogacy in the United Kingdom that have grown up, which are, I suggest, a direct and inevitable result of the formulation of the law. Because surrogacy agreements are wholly unenforceable, and because the surrogate is always and incontrovertibly the legal mother, prospective intended parents without an intricate knowledge of the law could be forgiven for thinking that there is an inherent uncertainty in entering an arrangement in the United Kingdom. Additional myths that arise about what payments can be made and how legal parenthood can eventually be achieved (or not) only add to this. A quick internet search will reveal surrogacy 'packages' available as options in the United States, Canada, Russia, Georgia, the Ukraine, and Greece, among other destinations. While some of the potentially more concerning surrogacy destinations have closed their doors to foreign intended parents (including India, Thailand, Nepal, Mexico, and others), the certainty that is promised in these packages is what will inevitably continue to attract prospective parents unless there is something to keep them at home. Hopefully, more transparent acknowledgement from government that surrogacy is just one of a number of available assisted conception options, with the promotion of centralized guidance with a particular 'pathway' through surrogacy outlined in it, will help to do this in advance of any law reform.

However, law reform is still needed and it must be drafted both to be pragmatic in recognizing the extent of surrogacy and the problems with it, as well as ethically concerned to facilitate intended parents' reproductive liberty, recognize surrogates' autonomy, and do these with respect for the best interests of children.[51] More empirical evidence would be useful, but we already see that there are very few disputed cases in the United Kingdom, that surrogates are proud of what they do and often do it multiple times, and that children born from surrogacy do well.[52] For all these reasons, a law that reverses the presumption of motherhood in surrogacy, or at least provides for a formal transfer of legal parenthood to take place at birth, with the surrogate's advance consent, would be preferred. This does justice to the intended parents' reproductive aims, while respecting the surrogate's autonomy and capacity to make decisions, and is in the best interests of children and families as it promotes legal and social certainty from day one of a child's life. It would also remove the need for either the rubber-stamping of parental order applications that occurs in the majority of cases, or the more detailed scrutiny that happens in others, saving both the physical and the emotional costs. Additionally, though it might be expected that some intended parents might still travel overseas for surrogacy, if they were recognized as the legal parents under UK law, many of the conflicts of law and immigration problems faced by parents in the past may be avoided, also in the best interests of the children concerned.

50 See n 1, above.

51 K Wade, 'The Regulation of Surrogacy: A Children's Rights Perspective' (2017) 29 Child and Family Law Quarterly 113.

52 The longitudinal study of Susan Golombok et al at the Cambridge Centre for Family Research attests to this, the latest instalment being a study of surrogate-born children as teenagers. For a summary, see V Jadva, 'Surrogates and Intended Parents in the UK' (2016) 4(3) Journal of Medical Law and Ethics 215.

18

Ageing and Fertility

Legal and Ethical Perspectives

Pia Jolliffe and William Jolliffe

I. Introduction

Around the world, fertility decline and population ageing are major challenges facing humanity. Falling fertility reduces the percentage of younger people, while falling mortality rates increase life expectancy. Depopulation rather than overpopulation is a challenge faced by many rich and poor countries around the world. There is a real concern about how taxpayers will finance the rising medical costs for an ageing population and whether the population will remain at the same level.[1]

This chapter starts out with some facts about the relationship between fertility and population ageing, focusing on the 'demographic deficit' and its economic consequences. The chapter then turns to the legal and ethical issues related to these demographic developments. In particular, we discuss how population control and family planning policies try to enhance or curb fertility by laws, stipends, and regulations. We focus on reproductive medicine and concentrate on the moral issues that may shape fertility decisions at the individual level of society. The chapter concludes with a reflection on these issues in the light of our Christian faith.

II. Demographic Background

There is a worldwide drop in fertility rates and a decline in population growth.[2] Usually it is presumed that a total fertility rate of 2.1 children per woman is necessary for one generation to replace the previous one. However, this standard of 2.1 births per woman applies to countries with high health-care standards. In regions that are more prone to diseases and natural disasters, child mortality rates are higher. A woman may need to give birth to more than 2.1 children to ensure that more than 2.1 children survive to adulthood.[3]

Why this fertility decline? In his book *The Demographic Crash* (2001), Michel Schooyans (Pontifical Academy for Life) identifies two kinds of causes for the global drop in fertility: first, an unfavourable environment; and, second, anti-natal techniques. The environment for fertility is 'unfavourable' because men and women marry later and thus the median

[1] IR Dowbiggin, *The Sterilization Movement and Global Fertility in the Twentieth Century* (Oxford University Press, 2008), 1.

[2] M Schooyans, *The Demographic Crash: From Fatalism to Hope* (Central Bureau, CCVA, 2001), 4.

[3] M Schooyans, *Pour Comprendre Les Évolutions Démographiques* (3rd edn, Association Pour la Recherche et l'Information Démographiques (APRD), 2011), 27.

Pia Jolliffe and William Jolliffe, *Ageing and Fertility* In: *Philosophical Foundations of Medical Law*. Edited by: Andelka M Phillips, Thana C de Campos, and Jonathan Herring, Oxford University Press (2019).
DOI: 10.1093/oso/9780198796558.003.0019

age at which women have their children increases. For example, according to research published in 2016, in Japan only 2 per cent of children were born out of wedlock and only 6 per cent of married couples remained childless. However, since the 1980s, the percentage of unmarried men and women has risen and—consequently—the number of births declined.[4]

This has been accompanied by a general drop in marriages and an increase in women's access to higher education. While higher education is of immense value, it may discourage women from early childbearing. This is so not least because highly educated women may aspire for a career to support their household income. Yet, in many societies, it is still difficult to combine an active participation in the workforce with motherhood and other forms of caring. Indeed, women often find it difficult to access permanent positions with high levels of protection. Those who strive to combine family work with paid employment often find themselves in residual, marginal, underpaid positions with low levels of protection. Credit policies may also have an impact on family life when they entice large segments of the population to access credit which is often spent on consumer goods rather than on goods favourable to the family, such as well-prepared food, medical care, and education. As a consequence, children are easily perceived as an economic burden, not least because many parents need to work hard to pay for child care. Monsignor Schooyans also suggests that migration from rural to urban lifestyles impacts on fertility rates because in cities country solidarity cannot be taken for granted. The image of the family has also suffered from the mass media who shower on children and young people a range of often contradictory and ambiguous messages. These messages are often shaped by secularized ideology and the culture of death.[5] For example, Mexico and Brazil are famous for *telenovelas* which promote family planning. During the 1970s and 1980s, Miguel Sabido produced in Mexico five family-planning soap operas and it is estimated that during the same period Mexico's population growth rate decreased by 34 per cent. In Brazil, the rise of *telenovelas* was accompanied by a decline in fertility rates from over 6.0 children per woman in 1960[6] to 1.8 in 2016.[7]

Anti-natal techniques are symbolic of the culture of death and all anti-natal techniques have a direct negative effect on fertility. On the one hand, there are 'provisional' techniques such as contraception, abortion, and intra-uterine devices (IUD). On the other hand, there are definitive techniques such as infanticide and sterilization. In particular, female infanticide is a big concern in societies that fear the transmission of life to such an extent as to use force to curb it. This has sadly been reported in China. Sterilization is another way to forcibly curb fertility in poor regions of the world, such as Peru and Thailand. Local authorities often offer sterilization as a 'service' to women who are ignorant and often illiterate, convincing them that the procedure is 'benign' and 'for their own good'.[8]

A consequence of the worldwide fertility decline is population ageing.[9] For example, by 2015, the entire European Union was affected by population ageing due to increased life

[4] I Fassbender, 'Enhancing Autonomy in Reproductive Decisions? Education about Family Planning and Fertility as a Countermeasure against the Low Birthrate' (2016) 28 Contemporary Japan 123, 125.

[5] O Tarzia, 'Introduction' in *Woman and Man the Humanum in Its Entirety* (Libraria Editrice Vaticana, 2010), 185–6.

[6] S Baston, 'Declining Fertility, Television and the (Mis)Representation of Motherhood' in A Buchanan and A Rotkirch (eds), *Fertility Rates and Population Decline: No Time for Children?* (Palgrave Macmillan, 2013), 185–6.

[7] Population Reference Bureau, '2016 World Population Data Sheet' (2016), 12.

[8] Schooyans (n 2) 28–30.

[9] United Nations, 'World Population Ageing Report 2015' (2015), 4.

expectancy and generally low fertility. Between 1994 and 2014, the proportion of those aged 65 or over in the European Union increased by 4 per cent, while there was a decline of 3 per cent in the proportion of younger people (age 0–14).[10]

Declining fertility and population ageing also have economic consequences. Sarah Harper suggests that around the world there may be a change in the support ratio between working adults in their middle years of economic productivity and elderly dependants. This is being referred to as the 'demographic deficit'. Among demographers there are two arguments concerning the consequences of this 'demographic deficit'. Some presume that falling fertility leads to a decline in economic activity. Others think that the fertility decline in most regions of the world is leading to population ageing, causing an economic burden on pension and health care.[11]

The first argument has been contested by those who claim that in a knowledge-based society aggregate demand depends on income rather than on the number of people. Some have pointed out that an increased demand for elder care services will even drive the economy. Also, men and women are likely to stay in the labour market and be economically productive for much longer than in previous decades. In light of this, some argue that by 2050, being 60 may no longer be a useful definition for 'old age'.[12]

The idea of people remaining economically active longer relates to the above argument according to which falling fertility is leading to ageing population with the economic burden of pension and health care. So, delaying retirement and postponing demand for pensions may be important for countries where early retirement rates are generally high. It is also important to bear in mind old peoples' informal productivity,[13] for example, volunteering.

In poor countries, there has been a hypothesis that the desire for security in old age is the cause of high fertility. Different theoretical modules and arguments exist which support or challenge the assumed relationship between old age security and fertility. Already in 1990, the International Labour Office in Geneva published a research paper that discussed these arguments.[14] The authors of this paper found that the general case for the importance of the old age motive in developing countries is grounded on four observations. First, what men and women say about their responsibilities for childbearing. Second, there are few possible alternatives to children for ensuring support for any predictable or unpredictable times of disability and old age; therefore (third), the dependence of elderly and disabled parents on their adult sons and daughters. Fourth, developing countries in particular are generally marked by an association between high fertility and the absence of old age pension programs. Conversely, industrialized countries with below-replacement fertility need to develop programs and policies to secure the well-being of an ageing population.[15]

There are reasons for questioning the importance of the old age support motive. First of all, the above reasons often stem from interviews where answers given depend on the research context, the personality of the researcher, the order of questions, the way in which they are phrased, the tone of the interviewer's voice, and the extent to which research

[10] European Union, 'Short Analytical Web Note 3/2015', 8.

[11] S Harper, 'Falling Fertility, Ageing and Europe's Demographic Deficit' in Buchanan and Rotkirch (n 6) 224–6.

[12] S Harper, 'The Capacity of Social Security and Health Care Institutions to Adapt to an Ageing World' (2010) 63 International Social Security Review 177, 178.

[13] S Harper and GW Leeson, 'The Global Ageing Survey (GLAS)—Ageing and Later Life', 4.

[14] JB Nugent and R Anker, *Old Age Support and Fertility* (International Labour Office, 1990).

[15] Ibid 3.

participants understand concepts and words which are often translated. Social research also evidences a general shift in old age support due to changing norms and values about family and community life. It has also been argued that parents aspire to transfer cash and bequests to their children rather than to receive benefits from them.[16]

So, there exists a relationship between falling fertility and population ageing. The next section turns to the legal and ethical issues that arise out of these demographic developments.

III. Legal and Ethical Perspectives

This section discusses legal and ethical perspectives related to the global phenomenon of older populations and fertility decline. First, we draw attention to ethical issues related to population control and family planning. This is followed by a discussion of the ethical issues related to reproductive medicine in the light of our Christian faith.

A. Population Control and Family Planning

The social context in which men and women make decisions about childbearing is profoundly shaped by different conditions that affect fertility, both directly and indirectly. The arising social and political ethical questions concern nations, their sovereignty, and their populations, as well as the relations among nations.[17]

Already in the eighteenth century, fertility control, or rather 'check on population', was the topic of Thomas R Malthus's famous *Essay on the Principle of Population*.[18] In this essay, Malthus made two basic assertions: first, 'that food is necessary for the existence of man'; second, 'that the passion between the sexes is necessary, and will remain nearly in its present state'. Taking these assumptions as certainties, Malthus concluded that the future of humankind depends on the ratio between the number of people in the world and the resources needed for their survival.[19] In order to balance human reproduction and food production, Malthus argued for 'checking' population. In the first published version of his essay, Malthus distinguished between two types of 'checks': active and preventive 'checks' of misery or of vice. For example, active checks of misery are phenomena like disease or hunger, and warfare would be an active check on vice. Preventive checks of misery include postponing marriage and celibacy; among preventive checks upon vice he listed abortion and birth control. Indeed, contraception (even within marriage) was morally unacceptable for Malthus, himself an Anglican, and for the majority of his readers. In a later version of his essay, Malthus even spoke more positively of a new check upon population, namely 'moral restraint'. This means postponing marriage until people can support a family, and chastity until they marry.[20]

16 Harper and Leeson (n 13) 7.
17 Schooyans (n 2) 53.
18 TR Malthus, *An Essay on the Principle of Population* (Oxford University Press, 2008).
19 Ibid 12–13.
20 Ibid xviii.

Malthus's essay has influenced population debate to this day, especially among those who argue that governments should encourage fertility control. For example, one of the pioneering eugenicists in England, Havelock Ellis, used Malthus's theory to justify birth control. In 1912, the Feeble-Minded Persons (Control) Bill was proposed to Parliament. GK Chesterton commented:

> The first of the Eugenic Laws has already been adopted by the Government of this country and passed with the applause of both parties through the dominant House of Parliament... What is novel and what is vital is this: that the defence of this crazy Coercion Act is a eugenic defence. It is not only openly said, it is eagerly urged the aim of the measure is to prevent any person whom these propagandists do not happen to think intelligent from having any wife or children.[21]

Havelock Ellis, in turn, was the primary Neo-Malthusian influence on Margaret Sanger, the founder of the International Planned Parenthood Federation. Like Malthus, Ellis and Sanger point to the need for population control, especially among the poor and marginalized. However, in contrast to Malthus, they insist on the use of contraception and abortion as a means of family planning. Sanger is often celebrated as a key figure of feminism and women's liberation. Yet, her feminism was severely compromised by her association with the eugenics movement: for her, women's liberation meant achieving eugenic aims. She was therefore unable to include all women in her vision of freedom. Sanger was interested in the eugenic restructuring of family life by rational control of female fertility.[22] Although she promoted general education in the physical functioning of the human body,[23] she doubted women's and men's ability to harmonize the biological functioning of their bodies with their wishes for family planning. Instead, she promoted general education about the use of contraception: 'continence must give way, as a method of birth control, to contraceptives'.[24] Margaret Sanger is also known for her institutional leadership. In 1921, she founded the American Birth Control League. From the beginning, this institution was motivated by eugenic concerns, such as the conviction of the necessity of sterilization of the weak and feeble-minded.

Out of the American Birth Control League eventually developed, in 1942, the Planned Parenthood Federation of America (PPFA). From the 1950s onwards, the PPFA emphasized population control. It received massive financial support from businessmen such as John D Rockefeller, who supported Sanger and the PPFA with an estimated $396,000 between 1940 and 1955.[25] Indeed, around the world, faster economic growth was promised if fertility was controlled, and many other international agencies started offering assistance to governments of poor countries in setting up national family-planning programs.

The world seems to be divided into those countries with high population growth and those with low birth rates. Particularly among the poor and disadvantaged, women's and men's fertility is frequently targeted by governments implementing population-control policies shaped by neo-Malthusian and eugenic ideas. For example, in India, sterilization

[21] GK Chesterton, *Eugenics and Other Evils* (Cassell, 1922), 19–21.
[22] A Franks, *Margaret Sanger's Eugenic Legacy: The Control of Female Fertility* (McFarland, 2004), 29.
[23] M Sanger, *What Every Girl Should Know* (Haldeman-Julius Co, 1922).
[24] M Sanger, *The New Motherhood* (Jonathan Cape, 1922), 137.
[25] Franks (n 22) 37.

became after 1952 the main means of fertility control. In contrast to other countries, mass sterilization has been targeted at men to the extent that, at different times and in different states, the 'acceptance' of vasectomy was a determinant for the allocation of public housing and jobs.[26] Even in 2014, local governments offered women incentives, such as cars and electrical goods, to volunteer for sterilization at family planning camps.[27] By 2016, the Indian Supreme Court ordered the government to close sterilization camps across the country. This decision was the result of the work of human rights and health activists like Devika Biswas, who submitted a petition to the Supreme Court based on her observations of mass sterilization in the village of Kaparfora in the northern Indian state of Bihar.[28]

Conversely, in the wake of fertility decline, many governments develop policies to encourage childbearing; for example: Japan, which had in 2016 a total fertility rate of 1.5 children per woman, 27 per cent of the population were older than 65 and only 13 per cent were younger than 15.[29] Since the 1990s, the low birth rate turned into a major policy issue. Policymakers introduced various measures to prevent a much-feared collapse of state social insurance programs due to a lack of taxpayers in the future. These measures include education programmes that provide information about fertility and ageing. They also emphasized the importance of planning one's life and of overcoming obstacles to building a family.[30]

The above examples highlight attempts at national and international levels to regulate fertility behaviour. Yet, it is difficult to establish a relationship between the law that regulates issues such as abortion, sterilization, and mothers' care of children on the one hand, and peoples' actual fertility behaviour on the other hand.[31] Reviews of the empirical evidence regarding the effects of policies on fertility suggest that these policies have some positive impact on fertility; however, this impact is rather small and affects the timing of births rather than the total number of births.[32] The evidence suggests that a whole array of ethical and other motives seems to shape the fertility behaviour of men and women in an ageing society.

B. Ethical Issues in Reproductive Medicine

The development of assisted reproductive technology has given the impression that pregnancy is possible at any stage of the life course. This is endorsed by the popular media. For example, on 15 April 2015, the *Mail Online* reported about a woman aged 57 who conceived 'thanks to IVF' beyond menopause and gave birth to a daughter.[33]

[26] R Whelan, *Choices in Childbearing: When Does Family Planning Become Population Control?* (Committee on Population and the Economy, 1992), 28.

[27] J Burke, 'India Mass Sterilisation: "My Wife Died in Tremendous Pain"', *The Guardian* (2014), http://www.theguardian.com/world/2014/nov/12/india-mass-sterilisation-wife-died-tremendous-pain accessed 15 July 2019.

[28] V Doshi, 'Will the Closure of India's Sterilisation Camps End Botched Operations?', *The Guardian* (26 October 2016), https://www.theguardian.com/global-development/2016/oct/26/will-closure-india-sterilisation-camps-end-botched-operations-supreme-court accessed 15 July 2019.

[29] Population Reference Bureau (n 7) 13.

[30] Fassbender (n 4) 124–9.

[31] H Schubuell, 'Law Affecting Contraception, Abortion and Sterilisation in Europe"' in *Law and Fertility in Europe: A Study of Legislation Directly or Indirectly Affecting Fertility in Europe* (Ordina Editions, 1975), 55.

[32] AH Gauthier, 'Family Policy and Fertility: Do Policies Make a Difference?' in Buchanan and Rotkirch (n 6) 269.

[33] L Waterlow, 'Britain's Oldest Mother Says German Woman Pregnant with Quads at 65 Is "Selfish", as She Reveals Her Regrets at Not Starting a Family before She Turned 57', *Mail Online* (15 April 2015), http://www.

However, these media images distort the reality of infertility being intimately related to women's age. Women have only a certain number of ovaries. This number is fixed at birth. Women´s fecundity typically declines progressively with rising age, and quicker from 35 years of age onwards. Importantly, as both men and women age, it takes longer to conceive a child. Indeed, because of the social changes outlined above, today, couples are often in their 30s when they feel ready to conceive a child. However, the older couples are, the more likely they are to have lost the opportunity to conceive naturally: as men age, their semen volume declines. In parallel, the most common factors related with ageing women's infertility are secondary amenorrhea, polycystic ovary syndrome, uterine myomas, and endometriosis.[34]

In vitro fertilization (IVF) is frequently suggested as a remedy for infertile couples. IVF involves several stages. First, the ovaries are stimulated so as to provoke super-ovulation. The reason for this production of a multitude of ripe ova (rather than one ripe ovum as would normally be the case) is the idea that the chances of achieving a pregnancy are higher if more than one embryo is put into the uterus. The ripened ova are collected by passing an ultrasound probe and a needle into the vagina. In this way, the ovaries are visualized and a needle is guided through the top of the vagina to collect twelve or more ova. The sperm is normally generated by masturbation and added separately to each ovum. In general, several embryos are created through this process. One or two embryos are then transferred into the womb. This transfer usually only takes place after the embryos have been screened under a microscope and 'high quality' ones have been selected. Two weeks after this transfer, it is possible to conduct a pregnancy test to see if the IVF treatment has worked.[35] Importantly, there are a number of embryos left over. These so-called 'spare' embryos are either frozen and stored for future use by the biological parents or by another couple. Sometimes, parents give permission for the embryos to be used in research and many embryos are immediately destroyed. Ethicists have observed that jurists and legislators have largely failed to treat the in-vitro embryo as a person. Accordingly, the question of the in-vitro embryo's legal status has been evaded.[36]

IVF was problematic from the beginning. The method was developed by the British medical doctor Robert Edwards and the gynaecologist Patrick Steptoe. In 1969, they managed to fertilize an ovum in a glass outside a woman's body. Between 1972 and 1974, they transferred fertilized embryos to their mothers. However, the embryos died and no complete pregnancy and birth resulted. In 1977, the first artificial insemination worked and the first child (Louise Brown) was born after an in-vitro fertilization. Importantly, the Medical Research Council rejected Edward´s and Steptoe's proposal for research funding not because they were against IVF in general, but because the Council was worried about the lack of ethical standards of their research projects. In consequence, IVF research between

dailymail.co.uk/femail/article-3039625/Britain-s-oldest-mother-says-German-woman-pregnant-quads-65-selfish-reveals-regrets-not-starting-family-turned-57.html accessed 15 July 2019.

[34] F Petraglia, GI Serour, and C Chapron, 'The Changing Prevalence of Infertility' (2013) 123 International Journal of Gynecology & Obstetrics S4, S3–S6.

[35] A Sutton, *Infertility and Medically Assisted Conception* (Catholic Truth Society, 2003), 20–3.

[36] J Keown, *The Law and Ethics of Medicine: Essays on the Inviolability of Human Life* (Oxford University Press, 2012), 299.

1971 and 1978 was entirely funded by private foundations, such as the Ford and Rockefeller Foundation and the Population Council.[37]

Research demonstrates that women's age is an important factor in predicting the results of assisted reproductive technologies.[38] According to the consultant obstetrician and gynaecologist Hans Evers (Maastricht University), women above the age of 42 have only a 5 per cent rate of successful pregnancy after an IVF treatment and those above 44 only 2 per cent. Therefore, Evers suggests the use of donated ova rather than IVF for women above the age of 42 years. Yet, the use of donor eggs raises ethical issues, too. Indeed, some researchers suggest the use of donor eggs from women in their 20s or 30s, as an alternative to IVF for older women. There are real moral concerns related to pregnancy risks and often unequal power relations between those who donate ova and those who receive them. In spite of the low success rates of IVF and donor eggs, the number of IVF children is rising.[39]

As a matter of fact, IVF and other reproductive technologies raise a myriad of ethical concerns. First of all, more IVF means rising numbers of failed attempts to conceive a child, as well as rising numbers of remaining embryos who have no use, who are orphaned and eventually disposed of:

> In the usual practice of in vitro fertilization, not all of the embryos are transferred to the woman's body; some are destroyed ... By acting in this way the researcher usurps the place of God; and, even though he may be unaware of this, he sets himself up as the master of the destiny of others inasmuch as he arbitrarily chooses whom he will allow to live and whom he will send to death and kills defenceless human beings.[40]

Similar concerns are related to embryo-cryopreservation, a practice used by women who want to become mothers after the onset of their menopause:[41]

> The *freezing of embryos*, even when carried out in order to preserve the life of an embryo—cryopreservation—*constitutes an offence against the respect due to human beings* by exposing them to grave risks of death or harm to their physical integrity and depriving them, at least temporarily, of maternal shelter and gestation, thus placing them in a situation in which further offences and manipulation are possible.[42]

Indeed, there is a general ethical concern when human problems, frustrations, and unintended consequences of personal life choice (such as remaining single and therefore being childless) are being treated as medical problems. To be sure, the pathologizing of human problems—such as unintended infertility—render human affairs into cases that need as a remedy medicalization and technology. Healing thus becomes a technical and medical

[37] S Kummer, 'Leben aus dem Labor. 40 Jahre Reproduktionsmedizin-Eine Übersicht' (2017) 24 Imago Hominis 15, 19.
[38] Petraglia et al (n 34) S6.
[39] IMABE, 'Reproduktionsmedizin: Experte rät Frauen ab 42 Jahren von IVF ab' (April 2017), https://www.imabe.org/index.php?id=2387 accessed 15 July 2019.
[40] Congregation for the Doctrine of the Faith, 'Instruction on Respect for Human Life in Its Origin and on the Dignity of Procreation Replies to Certain Questions of the Day', 5,http://www.vatican.va/roman_curia/congregations/cfaith/documents/rc_con_cfaith_doc_19870222_respect-for-human-life_en.html accessed 15 July 2019.
[41] Kummer (n 37) 27–30.
[42] Congregation for the Doctrine of the Faith (n 40) 6.

rather than a psychological and spiritual issue. Pope Benedict XVI said in his address to participants at the General Assembly of the Pontifical Academy for Life:

> I would therefore like to remind spouses in a condition of infertility, that this does not thwart their matrimonial vocation. Spouses are always called by their baptismal and matrimonial vocation itself to cooperate with God in the creation of a new human life. The vocation to love is in fact a vocation to the gift of self, and this is a possibility that no physical condition can prevent. Therefore, whenever science finds no answer, the answer that gives light comes from Christ.[43]

IV. Concluding Remarks

Perhaps it may be wise to pause at this point for some concluding reflections and remarks. As outlined in our chapter, population ageing is a consequence of a global fertility decline. This fertility decline, in turn, is the result of various factors, including changing patterns of family life and anti-natal techniques. Legal and ethical perspectives on these issues are manifold and, in this chapter, we concentrated on the question of when fertility control becomes population control, and on ethical issues around in vitro fertilization, which is promoted as a remedy to infertility often caused by old age. In short, we found that population control and fertility control have been policy concerns throughout the building of modern nation states. The attempt to either curb or encourage childbearing has been and continues to be a major concern of governments across the globe. Importantly, anti-natal techniques (like vasectomy) as well as pro-natal techniques (like in vitro fertilization) give rise to ethical concerns. In this chapter, we discussed them in the light of the teaching of the Catholic Church.

Accordingly, assisted reproductive technologies, like IVF, are not morally wrong because the church says so. Instead, the church says they are immoral,[44] because they are wrong according to eternal and natural law. Eternal law encompasses everything that is created by God.[45] It includes and supersedes natural law:

> The creation is a 'compass'. In the past, people spoke of a natural law. Today, this idea has become a laughingstock, and it is doubtless true that it has often been misused in the past; nevertheless, the kernel [*sic*][46] still holds good. There exists something that is 'naturally' right, thanks to the compass provided by the creation, something that makes possible an international law that transcends the boundaries of those laws that are promulgated by individual states. There exists something that is 'naturally' right, antecedent to our legislation, and hence it is simply impossible for *everything* that occurs to men to be 'right'. It is possible for laws to exist that are indeed valid legal statutes but which in fact represent

43 Benedict XVI, 'Address to Participants at the General Assembly of the Pontifical Academy for Life' (2013) 123 International Journal of Gynecology and Obstetrics S2.

44 H Watt, 'Ethical Reproductive Technologies: Misplaced Hope?' in H Watt (ed), *Fertility & Gender: Issues in Reproductive and Sexual Ethics* (Anscombe Bioethics Centre, 2011), 202.

45 T Aquinas, 'Summa Theologiae IaIIae 93: The Eternal Law' in RW Dyson (ed), *Aquinas: Political Writings* (Cambridge University Press, 2002), 108.

46 Pope Benedict refers to a kernel of truth about natural law.

injustice rather than 'justice'. Since it is God's creation, nature itself is a source of law. It indicates boundaries that must not be transgressed.[47]

Bibliography

Aquinas, T, 'Summa Theologiae IaIIae 93: The Eternal Law' in RW Dyson (ed), *Aquinas: Political Writings* (Cambridge University Press, 2002).

Baston, S, 'Declining Fertility, Television and the (Mis)Representation of Motherhood' in A Buchanan and A Rotkirch (eds), *Fertility Rates and Population Decline: No Time for Children?* (Palgrave Macmillan, 2013).

Benedict XVI, *The God of Jesus Christ: Meditations on the Triune God* (Ignatius Press, 2008).

Benedict XVI, 'Address to Participants at the General Assembly of the Pontifical Academy for Life' (2013) 123 International Journal of Gynecology and Obstetrics S2.

Burke, J, 'India Mass Sterilisation: "My Wife Died in Tremendous Pain"', *The Guardian* (2014), http://www.theguardian.com/world/2014/nov/12/india-mass-sterilisation-wife-died-tremendous-pain accessed 15 July 2019.

Chesterton, GK, *Eugenics and Other Evils* (Cassell, 1922).

Congregation for the Doctrine of the Faith, 'Instruction on Respect for Human Life in Its Origin and on the Dignity of Procreation Replies to Certain Questions of the Day' (1987), http://www.vatican.va/roman_curia/congregations/cfaith/documents/rc_con_cfaith_doc_19870222_respect-for-human-life_en.html accessed 15 July 2019.

Doshi, V, 'Will the Closure of India's Sterilisation Camps End Botched Operations?', *The Guardian* (26 October 2016), https://www.theguardian.com/global-development/2016/oct/26/will-closure-india-sterilisation-camps-end-botched-operations-supreme-court accessed 15 July 2019.

Dowbiggin, IR, *The Sterilization Movement and Global Fertility in the Twentieth Century* (Oxford University Press, 2008).

European Union, 'Short Analytical Web Note 3/2015', https://ec.europa.eu/eurostat/documents/3217494/6917833/KE-BM-15-003-EN-N.pdf/76dac490-9176-47bc-80d9-029e1d967af6 accessed 29 August 2019.

Fassbender, I, 'Enhancing Autonomy in Reproductive Decisions? Education about Family Planning and Fertility as a Countermeasure against the Low Birthrate' (2016) 28 Contemporary Japan 123.

Franks, A, *Margaret Sanger's Eugenic Legacy: The Control of Female Fertility* (McFarland, 2004).

Gauthier, AH, 'Family Policy and Fertility: Do Policies Make a Difference?' in A Buchanan and A Rotkirch (eds), *Fertility Rates and Population Decline: No Time for Children?* (Palgrave Macmillan, 2013).

Harper, S, 'The Capacity of Social Security and Health Care Institutions to Adapt to an Ageing World' (2010) 63 International Social Security Review 177.

Harper, S, 'Falling Fertility, Ageing and Europe's Demographic Deficit' in A Buchanan and A Rotkirch (eds), *Fertility Rates and Population Decline: No Time for Children?* (Palgrave Macmillan, 2013).

Harper, S and Leeson, GW, 'The Global Ageing Survey (GLAS)—Ageing and Later Life. United Kingdom and Europe' (Oxford Institute of Ageing, 2007).

IMABE, 'Reproduktionsmedizin: Experte Rät Frauen Ab 42 Jahren von IVF Ab' (April 2017), https://www.imabe.org/index.php?id=2387 accessed 15 July 2019.

Keown, J, *The Law and Ethics of Medicine: Essays on the Inviolability of Human Life* (Oxford University Press, 2012).

Kummer, S, 'Leben Aus Dem Labor. 40 Jahre Reproduktionsmedizin-Eine Übersicht' (2017) 24 Imago Hominis 15.

Malthus, TR, *An Essay on the Principle of Population* (Oxford University Press, 2008).

Nugent, JB and Anker, R, *Old Age Support and Fertility* (International Labour Office, 1990).

[47] Benedict XVI, *The God of Jesus Christ: Meditations on the Triune God* (Ignatius Press, 2008), 46.

Petraglia, F, Serour, GI, and Chapron, C, 'The Changing Prevalence of Infertility' (2013) 123 International Journal of Gynecology & Obstetrics S4.

Population Reference Bureau, '2016 World Population Data Sheet' (2016).

Sanger, M, *The New Motherhood* (Jonathan Cape, 1922).

Sanger, M, *What Every Girl Should Know* (Haldeman-Julius Co, 1922).

Schooyans, M, *The Demographic Crash: From Fatalism to Hope* (Central Bureau, CCVA, 2001).

Schooyans, M, *Pour Comprendre Les Évolutions Démographiques* (3rd edn, Association Pour la Recherche et l'Information Démographiques (APRD), 2011).

Schubuell, H, 'Law Affecting Contraception, Abortion and Sterilisation in Europe' in *Law and Fertility in Europe: A Study of Legislation Directly or Indirectly Affecting Fertility in Europe* (Ordina Editions, 1975).

Sutton, A, *Infertility and Medically Assisted Conception* (Catholic Truth Society, 2003).

Tarzia, O, 'Introduction' in *Woman and Man: The Humanum in Its Entirety* (Libraria Editrice Vaticana, 2010).

United Nations, 'World Population Ageing Report 2015' (2015).

Waterlow, L, 'Britain's Oldest Mother Says German Woman Pregnant with Quads at 65 Is "Selfish", as She Reveals Her Regrets at Not Starting a Family before She Turned 57', *Mail Online* (15 April 2015), http://www.dailymail.co.uk/femail/article-3039625/Britain-s-oldest-mother-says-German-woman-pregnant-quads-65-selfish-reveals-regrets-not-starting-family-turned-57.html accessed 15 July 2019.

Watt, H, 'Ethical Reproductive Technologies: Misplaced Hope?' in H Watt (ed), *Fertility & Gender: Issues in Reproductive and Sexual Ethics* (Anscombe Bioethics Centre, 2011).

Whelan, R, *Choices in Childbearing: When Does Family Planning Become Population Control?* (Committee on Population and the Economy, 1992).

19

The Emergence of Family Agreements in an Ageing World

Pip Coore

I. Introduction

In life, one thing is certain: we will all age. As the global population ages, the number of people affected by age-related illnesses requiring ongoing, extended care will dramatically increase.[1] Currently, limited places in aged care facilities, coupled with government policies encouraging people to remain in the community as they age, puts new pressures on families to retain the caring role for their older relatives.[2] This is creating a situation where life comes full circle; where the older parent(s) becomes the dependant and the adult child, particularly the daughter,[3] becomes the carer.[4]

As reliance on families to care for their older relatives increases, many families are choosing to enter into family agreements for legal protection.[5] Family agreements are, in essence, arrangements whereby an older person transfers property to someone in exchange for a promise of 'care for life'[6] ('Family Agreement'). Typically, Family Agreements are made between an older parent and their adult child,[7] and they are mostly made orally and without legal advice.[8]

Although Family Agreements are intended to safeguard older people and their caregiving adult child from harmful outcomes, there is currently no legislation governing or regulating them,[9] there is little written about them, and there

[1] CT Kulik, S Ryan, S Harper, et al, 'Aging Populations and Management: From the Editors' (2014) 57(4) Academy of Management Journal 929.

[2] B Herd, 'The Family Agreement: Legal Good Sense or Social Bad Taste for the Aged?' (2002) 27(2) Alternative Law Journal 72; B Herd, 'The Family Agreement—A Collision between Love and the Law?' (2002) 81 Reform 23.

[3] L Pickard, 'A Growing Care Gap? The Supply of Unpaid Care for Older People by Their Adult Children in England to 2032' (2015) 35(1) Ageing and Society 96.

[4] Commonwealth of Australia, Official Committee Hansard, House of Representatives, Standing Committee on Legal and Constitutional Affairs, 'Older People and the Law' (2007), http://parlinfo.aph.gov.au/parlInfo/search/display/display.w3p;query=Id%3A%22committees%2Fcommrep%2F10278%2F0000%22 accessed 15 July 2019.

[5] Herd, 'The Family Agreement' (n 2).

[6] Herd, 'The Family Agreement: Legal Good Sense?' (n 2); Herd, 'The Family Agreement—A Collision' (n 2); MI Hall, 'Care for Life: Private Care Agreements between Older Adults and Friends or Family Members' (2003) 2 Elder Law Review 1.

[7] R Lewis, *Elder Law in Australia* (LexisNexis Butterworths, 2004), para 10.36.

[8] Hall (n 6); Australian Government, Australian Law Reform Commission, 'Elder Abuse—A National Legal Response: Final Report' (2017), https://www.alrc.gov.au/sites/default/files/pdfs/publications/elder_abuse_131_final_report_31_may_2017.pdf accessed 15 July 2019.

[9] The Parliament of the Commonwealth of Australia, House of Representatives Standing Committee on Legal and Constitutional Affairs, 'Older People and the Law' (2007), http://www.aph.gov.au/Parliamentary_Business/Committees/House_of_Representatives_Committees?url=laca/olderpeople/report.htm accessed 15 July 2019.

Pip Coore, *The Emergence of Family Agreements in an Ageing World* In: *Philosophical Foundations of Medical Law*. Edited by: Andelka M Phillips, Thana C de Campos, and Jonathan Herring, Oxford University Press (2019).
DOI: 10.1093/oso/9780198796558.003.0020

is limited information available to guide families wishing to enter into Family Agreements.[10]

In the absence of specific legislation governing and regulating Family Agreements,[11] families are entering into agreements that exist beneath the law's radar.[12] This unregulated family contracting may breed potential disadvantages for all family members. Therefore, the purpose of this chapter is to shed some light on this little-known area of family care to better understand whether (if at all) Family Agreements are adequately protecting older people and their caregiving adult child from harmful outcomes. In doing so, this chapter identifies ways in which the law has responded to population ageing and outlines areas that require further attention.

This chapter largely deals with the relationship of care between an older parent and their adult child ('the Caring Relationship'). Although there is no legal age at which a person becomes 'old',[13] the phrase 'older person' is commonly used by gerontologists to describe persons over the age of 65.[14] This chapter adopts that description. Due to the limited literature on Family Agreements, this chapter mainly considers the position in the United Kingdom, Australia, and Canada.

II. An Ageing World

The rapidly ageing population is a 'global phenomenon'.[15] The United Nations observed that, in 2017, there was an estimated 962 million people aged 60 or over worldwide, which is 13 per cent of the global population.[16] The United Nations predicts this number will increase to 1.4 billion in 2030 and 2.1 billion in 2050.[17] In 2016, more than 15 per cent of the total population was aged 65 and over in the United Kingdom[18] and Australia.[19] By 2040, it is projected that 24.2 per cent of the United Kingdom's population[20] and 20 per cent of Australia's

[10] Alzheimer's Australia, Submission No 55 to the Parliament of Australia House of Representatives Inquiry into Older People and the Law (2006), 20, https://www.aph.gov.au/Parliamentary_Business/Committees/House_of_Representatives_Committees?url=laca/olderpeople/subs.htm accessed 15 July 2019.

[11] Australian Committee (n 9).

[12] Herd, 'The Family Agreement: Legal Good Sense?' (n 2) 74.

[13] A Brammer and S Biggs, 'Defining Elder Abuse' (1998) 20(3) Journal of Social Welfare and Family Law 285, 295.

[14] Ibid 294.

[15] United Nations, Department of Economic and Social Affairs, Population Division, 'World Population Ageing 2015 (2015), https://www.un.org/en/development/desa/population/publications/pdf/ageing/WPA2015_Report.pdf accessed XXXX; GW Leeson, 'Increasing Longevity and the New Demography of Death' [2014] International Journal of Population Research; Kulik et al (n 1).

[16] United Nations, Department of Economic and Social Affairs, Population Division, 'World Population Prospects: The 2017 Revision' (2017), https://esa.un.org/unpd/wpp/Publications/Files/WPP2017_KeyFindings.pdf accessed 15 July 2019.

[17] Ibid.

[18] Office for National Statistics, 'Overview of the UK Population: July 2017' (2017), https://www.ons.gov.uk/peoplepopulationandcommunity/populationandmigration/populationestimates/articles/overviewoftheukpopulation/july2017 accessed 15 July 2019.

[19] Australian Government, Australian Institute of Health and Welfare, 'Older Australia at a Glance' (2017), https://www.aihw.gov.au/reports/older-people/older-australia-at-a-glance/contents/demographics-of-older-australians/australia-s-changing-age-and-gender-profile accessed 15 July 2019.

[20] Age UK, 'Later Life in the United Kingdom' (2018), 3, https://www.ageuk.org.uk/globalassets/age-uk/documents/reports-and-publications/later_life_uk_factsheet.pdf accessed 15 July 2019, citing 'National Population Projections for the UK, 2014-Based' (Office for National Statistics, 2015).

population[21] will be aged 65 and over.

In addition to global population ageing, life expectancy has also significantly increased.[22] Between 2014 and 2016, life expectancy in the United Kingdom was 79.2 years for males and 82.9 years for females.[23] For the same period in Australia, life expectancy was 80.4 years for males and 84.6 years for females.[24] The reasons for this increase in life expectancy includes, but is not limited to, improved health care and lifestyles,[25] safer working environments, and medical and technological advances.[26]

A. Dementia

Although living for longer is to be celebrated,[27] and although ageing does not automatically result in a decline in health,[28] increased life expectancy may also mean longer stretches of frailty, disability, and dependence,[29] particularly due to the increasing rates of dementia.[30]

Today, dementia is ranked ahead of some cancers, cardiovascular disease, and stroke as one of the main causes of disability among older people.[31] More than 46 million people worldwide have dementia,[32] and this number is expected to increase to 135.1 million by 2050.[33] In the United Kingdom and Australia, one in every fourteen people,[34] and one in every ten people respectively,[35] aged 65 and over has dementia.

The dramatic shift in the age structure of the population presents many challenges for governments, particularly in relation to the provision of health and aged care services.[36] Alarmingly, the House of Lords Select Committee on Public Service and Demographic

21 Australian Bureau of Statistics, 'Population Projections, Australia, 2012 (Base) to 2101' (2013), http://www.abs.gov.au/ausstats/abs@.nsf/lookup/3222.0Media%20Release12012%20(base)%20to%202101 accessed 15 July 2019.

22 Leeson (n 15); United Nations (n 16).

23 Office for National Statistics, 'National Life Tables, UK: 2014 to 2016' (2017), https://www.ons.gov.uk/peoplepopulationandcommunity/birthsdeathsandmarriages/lifeexpectancies/bulletins/nationallifetablesunitedkingdom/2014to2016 accessed 15 July 2019.

24 Australian Bureau of Statistics, 'Life Tables, States, Territories and Australia, 2014–2016' (2017), http://www.abs.gov.au/ausstats/abs@.nsf/Latestproducts/3302.0.55.001Main%20Features22014-2016?opendocument&tabname=Summary&prodno=3302.0.55.001&issue=2014-2016&num=&view= accessed 15 July 2019.

25 Office for National Statistics (n 18).

26 Australian Bureau of Statistics (n 24).

27 House of Lords, Select Committee on Public Service and Demographic Change, Report of Session 2012–13, 'Ready for Ageing?' (2013), http://www.cpahq.org/cpahq/cpadocs/UK%20Parliament%20HOL%20Ready%20for%20the%20Ageing.pdf accessed 15 July 2019.

28 J Herring, *Older People in Law and Society* (Oxford University Press, 2009).

29 Kulik et al (n 1).

30 Herring (n 28).

31 Alzheimer's Society, 'Facts for the Media' (2018), https://www.alzheimers.org.uk/info/20027/news_and_media/541/facts_for_the_media accessed 15 July 2019; Access Economics, Report Prepared for Alzheimer's Australia, 'Keeping Dementia Front of Mind: Incidence and Prevalence 2009–2050' (2009), https://www.dementia.org.au/sites/default/files/20090800_Nat__AE_FullKeepDemFrontMind.pdf accessed 15 July 2019.

32 Alzheimer's Disease International, 'World Alzheimer Report 2015, The Global Impact of Dementia: An Analysis of Prevalence, Incidence, Cost and Trends' (2015), https://www.alz.co.uk/research/WorldAlzheimerReport2015.pdf accessed 15 July 2019.

33 Ibid.

34 Alzheimer's Society, 'What Is Dementia?' (2017), https://www.alzheimers.org.uk/download/downloads/id/3416/what_is_dementia.pdf accessed 15 July 2019.

35 Professor L Brown, E Hansnata, and HA La, Report Prepared for Alzheimer's Australia, 'Economic Cost of Dementia in Australia: 2016–2056' (2017), https://www.dementia.org.au/files/NATIONAL/documents/The-economic-cost-of-dementia-in-Australia-2016-to-2056.pdf accessed 15 July 2019.

36 Australian Committee (n 9); House of Lords Committee (n 27).

Change concluded that the UK Government is 'woefully underprepared' for the rapidly ageing population.[37] Further, it was commented that: 'Publicly funded care alone has never met all the needs of older people who are frail, vulnerable, ill or isolated.'[38] More recently, the King's Fund found that: 'The social care system in its current form is struggling to meet the needs of older people.'[39]

III. Family Caring

As government support is diminishing, there is an 'increasingly divergent picture' of families providing unpaid care for their older relatives.[40] In 2015, there was an estimated 6.8 million people providing unpaid care in the United Kingdom, which saved the public purse £15.1 million per hour and had an economic value of £132 billion.[41] In the same year, there was an estimated 2.86 million unpaid carers in Australia providing 1.9 billion hours of unpaid care, which had an estimated replacement value of $60.3 billion.[42]

Despite previous care literature suggesting that spouses provide the majority of care for older people,[43] recent research suggests that adult children, particularly daughters, are the main source of care for older people.[44] Unlike many cultures, co-residence of older parents with their adult children is not traditionally common in England and Australia.[45] However, due to the increase in life expectancy of older people, the need for older people to co-reside with their family members is increasing.[46] As many older people wish to remain in the community as they age, it is observed that much of the care provided by family members takes place in the context of co-residence of the older parent with their adult child.[47]

In many instances, an adult child will persuade their older parent to sell their home and put the settlement proceeds towards a new home they purchase together.[48] Alternatively, the settlement proceeds are often used towards extending the adult child's existing home to incorporate a self-contained flat for either or both older parents to reside in.[49] This living

[37] House of Lords Committee (n 27) 7.

[38] Ibid 14.

[39] R Humphries, R Thorlby, H Holder, et al, 'Social Care for Older People: Home Truths' (The King's Fund and Nuffield Trust, 2016), 3, https://www.nuffieldtrust.org.uk/research/social-care-for-older-people-home-truths accessed 15 July 2019.

[40] Carers UK, 'Caring & Family Finances Inquiry: UK Report' (2014), 128, http://www.carersuk.org/for-professionals/policy/policy-library/caring-family-finances-inquiry accessed 15 July 2019.

[41] L Buckner and S Yeandle, 'Valuing Carers 2015: The Rising Value of Carers' Support' (Carers UK, 2015), http://www.carersuk.org/for-professionals/policy/policy-library/valuing-carers-2015 accessed 15 July 2019.

[42] Deloitte Access Economic, 'The Economic Value of Informal Care in Australia in 2015' (Carers Australia, 2015), http://www.carersaustralia.com.au/storage/Access%20Economics%20Report.pdf accessed 15 July 2019.

[43] L Pickard, R Wittenberg, A Comas-Herrera, et al, 'Care by Spouses, Care by Children: Projections of Informal Care for Older People in England to 2031' (2007) 6(3) Social Policy & Society 353.

[44] Pickard (n 3).

[45] J Herring, *Family Law* (6th edn, Pearson, 2013), 702; S Field, 'Issues Facing Older Australians: Legal, Financial and Societal' (2005) 1 Journal of International Aging Law and Policy 95.

[46] JM Latorre Postigo and R López Honrubia, 'The Co-Residence of Elderly People with Their Children and Grandchildren' (2010) 36(4) Educational Gerontology 330.

[47] LE Pezzin, RA Pollak, and BS Schone, 'Efficiency in Family Bargaining: Living Arrangements and Caregiving Decisions of Adult Children and Disabled Elderly Parents' (2007) 53(1) CESifo Economic Studies 69, 70.

[48] Field (n 45); ALRC Final Report (n 8).

[49] Herd, 'The Family Agreement: Legal Good Sense?' (n 2).

arrangement is commonly known as the 'granny flat' scenario,[50] and is usually associated with the promise that the adult child will care for their older parent(s) for life.[51]

Although it is widely acknowledged that families are the main source of care for older people,[52] it is commented that the literature on long-term care 'pays little attention to the family'[53] and the relationship between an adult child and their older parent.[54] In response to our 'inescapable demographic destiny',[55] and with the debate raging over how care for older people is to be financed,[56] the question of who will care for older people is significant and highlights the need for a legal framework that will support family caregivers who choose to care for their older parents.[57]

A. Filial Obligations

In many regions around the world, such as Singapore, China, the United States, and Canada, adult children have a legal duty to care for their parents under filial responsibility laws.[58] These laws, also known as filial support laws, emanated from the Elizabethan Poor Laws during the sixteenth century,[59] although the duty of children to support their parents can be traced back to the third century in Roman society.[60]

In 1948, England repealed its filial support laws.[61] As a result, no such laws exist in the United Kingdom.[62] In response to the rapidly ageing population, Herd argued that legislation compelling the performance of filial obligations should be investigated in Australia.[63] The Australian House of Representatives Standing Committee on Legal and Constitutional Affairs ('the Australian Committee') agreed that filial support laws are 'worth investigating'.[64] However, the Australian Committee emphasized that legislating a duty to care, particularly in the context of familial relationships, is 'problematic'.[65] In any event, the Australian Government did not accept the Australian Committee's recommendation to further investigate the implementation of filial support laws.[66] As a result, no filial support laws exist in Australia.

50 Ibid 72; Herd, 'The Family Agreement—A Collision' (n 2) 24; ALRC Final Report (n 8) para 6.8; Field (n 45) 104.

51 Herd, 'The Family Agreement: Legal Good Sense?' (n 2); Herd, 'The Family Agreement—A Collision' (n 2); Hall (n 6).

52 Carers UK (n 40); Pickard (n 3); Pickard et al (n 43); J Herring, *Caring and the Law* (Hart Publishing, 2013), 187.

53 Pezzin et al (n 47) 72.

54 Herring (n 52) 188.

55 Australian Committee (n 9) vii.

56 J Herring, *Family Law* (7th edn, Pearson, 2015), 723.

57 Alzheimer's Australia (n 10) 20.

58 GHY Ting and J Woo, 'Elder Care: Is Legislation of Family Responsibility the Solution?' (2009) 4 Asian Journal of Gerontology & Geriatrics 72.

59 Elizabethan Act for the Relief of the Poor, 43 Eliz 1, c 2 (1601).

60 J Van Houtte and J Breda, 'Maintenance of the Aged by Their Adult Children: The Family as a Residual Agency in the Solution of Poverty in Belgium' (1978) 12(4) Law & Society Review 645.

61 National Assistance Act, 1948, 11 and 12 Geo 6, c 29.

62 Herring (n 56) 723.

63 Hansard (Cth) (n 4) 4 per Herd.

64 Australian Committee (n 9) para 4.68.

65 Ibid.

66 House of Representatives Standing Committee on Legal and Constitutional Affairs, 'Older People and the Law: Government Response' (2009), 23, http://www.aph.gov.au/Parliamentary_Business/Committees/House_of_representatives_Committees?url=laca/reports.htm accessed 15 July 2019.

Many legal commentators have encouraged the repeal of all remaining filial support laws,[67] as they are viewed as archaic and not suitable for enforcement in contemporary societies that have assumed public responsibility for the care of their indigent elderly.[68] Herring argues strongly against creating legally enforceable obligations on adult children to support their older parents.[69] Instead, Herring suggests that the law 'can uphold, bolster or reinforce the obligation in other ways, free of direct enforcement'.[70] Herring argues that a preferable response is for the law to offer benefits or advantages to those family members who fulfil their care obligations.[71] One example of such benefits is tax concessions.[72] Herring comments that: 'A tax credit similar to that available to those caring for children could be offered to those caring for relatives in need.'[73] Similarly, Herd argues that 'children who take on the caring role should receive some tax recognition and concessions'.[74]

B. Reciprocity

Aside from whether adult children have a legal duty to care for their older parents, it is argued that they have a moral obligation to do so.[75] Although there are a number of ways this moral obligation could be established,[76] it is typically established on a norm of reciprocity; whereby adult children owe their elderly parents something in return for all that they have done for them.[77]

The phenomenon of families caring for their older relatives is not a new concept.[78] Traditionally, societies supported older people via a system of 'intergenerational reciprocity', whereby adults provided for their young children and, when those children grew up, they cared for their older parents.[79] From 1950 onwards, women, who were traditionally the main caregivers, increasingly engaged in employment outside the home.[80] This shift away from family care challenged the viability of traditional intergenerational reciprocity, which encouraged the further development of aged care facilities.[81] However, currently, limited available places in aged care facilities puts new pressures on families to provide care for their older relatives that aged care services cannot meet.[82]

[67] CD Byrd, 'Relative Responsibility Extended: Requirement of Adult Children to Pay for Their Indigent Parent's Medical Needs' (1988) 22(1) Family Law Quarterly 87.

[68] TA Kline, 'A Rational Role for Filial Responsibility Laws in Modern Society?' (1992) 26(3) Family Law Quarterly 195.

[69] J Herring, 'Together Forever? The Rights and Responsibilities of Adult Children and Their Parents' in J Bridgeman, H Keating, and C Lind (eds), *Responsibility: Law and the Family* (Ashgate Publishing Group, 2008).

[70] Ibid 56.

[71] Ibid.

[72] Ibid. See also Herd, 'The Family Agreement: Legal Good Sense?' (n 2); Herd, 'The Family Agreement—A Collision' (n 2); and Hansard (Cth) (n 4) 5 per Herd.

[73] Herring (n 69) 56.

[74] Hansard (Cth) (n 4) 5 per Herd.

[75] Herring (n 56).

[76] Ibid.

[77] MC Stuifbergen and JJM Van Delden, 'Filial Obligations to Elderly Parents: A Duty to Care?' (2011) 14 Medicine, Health Care and Philosophy 63, 64.

[78] Herd, 'The Family Agreement: Legal Good Sense?' (n 2).

[79] Kulik et al (n 1) 929.

[80] Herd, 'The Family Agreement: Legal Good Sense?' (n 2); Herd, 'The Family Agreement—A Collision' (n 2).

[81] Ibid.

[82] Ibid; D De Vaus, 'Children's Responsibilities to Elderly Parents' (1996) 45 Family Matters, Australian Institute of Family Studies 16, https://aifs.gov.au/sites/default/files/fm45dd.pdf accessed 15 July 2019.

IV. Preventative Legal Tools

Today, many adult children cannot afford to reduce their working hours to care for their older parents without compensation.[83] In observance of this, it is argued that uncompensated caring is unrealistic and will therefore be replaced with the notion of compensated caring.[84] This is what Herd describes as 'the genesis' of the Family Agreement, which is 'the transformation of a cultural duty into a compensatable, contractual obligation of care'.[85] Family Agreements are described as:

> an arrangement between an older person and another party or parties (usually family members or carers) whereby the older person provides a benefit to the other party in exchange for continuing (or lifelong) care. The benefit can take various forms, for example a transfer of property or a compensatory payment.[86]

Due to their private nature,[87] there is little statistical or empirical evidence of families formalizing or documenting Family Agreements.[88] However, anecdotal evidence suggests that families are undoubtedly entering into Family Agreements, albeit on an informal or oral basis.[89] In response to the dramatic shift in age structure of the population, and the preference of older people to remain in a familial and familiar environment as they age, it is expected that the usage rate of Family Agreements will increase.[90]

A. The Granny Flat Scenario

One common derivative of Family Agreements is the 'granny flat' scenario,[91] which, as discussed above, involves an older parent using their life savings, or the proceeds from the sale of their previous home, to build a self-contained residence on their adult child's property.[92] In the granny flat scenario, it is common for the title of the property to remain in the name of the adult child.[93] However, as Field notes: 'The problems associated with this transfer of money, without an associated transfer of title, are all too obvious.'[94] In many instances, the family home constitutes the majority of the assets of the older parent.[95] Therefore,

[83] Herd, 'The Family Agreement: Legal Good Sense?' (n 2); Herd, 'The Family Agreement—A Collision' (n 2); Lewis (n 7) para 10.37; British Columbia Law Institute, Committee on Legal Issues Affecting Seniors, 'Private Care Agreements between Older Adults and Friends of Family Members' (2002), Report No 18, http://www.bcli.org/sites/default/files/Private_Care_Agreements_Between_Older_Adults_and_Friends_or_Family_Members.pdf accessed 15 July 2019.

[84] Herd, 'The Family Agreement: Legal Good Sense?' (n 2); Herd, 'The Family Agreement—A Collision' (n 2); British Columbia Law Institute (n 83).

[85] Herd, 'The Family Agreement—A Collision' (n 2), 24.

[86] Australian Committee (n 9) para 4.2.

[87] R Monro, 'Family Agreements All with the Best of Intentions' (2002) 27(2) Alternative Law Journal 68.

[88] Herd, 'The Family Agreement: Legal Good Sense?' (n 2); Herd, 'The Family Agreement—A Collision' (n 2).

[89] Ibid; Hall (n 6); Australian Committee (n 9).

[90] Herd, 'The Family Agreement: Legal Good Sense?' (n 2); Herd, 'The Family Agreement—A Collision' (n 2); Australian Committee (n 9).

[91] Ibid.

[92] Australian Committee (n 9); Field (n 45).

[93] Field (n 45).

[94] Ibid 104.

[95] Field (n 45).

the transfer of an older parent's property to their adult child without the simultaneous transfer of the title leaves the older parent vulnerable to elder abuse, particularly financial elder abuse.

B. Financial Elder Abuse

Research suggests that financial abuse is the most common type of elder abuse in Australia[96] and the second most common type of elder abuse in the United Kingdom.[97] Moreover, older people with dementia are particularly vulnerable to financial abuse.[98] Despite this, there are currently no laws dealing specifically with financial abuse,[99] and thus no statutory definition exists. As a result, many agencies have developed working definitions of financial abuse.[100] One commonly accepted definition is 'the illegal or improper use of a person's finances or property by another person with *whom they have a relationship implying trust*'.[101] Unlike other definitions of financial abuse, this definition is more worthy of consideration as it explicitly recognizes a relationship where there is an expectation of trust, which is arguably at the heart of the Caring Relationship.

Disturbingly, the main perpetrators of financial abuse are trusted family members.[102] Although many family carers act with honesty and integrity,[103] research suggests that people in positions of trust have a greater opportunity to commit financial abuse.[104] Given the majority of care for an older person is provided by a 'trusted' family member, there is a concern that financial abuse within the Caring Relationship will increase as the usage rates of Family Agreements increase.

Due to the inherent belief that 'family relationships should be preserved at any cost',[105] many older people are reluctant to engage with the legal system when they experience financial abuse.[106] As a consequence, financial abuse is likely to be discovered after the older person's assets have been 'squandered', with little recourse to get them back.[107]

[96] D Bagshaw, V Adams, L Zannettino, et al, 'Elder Mediation and the Financial Abuse of Older People by a Family Member' (2015) 32(4) Conflict Resolution Quarterly 443; ALRC Final Report (n 8) para 2.51.

[97] M O'Keeffe, A Hills, M Doyle, et al, 'UK Study of Abuse and Neglect of Older People: Prevalence Survey Report' (National Centre for Social Research and King's College London, 2007), https://www.kcl.ac.uk/sspp/policy-institute/scwru/pubs/2007/okeefeetal2007ukstudyprevalence.pdf accessed 15 July 2019.

[98] Ibid; Bagshaw et al (n 96).

[99] Australian Committee (n 9) para 2.13.

[100] G Fealy, N Donnelly, A Bergin, et al, 'Financial Abuse of Older People: A Review' (National Centre for the Protection of Older People, University College Dublin, 2012).

[101] Elder Abuse Prevention Unit, 'Financial Abuse' (2014), https://www.eapu.com.au/elder-abuse/financial-abuse accessed 15 July 2019 (emphasis added).

[102] D Bagshaw, S Wendt, L Zannettino, et al, 'Financial Abuse of Older People by Family Members: Views and Experiences of Older Australians and Their Family Members' (2013) 66(1) Australian Social Work 86; O'Keeffe et al (n 97); House of Commons Health Committee, 'Elder Abuse: Second Report of Session 2003–04' (2004), http://www.publications.parliament.uk/pa/cm200304/cmselect/cmhealth/111/111.pdf accessed 15 July 2019.

[103] Carers Queensland, Submission No 81 to the Parliament of Australia House of Representatives Inquiry into Older People and the Law (2006), https://www.aph.gov.au/Parliamentary_Business/Committees/House_of_Representatives_Committees?url=laca/olderpeople/subs.htm accessed 15 July 2019.

[104] City of London Police, 'Assessment: Financial Crime against Vulnerable Adults' (Social Care Institute for Excellence, 2011), https://www.scie.org.uk/publications/reports/report49.asp accessed 15 July 2019.

[105] Monro (n 87) 71.

[106] Ibid; Herd, 'The Family Agreement: Legal Good Sense?' (n 2); L Kyle, 'Out of the Shadows: A Discussion on Law Reform for the Prevention of Financial Abuse of Older People' (2013) 7(4) Elder Law Review 1.

[107] State Trustees Victoria, Submission No 138 to the Australian Law Reform Commission (2016), 8, https://www.alrc.gov.au/sites/default/files/subs/138._state_trustees_victoria.docx accessed 15 July 2019.

C. Enduring Documents

One way in which the law has responded to population ageing is through the implementation of preventative legal tools, such as enduring documents.[108] In the United Kingdom, this instrument is called a Lasting Power of Attorney[109] and, in Australia, it is called an Enduring Power of Attorney.[110] Under these instruments, an older person can appoint an attorney to make decisions, including financial decisions, on their behalf that, significantly, is not revoked upon the older person losing capacity.[111]

Typically, older people appoint their family members as attorneys,[112] particularly those they are in a caring relationship with.[113] The assumption underpinning enduring documents is that families will always act in the best interests of the older person, particularly when they lack capacity.[114] In the United Kingdom, the 'best interests' principle is relevant to all decisions involving the care or treatment of the older person.[115] However, Herring has outlined several criticisms of the 'best interests' principle.[116] One of these criticisms is that decisions are made after taking into account what is in the best interests of the older person, as an individual, without considering the interests of those who care for them.[117] Herring argues that the failure to consider the interests of the caregiver is 'inappropriate',[118] as they will often be impacted by such decisions.[119] It is therefore not surprising that an enduring document is described as an *individual* planning tool.[120] As Brick comments:

> the purpose of prevention in old age is to enable the *individual* to prepare for it, to better control and handle its side effects, so as to ensure the *individual's* autonomy and beliefs be fulfilled even in situations of declined capabilities.[121]

However, Herring suggests that '[n]o one can be truly independent',[122] and therefore argues that the law should stop treating older people as solely independent individuals, but seek to recognize and promote caring relationships.[123]

The Australian Law Reform Commission (ALRC) has recently commented that although enduring documents play an important role in protecting an older person from abuse, they may facilitate abuse by the very person appointed to protect the older person.[124] In other words, attorneys are using enduring documents as a 'licence to loot'.[125]

108 I Doron and I Gal, 'The Emergence of Legal Prevention in Old Age: Findings from an Israeli Exploratory Study' (2006) 21 Journal of Cross Cultural Gerontology 41.
109 See Mental Capacity Act (2005), s 9.
110 In a Queensland context, see Powers of Attorney Act 1998 (Qld), s 32.
111 Mental Capacity Act (2005) (UK), s 9(1); Powers of Attorney Act 1998 (Qld), s 32(2).
112 A-L McCawley, C Tilse, J Wilson, et al, 'Access to Assets: Older People with Impaired Capacity and Financial Abuse' (2006) 8(1) Journal of Adult Protection 20.
113 Herring (n 52) 168.
114 McCawley et al (n 112).
115 Mental Capacity Act 2005, s 5.
116 Herring (n 28).
117 Ibid 68.
118 Ibid.
119 Herring (n 28) 96. See also Chapter 2 (this volume).
120 Doron and Gal (n 108).
121 Ibid 43, citing I Brick, 'Prevention in Old Age: The Welfare Perspective' (1985) 32 Gerontology 5 (emphases added).
122 J Herring, 'The Disability Critique of Care' (2014) 8 Elder Law Review 1, 13.
123 Chapter 2 (this volume).
124 ALRC Final Report (n 8).
125 *MJ, JM v The Public Guardian* [2013] EWHC 2966 (COP) per (the then) Judge Denzil Lush, para 98.

Arguably, Family Agreements are also a preventative legal tool as they enable a person 'to prepare for old age'.[126] However, the significant difference between enduring documents and Family Agreements is that Family Agreements encourage and facilitate families to discuss, and document, their expectations regarding the provision and receipt of future care for their older parent(s) before they lose decision-making capacity, rather than focusing solely on the older person as an individual. Family Agreements are therefore challenging individualistic-based legal tools as they consider the interests of those caring for the older person.

V. Family Agreements: The Way Forward?

For many people, documenting a caring relationship between family members is 'distasteful'.[127] However, the law has already challenged the cultural aversion of contracting with family members with the acknowledgment of, and legislative support for, pre-nuptial agreements and cohabitation agreements.[128] In the context of cohabitation agreements, Reece observed: 'Making a [living together] agreement prompts you to discuss how your living together will work in practice and what your expectations of each other are.'[129] In the context of Family Agreements, Carers Queensland commented: 'The most beneficial thing about such agreements is that they provide an avenue for people to discuss and consider their, often previously unstated, expectations and assumptions regarding the provision and receipt of future care for older people.'[130]

Family Agreements are said to safeguard older people from harmful outcomes, particularly when they have transferred a substantial asset to their adult child in exchange for care.[131] Yet, the current legal status of Family Agreements is 'unclear'.[132] Hall comments that a significant problem with Family Agreements is that they tend to be nothing more than a very general and vague promise of the adult child to take care of their older parent for the rest of their life.[133] The Victorian Government commented: 'The informality and familial nature of these agreements may make it difficult for the law to recognise and/or enforce them as contracts, and common law presumptions may assume that the transfer of property is a gift with no obligations attached.'[134]

[126] Doron and Gal (n 108) 42.

[127] Herd, 'The Family Agreement: Legal Good Sense?' (n 2) 73.

[128] Herd, 'The Family Agreement—A Collision' (n 2).

[129] H Reece, 'Leaping without Looking' in R Leckey (ed), *After Legal Equality: Family, Sex, Kinship* (Routledge, 2014), 119, citing Advice Services Alliance 2004, 'livingtogether agreements', https://www.advicenow.org.uk/articles/living-together-agreements accessed 17 March 2013.

[130] Carers Queensland (n 103) 5.

[131] Office of the Public Advocate, Submission No 76 to the Parliament of Australia House of Representatives Inquiry into Older People and the Law (2006), 8, https://www.aph.gov.au/Parliamentary_Business/Committees/House_of_Representatives_Committees?url=laca/olderpeople/subs.htm accessed 15 July 2019.

[132] New South Wales Ministerial Advisory Committee on Ageing, Submission No 103 to the Parliament of Australia House of Representatives Inquiry into Older People and the Law (2006), 5, https://www.aph.gov.au/Parliamentary_Business/Committees/House_of_Representatives_Committees?url=laca/olderpeople/subs.htm accessed 15 July 2019.

[133] Hall (n 6).

[134] Victorian Government, Submission No 121 to the Parliament of Australia House of Representatives Inquiry into Older People and the Law (2006), 29, https://www.aph.gov.au/Parliamentary_Business/Committees/House_of_Representatives_Committees?url=laca/olderpeople/subs.htm accessed 15 July 2019.

Due to the majority of Family Agreements being made on an informal and oral basis, they are rarely being prepared and executed as full legal contracts.[135] This is leading to ambiguous arrangements[136] that are breaking down behind closed family doors.[137] In recognition of this, the ALRC concluded that the current law inadequately protects the rights of an older person when a Family Agreement breaks down.[138] The same may also be true for the caregiving adult child.

In 2002, the British Columbia Law Institute recommended, among other things, that legislation empowering courts to intervene or set aside Family Agreements would be useful.[139] In 2007, the Australian Committee, in supporting this legislative recommendation, agreed that there may be a need for a specific mechanism to equitably resolve disputes that arise under Family Agreements.[140] Therefore, the Australian Committee recommended that there should be an investigation of legislation regulating Family Agreements.[141] In doing so, the Australian Committee suggested that requiring formalization of Family Agreements in writing would be desirable,[142] and that registration of Family Agreements could reduce uncertainty and would assist the courts in cases where disputes arise.[143] In 2009, the Australian Government accepted this recommendation in principle,[144] agreeing that 'the role of family agreements and the issues of how the scope for abuse can be limited or ameliorated need to be further studied'.[145] Yet, despite this, no such legislation exists.

In 2017, the ALRC, after undertaking an inquiry into 'Protecting the Rights of Older Australians from Abuse',[146] recommended that tribunals should have jurisdiction to resolve disputes within families with regard to residential property under Family Agreements.[147] Further, the ALRC recommended that the *Social Security Act 1991* (Cth) should be amended to require that the granny flat scenario is expressed in writing in order for the older person to be entitled to receive the Age Pension.[148]

In light of these recommendations, and in response to the ageing population, lawmakers and policymakers need to further consider the regulation of family care relationships so as to ensure the rights of older people and their caregiving family members are protected from harmful outcomes, particularly as Family Agreements are increasingly being entered into.[149]

135 Australian Committee (n 9).
136 Monro (n 87) 69.
137 Herd, 'The Family Agreement: Legal Good Sense?' (n 2).
138 Australian Law Reform Commission, Australian Government, 'Elder Abuse: Issues Paper' (2016), para 117, https://www.alrc.gov.au/publications/elder-abuse accessed 15 July 2019.
139 British Columbia Law Institute (n 83).
140 Australian Committee (n 9) para 4.43.
141 Australian Committee (n 9).
142 Ibid para 4.41.
143 Ibid para 4.42.
144 Australian Committee, 'Government Response' (n 66) 21.
145 Ibid.
146 Australian Government, Australian Law Reform Commission, 'Elder Abuse' (2017), https://www.alrc.gov.au/inquiries/elder-abuse accessed 15 July 2019.
147 ALRC Final Report (n 8) Recommendation 6-1.
148 Ibid Recommendation 6-2.
149 Herd, 'The Family Agreement: Legal Good Sense?' (n 2); Herd, 'The Family Agreement—A Collision' (n 2); Hansard (Cth) (n 4) 5 per Herd; Australian Committee (n 9); British Columbia Law Institute (n 83).

Bibliography

Access Economics, Report Prepared for Alzheimer's Australia, 'Keeping Dementia Front of Mind: Incidence and Prevalence 2009–2050' (2009), https://www.dementia.org.au/sites/default/files/20090800_Nat__AE_FullKeepDemFrontMind.pdf accessed 15 July 2019.

Age UK, 'Later Life in the United Kingdom' (2018), https://www.ageuk.org.uk/globalassets/age-uk/documents/reports-and-publications/later_life_uk_factsheet.pdf accessed 15 July 2019.

Alzheimer's Australia, Submission No 55 to the Parliament of Australia House of Representatives Inquiry into Older People and the Law (2006), https://www.aph.gov.au/Parliamentary_Business/Committees/House_of_Representatives_Committees?url=laca/olderpeople/subs.htm accessed 15 July 2019.

Alzheimer's Disease International, 'World Alzheimer Report 2015, The Global Impact of Dementia: An Analysis of Prevalence, Incidence, Cost and Trends' (2015), https://www.alz.co.uk/research/WorldAlzheimerReport2015.pdf accessed 15 July 2019.

Alzheimer's Society, 'What Is Dementia?' (2017), https://www.alzheimers.org.uk/download/downloads/id/3416/what_is_dementia.pdf accessed 15 July 2019.

Alzheimer's Society, 'Facts for the Media' (2018), https://www.alzheimers.org.uk/info/20027/news_and_media/541/facts_for_the_media accessed 15 July 2019.

Australian Bureau of Statistics, 'Population Projections, Australia, 2012 (Base) to 2101' (2013), http://www.abs.gov.au/ausstats/abs@.nsf/lookup/3222.0Media%20Release12012%20(base)%20to%202101 accessed 15 July 2019.

Australian Bureau of Statistics, 'Life Tables, States, Territories and Australia, 2014–2016' (2017), http://www.abs.gov.au/ausstats/abs@.nsf/Latestproducts/3302.0.55.001Main%20Features22014-2016?opendocument&tabname=Summary&prodno=3302.0.55.001&issue=2014-2016&num=&view= accessed XXXX.

Australian Law Reform Commission, Australian Government, 'Elder Abuse: Issues Paper' (2016), https://www.alrc.gov.au/publications/elder-abuse accessed 15 July 2019.

Australian Government, Australian Law Reform Commission, 'Elder Abuse' (2017), https://www.alrc.gov.au/inquiries/elder-abuse accessed 15 July 2019.

Australian Government, Australian Law Reform Commission, 'Elder Abuse—A National Legal Response: Final Report' (2017), https://www.alrc.gov.au/sites/default/files/pdfs/publications/elder_abuse_131_final_report_31_may_2017.pdf accessed 15 July 2019.

Australian Government, Australian Institute of Health and Welfare, 'Older Australia at a Glance' (2017), https://www.aihw.gov.au/reports/older-people/older-australia-at-a-glance/contents/demographics-of-older-australians/australia-s-changing-age-and-gender-profile accessed 15 July 2019.

Bagshaw, D, Adams, V, Zannettino, L, and Wendt, S, 'Elder Mediation and the Financial Abuse of Older People by a Family Member' (2015) 32(4) Conflict Resolution Quarterly 443.

Bagshaw, D, Wendt, S, Zannettino, L, and Adams, V, 'Financial Abuse of Older People by Family Members: Views and Experiences of Older Australians and Their Family Members' (2013) 66(1) Australian Social Work 86.

Brammer, A and Biggs, S, 'Defining Elder Abuse' (1998) 20(3) Journal of Social Welfare and Family Law 285.

British Columbia Law Institute, Committee on Legal Issues Affecting Seniors, 'Private Care Agreements between Older Adults and Friends of Family Members' (2002), Report No 18, http://www.bcli.org/sites/default/files/Private_Care_Agreements_Between_Older_Adults_and_Friends_or_Family_Members.pdf accessed 15 July 2019.

Brown, L, Hansnata, E, and La, HA, Report Prepared for Alzheimer's Australia, 'Economic Cost of Dementia in Australia: 2016–2056' (2017), https://www.dementia.org.au/files/NATIONAL/documents/The-economic-cost-of-dementia-in Australia-2016-to-2056.pdf accessed 15 July 2019.

Buckner, L and Yeandle, S, 'Valuing Carers 2015: The Rising Value of Carers' Support' (Carers UK, 2015), http://www.carersuk.org/for-professionals/policy/policy-library/valuing-carers-2015 accessed 15 July 2019.

Byrd, CD, 'Relative Responsibility Extended: Requirements of Adult Children to Pay for Their Indigent Parent's Medical Needs' (1988) 22(1) Family Law Quarterly 87.

Carers Queensland, Submission No 81 to the Parliament of Australia House of Representatives Inquiry into Older People and the Law (2006), https://www.aph.gov.au/Parliamentary_Business/Committees/House_of_Representatives_Committees?url=laca/olderpeople/subs.htm accessed 15 July 2019.

Carers UK, 'Caring and Family Finances Inquiry: UK Report' (2014), http://www.carersuk.org/for-professionals/policy/policy-library/caring-family-finances-inquiry accessed 15 July 2019.

City of London Police, 'Assessment: Financial Crime against Vulnerable Adults' (Social Care Institute for Excellence, 2011), https://www.scie.org.uk/publications/reports/report49.asp accessed 15 July 2019.

Commonwealth of Australia, Official Committee Hansard, House of Representatives, Standing Committee on Legal and Constitutional Affairs, 'Older People and the Law' (2007), http://parlinfo.aph.gov.au/parlInfo/search/display/display.w3p;query=Id%3A%22committees%2Fcommrep%2F10278%2F0000%22 accessed 15 July 2019.

Deloitte Access Economic, 'The Economic Value of Informal Care in Australia in 2015' (Carers Australia, 2015), http://www.carersaustralia.com.au/storage/Access%20Economics%20Report.pdf accessed 15 July 2019.

De Vaus, D, 'Children's Responsibilities to Elderly Parents' (1996) 45 Family Matters, Australian Institute of Family Studies 16, https://aifs.gov.au/sites/default/files/fm45dd.pdf accessed 15 July 2019.

Doron, I and Gal, I, 'The Emergence of Legal Prevention in Old Age: Findings from an Israeli Exploratory Study' (2006) 21 Journal of Cross Cultural Gerontology 41.

Elder Abuse Prevention Unit, 'Financial Abuse' (2014), https://www.eapu.com.au/elder-abuse/financial-abuse accessed 15 July 2019.

Fealy, G, Donnelly, N, Bergin, A, Treacy, MP, and Phelan, A, 'Financial Abuse of Older People: A Review' (National Centre for the Protection of Older People, University College Dublin, 2012).

Field, S, 'Issues Facing Older Australians: Legal, Financial and Societal' (2005) 1 Journal of International Aging Law and Policy 95.

Hall, MI, 'Care for Life: Private Care Agreements between Older Adults and Friends or Family Members' (2003) 2 Elder Law Review 1.

Herd, B, 'The Family Agreement—A Collision between Love and the Law?' (2002) 81 Reform 23.

Herd, B, 'The Family Agreement: Legal Good Sense or Social Bad Taste for the Aged?' (2002) 27(2) Alternative Law Journal 72.

Herring, J, 'Together Forever? The Rights and Responsibilities of Adult Children and Their Parents' in J Bridgeman, H Keating, and C Lind (eds), *Responsibility: Law and the Family* (Ashgate Publishing Group, 2008).

Herring, J, *Older People in Law and Society* (Oxford University Press, 2009).

Herring, J, *Caring and the Law* (Hart Publishing, 2013).

Herring, J, *Family Law* (6th edn, Pearson, 2013).

Herring, J, 'The Disability Critique of Care' (2014) 8 Elder Law Review 1, 13.

Herring, J, *Family Law* (7th edn, Pearson, 2015).

House of Commons Health Committee, 'Elder Abuse: Second Report of Session 2003–04' (2004), http://www.publications.parliament.uk/pa/cm200304/cmselect/cmhealth/111/111.pdf accessed 15 July 2019.

House of Lords, Select Committee on Public Service and Demographic Change, Report of Session 2012–13, 'Ready for Ageing?' (2013), http://www.cpahq.org/cpahq/cpadocs/UK%20Parliament%20HOL%20Ready%20for%20the%20Ageing.pdf accessed 15 July 2019.

House of Representatives Standing Committee on Legal and Constitutional Affairs, 'Older People and the Law: Government Response' (2009), http://www.aph.gov.au/Parliamentary_Business/Committees/House_of_representatives_Committees?url=laca/reports.htm accessed 15 July 2019.

Humphries, R, Thorlby, R, Holder, H, Hall, P, and Charles, A, 'Social Care for Older People: Home Truths' (The King's Fund and Nuffield Trust, London, 2016), 3, https://www.nuffieldtrust.org.uk/research/social-care-for-older-people-home-truths accessed 15 July 2019.

Kline, TA, 'A Rational Role for Filial Responsibility Laws in Modern Society?' (1992) 26(3) Family Law Quarterly 195.

Kulik, CT, Ryan, S, Harper, S, and George, G, 'Aging Populations and Management: From the Editors' (2014) 57(4) Academy of Management Journal 929.

Kyle, L, 'Out of the Shadows: A Discussion on Law Reform for the Prevention of Financial Abuse of Older People' (2013) 7(4) Elder Law Review 1.

Latorre Postigo, JM and López Honrubia, R, 'The Co-Residence of Elderly People with Their Children and Grandchildren' (2010) 36(4) Educational Gerontology 330.

Leeson, GW, 'Increasing Longevity and the New Demography of Death' [2014] International Journal of Population Research 1–7.

Lewis, R, *Elder Law in Australia* (LexisNexis Butterworths, 2004).

McCawley, A-L, Tilse, C, Wilson, J, Rosenman, L, and Setterlund, D, 'Access to Assets: Older People with Impaired Capacity and Financial Abuse' (2006) 8(1) Journal of Adult Protection 20.

Monro, R, 'Family Agreements All with the Best of Intentions' (2002) 27(2) Alternative Law Journal 68.

New South Wales Ministerial Advisory Committee on Ageing, Submission No 103 to the Parliament of Australia House of Representatives Inquiry into Older People and the Law (2006), https://www.aph.gov.au/Parliamentary_Business/Committees/House_of_Representatives_Committees?url=laca/olderpeople/subs.htm accessed 15 July 2019.

Office for National Statistics, 'National Life Tables, UK: 2014 to 2016' (2017), https://www.ons.gov.uk/peoplepopulationandcommunity/birthsdeathsandmarriages/lifeexpectancies/bulletins/nationallifetablesunitedkingdom/2014to2016 accessed 15 July 2019.

Office for National Statistics, 'Overview of the UK Population: July 2017' (2017), https://www.ons.gov.uk/peoplepopulationandcommunity/populationandmigration/populationestimates/articles/overviewoftheukpopulation/july2017 accessed 15 July 2019.

Office of the Public Advocate, Submission No 76 to the Parliament of Australia House of Representatives Inquiry into Older People and the Law (2006), https://www.aph.gov.au/Parliamentary_Business/Committees/House_of_Representatives_Committees?url=laca/olderpeople/subs.htm accessed 15 July 2019.

O'Keeffe, M, Hills, A, Doyle, M, et al, 'UK Study of Abuse and Neglect of Older People: Prevalence Survey Report' (National Centre for Social Research and King's College London, 2007), https://www.kcl.ac.uk/sspp/policy-institute/scwru/pubs/2007/okeefeetal2007ukstudyprevalence.pdf accessed 15 July 2019.

Pezzin, LE, Pollak, RA, and Schone, BS, 'Efficiency in Family Bargaining: Living Arrangements and Caregiving Decisions of Adult Children and Disabled Elderly Parents' (2007) 53(1) CESifo Economic Studies 69.

Pickard, L, 'A Growing Care Gap? The Supply of Unpaid Care for Older People by Their Adult Children in England to 2032' (2015) 35(1) Ageing and Society 96.

Pickard, L, Wittenberg, R, Comas-Herrera, A, King, D, and Malley, J, 'Care by Spouses, Care by Children: Projections of Informal Care for Older People in England to 2031' (2007) 6(3) Social Policy and Society 353.

Reece, H, 'Leaping without Looking' in R Leckey (ed), *After Legal Equality: Family, Sex, Kinship* (Routledge, 2014).

State Trustees Victoria, Submission No 138 to the Australian Law Reform Commission (2016), https://www.alrc.gov.au/sites/default/files/subs/138._state_trustees_victoria.docx accessed 15 July 2019.

Stuifbergen, MC and Van Delden, JJM, 'Filial Obligations to Elderly Parents: A Duty to Care?' (2011) 14 Medicine, Health Care and Philosophy 63.

The Parliament of the Commonwealth of Australia, House of Representatives Standing Committee on Legal and Constitutional Affairs, 'Older People and the Law' (2007), http://www.aph.gov.au/Parliamentary_Business/Committees/House_of_Representatives_Committees?url=laca/olderpeople/report.htm accessed 15 July 2019.

Ting, GHY and Woo, J, 'Elder Care: Is Legislation of Family Responsibility the Solution?' (2009) 4 Asian Journal of Gerontology and Geriatrics 72.

United Nations, Department of Economic and Social Affairs, Population Division, 'World Population Ageing 2015' (2015), http://www.un.org/en/development/desa/population/publications/pdf/ageing/WPA2015_Report.pdf accessed 15 July 2019.

United Nations, Department of Economic and Social Affairs, Population Division, 'World Population Prospects: The 2017 Revision' (2017), https://esa.un.org/unpd/wpp/Publications/Files/WPP2017_KeyFindings.pdf accessed 15 July 2019.

Van Houtte, J and Breda, J, 'Maintenance of the Aged by Their Adult Children: The Family as a Residual Agency in the Solution of Poverty in Belgium' (1978) 12(4) Law and Society Review 645.

Victorian Government, Submission No 121 to the Parliament of Australia House of Representatives Inquiry into Older People and the Law (2006), https://www.aph.gov.au/Parliamentary_Business/Committees/House_of_Representatives_Committees?url=laca/olderpeople/subs.htm accessed 15 July 2019.

20

The Problem of Mental Capacity in Self-Harming Egosyntonic Disorder

Camillia Kong

> Right before I swallowed the pills, I went to see my husband at work. I used to go there and, sort of like, bother him. He was just like, 'It's over, that's it.' Then I just felt so alone, more alone than I've ever, ever felt. And I just said, I'd just rather be dead than feel this way. And I'd rather feel dead than hurt, and I can't take the hurt anymore. I knew that I didn't know what was going to happen, I took a lot of pills, and I figured it would probably hurt, the way that I would die. But I figured that it would be *over*, instead of every day just living with pain. *Every day*. I couldn't take it anymore.[1]

Kate describes her feelings right before she attempted suicide after her husband had left her. She had a diagnosis of borderline personality disorder (BPD) and a history of self-harm. Consider Kate's case alongside the controversial suicide of Kerrie Wooltorton in 2007 by ethylene glycol toxicity. Ms Wooltorton had a history of self-harm and depression; she was diagnosed with 'untreatable' BPD and had previous admissions under the Mental Health Act. In nine previous attempted suicides, she had accepted life-saving treatment. Ms Wooltorton had prepared an advance directive three days beforehand. This advance directive was submitted to clinical staff fully conscious and alert, stating that she refused treatment, but wished to die where she would not be alone and could be made comfortable. Judging her to be competent, the clinician in charge complied with Ms Wooltorton's wishes. She died the following day.

The Wooltorton case raised all sorts of complex issues around mental capacity assessment[2] and the validity of advance decisions.[3] Sheila McLean nonetheless concluded that the case was 'in essence only about a straightforward refusal of consent by a competent adult person' and however uncomfortable one might be with the outcome, Ms Wooltorton as a capacitous adult had the right to have her treatment refusal respected.[4] But this conclusion

[1] J Young, JS Klosko, and ME Weishaar, *Schema Therapy: A Practitioner's Guide* (Guildford Press, 2003), 320.

[2] A David and N Kapur, 'Mentally Disordered or Lacking Capacity? Lessons for Managing Serious Deliberate Self Harm' (2010) 341 British Medical Journal 587; G Richardson, 'Mental Capacity in the Shadow of Suicide: What Can the Law Do?' (2013) 9 International Journal of Learning and Change 87.

[3] N Kapur, C Clements, N Bateman, et al, 'Advance Directives and Suicidal Behaviour' (2010) 341 British Medical Journal c4457.

[4] S McLean, 'Advance Directives and the Case of Kerrie Wooltorton', BMJ Group Blogs (1 October 2009), http://blogs.bmj.com/bmj/2009/10/01/sheila-mclean-on-advance-directives-and-the-case-of-kerrie-wooltorton/ accessed 15 July 2019.

Camillia Kong, *The Problem of Mental Capacity in Self-Harming Egosyntonic Disorder* In: *Philosophical Foundations of Medical Law*. Edited by: Andelka M Phillips, Thana C de Campos, and Jonathan Herring, Oxford University Press (2019).
DOI: 10.1093/oso/9780198796558.003.0021

ignores the core ethical dilemma behind determining mental capacity in such cases, where chronic self-harming and suicidality are behaviours that are constitutive of an enduring egosyntonic disorder. Egosyntonic disorders mean that the nature of the impairment and its indicative behaviours accord with the individual's selfhood and personal identity. By contrast, egodystonic disorders occur where disordered behaviours are viewed as disconnected from and in conflict with the individual's sense of self.

The concept of mental capacity functions as a gatekeeper for the right of personal autonomy, namely the right to make one's own decisions about care and treatment. Under the Mental Capacity Act 2005 in England and Wales (MCA), mental capacity is decided according to a functional test based on the ability to: (1) understand; (2) retain; (3) use and weigh; and (4) communicate information that is relevant to a specific decision. In theory, these value-neutral criteria are designed such that assessors refrain from judging the wisdom and goodness of individuals' decisions. These functional criteria are nonetheless problematic: autonomy is presumed to be *individualistic* and *value-neutral*, which then precludes explicit engagement with the more substantive evaluative judgments that are needed to articulate what may be incapacitous in the decision making expressed in self-harming egosyntonic disorders.[5]

In this chapter, I argue that a relational approach to the question of mental capacity will help clarify the substantive evaluative judgments needed in such problematic cases. Specifically, I suggest that the concept of capacity should operationalize a model of relational autonomy which illuminates the importance of *mutual recognition* in the development of self-narratives that are consistent with autonomy. Section I provides a brief overview of the diagnosis of BPD. Section II critically assesses the authenticity approach as a possible alternative framework for capacity assessment in self-harming egosyntonic disorders and claims that the authenticity approach ultimately remains overdetermined by the clinical diagnostic criteria. Section III explores how relations-to-self conducive to autonomy or heteronomy are inculcated through an intersubjective process of recognition or misrecognition. I examine the subjective and intersubjective possibilities of active resistance and narrative repair in section IV, concluding with its implications for capacity assessment in section V.

I. About Borderline Personality Disorder

Although the diagnosis remains deeply controversial,[6] 'personality disorder' in the Diagnostic and Statistical Manual of Mental Disorders 5 (DSM-5) is defined by enduring patterns of experience and behaviour in areas of: (1) thinking; (2) feeling; (3) interpersonal relationships; and (4) impulse control. These patterns depart from cultural norms and

[5] Elsewhere, I have argued more fully for a relational account of capacity and suggested how more substantive judgments inevitably motivate mental capacity assessments. See C Kong, *Mental Capacity in Relationship: Decision-Making, Dialogue, and Autonomy* (Cambridge University Press, 2017); C Kong, 'Beyond the Balancing Scales: The Importance of Prejudice and Dialogue in *A Local Authority v E and Ors*' (2014) 26 Child and Family Law Quarterly 216.

[6] KL Lewis and BFS Grenyer, 'Borderline Personality or Complex Posttraumatic Stress Disorder? An Update on the Controversy' (2009) 17 Harvard Review of Psychiatry 322; ES Gritti, DB Samuel, and M Lang, 'Diagnostic Agreement between Clinicians and Clients: The Convergent and Discriminant Validity of the SWAP-200 and MCMI-III Personality Disorder Scales' (2016) 30 Journal of Personality Disorder 796.

expectations, are pervasive and inflexible, and generate distress or impairment. Pathological personality traits in BPD fall into more specific impairments in self- and interpersonal functioning. Impairments in self-functioning revolve around issues of identity (such as poorly developed or unstable self-image that is often connected to excessive self-criticism, feelings of emptiness, and dissociative states) and self-direction (such as unstable goals, aspirations, and values). Impairment in interpersonal functioning involves hypersensitivity and fears of abandonment and rejection. Together, these impairments are expressed in emotionally dysregulated, maladaptive behaviours, such as risky behaviour, repeated self-mutilation with non- and parasuicidal intent, and suicide attempts.

BPD and its symptoms present a conundrum on two fronts. First, the *enduring persistence of the unstable self* reveals that BPD selfhood rests on a paradox: on the one hand, individuals can switch between, or even experience concurrent, psychological states of emptiness, dissociation, and emotively charged self-punishment. On the other hand, this instability remains enduring and 'stable', so that such instability *constitutively defines* BPD selfhood and personal identity. Second, maladaptive coping behaviours of BPD appear to be *consistent* expressions of the unstable self. Reasons behind intentional self-mutilation include the expression of anger, self-punishment, distraction from emotional distress, and a desire to regain normal feelings.[7] Indeed, self-punishment and anger towards oneself (rather than towards others) are often the predominant motives behind non-suicidal self-mutilation,[8] while the desire to decrease one's burden on others largely motivates suicide attempts in BPD.[9] The self-punitive intentions behind self-mutilating, suicidal behaviour in BPD appear to be entirely consistent expressions of individuals' personal identity based on self-abnegating narratives and values. Further complications emerge when considering the overwhelming evidence that the emergence of BPD is closely connected to trauma and adverse childhood experiences of abuse, physical and/or emotional neglect, and invalidation (hence why some prefer the less pejorative diagnosis of post-traumatic stress disorder).[10]

II. The Authenticity Approach to Capacity

Functional tests of capacity, such as the approach adopted in the MCA, are designed to presume capacity in the first instance and thereby safeguard the self-determination of individuals with impairments. Although the inquest found that the clinical staff had assessed her decision-making competence appropriately, determining capacity in situations like

[7] MZ Brown, KA Comtois, and MM Linehan, 'Reasons for Suicide Attempts and Nonsuicidal Self-Injury in Women with Borderline Personality Disorder' (2002) 111 Journal of Abnormal Psychology 198.

[8] Ibid 200; O Guralnik and D Simeon, 'Psychodynamic Theory and Treatment of Impulsive Self-Mutilating Behaviors' in D Simeon and E Hollander (eds), *Self-Mutilating Behaviors: Assessment and Treatment* (American Psychiatric Press, 2001), 175–97.

[9] Brown et al (n 7) 200.

[10] B van der Kessel, *The Body Keeps the Score: Brain, Mind, and Body in the Transformation of Trauma* (Penguin, 2015); B van der Kolk, JC Perry, and JL Herman, 'Childhood Origins of Self-Destructive Behavior' (1991) 148 American journal of Psychiatry 1665; M Linehan, *Cognitive-Behavioral Treatment of Borderline Personality Disorder* (Guildford, 1993); GL Gladstone, GB Parker, PB Mitchell, et al, 'Implications of Childhood Trauma for Depressed Women: An Analysis of Pathways from Childhood Sexual Abuse to Deliberate Self-Harm and Revictimization' (2004) 161 American Journal of Psychiatry 1417; P Soloff, KG Lynch, and TM Kelly, 'Childhood Abuse as a Risk Factor for Suicidal Behavior in Borderline Personality Disorder' (2002) 16 Journal of Personality Disorders 201.

the Wooltorton case is not straightforward precisely because self-mutilating, suicidal behaviours are constitutive of disordered borderline selfhood. The functional route towards capacity is insufficiently equipped to cope with egosyntonic disorders of this kind on two levels. First, it is questionable that an entirely functional focus is achievable if self-harm is a constitutive feature of the diagnosis:[11] consider by analogy the problematic question of capacity among those with eating disorders, such as anorexia nervosa (AN). AN is constitutively defined by an overriding fear of weight gain and refusals of treatment or food are core symptoms of the disorder. Medico-juridical practitioners consequently struggle to assess capacity about AN treatment refusals without appealing to the diagnostic criteria for eating disorders ('by definition, an eating disorder entails a refusal of treatment and food'). By the same logic, individuals with BPD may be unable to make capacitous choices related to self-harm and suicide because such behaviours are constitutive features of how the disorder manifests itself ('by definition, BPD entails self-harming and suicidal behaviour'). The reasoning behind capacity adjudications in both cases would collapse into status-based assessments, meaning the functional approach itself may fail by its own standards when assessing the capacity of self-harming behaviours that constitutively define the diagnostic criteria.[12]

Second, and more fundamentally, whether a functional approach can accurately pinpoint what might be incapacitous about decision making in self-harming egosyntonic disorders is doubtful. The case of AN is again helpful here. Jacinta Tan et al revealed that individuals with AN often pass functional tests of capacity (like the MacCAT-T) with flying colours, displaying relevant knowledge about their disorder and making decisions in a rational, logically consistent manner.[13] By the lights of a purely functional test, many AN patients at risk of death would be found to have capacity to refuse life-preserving treatment as a result.[14] Tracking the problematic nature of AN decision making therefore requires going beyond the functional test, towards an examination of concepts such as personal identity, values, and authenticity. Even in cases where ambivalence towards or conflict with the eating disorder is expressed, treatment is typically difficult because it involves challenging core parts of an individual's perceived identity and values, making it tantamount to becoming a different person altogether.[15]

To determine the decision-making capacity of AN patients, Tan et al appeal to a distinction between 'pathological' and 'non-pathological' values, 'pathological' values denoting those which arise from a mental disorder, such as the overriding importance of thinness above all else or a preference to risk death or disability rather than weight gain.[16] The concept of mental disorder further distinguishes pathological values from eccentric, unreasonable

[11] Indeed, BPD is the only personality disorder which includes self-injurious or suicidal behaviour among its diagnostic criteria: M Berk, M Grosjean, and H Warnick, 'Beyond Threats: Risk Factors for Suicide in Borderline Personality Disorder' (2009) 8 Current Psychiatry 33.

[12] Kong, 'Beyond the Balancing Scales' (n 5) 232.

[13] JOA Tan, PT Hope, DA Stewart, et al, 'Competence to Make Treatment Decisions in Anorexia Nervosa: Thinking Processes and Values' (2006) 13 Philosophy, Psychiatry, and Psychology 267 (page numbers refer to PMC version: https://www.ncbi.nlm.nih.gov/pmc/articles/PMC2121578/#__ffn_sectitle accessed 15 July 2019.

[14] Although the law certainly does not necessarily defer to this position: *A Local Authority v E and Others (Medical treatment: Anorexia)* [2012] EWHC 1639 (COP); [2012] MHLO 55; *The NHS Trust v L* [2012] EWHC 2741 (COP); [2012] MHLO 159.

[15] T Hope, J Tan, A Stewart, et al, 'Anorexia Nervosa and the Language of Authenticity' (2011) 41 Hastings Center Report 19, 25.

[16] Tan et al (n 13).

values, making 'authenticity' equivalent to the autonomous, non-disordered self. Although proponents of this view are rightly hesitant to argue that authenticity is necessarily coextensive with capacity,[17] the concept has nonetheless been deployed to illustrate how the ideal of autonomy should be *independent* of mental disorder, where authentic views, in other words, are those 'that she would have (or did have) if she did not suffer from the mental disorder'.[18] Consequently, '[i]f value or value system can be determined to arise from a mental disorder then it is "pathological"'.[19] Particular decisions determined by pathological values diverge from the 'authentic', non-disordered person and may therefore fail to demonstrate decision-making competence.

Aspects of this research are applicable to issues of self-mutilating and suicidal behaviour in BPD. Tan et al rightly highlight ambiguities about the authenticity of egosyntonic disorder, a point which tends to be overlooked in a purely functional approach to capacity. Moreover, attending to these ambiguities would lend itself towards a more scalar rather than binary view of decision-making capacity, offering greater leeway for the provision of positive support that fits somewhere between coercive treatment and strict non-intervention.[20] This grey area is important given the significant mortality rates of individuals diagnosed with AN and BPD.[21]

Yet, an authenticity approach to capacity raises its own problems on several fronts. First, the distinction between pathological and non-pathological values hinges on a strict adherence to how mental disorder is clinically defined, thus committing itself to questionable assumptions about the scientific objectivity of diagnoses. As mentioned earlier, the BPD diagnosis is both deeply controversial and stigmatizing: not only is its criteria contested by both clinicians and patients,[22] but it contains implicit, value-laden views about gender, untreatability, and intentionality of behaviour (ie 'attention-seeking' and 'manipulative', 'difficult', 'irresponsible', 'psychological vampires').[23] In other words, BPD carries the burden of being perceived as an untreatable disorder on the one hand, yet as expressing fully intentional, controllable behaviours that individuals can and should be accountable for on the other. To pathologize certain behaviours and presume their inauthentic source overlooks implicit assumptions within the BPD diagnosis which demand further critical scrutiny.[24]

Second, the complex phenomenology behind the egosyntonicity of BPD cannot be captured if the authentic self is separated from the disordered self. It may be the case that we

[17] Hope et al (n 15) 28.

[18] Tan et al (n 13) 20.

[19] Ibid 21.

[20] Kong, *Mental Capacity in Relationship* (n 5) ch 5; Richardson (n 2).

[21] According to Klaus Lieb et al, '10% of [BPD] patients commit suicide, a rate almost 50 times higher than in the general population': K Lieb, MC Zanarini, C Schmahl, et al, 'Borderline Personality Disorder' (2004) 364 Lancet 453; M Pompili, P Girardi, A Ruberto, et al, 'Suicide in Borderline Personality Disorder; A Meta-Analysis' (2005) 59 Nordic Journal of Psychiatry 319; J Arcelus, AJ Mitchell, J Wales, et al, 'Mortality Rates in Patients with Anorexia Nervosa and Other Eating Disorders: A Meta-Analysis of 36 Studies' (2011) 68 Archives of General Psychiatry 742.

[22] Linehan (n 10) 3–26; N Rüsch, A Hölzer, C Hermann, et al, 'Self-Stigma in Women with Borderline Personality Disorder and Women with Social Phobia' (2006) 194 Journal of Nervous & Mental Disease 766; M Crowe, 'Never Good Enough—Part 1: Shame or Borderline Personality Disorder?' (2004) 11 Journal of Psychiatric and Mental Health Nursing 327.

[23] NN Potter, *Mapping the Edges and the In-Between: A Critical Analysis of Borderline Personality Disorder* (Oxford University Press, 2009); C Shaw and G Proctor, 'Women at the Margins: A Critique of the Diagnosis of Borderline Personality Disorder' (2005) *15* Feminism and Psychology 483; L Bowers, *Dangerous and Severe Personality Disorder: Response and Role of the Psychiatric Team* (Routledge, 2002).

[24] Potter (n 23).

might question whether the disordered self is indeed authentic, particularly in cases of extreme ambivalence or value conflict. But egosytonicity becomes a difficult issue when the disordered self is subjectively perceived to be the authentic self: the self may not disown the values that are, from the outside, viewed as pathological, disordered, or self-destructive. Indeed, disordered behaviour may be an appropriate response to the way one sees the world, fully consistent with one's identity.[25] If we no longer rely on the clinical diagnostic criteria, the pathological / non-pathological distinction must rely on what it means to be authentic / inauthentic. Yet, this becomes a circular argument if authenticity depends on whether or not one has a mental disorder.[26] It thus becomes unclear what the pathological / non-pathological distinction brings to the table to improve mental capacity adjudications of egosyntonic self-harming and suicidal behaviour in BPD. Indeed, it seems to collapse into a status-based test, failing in similar ways to that of the functional test.

We therefore need an approach to mental capacity that can capture the phenomenology of egosyntonic disorder, yet avoids overdetermination by the diagnostic criteria. In the next section, I argue that mental capacity in such cases needs to attend to the *social and relational process* of how autonomous or heteronomous selfhood develops in the first place. This analytical focus will help clarify the self-understanding and self-narratives that are consonant with autonomy, giving it two advantages over a narrow focus on authenticity or pathological values: first, this approach looks at *how* autonomy competencies develop *irrespective of pathology*; second, *cohesive, integrated* self-narratives (which egosyntonic disorders often reveal) will not necessarily reflect the possession of autonomy competencies. Instead, the *substantive content* of these self-narratives will indicate whether certain ways of valuing oneself have been internalized.

III. Relational Autonomy and Mutual Recognition

The concept of mental capacity assumes the value of autonomy as a core pillar of medical law and clinical practice. This emphasis on individual autonomy has its critics (as we see in this volume): Jonathan Herring, for example, questions why autonomy rather than care should be the lens through which interpersonal obligations are viewed. Others, such as Charles Foster, believe that values such as dignity rather than autonomy often bear the normative burden in ethically fraught medico-juridical scenarios. The tragic outcome of the Wooltorton case provides obvious reasons why one might question the pre-eminent weight accorded to the autonomy ideal in mental capacity law and medical law more generally. However, these worries do not warrant a complete dismissal of autonomy, though they do highlight the need for significant refinements as to how the concept is operationalized in medical law cases involving potentially fatal egosyntonic disorders.

Bioethical theory and medico-juridical practice tend to take as their point of departure the liberal conception of autonomy defined as personal independence, where the self is

[25] cf *Wye Valley NHS Trust v Mr B* [2015] EWCOP 60.

[26] Hope et al (n 15) acknowledge that this argument would be circular and rightly scale back the claims that disordered personal identity would be inauthentic. However, how this coheres with Tan's claims in 'Competence to Make Treatment Decisions' (particularly the version published on PMC) is unclear, where the pathological / non-pathological values distinction lends itself to circular reasoning.

sovereign over one's body and mind.[27] Deference to an individual's choices, preferences, and wishes is required so long as certain criteria are met: (1) *procedural conditions*: one's choices reflect a consistent hierarchical order (that first-order choices cohere with higher-order desires and values); and (2) *authenticity conditions*: an individual's values accord with her sense of personal identity and selfhood (that one takes 'ownership' of one's higher-order preferences). But as we have seen so far, those with egosyntonic disorders often meet both conditions: individuals with BPD may engage in repetitive self-mutilating behaviour (such as cutting) and this not only accords with their higher-order preferences (ie relief of pain or distress, desire to self-punish), but likewise conforms to their core personal identity (ie as deserving punishment due to one's worthlessness). Alternatively, an attempt to isolate what is potentially 'authentic' in the BPD self is difficult without understanding what has gone awry in the *development* of personal identity. For many with BPD, traumatic, abusive childhood experiences have affected their self-constitution, with self-destructive coping mechanisms and decisions manifesting themselves later in life. An individual's disordered motivational structure and self-understanding can hinge on relational, socializing influences. Closer scrutiny of these influences will add much-needed nuance to the issue of whether self-mutilating or suicidal behaviours reflect capacitous and, indeed, autonomous decision making.

Feminist models of relational autonomy have particular relevance here. Theories of relational autonomy focus precisely on the question of how pernicious socialization can affect the development or expression of personal identity and key autonomy competencies, either in a causal or a constitutive sense.[28] Autonomy competencies are socially acquired rather than the result of monological introspection and include an 'ingrained disposition to consult the self, a capacity to discern the import of felt self-referential responses as well as independent beliefs, values, and goals, and a capacity to devise and carry out conduct congruent with the self', particularly in determining whether certain situational constraints are appropriate or addressing discord within oneself.[29] Based on this definition, integration or consistency between one's sense of self and one's values isn't the main focus. What matters, rather, is the *process* behind our self-constitution—namely, the complex interaction between social / relational context and individual dispositional traits—which may or may not encourage and establish autonomy competencies in our personal identity.[30] The process behind self-constitution will involve both passive and active factors that contribute to or obstruct the development of key autonomy skills.

Passive determinants of autonomy denote the socializing influences and narratives one cannot control. More specifically, an intersubjective process called *mutual recognition* makes our autonomy 'vulnerable to disruptions in one's relationships to others'.[31] Through mutual recognition, attitudes of others come to mediate our own *intrapersonal*,

[27] JS Mill, *On Liberty* (Penguin, 1974), 69, mentioned by MacDonald J in *Kings College Hospital NHS Foundation Trust v C & V* [2015] EWCOP 80.

[28] I explore the debate between causal and constitutive accounts in Kong, *Mental Capacity in Relationship* (n 5) ch 3.

[29] DT Meyers, *Self, Society, and Personal Choice* (Columbia University Press, 1984), 83–4.

[30] DT Meyers, 'Intersectional Identity and the Authentic Self?: Opposites Attract!' in C Mackenzie and N Stoljar (eds), *Relational Autonomy; Feminist Perspectives on Autonomy, Agency, and the Social Self* (Oxford University Press, 2000), 154.

[31] J Anderson and A Honneth, 'Autonomy, Vulnerability, Recognition, and Justice' in J Christman and J Anderson (eds), *Autonomy and the Challenges to Liberalism* (Cambridge University Press, 2005), 130.

relations-to-self and frame our choices accordingly.[32] We internalize modes of mutual recognition or misrecognition within the developmental process. Some relations-to-self are prone towards indecisive, doubtful, punitive, or hateful attitudes towards oneself; other intrapersonal attitudes reveal more *nurturing* relation-to-self, constituted by a positive vision of one's identity and agency. Three modes of recognition are significant in cultivating nurturing relations-to-self that are amenable to autonomy.[33]

First, respectful recognitional bonds are expressed when others treat us as worthy of respectful treatment, as individuals whose reasons deserve consideration. When internalized as *self-respect*, we likewise regard ourselves as persons of worth and valid reasons, and object to others' arbitrary disregard for our physical integrity, reasons, and personal characteristics. Degrading treatment by others, once internalized, will manifest itself in the intrapersonal acceptance of others' disregard as deserved (ie an appropriate response in keeping with one's sense of self). Or even if one objects, one will lack the internal resources to mount resistance in situations where such treatment has fallen short of respect.

Second, mutual recognition based on trust becomes internalized as *self-trust*. This intrapersonal attitude implies an open, confident relationship with conative aspects of our agency, such as our perceptions, emotions, desires, and impulses. Self-trust develops when those around us treat our particular conative expressions as legitimate and valuable. Relational contexts and socializing narratives that validate our conative responses help nurture an *intrapersonal* framework of safety and compassion towards ourselves—we become attuned to and openly explore these facets of our identity. Without experiencing recognitional bonds founded on trust, our relationship to the conative dimensions of our own agency can go awry in two ways: we can disown or distrust them—and thereby become uncertain about the crucial role these play in our practical actions and choices—or they can become underdeveloped, dysregulated, and inflexible—where an orientation of psychological rigidity rather than reflexivity towards our conative responses characterizes our agency.

Finally, mutual recognition that affirms the positive contributions of our activities, goals, and role to a defined group or community becomes internalized as an intrapersonal attitude of *self-esteem*. We gain a sense of our intrinsic value and belonging. By contrast, a sense of interpersonal disconnection, displacement, and personal insignificance pervades where self-esteem is lacking.

Studies have shown repeatedly that individuals with BPD have little or no experience of these modes of mutual recognition required to acquire autonomy competencies. Trauma, abuse, and adverse childhood experiences are prevalent among those later diagnosed with BPD. These experiences typically include a family context that is: (1) unsafe and unstable (particularly in cases of abuse, neglect, or abandonment); (2) depriving (in terms of parental nurturing, guidance, or protection); (3) harshly punitive and rejecting (highly critical, unforgiving, and punishing); and (4) subjugating (in that the needs and emotions of the child are suppressed through active discouragement or withdrawal).[34]

[32] Ibid 131.

[33] I adapt the recognitional framework of Axel Honneth to the context of impairment. See A Honneth, *The Struggle for Recognition: The Moral Grammar of Social Conflicts* (MIT Press, 1996).

[34] Young et al (n 1) 312–13.

Such a family environment embodies modes of *misrecognition*, as illustrated well in the therapeutic dialogue between Kate (from the beginning of the chapter) and Jeffrey Young (the founder of Schema Therapy). Kate was physically and sexually abused by her brother and she was blamed for, rather than protected from, his behaviour when she told her parents. Kate's lack of self-respect put her in a double-bind—she could neither defend herself against her mother's cutting criticisms of her nor even think she was *deserving* of such a defence: 'That's what prevents me from sticking up for myself and taking care of myself, because I just don't feel like I have the right. And I don't think that anyone has the right to want to take care of me, because I don't deserve it.'[35] She had little opportunity to develop self-trust, given that her conative responses to situations were repeatedly invalidated to the point that they would incite punitive, volatile recriminations. For example, Kate's mother frequently berated her for being 'miserable'. 'She told me she didn't like me, that I was just hopeless, that I was just so miserable she couldn't stand it . . . I just believed it, because it was true.'[36] Kate also lacked self-esteem—her activities were met with ambivalence and lack of care, and any sense of intrinsic belonging or subjective value was absent. When asked about the origin of her feelings of 'being no good or worthless', Kate stated, 'I've just always felt them, just from my family life, just not really feeling that I was important, or like I made a difference, or that I was significant in my family . . . [T]hey just never listened to me, never acknowledged me. I could do whatever I wanted, whenever I wanted.'[37]

Ultimately, individuals with BPD have failed to experience the intersubjective, recognitional bonds of respect, trust, and esteem which help cultivate nurturing intrapersonal relation-to-self. Misrecognition becomes part and parcel of one's way of relating to oneself. Due to emotional deprivation and abuse, many individuals believe they have no right to express their needs and feelings, and deserve punishment when they do so.[38] BPD individuals internalize and identify with self-abnegating narratives, viewing themselves as inherently worthless and irredeemably bad. Kate described herself as 'not really a whole person, whatever a whole person is, I don't even know. I just know that I look at other people, and I just don't see myself equal to anybody'.[39] Like Kerrie Wooltorton, she engaged in self-mutilating behaviour, culminating with an attempted suicide via drug overdose. Describing that incident, Kate stated: 'I just felt that I was no good, that I was worthless . . . I was just nobody.'[40]

The broader relational, social context therefore determines whether a certain manner of valuing oneself has been inculcated. In ideal circumstances, this culminates in nurturing relations-to-self which function as the necessary scaffolding on which our autonomy competencies can be developed and exercised.[41] Such attention to the socializing process behind developing autonomy competencies points to a key difference from both functional and authenticity approaches to capacity. The latter approaches remain relatively neutral towards the question of *which* self-conceptions can be seen as expressing autonomous—and therefore—capacitous decisions. But even if authenticity is coextensive with

[35] Ibid 318.
[36] Ibid 317.
[37] Ibid 316.
[38] Ibid 345.
[39] Ibid 315.
[40] Ibid 316.
[41] I discuss this in some depth in C Kong, 'Nurture before Responsibility: Self-in-Relation Competence and Self-Harm', (2019) 26 Philosophy, Psychiatry, and Psychology 1.

non-pathological values, it remains unclear why a person's skewed valuing cannot fulfil this criterion, particularly if one feels fully 'responsible' for one's values and decisions which are consistent with one's sense of self. This is especially the case if clinical opinion is split as to whether or not one suffers from a mental disorder. By contrast, a relational approach to autonomy posits that not all self-narratives can be said to be consonant with autonomy. Different modes of recognition capture the more passive process of constituting an autonomous or heteronomous self and likewise provide crucial content by which *normatively acceptable* intrapersonal narratives can be judged.

IV. Narrative Repair

Alongside this passive process is a more active dimension of autonomous self-constitution, where individuals reflexively adjust and claim responsibility for the ways in which relational, social influences have shaped one's cognitive and motivational structure. Thus, one does not automatically submit to such influences, but responds to them so that the self is dynamic rather than fixed and rigid. This becomes particularly important in the case of BPD. The diagnostic criteria suggest that individuals struggle with unstable, empty selfhood, even as the lens through which they view themselves is often highly rigid and self-abnegating, with inflexible expectations about their and others' behaviour. This implies difficulty engaging with the more active dimension of autonomous self-constitution.

For example, Kate describes to Young that 'I know I'm just supposed to be myself, but this is just really hard for me' due to this sense of expectation of what *others* expect her to do or be like, such as 'intelligent and articulate', 'without too much emotion'.[42] She states explicitly:

> I don't know what it is that I am. I think I'm just a miserable person deep down. That's just what I think . . . I start to emulate people, and just sort of like change myself, and I can be whoever and whatever I want. But what I've found is that it's just made me feel worse, more empty . . . because I don't know what *I* expect. I don't know what *I* want. I don't know what's important to *me*. I don't know. I'm 27 years old and I have no clue.[43]

Instability in one's personal identity and phenomenological experience of selfhood (ie feelings of emptiness and confusion about one's identity, as Kate describes; dissociative experiences in the midst of self-harming behaviour) can be attributable partly to the challenge of actively constituting an autonomous self. The simultaneous emptiness and rigidity of BPD selfhood means the process of developing a dynamic yet stable practical identity cannot be carried out in isolation, through one's own monological introspection.[44] Individuals' core sense of themselves can be heavily invested in self-abnegating narratives: no matter how harmful or inconsistent with autonomy these may be, they are still familiar. The alternative—ie the dialogical process of constituting one's identity through unfamiliar narratives and perspectives—is often daunting and terrifying.

42 Young et al (n 1) 319.
43 Ibid.
44 Indeed, this is the case for all individuals engaged in the active process of self-constitution. But the need for supportive others is especially so in cases where self-abnegating narratives are pervasive.

Where nurturing relations-to-self are lacking, overturning the pernicious narratives which distort our self-understanding will demand 'narrative repair'—a process of dialogical engagement with others who can help us identify and reflect on these distortions, create distance between our sense of self and dominant, self-abnegating narratives, and highlight intra-psychical tensions so as to encourage a practical identity which actively resists harmful socialization.[45] In other words, this process attempts to undo the internalization of misrecognition so that harmful self-constituting narratives become *egodystonic*—alien to ourselves and external to our practical identity.

Narrative repair as active resistance forms a crucial part of Schema Therapy approaches for treating BPD, for example. Through therapeutic dialogue and experiential work, individuals are encouraged to confront and undo their identification with the self-punitive mode of their identity. The self-punitive voice comes to be known as the 'Punitive Parent', thus distancing it from the self. For example, Young enjoins Kate to visualize herself as 'Angry Kate', and coaches her to respond to her father and challenge his mistreatment of her:

KATE: (*to father in image*) I'm just tired of [my brother] taking everything out on me, and beating me, and having you yell at me.
YOUNG: (*coaching Kate*) 'It's not fair.'
KATE: (*Repeats.*) It's not fair.
YOUNG: (*still coaching*) 'And that's why I want to destroy my room. Because I'm so angry at you for doing this.'
KATE: I just want you all to die.[46]

But the process of externalizing the internalized 'Punitive Parent' from one's sense of self is difficult, as evident in Kate's feelings following this challenge:

YOUNG: OK, that's good that you said that, Kate. Now, are you feeling bad about yourself or saying it, or does it feel like a relief?
KATE: No. (*Cries.*) It's wrong.
YOUNG: Can you be the part of you that feels that's wrong right now? Is that your father now, telling you that?
KATE: (*Nods yes.*) ... 'It's wrong for you to think those things and to feel those thing, and to be angry, and to want me dead, to want us dead. We take care of you.'[47]

This exchange demonstrates in concrete terms how the punitive voice starts to become uncoupled with, and externalized from, the BPD individual through dialogical prompts. Kate initially says 'it's wrong' for her to be angry, but Young encourages her to identify that voice with something outside herself—calling it the Punitive Parent—in order to cultivate strategies of protection and resistance against harmful, abusive narratives. Importantly, the dialogue continues by bringing in an external, nurturing narrative which counters the Punitive Parent voice. In these visualization strategies, the Schema therapist is brought into the image

[45] HL Nelson, *Damaged Identities, Narrative Repair* (Cornell University Press, 2001).
[46] Young et al (n 1) 343.
[47] Ibid.

or scenario to actively *intervene, speak up for*, and *protect* the BPD individual. Young asks Kate to bring him into the image to speak to her father, to protect her from him in the scene:

YOUNG: Now I'm going to speak up for you to the Punitive Father: 'Look, it's not wrong for Kate to be angry with you. You don't give her the normal amount of attention and caring that a father gives, and your wife is no better. She doesn't give her the attention, either. No wonder she's angry. No wonder she hates all of you. What do you do to make her care about you? What do you do to make your daughter love you and feel close to you? All you do is get angry with her and blame you and feel close to you? All you do is get angry with her and blame her for things. Even when her brother beats her, you still blame her. Do you expect her to love you for that and be happy? Is that fair?'[48]

When Kate is asked about how she feels about Young saying those things on her behalf, she refers to her guilt and fear that once he leaves the image she is going to be beaten up by her brother 'for sticking up for myself'.[49] Young then asks Kate to visualize a kind of wall or barrier to protect herself from her brother in the image, encouraging her to replicate the protective interventions Young uses against her father.

If certain core attitudes towards oneself are externalized, one might ask whether this process of narrative repair exacerbates rather than ameliorates the instability of selfhood that is characteristic of BPD: does this not create a vacuum of values which would amplify the sense of emptiness of BPD selfhood? Importantly, alongside these strategies of externalization is the promotion of recognitional 'counter-stories'; stories of narrative repair reflect the modes of recognition that are necessary to encourage nurturing relations-to-self and promote autonomy competencies. These include the encouragement of individuals' exploration of their conative responses, needs, and values. For example, Kate describes the significance and meaning of the moment she discovered her favourite colour:

KATE: I was so excited ... because I had a favorite color. And it was something that I actually pointed to.

YOUNG: And you knew it was *you*.

KATE: Yes. (*Cries.*) I was 27 years old and that was it. This is the color that I really like, not because somebody says it's the color I should like, or somebody that I want to be like likes it, it's just – to *me* – it's very pleasing. So I was real proud of myself (*laughs*).

YOUNG: That's wonderful. So you were able to find the part of yourself that's real, as oppose to the part that's trying to be what everyone else wants you to be ...

KATE: And it's funny, but, whenever I see that color, I just want to hang on to it, because it's something that I know that I like and it's important to me. Because there are so few things that I know that I like and that I want.[50]

This passage illustrates well how actively engaging in the process of narrative repair through intersubjective dialogue premised on recognitional bonds helps strengthen one's subjective autonomy competencies: alternative tracks of self-understanding are revealed and one's

[48] Ibid 343.
[49] Ibid 344.
[50] Ibid 369–70.

conative responses—such as one's favourite colour—experience subjective validation and trust. We eventually gain a clearer, more determined stance towards the social values and norms that are consistent with ourselves, and begin to assert our agency in the process of self-constitution. These emotions and preferences then become potential topics of examination through intersubjective dialogue. Previously self-consistent narratives and social norms are subject to critical reflection with others, where we examine our beliefs about ourselves with others, actively confront contradictory commitments, and address value conflict in our lives.

This does not mean that all contradictions within oneself are resolved: the ideal of integration is not necessarily the goal of constituting the autonomous self since individuals with self-abnegating egosyntonic disorders may well embody such an ideal. Integration in and of itself fails to track the complex interaction between external obstacles (ie socializing narratives, modes of misrecognition) and internal impediments (ie self-abnegating attitudes and beliefs, inflexibility, timidity) which prevent the development of autonomy competencies. Rather, the focus is on cultivating an open, flexible practical orientation, both *intrapersonally* and *interpersonally*, so that we become more sensitive and understanding of discord within ourselves, as well as more attuned and proactive towards the socializing narratives surrounding us.

V. Back to the Question of Capacity

This discussion has two implications on assessments of mental capacity: first, the concept of capacity must presume and operationalize a more nuanced interpretation of autonomy, especially if it is to understand how the relational and environmental context contributes to the development of egosyntonic, self-mutilating behaviours as evidenced in disorders such as BPD. Second, even as capacity assessments in medico-juridical practice themselves are outside the intersubjective process of autonomous self-constitution, they are nonetheless well placed to identify the potential need for a process of narrative repair in the first instance.

First, individuals' self-conception premised on self-abnegation or self-hatred would not be considered an appropriate expression of autonomy competencies from the theoretical standpoint I have discussed thus far: it would instead alert us to the absence of crucial recognitional mechanisms that are necessary for the development of autonomy. Attunement to this developmental aspect enables us to acknowledge ways in which *authentic* selves can also be steeped in self-abnegation and self-hatred; or to state it differently, how highly negative self-constituting narratives may be *authentic* (or *egosyntonic*), but not necessarily expressive of *autonomy*. On the one hand, this enables us to accommodate more evaluative judgments about the narratives which lie behind the self-constitution of egosyntonic, self-mutilating, and suicidal behaviours: the narrative that one deserves to be punished due to some inherent worthlessness might be authentic, but capacity assessors should rightly hesitate about *endorsing and validating* those narratives through capacity adjudications. On the other hand, a more nuanced view of relational autonomy enables a more scalar rather than either-or view of capacity: individuals may experience strong intrapersonal integration, but embody heteronomy; equally, their ability to exercise self-determination in discrete parts of their lives may deserve respect and recognition. Some degree of practical judgment is needed to resolve the question of capacity as a result. A functional approach may well conclude that BPD individuals choosing to engage in self-mutilating or suicidal behaviour reflects decision-making capacity—as the clinicians had in the Wooltorton case. But if a relational concept of autonomy is operationalized in capacity, then the criteria would require further understanding of the individual's 'practical orientation' towards the decision—more specifically, how this choice reflects certain subjective narratives and a particular understanding of the self.

Returning to Kate's attempted suicide at the beginning of this chapter, it might be true that capacity assessments are by their very nature hampered by urgent time constraints, discrete and relatively unsituated judgments. Especially in emergency situations, a clinician with little or no history of the patient often assesses capacity. At the very least, any assessment of Kate's decision to refuse life-preserving treatment would require some very basic attunement to her self-constituting narratives, to be reflexively aware about how the phenomenology of egosyntonic disorders like BPD eludes conventional definitions of liberal autonomy and authenticity. In no way does this imply that capacity assessors in medico-juridical practice should automatically discount her view and coercively treat her against her wishes in the name of her best interests. It might mean some follow-up clarification of how her decisional capacities and her self-mutilating or suicidal behaviour reflect certain socially acquired self-abnegating but intrapersonally consistent narratives.[51] This more nuanced understanding of autonomy should help us move towards a more complex understanding of the decisional pitfalls of individuals with self-harming egosyntonic disorders.

Second, individuals' active confrontation of self-abnegating narratives through narrative repair requires a surrounding community that helps support their resistance; these communities are themselves 'a social achievement and not a social given'.[52] Many individuals with BPD, let alone mental disorder more generally, have not been fortunate enough to experience the type of narrative repair discussed in the previous section. Capacity assessors are unable to carry out the intensive process of narrative repair, simply due to the intrinsic constraints of their task. But, as I have argued elsewhere,[53] capacity assessments can nonetheless provide an important check on those who can and should be engaged in this process in two ways. Because it isn't a social given, assessors can, first, detect when narrative repair might be necessary and appropriate, and identify when one has been disadvantaged from developing a supportive community of resistance.[54] Moreover, the very language of the assessment could help *initiate* that process of narrative repair, so as to ensure that the reasoning behind the assessment of capacity is itself consistent with recognitional mechanisms intended to cultivate nurturing relations-to-self. When done effectively, capacity assessment can itself function as part of an autonomy-enhancing normative framework for the medico-juridical treatment of individuals with self-harming egosyntonic disorders like BPD.

One might argue that this relational approach represents an overly substantive approach which would result in unwarranted paternalistic interventions in the lives of, not just those with BPD, but anyone with self-abnegating narratives. The straightforward response would

51 As was demonstrated well by the judgment by Macdonald J in the 'sparkly case': *King's College Hospital NHS Foundation Trust v C and Anor* [2015] EWCOP 80.

52 M Fricker, *Epistemic Justice: Power and the Ethics of Knowing* (Oxford University Press, 2009), 54.

53 Kong, *Mental Capacity in Relationship* (n 5) chs 6, 7.

54 eg Bodey J's recommendations in *A Local Authority v A and Another* [2010] EWHC 1549 (Fam).

be to simply uphold the MCA's diagnostic threshold which stipulates impairment of the mind must be present to trigger the functional test of capacity. But this would be a weak and unsatisfactory evasion of this objection. From one direction, I think it is necessary to bite the bullet that the line between disorder and non-disorder will become more fluid with such an approach—and this is important if we are to be serious about the safeguards, supports, and positive duties that are necessary for the *promotion* rather than the mere *respect* of autonomy, particularly to enable the decisional capacity of individuals with impairments. From another direction, it is important to draw critical attention to the contentious value-neutral presumptions of the functional test of capacity: the problematic egosyntonic nature of self-harm and suicidality in BPD provides a clear example of shortcomings from such an approach, ranging from the absence of sufficiently evaluative criteria to track what is disordered about such behaviour, to an illusory eschewal of status-based judgments. Equally, there should be caution in uncritically endorsing overly substantive claims about the nature of disorder, as seen in the temptation to conflate pathology with inauthenticity in the authenticity approach to capacity. The relational approach tries to achieve the right balance, injecting just enough content to the criteria of capacity so as to distinguish between self-conceptions which reflect socially acquired autonomy competencies, and those which have internalized narratives of misrecognition. Capacity as a concept should not be value-neutral about the types of narratives that are consonant with autonomy and should demand critical reflection on those intrapersonal narratives that are implicitly endorsed in the practice of capacity assessment.

VI. Conclusion

This chapter has argued that the complex phenomenology of self-harming, egosyntonic disorders, such as BPD, demands a more nuanced approach to mental capacity. Individualistic and procedural assumptions in our current functional model of mental capacity fail to pinpoint why decision-making capacity is problematic in such cases, while authenticity-based accounts tend to rest on circular accounts of authenticity and mental disorder. Both struggle because there is a reluctance to engage in some of the knottier evaluative content around what it means to be a *capacitous and autonomous self*. Instead, we should not shy away from the more substantive criteria of capacity which is embedded in a more relational approach, where we consider the normative content of relations-to-self that are characteristic of autonomy or heteronomy, irrespective of diagnostic criteria and psychopathology.

Moreover, this relational approach signals to capacity assessors when narrative repair might be necessary to overturn deeply self-abnegating narratives which can motivate self-mutilation and suicide attempts. Capacity assessment involves an overwhelming focus on the individual undergoing assessment, where it is up to *that person* to prove or disprove her decision-making capacity. But a relational approach pushes against this impulse, suggesting that the social and care environment has a significant role to play in enabling and supporting how we *become* capacitous decision-makers who value and respect ourselves in particular ways. Attentiveness to the complex development of autonomous, self-nurturing narratives may be a key ingredient to providing positive support to those self-harming egosyntonic disorders. The reasons behind suicidal behaviours in these disorders are complex and multi-layered, and, indeed, there are cases where interventions may not be ethically warranted.

But it is important to ensure capacity assessors are equipped with as many resources which attend to these complexities, with a framework which enables a deeper understanding of individual narratives and the *sources* of such narratives, to make the best types of judgments in such difficult cases.

21

Medical Privacy and Big Data

A Further Reason in Favour of Public Universal Health-Care Coverage

*Carissa Véliz**

Most people are completely oblivious to the danger that their medical data undergoes as soon as it goes out into the burgeoning world of big data. Medical data is financially valuable, and your sensitive data may be shared or sold by doctors, hospitals, clinical laboratories, and pharmacies—without your knowledge or consent.[1] Medical data can also be found in your browsing history, the smartphone applications you use, data from wearables, your shopping list, and more. At best, data about your health might end up in the hands of researchers on whose goodwill we depend to avoid abuses of power.[2] Very likely, it will end up with data brokers who might sell it to a future employer, or an insurance company, or the government. At worst, your medical data may end up in the hands of criminals eager to commit extortion or identity theft. In addition to data harms related to exposure and discrimination, the collection of sensitive data by powerful corporations risks the creation of data monopolies that can dominate and condition access to health care.

This chapter aims to explore the challenge that big data brings to medical privacy. Section I offers a brief overview of the role of privacy in medical settings. I define privacy as having one's personal information and one's personal sensorial space (what I call *autotopos*) unaccessed. Section II discusses how the challenge of big data differs from other risks to medical privacy. Section III is about what can be done to minimize those risks. I argue that the most effective way of protecting people from suffering unfair medical consequences is by having a public universal health-care system in which coverage is not influenced by personal data (eg genetic predisposition, behavioural data, etc).

I. Medical Privacy

Privacy consists in having one's personal information and one's personal sensorial space (what I call *autotopos*[3]) unaccessed.[4] Personal information is the kind of information that

* This chapter has been written with the support of the Wellcome Trust (grant number WT104848/Z/14/Z).

[1] A Tanner, *Our Bodies, Our Data: How Companies Make Billions Selling Our Medical Records* (Beacon Press, 2017), 1.

[2] Ibid.

[3] From the Greek *auto* (self) and *topos* (place or space). My thanks to Roger Crisp for suggesting the term.

[4] The adjective 'unaccessed' is not found in dictionaries, but there is no suitable existing term to convey in one word the property of not having been accessed. 'Inaccessible' denotes the property of not being able to be accessed, which is different from being accessible yet not actually accessed. Analogous differentiations exist in English that use the same prefixes (eg indisputable/undisputed, inalterable/unaltered, etc).

Carissa Véliz, *Medical Privacy and Big Data* In: *Philosophical Foundations of Medical Law*. Edited by: Andelka M Phillips, Thana C de Campos, and Jonathan Herring, Oxford University Press (2019). © Andelka M Phillips, Thana C de Campos, and Jonathan Herring
DOI: 10.1093/oso/9780198796558.003.0022

someone in a certain society would not want to share with just anyone, or information an individual is particularly sensitive about. The autotopos is the kind of sensorial space that people in a certain society would not want just anyone, other than themselves (and perhaps a very limited number of other people chosen by them), to access. One's autotopos is accessed when someone sensorially enters a culturally established personal zone of one. That is, when another (through direct or indirect perception, such as cameras and microphones) sees, hears, smells, or touches one in a zone in which there are cultural expectations to be free from the eyes, ears, touch, and presence of others (eg in the toilet). One's autotopos is also accessed when one is witnessed engaging in some activity or being the subject of some event that typically evokes the desire to have no witnesses or very few chosen witnesses (eg being naked).[5]

Medical privacy refers to having personal information about one's health status unaccessed and having one's autotopos unaccessed in the context of medical settings. Some scholars, such as Anita Allen, include within medical privacy things like 'associational privacy (eg intimate sharing of death, illness, and recovery); proprietary privacy (eg self-ownership and control over personal identifiers, genetic data, and biospecimens); and decisional privacy (eg autonomy and choice in medical decision making).'[6] This over-inclusion is mistaken. What Allen calls 'associational privacy' can be explained through a combination of informational and sensorial access: we do not want non-intimate people to *see* us when we are ill or dying; we do not want them to *know* about our illnesses. Similarly, with so-called 'proprietary privacy', if we worry about the information that genetic data carries and the possible consequences of that information getting shared inappropriately, then it is a matter of privacy, but one that is covered by informational privacy. If the worry is rather financial (ie about who should profit from patients' genetic data), then it is a proprietary issue, not a privacy one. Finally, what Allen calls 'decisional privacy' is rather a matter having to do with the interest we have in being allowed to do as we please without interference.[7] In other words, it is a matter of freedom and autonomy, not privacy.

One might wonder what makes the two species—informational and sensorial access—part of the genus of privacy. The unity of the category of privacy is founded on the notion of being personally unaccessed and the kinds of interests we have in not being accessed by others. Privacy protects us from: (1) certain kinds of harms that may come about as a result of other people having access to our personal life (eg discrimination, identity theft, etc); (2) the demands of sociality; (3) being judged and possibly ridiculed by others (and thus from self-conscious negative emotions such as shame and embarrassment); and (4) the discomfort of being watched, heard, and so on.[8]

The medical context is an important home for privacy. Visits to the doctor's office or the hospital create moments of great vulnerability for patients and their families. People typically do not like just anyone knowing about their diseases (particularly when it comes to certain kinds of diseases that carry more stigma with them), and we do not like being seen at our worst—when we are sick, worried, and stripped down of makeup and our everyday attire. Yet, privacy losses are inevitable in medical contexts. For patients to get adequate

[5] C Véliz, 'On Privacy' (DPhil thesis, University of Oxford, 2017), ch 4.

[6] A Allen, 'Privacy and Medicine' in EN Zalta (ed), *The Stanford Encyclopedia of Philosophy* (winter 2016 edn), https://plato.stanford.edu/archives/win2016/entries/privacy-medicine/ accessed 15 July 2019.

[7] WA Parent, 'Privacy, Morality, and the Law' (1983) 12 Philosophy and Public Affairs 269.

[8] Véliz (n 5).

care, they have little choice but to surrender both sensitive information about themselves and access to their bodies to health-care professionals. Likewise, for subjects to participate in health research, they must give up some degree of informational and sensorial privacy. It is the duty of health-care professionals and researchers, however, to minimize privacy losses, to show consideration towards patients and subjects, and to avoid any unnecessary exposure.

Thus, health-care professionals take care to protect patients' autotopos. Sensorial privacy is protected through bedside manners (eg looking away while the patient undresses), and other practices designed to limit exposure to patients' autotopos (eg the use of hospital gowns, curtains, etc).

Similarly, confidentiality protects informational privacy. Confidentiality refers to the moral duties of non-disclosure of information shared in the context of a fiduciary, contractual, or professional relationship, such as that of the lawyer–client relationship or the doctor–patient one. The Hippocratic Oath, which set the historical foundations of medical ethics, already took into account privacy, and included a vow not to speak of what is seen and heard in the course of treatment.[9] In addition to being a means of respecting a patient's right to privacy, confidentiality protects a patient's autonomy by sheltering them from external interference and possible criticism about their decisions.[10] Confidentiality also protects patients from possible stigmatization and discrimination (eg at work, or within the family). It makes it more likely that patients will seek medical care (thus keeping medical costs lower through routine check-ups that allow prompt medical attention), be honest with doctors (making medical care more accurate), and be more willing to participate in health research. [11]

In the context of medical research, ethics committees and institutional review boards make sure research subjects' privacy is adequately protected. Confidentiality requires that research subjects not be identifiable. To fulfil that objective, researchers anonymize data through aggregating it and using 'identifiers' (as opposed to names).[12] Further protection of privacy is traditionally afforded to research subjects through the use of informed consent. In order to give consent, participants must know what data will be collected about them, and how it will be managed. Subjects should also be informed of their right to withdraw from research at any time, and they should be told what would happen to their data in that scenario (ideally, data should be destroyed).

Anonymization and informed consent have never been perfect tools for protecting privacy. Genetic data, for example, resists anonymization because it is unique to each individual. Similarly, in some cases, it is impossible to extract valid informed consent (eg if a research subject is incapacitated). Notwithstanding their very significant limitations, however, it is widely accepted that they are usually good enough tools for protecting privacy, particularly given that they can be complemented with other good practices to compensate for their shortcomings. For instance, a study using genetic data can be kept in a

[9] 'Oath of Hippocrates' in WT Reich (ed), *Encyclopedia of Bioethics* (Macmillan, 1995), 2632.

[10] Allen (n 6).

[11] For more on the legal nature of confidentiality, see J Herring, *Medical Law and Ethics* (6th edn, Oxford University Press, 2016), 224.

[12] Cited by Anita Allen (n 6); Institute of Medicine, Committee on the Role of Institutional Review Boards in Health Services Research Data Privacy Protection, *Protecting Data Privacy in Health Services Research* (National Academies Press, 2000), https://www.nap.edu/read/9952/chapter/1 accessed 15 July 2019.

closed environment (eg using computers that are not connected to the internet, and in a locked room to which only authorized researchers have access, etc) to make sure that data is not linked to other data that could expose individuals. Similarly, in cases in which informed consent from a patient is not possible, consent from family members can act as a proxy. As it will become apparent in the next section, big data complicates the use of both anonymization and informed consent to the point of risking making them null.

After this brief overview of the role of privacy in medical settings, I will go on to detail the opportunities and privacy perils that big data presents in medical settings.

II. The Challenge of Big Data for Medical Privacy

The arrival of big data promises to revolutionize medicine. With technological innovation, however, often come new ethical challenges. As we find ourselves in novel situations, the need to foresee possible risks and benefits becomes crucial to make the most of available technologies, while avoiding as many negative consequences as possible.

In what follows, I will cover some of the medical advantages that big data may offer, before going on to explore possible privacy pitfalls and suggestions to minimize risks.

A. Big Data in Medicine

The most influential definition of big data outlines it in terms of three dimensions: volume (scale), velocity, and variety.[13,14] Big data's value rests in its capacity to combine large amounts of information, faster than ever, and from a variety of sources, into a single dataset that can allow the identification of correlations that would otherwise remain undetected.[15]

Data aggregated from sources outside of traditional medical settings can be very valuable for medical purposes. At Johns Hopkins, for example, researchers could predict the location and time of a flu outbreak based on tweets.[16] At Boston Children's Hospital, researchers could predict, track, and map obesity rates in a neighbourhood using Facebook 'likes'.[17]

It is widely believed that big data holds incredible potential to advance the diagnosis, treatment, and prevention of diseases through resolving some current problems in medicine. Randomized controlled trials (RCTs) have been crucial in the development of rigorous

[13] D Laney, '3D Data Management: Controlling Data Volume, Velocity and Variety' (2001) 6 META Group Research Note.

[14] Laney's conceptualization has become the classic definition. Subsequent approaches have added other elements to big data. See eg M Ali-ud-din Khan, MF Uddin, and N Gupta, 'Seven V's of Big Data: Understanding Big Data to extract Value' (Proceedings of Zone 1 Conference of the American Society for Engineering Education, Bridgeport, CT, April 2014), doi: 10.1109/ASEEZone1.2014.6820689. In their paper, Khan et al add validity, volatility, veracity, and value to elements of big data. Most of these components, however, seem more normative than descriptive. Sometimes, data used in big data analyses have little veracity or validity, leading to errors. While it is important to emphasize the desirability of features such as veracity and validity to create value, they do not seem intrinsic to a definition of big data. Inaccurate data can still form part of big data.

[15] JH Thorpe and EA Gray, 'Big Data and Public Health: Navigating Privacy Laws to Maximize Potential' (2015) 130(2) Public Health Reports 171.

[16] DA Broniatowski, MJ Paul, and M Dredze, 'National and Local Influenza Surveillance through Twitter: An Analysis of the 2012–2013 Influenza Epidemic' (2013) 8(12) PLoS One e83672.

[17] R Chunara, L Bouton, JW Ayers, et al, 'Assessing the Online Social Environment for Surveillance of Obesity Prevalence' (2013) 8 PLoS One e61373.

medicine by providing evidence on the efficacy and safety of drugs and interventions of various kinds. However, RCTs are expensive; their findings are both too broad (given problems of statistical sampling, a treatment found to be beneficial in a trial may not be beneficial for any given individual) and too narrow (trial population and setting may not be representative of the general practice); the randomization of patients may be ethically dubious, as some patients will receive better treatment than others, whether the better treatment is the existing care or the intervention being tested; and there are usually long delays before RCT results can translate into common practice. Big data aspires to solve these issues by having access to inexpensive data—generated as a by-product of patient care and people's day-to-day lives—that is specific to individuals and that assembles information from large groups of people, therefore being adequately narrow and broad. Big data research also avoids the ethical dubiousness of randomization, and treatment could potentially be much more immediately available.[18]

Big data may thus greatly advance personalized medicine. At least for some kinds of diseases, such as cancer, treatments are sometimes only effective in a small number of patients. There are many different varieties of cancer, and people with different genomes react differently to drugs. Big data holds the promise of being able to develop precision medicine on the basis of genomic profiles.[19] Rather than prescribe a drug tested on a small sample of the population in the hopes that a patient will react the way most people did in the sample, analyses based on big data will not have to hope for the best. Instead of working from a mere sample of the population, all subjects can be profiled individually, and the drug that has been shown to work better for people closest to a patient's profile can be prescribed.

Finally, big data may uncover hitherto unsuspected correlations by taking into account data about people's living environments, their responsibility for their health (exercise, eating, and drinking habits, etc), social relations, and more.

Although the promise of big data in medicine is great, it is worth taking into account that, so far, it is mainly just a promise, and one that has been there for many years. For all their limits, RCTs are still the best source of medical evidence we have, and there is a chance big data may never live up to its many expectations. As Sir Richard Peto, Professor of Medical Statistics and Epidemiology at the University of Oxford, points out: 'You need large-scale, randomized evidence to answer a lot of questions, and I think the claim that database analysis will do so isn't justified.'[20]

B. Privacy and Other Derivative Risks

All the possible medical benefits of big data, assuming they will come, will arise as a result of having more data about patients. With more data, however, come more privacy risks. Any time data is collected, there is a risk that information may be abused or may end up in the wrong hands. In the past, however, risks were partly minimized by technological limits. When health records or data from studies were collected and stored in paper in hospitals

[18] DC Angus, 'Fusing Randomized Trials with Big Data: The Key to Self-learning Health Care Systems?' (2015) 314 Journal of the American Medical Association 767.
[19] J Andreu-Perez, CC Poon, RD Merrifield, et al, 'Big Data for Health' (2015) 19(4) IEEE Journal of Biomedical Health and Informatics 1193, 1197.
[20] Quoted by Tanner (n 1) 164.

and doctors' offices, they were usually kept under lock and key in a cabinet, and the possibility of it reaching a great number of people was highly unlikely. As soon as health records become electronic, and are stored in computers with internet access, the risk of data breaches, leaks, and misuses increases. Any data kept on a device connected to the internet is potentially hackable. And any hacked data can end up being exposed and possibly sold on the dark web. Data breaches are common in medical settings. Just in 2015, a particularly bad year, over 112 million health records were breached in the United States alone.[21] While the number of people (health records) affected was lower in 2017, the number of healthcare data security incidents was higher than in past years, and seems to be on the rise, which suggests that patients' health records are increasingly at risk.[22]

In addition to the risk of having Electronic Health Records (EHRs), privacy risks are exacerbated by big data through the amount of data collected and the sources it comes from. Medical data not only comes from traditional sources like EHRs and genetic and microbiomic sequencing data, but also from smartphone applications, data brokers, social networks, internet searches, environmental data (eg air quality data), ambient sensors, wearables, etc.[23] Health data reaches beyond the doctor's office and the hospital into everyday life. Big data will be able to correlate relationships between health and buying habits, movement tracking, sleeping habits, social relations, and more. The objective is to be able to answer questions such as: Do Facebook friends influence one's life choices? Is using a bicycle to get to work healthier than walking? Is the air in some cities so polluted that it can affect life expectancy?[24]

Thus, data that may be used for medical (and other) purposes can include data that subjects voluntarily give up, data inferred from aggregated data, data that individuals may have no knowledge is being collected, and data that could potentially be collected against the wishes of data subjects (eg browsing history). All this information can be stored indefinitely, which, in time, allows data to be used for purposes other than that for which it was collected.[25] Some of these uses can hurt data subjects.

Inappropriate uses of medical data abound and will probably increase as the data economy expands. Private corporations' use of medical data is an important concern when companies get involved with health care. For example, Google's DeepMind has been involved with the NHS in the United Kingdom to develop a clinical application for kidney injury. Millions of medical records were shared with the company without informing patients or asking for their consent. Many months later, the United Kingdom's Information Commissioner's Office ruled it unlawful.[26] Even though DeepMind had made public assurances that the medical data would not be linked to Google accounts, products, or services, there was never any legal guarantee that they would keep their word. The company has

[21] D Munro, 'Data Breaches in Healthcare Totaled over 112 Million Records in 2015', *Forbes* (31 December 2015), https://www.forbes.com/sites/danmunro/2015/12/31/data-breaches-in-healthcare-total-over-112-million-records-in-2015/#5118fabc7b07 accessed 15 July 2019.

[22] HIPAA Journal post, 'Largest Healthcare Data Breaches of 2017' (4 January 2018), https://www.hipaajournal.com/largest-healthcare-data-breaches-2017/ accessed 15 July 2019.

[23] Andreu-Perez et al (n 19) 1194.

[24] GM Weber, KD Mandl, and IS Kohane, 'Finding the Missing Link for Big Biomedical Data' (2014) 311 Journal of the American Medical Association 2479.

[25] Thorpe and Gray (n 15).

[26] J Powles, 'Why Are We Giving Away Our Most Sensitive Health Data to Google?', *The Guardian* (5 July 2017), https://www.theguardian.com/commentisfree/2017/jul/05/sensitive-health-information-deepmind-google accessed 15 July 2019.

recently been accused of breaking its promise after it announced that Google would absorb DeepMind's medical division.[27] At the moment, because it is not in the position of a health-care professional, Google does not owe duties of confidentiality to patients. People's medical data could be used for all sorts of purposes: to be sold to third parties, for targeted marketing, for personalized pricing (ie selling certain products at a higher price to people who want or need them the most), or for developing Artificial Intelligence tools that can be applied in unknown ways in the future. It has been suggested that DeepMind's interest in helping develop this application relied from the start on acquiring data for its machine-learning commercial research projects.[28] A corporation may use sensitive data surrendered in the belief that it might help patients in questionable ways.

A related significant concern that is not directly about privacy, but rather a derivative worry about the power that comes with access to private data, is that big corporations that have more financial and technological capabilities than governments will monopolize access to health care. Dominance in data collection leads to monopolies, and dominance in the collection of sensitive data can lead to particularly problematic monopolies. Google, for example, could hold a monopolistic position of power over health analytics on account of being the institution holding more data on individuals around the world.They may develop the most advanced algorithms for medical diagnosis with that data, and other possible competitors who do not have as much data will not stand a chance against the titan. As things stand, DeepMind is getting patients' data for free, and yet it could potentially retain full power over the knowledge and algorithms that it develops from its collaboration with the NHS—as well as the profits.[29] If we allow corporations to hold power over data and access to health care, prices could soar, and medical attention could be given to individuals only under unacceptable data deals (eg in addition to payment, forcing patients to give up all of their personal data in exchange for medical care).

Other privacy-related risks of big data include people being discriminated against at their workplace on account of their medical history (eg for suffering from a certain disease, or because they are pregnant). Insurance companies could also take advantage of medically relevant information to charge some people more than others (eg penalize those who do not exercise enough, or worse, those who have genes that are deemed risky). Pharmaceutical companies could engage in price discrimination by identifying people who desperately need a medicine that can only be bought from them and charge more for it. Criminals can also extort patients, threatening to expose sensitive images or information about them if they do not give up money. In 2017, a criminal group gained access to data from a cosmetic surgery clinic and extorted patients, asking for a bitcoin ransom. Hackers ended up publishing more than 25,000 private photos, including nude ones, and personal data including passport scans and national insurance numbers.[30] Another common criminal act

[27] M Murphy, 'Privacy Concerns as Google Absorbs DeepMind's Health Division', *The Telegraph* (13 November 2018), https://www.telegraph.co.uk/technology/2018/11/13/privacy-concerns-google-absorbs-deepminds-health division/ accessed 15 July 2019.

[28] J Powles and H Hodson, 'Google DeepMind and Healthcare in an Age of Algorithms' (2017) 7(4) Health and Technology 351, https://link.springer.com/article/10.1007/s12553-017-0179-1 accessed 15 July 2019.

[29] Ibid.

[30] A Hern, 'Hackers Publish Private Photos from Cosmetic Surgery Clinic', *The Guardian* (31 May 2017), https://www.theguardian.com/technology/2017/may/31/hackers-publish-private-photos-cosmetic-surgery-clinic-bitcoin-ransom-payments accessed 15 July 2019.

is medical identity theft, committed by uninsured individuals who need medical care and steal another person's identity to get it.[31]

In a nutshell, the challenge for big data in medicine is to develop personalized medicine with the knowledge and consent of data subjects, protecting people's privacy, and minimizing risks that stem from the collection and use of sensitive data. In what follows, I explain why anonymization and consent are necessary but insufficient tools to meet this challenge.

C. The Limits of Anonymization and Consent in the Context of Big Data

As mentioned in section I above, medical ethics has relied on anonymization and informed consent to protect people's privacy. Big data, however, makes both of these tools difficult, if not impossible, to implement. Let us consider anonymization first.

Anonymization has always been a challenge. Studies that involve photographs, for example, or genetic data, can be hard or impossible to anonymize.[32] But, for the most part, other kinds of data could be more easily anonymized by stripping away information that could identify individuals. The use of big data, however, makes anonymization a near impossible feat, because the more data points we have about individuals, the easier it is to identify them. [33] There is usually only one individual of your height who works and lives where you do, for example. It only takes two or three data points to identify anyone.[34] Given the increasing amount of publicly available data that we have on people, re-identification will continue to get easier.[35] Furthermore, for data to reveal insights, it must be linked to the correct person to ensure appropriate diagnosis and treatment.[36] Therefore, every person must be uniquely tagged with a medical identifier, making it all the more easy to re-identify individuals.

Even if it were possible to anonymize data in a secure way, the analysis of aggregated data can also result in group-level harms such as stigmatization and discrimination. Such harms can impact everyone in a given group and not only the people who might have consented to research.[37]

Such are the limits of anonymization in the context of big data. Let us now turn to consent. Big data is designed to reveal unforeseen correlations, which implies that there will be a significant degree of uncertainty about future findings. Even if data subjects were to agree to give up their data, consent cannot be fully informed because subjects cannot be told about future uses and consequences of their data, as not even researchers can know what kinds of correlations may be unveiled, and they often cannot guarantee how this data will be used.[38]

[31] Tanner (n 1) 98.

[32] Nuffield Council on Bioethics, *The Collection, Linking and Use of Data in Biomedical Research and Health Care: Ethical Issues* (Nuffield Council on Bioethics, February 2015).

[33] Weber et al (n 24).

[34] YA de Montjoye, CA Hidalgo, M Verleysen, et al, 'Unique in the Crowd: The Privacy Bounds of Human Mobility' (2013) 3 Scientific Reports 1376; YA de Montjoye, L Radaelli, VK Singh, et al, 'Identity and Privacy. Unique in the Shopping Mall: On the Reidentifiability of Credit Card Metadata' (2015) 347 Science 536.

[35] Tanner (n 1) 91.

[36] Andreu-Perez et al (n 19) 1204.

[37] BD Mittelstadt and L Floridi, 'The Ethics of Big Data: Current and Foreseeable Issues in Biomedical Contexts' (2016) 22(2) Science and Engineering Ethics 303.

[38] Ibid.

One might be tempted to think that consent is unnecessary because the risks involved in big data research are minimal. However, given the uncertainty over what kinds of information may be revealed in the future on the basis of collected data, and given the possibility of leaks and hacks, it is hard to make a case that the risks are indeed minimal.[39]

Anonymization and informed consent, then, cannot protect medical privacy in the digital age, and they do nothing to avoid concerns about power that result from the collection of sensitive data. If the traditional tools of medicine are insufficient to protect patients in big data contexts, how can risks be minimized? I turn to this question next.

III. Minimizing Risks

Part of what made anonymization and consent appropriate tools in the past were complementary practices that could strengthen protection, such as keeping paper files in a locked cabinet to which only approved researchers had access. In what follows are some complementary practices that can help minimize risks in the era of big data.

Data practices must be better regulated to protect data subjects.[40] Inappropriate uses of data, including the re-identification of individuals in anonymized databases and discrimination, should be made illegal. Similarly, we should make it illegal to link health information from research databases to other data resources if data subjects have not given their explicit consent.[41] If risks will be imposed on data subjects (eg by inferring sensitive information from non-sensitive information, or by storing data in a way that could allow for identification and misuse), medical data should not be used from people who have not agreed to be research subjects, as when data is analysed from social media or open web forums, or when doctors, hospitals, or pharmacies share medical data with data analysis companies without patients' knowledge. Policing such behaviour, however, can be quite a challenge, and even with strong regulations in place, risks from privacy losses do not disappear. For this reason, limits to how data is used are not enough, and further limits on the *access* to data should be put in place.

Consent has always been a valuable guardian of access to data, but its practice must be updated to fit big data contexts. One possibility is to put the onus on patients—to give them control of their data and make them responsible for it. Even acknowledging that the kind of consent being secured is limited and not fully informed due to the uncertainty surrounding big data, individuals could be asked for consent for each use of their data. This approach is incredibly burdensome, however, both for institutions and individuals. . Making individuals responsible for their health data will likely result in them being overwhelmed with consent requests, which may lead to them oversharing and regretting it when it is too late to

[39] Ibid.

[40] The General Data Protection Regulation (GDPR) is a step in the right direction, but it might not be enough to protect data subjects' medical data; it is too early to tell, as much depends on how the Regulation will be interpreted and enforced. The recommendations here go beyond the GDPR and are specific to medical data. See Council Regulation (EU) 2016/679 of 27 April 2016 on the protection of natural persons with regard to the processing of personal data and on the free movement of such data, and repealing Directive 95/46/EC (General Data Protection Regulation) [2016] OJ 2 119/1, http://eur-lex.europa.eu/legal-content/EN/TXT/?qid=1525272154893&uri=CELEX:32016R0679 accessed 15 July 2019.

[41] IS Kohane and RB Altman, 'Health-Information Altruists—A Potentially Critical Resource' (2005) 353(19) New England Journal of Medicine 2074.

recall their data. A more promising proposal is 'tiered' consent, in which data subjects can choose specific future uses of their data (eg someone can decide their data can be used only for cancer research).[42] Along these lines, researchers in the United Kingdom have developed an interface that allows patients to give 'dynamic consent' to the use of their data—that is, that allows them to engage in research studies and change their consent preferences at any time in narrow and broad ways.[43]

Another option is to have consent models mediated by third parties that negotiate agreements on behalf of data subjects. Data trusts could be modelled after labour unions. This proposal could work quite well, if people were to organize and data experts, ethicists, and lawyers could advise data trusts. Related to consent, if private corporations are to responsibly manage sensitive data about people from which medical information may be inferred, they should have similar fiduciary and confidentiality responsibilities as doctors currently have. If a company betrays the trust of users by misusing their medical data, they should lose their licence to manage medical data.

Companies and institutions should invest in research, software, and infrastructure to manage medical data in the safest way possible. Encryption of data is a must, and security methods such as differential privacy[44]—whereby mathematical noise is inserted into a database to camouflage individual data records—should be implemented. There should also be plans to delete data once it has been used. Only then can patients' consent be valid, as only then will they know how their data will be used. Without an expiry date, data can be used in any way in the future. Data deletion is also an effective way to minimize the risks of misuse.[45]

Apart from making bad practices illegal, giving patients some degree of control over their data through some form of consent, holding corporations to respect fiduciary duties and confidentiality, implementing the best possible security protocols, and deleting data, regulation must ensure that private companies do not monopolize medical data. Above and beyond the risks that can spill outside the doctor's office, medical risks are perhaps the most important to take into account in the context of medical settings. For big data to be a positive force in medicine, we must ensure that all data subjects on whose data it relies can benefit equally from it. Privacy risks are an obstacle to this objective because people can be discriminated against on account of data about them—they can be denied services, or charged more for them. Data risks related to monopolies can also make prices increase, allowing data titans to unduly privately benefit from data they have harvested from the public.

These risks provide a strong argument in favour of having universal health care.[46] The most effective way of protecting people from suffering unfair consequences in medical settings is by having public universal health care coverage in which citizens contribute to the system through taxes and not through dues based on data about them. Such a system would

[42] Mittelstadt and Floridi (n 37).

[43] J Kaye, EA Whitley, D Lund, et al, 'Dynamic Consent: A Patient Interface for Twenty-First Century Research Networks' (2015) 23 European Journal of Human Genetics 141.

[44] C Dwork, 'Differential Privacy' in M Bugliesi et al (eds), *Automata, Languages and Programming* (Springer, 2006), vol 4052.

[45] C Véliz, 'Tus datos son tóxicos', *El País* (8 April 2018), https://elpais.com/tecnologia/2018/04/06/actualidad/1523030681_007734.html accessed 15 July 2019.

[46] There are other arguments in favour of universal health care, but those are outside the scope of this chapter. For an overview of some of these arguments, see N Daniels, 'Justice and Access to Health Care', *Stanford Encyclopedia of Philosophy* (winter 2017 edn), https://plato.stanford.edu/entries/justice-healthcareaccess/ accessed 15 July 2019.

do nothing to prevent work discrimination or extortion resulting from medical data misuses, but it can minimize medical identity theft and, most importantly, it can guarantee that people will not suffer unfairness in access to health care on account of health data monopolies or discrimination.

A strong public and universal health-care system not only provides the most robust protection citizens can get to ensure fair access to medical care—it is also the kind of entity that has enough power to negotiate fair deals with corporations. The NHS, for instance, has enough data about patients, enough medical technology, and enough connections to research institutions to be able to collaborate with corporations without buckling under their weight. In the future, it ought to hire expert lawyers in order to negotiate a better deal with companies like Google so that patients' interests are better protected. Medical data is both very sensitive and very valuable, and health-care institutions should not be giving it out without patients' consent and without ensuring that they will retain some power over the resulting technology.

A. Some Objections

1. The Personal Responsibility Objection

I have argued that privacy risks are dangerous in relation to medical data because they may result in people being treated differently from each other on the basis of personal information about them. But it could be objected that people ought to be treated differently in virtue of how responsible they are for their health conditions. In other words, it could be argued that we should welcome big data analyses even when they come at the cost of losing medical privacy because they will enable accurate attribution of responsibility within health-care settings, so that patients who are less responsible for their disease get more benefits, and patients who are more responsible get less, and that would be fairer than all patients being treated equally even when some of them might be responsible for their own misfortune. However, it will be hard to make sure institutions are not discriminating against people on the basis of information that should not be taken into account, such as genetic make-up, or race. Moreover, the attribution of responsibility is bound to be very controversial. First, algorithms on which big data depend can and do make mistakes.[47] Second, this kind of assessment is not a purely scientific determination, but a value-laden philosophical task that depends on how we conceptualize responsibility.

Furthermore, health is largely a matter of luck: a combination of having the right genes, living in a healthy environment, having had the right education, etc. Cancer, for instance, is the most common cause of death in the world, and a recent study suggests that most cancers are the result of random mutations.[48] Given the weight of luck in health status, an important factor for ensuring all citizens have a fair equality of opportunity is providing universal access to health care. Maintaining health contributes to being able to access the wide range of opportunities available in a given society. If we want to protect equality of opportunity, then

[47] For a good compendium of such mistakes, see C O'Neil, *Weapons of Math Destruction* (Kindle edition, Penguin, 2016).

[48] C Tomasetti, L Li, and B Vogelstein, 'Stem Cell Divisions, Somatic Mutations, Cancer Etiology, and Cancer Prevention' (2017) 355(6331) Science 1330.

offering universal access to health care will contribute to setting off the inequalities that are brought about by sheer luck.

2. The Free Rider Objection

I am proposing two courses of action that may seem in tension with each other. On the one hand, I am proposing asking for informed consent for the collection of medical data, and at the same time, I am defending a universal system of public health care. Believers in desert (ie, roughly, that people should get what they deserve) might want to object that it would be unfair for people who do not give their consent for the collection of their medical data to benefit from a medical system that depends on that data to advance knowledge.

This objection, I suspect, comes from underestimating the cost of donating data; since there is no phenomenological feeling to have one's data collected (it is not a bodily-invasive procedure, it does not physically hurt), it is understandable for someone to think that people who do not donate their data are just being selfish. But the risks of sharing medical data are real, as examples show, and they are likely to become riskier as time goes by and there is more data about people to be aggregated. Donating medical data should thus be thought analogous to participating in clinical research: because it is a risky endeavour, subjects should not be compelled to participate. Participation should always be free, and withdrawal from participation without reprisal must always be an option. Importantly, according to the Declaration of Helsinki, regarded by most as one of the main guidelines for medical research: 'While the primary purpose of medical research is to generate new knowledge, this goal can never take precedence over the rights and interests of individual research subjects.'[49]

People who do not donate their medical data are no worse than people who have not participated in medical research and yet benefit from medical advancements. To recruit data subjects, researchers should do what clinical researchers do to convince people to participate in research: make sure appropriate safety measures are put in place (which, in the case of data, has to include a plan to delete data), ask for informed consent, and give people sufficient compensation to make it worth their while to participate.

3. The Brakes to Innovation Objecton

A third objection to making an effort to protect privacy in medical settings is that limiting the access to and management of medical data will put a brake on data-driven innovation.[50] Ethical limits, however, should not be considered undue obstacles to innovation. In the long run, unethical practices breed distrust and resentment, and a backlash could end up being much more of a barrier to innovation. As an (extreme) analogy, doctors killing healthy people in order to transplant their organs might save lives in the short term, but it will not lead us to the kind of society we want to live in. And it would be a matter of time before people stopped going to the doctor. Privacy is a right for good reasons, and rights are meant to serve as 'red lines' that should not be crossed, even when short-term benefits for violating them might be tempting. Furthermore, as I suggested before, it is still unclear to what extent big data has the capacity to bring about significant medical benefits. The burden

[49] World Medical Association Declaration of Helsinki—Ethical Principles for Medical Research Involving Human Subjects (adopted by the 18th WMA General Assembly 1964) (Note of Clarification added 2002), art 8.

[50] N Price, and G Cohen, 'Privacy in the Age of Medical Big Data', *Nature Medicine* 25, 37–43, 2019.

of proof is on big data to show its worth; in the meantime, especially given the lack of proper regulation, patients should not be forced to gamble with their most sensitive data in exchange for uncertain future benefits.

IV. Conclusion

Big data promises to significantly enhance the power of medicine to diagnose, treat, and prevent diseases. With this promise, however, come significant privacy risks to data subjects who could suffer unfair discrimination, exposure, extortion, and limited access to health care. To minimize these risks, inappropriate uses of data should be outlawed, and consent must be sought from data subjects, even if it is a limited form of consent such as tiered consent. Companies managing sensitive information must also be held to respect fiduciary duties and confidentiality regarding medical data. Security measures like encryption and other cryptographic methods such as differential privacy should be implemented. Data should be deleted after use. Finally, corporations should not be allowed to hold complete power over medical big data. If corporations monopolize medical big data, the best treatments in medicine may only be available to the rich, or to ordinary people under unfair data deals. As things stand, there do not seem to be enough structures to guarantee that public goods and interests will prevail above private interests in the use of big data for medical purposes. If, however, public health-care systems manage to negotiate control over data—through harnessing the weight of the data they have, their connections to research institutions, the trust of their patients (if they manage to keep it), the ability of government to regulate medical settings, and hiring top lawyers to represent the public's interest—fruitful collaborations between the private and public sectors may ensue, and patients may have their privacy and interests better protected. Medical big data can only be successful and ethical if it respects people's right to privacy.

Bibliography

Andreu-Perez, J, Poon, CC, Merrifield, RD, Wong, ST, and Yang, GZ, 'Big Data for Health' (2015) 19(4) IEEE Journal of Biomedical Health and Informatics 1193.

Angus, DC, 'Fusing Randomized Trials with Big Data: The Key to Self-Learning Health Care Systems?' (2015) 314(8) Journal of the American Medical Association 767.

Broniatowski, DA, Paul, MJ, and Dredze, M, 'National and Local Influenza Surveillance through Twitter: An Analysis of the 2012–2013 Influenza Epidemic' (2013) 8(12) PLoS One e83672.

Chunara, R, Bouton, L, Ayers, JW, and Brownstein, JS, 'Assessing the Online Social Environment for Surveillance of Obesity Prevalence' (2013) 8(4) PLoS One e61373.

Daniels, N, 'Justice and Access to Health Care', *Stanford Encyclopedia of Philosophy* (winter 2017 edn), https://plato.stanford.edu/entries/justice-healthcareaccess/ accessed 15 July 2019.

de Montjoye, YA, Hidalgo, CA, Verleysen, M, and Blondel, VD, 'Unique in the Crowd: The Privacy Bounds of Human Mobility' (2013) 3 Scientific Reports 1376.

de Montjoye, YA, Radaelli, L, Singh, VK, and Pentland, AS, 'Identity and Privacy. Unique in the Shopping Mall: On the Reidentifiability of Credit Card Metadata' (2015) 347(6221) Science 536.

Dwork, C, 'Differential Privacy' in Bugliesi, M, Preneel, B, Sassone, V, and Wegener, I (eds), *Automata, Languages and Programming* (Springer, 2006), vol 4052.

Hern, A, 'Hackers Publish Private Photos from Cosmetic Surgery Clinic', *The Guardian* (31 May 2017), https://www.theguardian.com/technology/2017/may/31/

hackers-publish-private-photos-cosmetic-surgery-clinic-bitcoin-ransom-payments accessed 15 July 2019.

Herring, J, *Medical Law and Ethics* (6th edn, Oxford University Press, 2016).

HIPAA Journal post, 'Largest Healthcare Data Breaches of 2017' (4 January 2018), https://www.hipaajournal.com/largest-healthcare-data-breaches-2017/ accessed 15 July 2019.

Institute of Medicine, Committee on the Role of Institutional Review Boards in Health Services Research Data Privacy Protection, *Protecting Data Privacy in Health Services Research* (National Academies Press, 2000), https://www.nap.edu/read/9952/chapter/1 accessed 15 July 2019.

Kaye, J, Whitley, EA, Lund, D, et al, 'Dynamic Consent: A Patient Interface for Twenty-First Century Research Networks' (2015) 23 European Journal of Human Genetics 141.

Khan, MA-u-d, Uddin, MF, and Gupta, N, 'Seven V's of Big Data: Understanding Big Data to Extract Value' (Proceedings of Zone 1 Conference of the American Society for Engineering Education, 2014), doi: 10.1109/ASEEZone1.2014.6820689.

Kohane, IS and Altman, RB, 'Health-Information Altruists—A Potentially Critical Resource' (2005) 353(19) New England Journal of Medicine 2074–7.

Laney, D, '3D Data Management: Controlling Data Volume, Velocity and Variety' (2001) 6 META Group Research Note.

Mittelstadt, BD and Floridi, L, 'The Ethics of Big Data: Current and Foreseeable Issues in Biomedical Contexts' (2016) 22(2) Science and Engineering Ethics 303–41.

Munro, D, 'Data Breaches in Healthcare Totaled over 112 Million Records in 2015', *Forbes* (31 December 2015), https://www.forbes.com/sites/danmunro/2015/12/31/data-breaches-in-healthcare-total-over-112-million-records-in-2015/ - 5118fabc7b07 accessed 15 July 2019.

Murphy, M, 'Privacy Concerns as Google Absorbs DeepMind's Health Division', *The Telegraph* (13 November 2018), https://www.telegraph.co.uk/technology/2018/11/13/privacy-concerns-google-absorbs-deepminds-health-division/ accessed 15 July 2019.

Nuffield Council on Bioethics, *The Collection, Linking and Use of Data in Biomedical Research and Health Care: Ethical Issues* (Nuffield Council on Bioethics, February 2015).

'Oath of Hippocrates' in WT Reich (ed), *Encyclopedia of Bioethics* (Macmillan, 1995).

O'Neil, C, *Weapons of Math Destruction* (Kindle edn, Penguin, 2016).

Parent, WA, 'Privacy, Morality, and the Law' (1983) 12(4) Philosophy and Public Affairs 269.

Powles, J, 'Why Are We Giving Away Our Most Sensitive Health Data to Google?', *The Guardian* (5 July 2017), https://www.theguardian.com/commentisfree/2017/jul/05/sensitive-health-information-deepmind-google accessed 15 July 2019.

Powles, J and Hodson, H, 'Google DeepMind and Healthcare in an Age of Algorithms' (2017) 7(4) Health and Technology 351, https://link.springer.com/article/10.1007/s12553-017-0179-1 accessed 15 July 2019.

Tanner, A, *Our Bodies, Our Data: How Companies Make Billions Selling Our Medical Records* (Beacon Press, 2017).

Thorpe, JH and Gray, EA, 'Big Data and Public Health: Navigating Privacy Laws to Maximize Potential' (2015) 130(2) Public Health Reports 171.

Tomasetti, C, Li, L, and Vogelstein, B, 'Stem Cell Divisions, Somatic Mutations, Cancer Etiology, and Cancer Prevention' (2017) 355(6331) Science 1330.

Véliz, C, 'On Privacy' (DPhil Thesis, University of Oxford, 2017).

Véliz, C, 'Tus datos son tóxicos', *El País* (8 April 2018), https://elpais.com/tecnologia/2018/04/06/actualidad/1523030681_007734.html accessed 15 July 2019.

Weber, GM, Mandl, KD, and Kohane, IS, 'Finding the Missing Link for Big Biomedical Data' (2014) 311 Journal of the American Medical Association 2479.

World Medical Association Declaration of Helsinki—Ethical Principles for Medical Research Involving Human Subjects (adopted by the 18th WMA General Assembly 1964) (Note of Clarification added 2002).

22

The Age of Personalized Medicine—From Patients to Consumers

The Digital Environment, Clickwrap Contracts, and Implications for Autonomy

Andelka M Phillips

As individuals, we all should be able to exercise our autonomy by making choices for ourselves. In the context of the practice of medicine, the principle of autonomy is one of the most significant ethical principles and respect for this principle is provided by the requirement to provide informed consent to undergo medical treatment and also the right of patients to refuse to undergo treatment. Our world today is experiencing rapid technological change, with many new products and services. This is the age of big data, Personalized and now Precision Medicine. It is also an age where many developments can be viewed as consumer-focused health-care services creating new markets, which challenge traditional paradigms, especially the paradigm of the doctor–patient relationship and the medical clinic, as the main providers of medical services. Many of these products and services are marketed and sold online to the public internationally, with little specific industry regulation. The mode of sale and lack of oversight mean that businesses often rely on their electronic contracts, available on their websites, to govern their relationships with their consumers. This chapter will explore the implications that the proliferation of electronic contracts and the designed environment of websites have on the exercise of individual autonomy when accessing services online. It does this in a specific context, that of Personalized Medicine, focusing on the example of direct-to-consumer genetic testing services (hereafter DTC, also referred to as personal genomics or commercial genomics), which have created a market for genetic tests as consumer services.[1] Very few tests on the market have been approved by any regulatory body[2] and their clinical utility is

[1] AM Phillips, *Buying Your Self on the Internet: Wrap Contracts and Personal Genomics* (Edinburgh University Press, 2019); AM Phillips, 'Reading the Fine Print When Buying Your Genetic Self Online: Direct-to-Consumer Genetic Testing Terms and Conditions' (2017) 36(3) New Genetics and Society 273–95, http://dx.doi.org/10.1080/14636778.2017.1352468 accessed 15 July 2019; AM Phillips, 'Genetics Goes Online—Privacy in the World of Personal Genomics' (October 2018), Privacy Laws & Business International Report, 19–21; AM Phillips, 'Only a Click Away—DTC Genetics for Ancestry, Health, Love ... and More: A View of the Business and Regulatory Landscape' (2016) 8 Applied & Translational Genomics 16–22, https://doi.org/10.1016/j.atg.2016.01.001 accessed 15 July 2019; and AM Phillips, 'Genomic Privacy and Direct-to-Consumer Genetics—Big Consumer Genetic Data—What's in that Contract?' (presented at GenoPri'15 (The 2nd Workshop on Genome Privacy and Security) and published as part of IEEE Conference Proceedings 2015), https://www.computer.org/csdl/proceedings/spw/2015/9933/00/9933a060.pdf accessed 15 July 2019.

[2] 23andMe, '23andMe Granted Authorization by FDA to Market First Direct-to-Consumer Genetic Test Under Regulatory Pathway for Novel Devices', Press Release (19 February 2015), https://mediacenter.23andme.com/press-releases/fdabloomupdate/ accessed 15 July 2019; C Humer and J Steenhuysen, '23andME Launches New Consumer Test Service to Check for Genetic Disorders', *Scientific American* (2015), http://www.scientificamerican.com/article/23andme-launches-new-consumer-test-service-to-check-for-genetic-disorders/ accessed 15 July

Andelka M Phillips, *The Age of Personalized Medicine—From Patients to Consumers* In: *Philosophical Foundations of Medical Law*. Edited by: Andelka M Phillips, Thana C de Campos, and Jonathan Herring, Oxford University Press (2019).
DOI: 10.1093/oso/9780198796558.003.0023

questionable.[3] For instance, although 23andMe has received approval from the US Food and Drug Administration (FDA) for a small number of its health tests, the approval for its BRCA testing came with a number of controls. This included the recommendation that consumers will need to have additional testing in a clinic before making decisions about treatment options.[4] Furthermore, as these services are sold internationally, physical samples of DNA and genetic data generated from those samples is often being processed and stored in countries other than where the consumer resides. It should be noted that the UK House of Commons' Science and Technology Committee has launched an enquiry into commercial genomics in early 2019[5] and we may see regulatory reform in the United Kingdom in light of this, but as the review will be completed after submission of this chapter, it is not possible to consider the Committee's recommendations herein.

Please note that this is an exploratory chapter; I am not purporting to be able to solve all the complex issues and challenges raised by consumerism of medicine. Instead, the aim herein is to draw attention to the manner in which interface design and electronic contracts can impact upon our abilities to make informed choices and exercise our autonomy. This chapter draws upon my related research, which included a review of the electronic wrap contracts of seventy-one companies that provide genetic tests for health purposes.[6]

I. What Does Autonomy Mean?

Autonomy is discussed in a number of other chapters in this book (see, for instance, the chapters by Thana C De Campos, Charles Foster, and Robert Gay). As Gay writes:

> Respect for autonomy implies that a person can freely choose what should be done on his or her behalf, and have that choice respected or, at the very least, implies allowing the person to refuse that something be done to him or to her in the context of health care. We might suggest that a paradigm example of the application of this principle is the ethical and legal requirement for sufficient informed consent . . .[7]

2019; US Food and Drug Administration, 'FDA Allows Marketing of First Direct-to-Consumer Tests that Provide Genetic Risk Information for Certain Conditions', Press Release (6 April 2017), https://www.fda.gov/newsevents/newsroom/pressannouncements/ucm551185.htm accessed 15 July 2019.

---

[3] J Karow, '23andMe DTC Breast and Ovarian Cancer Risk Test Misses Almost 90 Percent of BRCA Mutation Carriers', GenomeWeb (5 April 2019), https://www.genomeweb.com/molecular-diagnostics/23andme-dtc-breast-and-ovarian-cancer-risk-test-misses-almost-90-percent-brca#.XKfbrS1L1PU accessed 15 July. 2019; see Limitations of HBOC Direct-To-Consumer Genetic Screening: False Positives, False Negatives and Everything in Between' Abstract 27 presented at the ACMG Annual Clinical Genetics Meeting, 4th April 2019, Washington State Convention Center https://acmg.expoplanner.com/index.cfm?do=expomap.sess&event_id=13&session_id=10875 accessed 3 August 2019.

[4] FDA, 'FDA Authorizes, with Special Controls, Direct-to-Consumer Test that Reports Three Mutations in the BRCA Breast Cancer Genes', FDA News Release (6 March 2018), https://www.fda.gov/NewsEvents/Newsroom/PressAnnouncements/ucm599560.htm accessed 15 July 2019.

[5] Science and Technology Committee (Commons), Commercial Genomic Inquiry (March 2019), https://www.parliament.uk/business/committees/committees-a-z/commons-select/science-and-technology-committee/inquiries/parliament-2017/commercial-genomics-17-19/ accessed 15 July 2019; please note that I am making a submission to this Committee and meeting with its chair.

[6] See n 1.

[7] See Chapter 1, this volume.

Even when we are at our most vulnerable, we are still expected to exercise our autonomy by providing informed consent to appropriate treatment where it is offered. Although we do not have a right to demand any kind of medical treatment, we can decide not to undertake treatment. Although in some contexts we may favour a different approach from autonomy and when we consider issues of well-being relational autonomy has much to offer, informed consent is a useful requirement in the context of the practice of medicine.

In Thana de Campos's chapter in this volume (Chapter 5), she explores some of the critiques of autonomy. However, the focus herein is different. I am not advocating for giving autonomy prominence over any other ethical principle, but what I wish to do is to draw attention to the ways in which new services offered via the internet can influence our exercise of autonomy and our ability to make informed choices and provide informed consent. It is hoped that this work will encourage readers to think about how new and emerging consumer-focused health-care services offered online are framed and how we might need to do things differently. This is an important topic, because regardless of critiques, it is still generally accepted that an individual must give their consent to medical treatment and were a person to have a genetic test in a medical setting he or she would generally be required to provide informed consent prior to testing.

Furthermore, in the context of services that utilize personal data, in Europe especially, the General Data Protection Regulation (GDPR) sets a high standard for consent in the context of processing personal data.[8] Under article 4, genetic data is included within the definition of personal data and as DTC companies collect and process both genetic data and other forms of personal data, they should be complying with the provisions of the GDPR (it is also included in article 9 as discussed below). Consent is defined in article 4(11) as 'any freely given, specific, informed and unambiguous indication of the data subject's wishes by which he or she, by a statement or by a clear affirmative action, signifies agreement to the processing of personal data relating to him or her'. For UK citizens, the United Kingdom's Data Protection Act 2018 sets a similar standard[9] and the United Kingdom's Information Commissioner's Office (ICO) has indicated that businesses marketing their services to UK consumers need to comply with both the GDPR and the Data Protection Act.[10]

Genetic data is also included under article 9 of the GDPR in the prohibition on processing of special categories of data. Article 9 provides for a number of exceptions to this prohibition, but in the context of DTC, the most relevant exceptions are the 'explicit consent' of the data subject as set out in article 9(2)(b) and the research exemption set out in article 9(2)(j). Although article 4(11) provides the general definition of consent to data processing, article 7 also imposes a number of conditions in relation to consent, including that where

> the data subject's consent is given in the context of a written declaration which also concerns other matters, the request for consent shall be presented in a manner which is clearly distinguishable from the other matters, in an intelligible and easily accessible form, using

[8] Council Regulation (EU) 2016/679 of 27 April 2016 on the protection of natural persons with regard to the processing of personal data and on the free movement of such data, and repealing Directive 95/46/EC (General Data Protection Regulation), [2016] OJ 2 119/1, http://eur-lex.europa.eu/legal-content/EN/TXT/?qid=1525272154893&uri=CELEX:32016R0679 accessed 15 July 2019.

[9] See Data Protection Act 2018, Pt 4, s 84, https://www.legislation.gov.uk/ukpga/2018/12/pdfs/ukpga_20180012_en.pdf accessed 15 July 2019.

[10] See ICO, 'Guide to Data Protection', https://ico.org.uk/for-organisations/guide-to-data-protection/ accessed 15 July 2019.

clear and plain language. Any part of such a declaration which constitutes an infringement of this Regulation shall not be binding.

Therefore, genetic testing services offered to individuals based in the European Union need to meet the GDPR's requirements for consent, and this is quite a high standard. Given the commercial nature of DTC services, it is also unlikely that they could rely on the research exception, although if they were able to use it, they would still need to meet the consent requirements for the initial genetic test and it is likely that a new consent would be required for any secondary research using consumers' data. As the GDPR is also exerting a strong influence on the reform of data protection law globally, with countries such as New Zealand, Singapore, Japan, and Brazil[11] as well as others also reforming their law, it is likely that companies offering genetic testing services in other countries will also have to meet similar standards for consent.

The GDPR provides people with a number of rights in relation to their personal data and this also includes the right to erasure and the right to withdraw consent, which means that businesses handling personal data should also provide options for consumers to have their data deleted. While this may be challenging, DTC companies could provide an option for consumers to have their data deleted after a test is performed. Guardiome is an interesting example here, as they provide a whole genome-sequencing service, where their consumers receive their genomic sequence data on a device and at present Guardiome does not store or share their consumers' data.[12] This example shows that it is possible for DTC companies to make their services more privacy friendly and it is hoped that other companies will start to provide more privacy-centred services.

In the United Kingdom, the Human Tissue Act 2004 (which is enforced by the Human Tissue Authority) governs the use of human tissue and organs and it also has applicability to genetic tests. Section 45 of the Act makes it a criminal offence to perform genetic analysis without appropriate consent. The Human Tissue Authority has also released guidance in the form of Codes of Practice on Consent and the latest version of its Code of Practice on Consent suggests that: 'commercial organisations offering services related to the removal, storage and use of human tissue and cells must ensure that materials provided to customers to aid their decision-making, such as marketing and advertising materials, are accurate and abide by the Advertising Standards Agency's guidelines'.[13] If we consider this in the

[11] M Ramey, 'Brazil's New General Data Privacy Law Follows GDPR Provisions', *Inside Privacy* (20 August 2018), https://www.insideprivacy.com/international/brazils-new-general-data-privacy-law-follows-gdpr-provisions/ accessed 15 July 2019 (the English version of the new Brazilian legislation is available at https://www.pnm.adv.br/wp-content/uploads/2018/08/Brazilian-General-Data-Protection-Law.pdf) accessed 15 July 2019; H Lovells, 'Changes in Japan Privacy Law to Take Effect in Mid-2017', LEXOLOGY (1 February 2017), https://www.lexology.com/library/detail.aspx?g=efa0a2b0-b73e-456c-b4fa-26a268e9e751 accessed 15 July 2019; New Zealand Privacy Commissioner, 'Privacy Law Reform', https://www.privacy.org.nz/the-privacy-act-and-codes/privacy-law-reform/ accessed 15 July 2019; 'Singapore Personal Data Protection Reforms in Force from Next Year', *Out-Law* (3 September 2018), https://www.out-law.com/en/articles/2018/september/singapore-personal-data-protection-reforms/ accessed 15 July 2019.

[12] Guardiome, https://www.guardiome.com/omics-lab accessed 10 September 2019; and T Ray and UG Thomas, 'Startup Guardiome Emphasizes Privacy in New WGS Consumer Offering', GenomeWeb (29 December 2015), https://www.genomeweb.com/sequencing-technology/startup-guardiome-emphasizes-privacy-new-wgs-consumer-offering#.XLZXo3ZR1PU accessed 15 July 2019.

[13] See Phillips, *Buying Your Self on the Internet* (n 1) ch 3, citing Human Tissue Authority, 'Code A: Guiding Principles and The Fundamental Principle of Consent' (version updated 3 April 2017), 11, para 40, https://www.hta.gov.uk/hta-codes-practice-and-standards-0 accessed 15 July 2019; the previous version of this code was substantially similar. See Human Tissue Authority, 'Code of Practice 1—Consent' (Version 14.0, updated July 2014),

context of the provision of DTC genetic tests for health purposes, DTC companies should be making sure that both content on their websites and claims made in advertising are not misleading and are transparent about the respective risks, benefits, and limitations of testing. The need for unbiased marketing and transparency has also been stressed in much of the policy guidance on DTC to date.[14] Websites can be useful platforms for providing consumers with helpful information about genetic testing, but there is much room for improvement here, as previous studies have raised concern over the manner in which information regarding the respective risks and benefits of testing is provided,[15] together with the provision of information regarding companies' data privacy practices and consumers' understanding of that information.[16]

II. The Example of Direct-to-Consumer Genetic Tests for Health Purposes

The DTC industry is an interesting example, as it has created a new market for genetic tests, where people can order a genetic test from their homes without the involvement of a medical practitioner. The industry has developed over the last two decades[17] and it offers a diverse range of tests, which include tests for a wide array of health conditions, ancestry, and more dubious tests, such as tests for child talent, paternity, and infidelity.[18] Typically, a consumer will purchase the test online and then the company will send the consumer a sample collection kit, normally for a saliva sample or cheek swab. The consumer will the send this back to the company for analysis and receive test results through a web interface. It should be noted that the industry currently does not have harmonized standards and this applies to both tests for health purposes and ancestry testing. Therefore, it is possible to obtain contradictory disease risk estimates from different companies,[19] and many tests currently offered

archived content available at https://web.archive.org/web/20170120025305/https://www.hta.gov.uk/sites/default/files/Code_of_practice_1_-_Consent.pdf accessed 15 July 2019.

[14] See, for instance, Human Genetics Commission, 'A Common Framework of Principles for Direct-to-Consumer Genetic Testing Services' (Department of Health, 2010), archived content available at https://webarchive.nationalarchives.gov.uk/20120504102236/http://www.hgc.gov.uk/Client/document.asp?DocId=280&CAtegoryId=10 accessed 15 July 2019; European Academies Science Advisory Council (EASAC) and the Federation of European Academies of Medicine (FEAM), 'Direct-to-Consumer Genetic Testing: Summary Document' (EASAC-FEAM Project on Direct-to-Consumer Genetic Testing, October 2012), https://www.easac.eu/fileadmin/PDF_s/reports_statements/Easac_12_DTCGT-Lay_Web.pdf accessed 15 July 2019; European Society of Human Genetics, 'Statement of the ESHG on Direct-to-Consumer Genetic Testing for Health-Related Purposes' (2010) 18(12) European Journal of Human Genetics 1271–73.

[15] A Singleton, LH Erby, KV Foisie, et al, 'Informed Choice in Direct-to-Consumer Genetic Testing (DTCGT) Websites: A Content Analysis of the Benefits, Risks, and Limitations' (2012) 21(3) Journal of Genetic Counseling 433–9; JA Hall, R Gertz, J Amato, et al, 'Transparency of Genetic Testing Services for "Health, Wellness and Lifestyle": Analysis of Online Prepurchase Information for UK Consumers' (2017) 25(8) European Journal of Human Genetics 908–17.

[16] E Christofides and K O'Doherty, 'Company Disclosure and Consumer Perceptions of the Privacy Implications of Direct-to-Consumer Genetic Testing' (2016) 35(2) New Genetics and Society 101–23; J Hazel and C Slobogin, 'Who Knows What, and When?: A Survey of the Privacy Policies Proffered by U.S. Direct-to-Consumer Genetic Testing Companies' (19 April 2018, last revised 18 October 2018), Cornell Journal of Law and Public Policy and Vanderbilt Law Research Paper No 18, https://ssrn.com/abstract=3165765 accessed 15 July 2019.

[17] S Hogarth and P Saukko, 'A Market in the Making: The Past, Present and Future of Direct-to-Consumer Genomics' (2017) 36(3) New Genetics and Society 197–208, 197.

[18] Phillips, 'Reading the Fine Print' (n 1).

[19] US Government Accountability Office, (GAO) Direct-To-Consumer Genetic Tests: Misleading Test Results Are Further Complicated by Deceptive Marketing and Other Questionable Practice (GAO-10-847T,

may require further confirmatory testing in a clinic before decisions can be made about a particular individual's treatment. A recent study by Esplin et al found that 23andMe's BRCA test 'misses almost 90 percent of BRCA mutation carriers, both in those with and those without a personal or family history of cancer'.[20] While this study was focused on clinical utility, the authors questioned how useful overall such testing was for individuals with genuine health concerns, given that both those who receive positive and those who negative test results would require further testing to confirm their results. It should be noted that it is also possible to obtain contradictory ethnicity estimates.[21]

While the focus herein is on DTC tests for health purposes and these services together with DTC ancestry tests have received the bulk of academic attention to date, it should be stressed that most DTC companies are not restricted to offering only one type of test. While there remains a lack of industry-specific oversight, this also allows unscrupulous entities to operate. For example, it has recently emerged that vulnerable groups have been targeted in Louisville, Kentucky, where vans have driven to some of the most impoverished neighbourhoods and offered individuals $20 for cheek swabs of DNA.[22] In response to this, Kentucky's Attorney General has now issued a scam alert and it appears that this scam together with another is targeted towards identity theft and Medicaid fraud.[23] I also wish to stress that while less attention has been devoted to more dubious types of tests, such as those for child talent, 'peace of mind' paternity, and infidelity, we do need more research on these tests and regulators should play a role in protecting the public from these services.

Furthermore, several of the most prominent DTC companies are engaging in secondary health research using data collected from consumers.[24] Companies are also increasingly partnering with other entities in order to conduct medical research with 23andMe, entering

2010) Testimony before the Subcommittee on Oversight and Investigations, Committee on Energy and Commerce, House of Representatives, 1–8, http://www.gao.gov/assets/130/125079.pdf accessed 15 July 2019; J Cussins, 'Direct-to-Consumer Genetic Tests Should Come with a Health Warning', Pharmaceutical Journal (15 January 2015), https://www.pharmaceutical-journal.com/opinion/comment/direct-to-consumer-genetic-tests-should-come-with-a-health-warning/20067564.article?firstPass=false accessed 15 July 2019.

---

[20] J Karow, '23andMe DTC Breast and Ovarian Cancer Risk Test Misses Almost 90 Percent of BRCA Mutation Carriers', GenomeWeb (5 April 2019), https://www.genomeweb.com/molecular-diagnostics/23andme-dtc-breast-and-ovarian-cancer-risk-test-misses-almost-90-percent-brca#.XKfbrS1L1PU accessed 15 July 2019.

[21] KV Brown, 'How DNA Testing Botched My Family's Heritage, and Probably Yours, Too', GIZMODO (16 January 2018), https://gizmodo.com/how-dna-testing-botched-my-familys-heritage-and-probab-1820932637 accessed 15 July 2019; see also WD Roth and B Ivemark, 'Genetic Options: The Impact of Genetic Ancestry Testing on Consumers' Racial and Ethnic Identities' (2018) 124(1) American Journal of Sociology 150–84; WD Roth, 'Genetic Ancestry Tests Don't Change Your Identity, But You Might', *The Conversation* (5 July 2018), https://theconversation.com/genetic-ancestry-tests-dont-change-your-identity-but-you-might-98663 accessed 15 July 2019.

[22] P Ashley, 'Residents Concerned about DNA-for-Cash Transactions in Louisville', Wave 3 News (1 April 2019), http://www.wave3.com/2019/04/01/residents-concerned-about-dna-for-cash-transactions-louisville/ accessed 15 July 2019.

[23] Office of the Attorney General of Kentucky, 'Beshear: Fraudulent Medical Billing Scams Targeting Kentuckians', Scam Alert (9 April 2019), https://ag.ky.gov/scams/Pages/Current-Scam-Alert.aspx accessed 15 July 2019; 'Kentucky AG on DNA-for-Cash Scheme', GenomeWeb (12 April 2019), https://www.genomeweb.com/scan/kentucky-ag-dna-cash-scheme#.XLUk5i9L10s accessed 15 July 2019; M Glowicki, 'Beshear Urges Those Who Received Money for DNA Samples to Call Fraud Hotline', Louisville Courier Journal (8 April 2019), https://www.courier-journal.com/story/news/crime/2019/04/08/kentucky-ag-asks-dna-cash-customers-call-fraud-hotline/3405027002/ accessed 15 July 2019; KV Brown, 'Scammers May Be Using DNA Testing to Defraud Medicare and Steal Identities', *Bloomberg* (18 April 2019), https://www.bloomberg.com/news/articles/2019-04-17/scam-dna-tests-may-be-new-target-for-health-fraud-states-warn accessed 15 July 2019.

[24] AM Phillips, 'Only a Click Away—DTC Genetics for Ancestry, Health, Love … and More: A View of the Business and Regulatory Landscape' (2016) 8 Applied & Translational Genomics 16–22.

into at least fifteen partnerships to date[25] (the most recent being with GlaxoSmithKline[26]) and Orig3n entering a partnership with the Chinese insurer ZhongAn Online P&C Insurance Co, Ltd.[27] Thus, there is real potential for data sharing in this context and companies marketing their services to EU consumers do have work to do in order to ensure compliance with the GDPR.

Prior to the advent of DTC services, genetic tests for health purposes were only offered in a clinical setting and, today, if a patient undergoes a genetic test in a clinic, as well as having to provide informed consent to undergo testing, they will also have genetic counselling both prior to and after the test. This counselling assists patients in understanding what test results mean for them, including the limitations of such tests. While a number of genetic tests are useful in clinical practice, there is a lack of validation and clinical utility for many tests for common, complex diseases.[28] Concern has been expressed regarding the limitations of tests. One of the reasons for this is that tests have not been standardized for many complex diseases and it is possible to obtain contradictory risk estimates for the same disease or condition from different companies.[29] Recent research has also found a relatively high level of false positive results in DTC offerings[30] and concern has also been expressed regarding the nature of information provided by DTC companies about their services.[31]

[25] M Sullivan, '23andMe Has Signed 12 Other Genetic Data Partnerships beyond Pfizer and Genentech', *VentureBeat* (14 January 2015), https://venturebeat.com/2015/01/14/23andme-has-signed-12-other-genetic-data-partnerships-beyond-pfizer-and-genentech/ accessed 15 July 2019; C Lagorio-Chafkin, '23andMe Exec: You Ain't Seen Nothing Yet', *Inc* (7 January 2015), http://www.inc.com/christine-lagorio/23andMe-new-partnerships.html accessed 15 July 2019.

[26] L Geggel, '23andMe Is Sharing Its 5 Million Clients' Genetic Data with Drug Giant GlaxoSmithKline', *Livescience* (26 July 2018), https://www.livescience.com/63173-23andme-partnership-glaxosmithkline.html accessed 15 July 2019; GlaxoSmithKline, 'GSK and 23andMe Sign Agreement to Leverage Genetic Insights for the Development of Novel Medicines' (25 July 2018), https://www.gsk.com/en-gb/media/press-releases/gsk-and-23andme-sign-agreement-to-leverage-genetic-insights-for-the-development-of-novel-medicines/ accessed 15 July 2019.

[27] S Hurst, 'Chinese E-Insurer Zhong An Has Teamed Up with BioTech Company Orig3n for Health Tech Solutions', *CROWDFUND INSIDER* (2 August 2018), https://www.crowdfundinsider.com/2018/08/137259-chinese-e-insurer-zhongan-has-teamed-up-with-biotech-company-orig3n-for-health-tech-solutions/ accessed 15 July 2019.

[28] A Regalado, '23andMe Thinks Polygenic Risk Scores Are Ready for the Masses, But Experts Aren't So Sure', *MIT Technology Review* (8 March 2019), https://www.technologyreview.com/s/613095/23andme-thinks-polygenic-risk-scores-are-ready-for-the-masses-but-experts-arent-so-sure/ accessed 15 July 2019; MC Cornel, CG van El, and P Borry, 'The Challenge of Implementing Genetic Tests with Clinical Utility While Avoiding Unsound Applications' (2014) 5(1) Journal Community Genetics 7–12; JP Annes, MA Giovanni, and MF Murray, 'Risks of Presymptomatic Direct-to-Consumer Genetic Testing' (2010) 363 New England Journal of Medicine 1100–1.

[29] US Government Accountability Office, 'Direct-To-Consumer Genetic Tests: Misleading Test Results Are Further Complicated by Deceptive Marketing and Other Questionable Practice', GAO-10-847T (2010), https://www.gao.gov/products/GAO-10-847T accessed 15 July 2019.

[30] S Tandy-Connor, J Guiltinan, K Krempely, et al, 'False-Positive Results Released by Direct-to-Consumer Genetic Tests Highlight the Importance of Clinical Confirmation Testing for Appropriate Patient Care' (2018) 20 Genetics in Medicine 1515–21.

[31] NP Lewis, D Treise, SI Hsu, et al, 'DTC Genetic Testing Companies Fail Transparency Prescriptions' (2011) 30 New Genetics and Society 291–307; LI Laestadius, JR Rich, and PL Auer, 'All Your Data (Effectively) Belong to Us: Data Practices among Direct-to-Consumer Genetic Testing Firms' (2016) 19 Genetics in Medicine 513–20; J Hazel and C Slobogin, 'Who Knows What, and When?: A Survey of the Privacy Policies Proffered by U.S. Direct-to-Consumer Genetic Testing Companies' (19 April 2018, last revised 18 October 2018), Cornell Journal of Law and Public Policy and Vanderbilt Law Research Paper No 18-18, https://ssrn.com/abstract=3165765 accessed 15 July 2019.

III. Consent and Contracting Online

As noted above, DTC services can be viewed as one example of Personalized Medicine. Personalized Medicine encompasses many things, but a useful way of conceptualizing it is that these are innovations that are centred around tailoring treatment to individuals, rather than diseases.[32] Meanwhile, Precision Medicine goes one step further and can be described as 'an emerging approach for disease treatment and prevention that takes into account individual variability in genes, environment, and lifestyle for each person'.[33] While the idea of Personalized Medicine has broad appeal, the reality of tailoring medical treatment to individuals in reality is far more challenging, and as Dickenson et al write: 'it is extremely unlikely that completely individualized treatments are ever going to be feasible. Many commentators and clinicians acknowledge that the best aspiration is to deliver diagnoses and treatments stratified into patient groups by genomic science'.[34] Nevertheless, services such as DTC genetic tests challenge both doctor–patient relationships and the very nature of how medical services are offered. In the context of medical treatment, an individual is no longer solely a patient: he or she may also be a consumer simultaneously. Doctors can also be seen as service providers. This has also expanded the range of entities that provide health and medical services and the lines between what distinguishes medical services from other types of services are beginning to blur. This raises a number of difficult issues, but the aim herein is to shed light on how our autonomy as individuals is impacted by developments in consumer-focused health care. Sometimes, the services offered may not be new in themselves, but the mode of access is different. For others, though, the service itself may be novel. While the focus herein is on the example of DTC genetic tests, wearable devices, such as smart watches and fitness bands, raise similar issues.

The internet is increasingly an integral part of everyday life for many people. Most of us will use it for both work and leisure. However, what is often overlooked is that the way in which the internet and e-commerce have evolved to date has given increased prominence to contract law in regulating relationships between companies and consumers and also in regulation of new products and services, where industry-specific legislation is lacking. Whether you are visiting a website, installing software, or purchasing a product or service online, you are forming contractual relationships. Every website you encounter will have its own contract in the form of terms of use, terms of service, or terms and conditions. These are electronic contracts, typically clickwrap or browsewrap, which have evolved from shrinkwrap licences. They are also mass standard form contracts (sometimes referred to as boilerplate) and are also forms of contracts of adhesion.[35] A clickwrap contract will usually display the terms of the contract on the screen and require the user to scroll through the terms before clicking on a button, which may be labelled 'I Agree' or 'I Accept'. In contrast, browsewrap contracts have the document title as a hyperlink without the terms displaying on the screen, meaning that it is possible to accept the terms without seeing them.[36]

[32] J Herring, *Medical Law and Ethics* (7th edn, Oxford University Press, 2018), 12.

[33] US National Library of Medicine, 'What Is Precision Medicine?', *Genetics Home Reference*, https://ghr.nlm.nih.gov/primer/precisionmedicine/definition accessed 15 July 2019.

[34] D Dickenson, B van Beers, and S Sterckx, 'Introduction' in B van Beers, S Sterckx, and D Dickenson (eds), *Personalised Medicine, Individual Choice and the Common Good* (Cambridge University Press, 2018), 3.

[35] NS Kim, *Wrap Contracts: Foundations and Ramifications* (Oxford University Press, 2014), 39–44; NS Kim, 'Exploitation by Wrap Contracts-Click "Agree"' (2014) 39(2) California Bar IP Journal, New Matter 10–17.

[36] NS Kim, *Wrap Contracts: Foundations and Ramifications* (Oxford University Press, 2014), 41–4.

Consider your own interaction with websites. Very few of us will have read all the terms of all the contracts we encounter online. We are also unlikely to have read all the privacy policies we encounter and as these documents are often linked together and seek to incorporate terms by reference, this is problematic. It means that in order to understand our rights and obligations in the context of a particular transaction with a business online, we should have, in fact, read all of these documents.

A number of studies have investigated the amount of contracts and privacy policies individuals encounter online, together with the time it would take to read these documents, as well as the readability of these documents. A few examples are discussed below to highlight the nature of people's interactions with these documents. Cranor and McDonald's 2008 study estimated that it would take 201 hours a year for the average American consumer to read all the privacy policies they encountered online.[37] As more people are now accessing a greater number of services online, this figure is now likely to have increased.

The Norwegian Consumer Council (NCC) in its APPFAIL campaign estimated that the average smartphone contained 250,000 words of contracts or privacy policies.[38] The NCC's APPFAIL report examined the contracts and privacy policies of twenty popular smartphone applications in order to assess their compliance with EU data protection and consumer protection law. This report included discussion of the issue of informed consent, and the NCC suggested that: 'If terms are very difficult to read as they are very long, ambiguous or written in overly technical, complex or vague language, a strong case can be made that informed consent is not possible for most consumers.'[39] Other studies have identified similar problems in relation to the length of contracts encountered by consumers. For example, according to Quartz, those who own five Apple devices will have entered into 'at least 30 contracts, totalling more than 100,000 words'.[40] Meanwhile, the work of the Australian consumer group CHOICE, which investigated the contracts of e-readers, using the example of the Kindle found that the device contained eight documents, which when combined exceeded 73,000 words in length and took the actor they hired to read them 9 hours to read aloud.[41] While this may not seem problematic for products that are trivial, when they relate to more sensitive products and services, more caution is needed.

[37] AM McDonald and LF Cranor, 'The Cost of Reading Privacy Policies' (2008) 4 Journal of Law and Policy for the Information Society 543–68 ; and see their more recent related work: JR Reidenberg, T Breaux, LF Cranor, et al, 'Disagreeable Privacy Policies: Mismatches between Meaning and Users' Understanding' (2015) 30 Berkeley Technology Law Journal 39–88; and F Schaub, R Balebako, and LF Cranor, 'Designing Effective Privacy Notices and Controls' (2017) 21 IEEE Internet Computing 70–7.

[38] See Phillips, *Buying Your Self on the Internet* (n 1) ch 1, citing Norwegian Consumer Council, '250,000 Words of App Terms and Conditions' (24 May 2016), https://www.forbrukerradet.no/side/250000-words-of-app-terms-and-conditions/ accessed 15 July 2019; Norwegian Consumer Council, 'APPFAIL Threats to Consumers in Mobile Apps' (March 2016), https://www.forbrukerradet.no/undersokelse/2015/appfail-threats-to-consumers-in-mobile-apps/ accessed 15 July 2019.

[39] Phillips, *Buying Your Self on the Internet* (n 1) ch 4, citing NCC (n 38) 24.

[40] C Groskopf, 'CLICK "I AGREE" Apple Fans Have Click-Signed More than 100,000 Words of Legal Contracts', *Quartz* (5 November 2016), https://qz.com/797928/apple-fans-have-click-signed-more-than-100000-words-of-legal-contracts/ accessed 15 July 2019. This is also mentioned in the chapter AM Phillips, 'Will My Genes Really Help Me Fit into Those Jeans? Personal Genomics and Wrap Contracts' in L Edwards, B Schafer, and E Harbinja (eds), *Future Law: Emerging Technology, Ethics and Regulation* (forthcoming, Edinburgh University Press, 2020).

[41] E Hunt, 'Amazon Kindle's Terms "Unreasonable" and Would Take Nine Hours to Read, Choice Says', *The Guardian* (15 March 2017), https://www.theguardian.com/australia-news/2017/mar/15/amazon-kindles-terms-unreasonable-and-would-take-nine-hours-to-read-choice-says accessed 15 July 2019; CHOICE, 'Nine Hours of "Conditions Apply"', https://www.choice.com.au/about-us/media-releases/2017/march/nine-hours-of-conditions-apply accessed 15 July 2019. The videos are available at https://www.youtube.com/watch?v=6QZml7sPbVU&feature=youtu.be accessed 15 July 2019.

IV. How Can We Exercise Our Autonomy When Behaving as Automatons?

In their book *Re-Engineering Humanity*, Frischmann and Selinger suggest that contracts are often designed so as to blend into the website to enable a seamless transaction and that this has an impact on the ability of an individual to make an informed choice about whether or not to use these services. As they write:

> Designers arrange the digital contracting environment to create a practically seamless, transaction cost minimized user experience. Rather than requiring people who intend to use online services to read lengthy pages filled with boilerplate legal jargon ... a simple click of the mouse, with mere conspicuous notice of the existence of terms suffices to manifest consent for entering legally binding contractual relationships.[42]

They 'claim that the electronic contracting environment should be understood as a techno-social tool for engineering human beings to behave automatically, like simple machines'.[43] Meanwhile, the NCC in their *2018 Deceived by Design* report discuss the issue of nudging and the use of dark patterns in interface design, which steer users towards choosing less privacy-friendly options.[44] Dark patterns is a term coined by Harry Brignull.[45] NCC characterizes these as exploitative design choices, which can 'push consumers toward choices that benefit the service provider'.[46] *Dark patterns* are also 'ethically problematic, because they mislead users into making choices that are not in their interest, and deprive them of their agency'.[47] It should be noted that in April 2019, a US bill entitled the Deceptive Experiences to Online Users Reduction (DETOUR) Act was proposed, which would ban certain some of these practices if passed.[48] This legislation if it is enacted could assist with improving how businesses operate in this context, but as it is currently framed it would only apply to organizations, which had more than 100 million users and this legislation would be much more beneficial for the public if this figure was lowered.

The idea that in the online environment we may in fact have decreased agency due to certain design features has increased significance when we consider new services, such as DTC, that are complex. Consider the difference between an individual purchasing a DTC test online without any involvement of a medical practitioner and the experience of an individual undergoing genetic testing in a clinic with access to support from both genetic counsellors and physicians. If there was no question of disparity of information or understanding in this

[42] BM Frischmann and E Selinger, *Re-Engineering Humanity* (Cambridge University Press, 2018), 60; see also BM Frischmann and E Selinger, 'Engineering Humans with Contracts' (September 2016), Cardozo Legal Studies Research Paper No 493, https://papers.ssrn.com/sol3/papers.cfm?abstract_id=2834011 accessed 15 July 2019.

[43] Frischmann and Selinger, *Re-Engineering Humanity* (n 42) 61.

[44] NCC, 'Deceived by Design' (June 2018), https://www.forbrukerradet.no/undersokelse/no-undersokelsekategori/deceived-by-design/ accessed 15 July 2019.

[45] Phillips, *Buying Your Self on the Internet* (n 1) ch 5; citing Dark Patterns, 'What Are Dark Patterns?', https://darkpatterns.org/ accessed 15 July 2019.

[46] NCC (n 44) 4.

[47] Ibid 7.

[48] Please see S. 1084: Deceptive Experiences To Online Users Reduction Act https://www.govtrack.us/congress/bills/116/s1084/text accessed 10 September 2019; see also Andelka M Phillips, 'All Your Data Will Be Held Against You: Secondary Use of Data from Personal Genomics & Wearable Tech' in Susan Sterett and Lee Demetrius Walker (eds), *Research Handbook On Law And Courts* (Edward Elgar Publishing, forthcoming October 2019).

context, we might not think about this in the same way, but we have developed governance mechanisms in medical law in order to protect patients and ensure high standards in the provision of medical services. Even in other situations where products and services sold online are of a less complex nature, we are starting to see a shift in how regulators and the public view interface design. Concern over the impact of screen use and addictive elements in application design are leading to calls for improved oversight and changing the way we do things.[49] This is timely, and I should suggest that it should also be seen as an opportunity. New services and products offered online have evolved in a particular manner, but that does not mean this is the only way things could be done. DTC companies that wish to do respected and responsible medical research and want to retain consumer trust should consider how they can truly achieve compliance with applicable law, such as the GDPR, but also how to help their consumers. Interfaces could be designed that allow for speed bumps to slow the process of decision making down, rather than rushing consumers into a purchase.

V. What Exactly Are You Agreeing To?

A number of experiments that have involved the inclusion of problematic clauses in order to assess how people interact with these contracts further highlight both consumers' lack of reading of electronic contracts and the types of things that companies could bury in their fine print. These range from Purple's Community Service clause, which involved 1,000 hours of community service, including requirements to clean public toilets and hug strangers,[50] to GameStation's Immortal Soul clause,[51] or F-Secure's Herod clause.[52] In the Purple example: 'All users were given the chance to flag up the questionable clause in return for a prize, but remarkably only one individual, which is 0.000045% of all Wi-Fi users throughout the whole two weeks managed to spot it.'[53] In the GameStation example, which

[49] See eg the work of T Harris, 'How Technology Is Hijacking Your Mind—From a Magician and Google's Design Ethicist', *Thrive Global* (19 May 2016), https://www.thriveglobal.com/stories/8466-how-technology-is-hijacking-your-mind-from-a-magician-and-google-design-ethicist accessed 15 July 2019; see also Harris's website for other papers, http://www.tristanharris.com/essays/ accessed 15 July 2019; see also Center for Humane Technology, http://humanetech.com accessed 15 July 2019; and A Atler, *Irresistible: The Rise of Addictive Technology and the Business of Keeping Us Hooked* (Penguin, 2017), ch 1; see also S Collins, 'Call for Guidelines on Children's Screen Use', *The New Zealand Herald* (2 April 2019), https://www.nzherald.co.nz/national-video/news/video.cfm?c_id=1503075&gal_cid=1503075&gallery_id=205318 accessed 15 July 2019; and S Weale, 'Experts Call for Official Guidelines on Child Screen Use', *The Guardian* (25 December 2016), https://www.theguardian.com/society/2016/dec/25/experts-call-for-official-guidelines-on-child-screen-use accessed 15 July 2019; H Chowdhury, '"Addictive" Messenger Kids App Gives Children as Young as 6 New Way to Initiate Friend Requests', *The Telegraph* (14 August 2018), https://www.telegraph.co.uk/technology/2018/08/14/addictive-facebook-messenger-kids-app-children-young-6-add-friends/ accessed 15 July 2019; S Gibbs, 'Apple Investors Call for Action over iPhone "Addiction" among Children', *The Guardian* (8 January 2018), https://www.theguardian.com/technology/2018/jan/08/apple-investors-iphone-addiction-children accessed 15 July 2019; 'China Regulator to Set Time Limits on Hot Short-Video Apps', *Bloomberg* (29 March 2019), https://www.bloomberg.com/news/articles/2019-03-29/china-regulator-to-set-time-limits-on-popular-short-video-apps accessed 15 July 2019.

[50] See Phillips, *Buying Your Self on the Internet* (n 1) ch 1, citing Purple, '22,000 People Willingly Agree to Community Service in Return for Free WiFi' (13 July 2017), https://purple.ai/blogs/purple-community-service/ accessed 15 July 2019.

[51] M Perton, 'Read Fine Print or GameStation May Own Your Soul', *Consumerist* (16 April 2010), http://consumerist.com/2010/04/16/read-fine-print-or-gamestation-may-own-your-soul/ accessed 15 July 2019.

[52] T Fox-Brewster, 'Londoners Give Up Eldest Children in Public Wi-Fi Security Horror Show', *The Guardian* (29 September 2014).

[53] D Tuffley, 'How Not to Agree to Clean Public Toilets When You Accept Any Online Terms and Conditions', *The Conversation* (23 July 2017), https://theconversation.com/how-not-to-agree-to-clean-public-toilets-when-you-accept-any-online-terms-and-conditions-81169 accessed 15 July 2019.

was actually a prank for April Fool's Day, the immortal soul clause included an opt out. Those who ticked the box to opt out were to receive a £5 voucher.[54] However, only around 12 per cent of GameStation's customers opted out, meaning that more than 80 per cent failed to read the clause.[55] Obar and Oeldorf-Hirsch also included a child assignment clause in their recent research on undergraduate students' interaction with the contract and privacy policy of a fictitious social network.[56] In Obar and Oeldorf-Hirsch's study, a mere 1.7 per cent (9 out of 543) of those surveyed 'mentioned the child assignment clause'.[57] Obar and Oeldorf-Hirsch found that a sense of information overload may also be having an impact on how people engage with these policies online.[58]

In my review of seventy-one contracts from companies that provide DTC tests for health purposes, a number of contractual terms were identified which are problematic from a consumer protection perspective and could potentially be challenged on the grounds of unfairness under UK and EU consumer protection legislation.[59] These included: clauses that permit the DTC company a broad power to alter the terms of their contract without notice to the consumer (unilateral alteration clause); together with clauses that deemed consent to acceptance of terms through use of the service or visiting the website. I have suggested elsewhere that such terms are challengeable under both EU and UK law on the grounds of unfairness.[60] In the context of DTC specifically, clauses that allow a company broad power to alter terms without notice to the consumer are particularly problematic, given the sensitive nature of these services. These clauses can also lead to uncertainty regarding the exact content of the contract in its entirety, as where terms can change at any time it will be difficult for the consumer to have any certainty about what the terms of the contract are. As contracts also often refer to privacy policies, clauses of this type are also likely to be problematic from a data protection standpoint. In relation to clauses that deem consent to terms or privacy policies through either use of the service or visiting the website, these are also problematic from both consumer protection and data protection perspectives. It is unlikely that deeming consent through visiting a website or using a service will comply with the consent requirements set by the GDPR. Furthermore, consent to altered terms is also often deemed through continued use of the service or the website and this is also unlikely to be deemed as compliant with the GDPR.

A further issue in this context is the language used in online wrap contracts and privacy policies and how this impacts upon the exercise of autonomy and the ability of a consumer to make an informed choice. Becher and Benoliel's recent study assessed the readability of the wrap contracts used by 500 of the most popular American websites.[61] Their results suggest that most of these contracts are not readable by the average consumer with most being

[54] Perton (n 50).

[55] J Brownlee, 'GameStation EULA Collects 7,500 Souls from Unsuspecting Customers', Geek.com (16 April 2010), https://www.geek.com/games/gamestation-eula-collects-7500-souls-from-unsuspecting-customers-1194091/ accessed 15 July 2019.

[56] JA Obar and A Oeldorf-Hirsch, 'The Biggest Lie on the Internet: Ignoring the Privacy Policies and Terms of Service Policies of Social Networking Services' [2018] Information, Communication & Society 1.

[57] Ibid.

[58] Ibid.

[59] Phillips, 'Reading the Fine Print' (n 1) 273–95; see also Phillips, *Buying Your Self on the Internet* (n 1) ch 5.

[60] Ibid.

[61] U Benoliel and SI Becher, 'The Duty to Read the Unreadable' (January 11, 2019) 60 Boston College Law Review 1–37 Forthcoming, available at SSRN: https://ssrn.com/abstract=3313837 or http://dx.doi.org/10.2139/ssrn.3313837

written in language similar to that of academic journal articles.[62] Other work by Conklin and Hyde, which investigated the readability of insurance policies found that of seven policies considered, 'the easiest requiring 14 years of education and the most difficult requiring a PhD-level education.'[63] If we consider this in the context of the provision of DTC genetic tests for health purposes, which are complex in nature, there is a significant likelihood that consumers would have difficulty understanding the language used in these contracts even if they have time to read them and this should support the need for reform of governance of this industry, especially in relation to contracts and privacy policies, but also in relation to the provision of information about DTC tests.

VI. Repurposing Genetic Data

The example of DTC is useful here as it demonstrates some of the ways in which our personal information can be repurposed. Privacy is a significant issue in this context, as once an individual undergoes a genetic test, the results of that test in the form of digitized genetic data can be stored potentially indefinitely. They can also serve as a unique identifier for the individual and also be used to trace family members. For example, a number of DTC companies offer family-finder features in their ancestry testing services, which can connect individuals with unknown relatives and lead to significant revelations, such as unknown paternity. A recent news article discussed the experience of a woman who, through using 23andMe, found out not only about her biological donor father's genetic profile, but a large number of siblings (a total of thirty siblings), some of whom did not know they were donor conceived before using 23andMe's service.[64] While for some people, this may be a positive experience, it is also something that can have a very significant impact on individuals and there needs to be more information provided to the public regarding this.

In 2018, there was also much press coverage of the use of the genetic genealogy database GEDmatch in the investigation for the Golden State Killer case.[65] It is important to understand that GEDmatch is not a DTC company, but a database that allows users to upload genetic data from other services. It previously allowed for this type of use by law enforcement in its site user policy, but it should be noted that it changed this policy in May 2019, opting its users out of law enforcement matching by default.[66] In the Golden State Killer

62 Ibid at 21.

63 Phillips, *Buying Your Self on the Internet* (n 1) 7, citing K Conklin and R Hyde, 'If small print 'terms and conditions' require a PhD to read, should they be legally binding?' The Conversation (10 May 2018) https://theconversation.com/if-small-print-terms-and-conditions-require-a-phd-to-read-should-they-belegally-binding-75101 accessed 10 September 2019; see also K Conklin, R Hyde, and F Parente, 'Assessing plain and intelligible language in the Consumer Rights Act: a role for reading scores?' (2018) Legal Studies ISSN 1748-121X (in Press) http://eprints.nottingham.ac.uk/51073/ accessed 10 September 2019.

64 'Only Sort of an Only Child' (1 April 2019), https://www.genomeweb.com/scan/only-sort-only-child accessed 15 July 2019; see A Hassan, '2 Bay Area Women Linked to 28 Siblings Following DNA Test', ABC (30 March 2019), https://abc7news.com/society/2-bay-area-women-linked-to-28-siblings-following-dna-test/5225970/ accessed 15 July 2019.

65 AM Phillips, 'Genetics Goes Online—Privacy in the World of Personal Genomics', *PL&B International* (October 2018), http://www.andelkamphillips.com/wp-content/uploads/2018/10/Genetics.pdf accessed 10 September 2019.

66 Adam Vaughan, 'DNA database opts a million people out from police searches' *New Scientist* (20 May 2019) https://www.newscientist.com/article/2203857-dna-database-opts-a-million-peopleout-from-police-searches/ accessed 21 June 2019.

investigation, law enforcement created a profile on GEDmatch in order to find relatives of a potential suspect based on DNA samples collected at crime scenes some thirty years earlier. Through the use of the database, a suspect, James DeAngelo, was subsequently arrested and proceedings are ongoing.[67] It should be noted here, though, that DeAngelo has been cleared in relation to two murder charges on the basis that his DNA did not match.[68] As of April 2019, there has been a further recent development in these proceedings, with prosecutors seeking to use the death penalty.[69] Regardless of whether DeAngelo is ultimately convicted of the other charges against him, the manner in which this investigation was conducted should cause concern, especially in relation to privacy rights, but also in relation to other rights of suspects and innocent relatives, as well as how serious the consequences can be for individuals here. Since the Golden State Killer investigation coverage, it has emerged that a further 100 profiles from cold cases have been uploaded to GEDmatch and then in early 2019 the DTC company, FamilyTreeDNA, has revealed that it has been collaborating with the US Federal Bureau of Investigation (FBI) to investigate violent crime.[70] These examples demonstrate the potential for genetic data collected by DTC companies to be used for secondary research purposes that might not be in consumers' best interests and could also impact upon their rights. It is vital to remember the premise of innocence until proof of guilt and also the right to a fair trial.

While law enforcement and other entities are likely to want to utilize new sources of data in investigations, we need to consider carefully how appropriate it is to use commercial private databases for criminal investigations. Given recent developments in research on DNA transfer, it is also important that investigators and courts are not overly reliant on DNA evidence, as it is quite possible for innocent people to leave DNA traces in places, on objects, and even on other people without their knowledge. The case of Lukis Anderson, who was wrongly charged due to DNA transfer, where his DNA was found on a murder victim he in fact never met,[71] highlights the need for more caution and education here.

67 See Phillips, *Buying Your Self on the Internet* (n 1) ch 4, citing: M Thielking, 'Lawmakers Press Genetic Testing Companies for Details on Their Privacy Policies', *STAT* (21 June 2018), https://www.statnews.com/2018/06/21/congress-genetic-testing-companies-privacy-policies/ accessed 15 July 2019; R Becker, 'Golden State Killer Suspect Was Tracked Down through Genealogy Website GEDmatch', *The Verge* (26 April 2018), https://www.theverge.com/2018/4/26/17288532/golden-state-killer-east-area-rapistgenealogy-websites-dna-genetic-investigation accessed 15 July 2019; and T Hesman Saey, 'Why Using Genetic Genealogy to Solve Crimes Could Pose Problems', *ScienceNews* (7 June 2018), https://www.sciencenews.org/article/why-police-using-genetic-geneaology-solve-crimes-poses-problems?mode=pick&context=2782&tgt=nr accessed 15 July 2019; M Molteni, 'The Key to Cracking Cold Cases Might Be Genealogy Sites', *Wired* (1 June 2018), https://www.wired.com/story/police-will-crack-a-lot-more-cold-cases-with-dna/ accessed 15 July 2019; GEDmatch, https://www.gedmatch.com/tos.htm accessed 15 July 2019.

68 T Lapin, '"Golden State Killer" Cleared of 1978 Double-Murder Cold Case', *New York Post* (14 June 2018), https://nypost.com/2018/06/14/golden-state-killer-cleared-of-1978-double-murder-cold-case/ accessed 15 July 2019; Associated Press, 'DNA Clears Accused Golden State Killer Joseph DeAngelo of 1975 Murder', *NBC News* (10 January 2019), https://www.nbcnews.com/news/us-news/dna-clears-accused-golden-state-killer-joseph-deangelo-1975-murder-n956566?cid=sm_npd_nn_tw_ma accessed 15 July 2019.

69 D Smith and S Stanton, 'Prosecutors to Seek Death Penalty in Golden State Killer Case', *The Mercury News* (10 April 2019), https://www.mercurynews.com/2019/04/10/prosecutors-to-seek-death-penalty-in-golden-state-killer-case/ accessed 15 July 2019; K Dowd, 'Golden State Killer Suspect Appears in Court Nearly One Year after Arrest', *San Francisco Chronicle* (10 April 2019), https://www.sfgate.com/bayarea/article/joseph-deangelo-hearing-sacramento-trial-13757418.php accessed 15 July 2019.

70 M Haag, 'FamilyTreeDNA Admits to Sharing Genetic Data with F.B.I.', *The New York Times* (4 February 2019), https://www.nytimes.com/2019/02/04/business/family-tree-dna-fbi.html accessed 15 July 2019.

71 K Worth, 'Framed for Murder by His Own DNA', *Wired* (19 April 2018), https://www.wired.com/story/dna-transfer-framed-murder/ accessed 15 July 2019; see also RAH Van Oorschot and MK Jones, 'DNA Fingerprints from Fingerprints' (1997) 387(6635) Nature 767; and PA Smith, 'When DNA Implicates the Innocent' (2016) 314(16) Scientific American 11–12.

If using commercial genetic databases for criminal investigation is to be permitted, there should be much more public discussion of the issues at stake. In the United Kingdom, it is also an offence under the Human Tissue Act to analyse DNA without appropriate consent and at present it is likely that the consent mechanisms used by DTC companies may not meet the requirements of either the GDPR or the Human Tissue Act.

VII. Conclusion

In conclusion, the aim herein has been to draw attention to the impacts of electronic contracts and website design on the exercise of individual autonomy when making decisions about whether to purchase DTC genetic tests for health purposes. Given that most genetic tests for complex diseases have not yet been standardized and often lack clinical utility, allowing these services to be offered commercially without the involvement of physicians is concerning. When an individual has a genetic test in a medical clinic, they will have more support, especially in relation to understanding the implications of test results for their health, which is often not present with DTC services. There are also significant privacy risks in the context and wide potential for secondary use of genetic data by entities outside the health-care sector, which need more attention. It is also hoped that this chapter will encourage readers to think beyond this example to other new internet-based medical services and consider how we might approach things differently. Although e-commerce has made many services much more available, given the complex nature of genetic tests for health purposes, and the special characteristics of sequenced genetic data, taking a more cautious approach to governance in this context is desirable.

Index

For the benefit of digital users, indexed terms that span two pages (e.g., 52–53) may, on occasion, appear on only one of those pages.

Note: Tables are indicated by *t* following the page number.